THE LETTERS OF
George Meredith

EDITED BY C. L. CLINE

———

VOLUME I

OXFORD

AT THE CLARENDON PRESS

1970

Oxford University Press, Ely House, London W. 1

GLASGOW NEW YORK TORONTO MELBOURNE WELLINGTON
CAPE TOWN SALISBURY IBADAN NAIROBI DAR ES SALAAM LUSAKA ADDIS ABABA
BOMBAY CALCUTTA MADRAS KARACHI LAHORE DACCA
KUALA LUMPUR SINGAPORE HONG KONG TOKYO

CONTENTS

A LIST OF LETTERS

VOLUME I

1861

1864

A LIST OF LETTERS

A LIST OF LETTERS

ACKNOWLEDGEMENTS

THE obligations that I have incurred in the course of editing the letters of George Meredith are many and great. I must first of all thank the George Meredith Estate Trustees for their permission to publish the letters. But only the generosity of a host of individuals and institutions enabled me to avail myself of this permission.

In England the largest collections of Meredith letters belong (or belonged, in one instance, formerly) to the following: the Garrick Club (the Hardman letters, now in the British Museum), the Maxse family (the Maxse letters), the Lawrence family (the letters to the Misses Lawrence and Sir Trevor and Lady Lawrence), Mrs. G. B. Foster (the letters to Lady Ulrica Duncombe), Mrs. J. G. Gordon (the letters to Alice Brandreth Gordon, later Mrs. and Lady Butcher), Lady Halsey and Lady Bryant (the letters to the Walter Palmers), the Meynell family (the letters to Alice and Wilfrid Meynell), the British Museum, and the Bodleian Library. Often my obligation goes far beyond permission to print the letters. Mrs. Foster not merely consented to allow the letters to Lady Ulrica Duncombe to be photographed but generously sent the original letters to me. Had I been forced to work from photographic copies, I should never have been able to piece together the various parts of many of the letters, as I trust I have done. Mrs. Gordon was equally kind in sending the Alice Gordon-Butcher letters to me for indefinite loan. Mrs. Sowerby (the former Olivia Meynell) brought the letters written to the Meynells—later acquired by The University of Texas at Austin—to my London hotel and left them for my use. The late General Sir Ivor Maxse and Mr. and Mrs. John Maxse received me hospitably and allowed me to photograph the letters written to Admiral Maxse. Later when it developed that other letters were among the Maxse Papers, subsequently deposited in the West Sussex Record Office, I was permitted (through Francis W. Steer, Esq., and the W.S.R.O.) to have copies of them made. Lady Bryant, who first responded to my inquiry, put me in communication with Lady Halsey, who had custody of the letters to the Walter Palmers and who was most gracious to me on more than one visit to the Golden Parsonage. Finally, I should never have been able to trace and obtain access to the Lawrence family letters without the interest and assistance of the late Judge A. A. Gordon Clark ('Cyril Hare') and Mrs. Gordon Clark (the former Barbara Lawrence), whose hospitality at Berry's Croft, near Meredith's Box Hill cottage, will always remain among my most pleasant memories.

To all of the above I wish to record my special thanks.

In the beginning it was apparent to me that no definitive edition of Meredith's letters could be undertaken without the co-operation of the authorities of Yale University, possessor of the richest single Meredith collection, formed originally by Mr. Frank Altschul. I am grateful therefore to the Library Committee and other authorities of Yale University for their co-operation and to Miss Marjorie Gray Wynne of the Yale Library for more than an impersonal interest in the project as it developed. The University of Texas at Austin acquired several hundred Meredith letters as they became available in the market, and I am greatly indebted to the various authorities for their support.

For permission to use other Meredith letters, I am indebted in varying degrees, as will appear in the accreditation at the head of each letter, to the following: Mrs. Helen Rossetti Angeli; Professor Donald Baker; Mrs. Katherine K. Benoliel; Mrs. A. A. Gordon Clark; the late Professor L. L. Click; Alan Clodd, Esq.; the late Sir Sydney Cockerell; Miss Irene Cooper Willis and Lloyds Bank; Walter R. Cresswell, Esq.; the late Richard H. P. Curle, Esq.; Professor Arthur Kyle Davis, Jr.; Dr. Myles Dillon; Mr. L. D. Feldman; David Garnett, Esq.; Algernon C. Gissing, Esq.; Professor David Bonnell Green; A. R. B. Haldane, Esq.; Sir Rupert Hart-Davis; Mrs. Harold Hartley; Professor Charles J. Hill; Miss Anne Karminski; Mrs. C. H. Kellaway; E. McLysaght, Esq.; Professor Leslie A. Marchand; Simon Nowell-Smith, Esq.; the late Colonel Mortimer Ruffer and Mrs. Ruffer; Noel Sharp, Esq.; Mr. Robert H. Taylor; Mrs. Janet Camp Troxell; the Arents Tobacco Collection, the New York Public Library; the Samuel and Mary R. Bancroft Collection, the Wilmington Society of Fine Arts; the Bapst Library, Boston College (and Miss Martha Dubay); the Berg Collection, the New York Public Library; Messrs. Bradbury and Agnew (and the late Alan G. Agnew and Peter Agnew, Esq.); the Keeper of the Brotherton Library, the University of Leeds; Brown University; the University of California, Berkeley; the University of California, Los Angeles; the Central Library, Manchester; the University of Chicago; the Mary Helen Cochran Library, Sweet Briar College; Columbia University; the Library of Congress; Dartmouth College;

ACKNOWLEDGEMENTS

Dickinson College; the Edward Laurence Doheny Memorial Library, St. John's Seminary (and Miss Lucille V. Miller); Duke University; the Fales Library Division of Special Collections, New York University Libraries; the Fitzwilliam Museum, Cambridge; the Free Library of Philadelphia (and Miss Ellen Shaffer); the Harvard College Library (and Miss Carolyn Jakeman and the late William A. Jackson); the Historical Society of Pennsylvania; the Huntington Library; the University of Illinois; the Lilly Library, Indiana University (and Mr. David Randall and Miss Doris M. Reed); the University of Liverpool (and D. F. Cook, Esq.); the University of London (and J. H. P. Pafford, Esq.); McGill University; Messrs. Macmillan; the Massachusetts Historical Society; the Pierpont S. Morgan Library (and Mr. Herbert Cahoon and Mr. Frederick B. Adams, Jr.); Miss Winifred A. Myers; the National Library of Australia; the National Library of Scotland; the National Library of Wales; the State University of New York at Buffalo; the Morris L. Parrish Collection, Princeton University (and Mr. Alexander D. Wainwright); the Carl H. Pforzheimer Library (and Mr. Carl H. Pforzheimer, Jr.); the University of Rochester; Rutgers University; Stadt-und Universitätsbibliothek, Frankfurt-am-Main; Professor Lionel Stevenson; Trinity College, Cambridge; the University Library, Liverpool; and Wellesley College.

For assistance of various kinds I also wish to thank the following: the Revd. Michael Adie; Mr. Frank Altschul; Mrs. Winifred M. Ashton; the Chief of Establishments, the Bank of England; Professor Joseph O. Baylen; the late Vanessa Bell; Hubert Bennett, Esq.; Miss Nellie Bonaparte Wyse; the late Professor Bradford A. Booth; M. A. F. Borrie, Esq.; Mrs. Ursula Bridge; B. P. C. Bridgewater, Esq.; Francis Bywater, Esq.; Messrs. Christie, Manson and Woods; Messrs. Constable (and Ralph Arnold, Esq.); Anthony Curtis, Esq.; P. J. Dobell, Esq.; Professor Leon Edel; the Folger Shakespeare Library; Dr. Adam Fox; Mrs. M. E. Campbell Fraser; Mr. Stephen Gál; Philip Gosse, Esq.; G. Kenneth Graham, Esq.; Mr. C. Hartley Grattan; Professor Gordon S. Haight; Mrs. Aurelia Brooks Harlan; Professor L. T. Hergenhan; P. Hogg, Esq.; Mrs. Madeline House; the Bishop of Jarrow; Professor Harvey Kerpneck; Professor Cecil Lang; F. L. Lucas, Esq.; Messrs. Maggs Bros.; Lady Mander (for innumerable kindnessess); David I. Masson, Esq.; Sir Francis Meynell; Professor Francis Mineka; Miss Eleanor L. Nicholes; I. G. Philip, Esq.; Miss Eva L. Pinthus; Sir John Pollock; A. B. Rogers, Esq.;

the late Siegfried Sassoon, Esq.; Commander E. S. Satterthwaite, R.N.; Robert Sencourt, Esq.; Mr. Morris Schertz; M. A. Smith, Esq.; Dudley Sommer, Esq.; Professor James Stone; Graham Storey, Esq.; F. P. Lake Sydenham, Esq.; the present Lord Tennyson; Mrs. Christine Campbell Thompson; Mrs. Margaret Farrand Thorp; P. D. F. Varrall, Esq.; and Cecil Woolf, Esq.

It is impossible to express sufficiently my sense of obligation of another sort to Professors Phyllis Bartlett and Geoffrey Tillotson, both of whom read in its entirety the manuscript in its first state, before numerous additions were made to it, and who saved me from numerous errors and made valuable suggestions about the editing. I can only say, with Meredith, 'You will know me grateful.'

Readers of Meredith's letters will see how often reference to Professor Lionel Stevenson's biography, *The Ordeal of George Meredith*, has obviated the necessity of long explanatory notes. Even so, I have leaned heavily upon Professor Stevenson's work and have quoted a large number of excerpts from it. I wish to thank him for his permission to print these excerpts and for his scholarly knowledge of Meredith, always at my disposal.

I must also thank various of my colleagues who have rendered assistance with their specialized knowledge: the late Professor Raphael Levy, for his assistance with the Provençal language; to the late Professor Harry Leon, for his thorough knowledge of classical languages and literatures; to Professors Helmut Rehder, George Schulz-Behrend, and Donald Sellstrom for assistance with their knowledge of German and French literatures. Throughout what proved to be a much longer task than I had foreseen I have had the indefatigable assistance of three matchless reference librarians—Miss Kathleen Blow, Miss Ruth Hale, and Miss Goldia Hester. Unfailing too in courtesy and aid have been the Stark Librarians of The University of Texas at Austin, Mrs. Ann Bowden and Mrs. June Moll. To these and to many other librarians in the United States and in England I wish to make acknowledgement.

A grant from the American Philosophical Society enabled me to spend one summer in England, and various grants from The University of Texas at Austin have supported the project. My obligation to both is great.

And finally I would record my gratitude to my wife for her assistance and her understanding.

EDITORIAL PRINCIPLES

I HAVE no quarrel with editors who believe that letters should be reproduced exactly as written. I have nevertheless preferred ease of reading to literal representation in rendering the text of Meredith's letters, especially as I believe that nothing of his personality is lost in so doing, as would not be true, for example, of Thackeray. The following principles have governed the editing of the letters:

1. Abbreviations of words ordinarily printed in lower-case type today have been silently expanded, except for a few commonly accepted ones. The symbol & has been replaced with the conjunction it represents except in the names of firms which themselves use the symbol.

2. Abbreviations of proper names, titles of books and magazines, and the like have been expanded within square brackets.

3. Titles of books and periodicals have been consistently printed in italics.

4. The headings, salutations, and conclusions of the letters have been standardized according to Meredith's usual, but not invariable, practice.

5. Undated letters or letters dated with the day of the week only have been dated, whenever possible, within square brackets. If the date is conjectural, it is preceded by a question mark. Letters incorrectly dated by Meredith have been printed with his date, followed by the correct date, when it can be supplied, in square brackets. For incorrectly dated letters obtained from printed sources, however, notice is taken of the incorrect date in the designation of the source of my text, with the correct date, when ascertainable, printed within square brackets in the heading of the letter.

6. I have thought it pointless to preserve Meredith's infrequent misspellings—usually of proper names—although I have retained a few of his eccentricities of spelling. In his later years, for example, he consistently refused to drop the *e* before the participal ending *ing*, and I have chosen to follow his practice.

7. I have tampered very little with Meredith's punctuation, although I have supplied end punctuation when it is omitted or an occasional interior mark of punctuation when it is demanded by clarity. Marks of

ellipsis within the text of letters are always those of Meredith or the published source which I am following. In footnotes they are mine.

8. The source of my text is always recorded, whether manuscript or printed, preceding the letter itself. When my text is derived from the original letter or a photographic reproduction and the letter has been previously published, I have so indicated, but I have thought it superfluous to record all of the various publications of the letters.

9. I have attempted to identify all of the persons, places (when not obvious), events, and allusions that appear in the letters. Needless to say, I have not always succeeded.

10. Identifications of persons to whom Meredith wrote letters have usually been made at the point of the first letter, although a brief identification may be made at the point of the first reference. When the identification is not made at the point of the first letter, the principal reference in the Index is printed in boldfaced type. I have attempted to minimize cross references, believing that the reader will find it more convenient to consult the Index than to be bothered by frequent cross references, but some cross references and repeated identifications, especially of nicknames and given names, seem unavoidable. Nicknames and recurring given names nevertheless usually appear in the Index.

11. Most of Meredith's letters which survive in the original survive without envelopes, although naturally a number of envelopes have survived. I have taken no account of them, however, unless they supply information, such as date or place, not supplied by the letter itself.

12. Letters printed without conclusion and signature have been derived from sources which omit conclusion and signature. Often these sources are book catalogues or books printing excerpts only, but frequently the source is *Letters*, where it is not always possible to determine the reason for the omission. The layout of the page is probably the main but not the sole reason.

INTRODUCTION

ON the morning of 18 May 1909 George Meredith died at the age of 81. Crippled in body and immobile, he was bright in mind and cheerful in outlook to the end.

Throughout the world, newspapers and journals chronicled the event and paid tribute to the great man dead. For Meredith stood almost without rival at the head of letters in the English-speaking world, the acknowledged dean, the oracle, the Grand Old Man. His own explanation of the honours that came his way in his later years—that 'great age in a known man stirs the English'—may have contained an element of truth but was certainly not the whole truth. The world had been slow to recognize his merits, and however imperfectly it understood them, it had belatedly done its best to atone for its earlier indifference. In 1892, at the death of Tennyson, he had been elected President of the Society of Authors, an office that carried with it implicit acknowledgement that he was England's most distinguished author. In the same year the University of St. Andrews had conferred upon him the honorary degree of LL.D., and only physical infirmity prevented his receiving an honorary degree from Oxford in 1899. In 1905 came official recognition: he became the twelfth member of the recently founded Order of Merit, strictly limited to twenty-four members, and his portrait, drawn by order of the King, was hung at Windsor Castle among the portraits of the other members of the order—all admirals, generals, or statesmen. On his eightieth birthday, in 1908, the newspapers and journals of England and America vied with one another in honouring him. His death in the following year called forth even greater tributes.

Simultaneously, however, as Professor Stevenson remarks in *The Ordeal of George Meredith*, an unseemly dispute arose. In spite of Meredith's known dislike of ostentatious funerals, the Society of Authors demanded that he be buried in the Poets' Corner of Westminster Abbey. But Westminster Abbey is holy ground, and Meredith was a Freethinker whose unorthodox religious views had often been publicized, and the Dean of Westminster was adamant in his refusal. A compromise was arranged: the body was cremated, in accordance with one of Meredith's several expressed wishes, the ashes were buried in Dorking Cemetery beside the body of his second wife, and a memorial service was held in Westminster Abbey.

When three years later *Letters of George Meredith*, Collected and Edited by His Son, appeared in two volumes handsomely printed on heavy wove paper and bound in green, with gold stamping and the monogram GM intertwined in gold on the front cover of each volume, they might have seemed to be a kind of posthumous crown or elaborate wreath placed upon the grave of the dead man. In reviewing the collection, *The Times Literary Supplement* concluded by saying: 'It is something to say that one is taken into the intimacies of a mind so rich, so full, that one wonders where there is another mind so rich, outside Shakespeare, in English literature.'

Meredith's only surviving son, William Maxse Meredith, was a partner in the publishing firm of Messrs. Constable, for which he had been active over a dozen years, among other things, in bringing out new editions of his father's works. Meredith's ashes were hardly cold in Dorking Cemetery before Will Meredith set about collecting and planning the publication of his father's letters. Two months after his father's death he sent the following letter to the press:

Sir,—

I beg you to allow it to be made known through the columns of your paper that it is intended to publish a collection of the letters of the late Mr. George Meredith, under the direct supervision of Lord Morley of Blackburn, and that I should be grateful if any one possessing letters will be so kind as to forward them to me at 10, Orange Street . . . when I will have them very carefully copied and returned without delay.—Believe me, yours faithfully,

W. M. Meredith

The response was apparently gratifying, as a good many letters were published by Will Meredith which must have come by way of this appeal. Some refusals and evasions he naturally encountered. Henry James, for example, preferred to keep 'unventilated' the few letters he had received from Meredith, and the Preface to *Letters* is a tacit admission of others.

Perhaps the unkindest cut of all came from the Misses Lawrence, friends of the Merediths since 1873, who took the old-fashioned attitude that letters were private communications between friends and that the public had nothing to do with them. As the Misses Lawrence had been intimate friends of Meredith and admitted having some 135 or 140 of his letters, Will Meredith understandably persisted. 'I am very anxious, as I know Lord Morley is also,' he wrote, 'that the volume should show my father's mind and his views and opinions in their full force.' The name of Morley gave the Misses Lawrence pause; indeed, they wrote in some distress to Morley, asking whether they were wrong to withhold the letters, as their instinct counselled, or whether they should compromise and send copies of several representative letters to Will. Morley's reply was blunt: 'I have been too busy to acquaint myself with the present position of the question of Mr. Meredith's letters', he wrote. 'Had you not better write to Will? I have no charge in the matter.' Morley, then, was but a screen behind which Will Meredith—at least in the beginning—operated, and the sole responsibility for the edition was his. This responsibility was confirmed when he took exception to a statement by the reviewer of *Letters* in the *TLS* who said that he fancied a change in the editorial hand could be detected a short way into the letters. The reviewer, Will Meredith replied, had evidently not read the title-page.

There are 767 letters in *Letters*. It seems clear that in publishing it, Will Meredith had two purposes in mind: (1) to produce a book that would be profitable both to the Meredith heirs and to Messrs. Constable and (2) to exhibit his father to best advantage through a selection of his letters. With the second purpose in mind, he did not attempt to publish all of the letters to which he had access. He rejected many of those written to himself, usually short letters of business, and he rejected some forty or fifty of the letters to Admiral Maxse, for one reason or another. And doubtless the same principle of selection was applied throughout and accounted for many other rejections. Meredith was not a man of independent means, like Walpole, writing for the amusement of himself and his friends, or Byron, writing more for posterity than for the recipients of his letters. He was, up until 1882, when a reversion fell in and made him relatively secure, a hard-pressed man who wrote novels and poetry in the spare time left over from performing the regular duties connected with two—and for a while three—regular jobs. Only after these duties were performed and his daily stint of writing was done was he free to write letters. Inevitably, then, many were short and hastily written, and Will Meredith excluded almost all of these.

Scholars have always felt, with reason, that relatives make the poorest biographers and editors of memoirs and family letters. They are protective and often deliberately attempt to falsify the image or—

in photographer's terms—to retouch it until little resemblance to the original remains. Although, by his selection of letters, Will Meredith was to a degree protective, he had no need to falsify the image, and in this respect might have been regarded as the ideal editor of his father's letters. Yet it is precisely at this point that, in the opinion of Henry James, he failed. 'What lacerates me perhaps most of all in the Meredith volumes', James wrote to Edmund Gosse (Percy Lubbock, *The Letters of Henry James*, N.Y., 1920, ii. 250), 'is the meanness and poorness of the editing—the absence of any attempt to project the Image (of character, temper, quantity and quality of mind, general size and sort of personality) that such a subject cries aloud for; to the shame of our purblind criticism. For such a Vividness to go a-begging. . . .'

We have now had more than half a century in which to discover other defects in *Letters*: they are many and serious, though in fairness it should be said that they are deficiencies that are largely common to nineteenth- and early twentieth-century editions of letters. Explanatory notes that should have been easy for Will Meredith to write at the time are few and far between. Indeed, after fifty or so pages they almost cease to exist, so that the *TLS* reviewer was not without justification in suspecting another editorial hand. Even the few notes are apt to be inaccurate. Further, few pains were taken with the chronology: letters are often dated with the year only or the month and year only, and the dates, again, are not infrequently wrong. Far worse, the text is highly inaccurate. The early handwriting of Meredith was firm and beautiful but not always easily legible. The later handwriting was infirm, crabbed, and often illegible, and an almost intuitive knowledge of Meredith's habits of expression is necessary to the reading of many of these letters. It is easy enough, I think, to account for the inaccuracies of the text in the published edition. Since the letters that are only legible to one thoroughly familiar with Meredith's hand and mind are as a rule more accurately transcribed than those in which the hand-writing offers no great problem, it seems clear, as implied in Will Meredith's advertisement, that he simply turned the letters over to a copyist, who struggled through them as best she could, putting aside those of which she could make nothing and getting assistance on them the next time Will was available. As Will was separated from his wife and was living in provincial hotels, usually in Devon, during the time of the editing, he was probably available very little. The inaccessibility of reference books in provincial towns may also have contributed to the slothfulness of the editing. The final defect in *Letters*, however, rests squarely upon his shoulders. Like his predecessors, nineteenth-century editors in general, he felt no obligation to print the letters as they were written: portions of letters are omitted without indication, names are omitted or indicated by initials only, and the text is sometimes edited for some particular reason, usually personal. That the punctuation is also edited seems to me a venial sin.

Any present-day editor of Meredith's letters must have mixed feelings about his obligation to Will Meredith. Undoubtedly he collected, printed, and so preserved numerous letters that might otherwise have been lost sight of for all time. On the other hand, he did one grave disservice to posterity: the originals of all the published letters to Frederick A. Maxse, John Morley, and Frederick Greenwood have disappeared from sight since they came into his hands. Far from returning letters promptly, as promised, he apparently did not return the letters to these correspondents at all. Searches of the premises of Messrs. Constable, to whom I fear I made myself a nuisance, inquiries of the survivors of these correspondents, appeals to the public through the columns of literary publications, inquiries of and by dealers in manuscripts, inquiries of public libraries and the private libraries known to me—all resulted in nothing. In the beginning the originals of the published letters to the Leslie Stephens were among those missing, and I confess that I long cherished the notion of a croquet box or a dusty bundle that might some day turn up somewhere; but the discovery of the Leslie Stephen letters in the hands of a private collector, several years ago, removed even that hope. In view of Will Meredith's deficiencies as editor and the importance of the three correspondents, the loss is serious. Fortunately, it was mitigated, just before going to press, by the further discovery of typed copies of the Maxse letters containing the omissions.

A year after the appearance of *Letters*, Thomas J. Wise printed *Letters from George Meredith to Edward Clodd and Clement K. Shorter*, a paper-back pamphlet containing a dozen letters and 'limited to thirty copies'. In common with all of Wise's publications, the number is suspect. In 1919, 1922, and 1924 respectively, Maurice Buxton Forman issued in similar format *Letters from George Meredith to Richard Henry Horne* (five letters), *Letters from George Meredith to A. C. Swinburne and Theodore Watts-Dunton* (twelve letters), and *Letters from George Meredith to Various Correspondents* (Vizetelly,

William Reeves, Frederick Sandys, Janet Ross, William Watson, Norman MacColl, Nora Senior, Luigi Ricci, Ford Madox Hueffer, and an Unnamed Correspondent—a total of seventeen letters). All were privately printed and supposedly limited to thirty copies. In 1919 Lady Butcher published her *Memories of George Meredith*, which contained a selection of Meredith's letters to her, not always accurately transcribed and frequently undated. In the same year S. M. Ellis, a relative of Meredith, published *George Meredith: His Life and Friends in Relation to His Work*. Ellis had permission to quote copyright material in his book, but when the Meredith Trustees found that more than a third of the book was comprised of copyright material, they took legal steps to enjoin sale of it. Contained in it were a number of Meredith's letters hitherto unavailable elsewhere. In the revised edition these letters were for the most part deleted. Finally, in 1923 appeared *The Letters of George Meredith to Alice Meynell*, beautifully and usually accurately printed by the Nonesuch Press and impeccably edited. Such, then, is the corpus of Meredith's published letters. Of course scattered letters are to be found in magazines, books, and newspapers, but except for the letters written to Hilda de Longueuil and published by R. E. Gordon George in the *Nineteenth Century* (February 1928) and by the same author under the name of Robert Esmonde Sencourt in *The Life of George Meredith* (1929), they have little sequence.

It has been my intention to bring together all of these printed letters and to add to them all of the unprinted letters that I could find and to publish them, for the convenience of anyone interested, in a body. In so doing, my primary consideration has always been to produce an accurate text, so that whenever possible I have worked from the original letter or a photographic copy of it even though it may have been previously printed. This naturally entailed writing to hundreds of public libraries and scores of private collectors; it also meant tracing or trying to trace the survivors of all known friends of Meredith; and it meant numerous visits to various libraries and to private holders of Meredith's letters in the United States and in England. Withal, the locating and obtaining of access to letters of Meredith all over the world was the most time-consuming of all the phases of the task. The difficulty of it has nevertheless been greatly reduced by the early interest of Mr. Frank Altschul in Meredith, which resulted in the great Altschul Collection of Meredith at Yale University, and by the acquisition of some hundreds of Meredith's letters by The University of Texas since the inception of the project. In comparison with the 767 letters appearing in *Letters*, slightly more than 2600 appear in this edition.

After an accurate text I have tried to provide an accurate chronology and such annotations as may be required to make the letters comprehensible to readers who may not always be Meredithians or Victorian specialists. I have therefore identified as many as possible of the people, books, and events alluded to in the letters. But even after laying under heavy tribute the libraries of the University of Texas, Yale, Harvard, and Cornell Universities, the New York and Boston Public Libraries, the Huntington Library, the Bodleian Library, and the British Museum, there have been times, regretted by no one so much as by me, when I had to admit failure.

I shall end by confessing that for me Meredith is a great novelist, occasionally a great poet, and a man of the greatest intellect among the Victorians, rivalled only in this respect by George Eliot. As such he has seemed to me deserving of an edition of his letters, as nearly complete as I could make it, accurately transcribed and properly edited. And this I have tried to do.

C. L. CLINE

ABBREVIATIONS AND SHORT TITLES

AC	*Altschul Catalogue.* (See Bibliography, Coolidge)
Boase	Frederic Boase (ed.), *Modern English Biography* (Truro, 1892, 1921)
BM	British Museum
BMC	*British Museum Catalogue*
CBEL	The *Cambridge Bibliography of English Literature* (Cambridge, 1940)
CHEL	The *Cambridge History of English Literature* (Cambridge, 1933)
C. & H.	Chapman & Hall
DNB	The *Dictionary of National Biography*
Ellis	S. M. Ellis, *George Meredith: His Life and Friends in Relation to His Work* (1919)
EC	The *English Catalogue*
EH	George Meredith, *Evan Harrington* (1860)
FR	The *Fortnightly Review*
HP	*The Hardman Papers.* (See Bibliography, Ellis)
IJ	The *Ipswich Journal*
ILN	The *Illustrated London News*
L. & M.	*The Letters and Memoirs of Sir William Hardman.* (See Bibliography, Ellis)
Letters	*Letters of George Meredith*, Collected and Edited by His Son (1912)
MVP	*A Mid-Victorian Pepys.* (See Bibliography, Ellis)
Modern Love, etc.	*Modern Love and Poems of the English Roadside*
OaW	*Once a Week*
PMG	The *Pall Mall Gazette*
P.O.D.	*Post Office Directory*
TLS	*The Times Literary Supplement*
Venn	J. A. Venn (ed.), *Alumni Cantabrigienses* (1940–54)
Whitaker	*Whitaker's Almanack*

SELECTED BIBLIOGRAPHY

Books in English published in London, books in French published in Paris, books in German published in Berlin unless otherwise noted.

ARTHUR, SIR GEORGE (ed.), *The Letters of Lord and Lady Wolseley* (1922)

AUSTIN, ALFRED, *The Autobiography of Alfred Austin* (1911)

BATTERSEA, CONSTANCE, *Reminiscences* (1922)

BAYLEN, JOSEPH O., 'George Meredith and W. T. Stead: Three Unpublished Letters', *Huntington Library Quarterly*, xxiv (1960)

——'George Meredith and W. T. Stead: Two Unpublished Letters', *Texas Studies in Literature and Language*, Spring (1962)

BENECKE, ADELAIDE (Mrs. ALFRED), *Memories of the Past* (privately printed, 1900)

BOASE, FREDERIC, *Modern English Biography* (Truro, 1892, 1921)

BOOTH, BRADFORD A., *The Letters of Anthony Trollope* (Oxford, 1951)

BRACKENBURY, GEN. SIR HENRY, *Some Memories of My Spare Time* (1909)

BRIGHT, J. S., *History of Dorking* (Dorking, 1884)

BURNAND, (SIR) FRANCIS, *Records and Reminiscences* (1904)

BUTCHER, LADY, *Memories of George Meredith* (N.Y., 1919)

CARR, J. COMYNS, *Coasting Bohemia* (1914)

——*Some Eminent Victorians* (1908)

CARR, MRS. J. COMYNS, *Mrs. J. Comyns Carr's Reminiscences* (?1926)

CLINE, C. L., 'The Betrothal of George Meredith to Marie Vulliamy', *Nineteenth Century Fiction*, xvi (1961)

CLODD, EDWARD, *Grant Allen: A Memoir* (1900)

——*Memories* (1916)

COHEN, LUCY, *Lady De Rothschild And Her Daughters, 1821–1931* (1935)

COLVIN, (SIR) SIDNEY, *Memories and Notes of Persons and Places* (N.Y., 1921)

CONNELL, JOHN (JOHN HENRY ROBERTSON), *W. E. Henley* (1949)

COOLIDGE, BERTHA, *A Catalogue of the Altschul Collection of George Meredith in the Yale University Library* (privately printed, 1931)

DOUGHTY, OSWALD, *A Victorian Romantic: Dante Gabriel Rossetti* (1960)

——and J. R. WAHL, *Letters of Dante Gabriel Rossetti* (1966)

EDEL, LEON AND DAN H. LAURANCE, *A Bibliography of Henry James* (1957)

ELLIS, S. M., George Meredith: *His Life and Friends in Relation to His Work* (1919)

——*The Letters and Memoirs of Sir William Hardman* (1925)

——*A Mid-Victorian Pepys* (1923)

——*William Harrison Ainsworth and his Friends* (1911)

——*The Hardman Papers* (1930)

EVERETT, EDWIN M., *The Party of Humanity: 'The Fortnightly Review' and its Contributors, 1865–1874* (Chapel Hill, 1939)

FORMAN, MAURICE BUXTON, *A Bibliography of George Meredith* (Edinburgh, 1922)

——*George Meredith and 'The Monthly Observer'* (privately printed, 1911)

——*Letters from George Meredith to Richard Henry Horne* (privately printed, 1919)

——*Letters from George Meredith to A. C. Swinburne and Theodore Watts-Dunton* (privately printed, 1922)

——*Letters from George Meredith to Various Correspondents* (privately printed, 1924)

——*Meredithiana* (Edinburgh, 1924)

GALLAND, RENÉ, *George Meredith: les cinquante premières années* (1923)

GWYNN, STEPHEN AND GERTRUDE M. TUCKWELL, *The Life of the Rt. Hon. Sir Charles W. Dilke* (1917)

HAIGHT, GORDON S. (ed.), *The George Eliot Letters* (New Haven, 1955)

——'George Meredith and the Westminster Review', *Modern Language Review*, liii (1958)

HAKE, THOMAS AND ARTHUR COMPTON-RICKETT, *The Life and Letters of Theodore Watts-Dunton* (1916)

HALDANE, ELIZABETH S., *From One Century to Another* (1937)

HAMMERTON, J. A., *George Meredith in Anecdote and Criticism* (1909)

HERGENHAN, L. T., *A Critical Consideration of the Reviewing of the Novels of George Meredith, from 'The Shaving of Shagpat' to 'The Egoist'* (Univ. of London dissertation, 1960)

HIRST, F. W., *Early Life and Letters of John Morley* (1927)

History of 'The Times', The (1939)

HUDSON, RICHARD B., 'Meredith's Autobiography and *The Adventures of Harry Richmond*', *Nineteenth Century Fiction*, ix (1954)

HYNDMAN, H. M., *The Record of an Adventurous Life* (New York, 1911)

LE GALLIENNE, RICHARD, *George Meredith: Some Characteristics* (1890)

JENKINS, ROY, *Sir Charles Dilke* (1958)

JOHNSON, EDGAR, *Charles Dickens* (N.Y., 1952)

LANG, CECIL Y., *The Swinburne Letters* (1959)

Letters of George Meredith to Alice Meynell, 1896–1907 (1923)

LEWIN, T. H., *The Lewin Letters* (1909)

LINDSAY, JACK, *George Meredith: His Life and Work* (1956)

LUCAS, E. V., *The Colvins and Their Friends* (N.Y., 1928)

LUCAS, REGINALD, *Lord Glenesk and the 'Morning Post'* (1910)

McCABE, JOSEPH, *Edward Clodd, A Memoir* (1932)

McKAY, GEORGE L., *A Stevenson Library: Catalogue of a Collection of Writings by and about Robert Louis Stevenson formed by Edwin J. Beinecke* (New Haven, 1958)

MACKAY, MONA, *Meredith et la France* (1937)

MAITLAND, FREDERIC WILLIAM, *The Life and Letters of Leslie Stephen* (1906)

MATZ, B. W., 'George Meredith as Publisher's Reader', *FR*, xcii (1909)

Maxse Papers, The: A Catalogue, (ed.) Francis W. Steer (Chichester, 1964)

MEREDITH, W. M., *Letters of George Meredith*, Collected and Edited by His Son (1912)

MEYNELL, VIOLA, *Alice Meynell: A Memoir* (1929)

MILNER, VISCOUNTESS, *My Picture Gallery: 1886–1901* (1951)

MONYPENNY AND BUCKLE, *The Life of Benjamin Disraeli* (1910–20)

MOORE, T. AND D. C. STURGE, *Works and Days from the Journal of Michael Field* (1933)

O'SHEA (PARNELL), KATHERINE, *Charles Stewart Parnell: His Love Story and Political Life* (1914)

PALMER, GLADYS, *Relations and Complications* (c. 1929)

QUILTER, HARRY (ed.) George Meredith, *Jump to Glory Jane* (1892)

RAY, GORDON NORTON, *The Letters and Private Papers of William Makepeace Thackeray* (Cambridge, Mass., 1946)

Recreations of the Rabelais Club, 1882–1885 (printed for members)

ROSS, JANET DUFF GORDON, *The Fourth Generation* (1912)

SALT, HENRY S., *Seventy Years Among Savages* (1921)

SCOTT, J. W. ROBERTSON, *The Story of the 'Pall Mall Gazette'* (Oxford, 1950)

SENCOURT, ROBERT ESMONDE, *The Life of George Meredith* (1929)

SEWELL, FATHER BROCARD, *Two Friends: John Gray and André Raffalovich* (1963)

SHARP, ELIZABETH A., *William Sharp (Fiona Macleod): A Memoir* (1912)

SHORTER, CLEMENT K., *C.K.S.: An Autobiography* (1923)

STEUART, JOHN A., *Robert Louis Stevenson: A Critical Biography* (Boston, 1924)

STEVENSON, LIONEL, *The Ordeal of George Meredith* (N.Y., 1953)

SULLY, JAMES, *My Life and Friends: A Psychologist's Memories* (1918).

SYMONS, ARTHUR, 'George Meredith: With Some Unpublished Letters', *FR*, cxix (1923)

TINSLEY, WILLIAM, *Random Recollections of an Old Publisher* (1900)

TOBIN, A. J. AND ELMER GERTZ, *Frank Harris: A Study in Black and White* (Chicago, 1931)

TREVELYAN, G. M., *British History in the Nineteenth Century* (1934)

WATERFIELD, GORDON, *Lucie Duff Gordon* (N.Y., 1937)

WAUGH, ARTHUR, *A Hundred Years of Publishing* (1930)

WINSTEN, STEPHEN, *Salt and His Circle* (1951)

WISE, THOMAS J., *Letters from George Meredith to Edward Clodd and Clement K. Shorter* (privately printed, 1913)

CHRONOLOGY OF
GEORGE MEREDITH

1828	Birth on 12 February at Portsmouth
1842–4	Schooling at the Moravian School at Neuwied on the Rhine
1845	Apprenticeship to Richard S. Charnock, solicitor
1849	Marriage to Mary Ellen Peacock Nicolls, 9 August
1851	*Poems*
1853	Birth of a son, Arthur Gryffydh, 13 June
1856 [1855]	*The Shaving of Shagpat: An Arabian Entertainment*
1857	*Farina: A Legend of Cologne*
1858	Elopement of Mary Ellen Meredith with Henry Wallis
1859	*The Ordeal of Richard Feverel*
1861	Death of Mary Ellen Meredith, October
1861	*Evan Harrington*
1862	*Modern Love . . . With Poems and Ballads*
1864	Marriage to Marie Vulliamy, 20 September
1864	*Emilia in England* (later renamed *Sandra Belloni*)
1865	*Rhoda Fleming*
1865	Birth of a son, William Maxse, 26 July
1867	*Vittoria*
1871	Birth of a daughter, Marie Eveleen, 10 June
1871	*The Adventures of Harry Richmond*
1876 [1875]	*Beauchamp's Career*
1877	Lecture on 'Comedy and Uses of the Comic Spirit', 2 February
1879	*The Egoist*
1880	*The Tragic Comedians*
1883	*Poems and Lyrics of the Joy of Earth*
1885	*Diana of the Crossways*
1885	Death of Marie Meredith, 17 September
1887	*Ballads and Poems of Tragic Life*
1888	*A Reading of Earth*
1891	*One of Our Conquerors*
1892	*Poems: The Empty Purse . . . and Verses*
1894	*Lord Ormont and His Aminta*
1895	*The Amazing Marriage*

1898	*Odes in Contribution to the Song of French History*
1901	*A Reading of Life*
1905	The Order of Merit conferred by order of the King
1909	Death, 18 May
1909	*Last Poems,* posthumous
1910	*Celt and Saxon,* posthumous novel

1. *To* R. M. HILL[1]

Text: *Letters of George Meredith*, Collected and Edited by His Son (1912), i. 3–4 (dated *8 July 1844*).

Neuwied
January 1, 1844[2]

My dear Hill,

   During the time that we've lived together, one feeling, whether in union, or shall I say enmity, no that is too harsh, has agitated our respective bosoms. It is fellowship. O may God grant that all may have the same feeling towards you to make your life happy. But true fellowship is not to be had without Christianity; not the name but the practice of it. I wish you the greatest of all things 'God's blessing', which comprehends all I would or could otherwise say.

Yours,
George Meredith

2. *To* R. H. HORNE[1]

MS.: Ashley Library, British Museum. Printed: *Letters from George Meredith to Richard Henry Horne* (privately printed, Cape Town, 1919), pp. 5–6; published: Maurice Buxton Forman, *A Bibliography of George Meredith* (Edinburgh, 1922), p. xx; excerpt published: Lionel Stevenson, *The Ordeal of George Meredith* (N.Y., 1953), p. 27.

7 Upper Ebury Street, Pimlico
March 8, 1849

Sir,

   You are a Poet and a Critic, and from certain of your writings I understand your sympathies in either phase to be with the young

---

1. [1] A schoolmate of GM's at the Moravian School at Neuwied on the Rhine which GM had entered on 18 Aug. 1842 (*Letters*, i. 3).
   [2] In one of his two personal copies of *Letters* (Bodleian Library) W. M. Meredith has altered the date from 8 July to 1 Jan., in keeping with his statement (i. 4) that GM left Neuwied on 7 Jan. 1844. If that statement is correct, this letter was written by GM at about the time of his departure, just short of his sixteenth birthday, but it is possible that Hill, not GM, was the one leaving school.
2. [1] In between 1844 and 1849 little is known of the life of GM. It is known that he was articled, on 3 Feb. 1846, to Richard S. Charnock, a solicitor of Paternoster Row, for five years; that he never took seriously to the study of law but began the writing of verse before he was nineteen; and that he was one of a small group who, in 1848–9, wrote, edited, and circulated among themselves a manuscript magazine called the *Monthly Observer*. By the age of twenty, then, it would seem that GM had determined upon a literary career, the first practical step of realizing which, perhaps, was this letter to Horne. (See Stevenson, pp. 16–27.)

Poet—As this is a fact seldom found even among literary men I have taken the liberty to address myself thus abruptly[2] to you—

I wish to lay before you certain Poems I have composed that I may obtain your opinion (In which I can trust) as to their merit—or more especially—the power of the Poetic Faculty in me.

If this request should occupy too much of your valuable time (the fruits of which I am very happy to have known) I shall of course be contented to understand such to be the case—but if you really can and will assist me with your advice I shall be exceedingly indebted and obliged to you.

In which case I would immediately forward you some finished specimens for perusal.

I have the honour to be / Sir / Your very obedient Servant,

George Meredith

3. *To* R. H. HORNE

MS.: Berg Collection, New York Public Library. Printed: *Letters from GM to RHH*, p. 7.

7 Upper Ebury Street, Pimlico
May 10, 1849

Dear Sir,

I have succeeded in obtaining Göthe's Minor Poems which you expressed a wish to have—on the day I had the honour of being introduced to you; will you therefore oblige me by accepting them— I am still in doubt whether you meant a translation of them or the originals which I *have* sent, but from your 'Geist des Felsen bei'm Drachenfels' and 'Dichters Antwort'[1] I presume you to be intimate with the German.

2. Richard Henry (or Hengist) Horne (1803–84), the man to whom he appealed for help, was at various times adventurer, editor, man of letters, and government employee. His report as commissioner charged with studying the employment of children in mines and factories in the early forties had inspired Elizabeth Barrett's poem, 'The Cry of the Children'. But it was as the author of *Orion, an Epic Poem in Ten Books* (3 edns. in 1843) that Horne had attracted the attention of GM. Horne was a prolific writer on a number of subjects in his day, but even *Orion* is now remembered only as a curiosity.

The sympathy with which GM's petition met and the value of Horne's aid to him may be gauged by the facts that GM's *Poems* (1851) appeared with a ten-line quotation from *Orion* on the title-page and that GM sent a copy to Horne, inscribed 'To R. H. Horne, Esq.ʳᵉ by whose generous appreciation and trusty criticism these "Poems" were chiefly fostered, George Meredith' (Forman, *Bibliography*, p. 10).

2 GM wrote *abrubtly.*

3. 1 These are presumed by Eri J. Shumaker (*A Concise Bibliography of the Complete Works of Richard H. Horne*, Granville, Ohio, 1943, p. vi) to be 'missing Horne items' in the bibliography, and I too have been unable to find them.

Meantime let me take this opportunity of thanking you for the
instruction you have already given me in the Art. I believe that I am
now *steadily* improving—I have but flickered heretofore.

With every respect / Believe me / Dear Sir / Most thankfully etc. etc.,

George Meredith

4. *To* MESSRS. CHAMBERS[1]

MS.: Huntington Library.

7 Upper Ebury Street, Pimlico,
London

June 4, 1849

Gentlemen:

I have sent you the enclosed Poem[2] in the hope that it will be acceptable to your Journal. It was written immediately on receipt of the
intelligence whereof it chaunts, and will I think even now, find many
an echo in hearts akin to the subject and the name which christens it.

If you are not overstocked with engagements for poetical contributions—I should be very glad to supply you regularly.

I have the honour to be / Gentlemen / Your obedient Servant,

George Meredith

5. *To* LEITCH RITCHIE[1]

MS.: Yale. Excerpt published: Forman, *Bibliography*, p. xxii.

7 Upper Ebury Street, Pimlico,
London

June 12, 1849

Dear Sir,

I am obliged by your acceptance of the Poem—Would a translation
of the life etc. etc. of *Kossuth the Magyar*[2] suit the columns of your

4. [1] Robert and William Chambers, proprietors of *Chambers's Edinburgh Journal.*
    [2] 'Chillianwallah', inspired by a battle in the second Sikh War (13 Jan. 1849) and
originally contributed by Meredith to the *Monthly Observer*. (See Note 1, Letter 2, and
Maurice Buxton Forman, *George Meredith and 'The Monthly Observer'*, privately printed,
1911.) Stevenson (p. 28) says that the poem was 'revised and shortened' on advice of
Horne.
5. [1] Leitch Ritchie (1800–65), novelist, journalist, editor. In 1849 he was co-editor of
Chambers's Journal.
    [2] Lajos or Louis Kossuth (1802–94), leader of the Hungarian insurrection of 1848–9.

journal? I could abridge it for one number even—or give it literally—Either as a translation or in the shape of an Essay I propose it—The accounts of the man now afloat are flimsy and unconnected and I think this would be acceptable.

May I beg you to substitute for *'hearts'* in the 7th line of the last verse of *'Chillianwallah' 'hopes'*—

Thus

'And the *hopes* of all will languish'

I have the honour to be / Dear Sir, / Very truly, Yours,

George Meredith

6. *To* FERENC (FRANCIS) PULSZKY[1]

Text: typed copy furnished by Mr. Stephen Gál of Budapest. Published: Eugene Horváth *Southeastern Affairs*, vii (1937), p. 207; B. G. Ívanyi, *TLS* ('Letters to the Editor'), 12 Nov. 1954.

[London]
June 30, 1849

Sir:

The very great sympathy which I feel to the cause and towards the people of Hungary, bade me to take this liberty of thus addressing you.

I read in the *Daily News* of yesterday 29 June that 'a body of fifty nine Hungarian Soldiers escaped from the Austrian Army in Italy, had arrived at Boulogne and were by order of the French minister to be shipp'd in the South Eastern Companies Steamer for Folkestone'.

Now I wish to ask—as the poor fellows arriving in England—whether any lodgment, place of abode, money or friends will be ready to meet them? And if not—the sympathy of our countrymen to their nation is sufficiently strong, to induce me to propose a subscription, to which I would heartily give my mite—Lord Dudley Stuart[2] and Mr. W. S. Landor[3] would I should imagine, be the first to head so noble

---

6. [1] Ferenc Pulszky (1814–97), writer, historian, statesman, sent in 1848 to London as Kossuth's representative to the British government. There with the help of leading authors, historians, and scientists he organized a Hungarian Propaganda Committee. Ívanyi sees in this letter 'signs of that intense intellectual curiosity and rigorous impartiality which were to distinguish the master of the dispassionate, realistic approach' and thinks that curiosity and impartiality account for GM's delay in completing the article on Kossuth. (See Note 1, following letter.)

[2] Lord Dudley Coutts Stuart (1803–54) acquired from his mother strong feelings of sympathy for the oppressed, especially the Poles (*DNB*). The assistance given the Emperor of Austria by Nicholas I of Russia in suppressing the Hungarian insurrection would have given Lord Dudley a more than normal interest in the insurrectionists.

[3] Landor had demonstrated his sympathy for the oppressed in 1808, when he raised a band of volunteers at his own expense and went to Spain to free it from Bonaparte (*Chambers's Biographical Dictionary*).

a charity or call it no charity—free offering and breaking of bread
from brother to brother I should rather say—For myself I am too
poor and too unknown to begin such a thing as this, otherwise I would
instantly set it afloat. If General Aulich[4] should occupy Fiume, we
could easily transmit money and Stores, besides these gallant Soldiers
to him—

I should be very glad to call on you, if your time is not too occupied,
and gain some little intelligence as to the campaign—as the *Wiener
Zeitung* from its false reports, is a continual source of irritation to me
and besides I wish to learn many things about Kossuth and to know
whether it is distance only which gives him the halo—

Trusting however you [will] let me know what (if any) arrangements have been made etc. etc.

I have the honour to be—Sir / with much respect and esteem—/
Your obedient Servant—

George Meredith

7. *To* LEITCH RITCHIE

Text: S. M. Ellis, *George Meredith: His Life and Friends in Relation to His Work* (1919),
p. 47; excerpt published: Forman, *Bibliography*, p. xxii, from which the heading of the
letter is taken.

22 John Street, Adelphi,
Strand, London
Care of T. L. Peacock, Esq.
November 30, 1849

[Dear Sir,]

I send you four sheet pages of *Kossuth*.[1] ... I trust it is not too late—
but the fact is I was determined to ascertain if the character of Kossuth
was as fine as ... I had imagined. ... You are at liberty to erase *all*
passages which suit not the purpose or politics of the Journal.

I accompany this with some Sonnets on Two Kings of England,[2]
which may if you like form a series.

---

4 Ludwig Aulich (1795–1849), Hungarian general and Minister of War; one of thirteen
generals executed by the Austrians after the Hungarian surrender (*New Century Cyclopedia
of Names*).

7. 1 On 9 Aug. 1849 GM and Mary Ellen Peacock Nicolls, daughter of Thomas Love
Peacock and widow of a young naval lieutenant, were married at St. George's, Hanover
Square. Brilliant, erratic, and six or seven years older than GM, she was one of the editor-
contributors conducting the *Monthly Observer*. Stevenson (p. 30) thinks that it was their
honeymoon that delayed the projected life of Kossuth until the defeat of the Hungarians
and the flight of Kossuth made it no longer topical.

2 One of these was doubtless 'John Lackland', published in *Poems* (1851). *Chambers's*
did not publish any of the sonnets.

I have been contemplating a sketch of the life of Hermann[3] who has lately died. There is as yet no English account.

8. *To* LEITCH RITCHIE

MS.: Yale. Excerpts published: Forman, *Bibliography*, pp. xxii, 7.

London
December 1, 1849

Dear Sir,

I find I have forgotten to enclose the Sonnets mentioned in my letter of yesterday's date containing the first four sheet pages of Kossuth and I send them herewith—I think they would do very well if taken in a series and I have a great many already finished. Let me know about the article on Hermann as early as you can as the sooner that is printed the better.

I have the honour to be / Dear Sir / Most faithfully yours,

George Meredith

9. *To* R. H. HORNE

Text: *Letters*, i. 5–6.

[1849 or 1850]

To R. H. H. with 'Daphne'[1]

That you will take the meaning of this verse
I know, deep-hearted friend and earnest man,
Poet! and thro' the simple picture see
The winged fancy rising from the flower!
Too delicate for me to touch, or do
Aught but suggest; send forth as Nature sends
The unfettered insects fluttering with delight
Thro' the long warm blue summer's day and folded
At eve behind some rainy leaf, while the woods
Sing wet with Tempest—On its wings alone

---

7. [3] Johann Gottfried Jakob Hermann (1772–1848), philologist and classical scholar of international reputation. Peacock speaks of him as one to whom he was 'especially indebted' (Carl Van Doren, *The Life of Thomas Love Peacock*, 1911, p. 16). *Chambers's* did not publish the article on Hermann, which may never have been written.

9. [1] GM's long poem 'Daphne', mentioned in Letter 11, was first published in *Poems* (1851).

Let it depend when once the warm-fingered sun
Has touched it into life—Enough for me
To paint the flower in all its natural hues
And plant it; this done, its fate is with the sky.
But you will know how in these after days,
First love still follows the fair, fleeting shape!
From the flush'd morning wave and woodland valley
Urging its wild pursuit, while[2] still in vain
Swift Nature lends her forces, still in vain
The old prophetic trees wave overhead—
Ah! happy he whose last inspired desire
Conquering its anguish shall have power to pluck
The never-fading laurel! Round his brows
Sweet Beauty hovers and a dawning gleam
Wakes ever on the leaves, for they are steep'd
I' the springs of day, and therefore do we mark
This strange foreshadowed crown of poet love,
The crown of poet passion. Thus to you
I dedicate, and in your hands I place
Daphne, the darling of my own first love.
So take her, part in friendship, but indeed
Chiefly a tribute to the noble lyre
Which sang of the giant bright whose starry limbs
Still scale the midnight Heavens and plant aloft
Heroic footsteps up untravelled space!
Live long and wear that constellated wreath.

10. *To* JAMES VIZETELLY[1]

MS.: The Historical Society of Pennsylvania.

Weybridge, Surrey[2]
Osborne's Hotel, Adelphi
January 15, 1850

Sir,
Mr. Horne has had the kindness to speak to you about a volume of

2 Professor Phyllis Bartlett, of Queen's College, has called my attention to the omission of *while*, necessary for the metre, in the printed text. The correction, which I owe to her, is made from the MS. in the Altschul Collection, Yale University.
10. 1 James Vizetelly (1817–97), with his brother Henry, engaged in both printing and publishing. Eventually Vizetelly & Company printed GM's *Poems*, with John W. Parker & Son as publisher.
2 The Merediths had taken lodgings at 'The Limes', Weybridge, across the Thames from Mary Ellen's father at Lower Halliford (Stevenson, p. 31). This letter was apparently written while GM was in London for a day or two.

Poems which I am desirous of publishing in the style of Tennyson[3]—
I should like to see you on the subject myself if you can hold yourself
disengaged to-morrow at 12 o'clock a.m. or I will (if this should not
suit you) attend any appointment you may make. I am

Your obedient Servant,
George Meredith

11. *To* JOHN W. PARKER[1]

MS.: Yale. Published: *Letters*, i. 7–8, with minor variants.

Weybridge
December 12, 1850

My dear Sir,

I send you a selection of Poems completed and a list of others from
which I intend selecting for the projected volume. Of the latter I prize
the 'Cassandra'[2] as my best work, but it is not yet finished. The 'Shipwreck of Idomeneus' is blank verse and 17 pages. The rest with exception of one or two of the Ballads are ready. Of the Poems I forward
you, I wish to have your opinion as early as you can give it—If you
think the specimens I forward you inferior to the 'requirements of the
age', 'not saleable' and so forth, I shall very likely be content to abide
by your decision for a time. Mr. Horne speaks very favourably of those
he has seen but he has only seen the classical Poem and a few others
and consequently insists on Ballad and modern ingredients which I
have endeavoured since then to supply—'Sorrows and Joys', 'The
Two Blackbirds', 'Infancy and Age'[3] are a selection from those published in *Household Words*. The two 'Blank verse metres' beginning
'How sweet on sunny afternoons'[4] are selections from half a dozen of
the sort, and will be *I* think the most original feature in the volume.

---

10. [3] Professor Geoffrey Tillotson has suggested to me that 'style' refers here to the manner of publication rather than of composition, and after examining original editions of
Tennyson's early publications, I am inclined to agree with him.

11. [1] Of John W. Parker & Son, 445 Strand. It is probable that GM addressed the father,
as senior partner, who had been superintendent of the Cambridge University Press
(1829–32) and had established his own business in London in 1832. In 1843 he was
joined by his son, John W. Parker, Junior (1820–60), who soon, if not from the beginning,
took over the negotiations with GM.

In May 1851 Parker published GM's *Poems* at the expense of the author. As the
correspondence shows (Letter 20) 500 copies were printed but only 100 bound. GM later
told Edward Clodd ('Some Recollections', *Fortnightly Review*, xcii, [July 1909] 23) that
he lost '£50 or £60 on the venture'.

[2] 'Cassandra' did not appear in *Poems*; it was first published in *Modern Love and
Poems of the English Roadside, with Poems and Ballads*, 1862.

[3] Not reprinted.   [4] Entitled 'Pastorals' in *Poems*.

Also 'London by Lamplight' has two or more numbers to follow (but shorter ones), if you think fit—Besides these I am writing a Ballad for *Household Words* which I think will be liked—I will tell you the subject when I see you. You will see that in the rape of Aurora I have followed the idea of Ariosto and invented a little mythology—The union of the Sun and the Dawn. And in 'Daphne' I have avoided mention of 'Dan Cupid'—I have other 'Pictures of the Rhine' but I thought six enough—

Thus far then I have explained the contents of the parcel, which as soon as you can peruse, do, and let me know your opinion thereon and thereafter, when I will have the pleasure of calling on you and consulting as to the birth and baptism of my firstborn of the Muse—

My dear Sir, / Yours very truly,

George Meredith

12. *To* JOHN W. PARKER

MS.: Berg Collection, New York Public Library. Excerpts published: Forman, *Bibliography*, p. 7, with variants.

Weybridge
Tuesday, December 17, 1850

Dear Sir,

I thank you for your very kind and candid exposition. Of course I can only feel obliged for the trouble you have taken—By publishing I scarcely expect any thing but loss; I know that a name must be successful before a book can. But to any achievement some first step must be made, both to the public and ourselves. In this first volume I hope to gain a *certain* position among those who best appreciate good poetry—Tennyson, whose name you quote, had, if I hear aright, but a doleful beginning—If I mistake not, none but 'the Judges' took notice of his maiden volume. I could cite many names—But this would be to no purpose now. True they encourage me to risk the publication, but in doing so I will not expect to see again what sum I may expend. You see, these Poems are on my mind; say that they have some little merit—I do not wish them therefore to die without one bold stroke to save themselves; if when left to themselves they have not vitality enough to survive, then I am content they should die.[1]

12. [1] For the sake of clarity I have inserted a semicolon after 'themselves'. Because of his irregular and incomplete education GM had not yet mastered the art of punctuation or the discipline of sentence-structure, and the deficiency is perhaps nowhere quite so obvious in the early letters as here.

And now I wish to ask you two things—supposing you to have time to read the Poems through; will you without reserve give me *your* opinion of their *merits*. Looking on them as the work of a young poet, one *not* to be discouraged and one who if like Apollo he misses the 'fleeting shape'[2] will be content with the laurels that some day or other he means to have*—Feel therefore especially certain that I can only feel grateful for all candid criticism—

Secondly (as I would rather you should publish for me than any other name and would therefore not willingly apply to any other person) will you tell me plainly whether (the whole risk etc. being mine) you would rather *not* publish my volume—The thing may happen naturally enough—either meagreness or over colouring or so forth and you have a name in the world. As for feeling offended which I think you fear I shall,—*that* is quite out of the question in any case and I shall perfectly understand your scruples—

I am / Dear Sir / Your obedient Servant,

George Meredith

* On looking this over I find I ought to have said 'hopes to have'.

13. *To* J. W. PARKER, JR.

MS.: Yale. Excerpts published: Forman, *Bibliography*, p. 8, with inaccuracies.

Weybridge
Monday morning, [December 23, 1850]

My dear Sir,

I am coming up to Town to spend the Christmas—and will call on you for the MSS. A literary friend of mine[1] has spoken to a printer[2] about the printing of my volume and the work will get up so as to do no discredit to your name. I say this presuming my fancy was groundless that you would object to publish it. But if in my last letter I did not thank you for the good sense, judgment, and kindly counsel of *your* letter to me—be sure it is not thrown away—I think I did not explain my meaning properly in my first letter to you—

If you should be out of Town will you leave out the parcel for me?

I am / My dear Sir / Yours very truly,

George Meredith

12. [2] Daphne.   13. [1] Horne.   [2] Vizetelly.

14. *To* JAMES VIZETELLY

Text (excerpt): American Art Association Catalogue (23 Apr. [n.y.]).

> Weybridge
> February 20, 1851

London by the lamplight I have quite cut to pieces. You will see I have transformed 'Midnight' into the 'Sleeping City' and 'Night' about half its original length stands now under the title of 'London by Lamplight'. 'Dusk of Eve' will not be published.

15. *To* JAMES VIZETELLY

MS.: University of Rochester.

> Weybridge
> [? February 1851]

Dear Sir,

I am coming up to Town on Wednesday—Pray endeavour to be disengaged in the morning and do *not* send any sheets, in the Interim, but have them ready by the time I come—

> Yours truly,
> George Meredith

16. *To* JAMES VIZETELLY

MS.: Yale. Printed: Bertha Coolidge, *A Catalogue of the Altschul Collection of George Meredith in the Yale University Library* (privately printed, 1931), p. 21.

> Weybridge
> [? February 1851]

Dear Sir,

I received this morning from Mr. Horne the proofs of 'Daphne' and the 'Wild Rose and Snowdrop' and am waiting to correct them when you send me a copy—I enclose you three more poems—'The Olive Branch', 'South West Wind in the Woodland' and 'Will o' the Wisp'. The rest shall shortly follow. Get these out of hand as soon as possible and I think there will be some chance of having the Poems out by the middle of next month—When I re-enclose the revised proofs to you do not make up any of the long slips into *pages* till the *order* in which they fall is settled—

Can you let me know how many pages the poems altogether that I have now sent would make?—and whether you think there would be room for the 'Shipwreck of Idomeneus'?[1]

Ever very faithfully,
George Meredith

17. *To* JAMES VIZETELLY

MS.: Yale. Published: Ellis, p. 55; printed: *Letters from George Meredith to Various Correspondents* (privately printed, Pretoria, 1924), p. 5.

Weybridge
[? February 1851]

My dear Sir,

If possible put the enclosed *Hexameters* among the 'pastorals'—that is to say, if not too late. Also 'Love in the Valley'—but separate the two—And put *neither first* among the pastorals—And let the Songs 'Spring'—'Autumn' be *last* among them. 'July' is to follow 'Antigone' and then 'Beauty Rohtraut'—[1]

I hope to hear from you to-morrow about 'Idomeneus' and that the volume will soon be finished.

Very truly,
George Meredith

18. *To* J. W. PARKER, JR.

Text: David Bonnell Green, 'George Meredith's "Austrian Poets": A Newly Identified Review Essay with Translations', *Modern Language Review*, liv (July 1959), 330–1.

Weybridge
March 18, 1851

My dear Sir,

Would you accept for *Fraser* some articles on the 'Austrian Poets'?[1] There are among them some rather remarkable men, not known as they deserve to be in England—The poets best known are Lenau

16. [1] Included in *Poems*.
17. [1] The directions were not carried out; probably it was too late.
18. [1] John W. Parker & Son were publishers of *Fraser's Magazine*, of which the younger Parker had been editor since about 1848. Green remarks (p. 331) that '*Fraser's* was apparently too "overpeopled and Malthusian" for a series of articles on the subject of Austrian poets and poetry, but room was found for one "compressed" article on the subject and "Austrian Poets" was published in the number for August 1852' (xlvi. 213–27).

(lately dead)² and Grillparzer,³ and neither of these have had a translator.⁴ Grillparzer is a great favourite with German scholars and deservedly—He is a dramatic Poet and Lenau a lyric Poet. I should propose to write a small sketch of the life of each, and a summary of their powers; giving a translation of the smallest and most characteristic of their poems, or in the dramatic poets, the most striking scene—

Now, these articles I propose, could be written in a series of twelve, of six, or even more compressed—

I shall be in town on the 24th and will call on you, but have the kindness to let me know by return of post, whether you could accept any, or one, and I will bring it with me—And—if it would not be requiring too much—would you tell me (supposing my proposition not practicable) what kind of subject *Fraser* is in want of? or haply she is overpeopled and Malthusian. For the Fact is, that, for the space of a few months, I want to obtain some literary engagement or labour of some kind, but do not want to change residence [*of*, crossed out] to London, which I should have to do in the event of throwing myself upon a Journal—and *then* where is Parnassus?

I regret that the 'poems' will not be out before the end of March⁵— when I see you I shall want to arrange with you about advertisements etc. and your advice as to the best papers and periodicals, to send copies; though trust me to be quite prepared for all the 'merciful' flaying alive so prevalent just now—worse than the worst days of Gifford and the *Quarterly*—Indeed Kingsley and one or two others are the only critics whose corrections I should attend to.

And now that May is coming, may we calculate on some of your company for that month? Or are you too much engaged and enamoured of motley in Hyde Park?

I presume that you received some 'proofs' from Vizetelly, as I desired him to send them—

Very truly, / My dear Sir, / Yours,

George Meredith

² Nikolaus Lenau (pseudonym of Nikolaus Niembsch von Strehlenau, 1802–50).
³ Franz Grillparzer (1791–1872). Professor Bartlett calls my attention to the fact that the MS. of the Grillparzer article is extant in a notebook in the Altschul Collection, Yale.
⁴ An error, as Green points out: 'a number of Grillparzer's plays had been translated in whole or in part, and a number of Lenau's poems had appeared in English periodicals' (p. 330 n.).
⁵ Actually it was May.

19. *To* CHARLES KINGSLEY[1]

Text (fragment): Margaret Farrand Thorp, *Charles Kingsley* (Princeton, 1937), p. 51, except for the last sentence, supplied by Mrs. Thorp from her notes.

Weybridge
[? April 1851]

I am driven with a spur to tell you the delight and admiration with which I read your last book *Yeast*, and the positive 'Education' I have derived from it. It was the very book I was in want of and likely to do me more good than any that I know. May it do a great service in the world. . . .

20. *To* JAMES VIZETELLY

MS.: Yale. Published: Forman, *Bibliography*, p. 8, with minor variants; N.Y. *Evening Post* (13 July 1907).

Weybridge
Thursday—noon, [May 22, 1851]

Dear Sir,

Will you have the kindness to send me your account for the printing (*500* copies) together with the binding of *100* volumes *immediately?* as I am anxious to know whether the amount has overstept my calculations, or not—I trust the publishing of the volume will not be delayed beyond *Saturday* and that I shall receive a volume from you on Sunday morning? Not receiving the Dedication and Title page has made me fear another delay—

Yours, very truly,
George Meredith

21. *To* JAMES VIZETELLY

MS.: Yale. Envelope postmarked *Weybridge* and *Chertsey, My 26 1851.*

Weybridge
[May 26, 1851]

Dear Sir,

I am sorry to say I discover a great many new and original mistakes in my book* of which both the MS. and proofs were utterly guiltless.

*I must also complain of non attention to my correction of proofs.

19. ¹ Charles Kingsley (1819–75), Rector of Eversley, whose novels, as well as articles contributed to the *Christian Socialist*, had given him an established literary position. *Yeast*, published in *Fraser's* (July–Dec. 1848), had been cut short at the request of the proprietors but was published in book form by them in 1851. (It was reviewed in the 19 Apr. issue of the *Athenaeum*.) Probably GM wrote this letter before sending Kingsley a copy of *Poems*.

I suppose it is of no service capitulating them now. I shall probably see you next week and will point them—With the printing I cannot but be very pleased—It is faultless and excellent—If you have a copy by you quite ready (bound etc.) send it *at once* to Dr. Mackay[1] at the *Illustrated News* for review in my name and you will oblige me very much.

Very truly, Dear Sir,
George Meredith

22. *To* J. Everett Millais[1]

Text: Admiral Sir William James, *The Order of Release* (1948), p. 174.

Weybridge, Surrey
[? May 1851]

I called on you this morning to tell you what great delight your paintings have given me. For, as I live in the country, I could not wait for an introduction to you, which I should otherwise have desired.

I left at your residence a book of my own just published, if you will oblige me by accepting it as a testimony of the admiration in which I hold your genius.

In 'Mariana' you have, as I understand, greatly conceived a great poet; in the 'Woodman's daughter' wonderfully embellished a small one. Both are exquisite.

23. *To* Edmund Ollier[1]

MS.: Berg Collection, New York Public Library. Envelope postmarked *Weybridge*, without date, and *Kingston, Jy 9 1851*. Excerpts published: Stevenson, p. 38; Ellis, pp. 56–57.

Weybridge, Surrey
[July 8 or 9, 1851]

My dear Sir,

Permit me to reply to your very kind letter. It is the appreciation you give that makes Fame worth working for; nor would I barter such communications for any amount of favourable Journal criticism, however much it might forward the popularity and sale of the book—

21. [1] Charles Mackay (1814–89), LL.D., editor of the *Illustrated London News* (1849–59) and song-writer.
22. [1] (Sir) John Everett Millais (1829–96), Pre-Raphaelite painter who exhibited three pictures at the Royal Academy in 1851. 'Mariana', which GM mentions, illustrated a scene from Tennyson's poem of the name, and 'The Woodman's Daughter' was suggested by Coventry Patmore's poem 'The Tale of Poor Maud'.
23. [1] Edmund Ollier (1827–86), son of the publisher of Shelley and Keats. He contributed verses to periodicals and edited *The Essays of Elia*, with a memoir of Lamb. Like GM at this time, Ollier was something of a disciple of Horne.

I prepared myself, when I published, to meet with injustice and slight—
knowing that the little collection or rather selection in my volume was
but the vanguard of a better work to come; and knowing, also, that
the severest criticism could scarcely be more unsparing than myself
on the faults that are freely to be found; knowing lastly, that a first
volume (of poetry) is with the Press a marked book; but some beginning must be made. The poems are all the work of extreme youth, and,
with some exceptions, of labour. They will not live, I think; but they
will serve their purpose in making known my name to those who look
with encouragement upon such earnest students of nature who are
determined to persevere until they attain the wisdom and inspiration
and self-possession of the poet. I trust that my next work will be a
nearer advance to that aim.

What you say of my blank octo-syllabic may be true, and is quite
just; but the 'S. W. Wind in the Woodland'—in which I used it—is
a subject which, in my opinion, would have been marred by rhyme—
Nor could I find any other (better) mode of giving my impression of
the reckless rushing rapidity, and sweeping sound of the great wind
among the foliage which I felt impelled to do in such manner that the
ear should only be conscious of swiftness, and no sweetness; and that
there should be no direct pause throughout. This (in my mind) the
hurrying measure of the four feet gives. The blank 'stanzas' are more
open to objection I admit. Believe me, I venerate English Poetry too
much to wish to make any innovation on the old majestic metre of
Epic, Pastoral, and Drama; I used it for a purpose; for such a purpose
I would use it again, but only for such a purpose and under such
a plea—

Trust me, / My dear Sir, / Yours very truly,

George Meredith

24. *To* ALFRED TENNYSON[1]

Text: Hallam, Lord Tennyson, *Tennyson and His Friends* (1912), p. 131, dated *January 1851.*

[Southend, Essex]
[? July 1851][2]

Sir:

When I tell you that it would have been my chief ambition in publish-

24. [1] Tennyson had already attained the position of highest distinction among the poets
of his day, as manifested by his succession to the laureateship in Nov. 1850, so that it was
natural that he should receive one of the complimentary copies of *Poems.* 'As Meredith
told me himself,' writes Lord Tennyson (p. 131), 'Tennyson replied with an exceedingly
kind and "pretty" letter, saying that there was one poem in the book he could have wished
he had written, and inviting Meredith to come to see him.' (For an account of GM's dis-
illusioning visit, see Stevenson, pp. 39–40.)

[2] Lord Tennyson's date for this letter, Jan. 1851, is obviously incorrect, antedating as

ing the little volume of poems you have received, to obtain your praise, you may imagine what pride and pleasure your letter gave me; though, indeed, I do not deserve so much as your generous appreciation would bestow, and of this I am very conscious. I had but counted twenty-three years when the book was published, which may account for, and excuse perhaps many of the immaturities. When you say you would like to know me, I can scarcely trust myself to express with how much delight I would wait upon you—a privilege I have long desired. As I suppose the number of poetic visits you receive are fully as troublesome as the books, I will not venture to call on you until you are able to make an appointment. My residence and address is Weybridge, but I shall not return to Town from Southend before Friday week. If in the meantime you will fix any day following that date, I shall gladly avail myself of the honour of your invitation. My address here is care of Mrs. Peacock, Southend, Essex. I have the honour to be, most faithfully yours,

George Meredith

25. *To* A. J. Scott[1]

MS.: University of Texas. Published: Maurice Buxton Forman, *Meredithiana* (Edinburgh, 1924), p. 307 (derived from C. Richardson's Catalogue No. 93, Manchester, 1924, p. 13), with inaccuracies.

Weybridge
Thursday, [? July–August 1851]

My dear Sir,

I regret much that I should have trusted to the Printer for sending you my volume. I have now desired Mr. Parker to forward one to Gloster Crescent, which he will not fail to do, I know.—The Printer's directions were to send to Dr. Gully,[2] Malvern.

it does the publication of *Poems*. The present Lord Tennyson informs me that the original letter cannot be found but that the date on his grandfather's copy is Jan. 1851. I suggest that *July*, in GM's hand, was misread as *Jany*, a usual Victorian abbreviation.

25. [1] A. J. Scott (1805–66), unorthodox minister and teacher, was Professor of English Language and Literature at University College, London, from 1848 to 1851, when he became the first Principal of Owens College, Manchester. A learned man and an eloquent lecturer, he preached on Sunday evenings and lectured on Wednesday evenings for a number of years. It is clear from this letter that GM had been attracted to his lectures and that there was a personal connexion with the Scott family.

[2] James Manby Gully (1808–83), M.D. Edinburgh, 1829, practised medicine in London (1830–42) and later at Malvern (1842–71). He was the author of *The Water Cure in Chronic Disease* (1846, 6th ed. 1859) and of *The Lady of Belleisle*, a drama produced at Drury Lane in 1839. Frederic Boase (*Modern English Biography*, Truro, 1892) says that he appears as Dr. Gullson in Charles Reade's *It Is Never Too Late to Mend* (1857). In 1861 George Eliot wrote of him as a quack (Gordon S. Haight, *The George Eliot Letters*, New Haven, 1954, ii. 472).

Since it is some time that you have received my letter, you will permit me to repeat that, the contents of the volume are the work of extreme youth, and I desire them to be considered more as *indications*, than accomplishments. For I would not have published at all without firm faith that I should one day produce better. In short, I would have given forth no volume bearing the title of *Poems* without full belief (and such a consciousness may be felt in all humility) that I was a Poet. I am therefore the more conscious how little I have done; the more anxious to know myself in the right path. My mistake has been in putting forth so many poems together, of so decidedly a sensuous and lyric tendency, as to mislead Critics about the quality of my mind and Muse. More concisely I may say—it all reads—too young. Therefore I fear I shall not get the advice I, at this moment, most want. Mr. Tennyson, Mr. Kingsley, and some others, have written me words of very great encouragement. The former 'thinks me a Poet', and the latter is, on his return from Germany, going to write a Review.[3] But to you, Sir, I am more bound (having had the privilege of some of your instruction) than to the rest. I, therefore, in looking over what you will read, perceive well the many shortcomings therein that will suggest themselves to you—too late for remedy. My hope is that, here and there, a chance light may break through, and hint of better things to come—about which indeed, I am now engaged.

Present my best regards to Mrs. Scott and Miss Ker,[4]—and my love to Johnny.[5] And Believe me / My Dear Sir, / Yours, / With the deepest respect,

George Meredith

26. *To* W. H. (error for W. CHARLES) KENT[1]

Text: typed copy of a bookseller's excerpt, Pierpont Morgan Library.

Lower Halliford, Chertsey
[? 1853 or 1854]

Enclosed is a short article of the kind I think you require. Not

25. [3] Kingsley had gone abroad at the end of July. His review appeared in the December issue of *Fraser's Magazine* (xliv. 629–31). After noting that *Poems* was a first book, he continued: 'It is something, to have written already some of the most delicious little love-poems which we have seen born in England in the last few years, reminding us by their richness and quaintness of tone of Herrick; yet with a depth of thought and feeling which Herrick never reached. Health and sweetness are two qualities which run through all these poems.'

[4] Mrs. Scott's sister. Scott had married Ann Ker in 1830.

[5] The *DNB* says that Scott's only son, John Alexander Scott (b. 1846), died in 1894.

26. [1] William Charles Mark Kent (1823–1902), author, journalist, and friend of Dickens,

knowing what I was writing for, and the ware wanted I may not have come up to the mark [etc.].

27. *To* J. W. PARKER, JR.[1]

MS.: Yale.

7 Norman Street, Dover
Friday, September 15, 1854

Dear Parker,

I was pertinacious in my efforts to see you before I came down here by the sea, as it is not likely I shall return for a month. If you find it politic to use my article[2] this month (which I hope will be the case), send the proofs down here at once. I am compelled to work tolerably hard as my law affairs are in confusion and remunerative only to lawyers. As for the E[ast] I[ndia] H[ouse], I doubt whether anything will be done this year. So I must even harness my Muse and make her a hack for some space of time. It's not bad schooling, they say. Provided only it lasts not too long, I shall be without much cause of complaint. I hope you have had a pleasant time. How I long for one glimpse of a glacier! One 'Umarmung des Berggeistes!' The Sea is something, but nothing to that. Ah, my dear fellow: you are lucky in much. Here am I in the midst of sickness—Mary unwell, Arthur but poorly, and I am inclined to croak a little.—But patience! We all draw different threads.

Hoping I shall see you when I come back,

Trust me, / Yours,
George Meredith

was editor of the *Sun* newspaper (1845–70), in which he reviewed GM's *Shagpat* on 8 Jan. 1856. It is possible that GM knew him as a fellow contributor to *Household Words*.

Clues to the date of this excerpt are too meagre to allow of preciseness. But it is known that GM and Mary Ellen went to live with T. L. Peacock at Lower Halliford in 1853, and the error in Kent's initials suggests a date appreciably earlier than that of Letter 33, in which GM addresses him as 'My dear Kent'.

27. [1] There is a hiatus of more than three years in the letters of GM that can be dated with certainty, and this letter contains the only first-hand information that we have about him since the summer of 1851. Meanwhile he had continued writing poetry, had published a few poems and articles (see Stevenson, pp. 43–46, and Green, op. cit.), had engaged in a lawsuit over his inheritance, and had been forced by poverty to move in with Mary's father, in whose house at Lower Halliford his son Arthur was born on 13 June 1853. Stevenson (p. 42) says that 'Peacock was ready to use his influence to get him an appointment in the East India House. . . . But he proved unexpectedly obstinate. His ambition for literary fame made him refuse flatly to consider an ignominious—even if lucrative—career at an office desk.' No doubt GM was full of reluctance, but on the basis of this letter it must be said that the idea was entertained as a possibility.

[2] 'Black Sea and Caspian', as is made clear by the following letter, which GM had submitted to Parker for *Fraser's Magazine*. It was not published in *Fraser's*, and I have been unable to trace it.

28. *To* J. W. Parker, Jr.

MS.: Yale.

7 Norman Street, Dover
Wednesday, [September 20, 1854]

Dear Parker,

In answer to your kind letter of this morning, I think you may as well send that article ('Black Sea and Caspian') to whichever Magazine you think preferable. I don't care which, as it doesn't go into *Fraser*. I will, as you direct, let you know what subjects I propose writing on, in future. Of course you are more than dosed with Eastern articles. What you do print are altogether excellent. What say you to an article on the *Songs of the Dramatists?*[1] for next month, about 8 or 10 pages. I have already written part—probably it would be shorter. Also what say you, this month, to an Ode to H. I. M. Napoleon 3rd[2] which, being here in view of Calais cliffs and Boulogne Lights, I am beginning to revolve seriously. Thus:

> Imperial by the People's will,
> And swaying with such sovereign skill
> Power that is a gorgeous pyre
>   To Sceptre's slaves of Ire—
> Thou etc. etc.

does the first note strike you? Say the word, and you shall have it. Old 'effusions' are rotting for want of Print. My Muse is somewhat pining. I have led her lately through many rough realities to freshen her up. If I find her over delicate, I have done with her. This is the turning point. Castalia is good tipple, but in Britain the Muse must be robust enough to sing on small beer. Vale! Vale!

Yours ever faithfully,
George Meredith

28. [1] Robert Bell (1800–67), journalist, editor, and miscellaneous writer, had undertaken an annotated edition of the English poets, of which 24 volumes were issued between 1854–7. On the occasion of the appearance of vol. x, a favourable review of the work appeared in *Fraser's*, l (Nov. 1854), 583–94. It was unsigned, but internal evidence as well as the evidence of this letter clearly points to GM as the author.
[2] The ode, if written, never appeared in *Fraser's*.

29. *To* TOM TAYLOR[1]

MS.: Yale.

25 Lower Belgrave Square
Tuesday, April 24, 1855

My dear Taylor,

Will you send the enclosed 'Three Maidens'[2] to your Betrothed, and see if she likes them sufficiently to wed them to music. The verses are made up of two refrains, as you will see. If she does not like them, I will send something else . . . but I am sure her heart is too full for labour of any sort, just now. Say, I will wait her leisure.

Mary is coming to Town this week and then going to the sea-side, so I fear I shall not see you next Sunday, as I cannot leave my dear boy alone in the house with servants.

Ever your affectionate
George Meredith

30. *To* J. W. PARKER, JR.

MS.: Yale. Printed: *Altschul Catalogue*, pp. 21–22.

8 Leicester Place, Leicester
Square
Wednesday, July 8, 1855[1]

Dear Parker,

I have ready for publication, a volume of Songs, which I purpose to call 'British Songs', as under that title they come best.[2] In consideration of our association together in my first attempt, I offer it to you. I need scarcely say that I am quite conscious of not proposing in this,

---

29. [1] Tom Taylor (1817–80), dramatist and editor of *Punch* (1874–80), was at this time Secretary to the Board of Health. He had known the Merediths from the time that they lived in lodgings at Mrs. Macirone's in Weybridge. On 19 June 1855 he was married to Laura Barker, a skilled musician and composer.

[2] Published in *Once a Week* (30 July 1859).

30. [1] The day of the month is almost certainly an 8, but if the day of the week is accurate, it would have to be the 4th or the 11th.

[2] In the Berg Collection of the New York Public Library there is an interleaved copy of *Poems* (Berg Copy 7), in which some sixty-odd additional poems have been copied or listed in a Table of Contents in the hand of GM. An interesting study of Berg 7 has been made by Professor Phyllis Bartlett (*Bulletin of the New York Public Library*, lxi. 396–415), who says (p. 414), 'It is probably safe to assume that six of these manuscripts would have been among the collection of British Songs that he offered to Parker in the summer of 1855, in the vain hope of ready cash, and then destroyed.' Such evidence of the date of composition of these poems as Miss Bartlett finds points to the years 1852–3.

any remarkable advantage to you. You will, probably, comprehend my motive, and that it springs neither from a feeling of conceit, nor from any considerations of self-interest.

But, knowing your appreciation of the poetical market just now, it is very improbable you will entertain my proposal when I add, that I must sell the book, having spent on it, latterly, valuable time. Should you, under these circumstances, not decide till you have seen the book, and care to see it, I will forward it to you.

Very faithfully yours,
George Meredith

31. *To* J. W. Parker, Jr.

MS.: Yale.

Lower Halliford, Chertsey
Monday Morning, [? *post* July 8, 1855][1]

Dear Parker,

I hear from Bell[2] that you have kindly offered us your chambers, for my reading of the first part of my 'Arabian Night' next week. He asked me to appoint a day, and I mentioned Friday evening. If this suits you both, and I hear nothing to the contrary, I shall be in the Strand at 8 o'clock. He tells me you invited me to dine with you on the occasion. Such a prelude would have been pleasant, but a previous appointment with a friend, whom I must meet on business matters, holds me engaged.

I am, Dear Parker, / Yours very faithfully,
George Meredith

31. [1] A highly conjectural date. All that we know for certain of *Shagpat*, to which the letter refers, is that it was published on 19 Dec. 1855 (dated 1856) and that the author's note on p. [v.] is dated 8 Dec. 1855.

Stevenson (pp. 44–47) apparently assumes that GM was at work on it between 1852–4. My theory is that it was written in the latter part of 1855, though in the absence of letters for 1852–3 proof is not possible.

[2] ? Robert Bell, whose *Songs of the Dramatists* GM had reviewed for *Fraser's* in Nov. 1854.

32. *To* CHARLES KENT

Text (excerpt): Anderson Auction Co. Catalogue (14–15 Dec. 1909), p. 141.

[? Lower Halliford, Chertsey]
[? October–November 1855][1]

... By the way, if you want amusement, I recommend you Kingsley's last novel, *Westward Ho*,[2] a story of Elizabeth and the Old Voyagers' Time—admirably written, worthy of Kingsley. Of course, there's not much repose in the book. . . . I like in it the fine manly English tone—absence of all sentimentality.

As for me I have just finished a book which I have sold to Chapman & Hall. An 'Arabian Entertainment' [etc., etc., etc., with reference to *The Shaving of Shagpat*].

33. *To* CHARLES KENT

Text: typed copy made by a bookseller, Pierpont Morgan Library.

[London]
[? December 1855][1]

My dear Kent,

You have by this time received *The Shaving of Shagpat*. I am anxious to have your opinion; and more anxious to know your condition.

If you are busy reject an interview, if not, I should wish to clasp[2] my hand into yours a moment before I go down home by the 9.00[2] p.m. train.

Ever,
George Meredith

32. [1] The only real clue to the date of this letter is contained in the second paragraph. *Shagpat* was published on 19 Dec., but we do not know exactly when GM finished it.
  [2] Published in 1855. The dedication is dated *February 1855*, and the book was reviewed in the *Athenaeum* for 31 Mar.
33. [1] This letter must have been written between 19 Dec., when *Shagpat* was published, and 8 Jan., when Kent's review of it appeared in the *Sun*.
  [2] I have adopted this reading from an excerpt printed in the American Art Association's Catalogue of the Collection of William F. Gable [n.d.] as more likely than that of the bookseller (*clap . . . 4.00*).

34. *From* MARY ELLEN MEREDITH *To* CHARLES KENT

MS.: University of Texas.

Lower Halliford, Chertsey
January 24, [1856]

Dear Mr. Kent,

I was quite sure that I was indebted to your friendly hand for the three *Suns* and I thought it very kind of you, for the review was so appreciative and full that I was very glad to have so many copies to lend among my friends. I am as much surprised as gratified to find the book so well received, for the work is so unlike modern literature that I expected it would not be understood. The first notice was in the *Spectator* and just of the kind I had expected from all sides, flippant, disparaging, ignorant, and assuming; I knew it required courage and honesty to review so unusual a book well and to these first favourable reviews I shall always feel it owes the most, whatever subsequent notices may say.

I hope your health is quite restored and that Mrs. Kent has that great reward for her devoted nursing and care of you. Pray remember me very kindly to her and believe me

Faithfully yours,
Mary Meredith

P.S. I should have explained that I did not know till Mr. Meredith came down this week where I should write to you.

M.M.

35. *To* CHARLES KINGSLEY

MS.: Library of Harvard College.

Lower Halliford, Chertsey
February 11, 1856

My dear Sir,

I send you a book I have written: an Arabian Story.[1] I should have sent before, but I did not know your address; hearing you were not at Eversley. At last I came across Mansfield,[2] who told me where you were to be found.

35. [1] *The Shaving of Shagpat.*
    [2] Charles Mansfield, a Cambridge friend of Kingsley and a brilliant young scientist.

I don't know whether you care much for the Arabians: to me they have always seemed one of the most marvellous people on Earth— possessing humour and passion beyond any. They have, certainly, less of the heroic than the classical races; and the heart of Romance is, therefore, wanting in them. They represent the mind in a state of childhood, where quick transitions are natural, and lofty aims unknown. Whether I have seized their spirit you will judge. It is a sort of work which not everyone has sympathy with, and I willingly excuse all who have none.

I am, My dear Sir / Your very faithful

George Meredith

36. *To* MR. CRACE[1]

MS.: Duke University.

Seaford, Sussex
Wednesday, October 15, [1856]

Again Jove hunts with Dian. In prose, that planet sides the moon of midnight, as before you left. I am here: shall here remain yet awhile, for here is peace. Peace indeed, I sometimes exclaim: the peace that maketh war on solitary men! Nevertheless, I can write better here than elsewhere, and am knocked up in London quite.

But ere I say more of myself, let me ask, and ask to hear how you all are now, My dear Mr. Crace? I was grieved to hear the relaxation had affected you so much. Alas! I dread to be told of the sum of pill-boxes used and yet in requisition. You have doctored them, have you not? Too trustful Mrs. Crace! I am tempted to ask her whether that is not a tender womanly flattery of hers—the affecting to believe your pills of real service to the health of the family. *Nos faiblesses!* We all have them. This of yours is a very murderous one; but innocently so. My chief doubt is that you will be your first victim.

—But anon, anon, Sir! We have looked on an eclipse together, have we not? These phenomena are for the intercourse of parted friends. It was somewhat redder than usual. Can you explain?—Thus does one point in the Heavens join the scattered people of earth, and become a bond.

36. [1] The recipient of this letter may have been a grandson or other relative of Frederick Crace (1779–1859), whose great collection of maps and views of London was purchased in 1880 from his son John Gregory Crace by the British Museum. The London *Post Office Directory* (1855) lists H. Winfield Crace, barrister, of 19 Buckingham St., Adelphi, about whom I know nothing. There was also John Dibble Crace, architect, of 15 Gloucester Place.

Today it has been 'blust'rous', as they say here. The water within a foot of our little one room, and surf raging up wrathful-white all along the shingle and breaking in feathery masses on the sulphur grey curtain of cloud. Great excitement, of course. A tile blown through the window close to a certain gentleman's head. Blatchington Beach[2] is battered to bits, and Amphitrite has her 'brachia longa' stretched all around us. Can London show anything like it?—I suppose you are both looking to Piccolomini's[3] reappearance on the 23rd? Great great is the temptation to come to Town and see her. As I must go into Hampshire shortly, I think I even may pass through Town for the purpose. If I do, I will call on you, be sure: sure myself of welcome.

But how, when you hear that Py. Pilcher[4] has reappeared in the Town? He has been discerned with the naked eye: the breeches being in such a state of frenzied firmitude they look as if buttoned by a forty-Jack Tar-power, and held together by stitches having the tenacity and desperation of virgins betrothed. What he does here—unless to exhibit and taunt our youth with the aforesaid, no man knoweth.

I must trouble you with a question, which you may be able to answer off-hand, or not. Perhaps on referring to Buffon, or a Naturalist friend, you may know. It is—what species of animals *cross* with other animals. Will the Lion with other than his own kind? I fancy none of the nobler races do. Yet the Horse does, as we know. This I should like to ascertain, and if you can help me, I am certain you will. How is the Zebra produced: In the same way as the mule? Will Leopards, Tigers, and the like, cross?—

I am hard at work. Doing more than I should to do it thoroughly well: but needs must. I still try to do justice to the Novel. Work now and sing in the Spring.

My little man talks of Miss Nelly now and then. 'She did not like me to kiss her, Papa.' 'No, my dear, nor me: wasn't it odd!' 'Very odd, Papa, it was!'

I really hope you are now all getting better. I received the *Athenaeums*. Thanks for them. Lemon[5] spoke to me yesterday about them. You did not mention anything of their being returned? . . . I would have returned them immediately. Is it still of use?—On another occasion, should one present, I will forward to any required address, but on no account let anyone of your friends be dispossessed for me.

Kindest regards to Mrs. Crace, and the little ones. I persist in having Nelly Crace kissed for me: my name being pronounced at the same

36. [2] Now part of Seaford.

[3] Maria Piccolomini (1836–99), opera singer.

[4] Pilchers abound, but I have been unable to identify one whose first name, presumably, was Percy.

Mark Lemon (1809–70), editor of *Punch*, I suppose.

time in awful tones. Mrs. Meredith begs to be remembered. When you see Lethbridge[6] and Cutten[7] mention me to them in all cordiality.

Your ever faithful
George Meredith

I read about the 'Case'.[8] It was well it was hushed up and 'burked'. But what a piquant morsel lost for Christmas gossip!

37. *From* MARY ELLEN MEREDITH
To EDWARD CHAPMAN[1]

MS.: University of Texas.

28A Manchester Street, Manchester Square
Tuesday morning, [? 1856][2]

Dear Mr. Chapman,

On my return yesterday evening I found a letter from George in which he directs me to ask you for the remainder of the money you were so kind as to advance to him.

I am obliged to go to the City this morning and shall not be back in time to see you today, will you therefore be so good as to forward the money to me here, as I am to make a payment, to which George is pledged, with it before 12 tomorrow. If you should find that you

---

⁶ William Lethbridge. (See note 2, Letter 281.)

⁷ Frederick Cutten, surveyor, of 21 Coleman St., is the only Cutten listed in the London *P.O.D.* of 1855.

⁸ It is conceivable, in view of the second paragraph, that Crace was a physician. In that event the 'case' may have been the dropping of charges against Mr. Snape, surgeon of the Surrey Lunatic Asylum, following the death of an inmate who had been subjected to a prolonged cold shower bath. But I should hardly expect GM to regard such a case as 'a piquant morsel'.

37. ¹ Edward Chapman (1805–80), founder, with William Hall, of Chapman & Hall, booksellers and publishers. They had published Dickens's *Pickwick Papers* and others of his novels and at the end of 1855—with considerably less profit to themselves—GM's *The Shaving of Shagpat*. But though *Shagpat* was a failure, Arthur Waugh (*A Hundred Years of Publishing*, 1930, p. 141) quotes Edward Chapman's daughter as remembering her father continually acclaiming the book as 'the finest Eastern story outside *The Arabian Nights*'. Waugh says that GM and Arthur had spent a holiday with the Chapmans at Folkestone in the summer of 1856.

² A conjecture made with little confidence. I know of no date at which either of the Merediths resided at this address nor of any connexion between them and the occupant of it listed in the London *P.O.D.*—John Bettyes, who is identified as jobmaster in 1856 and 1857 and as coachmaker in 1858 and 1859. Further, I cannot reconcile satisfactorily the content of the letter with that of the following. But the 'advance' must surely have been made against either *Shagpat* or *The Fair Frankincense* of the following letter; hence my date.

know any of the Parthenon Club[3] and can help us with them I think you will not need much asking to do so.

In haste, I am

Faithfully yours,
Mary Meredith

38. *To* EDWARD CHAPMAN

Text: *Letters*, i. 9–10.

Seaford, Sussex
December 15, 1856

My dear Mr. Chapman,

Will you send me, this week, the £25 for which I made application, to sum the £70 requested in advance, and so doing oblige your faithful poet. . . .

I remain here, as I can work better than elsewhere, though, engaged as I am, the DULNESS is something frightful, and hangs on my shoulders like Sinbad's old man of the Sea. I dream of Boltons, I promise myself a visit there at Christmas, just for a beguilement; but it is doubtful if I shall quit hard work for a day, till the book is finished. I will come Manuscript in hand. Tell Mrs. Chapman how much I should wish to see her; and Serious Meta,[1] daughter of the Sage; also frolicsome Florence;[1] not forgetting Reginald,[1] the Roysterer.

The name of this novel is to be *The Fair Frankincense*.[2] Tell me what you think of it?—There are to be two Prophets in the book, and altogether a new kind of villain; being Humbug active—a great gun likely to make a noise, if I prime him properly.

Have you, or do any of your people know of, a book of Hampshire Dialect? I have a Sussex. Ballads, or Songs, with the provincialisms will serve. Perhaps Mr. Frederic Chapman[3] may know of such a thing? Also a slang Dictionary, or book of the same with Gloss. And if you have, or can get these, will you forward them by post?

---

37. [3] Unless the members were the proprietors of the *Parthenon*, with which the *Literary Gazette* was merged in 1862, I am without suggestion. Possibly Mary was hoping for assistance in launching *The Fair Frankincense*.

38. [1] Meta, Florence, Reginald: children of the Chapmans. After the Folkestone holiday, Mrs. Gaye (Meta Chapman) says that 'there was always a knife and fork laid, in case Mr. Meredith should care to come and dine' (Waugh, loc. cit.).

[2] Stevenson (p. 55) thinks that there is little reason to doubt that this was the story published as *Farina: a Legend of Cologne* by Smith, Elder & Co. in Aug. 1857. But GM's description of the book here does not seem to me to fit *Farina*.

[3] Frederic Chapman (1823–95), Edward Chapman's cousin, had become a partner in the firm in 1847. (For a biographical sketch, see Biographical Section, pp. 1718–19.)

Mrs. Meredith is staying at Blackheath.[4] Don't wait to send by her, as I am anxious she should spend Christmas in town. Dulness will put out the wax lights, increase the weight of the pudding, toughen the turkey, make lead of the beef, turn the entire feast into a nightmare, down here, to one not head and heel at work. . . .

I am glad *Aurora Leigh* is so well received.[5] I have not read it, but the extracts promise. Confirm to me the news of Bailey's pension.[6] Will that £100 per ann. chain him to earth, or only give him firmer spring into the empyrean! I should like to spin on the talk; but the paper contracts, and the Grave Man of business frowns already at four pages of it. So farewell.

39. *To* W. C. BENNETT[1]

MS.: Yale. Published: *Letters*, i. 11, with inaccuracies and slight omissions.

Seaford, Sussex
April 27, 1857

Sir:

I have to thank you for your latest volume of poems; and in doing so, I must beg your excuse for omitting to acknowledge a previous single piece forwarded to me, and which I discover in the present collection. It is usual in such cases to say what we do like, and not what we don't like; but I presume a sufficient balance in you to hear both. I like your songs, and baby-ballads very much. I like your feeling for English scenery, and remarkable descriptive power. I do not like your idylls (e.g. the 'Boat race') because both the form, the matter, and the blank verse, recall Tennyson so strongly, and one expects more than imitation from you. By the way, the giving of a daughter to the conqueror in a Boat race is, if British, not customary. A girl might

---

[4] With Lady Nicolls, mother of her first husband.

[5] Mrs. Browning's *Aurora Leigh* was reviewed in the *Athenaeum* on 22 Nov., with numerous excerpts.

[6] Philip James Bailey (1816–1902), author of *Festus*, first published anonymously in 1839 by C. & H. Waugh (p. 81) says that he spent the best years of his life 'adding to it, developing it, and generally perfecting it'.

39. [1] W. C. Bennett, LL.D. (1820–95), whose *Queen Eleanor's Vengeance and Other Poems* (1857) is doubtless the volume of poems for which GM is thanking him. There was apparently no personal connexion between the two, and whether Bennett knew— what is only recently known to us—that GM was at this time the conductor of the Belles Lettres and Art section of the *Westminster Review* and for that reason sent him the book, I am unable to say. (Gordon S. Haight, in 'George Meredith and the *Westminster Review*', *Modern Language Review*, liii (Jan. 1958), 1–16, establishes GM's authorship of the section from Apr. 1857 until Jan. 1858. The twelve guineas which he received for each of the articles comprise his only known literary earnings during this period.)

give herself; but for a Papa so to stipulate implies unpleasant paternal contempt for the lover's physique, and a sort of calculation seldom made, I fancy. You see I speak freely.

It seems to me that your taste is not for what you succeed in best, viz. minute description; but that you might produce a first-rate Dutch home-story in ten syllabic eight-line, or say, six-line verse; but I am passing my boundary in affecting to advise, and must honestly ask you to pardon me for the impertinence.

I am, Sir / Yours very faithfully,
George Meredith

40. *To* EYRE CROWE[1]

Text: *Letters*, i. 8–9 (undated but placed between letters of 1850–6).

Seaford, Sussex
[? June 4, 1857][2]

My dear Crowe,

Will you come down here to us to-morrow? We shall be glad to have you. Come and stay a week. The weather is lovely. The heat quite sweltering. Come, and if you like, bring the Boulogne Fish-fays to give a truthful representation of nature. I should prefer you coming now, as I may not be here much longer, and the presence of the illustrious Francboise(y) is desirable.[3] Mrs. Meredith joins in kind regards. She says you must come under pain of her displeasure. Come, O Crowe! Here is fishing, bathing, rowing, sailing, lounging, running, pic-nicing, and a cook who builds a basis of strength to make us equal to all these superhuman efforts. So Come!

There is a train at ten a.m. first and second class, the latter costs to Newhaven 9s. 8d. In the evening there is one at 6 p.m. with a Third Class, the latter being 5s. 11d. It reaches Newhaven at 1/2 past 8. From Newhaven to Seaford is a walk of two miles. If you walk, go on to the

---

40. [1] Eyre Crowe (1824–1910), A.R.A., who exhibited regularly at the Royal Academy from 1848 till 1904. Ellis (p. 51) says that Crowe was among the visitors at The Limes, Weybridge, where GM and Mary had rooms for a time, and it is reasonable to suppose that the acquaintance began there.

[2] A brief excerpt from this letter appears in the Sotheby Catalogue for 25–28 Feb. 1919, where the date for it is given as 4/6/59. Since GM and Mary were not living together in 1859, as they were at the time of this letter, I conjecture that the figure *7* was read as *9*.

[3] I suppose *Franc-boise(y)*, like *franc gautier* (or *gontier*, as it appears in Rabelais), to be an extension of the literal meaning (an inhabitant of the forest, a sort of Robin Hood) and to mean something like *bon vivant*. But I can throw no light on 'the Boulogne Fish-fays'.

Hotel at Newhaven, anyone will direct you the way. You can go on the train. I may perhaps meet you; but on second thoughts this is unlikely as I may be over the hills at a pic-nic. But I shall be at home by the time you arrive. Let no excuse delay, and trust me.

Anticipatingly yours,
George Meredith

41. *To* EYRE CROWE

MS.: Yale.

7 Hobury Street
King's Road, Chelsea[1]
Wednesday, [? August–September 1857]

My dear Crowe,

I wish to be the first to give you good news of your brother,[2] as I suppose he may not have written to you personally by this mail, so that you may hear in a round-a-bout fashion.

He has got the appointment. Also that of Superintendent[?][3] of the Elphinstone College, and writer of Telegraph Précis for Government —equal on the whole to about a thousand a year. This is good?— Tell Dan[4] to have the Ruskin notes ready. Fix a Rendezvous for next Sunday morning, preparatory to——! I shall drop in on Friday. I dine tomorrow with Richard Cole[5] who received to-day the letter

41. [1] In the summer of 1857 Mary Ellen Meredith was visiting in Wales, and Stevenson (p. 58) thinks that there is no doubt that the artist Henry Wallis was with her. On 18 Apr. 1858 a son was born to her at Clifton, and though the father's name was registered as 'George Meredith, author', GM, as we shall see, denied paternity. In the autumn Mary went off to Capri with Wallis, and GM later refused to allow her to return to him (Stevenson, p. 58). Meanwhile he took lodgings for himself and Arthur at 7 Hobury Street, Chelsea, from which this is the first letter that he is known to have written.

[2] (Sir) Joseph Archer Crowe (1825–96), journalist and art historian. The *DNB* says that he had reported the Crimean War for the *Illustrated London News*, and upon his return received an offer to direct an art school in India, but as the art school 'did not prove available' turned to reporting the Indian Mutiny for *The Times*. Crowe's own account (in *Reminiscences of Thirty-five Years of My Life*, 1895, pp. 230–46), differs. He says that the position was that of Superintendent of the Sir Jamsetjee Jeejeebhoy School of Art and that he was advised to go to Bombay in order to be on the ground. On 15 Aug. 1857 he received the appointment, at a salary of 300 rupees per month. In addition, he supplied digests of Indian news to the Government and wrote for various newspapers in India, France, and England. The total income produced, however, was probably far short of £1000 per annum.

[3] Dubious reading: the letters are imperfectly formed at the end of a line.

[4] Presumably Austin Daniel, GM's old friend and associate of the *Monthly Observer* days who was employed in the Examiner's Office, East India House. Conceivably the 'Ruskin notes' were for use in the second of two notices of Ruskin that GM wrote for the *Westminster Review*.

[5] Possibly a son or other relative of (Sir) Henry Cole, under whom Joseph Crowe was trained in the School of Design, South Kensington. Cole had three sons, only two of

from your brother with intelligence etc.—Can't you and Dan drop in in the evening about 1/2 past eight?

Ever faithfully,
George Meredith

42. *To* EYRE CROWE

MS.: Free Library of Philadelphia.

7 Hobury Street, Chelsea
Monday, January 4, 1858

Thanks for your letter; dear old fellow!—You seem to be walking in Paradise with pigs. No happier fate can artist or mortal dream of for the season. It is not I that write to you, my Crowe! It is a pudding-bag . . . a quiescent receptacle for Roast Beef, Punch, and mince Pies. Philosophers tell us that the soul taketh the body's shape, which hath its nature impressed on our ethereal essence. If so, what an appearance am I presenting to the Angels! This is one of the severe penalties one pays for being born an Englishman. Hard must we strive to keep up with the colossal appetites and Giant fare of our countrymen. Heaven be thanked the Christmas week is over! The Rajah and Ranee[1] got on well at Putney, where a few people came not worth mentioning. I have seen Dan, and read him the Overture of the Novel, with which the Humourist was pleased.[2] You shall hear it when you come. It goes on so so. Everything I do is an Experiment, and till it's done, I never know whether 'tis worth a farthing. Ah! how charmingly the *Virginians*[3] is written. W. M. T[hackeray] is the most perfect Artist in Prose that I know of. And I feel a despair at his calm command of material. He is too good to be greatly popular, and I'm a little amused to think that he would rather be popular of the two, but can't help his genius. 'Tis Pallas strikes! I have not heard whether T. L. P[eacock] saw him at Halliford. There's no news. A little Village beats London hollow for that sort of thing . . . unless we move among them who guide the State, or, better still, among such as profess an acquaintance

whom—neither named Richard—I have been able to trace. In further support of my hypothesis, Henry Cole as a young man had lived in the house of T. L. Peacock, whose works he edited in 1875. A connexion between the Cole family and Meredith, then, is not far-fetched.

42. [1] Doubtless facetious titles conferred on unidentifiable friends.

[2] Dan, the Humourist, was presumably Austin Daniel, and the Novel would have been *The Ordeal of Richard Feverel.* (See Note 4, preceding letter.)

[3] Published in twenty-four monthly numbers (Nov. 1857–Sept. 1859).

with such, which Ourself doth not. I have seen none of the set but Dan, and him not for a fortnight. I suppose him vanquished by Christmas and recumbent.

How long are you to be away? Write and say when I may expect to see you. Do you want any books? I'll send down some, if you like. I got another copy of Octave Feuillet's *Proverbes*[4] on purpose for you. By the way, I'll send you with the post *German Love*[5] just published . . . The writing is beautiful . . . so German! It shall be my Crowe's Christmas box! I won't write your name in it, that if you don't like it, you may give it to some woman who will. It is a book women *must* like . . . a book to find them out. For women feel deeper than we do, though they don't think so deep. Hence their craving for a preacher, a poet—anything that will beget a thought upon their emotions, as this book will.

No more room, I find: so, good bye. Write soon and remember always

Your affectionate
George Meredith

43. *To* EYRE CROWE

MS.: Huntington Library.

7 Hobury Street, Chelsea
April 28, 1858

My beloved Old Crowe?

Pleasure struck me on beholding your handwriting: pleasure doubled by the letter itself, which vouched for one holding a place in the memory of the absent: but where pleasure should have culminated, it collapsed.

For the horrible reflection then arose:—What are we to reply to all this wealth of wit and gaiety? Where is in us this spontaneous ebullient force which carries us on a roaring torrent of laughters headlong we know not whither, until exhausted Nature sinks, owning the mastery of a diviner hand?—Even as Widdicomb[1] in the Ring, immortal, flicks the noble Horse, so our Crowe, with light careless touch, insouciant, conscious of power *makes* NATURE CIRCLE TO THE PUN.

---

[4] Octave Feuillet (1821–90), French novelist and playwright, whose *Proverbes* was just published.

[5] An English translation of F. Max Müller's *German Love*, originally published at Leipzig in 1857.

43. [1] A celebrated ringmaster at Astley's Amphitheatre.

Dan and I have, and still are jogging, round and round. We know we must. We know it will end only with what physical strength remains to us. Dan has scarce any breath left in his body. I gasp frightfully. You are away, too distant to hear our appeal, not too distant for the whip you wield![2]

I would I had one, too. How shall I amuse my Crowe? If I speak much, old fellow, I shall get to speaking of myself, and that is not a cheerful theme.[3] Politics have relapsed from the Bernard Tragedy[4] to the Jew-Farce.[5] Steam in the shape of Palaver is being let off about the average. You read about the ovation to James[6] at the Café Chantant the other night? How the light and generous Gaul hailed him and *vived* him, and pressed on him the reluctant weed and the enthusiastic cognac, a nice mess for a fellow to get into!

I have not been to the French Exhibition yet.[7] I have been nowhere: working hard, and doing pretty well; though not as *fast* as I should wish.

How long are you going to stay from us? Nothing would be more delightful than to have your French tongue and English heart in companionship in the air breathed by Molière, Montaigne, Béranger: but just now it cannot be. However, you now have Old Dick,[8] and if you manage well, you may make an interesting show of him: a lucrative one, if he could be got to go to the provinces.

Now Exhibiting a Real Live Englishman! on the broad grin!—

The Turkey-cocks of all France are challenged to match the crimson efflorescence of his Sanguineous constitution.

His virtue is: He is pleased with everything.

His peculiarity: He is faithful to his Begum.

His point of similarity: He is a jolly good fellow.

---

43. [2] Crowe was in France, at Fontenay aux Roses, near Paris, as appears later.

[3] An allusion, no doubt, to the break with his wife. (See Note 1, Letter 41.)

[4] Dr. Simon Bernard was tried (12–17 Apr.) for conspiring with Orsini to kill Napoleon III. In the face of strong evidence against him and a general belief in England that he was guilty, he was acquitted.

[5] In the General Election of 1847 Baron Lionel de Rothschild was returned to the House of Commons for the City of London but was not seated because of his inability to subscribe to the oath 'on the true faith of a Christian'. Subsequently Jewish Disabilities Bills were introduced in the Parliaments of 1848, 1849, 1851, 1853, 1856, 1857, and—at the time of this letter—1858. The result was always the same: the bills passed the Commons only to be rejected by the Lords—hence GM's phrase 'the Jew farce'. But 1858 was different: on 1 July the Lords adopted a bill which allowed each House to alter by resolution the form of the oath. (See Monypenny and Buckle, *The Life of Benjamin Disraeli*, 1914, iii. 66–79.)

[6] Edwin James (1812–82), actor turned barrister, was engaged in the defence of Dr. Bernard. Presumably his popularity in Paris was some measure of the unpopularity of Napoleon III. (In 1861, however, James was disbarred for professional misconduct.)

[7] i.e. Exhibition of French paintings.

[8] ? Richard Cole.

Translate that placard. It would take.

I know Fontenay aux Roses well: a very pretty place, very dusty in summer, but full of fun, according to Paul de Kock.[9] At present, full of Pun . . . eh?

If you are to stay from us any time, pray, write to me again. Don't be shocked at my dull reply. I'll get more news next time. I am ill, overworked, vexed. I'll do better by degrees. Take the good intent just now.

Dickens is reading for his own benefit, like Thackeray.[10] I've an idea of advertising 'Nights with Crowe'. If pressed for money, I shall, and if it takes, we'll buy the 'Tardies'.[11] Yes, and take walks to Meudon, and drink rare wine over Rabelais together. Oh, a glorious Future! Dream of it. Think it possible. But wherever you are, don't forget

Your affectionate
George Meredith

My little Arthur received his Crowe's message, and sends love in return. It was kind of you to call before you left.

[Marginal postscripts]:

I hope the French *people* are sensible about us, now that the officials are so venomous. Tell them we are their *friends*.
If you hear of any good new books, bring word of them.

44. *To* TOM TAYLOR[1]

Text: typed copy, Yale.

7 Hobury Street
[*ante* April 27, 1859]

My dear Tom,

I have not heard from Lucas.[2] When he writes I suppose he will give me an idea of the kind of tone he intends to adopt in the new

9 Paul de Kock (1793–1871), French novelist.
10 Thackeray had recently lectured in America and England on the four Kings George, whereas Dickens was giving dramatic readings from his own works.
11 Although the initial letter appears to be *T*, it is conceivably *J*. In any event, the context suggests that the Maison des Jardies, an hotel-restaurant, at Sèvres-Ville-d'Avray, within two or three miles of Meudon, is intended. It was once occupied by Balzac.
44. 1 Taylor was a member of the *Punch* staff and is known to have been helping the proprietors, Bradbury and Evans, launch their new periodical *OaW*. In looking around for contributors, he apparently thought of GM.
2 Samuel Lucas (1818–68), an experienced journalist and reviewer for *The Times*, was the first editor of *OaW*.

serial.³ If it is of the character of *Household Words*, I am not suited to contribute. Facts on the broad grin, and the tricky style Dickens encouraged, I cannot properly do. And if Lucas does not clear himself of that legacy, the publication must fail.⁴

Anthony Trollope is travelling, making postal arrangements in the West Indies, Cuba, and elsewhere.⁵ He will be back, I fancy, in about a month or so. Doubtless he will have plenty of matter besides the book he is doing for Chapman and Hall (Account of Jamaica, etc). I will have him spoken to on the subject at once, if you think proper. He *wants* a medium for light writing, I know.

His brother, Adolphus,⁶ whom you met at the Brownings, might prove a serviceable man. Shall I write to him? He is doing a work on the Dukes of Ferrara, out of which, and other of his Italian stories, good articles might come.

If Lucas is the right sort of man, and gets about him a staff of writers altogether different from Dickens's, public taste may go with him.

I should imagine it would be better to give up the title of *Household Words*, and start unencumbered. In this day a body of sterling writers can always *make* a publication. The very name of *H[ousehold] W[ords]* will be an incubus on original effort—the public (a faithful old beast in the main) will be thinking of its spoiled child.

Mrs. Tom is very disappointing.⁷ I trust to be indemnified for the suspense she causes me. There can't be much longer delay?

Yours ever faithfully,
(Signed) George Meredith

44. ³ i.e. magazine, *OaW*. The way in which it came to be established is this: Dickens, at the time of his separation from his wife, was editor of *HW*, a magazine owned jointly by himself and Bradbury & Evans, its publishers. Dickens published a graceless explanation of the separation in *HW* and sent a copy of it to *Punch*, also owned by Bradbury & Evans, in the expectation that it would be published there. When it was not, he quarrelled with Bradbury & Evans, and *HW* was put up for sale, in order to dissolve the partnership. Dickens returned to his former publishers, Chapman & Hall, and a new periodical, *All the Year Round* (first number 30 Apr. 1859), with Dickens as proprietor and editor, replaced *HW*. Bradbury & Evans, not to be outdone, initiated *OaW* under the editorship of Lucas.

⁴ Dickens confirmed GM's judgement. 'What fools they are!' he said. 'As if a mole couldn't see that their only chance was in a careful separation of themselves from the faintest approach or assimilation to *All the Year Round*' (Edgar Johnson, *Charles Dickens*, N.Y., 1952, ii. 946).

⁵ Anthony Trollope (1815–82) was just beginning to be known as a novelist, following publication of *The Warden* (1855) and *Barchester Towers* (1857), one of the novels which GM had reviewed favourably in the *Westminster Review* (Haight, op. cit., p. 10). Trollope was still employed in the postal service and in Nov. 1858 had been sent on an official mission to the West Indies, from which he returned in July 1859. (See Bradford A. Booth, *The Letters of Anthony Trollope*, Oxford, 1951, pp. 43, 46.)

⁶ Thomas Adolphus Trollope (1810–92) lived in Italy mostly and was a frequent contributor to English periodicals on Italian subjects.

⁷ A reference to her approaching confinement.

45. *To* MISS BARKER[1]

MS.: University of Texas.

7 Hobury Street
April 27, 1859

My dear Miss Barker,

I had the good news yesterday in the proclamation, and rejoiced that it was over and she was safe. God bless both of them, and the infant. They only wanted this to their happiness. It shall be a girl next time. I am desirous of seeing Mrs. Tom in her new character. Meantime I send my Arthur to have a glimpse at the New Wonder. He has instructions not to stay.

Many thanks to you, my dear Miss Barker, for the letter of this morning. Believe me

Very faithfully yours,
George Meredith

46. *To* SAMUEL LUCAS

Text: typed copy, Yale.

7 Hobury Street
June 4, [1859]

Dear Sir,

Enclosed are the songs for *Once a Week*.[1] You shall have more, if you want them.

I fancy the 'Song of Courtesy' might furnish an illustration to Millais[2]—unless the mention of 'bride-beds'[3] be thought too strong for our virtuous public. On looking at my Arabian story[4] I am doubtful about it, and yet more doubtful of my present powers of putting it

---

45. [1] Sister of Mrs. Tom Taylor. She had sent GM a note telling him of the birth of the Taylors' son, Wycliffe.

46. [1] Poems by GM which appeared in *OaW* in 1859 were the 'The Song of Courtesy' (9 July), 'The Three Maidens' (30 July), 'Over the Hills' (20 Aug.), 'The Last Words of Juggling Jerry' (3 Sept.), 'Autumn Even-Song' (3 Dec.), and 'The Crown of Love' (31 Dec.).

[2] *OaW* never developed a successful editorial policy, but Lucas recruited the best staff of artists in the business—Millais, Keene, Leech, Tenniel, Hablôt K. Browne, and others—mainly from the *Punch* stable.

[3] When Sir Gawain, the knight of courtesy, was led to the bridal-bed, his bride 'was yellow and dry as a snake's old skin . . . with a hog's bristle on a hag's chin', but when he kissed her, she turned into a beautiful maiden. The illustration, however, was by Tenniel.

[4] Apparently never completed.

into shape. I seem to have lost the style. But I will do my best, and as early as possible. At all events I will write something.

Trusting you are getting your ranks in order,

I am, Dear Sir / Very faithfully yours,

(Signed) George Meredith

47. *To* SAMUEL LUCAS

MS.: Yale.

7 Hobury Street, Chelsea, S. W.

July 4, 1859

My dear Lucas,

(Since I am permitted so to address your august person) I beg to say that my ear is not naturally defective; but that I defer to your classical superiority. I claim rather to be something of a metricist, as you would see, if you came across a boyish volume of poems of mine.[1] Am I to see the proofs? I wish to, especially as I want to turn a phrase or two in 'Juggling Jerry',[2] which piece, remember, must not be too rigidly criticised in its rhythm, being the supposed speech of a vagabond freethinker.

And now I am going to show you what an unwise contributor you possess. I don't like your first number.[3] It contains no piece of weight. It has too many small pieces. It has made no impression among the people I have met anywhere. Dasent's Norse-story[4] is all very well, but the Bear has no tail (to speak metaphorically). It is inconsequent. Reade's[5] may turn out tolerable. The 'Port-Natal' contributor[6] is interesting. So is Lewes's 'Tadpole'.[7] Bridges Adams[8] writes freshly, as he always does: but they are all mere bits. And as for the illustrations: the 'Bun-house'[9] is of the style of 'Welcome Guest'. Leech should

---

47. [1] *Poems* (1851).

[2] Published in *OaW* (3 Sept.), with an illustration by Hablôt K. Browne.

[3] The first number of *OaW* bore the date of 2 July 1859. Although it was always dated Saturday, the magazine was available on the preceding Tuesday or Wednesday.

[4] 'Audun and His White Bear (From the Old Norse)', by (Sir) G. W. Dasent (1817–96), assistant editor of *The Times* and a well-known Scandinavian scholar.

[5] *A Good Fight*, by Charles Reade (1814–84), later revised, expanded, and published as *The Cloister and the Hearth* (1861).

[6] 'Snakes and Their Prey', by Arthur Clarence (contributed from Port Natal).

[7] 'The Tail of a Tadpole', by G. H. Lewes (1817–78), miscellaneous writer and editor with whom George Eliot lived.

[8] 'English Projectiles', by W. Bridges Adams (1797–1872), a prolific inventor and writer on technological subjects.

[9] One of several plates contributed by John Leech (1817–64), of the *Punch* staff.

give something different from 'Punch'. Tenniel[10] is excellent, and I am
glad he is going to do mine. I suppose Editors hear the truth as little as
Kings, and it is as dangerous to tell it them. But an Editor who can
listen to it, of him one may predict that he must ultimately win the
public, as I sincerely hope you will. I cannot help thinking that *All the
Year Round* is right in having a number of long articles, and enclosing
the minor ones under a particular heading. I think also that a periodical
requires something in the shape of a staff of writers, or it will lack
homogeneity in the contributions. It will present a bundle of waifs,
and fail in showing that *plan* which is necessary for success.

Pardon all this. You are doubtless receiving congratulations, and
this poor voice of mine will indeed seem discordant. I, who write for
the public, listen to and ponder on any criticism I hear; and as one of
the public I speak to you.

Ever faithfully yours,
George Meredith

I will send fresh contributions shortly: and possibly some prose.

48. *To* SAMUEL LUCAS

Text: typed copy, Yale. Excerpt printed: *Altschul Catalogue*, pp. 78–79.

7 Hobury Street
Thursday morning, [July 7, 1859]

My dear Lucas,

I think the 'maidens'[1] may pass. As to the novel:[2] alas and woe's me!
I find I have offended Mudie[3] and the British Matron. He will not, or
haply, dare not put me in his advertised catalogue. Because of the
immoralities I depict! O canting Age! I predict a Deluge. Mudie is
Metternich: and after him—.[4] Meantime I am tabooed from all decent
drawing-room tables.

On re-reading portions, I can't but say there is dulness in the book
here and there: dulness and weakness. My fingers start to tear out those

---

[10] (Sir) John Tenniel (1820–1914), also of the *Punch* staff, illustrated 'Audun and His
White Bear'. Over a period of fifty years he contributed more than 2,000 cartoons to
Punch.

48. [1] 'The Three Maidens', a poem published in *OaW* (30 July) with an illustration by
Hablôt K. Browne.

[2] *The Ordeal of Richard Feverel*, published 20 June 1859.

[3] The lending library, which had subscribed for 300 copies and then had withdrawn
the book from its list upon 'urgent remonstrances of several respectable families, who
objected to it as dangerous and wicked and damnable', as GM wrote to Lucas on 3 Oct.
(Letter 50).   [4] '. . . the deluge'.

passages, nevertheless the main design and moral purpose I hold to. I have certainly made it too subtle, for none have perceived it. The fact is, that the 'System' does succeed through the young fellow's luck in finding so charming a girl. The strength of his pure love for a woman is a success—till the father strikes down his own fabric. The 'System', you see, had its origin not so much in love for his son, as in wrath at his wife, and so carries its own Nemesis. This is shown in the chapter 'Nursing the Devil'. But I did not insist on it and lecture my dear public. I thought providing a contrast sufficient—in the 'Unmasking of Ripton Thompson'. The moral is that no System of the sort succeeds with human nature, unless the originator has conceived it purely independent of personal passion. That was Sir Austin's way of wreaking his revenge. However, it requires twice reading to see this, and my fault has been that I have made the book so dull that it does not attract a second reading. At least not among newspaper critics—to whom all honour and glory! I would rather have Mudie and the British Matron with me than the whole Army of the Press.

By the way, your cutting short the concluding triplet of 'Sir Gawain'[5] was a mistake. I seem to end in a caper, and perform an *entrechat*, instead of going off with a certain sedateness.

When shall you use 'Juggling Jerry'?[6] I shall be going out of town at the end of next week. You had better send me proofs in a day or two, and don't be too rigorous about our friend's rhythm. I'll do what I can, but I do not wish to destroy the emphasis of his phrases. I have a companion picture or two, to follow, that I will send, possibly, and some further pieces.

With all deference to Brooks, I think his tale of an Election[7] horrid, damaging, damnable. Also *some* of the verse you print might be done by the yard. This is very impertinent, but I have assumed the privilege. I find myself criticized much in the same fashion, so it is my right. Wishing you continued success,

Your faithful contributor,
(Signed) George Meredith

48. [5] Subject of 'The Song of Courtesy', published in *OaW* (9 July).
　　As published the poem ended:

> Like the true knight, may we
> Make the basest that be
> Beautiful ever by Courtesy!

Meredith had written:

> Like the true knight, so may we
> Make the basest that there be
> Beautiful by Courtesy!

[6] Published in *OaW* (3 Sept.), with an illustration by Hablôt K. Browne.

[7] 'An Election Story', by Shirley Brooks (1816–74), in the second number (9 July). Brooks was a member of the *Punch* staff from 1851 and in 1870 succeeded Mark Lemon as editor.

49. *To* CAPTAIN FREDERICK A. MAXSE, R.N.[1]

MS.: Maxse Papers.[2]

Esher
September 9, 1859

My dear Captain Maxse,

I have been journeying about Hampshire for the last three or four weeks—pardon my delay in replying to you.

I hope you have received *The Shaving of Shagpat*. I told Mr. Fred[eric]k[3] Chapman to oblige me by forwarding it. But it is ten to one against your being able to read it. I have known kindly persistent people defeated very early in the opening pages. And in truth the main story is much too much spun out.

A sea-novel not being to your taste (and for reasons which you make perfectly clear to me), work sea-incidents, sea-life, into the narrative. You know the life of the sea, and can describe it. As to the question of Plot:—would you set about building a house without a design? Or what sort of ship would you produce by simply following the successive leaps of your fancy? A story may be artificial, but not out of nature. Nature, it is true, seldom finishes and rounds off what she gives us. We must—more or less; and because men require it. Which do you prefer—the music made by the wind passing among harp-strings, or a Symphony of Beethoven's? As an exceptional mind, possibly, you may find more food in the former: more gratification you must receive from the latter.

Again Plot keeps you to nature: that is, to the amount of nature originally conceived in your plot. It keeps you from dwelling too long and wearisomely on favourite scenes: it pushes you ahead: it shows you something to attain to, in the final development. Where there is no plot, no story, the author generally maunders. Look at the *Virginians*,[4] where he is forced to depend entirely upon character, and overworks it, distends it, makes it monstrous.

49. [1] This, as far as I know the first letter that GM ever wrote to the man who was to become one of his most intimate male friends, is also the first to be dated from Esher, where he took Copsham (or Copsome) Cottage, in which he was to live until his second marriage, in 1864. (For a biographical sketch of Maxse, see Biographical Section, p. 1715.)

[2] When I made copies of the *manuscript* letters of GM to Maxse, in 1955, they were in the possession of General Sir Ivor Maxse. Later these letters and other family papers were transferred to the West Sussex County Record Office, from which I secured *typed* copies of a number of letters, the originals of which had disappeared. 'Maxse Papers' will be used to designate both sources.

[3] GM always added a *k* to Chapman's given name.

[4] Thackeray's *The Virginians* had just ended with publication of the 23rd and 24th numbers in September. In Letter 42 GM thought it 'charmingly' written and showing a 'calm command of material' when only three parts had been published.

On the other hand you may (and I know one or two clever men who do) hang too much upon plot, so that the blood of this world has no free space to circulate, and the whole creation becomes cramped and stiff. That is an error of the other extreme. The best plan is, to know clearly what you are going to do when you sit down to write, to be quite certain you are going to do something, and to have that something *in your eye*. There can be no harm in sketching it out. Indeed, I think that to do so, and then take it into the mind, and let it grow and expand as it will, and gradually by a natural process correct and weed itself, is *the* thing to do. I fancy all *great* works to have been so composed. Don't mind speaking to your friends about it, as it developes, and don't refuse to listen to anybody's opinion; and do refuse to listen altogether to the opinion of one. The best critic is the Many, in matters of human nature. But I must tire you, and I think I have said sufficient. As a last counsel, follow (to use the Germanism) the Objective rather than the Subjective in your art: aim at being concrete rather than abstract. Solid stuff endures, while flimsy ideas rapidly return to their element. Do I give advice I do not myself pursue? None the less do I see what should be.

As a pendant to these remarks, let me add, that if you have a Becky Sharp, a Don Quixote, or even a Pickwick, waiting to be delivered, pray do not waste a moment. *They* will soon find their way in the world.

Believe me / My dear Captn Maxse / Very faithfully yours,

George Meredith

50. *To* SAMUEL LUCAS

MS.: Parrish Collection, Princeton. Excerpt printed (from a typed copy in the Altschul Collection): *Altschul Catalogue*, p. 78.

Piccadilly[1]
October 3, 1859

My dear Lucas,

Your letter reached me this morning. I have been spending some time in Surrey. Many thanks for your kind intention to stand forth and defend my moral character.[2] Apropos of Mudie: Chapman here wrote to ask about the 'exclusion' in question. Mudie, it appears, took 300 copies: (deigning to say that he had some hope of me etc.). He replied that he had advertised it as much and as long as he could, but that, in

---

50. [1] Presumably written on the premises of C. & H., 193 Piccadilly.
[2] i.e. against the imputation of Mudie's withdrawal of *The Ordeal of Richard Feverel*. Lucas's defence was a review of the novel in *The Times* (14 Oct.).

consequence of the urgent remonstrances of several respectable families, who objected to it as dangerous and wicked and damnable, he was compelled to withdraw it. Such is the case. There are grossly prurient, and morbidly timid, people, who might haply be hurt, and with these the world is well stocked.

What are you going to do with the poem 'The Head of Bran' ?[3] It is the best thing you have yet had of mine; but it is enough for me that you have to consider the multitude. No complaints, I assure you. Still——!

I have once or twice dipped my pen in ink for you: I have two or three really good Tales:[4] but they are tales of real life. Now when I imagine a story, I do as I like, invent incidents, shape events, and so forth: but the reality fascinates me. I feel that I can't beat it. And the truth is, I won't send what is not good, or suitable: and until I can mould these, or devise some fresh ones (I will presently put the spur) *Once a Week* shall have no prose from me. I want to see you to speak to you about it. If during the next week you have occasion to write to me, address to Messrs. Chapman & Hall, as my residence will be uncertain.

With loud and long applause of your love of 'fair play'

I am / My dear Lucas / Very faithfully yours,

George Meredith

51. *To* Samuel Lucas

MS.: Yale.

October 25, 1859

My dear Lucas,

Could I be anything but content?[1] In general I hold that, whether praised or blamed for what he writes, a man should keep his peace. But since we have spoken on the matter I am justified in saying that your notice is very generous.

As to the offer of B[radbury] & E[vans],[2] I would like to speak to you. I left my card the other day. I have some Indian ballads of Thoby Prinsep's,[3] whom you may know, and who allows me to do with them

[3] A poem, published in *OaW* (4 Feb. 1860), with an illustration by Millais.

[4] These tales were apparently never published.

51. [1] A reference to Lucas's review of *The Ordeal of Richard Feverel*. (See Note 2, preceding letter.)

[2] For the serial rights to *Evan Harrington*, published serially in *OaW* beginning with 11 Feb. 1860.

[3] Henry Thoby Prinsep (1792–1878), Indian civil servant for many years, author of numerous works on India, and a 'facile verse-writer'. Returning to England in 1843, he attracted a number of artists and writers to his circle by his interest, kindliness, and generosity (*DNB*).

as I please. They are good from the fact of their telling a story. I will call with them one day this week.

Faithfully yours,
George Meredith

52. *To* SAMUEL LUCAS

MS.: C. L. Cline. Excerpt printed (from a typed copy): *Altschul Catalogue*, p. 76.

Esher
Monday, [? *c.* October 31, 1859][1]

Dear Lucas!

Miss Courtenay / 25 Sloane St / S.W.

Thoby Prinsep / Sandown House / Esher / Surrey.

I left the addresses with Walford.[2]

I think we may put some fitting verses to the cobbler, but you mustn't be in a hurry for them.—I want to meet Tenniel. My object is to ask him what he thinks (or would think) about illustrating *The Shaving of Shagpat*.[3] He would do it capitally. I think it would suit him. Combined we should be sure of a publisher and a public. May I ask you to suggest it to him? The book abounds with pictures of all sorts, that only want the pencil.

Your faithful
George Meredith

52. [1] It is impossible to date this letter with certainty, but 31 Oct. 1859 is a reasonable guess. If GM made his promised call on Lucas (see preceding letter) on the 27th or 28th, he may have failed to find him but talked with Walford instead, mentioning the names of Louisa Courtenay, a journalist friend of the Duff Gordons, and Thoby Prinsep as possible contributors to *OaW*. Walford may then have passed on the names without the addresses to Lucas, who asked GM for them.

[2] Edward Walford (1823–97) was connected with *OaW* from 1859–66, first as subeditor and then as editor. He was a well-known antiquary and was author of a series of biographical and genealogical works.

[3] This refers to the second edn. of *Shagpat*, which was not published until 1865 and which contained a water-colour drawing of 'Bhanavar among the Serpents' by Frederick Sandys, not Tenniel.

53. *To* MISS JANET DUFF GORDON[1]

Text: W. M. Meredith's personal copy of *Letters*, with corrections in his hand (Bodleian Library). Published: *Letters*, i. 13–15; Janet Ross, *The Fourth Generation* (1912), pp. 51–52.

[Seaford]
[? Late November–Early December 1859]

Fitz[2] goes about the house and neighbourhood with a huge volume of Francatelli[3] in his hand. Thus have we colloquized:—

Fitz: Oyster soup is out of the question, with cod and oysters to follow. It must be brown. But if the veal doesn't come from Brighton! Good G—d! what a set of heathens these people are!

Poet: Eh? Oh, yes, brown, of course!

Fitz: You haven't the slightest idea of the difficulties.

Poet (mooning): She was dressed very becomingly in white sauce.

Fitz (taking it naturally): *À la Béchamel.* That's what I'm most anxious about. Do you think Ockenden[4] understood my directions? The potatoes to be sliced about half an inch: sauce poured over: then fresh layer—(becomes excited)—if well done, I know nothing better in the world than Potatoes *à la Béchamel*!

Poet (writes): And you are all I care for in the world, dearest Rose! I care for nothing but you on earth! (Answers a trebly repeated query) Oh, yes! I like Maintenon cutlets very much.

Fitz (rubbing his hands): I can trust to old Ockenden for them, thank Heaven.

Poet (getting awake): Your wife should be a good cook, Maurice?

Fitz: Well, if she's at all educated and civilized, she will be.

Poet: I know a marriageable young lady who hates potatoes, doesn't understand a particle of the great Science, and finishes her dinner in two minutes.

Fitz: Lord help the man who marries her!

53. [1] This letter clearly reflects GM's feelings toward Janet Duff Gordon, who was shortly to marry another man. (For a biographical sketch of her and her family, see Biographical Section, pp. 1715–16.)
[2] Maurice FitzGerald, nephew of Edward FitzGerald, a brilliant classical scholar and a *gourmet*. He lived, among other places, at Seaford and Esher.
[3] Charles Elmé Francatelli (1805–76), born in London of Italian parents, had studied cuisine in France. His career as chef included positions with a succession of nobility, Crockford's and the Reform Club, and even Queen Victoria herself. He was the author of *The Modern Cook* (1845), which went through numerous editions, and *The Cook's Guide* (1861).
[4] Ellis (p. 78) says that GM and FitzGerald lodged in Seaford with the village carpenter and wheelwright, Richard Ockenden, 'whose wife was a wonderful cook—and the chief attraction for a prolonged stay in Sussex'.

Poet: I think he'll be a lucky fellow.

Fitz: No accounting for tastes! (Pursues the theme) The pheasant opposite you. I'll take the plovers. Ockenden says the jelly has set. Fancy your not knowing how much a gill is!—a gill and a half of Maraschino. I think the jelly will be a success.

Poet: Upon my honour, you look as radiant as if you had just touched off an ode!

Fitz: We won't open the Champagne till the second course.

Poet: I stick to claret.—What's the matter?

Fitz (impatiently): I have asked you half a dozen times whether you think the Ratafias should garnish the Jelly!

Poet (indifferently): Just as you like. (Writes): But a misfortune now befell our hero.

Fitz (with melancholy): I've given up all hope of the plovers' eggs! Heigho! (Stretches himself in a chair in a state of absolute mental depression.)

Poet, regarding him, takes out notebook: writes: Life is a thing of circles, like Dante's hell. In the narrowest of them Despair may be as abysmal, Hope as great, as in the widest! The patriot who sees his country enslaved: the lover who wins a smile from his mistress one day, and hears the next that she has bestowed the like on another gentleman: these sorrow not, or joy not more violently than one who is deprived of plovers' eggs, expectant of them, or greets a triumphant dish of potatoes *à la Béchamel*!

54. *To* SAMUEL LUCAS

MS.: Yale. Excerpt printed: *Altschul Catalogue*, p. 81.

Seaford
December 6, 1859

My dear Lucas,

I am returning this week, and will leave further chapters[1] at the Office, as I pass through London.

I send to-day, a batch of stories for Christmas, for *Once a Week*; written expressly for it, as I think the week should be distinguished a little.[2] The stories are (intended to be) all fun. There is no ghost-

54. [1] For the serial, *EH*.

[2] The stories, four in number, were published in *OaW* for 24 Dec. under the title 'A Story-Telling Party' and were signed with a lower-case Greek gamma. GM had actually pilfered the stories from his friend Francis Burnand, who gives (*Records and Reminiscences*, 1904, i. 363–4) an amusing account of chancing upon *his* stories in *OaW* and demanding that, in return, GM recommend one of Burnand's stories to the editor. GM did so, and in the 12 May 1860 issue Burnand's 'Mr. Lorquison's Story' appeared. (For Burnand, see Note 1, Letter 178.)

walking, and picturing of the season, as we are accustomed to see, but there is something for people to laugh over and tell again, if they please. I think the stories rather amusing: but I have not worked them up, and purposely not. *Don't put my name.*

And now, if they suit you, I want to tell you that I require £10 for them, and shall be obliged if B[radbury] & E[vans] will, at your representation of acceptance of article, forward me the same to Esher, in a day or two. Address:

Copsham Cottage, / Esher, / *Surrey.*

I think I must say definitively, that I can't begin the serial before February. I am in doubt about the title. Lewes don't like it; and his judgment is worth something. Besides it binds me too much to a positive course, and tempts to extravagance in the unfolding of situations.

I will try and see you next week, and consult on it.

Pray don't forget to speak to B[radbury] & E[vans] on the matter before-mentioned. It will oblige me.

Ever faithful[ly] yours,
George Meredith

55. *To* SAMUEL LUCAS

Text: typed copy, Yale. Excerpt printed: *Altschul Catalogue*, p. 81.

Copsham Cottage, Esher, Surrey
[*c.* December 12, 1859]

My dear Lucas,

I have received and acknowledged the note from B[radbury] and E[vans]; and am greatly pleased at their promptness.[1]

Believe me I would save you perplexity, if I thought it wise to begin next month. But I have the fear that I should only cause you greater in the end. My work is at present a study: the incidents shape and are dependent on character: consequently they have to be thought over and worked with some labour. You will, I think, like the story; and perhaps you may as well set up the first part immediately. If it gets into my hands, I shall be cutting at it, correcting, polishing—unless I see it as a fact in print.

To-day or to-morrow you will get the two next chapters for 2nd number:

'On Board the Jocasta'
'The Funeral and the Family'

55. [1] The old ledgers of Bradbury & Evans show that on 9 Dec. pre-payment for the Christmas stories was remitted to GM. (See Note 2, preceding letter.)

and on Thursday or Friday, the two succeeding:

'On the Road'
'Mother and Son'

which will form No. 3.

The *stories*[2] want an illustration, if it's possible. They seem to me to swing off, and sound naturally—that is, as men tell them. I hope they'll amuse. Next Christmas we must have a regular number, and beat our rivals.[3] This year we give them the race to walk over. They pocket the money; but let's be patient, and in the end our principle will tell. I hate the unreality and awkward construction of their framework.

I will try to be at the Office to-morrow at 4 or a quarter past, and may stand a chance of seeing you.

Ever faithfully yours,
(Signed) George Meredith

56. *To* SAMUEL LUCAS

MS.: Yale. Printed: *Altschul Catalogue*, p. 81, with omission of the first paragraph.

Copsham Cottage, Esher
December 20, [1859]

My dear Lucas,

Enclosed is 'Temujin'.[1] I can't get Thoby Prinsep to append more than his initials—to be printed as you will see, at the close of the ballad.

But, Oh, Heaven! Why have you advertised me as a 'popular author'?[2] Isn't it almost a fraud on the public? Won't they stare when they behold this notorious child they are quite unacquainted with?—

For my part I think the title should be *Evan Harrington*, simply. But wait as long as you can. Tell me what you think.

Get in the poems[3] before the story begins.

---

55. [2] *All the Year Round*, conducted by Dickens.
   [3] *All the Year Round*, conducted by Dickens.

56. [1] H. Thoby Prinsep's 'Temujin', signed *HP.*, appeared in the 1 Dec. 1860 issue of *OaW*.

   [2] In a self-congratulatory Postscript to the 24 Dec. issue, the proprietors of *OaW* promised improvement of the literary, scientific, and artistic features of the magazine and stated that 'an important Serial by a Popular Author is already in the Artist's hands, and will appear before the end of January . . .'.

   [3] Two poems by GM appeared in *OaW* before the commencement of *EH*: 'The Crown of Love' (31 Dec. 1859) and 'The Head of Bran' (4 Feb. 1860).

And please don't hurry for *emotion*. It will come. I have it. But—
unless you have mysteries of the W[ilkie] Collins kind[4]—interest, not
to be false and evanescent, must kindle slowly, and ought to centre
more in *character*—out of which incidents should grow. I will consider
your requirements as much as I possibly can. Tell me whether you
intend to put in the last *two* chapters you have, in the 2nd number; or
only the 'On Board Jocasta'—it will guide me as to terminations.

Ever yours,
George Meredith

57. *To* SAMUEL LUCAS

MS.: Yale. Printed: *Altschul Catalogue*, pp. 81–82, with omission of the fourth paragraph.

Copsham Cottage, Esher
December 28, 1859

My dear Lucas,

You shall have the proofs in a day or two. I am thinking over the
title. I can't as yet hit on one better than what we have. The name of
the hero is too commonplace. If anything better should strike you,
pray let me hear. Much depends on a good heading.

Have you had the fourth chapter set up yet? Please do, and send it.

I am rather upset by what you say about lack of interest in the progress of the story. Doubtless in a 'Serial' point of view, there may be
something to say; but I fancy I am right in slowly building up for the
scenes to follow, and the book will, as a whole, be better for it. It has,
however, slightly unsettled me. Still I would not have you do otherwise
than speak openly. In the end I profit and am spurred by it. Still if you
see good points, mention them: Praise nourishes.

As to the *Cornhill Maga[zine]*: the first Number fairly entitles it to be
call[ed] the '*Old Fogies*'.[1] It reeks with old Fogydom.

Try and allow my 3rd number to occupy 7 1/2 or 8 pages. 'On the
Road' is rather long. I will leave it at the office on Friday. Read and
let me have your opinion. It develops the character of the hero partly:
the incidents subsequently affect him. But I wish to know how you
take it. It does not much move the tale. But do not yet insist on that
entirely, at present.

---

[4] Wilkie Collins's *The Woman in White* was running serially in *All the Year Round*
(26 Nov. 1859–25 Aug. 1860).
57. [1] The first number of the *Cornhill Magazine*, under the editorship of Thackeray, bore
a publication date of Jan. 1860, but like other magazines was available a few days before
publication date. GM's opinion contrasts with that of Trollope, who wrote to Thackeray:
'Putting aside my own contribution . . . I certainly do conceive that nothing equal to it of
its kind was ever hitherto put forth—' (Booth, op. cit., p. 55).

I must tell you that Lady Gordon,[2] in whose judgment I have great confidence, likes the Countess,[3] and would not have her cut short: says she is true to nature, and the best of the 3 chapters. I may clip to the extent of half a page or more, here and there. Further I can't promise.

Ever most faithfully yours,
George Meredith

58. *To* SAMUEL LUCAS

MS.: Yale. Printed: *Altschul Catalogue*, p. 82, with omissions.

Copsham Cottage, Esher
[? December 31, 1859, or
January 1, 1860]

My dear Lucas,

I thank you for your 'giftie' in the shape of the admirable critique of the poem. A man should derive great benefit from seeing himself as a jackass sees him. The end is gained—I'll be tender to Benson.[1]

In re Title.[2]

Gentle and Genteel.

Isn't *Gentility and a Gentleman* better?

But since Evans is in a hurry, and likes it as it stands, and I can work it out sufficiently in the main to be true to it, I really don't care to hold out. If you don't hear by Friday next, put it in Evans's hands and let us face our public boldly.

To-morrow I will despatch proofs of the first 3 chapters. They will need no Revise, I should think. Perhaps your sub, or somebody, will look and see there's no bad English, or absurdity.—I'll mark for Revise, when I want one.

What do you think of the Laureate's 'Sea-Dreams'?—!!: The Muse in a four-poster![3]

Copy you shall have very shortly. But try and spur me on without giving me the sense that I am absolutely due; for then I feel hunted, and may take strange leaps. I think we shall do, but I am in a sort of

57. [2] i.e. Duff Gordon (see Biographical Section, pp. 1715–16).
   [3] The Countess de Saldar in *EH*.
58. [1] Ralph A. Benson, a frequent contributor of poems to *OaW*. The 'giftie' was probably a criticism of GM's poem, 'The Crown of Love', published in the 31 Dec. issue of *OaW*.   [2] For *EH*.
   [3] Tennyson's 'Sea Dreams' was published in *Macmillan's Magazine* (Jan. 1860).

a knot just now. The endings of the numbers bother me. I can work out my idea; but shall I lead on the reader? That's my difficulty, till I get into the thick of it. After the first 4 numbers, the game will be clear.

Ever faithfully yours,
George Meredith

To you and *Once a Week* a successful New Year!

59. *To* SAMUEL LUCAS

MS.: Yale. Printed: *Altschul Catalogue*, p. 82, with omissions.

Copsham Cottage, Esher
Tuesday, [? January 3, 1860][1]

My dear Lucas,

Burnand[2] has fun in him. I have before tried to get him to send you something. Pray do as you like with the story.

What say you to these titles?—

The Substantial and the Essential (Bad, but better than *Shams and Realities*)—

All but a Gentleman

This, I think, hits the mark, all but—Say? In this title, 'Gentleman' is stressed differently. Thus the hero has and proves he has fine noble qualities, but with the stigma that clings to him there is one drawback. He is *all* but a gentleman.

The Tailor's Family

This binds to no special development and has not the rather provocative and offensive clang in the ear that 'gentleman' produces. It would allow my plot to work out. Speak?—Or *The Gentleman-Tailor's Family.*—

I have gone all wrong about the endings of the chapters for numbers, and am re-writing two. I am young at it. My idea and meaning was clear and safe; but I did not sufficiently *lead on*. But remember, I have called this a Comedy. To invent probabilities in modern daily

<hr>

59. [1] GM's Christmas stories appeared in the 24 Dec. issue of *OaW*. (See Note 2, Letter 54.) Burnand could not have seen them earlier than about 21 Dec. and probably did not see them until several days later. Theoretically this letter might have been written on 27 Dec. But on 28 Dec. (Letter 57) GM says that he is thinking over the title of his novel. That subject, taken up in Letter 58 (31 Dec. or 1 Jan.), I assume to be continued in this letter.

[2] With this letter GM sent Burnand's 'Mr. Lorquison's Story'. (See Note 2, Letter 54.)

life is difficult; you can't work up the excitement of melodrama and *Women in White*—at least till you are in full career.

Upon my honour, I work for my money!—

Yours ever faithfully,

George Meredith

60. *To* SAMUEL LUCAS

MS.: Yale. Printed: *Altschul Catalogue*, pp. 82–83, with omissions.

Copsham Cottage, Esher

Thursday, [? January 5, 1860]

Proofs of Chapters 1.2.3.
returned herewith.

My dear Lucas,

The later the day, the better the work. I can say no more.

I shall have that amount, or more, ready when you start. I will, as far as a man may say, keep up, and give you no anxiety.

I send a chapter (partly re-written) called 'My Gentleman on the Road'.[1] I particularly wish your opinion of it. I stress small incidents: but they best exhibit character: and remember (or such is my view) serial reading demands excitement enough to lead on, but, more and better, amusement of a quiet kind. The tension of the *W[oman] in W[hite]* is not exactly pleasant, though cleverly produced. One wearies of it. Be patient. By the way, if you know any instances of fine gentlemanly delicacy, communicate. It will help invention.

Tell me quickly how you think the chapter goes; I introduced it for the sake of 'showing' the hero.

That with the preceding chapter in your hands, will make the 3rd Number.

Who illustrates?

I have in my hands a capital translation of the old popular German ballad of Tannhäuser by Lady Duff Gordon.[2] She will let you have it for *O[nce] a W[eek]*, if you like:—about a column in length.

I will call on Evans next week, if possible, but I have full trust in him.

One thing I want you to ask him *now*. That is, to give me the permission to dispose (if in his gift, and not mine) of the first sheets to an American publisher. I'm horridly poor and £30 or £40 is a windfall. Will you do it? And let me know by return post.

60. [1] Chapter 6 of *EH*, published as a part of No. 3, 25 Feb.

[2] 'Tannhäuser', by L. D. G. (Lady Duff Gordon), with an unsigned introduction by Sir Alexander Duff Gordon, appeared in the 17 Aug. 1861 issue of *OaW*.

Or if Evans will do it for me, Field[s],[3] of the Boston firm, will (from what he said of *R[ichard] F[everel]*) gladly close for it. Besides, this story would catch the Yankee by the ear. We ought to get a *sum* for it.

Yours ever,
George Meredith

61. *To* SAMUEL LUCAS

MS.: Yale.

193 Piccadilly, London, W.
[*c.* January 17, 1860]

My dear Lucas,

I called this morning to see you in Cork Street.[1] Could not call again.

Let Evans keep the original heading,[2] an he likes it.

I will support it to the best of my ability.

Copy you shall [have] further on Friday. Meantime send fresh proofs, if you please.

Yours ever,
George Meredith

62. *To* F. M. EVANS[1]

Text: typed copy furnished by Messrs. Bradbury & Agnew. Published: *Letters*, i. 20.

Copsham Cottage, Esher
Saturday, January 21, 1860

My dear Sir,

I thank you for the £50 cheque on account.

I tried to call on you yesterday when I was in Town, but had no time. Perhaps you may as well, since you kindly undertake the task, write to Messrs. Harper's agents, or send to them; and come to the

---

[3] James T. Fields, of Ticknor & Fields, Boston.
61. [1] William Tinsley (*Random Recollections of an Old Publisher*, 1900, i. 323) says that Lucas lived in a 'charming home in Cork Street, where works of art and books abounded'.
   [2] For *EH*.
62. [1] Frederick Mullett ('Pater') Evans (1803 or 1804–69), with his partner William Bradbury, had entered into the printing business in 1830. In 1842 they purchased *Punch* and in 1843 became publishers, their first book being Dickens's *Christmas Carol* (Boase, *Modern English Biography*).

best terms you can.[2] The story (as you may tell them) will suit Yankee sentiment and Yankee principles. Exalt me tolerably, and in fine, I shall be quite satisfied that you will manage[3] it as well as it can be done: but there should be no loss of time.

Yours faithfully,
George Meredith

N.B. Perhaps, should it be needful, you may say that we are going to be guilty of no *impropriety* in this tale, and will never again offend young maids.[4]

63. *To* SAMUEL LUCAS

MS.: Yale. Excerpt printed: *Altschul Catalogue*, p. 83.

Copsham Cottage
Saturday, January 21, 1860

My dear Lucas,

Have the chapter 'Mother and Son',[1] (which I send) set up at once— read it, and tell me whether you think it of sufficient interest and length for No. 4. If not the 'Eccentric' must go with it. Decide then![2]

Keene will do capitally.[3] Shall I see proofs of the illustrations?—

I think *positively* the Dickens system of making the principal tale commence the number, far preferable to its being in the middle; and if you'll allow me I'll stipulate thereupon.[4] Please agree, and say so. It gives a look of solidity even to the advertisements. Aren't you going to put it in your bills? And have you heard any verification of the title having been used before?

Yours faithfully,
George Meredith

62. [2] For American rights to *EH*.

  [3] *Letters* reads *arrange*.

  [4] A reference to objections to *The Ordeal of Richard Feverel*.

63. [1] Chapter 7, published as No. 4, 3 Mar. 1860.

  [2] The word *then* may be *thou*, as transcribed in the *Altschul Catalogue*. But it is not italicized as in the *AC*.

  [3] Charles Keene (1823–91), whose drawings in *OaW* and *Punch* made him famous, was to illustrate *EH*.

  [4] The only innovation in *All the Year Round* was its commencement with a serial story by a well-known writer, who was not anonymous like the rest of the contributors but was advertised with the magazine. Dickens led off with *A Tale of Two Cities* and was followed by Wilkie Collins with *The Woman in White*. Lucas adopted Meredith's advice, and thereafter *OaW* began with a serial.

64. *To* SAMUEL LUCAS

MS.: Yale. Printed: *Altschul Catalogue*, p. 83, with omissions.

Copsham Cottage, Esher
Friday, [? January 27, 1860]

My dear Lucas,

I sent the proofs of Nos. 2 and 3, to the Office to-day: also MSS. for No. 5, being the chapters 'An Eccentric' and 'The Countess in Low. Society'.[1]

Are you sure you're not thinking of the quantity of matter as suitable for your editorial requirements, rather than the quality of the chapter in question? Looking over it I can't say it holds me much. Have the 8th and 9th chapters set up at once, and see whether it won't be better to finish the month with a larger supply. 'Tannhäuser' (with an introduction by Sir A. D. G.),[2] I send as well. Let the signature be L. D. G. Forward the proof to Lady Duff Gordon, Royal Hotel, Ventnor, Isle of Wight.

Ever yours,
George Meredith

65. *To* SAMUEL LUCAS

MS.: Yale.

Copsham Cottage, Esher
Sunday, [February 5, 1860]

Dear Lucas,

Botheration is our lot. I have written to Lover,[1] subscribing to what you propose;—apologizing etc.—Was ever such a damned nuisance?

Please let me have the last two chapters (proofs) by Wednesday next. I'm going to Ventnor for a couple of weeks, and should like to take them with me. Send also, if you can, proofs of 'Tannhäuser' and I will take them to Lady Gordon, to whom I am going. I will try and see you on Tuesday. Shall you be at Bouverie Street by about 4 p.m.?

Yours faithfully,
George Meredith

64. [1] Chapters 8 and 9, published as separate numbers.
[2] See Note 2, Letter 60.
65. [1] Samuel Lover (1797–1868), Irish novelist (*Rory O'Moore*, 1837), poet, and musician ('Molly Bawn'), had contributed a poem, 'The Bride of Galtrim', to *OaW* for 21 Jan. GM had probably been critical of it, as he was of many of the contributions to *OaW*.

66. *To* SAMUEL LUCAS

MS.: Yale. Printed: *Altschul Catalogue*, p. 83, with omissions.

[Copsham Cottage, Esher]
Monday morning, [February 6, 1860]

My dear Lucas,

In No. 3. 'The Funeral and the Family', where Evan and Andrew Cogglesby are talking, the footman is made to announce 'Dinner at 1/2 past 7'.—Put 6. That was a late hour for the period, and we may as well be as true as we can. May I trouble you?

Please also send the 1st number[1] that I may have it on Wednesday morning—if possible.

We will leave the artist to his devices. Just tell him from me (with a multitude of thanks) that it will be as well not to insist too much on the costume—especially in dealing with the younger people. Thackeray touches the question capitally in *Vanity Fair*. A young lady in a 'poke' is hardly presentable.[2]

Your faithful
George Meredith

67. *To* SAMUEL LUCAS

MS.: Yale. Printed: *Altschul Catalogue*, p. 22.

Copsham Cottage, Esher
Wednesday, [February 8, 1860]

My dear Lucas,

You haven't sent revises: I can't trust myself to go over the whole again; I send the one bit of correction.

If not too much to ask, revises had better be sent.

And please have the numbers forwarded to me, as they come out. I called for yesterday's. Keene's first illustration is as good as it could be. Send the next number to me, 'Royal Hotel / Ventnor / Isle of Wight'.[1]

Don't you think it would be as well to print the headings (and advertize here and there) of the chapters on the title-page?—

66. [1] i.e. the 11 Feb. issue of *OaW*, with the first number of *EH*.
   [2] In a footnote toward the end of Ch. VI of the first edn. of *Vanity Fair* Thackeray says that it was his intention to depict all of his characters in the costumes of the early years of the nineteenth century, but when he remembered the hideous costumes of the day and recalled that a lady was actually 'habited like this' [illustrating with an exaggerated poke bonnet], he decided to dress them in the current fashion.
67. [1] He was going to visit the Duff Gordons.

You shall have a part a week, or more.

I will have two chapters, and the remaining proofs in hand, in Bouverie Street on Friday. I go on *Saturday* to the Isle of Wight, for a week or so.

> Yours ever,
> George Meredith

68. *To* SAMUEL LUCAS

MS.: Yale. Printed: *Altschul Catalogue*, p. 83, with omissions.

> Copsham Cottage
> Thursday, [? February 9, 1860]

My dear Lucas,

Your advice is good. This cursed desire I have haunting me to show the reason for things is a perpetual obstruction to movement. I *do* want the dash of Smollett and know it. But remember that *full* half the *incident* of Smollett trenches on amusing matter not permitted me by my public.—I wish you had given me the spur on that point before.

Pray look ahead. There's in the next number a description of a cricket field. I will cut it in what pieces you please—especially the early part. But cricket fields are rather liked. I will attend to your suggestions if you will look over the number at once, and send them. The paragraph about 'eating and drinking' shall be cut out.

Then follows a chapter I have doubts of. 'The Comic Muse surveys the position.'[1] Pray, when it is set up, look at it just before it is sent. Speak out, for I am only anxious to do my duty by you, and will defer to my editor almost entirely.

We then come to Beckley-Court, and the intrigues of the Countess, the loves of Evan and Rose, etc., and then I think we shall do.

> Yours ever,
> George Meredith

Remember that in Smollett conduct is never *accounted* for. My principle is to show the events flowing from evident causes. To *naturalize* them to the mind of the reader, I have many temptations to incident which I reject because they seem to me out of nature.

Tell me distinctly whether the account you hear of the story is on the whole bad—or say, not tolerably good. Or is it *just* as you put it?

---

68. [1] Altered to 'The Countess Describes the Field of Action'.

69. *To* SAMUEL LUCAS

MS.: Yale.

Copsham, Esher
Sunday, [? March or April 1860]

My dear Lucas,
  Glad to hear you are back and well. The truth is I have been seriously knocked down, and I beg you will, in my name, ask Keene and Swain,[1] to both of whom I am doing great injustice, to excuse me, and name the circumstances to them. I am recovering and shall, I hope, soon regain what is lost. I am upset about my work.

Ever yours,
George Meredith

70. *To* SIR ALEXANDER DUFF GORDON

MS.: University of Texas.

[Copsham Cottage, Esher]
April 5, [? 1860][1]

My dear Sir Alec,
  May I beg of you to send by your invaluable messenger, this volume of Macaulay to Chapman & Hall, 193 Piccadilly. They want the book to-day, or I would not trouble you.

Most faithfully,
George Meredith

71. *To* FREDERICK A. MAXSE

Text: *Letters*, i. 15–17. Collated with the typed copy in the Maxse Papers, which supplies the date.

Copsham Cottage, Esher
April 20, [1860]

My dear Captain Maxse,
  I have been struck down by illness, and did not receive your pamphlet[1] till two days back. I have been happy to do my best with regard to corrections.

69. [1] Joseph Swain, a well-known wood-engraver who engraved the plates for Keene's drawings; head of the engraving department of *Punch*, with which he was connected for more than fifty years.
70. [1] Macaulay died on 28 Dec. 1859 and various selections from his works and books about him began to appear shortly later. I have no other basis for the dating of this letter. C. & H., however, were not Macaulay's usual publishers.
71. [1] *The Maxse Papers: A Catalogue*, ed. Francis W. Steer, Chichester, 1964, lists *A Word for Truth* (*Concerning Our Attitude towards France*), London, 1860, by An English Seaman, [Maxse] almost certainly the pamphlet under discussion, but I have not seen it.

I like the pamphlet. It goes with many of my views, and it is generous: a point on which I lay stress, for the popular principle is avowed selfishness and breeches pocket, or bare sentimentalism, in dealing with foreign relations.

I do not like the colloquial introduction. 'J. B.' [? John Bull] and the 'West End' are in my opinion beneath the dignity of an earnest address to one's countrymen. I have taken the liberty (for which I beg your excuse) to strike out one or two sentences.

But, may I ask, are you not under some influence yonder? Are you not prompted by some peculiar feeling—a private friendship? The sound to me, throughout, is that of one whose heart was moved by personal esteem. I mention this, because I think it will be a general impression; and I know enough of the French to be aware that some of them rise high with you in intimacy.

Anyhow I think the pamphlet must fail; for what might have floated will sink it. It says true and pregnant things: but have you forgotten that when you are putting your countrymen and friend flagrantly in the wrong, they never can see it unless you consent to relieve their eyes with the shady doings of the opposite party.

You have not toned down your picture. You put us in the wrong entirely. Even I, who feel with you, entertained a constant protest as I read on.

I think you should have devoted a page or two to a consideration of the sentiments of the different classes of Frenchmen towards England and to an exposition of the French character. And it would have been as well to have made an attempt philosophically to account for these epidemics of animosity on *both* sides. I believe that on ours it springs *solely* from panic, and the revulsions of humiliation and shame attendant thereon. Where have the French more enthusiastic admirers of their valour? of their intellect? of their wit? I think our hands are given heartily across Channel till this cursed uneasiness about our 'homes' makes the Briton draw back and clench his honest fist.

Of the Emperor I strongly approve your bold speaking. He has done great work and shown great-mindedness towards us. The veil of the 'Panic' is between us and him; but even should he become our foe, the Italian campaign must be seen in its true features sooner or later. It is worthy an Epic. About Savoy our singing has been small, but the political principle involved in the appropriation of this province,[2] and the danger to Switzerland, justify plain speaking.—Pardon me, I beg, and believe me, my dear Captain Maxse,

Yours very faithfully,
George Meredith

[2] Savoy was ceded to France by the Treaty of Turin (24 Mar. 1860).

72. *To* F. M. EVANS

Text: typed copy furnished by Messrs. Bradbury & Agnew.

Copsham Cottage, Esher
June 28, 1860

My dear Sir,

I beg to acknowledge the receipt of your cheque for £60 further on account for E[*van*] H[*arrington*].

The first day I have time to spare in town I will call on you.

Let me add that if you come to Esher again, I hope you will do me that favour.

Faithfully yours,
George Meredith

73. *From* MARY ELLEN MEREDITH
To EDWARD CHAPMAN

MS.: University of Texas.

Lower Halliford, Chertsey
July 4, 1860

My dear Mr. Chapman,

Can you lend me £10 till Michaelmas. In the event of my death between this and that Papa will repay it to you. I have no other security to you except my own assertion that I have never yet borrowed a penny without returning it at the specified time. If you can oblige me please send me a check here. I have let my house to Parker and taken a little cottage for boating at Weybridge so that what I have had to buy for that and the moving spare things from Richmond has taken up my loose cash and I never get in debt.

I am so vexed that the first letter I greet you with after your perilous journey to 'Foreign Parts' should be about money that I will not write to answer Mrs. Chapman's last kind letter now but shall do so by-and-bye on a sheet unalloyed by Mammon.

I should be glad to hear however how you like the place and how you performed the journey.

And with kindest love to all your family, believe me

Faithfully yours,
Mary Meredith

74. *From* MARY ELLEN MEREDITH
To EDWARD CHAPMAN

MS.: University of Texas.

Lower Halliford, Chertsey
July 8, 1860

My dear Mr. Chapman,

Many thanks for your kindness: the first two halves came safely. Never having written or seen an I.O.U., I think it better to send it now so that if not right you can send it to me to be corrected with the other half notes.

I am hard at work getting my boating cottage in order, in a few days I shall write to Mrs. Chapman. I am very glad you all like the place.

With love to all, believe me

Faithfully yours,
Mary Meredith

I have said October 1, because though I shall have the money on the 29th of September I may not be able to transfer it to you by that time.

75. *To* SAMUEL LUCAS

MS.: Yale.

[Copsham Cottage, Esher]
Friday, [? August 1860][1]

My dear Lucas,

I think Millais might catch a sentiment from one or two of the enclosed. I would rather not have my name to them, as they are productions of my coxcombical and too imitative youth. Initials, if you like. You see, I still intend to do something better. I have one or two ballads for you by and by. These may now be printed at once. After the story is concluded I shall have a good many more, of a different character. But do, pray, exclude some of your present versiclers.

75. [1] This letter must have been written while *EH* ('the story') was in process of publication. The only poem published by *OaW* during this time was 'The Meeting' (1 Sept.), signed *G.M.* and illustrated by Millais, and I think it certain that 'the enclosed' of the first sentence refers to poems. Inasmuch as 'the pretty piece of orange peel' which GM received while he was in St. Briavels in September may well have been in response to the invitation at the end of this letter, Aug. 1860 seems a likely date for it.

You're getting a bad reputation. In return for this pleasant counsel you may send me all the letters you have had in condemnation of your servant within the last week.

Ever yours,
George Meredith

76. *To* F. M. EVANS

Text: typed copy furnished by Messrs. Bradbury & Agnew.

Copsham Cottage
Wednesday, [September 5, 1860][1]

My dear Mr. Evans,

Evan Harrington is near a close. Don't you think it would be as well to get the 3 volumes ready at once? We shall have done no later than the first week in October. The season begins in November. It would scarcely be too early. Are you prepared for this? I will call the first day I find time to spare, but perhaps it would be better if you wrote your opinion immediately.

Oblige me also by sending a cheque for £80 to Chapman & Hall's to-morrow. That will make the sum received £250.

Faithfully yours,
George Meredith

77. *To* SAMUEL LUCAS

MS.: Yale. Excerpt printed: *Altschul Catalogue*, p. 83.

St. Briavels[1]
September 27, [1860]

My dear Lucas,

Herewith is the conclusion, which, please, send to printers at once.

It is finished as an actor finishes under hisses. I thank you immensely for the pretty piece of orange-peel you transferred to my care;[2] but I really had no curiosity to inspect specimens, knowing the kinds to be not various.

76. [1] The date is fixed by an entry in the old Bradbury & Evans ledgers: on 6 Sept. a cheque in the sum of £80 was drawn in favour of GM. Other cheques had been debited as follows: 19 Jan., £50; 20 Apr., £60; 9 June, £60; 25 June, £60—with the 6 Sept. cheque a total of £310, not £250 as GM calculates.

77. [1] In the Wye valley, Gloucestershire.

[2] Probably a letter from a reader. But L. T. Hergenhan (*A Critical Consideration of the Reviewing of the Novels of George Meredith, from 'The Shaving of Shagpat' to 'The Egoist'*, University of London dissertation, 1960) has found a number of hitherto unrecorded reviews of GM's novels. The *Daily News*, for example, said that interest was declining in the concluding chapters, and the *Glasgow Courier* (13 Sept.) hinted that enough of a good thing was as good as a feast.

If you have any more, simply register them and put them by for my cooler hours. I wish you were here. The country is charming, the host[3] capital, the solitary guest very anxious to quarrel with somebody— even his badgered Editor! Sincerely I am sorry for you mainly, and will do you more justice another time.

Yours ever,
George Meredith

78. *To* SAMUEL LUCAS

MS.: Yale. Printed: *Altschul Catalogue*, p. 83, with omission of the second paragraph.

The Orchard, St. Briavels,
Coleford
Sunday, [September 30, 1860]

My dear Lucas,

How is it I haven't had proofs of the last number?[1] I particularly wished for them, to add a little polish to the hurried close. It's vexatious. Are you all in a state of disgust with the story and anxious to shovel it off anyhow? Upon my honour—I see its demerits clearly, and the points I missed, and lengthiness I should have cut short, but I maintain that the story is true to its title, and that I avoided making the fellow a snob in spite of his and my own temptations. Hence probably the charge of dulness: but this comes of an author giving himself a problem to work out, and doing it as conscientiously as he could. The ground was excessively delicate. This is too late to dwell upon; but I shudder at the thought of the last number.—

To-morrow Hawkins and I propose a descent upon Usk. What think you of the Round Table as a Christmas title? Arthur sitting in state, if you like, and listening to stories of the modern world.[2] It may sound too remote for the public ear: but it gives an opening for chivalrous narrative, suitable to present popular feeling.

Faithfully yours,
George Meredith

[3] Edward Hawkins, Jr. (1814–67), of 13 Great Marlborough St. and The Orchard, St. Briavels, Coleford, Gloucestershire; son of Edward Hawkins of the British Museum. He took B.A. and M.A. degrees at Cambridge in 1837 and 1841, was admitted to Lincoln's Inn on 25 Jan. 1838, was called to the bar on 5 May 1842, and practised as a conveyancer until his death (J. A. Venn, *Alumni Cantabrigienses*). The connexion with GM was probably through the Duff Gordons, for in Letter 125 to Janet Ross GM refers to Hawkins as her 'Perfect Gentleman'.

78. [1] The letter is endorsed with this note: 'Proof sent to Esher and a duplicate to Coleford. Oct. 2. EW' [Edward Walford, sub-editor of *OaW*].

[2] Presumably nothing came of this proposal, which is outlined at length in the following letter.

79. *To* SAMUEL LUCAS

MS.: Yale.

Esher

Monday, [? October 8, 1860]

My dear Lucas,

The '*Round Table*' scheme[1] will be very difficult to suit to our men, and without vulgarizing Arthur, I scarcely see how it's to be done.— What do you say to the title '*The Old Stage Coach*'?—Mr. William Oldfangle, a stage-coachman of the period just before the introduction of steam; a very croaky old boy, who in the end overturns all his passengers: they take refuge at an inn and tumble into good humour, tell their stories, and separate on the best of terms with one another and the time to come. I can put into this set a jolly character. At all events, it is a framework, such as it is.

The idea of the Round Table is certainly more unique. To get modern stories it must be done in this way. The narrator must confess that he *did* eat Christmas pudding overnight, albeit of a romantic temperament. So much he accords to common sense and his physician. Still he believes that he did see Arthur and his court, and messengers come to the King from all parts of the world (Garibaldi's heroic deeds[2] being recited to the circle of Knights with applause). The Christmas amusements are related. Then a Bard strikes his harp. Then a Knight tells a *chivalrous* tale. Then King Arthur's *Dwarf* tells a story that *Harrison*[3] might do well. Then *Dumplin*, the King's jester, tells a *comic story*. And a modern one or two may come in. Finally, Merlin, as Old Moore,[4] in alternate verse and recitative, after comic-song fashion, winds up. And lo, the amazed narrator beholds Arthur and his Knights all put their hands to the round table, Merlin acting medium, and the table rises, they with it; the roof of the castle flies off, the table turns and ducks and soars and is lost among the stars. The narrator finds himself in an old ruin, or where you will.—Arthur is supposed, like

79. [1] See preceding letter.

[2] The heroic deeds of Giuseppe Garibaldi (1807–82) in 1848 and 1860 had won the admiration of liberals everywhere. In May 1860 his band of a thousand poorly equipped 'Red Shirts' landed in Sicily and within a month had conquered the island. In August, with an army of four thousand, he set out to conquer Naples, won the battle of Volturno, fought against an army twice the size of his own, and was for a time dictator of the Kingdom of Naples.

[3] A. Stewart Harrison, a frequent contributor to *OaW*: 'The Pythagorean—A Tale of the First Century' (28 Jan. 1860), 'The Old Player's Story' (28 July 1860), 'The Iceberg' (6, 13 Oct. 1860), etc.

[4] Francis Moore (1657–1715) 'practised physic in London, and in 1700 started "Old Moore's"' astrological almanac' (*Chambers's Biographical Dictionary*).

Barbarossa, to be waiting for the events to call him back. Each Christmas Eve he comes from Avalon to discuss the doings of mankind and feast with his Knights.

The difficulty is that every story must have a marked tone. You must admit that, either from its noble character, or rich buffoonery, Arthur would have listened to it. The King does not decline to give ear to events in humble life; but we cannot have them merely trivial. Now, can you reckon on your story tellers? I think I can undertake to do two, besides the framework. Perhaps a ballad, as well.

Harrison is very clever, and may be counted on. We want two other *good men.*

However, this is the scheme, and you will consider it. I will call on you to-morrow in Cork Street between 12 and 1.—On Thursday I shall be in Town again, and at your service for the evening.

The 'Old Stage Coach' will be more homely and easier; but we must be careful not to seem to be copying the enemy.⁵ It can be managed. I'm for the higher effort, if practicable.

Faithfully yours,
George Meredith

Understand that the general tone of the 'Round Table' is not to be burlesque; but of that mixture which pertains to dreams and indigestion—the mythus shines undistorted through it.

80. *To* F. M. EVANS

Text: typed copy furnished by Messrs. Bradbury & Agnew.

Esher
Friday, October 19, 1860

My dear Evans,

I return 7 sheets, corrected.¹ Without recasting the whole, I can't do much to better the performance. Be so good as to send the enclosed 'The Beggar's Soliloquy'² over to Lucas. I want a cheque next week for the remainder of the money due to me. It would be safer to send it by messenger to Chapman in Piccadilly.

Faithfully yours,
George Meredith

---

⁵ Dickens and *All the Year Round.*
80. ¹ For *EH* in book form.
  ² A poem, published in *OaW* (30 Mar. 1861), with an illustration by Charles Keene.

81. *To* MISS JANET DUFF GORDON[1]

MS.: Yale. Published: *Letters,* i. 18–19, with the postscript incorporated in the body of the letter and with minor variants; *The Fourth Generation,* p. 86, with omission of the postscript.

Copsham, Esher
Friday evening, [November 23, 1860]

My dear Janet,

Yesterday I went to Town, and of course forgot—not you—but your catalogue. I therefore called on Willis & What's his name and asked the latest period of the packing. Thereupon a melancholy man conducted me to an enormous box. 'That's choke full, sir, and we've got 40 volumes more to stow in—somehow—*I* don't know how.' This was my time to tell him that you had bought half of Mudie's library, and expected that as well to be got into said box.—Why, wouldn't my Henry do it?—Yes, but, my dear Janet, Willis & What's his name aren't in love with you, and they can't. Passion does not inspire them. As for your poet, he sinks to the lowest depths of prose, and suggests the necessity for a fresh box, a small one, in addition to the one of elephantine proportions and yet unequal stomach. You are to write to me, and say that you consent to this, and I will call on W. & W.—If this is clear, all right. But I feel utterly perplexed.

I have been, and am, knocked down again by the old illness.[2] I hope it won't last, for it's horridly dispiriting.

God bless you, my dear girl! If you don't make a good wife, I've never read a page of woman. He's a lucky fellow to get you, and the best thing he can do is to pray that he may always know his luck.— Watts[3] and Coutts[4] passed like doleful spectres this afternoon, in the fog. The hunt is Queenless evermore.

Your most faithful
George M.

Arthur 'hopes you're quite well'. He can't think of anything more to say, and on my telling him I've written so, he explodes with laughter.

81. [1] Janet was being married on 5 Dec. In *The Fourth Generation* (p. 85) she says of this letter: 'Mr. Ross wanted to give me jewels, but I asked him to let me spend the money in books, and we bought many at Willis and Sotheran's, who were to pack and send them out to Alexandria. My Poet [Meredith] mentioned some I ought to have, and as I was going to my mother at Ventnor, I begged him, when in London, to order them to be packed with the others.'

[2] The exact nature of the 'old illness' is never specified. It may have been the 'knot of nerves' mentioned in Letter 101 or the digestive ailment mentioned frequently a year or two later.

[3] G. F. Watts (1817–1904), the painter and sculptor, who lived for twenty-five years with GM's friend Thoby Prinsep and who frequently hunted with the Duc d'Aumale's harriers. (Aumale was a member of the exiled Orleans family, several of whom lived at nearby Claremont.)   [4] Identified by Janet Ross as the Duc d'Aumale's huntsman.

82. *To* MISS JANET DUFF GORDON

MS.: Yale. Excerpts published: *Letters*, i. 20–21, with initials only for the names *Izod* and *Clarke*.

Copsham, Esher
Thursday, [November 29, 1860]

My dear Orange Blossom!

Izod[1] has been at me, and with the best intentions in the world, no doubt, but on the Earth I lie, and imagination will picture the idea that I am going under it. Here is a cheerful theme to address to a sweet young bride! But if I am not better by Saturday I shall not witness the wreath on my Janet's head, nor see the fixing of the ring on her hand.

Williams[2] dined here last night. He and Chapman[3] and others were at Hickman's[4] a few days back. The conversation turned upon Esher's mighty loss. Hearken to the ensuing!

Hickman: 'Her first offer—wasn't it?'

Williams: 'A—ya—aaa—'

Chapman: 'Oh, no! She had one before.'

Omnes: 'Oh!'

Chapman: 'I heard it from Sir A[lexander].[5] Some fellow, he said, with no money, no position—nothing at all.'

Omnes: 'Lord! What an ass.'

Chapman: 'Sir A[lexander] was tremendously upset by it.'

Hickman: 'And she rejected him, of course!'

Chapman: 'I don't think she's one for a poor man.' (To Williams): 'Didn't you hear of it?'

Williams: 'A—ow—Miss Gordon? Yeaiow—es. I did hear —oooo —something.'

Hickman: 'Who could the fellow have been?'

Williams: 'Don't know 'm sure.'

A wag brays mildly. Williams goes home early. Chapman asks me next day whether Williams has ever been in love with Orange Blossom. I ask—why? 'Oh!' (he repeats foregoing conversation) 'Williams turned so *green*.'

---

82. [1] Charles William Izod, the Esher doctor.

[2] Presumably the Revd. William Rice Steuart Williams, of Esher Green. He had graduated B.A. (1844) and M.A. (1851) at Oxford.

[3] Frederic Cahpman, of C. & H. GM was now an employee of C. & H. having succeeded John Forster as reader of MSS. for the firm. Waugh (p. 142) says that he began in the winter of 1860 at a salary of £250 a year. But B. W. Matz, who joined the firm in 1880, says that GM read the first MS. in Aug. 1860 ('George Meredith as Publisher's Reader', *Fortnightly Review*, xcii (Aug. 1909), 284).

[4] Frederick D. Hickman.   [5] Janet's father.

It's nothing to laugh at:[6] but a curious scene. Naughty Sir Alec should not have let out so much. I have never breathed it.

I am distressed to hear such bad accounts of my dear Lady Gordon.[7] Come I will, if I can, but I am horribly unwell. (There's a rumour of the eldest Clarke girl[8] going to marry an elderly Ditton man.)

Your affectionate and faithful

George M.

Arthur's at school. The dear man longs to see you.

83. *To* MISS JANET DUFF GORDON

MS.: Yale. Published: *Letters*, i. 21–22, with omissions and variants; *The Fourth Generation*, p. 87.

Esher

Friday, November 30, 1860

My dearest Janet,

A thousand thanks for the photograph.[1] It is a good and a fitting present at this awful instant. It admirably represents the occasion. Looking on it, I see the corpse of the Maiden Janet. Just what she may henceforth give of herself, and no more. It isn't bad, it's pleasant to have, but it's Janet washed out, and decorated with soot. Behind it lies her free youth. She looks darkly forward on the children of Egypt. It's Janet half Copt already.[2]

How do you feel? *Do* write down half a page of your sensations, and hand them to me, under seal, with directions that I may read them a year hence and compare with results. Not that you're romantic, and I don't suppose you flutter vastly just when you're caught, but still, dear Orange blossom, you're a bit of a bird, like the rest.

By the way, why am I to have the photograph of Janet a wife, while Arthur takes the maiden?

Of course I'll send out my books and my poems to my best public. Unless I do them horridly, and I must soon get stronger, or I shall.

If I can come, as I trust to, I must return on Wednesday. I have all

82. [6] At least not to GM, who shared the feelings.

[7] Lady Duff Gordon was confined to her bed and indeed never fully recovered her health.

[8] T. O. Clarke, of Lilseworth, Esher, is the only Clarke listed in *Kelly* for 1859. Presumably this is one of his daughters.

83. [1] In *The Fourth Generation* (p. 86) Janet Ross writes: 'In London I was photographed and sent a copy to my Poet and one to [A. W.] Kinglake. It was very unlike, as are all photographs that have ever been done of me. Meredith answered by return of post. . . .'

[2] Janet was going to live in Alexandria.

the writing, on a paper, now on my shoulders.³ Thursday is contribution day. I shall return and spend a week with your mother later, when she is alone, and may want me.

And now, my dear, my future Copt, and my good friend forever, as I hope, farewell, till we meet. I pray fervently you may be happy.

I think of leaving Copsham, to live in two small town rooms, that I may save for Arthur's education. The safest address to me from Egypt, will be Chapman & Hall's, 193 Piccadilly.

God bless you!—My compliments to your elect.

Faithfully ever,
George Meredith

P.S. Esher's in mourning. I must quit the place before Tuesday. The shock will be fearful here.

84. *To* D. G. Rossetti¹

Text: copy made by Mrs. Janet Camp Troxell from the original letter in her possession.

Copsham Cottage, Esher, Surrey
Friday, November [1860]

My dear Rossetti,

Pardon my silence. I have been unable to reply fully, and so delayed.

You had better send the Poem² to me. I will give it my best attention. If I can recommend it, doubt not that I will do so.

But a poem on a Scriptural theme, you know how little chance it has with the British Public, be it never so good. Still your enthusiasm arouses my curiosity, and I may think more hopefully of it when I have read it. At all events, I can spare the author annoyance by reading it first, and taking the responsibility on myself. Illustrations from your hand, will add largely to its chances of sale: and *sale* as well as merit, is what we shall have to look to.

As to my own work,³ you speak too favourably of it. I was unfortunately knocked down by illness during composition; and the 'Weeks'⁴

³ This is GM's first reference to an additional job that he had taken on—the writing of a couple of columns of news notes and a leading article (or two) each week for the *Ipswich Journal*. In return he received £200 a year (Stevenson, p. 85). As the *Journal* was staunchly Tory and GM's political and social views were liberal or radical, the work became galling long before he could afford to resign it.

84. ¹ D. G. Rossetti (1828–82), known at this time as a leading Pre-Raphaelite painter. I do not know when or how the two men first met.

² Charles Jeremiah Wells's *Joseph and His Brethren* (1824), a new edition of which Rossetti planned. In 1861 Swinburne, through R. Monckton Milnes, tried to get an article on Wells into *Fraser's Magazine*. Cecil Y. Lang (*The Swinburne Letters*, New Haven, 1959, i. 45 n.) attributes Swinburne's interest to Rossetti's enthusiasm.

³ *EH*.   ⁴ i.e. *OaW*.

stayed not for me. I fell into slipshod, and had to scuffle on anyhow. The Countess, you see, has only one side of her character to the reader. The action was too quick, continuous: the space too short. It is a comedy, as I have said, and this should explain some of the short-comings of the work. The writing is atrocious. It is quite destitute of the *lumen purpureum* which I like to give. How a work without colour, can please you at all, astonishes me. Raikes is abominably vulgar. The idea of him came from the necessity for a contrast to Evan: and this from the title I gave the book, which tied me down. I am so disgusted that I can't even persuade myself to touch it up for the re-issue. The nausea is too strong. It must go forth much as it is. But for the question of money I would quash it altogether.

If I have health the next will be better.

I shall be most happy to make my bow to Mrs. Rossetti, when you are pleased to give me warning that I may.

Very faithfully yours,
George Meredith

85. *To* FREDERICK A. MAXSE

MS.: Maxse Papers.

Copsham Cottage, Esher
Friday, December 14, 1860

My dear Captain Maxse,

Pray send me what you have done: tell me nothing of your doubts; but wait for my opinion. We will then compare. I am glad you have taken to the sea. I am certainly busy, but my leisure is at your disposal. Without putting himself on a pedestal, one man may offer to be of use to another, in matters of this sort. I sometimes, like Boileau,[1] read what I have written, to my cook; and I have known one or two illiterate men who were useful critics. At least I have the satisfaction of knowing that you can hear an honest judgment, and then I shall not be con-demned to read affected nonsense. In fact, I shall begin very hopefully.

Faithfully yours,
George Meredith

85. [1] An error for Molière.

86. *To* F. M. EVANS

Text: typed copy furnished by Messrs. Bradbury & Agnew. Excerpt published: Stevenson, p. 82.

Esher
Sunday, December 23, 1860

My dear Evans,

I acknowledge thankfully receipt of cheque for the £50/0/0.[1]— I wish I could have done more for *Ev*[*an*] *Harrington*, for both our sakes: but I should have had to cut him to pieces, put strange herbs to him, and boil him up again—a tortuous and a doubtful process: so I let him go much as *Once a Week* exhibited him. We must take our luck and do better next time.

I'm to dine with you this week? Will Thursday suit you? Name your day early. Friday I'm engaged.

Faithfully yours,
George Meredith

87. *To* SAMUEL LUCAS

Text: *Letters*, i. 22–23. Excerpt published: Stevenson, p. 88.

Esher
[*c.* December 23, 1860]

My dear Lucas,

You sent proofs of the first story (The Highwayman),[1] but, if I haven't returned them, I have mislaid them. Send proofs of the second story[2] at once, as I have now time to finish it. By the way, I don't think your common pay should extend to me, and you are bound to heighten the scale. If you do, I will give you some very good stories, but I must have money. Evans, I am sure, will do this, upon your reputation.

As to those that I wrote for the occasion, they have not my stamp upon them, and I would prefer not to append my name. In the matter

---

86. [1] This must have been an advance: the ledgers show that a cheque drawn in favour of GM on 22 Dec. caused him to end the year owing the firm a balance of £47.

87. [1] This is apparently 'The Parish Clerk's Story', published anonymously in *OaW* (23 Feb. 1861). The old ledgers of Bradbury & Evans show a credit of five guineas to GM for the story.

[2] Whether this story is identical with 'Paul Bentley', mentioned below, of which no trace remains, is uncertain. The MS. of an unpublished GM story, 'The Friend of the Engaged Couple', 31 pp. in length, was found in John Lane's collection after his death and is now in the Altschul Collection. In the upper left corner of the first page the word 'yes' is pencilled, presumably by Lucas.

of verse, also, I shall rarely be able to give my time for the money I get for it. You have the option of rejecting. Consider whether you should not offer fitting inducements to contribute one's best?

I think you might at once put the 1st portion of 'Paul Bentley' into the artist's hands.

I wish you a sound digestion to your Christmas, and am, my dear Lucas, your faithful

George Meredith

88. *To* FREDERICK A. MAXSE

Text: typed copy, Maxse Papers.

Copsham Cottage, Esher
Wednesday, [late December
1860–early January 1861]

My dear Captain Maxse,

I have read your manuscript.[1] The title is excellent. First I object to the classical names. You wish to avoid social distinctions, but you defeat your purpose. Theages and Corybas and Alcides are not only at the very top of the social scale, by virtue of the appellation you bestow on them, but at least ten feet above the level of the earth. One can't grasp the reality of characters thus dignified. And consider what you do in producing such a speculative Alcides!—We have English names that will serve you. Randall, Duncan, Drummond, and such like. You state the position of your personages over and over again. The classical names are an obstruction simply.

Now, as to the story: as yet I get very little glimpse of it, and I confess the time[2] of the whole smacks to me too much of *Robt. Mornay*.[3] The 'Dream' is a little overdone with speculation. Your characters are in arbitrary contrast to one another, but are individually not sharply enough defined. Between Miranda and the narrator passages are to [   ],[4] but you have not sufficiently warmed the reader, by leading up to them. The chapters I have read give the effect of the doldrums, as far as story is concerned. We want a breeze to spring up, and keep expecting it. Certainly the Riff attack is good, and here you had your chance, but pardon me if I tell you I think you missed it. The little bit with Miranda there is bewildering rather than effective. And this, as

88. [1] For the context of this letter, see Letter 85.   [2] ? Misreading for *tone*.
[3] Maxse's earlier novel, published in 1859.   [4] Word (or part of a word) missing.

I think, because Mr. Alcides is such a very limp philosopher. He lacks passion. In a prominent character it should at least be latent.

What I would do—it's what I have done in my own case, or could I advise it so coolly?—would be to cut up the MS, re-write it, and see that each chapter has a point. You must keep striking on the key-note, and distinctly. If Alcides is to love Miranda, let us expect it. He need not be jealous even of Corybas. Love has a thousand disguises, but we must not be taken 'aback' towards the end of the book. I would bring the Riff scene (by resolute incision) into the third chapter. And avoid inflicting on your reader the languors of your Alcides quite so much. Remember that characters mainly (unless wonderfully struck out) are interesting to the world, not for themselves, but for the part they are playing.—I will gladly counsel further, if you please, and will pardon my plain-speaking. I will also see through Press.

Very faithfully yours,
George Meredith

89. *To* KENNETH CORNISH[1]

Text: cutting from a book catalogue issued by Alvin J. Scheuer (n.d.), sent by M. Buxton Forman to W. M. Meredith; Meredith Papers, George Meredith Estate Trustees.

Esher
March 19, 1861

Dear Sir,

I have now an explanation of the singular attitude you have latterly assumed towards me, and I confess that you have some justification for it, though I could have wished you to express yourself to me openly, which would have obviated the misunderstanding. The story was hastily sketched one morning and eagerly seized by you. It went on for seven numbers entirely because I hoped to better it and bring it to a telling point; certainly not that I wished to impose upon you objectionable matter. I beg to tell you that I am not a man to make money in that way. If you had stated plainly that it was a burden to pay for it beyond a certain rate, I should have assented to your terms with the

---

89. [1] Kenneth Henry Cornish, surgeon, of 5 Essex Court, Temple. *Churchill's London and Provincial Medical Directory* for 1860 gives the following information about him: Member Royal College of Surgeons (1857); Surgeon Royal Humane Society; Fellow Medical Society of London. After listing several contributions to *Lancet*, the entry concludes: 'Later editor of the Physical Science Dept. of the *Illustrated Inventor*. Inventor of some New Surgical Instruments.' *Churchill's Medical Directory* for 1877 adds: 'Edited various Scientific and Political journals, 1857–67.'

I have been unable to identify the journal that Cornish was editing in 1860, the probable date of GM's contribution. *The Illustrated Inventor*, a short-lived publication that suspended operations in 1859, did not publish any seven-part stories.

same readiness that you did to mine. As to Law, which I hear you have mentioned, it would take much to induce me to mix Literature with Law, or to drag a gentleman where I should dislike to appear myself.

In fact, legally I think you may claim the verdict, for I now (for the first time) remember you saying something about 3 or 4 numbers: though I did not think it, as I wrote, necessary to bind myself to that number, or understood it in the light of an agreement. I happened to want the money, when the story was finished. I asked for it and you continued silent. What could I think?

Oblige me by forwarding the sum that you compute as fair, by post: or let me know if you prefer to have the receipt from the hands of my messenger, and believe me, with much regret for a misunderstanding I cannot take all the blame for

Very faithfully yours,
George Meredith

90. *To* KENNETH CORNISH

Text (excerpt): Francis Edwards' Catalogue No. 301, sent by M. Buxton Forman to W. M. Meredith; Meredith Papers.

Esher
March 27, 1861

I am quite satisfied. I am glad that I wrote and that you have understood me. When I asked for £3 a page, it was not so much the worth of the matter that I had to consider, but the fact that in writing for you, I was obliged to put by a work on which I was engaged.... But I need not tell a literary man that hasty writing is rarely to be depended upon. [Etc.]

91. *To* W. C. BONAPARTE WYSE[1]

MS.: University of California, Los Angeles. Published: Ellis, pp. 115–16.

Esher, Copsham
Friday afternoon, [? April 1861]

My dear Wyse,

Hail to you! Glad must be the release from Coram:[2] into which smutty Elysium I was nigh penetrating yesterday, but had forgotten your number.—Now, listen; for this is a thing to be done.

91. [1] For a biographical sketch of Wyse, see Biographical Section, pp. 1716–17.
[2] Ellis (p. 115) says that 'Wyse was living in Guildford, when not at his rooms in Great Coram Street'.

Shoulder your knapsack to-morrow (Saturday) at 2 o'clock, or 3.—
March on the London road, asking for *Ripley*;³ walk through it and
straight on, whither leads the Bonapartian nose. I, meantime, will start
from Copsham at *3*, dining at 2: and on this road, about Ripley
Common I'll meet you, and bring you to me. Maxse, and another,
lunch with me on Sunday. Stay till Monday and I will walk back with
you, perhaps all the way, returning by rail. Isn't this a decent proposition? Respond to it, and encourage me.—I am hoarding up similes
from [? for] whomsoever I leave to the work of the paper. I must go
somewhere soon; for my work is *beastly*.

Why are you so sensitive about your verse? Let it have air and be
seen; or it will never have a skin to stand our atmosphere.

We have fine suns; but the East I do abominate. It blows my feathers
the wrong way 'intirely'.⁴

I am getting temporarily tired of my *Emilia*.⁵ I have read it to Lady
Duff,⁶ who is satisfied with it; but I am not. I have done little more to it
than what you heard. Two chapters. The dawdling dispirits me.

Not to have the same effect upon you, I conclude:

Your faithful
George Meredith

The distance from Guildford to Copsham is 12 1/2 miles: not too
much. The walk is charming, to my mind. Pray, come.

92. *To* W. C. Bonaparte Wyse

Text: Ellis, p. 116.

[Copsham Cottage, Esher]
[? April, 1861]

My dear Wyse,

I think it possible that I shall to-morrow walk *in the morning* to
Ripley and *dine* at the Talbot¹ at 2 p.m., so call there: ask: get an
answer. Have I made myself clear? This is the effect of the East wind.
'The parting of the Poets at the pond by the Lone Hut.'² Look out for
that title. The effect of your departing figure, with the East fretting

---

³ Approximately half-way between Esher and Guildford.
⁴ Mimicry of Wyse's brogue recurs frequently in letters to him.
⁵ The earliest reference I have found to *Emilia in England,* which was to give GM great
trouble before it was published in 1864.
⁶ i.e. Duff Gordon.
92. ¹ The Talbot, partly of the seventeenth century, still stands.
² The Hut Hotel at Wisley.

your rear, will linger with me till finally I go. If you are at the Talbot, we will visit Newark Abbey.[3] If not, I perhaps shall meet you on the road.

Only don't forget *to call at the Talbot.*

93. *To* W. C. BONAPARTE WYSE

MS.: University of California, Los Angeles. Published: Ellis, p. 117, with omissions.

Copsham
Saturday, [? April 27, 1861]

It's many a penny you'll pay to go
   To a town beneath the skies,
Where a gentleman dwells whom you may know
   By the name of Bonaparte Wyse.

I was a pote, and *he* was a pote,
   In this town of merchandize:
And we laughed at jests profane to quote,
   I and my Bonaparte Wyse.
We cracked our joke improper to quote,
   I and my Bonaparte Wyse.

   Chorus—Tol-loddi, tol-loddi;
         Tol-le-loddi—tolloddi—tollieo.[1]

Yesterday, being fair, I marched me to the vale of Mickleham.[2] An English Tempe! Was ever such delicious greenery? The nightingale saluted me entering and departing. The walk has made of me a new man. I am now bathed anew in the Pierian fount. I cannot prose. I took Keats with me, to read the last lines of *Endymion* on the spot of composition.[3]

Now, listen: come here by the afternoon train on Thursday next, and I will return with you for a day through Mickleham, and over the hills. Can you? Will you? Perhaps Maxse will join us. The cuckoo has been heard. And through the gates of his twin notes we enter the heart

92. [3] The E.E. ruins of Newark Priory, near Ripley.
93. [1] A parody of Poe's 'Annabel Lee'.
   [2] Along the river Mole, on a bend of which is situated the village of Mickleham, where GM was married to Marie Vulliamy in 1864.
   [3] In 1818 Keats was staying at the charming Fox and Hounds hotel—later renamed the Burford Bridge Hotel—at the foot of Box Hill and there completed *Endymion* after a moonlight walk in the vicinity.

of spring. We will have rare poetizing. No laughter, no base cynical scorn, but all honest uplifting of the body and soul of us to the calm-glowing central Fire of things. Even so, my friend.—Or, again: Will you, on Friday, bring Madame⁴ to Burford Bridge at a certain appointed hour, and let me meet you, and let us explore the vale, and sleep in the nightingale vale that night and roam about next day, and home at night, per train, each his way. These be propositions.

My kind regards to Madame. But that I know she will see this, I would say something sweet of her.

Box Hill is your station for Mickleham.

How are you? Give me a sonnet, by return.

Your faithful

George Meredith

94. *To* W. C. BONAPARTE WYSE

Text (excerpt): Ellis, p. 118.

Copsham

May 3rd, 4th, or 5th [*sic*], [1861]

I look'd for my poet—he came not!
    He came not, though much I expected him.
His breach of agreement I blame not,
    But Faith has forever rejected him!

    (*Chorus*—Through Eternity, 'Forever', etc.)

Yes, tho' the weather be December O!
    Is this a fair excuse, my Bonaparte,
For Friar's Omelettes kill'd in embryo,
    And breakfasts spoilt, or eaten on'y part?

Lo, the sweet sunshine to shame thee!
'Tis the weather for poets to forage in.
In the clouds I reproachfully name thee,
And they say—Here his promise has origin!
Of us, and in us, see his origin!
His misty, remarkable origin!

A friend has called to take me to Oatlands Park.¹ I may stay till Monday, and may then drop down on you. Maurice FitzG[erald]

⁴ The *DNB* says that Wyse married Ellen Linzee Prout of St. Mabyn, Cornwall, in 1864, but it is clear from this letter that the marriage occurred earlier.
94. ¹ Near Weybridge. The friend was James Sprent Virtue (1829–92), printer and publisher, who lived at Oatlands Park at this time.

wants us to go down to him at Littlehampton for a couple of days. He leaves in a week. Shall we? The country is nice. I'll if you'll. I want also to go to the Switzerland beyond Godalming. . . .[2]

95. *To* W. C. BONAPARTE WYSE

Text: Ellis, pp. 118–19.

Tuesday, May 7, 1861

O Corsican!—The naval man[1] and the poet of Copsham have combined to arrange an expedition over Mickleham, and along the hills of laughing Surrey, into the heart of pastoral Hampshire, it may be; and, to be complete, we want thee to join us. This, if the weather be not quite damnable.[2] Or say, in spite of the Gods of Air, if you please. I care not. I am for jollity and snapping of audacious fingers. What tho' Jove frown? The muse is our'n, and eke the pint of Bass: the comely pipe, the soothing lass, etc.

We start on Saturday: we lunch lightly at Copsham at 2 p.m. Then like arrows from the Tartar's bow, out we sally, and away we go: knapsack on back. Singing—Hey nonny nonny! What will you do? Reply at once. *I* say, come here. Meetings are always doubtful.

96. *To* MRS. JANET ROSS

MS.: Yale. Published: *Letters*, i. 23–27, with variants and with initials only for some of the names; *The Fourth Generation*, pp. 102–5, with omissions and variants.

Copsham, Esher
Friday, May 17, 1861

My dear Janet:

The little man[1] has been in great glee to answer you. He had paper and everything ready to do so a week before your letter came, and his reply is all his own, and from his heart. He must love you. Who could fail to love one so stanch and tender to him? Here have I waited silently, thinking much of you, and incurring I know not what con-

---

94. [2] i.e. Hindhead, elevation 895 feet.
95. [1] Maxse.
 [2] On 17 May (Letter 97) GM wrote to Wyse, 'Maxse starts with me, if it's tolerably fine, on Saturday'. From this, I infer that the trip mentioned here was postponed. The temperature in London on 9–11 May was respectively 42, 44, and 48 degrees, with overcast skies.
96. [1] i.e. Arthur.

demnation. I have not thought of you less because I withheld my pen. The truth is, my experiences are all mental—I see nothing of the world, and what I have to say goes into books. However, I am now compelled by my state of health to give up for a time. Your poet—dare I call myself that, after hearing the rhapsodic eulogies of old Alder?[2] I assure you, my dear, I cannot equal him. I might put him into rhythm, but that would spoil his hearty idiom. I feel quite a friendliness for old Alder after hearing him speak of you.—'I never saw a young lady like her and never shall *again*. She's a loss to Esher and to England:' etc. etc.—You are compared with Miss Gilbert and Miss Reynolds; and men are dared to say that either fair equestrian surpassed you on horseback. Apropos of the former lady, Landseer[3] has a picture of her in the Academy, leaning exhausted against the flanks of a mare couchant. 'Taming of the Shrew' the picture is named, and it is sufficiently bad. Millais has nothing. Hunt a 'Street wooing in Cairo',[4] of which you could judge better than I. Leighton[5] has a 'Paolo and Francesca'; painted just as the book has dropped and they are in no state to read more. You would scorn it; but our friendship never rested on common sentiments in art. I greatly admire it. I think it the sole English picture exhibiting passion, that I have seen. I have the delight to stand alone in my judgment of this, as of most things, and I shall see the world coming round to my opinion, and thinking it its own. Does that smack of the original George M?—Never mind.—Well: there is a *beautiful* portrait of Alice Prinsep by Watts.[6] Idealised, of course—showing more *in* her than she possesses; but my friend Maxse—one who is strong on points of feminine beauty (a naval man loose upon society) —thinks her superior to the picture in physique. He meets her out. He said to me, the first time, 'I think she thought me slow:'—the second:

---

[2] 'A retired, well-to-do butcher at Esher, who came out hunting with the Duc d'Aumale's harriers, but never jumped even a hurdle' (*The Fourth Generation*, p. 103).

[3] (Sir) Edwin Landseer (1802–73), famed for his pictures of animals, exhibited 'The Shrew Tamed' at the Royal Academy in 1861. 'Unfortunately,' says the *Annual Register*, 'the picture was suggestive of one of the social scandals of the hour, and the public were as much attracted by "The Pretty Horse-Breaker" as by the wonderful art of the painter.' Cyril Pearl (*The Girl with the Swansdown Seat*, N.Y., 1955, p. 129) explains that the picture was said to be a photographic likeness of the notorious Skittles, who, according to a letter, signed 'H' [? Matthew James Higgins ('Jacob Omnium')] in *The Times* (3 July 1862), first made her appearance in London 'early in the season of 1861'.

[4] 'A Street Scene in Cairo: the Lantern-maker's Courtship', by Holman Hunt (1827–1910).

[5] Frederick Leighton (1830–96), successively knight (1878), baronet (1886), and peer (1896).

[6] During the twenty-five years that G. F. Watts lived with the Prinseps, he painted various members of the family. The *DNB* says that Thoby Prinsep had three sons, whose names are given, and a daughter, unnamed. I suppose Alice to be the daughter, though there was at least one niece, May Prinsep, also painted by Watts. The *Annual Register* says that the portrait of Alice 'received most of the public approbation'.

'Is she at all stupid?' His conclusive judgment pronounces her an exquisitely plumed little poll parrot. She is being admired: people think she should wear more clothing. The effect is said to be that of a damsel such as you see at the booth of a country fair.—Maxse is a very nice fellow, with strong literary tastes. He was Naval *Aide-de-camp* to Lord Lyons[7] in the Crimea. I dare say you have heard of him. You would like him. He is *very* anxious to be introduced some day to Rose Jocelyn.[8] I tell him that Janet ROSS is a finer creature. If Rose satisfies him, how will not Janet! He has taken a cottage at Molesey,[9] and we make expeditions together on foot.—Talking of Rose, did you see the *Saturday*?[10] It says you are a heroine who deserve[s] to be a heroine. And yet I think I missed you. Your mother tells me that Mrs. Austin[11] speaks in very handsome terms of the performance generally, and of the portrait in particular.—I have not seen your mother for some days. She has had another attack, a very severe one. It wears my heart to think of her. And yet her constitution rallies from time to time, and I have still strong hopes of her ultimate recovery. She must not spend another winter in England.—The baby[12] is quite charming. Like you, but rosier, and with a tendency to be just as positive. She articulates admirably, and shows qualities equal to the physiological promise I have noted from the first. How I should wish Arthur to conquer a fair position in the world, and lead her away as a certain Janet was led! At present he is not brilliant, but he is decidedly hopeful. I don't want to force him yet. I wish to keep him sound and to instil good healthy habits of mind and body. In writing, spelling, and reading; in memory for what he acquires, few children surpass him. And he really thinks—without being at all instigated to think. I remained at Copsham for his sake and perhaps shall not quit it for some time to come. He will not go to a regular school till next year. I don't like the thought of his going; but it must be, and so I submit.

I have three works in hand. The most advanced is *Emilia Belloni*;[13] of which I have read some chapters to your mother, and gained her strong approval. Emilia is a feminine musical genius. I gave you once, sitting on the mound over Copsham, an outline of the real story it is taken from.[14] Of course one does not follow out real stories; and this

96. [7] Maxse was flag-lieutenant to Lord Lyons and later aide-de-camp to Lord Raglan.
  [8] The heroine of *EH*, modelled on Janet Ross.
  [9] On the Mole, just north of Esher.
  [10] The *Saturday Review*, which reviewed *EH* (19 Jan.) as 'a surprisingly good novel . . . a story new in conception, new in the study of character, fresh, odd, a little extravagant, but noble and original'.
  [11] Janet's grandmother, Sarah Austin. (See Biographical Section, 'The Duff Gordons', pp. 1715–16.)
  [12] Janet's sister Urania (Rany).   [13] i.e. *Emilia in England*.
  [14] The story owes something to the person and experiences of Emilia Macirone (Lady

has simply suggested Emilia to me.—Then, my next novel is called
A Woman's Battle.[15] Q[uer]y—good title?—I think it will be my best
book as yet. The third is weaker in breadth of design. It is called *Van
Diemen Smith*[16]—is interesting as a story. *Nous verrons.*—Last night
I went with Maxse to the House of Commons to hear the Debate on the
Constitution. I saw your friend Layard,[17] but did not hear him.
Eothen[18] was absent. Gladstone swallowed the whole Conservative
body with his prodigious yawns and eloquence alternately. I never saw
a man yawn so naïvely and excuseably. The truth is that there is some
honesty, but small stock of brains on the Conservative side. I could not
wait for Bright. I heard Horsman,[19] who is good enough, and seems
bidding for the Conservative leadership. He will perhaps get it; but he
is not the man to prop a sinking cause. It is clear that we in England
are going down to a lower circle. Natural development, no doubt.—

I have made friends with a nice fellow lately: a son of the Ambassador at Athens, Sir T. Wyse, whom your mother knew. He married
a Bonaparte—a daughter of Lucien—who is what all the Bonaparte
women are. Hence separation, and the father cares not to see or hear of
his children—two boys, Napoleon Wyse and Bonaparte Wyse. The
latter I know. He has nice tastes and is an odd mixture of Irishman and
Corsican. He wanted me to go to Athens with him. I may meet him
returning and come home through Provence. He is intimate with the
members of the new school of Provençal poets there, and wishes me to
know them. Mistral[20] I have read. He is really a fine poet. If I go I shall
have something to write to you about.

The dear good Bart[21] looks melancholy riding alone. It's rather sad
seeing him out. Otherwise he is as cheerful and of the same port as
of yore.

My dear, I have been thinking many a month of a Wedding present
for you. I don't like jewels, and books you have enough of. It has struck
me that a magnified photograph of your father and mother, Mossy[22]

Hornby), at whose mother's house, The Limes, Weybridge, the Merediths had boarded
for a time shortly after their marriage.
[15] Ellis (p. 218) says that this is the original title for the novel *Rhoda Fleming*. Though
'a woman's battle' fits the novel, no proof exists.
[16] Published as 'The House on the Beach' in the *New Quarterly Magazine* (Jan. 1877),
pp. 329–410; published in book form by Harper in America in 1877, but not republished
in England until 1895.
[17] (Sir) Austen Henry Layard (1817–94), excavator of Nineveh and politician.
[18] A. W. Kinglake (1809–91), author of *Eōthen* and later *The Invasion of the Crimea*.
He was a friend of the Duff Gordons, and Janet suspected the two men of being a bit
jealous of one another.
[19] Edward Horsman (1807–76), a Liberal politician whose views were more conservative than those of the Conservative leadership.
[20] Frédéric Mistral (1830–1914), Provençal poet.
[21] i.e., Sir Alexander Duff Gordon.
[22] Maurice, Janet's brother.

and Rany, would please you best. Your mother will sit when she is well enough. What say you?—

In conclusion, let me beg you to send to me and tell me anything that you want that I may have the pleasure to get it for you. I rejoice with all my soul that you are so happy. By the way, Maxse introduced me to the Comte de Paris[23] the other day; who said of your husband: 'Mr. Ross is a very clever man', in a tone of conviction and esteem. Of you he spoke as it pleased me to hear. The Orleanists seem looking up, owing to the Aumale pamphlet.[24] The Duke was chairman of the Literary Fund dinner last night, and spoke capitally.

Remember me to your husband very kindly. And please write soon and cordially forgive me. My heart is very much with you, and I am always at my Janet's service. God bless you!

Your faithful
George Meredith

97. *To* W. C. BONAPARTE WYSE

Text: Ellis, p. 119.

Friday, May 17, [1861]

I was hurt to find you gone yesterday. Why do you treat me so? It might happen that I should not see you ere you leave England, and then——?

Maxse starts with me, if it's tolerably fine, on Saturday.[1] On Sunday morning will you walk to St Martha's Chapel,[2] and we can spend the day together, and walk in such a direction that you can take the train home at night to Guildford. We will be at St Martha's Chapel towards 12 o'clock. If I don't find you there, I shall think there is bad blood in the world and, my dear old boy, I trust you will come. If it rains cats and dogs, of course, I won't hope it. But the cats without the dogs may give us a chance.

I went to the House—heard Gladstone, and was astounded at the prodigious nature of his yawns. These, with his eloquence, swallow the whole Conservative body.

96. ²³ Grandson of Louis Philippe; he lived with other members of the House of Orleans at Claremont, on the outskirts of Esher.

²⁴ A brochure printed in France, under the title *Lettre sur l'histoire de France*, and addressed to Napoleon III. It was strongly critical of the imperial government. (Aumale was a son of Louis Philippe.)

97. ¹ See Note 2, Letter 95.

² A famous Surrey landmark, a couple of miles SE. of Guildford. Originally a late Norman structure, it had long been in ruins until its restoration in 1848 (The Penguin *Surrey*, p. 230).

98. *To* W. C. Bonaparte Wyse

Text: Ellis, p. 119.

[Copsham Cottage, Esher]
[*c.* May 21 or 22, 1861]

My dear Friend,
    Only just received your letter—returned from walk with Maxse into Hampshire and Sussex—perfectly charming, and full of fun, etc. But, oh! how I cursed on St Martha's sacred ground.[1] In Hell I shall repent it. My dear fellow! I must see you somehow, so I will try, if possible, to run down on Thursday evening from Town, and I'll dine with you at seven, or if you have had dinner, take a chop. Don't *prepare* for me, as press of business makes me uncertain. God bless and prosper you in your expedition. Anyhow you have stuff in yourself to conquer a destiny. Grand-nephew of Napoleon—adieu!

99. *To* Frederick A. Maxse

MS.: Maxse Papers. Envelope postmarked *Kingston-on-Thames, My 26 61*.

[Copsham Cottage, Esher]
Friday, [May 24, 1861]

My dear Maxse,
    I went to Harris,[1] and am medicined. By the way, Arthur has a story called the 'King of the Medicines', who combats the 'King of the Illnesses'. I asked him which was to beat. He said, 'Oh, the King of the Medicines'. I replied that I was glad, and it has given me great faith in Harris. We shall see. He seems sensible, and talks encouragingly. Thanks for all your trouble.
    I returned comfortable, after a pleasant walk—no adventures of any kind.
    By this time you have walked under the lamps of May.[2] Invite me, I pray. To-morrow I go to Wyse. I return on Monday: shall be happy to come on Tuesday. . . .? And then you must come to me for two days. We dine on the lawn *at your* hour: and have coffee up in the fir-wood—nightingales in the beeches below.

98. [1] i.e. because Wyse did not meet him there as requested in the preceding letter.
99. [1] A common name in medical directories. Both Guy's and St. Bartholomew's hospitals had physicians of the name attached to their staffs at this time.
    [2] In 'Meditation under Stars' GM uses 'lamps' to represent stars.

Two letters from Kate.[3] She is not yet spliced. The accounts of young Dormer are extraordinary. He is really a fine *young* fellow. The woman's heart is becoming weak to such singular devotion. 'If he were not so young!' she already cries.

Your faithful
George M.

100. *To* W. C. BONAPARTE WYSE

MS.: Yale. Published: Ellis, pp. 119–20, with the omission of one sentence.

Friday, [May 24, 1861]

My dear Wyse,

I come to-morrow—(Saturday)—perhaps early, perhaps late; perhaps by rail, perhaps on foot. Anyhow, I come. Tell Elaine[1] I will write some verses, certainly.—Isn't the weather glorious?* Is there anything like pastoral England when the gods are kind to her?

> Yes, we'll pic-nic in the woods,
> And touch on the diviner moods,
> We will forget that we are clay
> And live the fulness of our day.
> On ladders of pure Niedersteiner,
> Or Burgundy, or simple Claret,
> (Than which on Earth there's nothing finer
> When waiters stand not by to mar it)
> We'll mount diviner and diviner.
> Until at last on men we glance
> Olympian-like, electively,
> And 'gin to laugh, and shout, and dance,
> And get lock'd up, effectively.

Mr. Wyse, Sir! I think I'll be early to-morrerr, if ye please, sir. I'll be 'bliged t'ye not to go out altogether for so long a time as last—at a stretch, ye understand, my worthy friend. With which, God bless ye!

George Meredith

Motto: Pluck up!

*[Written opposite this sentence]: Ha! ha! You can't be *cool* in this weather.

99. [3] Kate Terry, sister of Ellen, both of whom had already begun their acting careers. Nothing came of Kate's affair with young Dormer, mentioned below: she married Arthur Lewis in 1867. I am unable to identify Dormer.
100. [1] i.e. Ellen (Mrs. Wyse).

101. *To* W. C. BONAPARTE WYSE

MS.: Dartmouth College. Published: Ellis, p. 151, with variants.

[Copsham Cottage, Esher]
Friday, [May 31, 1861]

My dear Wyse,

How I miss you and regret not being with you. I saw the doctor yesterday, who says that the 'knot of the nerves' is irritated and has been long so. I must not smoke, I must not work; I must go to the college of the sunny Lazzaroni and live as the ephemerae live that I may not die like them. He says also that at the end of six weeks I must pack my knapsack and away to Switzerland or Tyrol. So haste on your mission. I meantime offer sacrifices—a kid. I send you the book of M. Aubanel's[1] lyrics. They are intensely Southern, arid, monotonous, impressive. When you see M. Mistral, pray tell him that it is my earnest wish to be introduced to him. *Mirèio,*[2] the more I look at it, strikes me as a consummate work in an age of very small singing. It has in some parts the pastoral richness of Theocritus and the rough vigour of Homer. I read your translation of the portion describing the mares of the Camargue to Maxse, who was delighted. He spoke of the poem to the Duc d'Aumale. The latter supposed the name of M. Mistral a *nom de plume*! He seemed astonished to learn that France held a living poet unknown to him and admired in England. Lady Gordon still has your copy. She is too ill to be seen, or I would give you her opinion. You know how highly I esteem her as a critic.

I am composing gently. Yesterday I met in Fleet Street Dante Rossetti, the artist. I went with him to his studio, and there he gave me a translation he has been at work on many years, viz. poems from the Italian poets up to Dante. Some are perfectly exquisite: as for the translation, it is so good that he will rank as poet as well as artist from the hour of the publication. Soon may we two drink this pure Italian wine together!

The Derby[3] is over, and England's annual culmination with it.

101. [1] Théodore Aubanel (1829–86), Provençal poet and dramatist.
  [2] Mistral's epic, *Mirèio,* published in 1859, won for him the poet's prize of the French Academy and the Cross of the Legion of Honour. So impressed was GM by the description of the Mares of Camargue, mentioned below, that he himself translated it and published it in *A Reading of Life* (1901). A few Meredithians have long known that GM also reviewed *Mirèio* in the *Pall Mall Gazette,* but Professor Phyllis Bartlett has only recently recovered the review from a clipping among the Meredith papers of the Altschul Collection. It was actually an unsigned review (*PMG,* 27 Mar. 1869, pp. 11–12) of an English translation of the poem by H. Crichton, published in 1869. GM's translation of the 'Mares' passage is part of the review, and his instructions to the printer of *A Reading of Life* to print the passage are extant with the clipping.
  [3] Derby Day was 29 May in 1861.

Exhausted the nation takes breath, and the more ardent spirits look forward to the Derby ensuing. And so on!—I send herewith a letter that reached Guildford open, for your brother. One for Madame is in my charge—shall be sent when I have her address. Hoping a few days will bring tidings of you,

Your friend,
George Meredith

102. *To* SAMUEL LUCAS

Text: typed copy, Yale. Printed: *Altschul Catalogue*, p. 162.

[Copsham Cottage, Esher]
[ante June 12, 1861]

My dear Lucas,

I send you some of the *Dyke Farm*.¹ About 4 chapters further to follow. Mind, I won't put my name, and I insist upon *proper payment.* And listen! I have three poems to make your mouth water.² But you shan't have them if you *don't pay the Muse better.* Consider the character of your publication! Is it not worth it?—One, Dante Rossetti will illustrate. Jones³ another. The third (being the 'Old Chartist'—the best you will have had) may suit Charles Keene's pencil. Upon my honour, my dear Editor, you are wrong to let your authors so much alone. *Give them a dinner.* I, faithful as I am, am nearly being snapt up Once a Week and lost to you forever.

Faithfully,
(Signed) George Meredith

103. *To* SAMUEL LUCAS

MS.: Yale. Printed: *Altschul Catalogue*, p. 22.

[Copsham Cottage, Esher]
Wednesday, June 12, [1861]

My dear Lucas,

I send you a subject that I intended for one of our Christmas set,

102. ¹ Nothing is known for certain about this work. Ellis (pp. 217–18) identifies it with *A Woman's Battle* and *Rhoda Fleming*, but *The Dyke Farm* was apparently to be less than novel length and was to be anonymous. GM always signed his name to novels.

² One of the three was 'Cassandra', which Rossetti was to illustrate. It was not published in *OaW* but in the volume *Modern Love* etc. (Apr.1862). The second was probably 'Phantasy' (published in *OaW*, 23 Nov. 1861). The third, as mentioned below, was 'The Old Chartist' (published in *OaW*, 8 Feb. 1862).

³ (Sir) Edward Burne-Jones (1833–98).

but found it scarce suitable.[1] It's amusing in its way. I won't put my name to it, and, as the cabman says, 'Leave it to you Sir.'

I will dine with you any day you like, if you fix the country. In town I will only dine on a Thursday. I wish you would come to me some day towards the end of next week: you can return at night, if you so decide. The woods here are delicious for evening walks etc. Name a day. I want to read to you some pieces that will please you, I fancy.

Faithfully yours,
George Meredith

Let me have *Dyke Farm* copy immediately that I may have it before me as I go on.

104. *To* W. C. BONAPARTE WYSE

Text (excerpt): Ellis, p. 152.

Copsham Cottage
Sunday, June 16, 1861

My very dear L. B. Pat!

Tell M. Mistral that Lady Gordon, an excellent critic, and one whose opinion I value more highly than that of most *men*, is astonished and delighted at the vigour and freshness of his poem. She has taught herself to read it in Provençale, and has now a fair appreciation of the beauty of the instrument M. Mistral touches so wonderfully. When known in England, *Mirèio* is certain to be highly appreciated.

I have spoken to Chapman and Hall about your projected book on Rabelais. I think you may look on it as determined, if only you keep to your resolution to work. . . .

Now tell me, why can't you go to Como through Tyrol? And meet me in Belgium quickly? . . . State when you will be at Como, and for what time. But you are more certain of me by catching me now. I, too, am slipping, and my nostril is turning seawards. The summer is on us, and the Goddess Amphitrite, whose long arms are round the margin of Earth, opens them invitingly for me. Yet do I lean to your companionship in preference, and if I make appointments I keep them. So count on me. I have been to the Doctor! He prohibits work; finds me perfectly sound, but with a drag on one organ—promises speedy cure; and has already set me up somewhat. My tabak is cut dolefully short.

---

103. [1] Nothing more is known of this contribution. Though *OaW* continued to publish poems by GM, it published no more prose, so far as we know. The ledgers of Bradbury & Evans record only payments for poems.

And I am to see fresh sights and drink novel air for a term of two months. God bless you! Don't lose heart. Write immediately.

Arthur's birthday was on Thursday, when he entered his ninth year. I spent the whole day in the woods with the dear little man. I wish I could only contrive to bring him abroad with me. Leaving him is all that bothers me.[1]

105. *To* W. C. BONAPARTE WYSE

Text: Ellis, p. 153.

[Copsham, Esher]
[*c.* June 26, 1861]

My dear Fellow,

I don't think I can start before Tuesday next, as there are things to be got ready for Arthur. I thank you for your readiness to meet my wishes. I suppose we shall be three days on the route—so meet on Friday or Saturday. I hope it won't annoy you our being so late. Arthur is at school, but will chirp when he hears the good news. . . . Zurich will do capitally. 'By the margin', etc.[1]

La-la-laity!

I have just polished 'Cassandra' to my satisfaction. Also, a new Poem—'The Patriot Engineer'.[2] 'Phantasy' is remoulded and made presentable. Best of all, my health is very promising. I shall not bring a hat, or a tail coat. I won't. If needs must in your society, I will buy one. To our quick and joyful meeting, my friend! In great haste, your aff[ectionate]

George Meredith

106. *To* F. M. EVANS

Text: typed copy furnished by Messrs. Bradbury & Agnew.

[Copsham, Esher]
Friday, June 28, [1861]

My dear Evans,

I must ask you for £40, further, as I have all sorts of expenses, bills, and what not, crowding on me. Will you send it to Chapman's on

104. [1] As it turned out, Arthur accompanied GM.
105. [1]   By the margin, willow-veiled,
              Slide the heavy barges trailed
              By slow horses. . . .
                              'The Lady of Shalott'
[2] Published in *OaW* (14 Dec.), with an illustration by Keene.

Tuesday next, not later than 12, noon! I start on Wednesday or Thursday. I will see if I can't hunt up matter for *Once a Week*. It reads dolefully just now.

Faithfully yours,
George Meredith

107. *To* SAMUEL LUCAS

MS.: Yale. Printed: *Altschul Catalogue*, p. 23.

Copsham Cottage, Esher
[*c.* July 1, 1861]

My dear Lucas,

I go to Switzerland on Thursday. But am I addressing a shade? You were—but are you still? Is't parturition of some great performance—some work upon the Saxons or the Normans? Or are we no longer to the taste of our Editor? Lord! what a deal you've lost! Now, if you want the *Dyke Farm* finished, write to me Poste Restante, Innsbruck, Tyrol; where I hope to be within a fortnight of this date. Say that you want to begin it and I'll sit down and finish it. I forward you two additional Chapters. I won't put my name.

I shall be absent about 2 months. I have a young fellow or two who may be trained to serve well. Them will I introduce to you by and by.

Lady Duff Gordon is going to the Cape on a sea voyage for health.[1] Will you, to oblige me, and *at once*, send her a cheque for her 'Tannhäuser'? I say nothing of the length of time it has been in your hands. I agree with you that it is a foolish thing to recommend anybody or anything to an Editor.—She leaves on the 12th of this month.

Your faithful
George Meredith

108. *To* W. C. BONAPARTE WYSE

Text (excerpt): Ellis, p. 153.

Copsham
[*c.* July 1, 1861]

My dear Poet,

I hope to be with you by the margin of Zürich's fair waters on Saturday, or Sunday. We start Thursday night; and come, I think, by

---

107. [1] Lady Duff Gordon sailed aboard the *St. Lawrence* and anchored at Cape Town on 17 Sept. after a voyage of nearly two months (Gordon Waterfield, *Lucie Duff Gordon*, N.Y., 1937, pp. 161, 165).

the Great Luxembourg Railway, which they say is more direct. Passports are here. All is ready. The delay has been caused by the newspapers, knickerbockers for Arthur—and knick-knacks. I am told by my doctor to get much tonic glacier air: to pass many mountain passes: to keep to the high land. Before we start together, I want to go to Hofwyl, to see a school to which Arthur may ultimately be sent.

I shall bring a knapsack. . . . I shall take to myself two months and perhaps a week more. Do try and give up so much time to me. . . . I shall proceed to the Hôtel de Belle Vue on arriving at Zürich.

109. *To* EDWARD WALFORD[1]

MS.: The Lilly Library, Indiana University.

Copsham
Tuesday, [July 2, 1861]

My dear Walford,
I have got a friend—a Conservative—to do the paper[2] . . . he being much to the taste of the Proprietor, who has not the honour of knowing you. Thanks to you for your kind offer to assist.—Is *Once a Week* going to be given up? I hear nothing of what may be wanted of me, and so forth. The impenetrable Editor recedes more and more. Nor do we deem him fleshly.

I go to Switzerland on Thursday. Lucas could have had the *Dyke Farm*, but he wouldn't send me proofs, and so it remains.

Your faithful
George Meredith

110. *To* F. M. EVANS

Text: typed copy furnished by Messrs. Bradbury & Agnew. Published: *Letters*, i. 27–28, with variants.

Zürich, Suisse
Tuesday, July 9, [1861]

My dear Evans,
Be so good as to send me £30, through your Banker, to Innsbruck, address Poste Restante; and please don't fail to do this within a couple of days after receipt of this letter, as your servant will require it.

109. [1] Although at the end of the letter GM has directed it to 'W. L. Walford, Esq.', there can be no doubt that it was written to Edward Walford, sub-editor of *OaW*, to which much of the letter pertains. (See Note 2, Letter 52.)
[2] i.e. the *Ipswich Journal*. I have no plausible guess as to the identity of the Conservative substitute.

Arthur is quite well, and bore his travelling like a man. He met with perfect kindness from everybody and remarks that 'these Germans are nice people'. He has it on his mind that he did not go to say good bye to Mrs. Orridge.[1] Let her know his compunction's visitings.

Write a word of *avis* that your banker has done the good deed, and also, if Lucas has not written, say whether he wants the continuation and conclusion of the *Dyke Farm*.

Zürich is a charming place, with a clear lake, fine hills, and Alps in the distance. The Swiss fleece you with admirable gravity. The great 'shots' of Stanz[2] parade the town with their prizes in their hats. . . . I shall send you something shortly. I am better already. I shall soon be eager for work.

Your faithful
George Meredith

111. *To* FREDERICK A. MAXSE

Text: typed copy, Maxse Papers. Published: *Letters*, i. 30–34, with omissions.

Meran, South Tyrol
Friday, July 26, [1861]

My dear Maxse,

Is it you who send the poem 'Tannhäuser'[1] to me here? And why? Do you think it very good?—O my dear fellow! I'll talk about that presently, but I wish you were with me or I with you: for my companion's a dear old boy, but we don't get on quite as travellers. And not only for that reason, but for many reasons. I want to see you, and shake your hand, and hear about your bubbles, and the life you go through. In fact, I begin to feel that I must see you and have a very strong affection for you, if you don't mind hearing that much, O my shame-faced Briton!—Well, I fear I shall not meet you at Baden Baden, even if you go there. I have been thrown out by money-arrangements failing, letters missing etc. I return by Botzen to Verona; thence to Milan, Turin, Dijon, Paris. The dear little man is quite well, making a collection of Tyrolese butterflies and beetles. He is at Landeck, about 80 miles in the rear of us; at the junction of the Inn and the Rosanna. The Rosanna, by the way, put me in mind of you—

---

110. [1] Daughter of Evans who was married to Robert Orridge, a barrister living at Esher.
  [2] Stans, capital of Nidwalden.
111. [1] Not Lady Duff Gordon's poem but *Tannhäuser; or the Battle of the Bards*, by Neville Temple and Edward Trevor (pseudonyms of Julian Fane and Edward Robert Bulwer Lytton, later 1st Earl of Lytton). It was praised by the *Saturday Review* (15 June) in spite of its frank imitation of Tennyson.

nay, sang of you with a mountain voice, somehow, I don't know how. Perhaps because it is both hearty and gallant, subtle, and *sea-green*. You never saw so lovely a brawling torrent. Clear, ice-cold, foaming. You shall have the verses it *inspired*.[2] Tell me: Would you like the dedication of my volume of Poems, when it's ready? Say, no, if you feel no. For my part I feel the honour will be mine.[3]

We walked from Innsbruck to Landeck in three days. Wyse does not walk in rain, or when it's to be apprehended; nor when there's a chance of nightfall; nor does he like it in the heat; and he's not the best hand in the world at getting up in the morning, and he's rather excitable. But still thoroughly kind and good. So we did not come at a great rate. From Landeck we took three days and a quarter to Meran, whence I write to you. The country is wonderful. Mountains holding up cups of snow to the fiery sun, who glares on them in vain. The peasantry are a noble race: pious, and with a strong smell. Priests abound and soap flies before them. I sigh, like Tannhäuser, for the Venusberg. The limbs of that lady are clean; and she is sweet and affable, and of a fair face, which cannot be said for one woman—not one single woman hitherto encountered by me.—Now, don't you think the writers of 'Tannhäuser', clever as they are and of marked poetic power, should have waited till they wore off Tennyson somewhat? Such is my opinion. There was to be a review in the *Times*. Has it appeared?—

Meran is southern in heat and luxury of growth of all kinds of fruits. The cicada goes all day like a factory wheel—poetic simile! The flies sting, and the sun is relentless. I begin to understand why Daphne fled into a laurel from the fiery fellow.[4] Still I like sun, as you do. Anything's better than the meagre days we got last year. This land abounds in falling waters, brooks, torrents, all ice cold. We drank at the wells every ten minutes, sat over the brooks naked legged, dipped our heads desperately. Here are crucifixes at every fifty yards. You go to a well and the pipe through which the water flows is through the body of a Christ. Hear you a droning noise on the wind, it issues from a body of peasants mumbling their rosaries as they march to work. They are invariably courteous. Wyse says, they remind him more of the Spaniards than do any other people. But they have not the same prolonged gravity of deportment. Nothing can be grander than the colossal mountains of porphyry and dolomite shining purple and rosy, snow-capped here and there, with some tumultuous river noising

111. [2] 'By the Rosanna. To F. M. [Frederick Maxse]', published in *OaW* (19 Oct.). The poem is dated from Stanzer Thal, Tyrol.
    [3] *Modern Love* etc. (1862), to which this refers, was 'Affectionately Inscribed to Captain Maxse, R.N.'   [4] i.e. Apollo.

below, and that eternal stillness overhead, save when some great peak gathers the thunders and bellows for a time. Then to see the white sulphurious masks curl and cover round it, and drip moisture on the hanging meadows, would task your powers of description, O my friend!

Do our loves prosper?

> Life is real—life is earnest![5]
> Tiddle lol de lol de lol.

But I wish you would fix soon; for as I told you, and as you feel, time goes, and the wheel is pleasant, but if you keep on the wheel you are grey before you know, and then the past looks horridly empty. Heigho! I have Art to solace me. If I saw you stick to that I would not preach. My health is better. I can do 30 miles per diem under this sun, without knocking up. Nevertheless the nerves are not yet right. One good sign is that I am very anxious to finish my *Emilia*; and have gentle prickings about other matters in my mind.

Meran is a glorious place. We look towards Italy. The country is like a garden. The Adige[6] flows on one hand, the Passer on the other. We have a Schwimm-bad here. The water is too cold for swimming. It stings. Wyse goes to it in the morning and remains naked somewhere in the neighbourhood all day. Adventures we have had none. The old boy is very desponding about his circumstances, and he won't buckle up to brave them. I suppose he knows best, so I say nothing.

My first sight of the Alps has raised odd feelings. Here at last seems something more than earth, and visible, if not tangible. They have the whiteness, the silence, the beauty and mystery of thoughts seldom unveiled within us, but which conquer Earth when once they are. In fact they have made my creed tremble.—Only for a time. They have merely dazzled me with a group of symbols. Our great error has been (the error of all religion, as I fancy) to raise a spiritual system in antagonism to Nature. What though yonder Alp does touch the Heavens? Is it a rebuke to us below? In you and in me there may be lofty virgin points, pure from what we call fleshliness. And so forth.— Wyse is lost in astonishment at me because I don't look out for a 'woman'. 'You're a pote, and I can't think how a pote can get on without one. I'd go mad.'—Mrs. W. is very kind to Arthur, and really in love with the Irish-Corsican. They spoon terribly. Perhaps I am

---

[5] GM had read Longfellow, as this quotation from 'A Psalm of Life' demonstrates, but was not an admirer of his poetry.
[6] Or Etsch.

getting old, for I don't envy them, though I feel a kind of emptiness—
an uncared-for feeling. A good friendship would satisfy me.—You
made an impression on Lady Duff [Gordon]. She likes you and takes
to you altogether.—How is it the Austrians get beaten by the French?
A finer set of men than the Austrian soldiers you can't see anywhere.
Their drill seems good. They don't expect war for some months.
I hear Benedek[7] has left Verona for Carlsbad.

Write to me, Poste Restante, Milan, Lombardy, Italy. And don't
fast, there's a dear fellow.

Your faithful
George Meredith

112. *To* F. M. EVANS

Text: *Letters*, i. 28–29.

Meran, South Tyrol, Austria
[*c.* July 29, 1861]

My dear Evans,

I wrote to you from Zürich, asking for £30 to be sent on immediately
to Innsbruck.[1] It has not come. I have calculated on it, and am therefore quite upset by the contretemps. I have an idea that the letter cannot have reached you, or something is wrong. I wrote to Chapman
from Landeck, but am losing faith in letters. So, to make sure, I write
to you again. Please send, on the day you get this, £20 to the Poste
Restante, Meran, Süd Tyrol, Austria. I am almost inclined to ask you to
telegraph to a banker here to hand the money to me at the hotel, Graf
v. Meran. The truth is I have made a mess of my money-arrangements
and am here without any, dependent on a civil landlord for wherewithal to make merry abroad. Don't fail to do something. I wish
Frederick[2] would see Fred Chapman and hear what he has done. If he
has sent the money in time for it to reach me here on Monday, then
please send £10 to Milan, Lombardy, Italy, Post Restante—in a
registered letter, or credit on a banker. If he has delayed, or has not
received my letter, then I don't object to the expense of a telegraph to
a banker here, telling him to hand me the money at my hotel.

In my letter from Zürich I wished you to tell me whether Lucas
wanted the conclusion of the *Dyke Farm*. I left word for him to speak

111. [7] Ludwig von Benedek (1804–81), Austrian general who distinguished himself in
campaigns in Italy and Hungary in 1847–8 and 1849 but was the goat in the Austro-
Prussian War in 1866.
112. [1] The ledgers of Bradbury & Evans show entries 'To Cash' in GM's account on 18
July, in the amount of £30, and 31 July, in the amount of £20, plus telegraph charges of
12s. 9d. The delay in the response to GM's letter of 9 July caused the first remittance to
arrive after his departure from Innsbruck.
[2] Evans's son, then associated with his father in the publishing business.

to that effect, in Bouverie St. What the deuce has come to you all? The
moment I leave England all's dead silent to rearward. I'm not of much
importance, but still I expect my country to make a little sign. I suppose, from Lucas's silence, he does not want the work in question. But
why doesn't he say so? Contributors used in this fashion, fall to the
ground. Pray, write and tell me some news. Is it true that *Once a Week*
is dead? Is the *Times* defunct? Send to Milan a paper or two of any
kind, with the latest news. I shall see you, I hope, in the latter end of
August.—The country about Meran is a great garden open to the
South. Arthur rests in one of the valleys more north, and is making
a collection of butterflies and beetles. He is quite well, and very much
astonished at the smiles he meets in the houses. His more poetical
impressions he keeps to himself.

113. *To* F. M. EVANS

Text: typed copy furnished by Messrs. Bradbury & Agnew. Published: *Letters*, i. 29–30
(dated *July 1861*).

Meran
Monday, July 5 [error for
August 5], 1861[1]

My dear Evans,
(Father and son!)

I have received the £20[2] forwarded here, and right thankfully.
Your letter to Innsbruck has not reached me; nor have I heard from
Lucas.

I shall see whether the long-named banker at Innsbruck won't forward the money here, otherwise I shall be put out of my route altogether.

My walks of about 30 miles a day under a fiery sun, have improved
me, and I think I can go to work now for another nine months. Have
you any idea of what Lucas's intentions were concerning the *Dyke
Farm*?

I have an autobiographical story in view for *O[nce] a W[eek]* when
Chapman's 3 volumes[3] are out of hand.

That is, if *O[nce] a W[eek]* survives. For I know nothing and hear
nothing. Nobody sends me a *Times* or a *Punch*! I am forgotten if

---

113. [1] Mrs. Winifred M. Ashton, librarian at Messrs. Bradbury & Agnew's, has kindly
verified for me the MS. reading of this date. GM wrote *July 5*, which was the day after
he left England. 5 Aug. was on a Monday in 1861, and this is clearly the date intended.

[2] See Note 1, preceding letter.

[3] i.e. *Emilia*. The autobiographical story—i.e., told in the first person—was *The
Adventures of Harry Richmond*. (See Note 4, Letter 273.)

I don't set to work all the agencies of science. You write me contemptuously short business paragraphs. It's clear to me that travelling is for great men alone. They have their country's eyes on them!

The bother is that if I only knew where Lucas is going to, I might come across him and put something stronger than a pen to his breast to make him out with what he means.

Arthur is quite well. He is here, and a mighty traveller, as you may suppose.

He says he is happy, and is catching butterflies.

Ever faithfully,
George Meredith

114. *To* FREDERICK A. MAXSE

Text: typed copy, Maxse Papers.

Meran
Tuesday, August 7, [1861][1]

My dear Maxse,

I start to-morrow for Bozen and Verona. Thence to Venice, to Milan, to Como, Lago Maggiore, over the Splügen to Berne, and on perhaps to Baden Baden. I hope so, for I want to meet you. You will be down, I suppose, among the distinguished visitors. I have been quite disappointed, in my walking-tour. Here is Arthur on my hands altogether. One comfort is, the little fellow is well and his mind is opening.

Take these verses for what they're worth.[2] If you think well they shall be published. Preserve them, then, for I have no copy.

Your faithful
George Meredith

115. *To* FREDERICK A. MAXSE

Text: typed copy, Maxse Papers. Published: *Letters*, i. 34–39, with omissions.

Milan
August 16, 1861

My dear Maxse,

Behold a pretty picture, which is to tell you I have been in Venice, which you know so well, which is a dream and a seduction to the soul of me. I wish you had been there with me—Now, mark the Campanile

---

114. [1] 7 Aug. was a Wednesday in 1861.   [2] See Letter 111 and Note 2.

above, for you are to have it reproduced one day in illustrious verse.
There did I conceive an Ode.—I have followed Byron's and Shelley's
footsteps there (in Venice) on the Lido.[1] Do you remember in 'Julian
and Maddalo', where the two, looking towards the Euganean hills, see
the great bell of the Insane Asylum swing in the sunset? I found the
exact spot. I have seldom felt melancholy so strongly as when standing
there. You know I despise melancholy, but the feeling came. I love
both those poets; and with my heart given to them I felt as if I stood in
a dead and useless time. So are we played with sometimes! At that
hour your heart was bursting with a new passion,[2] and the past was as
smoke flitting away from a fired-off old contemptible gun. Well,
I walked the Lido every day, and bathed with my little man in the
tepid Adriatic, and floated through the streets in my gondola, and
received charming salutes from barred windows: from one notably
where a very pretty damsel, lost in languor, hung with her loose-
robed bosom against the iron, and pressed amorously to see me pass,
till she could no further: I meantime issued order to Lorenzo, my
gondolier, to return, and lo, as I came slowly into view she as slowly
arranged her sweet shape to be seen decently, and so stood, but half
a pace in the recess, with one dear hand on one shoulder, her head
slightly lying on her neck, her drooped eyelids mournfully seeming
to say: 'No, no; never! though I am dying to be wedded to that wish
of yours and would stake my soul I have divined it!'—wasn't it
charming? This too, so intensely human from a figure vaporous, but
half discernible!

I have been alone with Arthur in Venice, which was a blessing, for
somehow or other dear old Wyse isn't at all the right sort of companion. He says he thinks it's his stomach. I tell him that it is not fair
for a man to throw his stomach in one's face. The fact is the dear old
boy (meaning excellently) is irritable exceedingly: tiffs twenty times
a day, and now and then a sulk. Then ensues reconciliation: 'Mardith!
I don't mind saying I'm sorry! and ye can judge of me 'ffection for ye
when ye see I don't hes'tate to sacrifice me praide, etc.' He owns still,
he thinks me in the wrong, when the next occasion recurs. You may
imagine this sort of schoolboy business is not to my taste. When one
does meet a woman, it's better to have her in petticoats.—Here (in
Milan) I met him again. He went last night to see his mother[3] on Lake
Como, at the Villa d'Este. I go to him to-morrow. Next day, I trust,
homeward by way of the Mont Cenis, to Paris. I shall rest in Paris

---

115. [1] In *Beauchamp's Career* (ch. V) GM attributes his own admiration of Byron in
Venice to Renée de Croisnel.
 [2] Maxse was in love with Cecilia Steel, whom he married on 22 Jan. 1862. Meanwhile
his father's objections to the marriage stood in the way.
 [3] Lady Wyse, who had been separated from Sir Thomas since 1828.

a day or two, according to the state of my funds. Will you write to me there, Poste Restante. I want to know where I can see you in London, for I have an immense longing to wring your hand. I will accept a dinner. That is to say, a dish of fish, an English steak, and *no wine*. I am much better in health; but, you see, I have been somewhat disappointed about the management of Arthur. I have been able to get only one week's walk, and the rest of the time the little fellow has been on my hands. But what a jolly boy and capital companion he is! Full of fun and observation, good temper and endurance. The tour has sown much fine stuff in him, but I am anxious at last to have him home. As for me, I believe I shall now be in condition for labour of the remunerative kind. The novelty has been worth the money in all ways. Could I but afford to rest and look on man for one year! *Non è possibile.* —You must see Arthur's Diary. He is at it now, at my elbow.

Yes! those bleeding tortured images by the wayside were painful and became exasperating—almost as much so as the sight of the crowds of white coats[4] through the whole of the Venetian territory. In Verona they have a garrison of 45,000 men. The population numbers 60,000. The soldiers have to keep to themselves, the officers are cut, and nothing so miserable and menacing can be fancied. Even the girls won't be spoken to. I saw an amusing scene of a couple of officers after two, who led them a terrible round and finally drew up at a melon-seller's. There they began chattering, wouldn't let Mr. Oberlieutenant get in a word; suddenly they turned round, fired a volley of contempt and virtuous indignation and retired into the applauding crowd. When Venus turns against Mars what shall the poor devil do? Better doff his casque.—Now about 'Tannhäuser'.[5] I think the review in the *Times* stupid. It's just a blow of the trumpet. The poem is a failure, and the young men ought to have been told so. It fails, because the central point (in action), the 'Battle', is absurdly weak even to silliness: because the theme, which is so glorious, is spoilt, in order to cry up and *preach*, a sort of cherubim chastity popular just now, and which is not the real thing: because it has no *character*, even done in outline. It contains, I think, no image, or scene, that the mind clings to. I don't care much for the passages you point out—'a drooping harebell' is in the 'Princess'. The revelation of Venus is poor, matched with the subject. To my mind the best parts are the departure of the pilgrims, and the return, especially that of the one being questioned. The filing by of the procession reminds me of the main point in V. Hugo's ballad 'Les Cymbaliers du Roi'. On re-reading the poem I am confirmed in a cloyed sensation I first experienced. The alliteration is really so persistent that the ears feel as if they had been horribly

115. [4] i.e. Austrian soldiers.   [5] See Note 1, Letter 111.

drummed on. Power of narrative, I see. Mimetic power of a wonderful kind, and *flow* of verse, also extraordinary. I am not touched by any new music in it. I do not find any comprehension of human nature, or observation, or sympathy with it. I perceive none of the subtleties, deep but unobtrusive, that show that a mind has travelled. Great windy phrases, and what I must term (for so they hit my sense) *encaustic* imageries do not satisfy me any longer, though I remember a period when they did. The passage

'or shall I call you men or beasts',

praised by the *Times*, shows the Muse puff-cheeked, and Elizabeth ridiculous. The scene was managed in order to bring her out. It does so with a vengeance. Don't you see how ill in accordance with the little bit of idea one gets of Elizabeth this is? She may be vehement without acting the virago. Such a creature would not have commenced with invective: she might have heated herself up to it: entreaty, self-abandonment, unconscious declarations of her love for the object of their wrath in unmeasured praise of him, excuse of him etc.; then, when her words seem not to be producing their effect, then a fiery line, if you like. But how stagey is the 'Or shall I call you etc.!' And this is the thing that attracts you?—

Something better has done that. Well, I will tell you what I think. You know I wish very earnestly to see you, a man made to understand and make happy any pure good woman, married to one. I don't think any son owes his parents more than the conscientious assurance that he has clearly thought over what he is about to do (in such a matter); seeing that men are the only possible judges in the case; and that the stake is all their own. To have found a suitable person and to give her up for anything on earth is like seeing a jewel on the shore and rejecting it on account of the trouble of conveying it home. But do you strongly recognize the jewel? Have you found her? A boy can't, but a man must reason, in these cases. You may know your love from its power of persisting and bearing delay. Passion has not these powers. If your love of this person is true and not one of your fancies, it will soon light you clear enough. I'm sorry the mother seems not so well-set as you might wish. Was the father of good repute in the service? What sort of a man? Do look up these things. And don't be hasty and think you are trusting your instinct by grasping suddenly at the golden apple. Can you bear poverty for her? Will she for you? Can she, even if she would? Think whether you are risking it, and remember that very few women bear it and retain their delicacy and charm. Some do. Can you think her one of the chosen? The great difficulty is to be honest with ourselves. If there comes a doubt, the wave of passion overwhelms it. Try and listen to your doubt. See whether you feel, not what we call love, but tenderness for her. Satisfy yourself on this point. And then determine to wait. You can, if your heart has conceived real tenderness. If not, should you marry her? You speak of securing her. You may secure her person, but how can you be yet sure of more? If continually you find her worthier, fix your mind to win her by the force of your love. Then should you have that divine delight, I ask you whether you can see any earthly obstacle in your way? You are on the highest pinnacles and may remain untouched, whatever is said or done. You will have pains and aches—agonies to go through. They serve to strengthen you. God bless you, my dear Maxse!

Believe me your faithful and affectionate

George Meredith

I shall be in Paris about the 21st or 22nd, or 23rd. Please write when you get this.

Did you get the Pome I sent?[6]

116. *To* W. C. Bonaparte Wyse

Text (excerpt): Ellis, p. 157.

Milan

August 17, [1861]

My dear Wyse,

Heartily glad to hear good news from you! . . . To-morrow I'll come by the 9:30 from Milan. This reaches Camerlata at 10:53, but don't fear my disturbing you at that hour. Why don't you meet me and save my looking foolish, when you know I can't [speak] Italian and can only just stumble in French; and Frenchwomen have in their souls (in spite of their soft smiles) no mercy for a wretch who looks foolish! I shall sleep at Camerlata, and start for Turin next day early.

Your faithful

George Meredith

117. *To* Samuel Lucas

MS.: Yale.

Copsham Cottage, Esher

Saturday, [August 24 or 31, 1861]

My dear Lucas,

I hear you wrote to Innsbruck, and that you won £5000000 at the Tables at Spa. What's your secret? for I lost at Wiesbaden, though I hit

115. [6] 'By the Rosanna'.

the *number* once and got multiplied 35 times. Write and say when you may be seen. What follows the *Silver Cord?*[1] If you want to hear some *Poems*!: come hither quickly.—I received none of the letters forwarded to Innsbruck—through some carelessness of the Austrians. Been through Tyrol and North Italy to Venice. Very pleasant—at the devil's heat. I walked 30 miles per diem in it for one week—unnumbered rivulets flowing from my cheeks: my little man was with me, and bore him right gallantly.

Your faithful
George Meredith

118. *To* WILLIAM HARDMAN[1]

MS.: Garrick Club. Published: *Letters*, i. 43, with inaccuracies.

Copsham, Esher
Sunday, [? September 22, 1861]

My dear Mr. Hardman,

Most certainly I will come, and with very great pleasure; bringing my bag to show that I'm in earnest about a bed.

By the way, do you know, it's dangerous to ask poets to sleep at a house. You ask them to dine, but never to sleep. For, if you do, it seems they are only to be got rid of by a ruse. Numerous cases might be cited. How if I tax your ingenuity?

I see the *Silver Cord* reviewed in the *Saturday* [*Review*];[2] and, as I think, fairly: but it's a question whether Brooks is still young enough to feel that. Please don't spare him yourself; but put him on his mettle; and his next work will be capital.

I am exceedingly sorry to lose you both. I can only hope that you will, whenever you think proper, come to this humble place as frankly as I accept the opening to your

HOSPITABLE TOWN MANSION.

Six o'clock is an excellent hour, and I have just enough faith in my appetite and honour to say I will be punctual.

My little man says he hopes he shall see you and Mrs. Hardman here soon. He also mutters something about a 'Pantomime', which I can't

117. [1] *The Silver Cord*, by Shirley Brooks, was running serially in *OaW*. It ended in the 31 Aug. number.

118. [1] For a biographical sketch of Hardman, see Biographical Section, pp. 1717–18.

[2] Shirley Brooks's *The Silver Cord* was reviewed by the *Saturday Review* (21 Sept.) as 'clever and entertaining, full of novelty, fertile in incident, witty and brilliant in style', but lacking coherence and probability and having no characters 'for whom any reader can pretend to care a straw'. Brooks was a friend of Hardman's.

comprehend. We both send greetings to Mrs. Hardman, whose behaviour in the boat, let me add, has proved her right to be a companion
of men!

[Signature cut away]

119. *From* ARTHUR G. MEREDITH *to* MRS. JANET ROSS[1]

MS.: Yale. Published: *Letters*, i. 39–41, with numerous variants.

Copsham Cottage
September 25, [1861]

My dear Janet,

I was very much pleased, to receive your letter but I am very sorry
you are not well. Zillah[2] goes to school with me and I like it very much
(*sic*).\Pat, a little while ago, went into the water to fetch sticks, but Jessy
spoilt him by catching hold of his ear and tried to make him dive.
Jessy is a much better dog than Pat. Our gardens are getting on very
well I have got a lot of peas for seed and some beetroot almost ready to
dig up. About three months ago I went on the continent with my papa.
I started from Dover to Ostend and going in the harbour I saw some
Belgian peasants picking perywinkles; they laughed at us and had such
rosy cheeks and I thought them very funny. Then I had a long day in
the train from Ostend to Coblentz. In the morning I saw a steamer
going to Mainz, and so we dressed and got in it. On each side of the
Rhine There are mountains that have old castles on them where the
robber knights used to live, and there was the Lurli rock, they fired
a gun and there were three echoes. In the morning the waiter at
Mentz took me upstairs to a high place and showed me a stork's nest
built on a chine. I went from Mentz to Zurich; where the lake of Zurich
was so clear that you could see to the bottom of it. The next day
I went up part of a mountain and dined; and I saw the Alps at a distance; there was a crow which came hopping along and was quite
tame, but another boy teased it, and so it flew away. From Zurich
I went to Munich and I crossed lake Constance. Coming In the
harbour I saw the statue of a lion in the water. I stopped at Munich
a day and at twelve o'clock I heard a nice band. The Bavarian soldiers
dress is blue which looks very pretty. There is a beautiful palace at
Munich I went into a beautiful garden called the English gardens
were I saw some fire flies which show a green light. From Munich

---

119. [1] This letter contains the only factual account of GM's trip to the Continent.
      [2] A niece of Miss Grange, GM's housekeeper.

I went to Innsbruck were there was a church with bronze kings and queens surrounding the Emperor Maximilian[3] and I saw the tomb of Andreas Hofer.[4] I went up to some high gardens and had a view of Innsbruck. From Innsbruck I went to Landeck were I caught some very pretty butterflys from Landeck I went to Meran were there are castles. I went to schloss Labenberg [Lebenberg] and shloss Guin [? Goyen] were there was a nice room, and I bathed in the Passier. From Meran I went to Verona and I went to the amphi theatre it is quite round and high. From Verona I went to Venice were I was very happy I went about in gondolars in the canals and bathed at the Liedo the water is so hot that you can stopp in a long while—I dine at tables d'hotes and had my own bottle of wine, lots of grapes; and lemonade on the place st. Mark. I went in the palace of st. Mark were there were some pictures I went from Venice to Milan and went into the great cathedral from Milan I went to Paris, over the Mount Cenis, I liked going over. At Paris I had breakfast at caffas I went to the Champs Elysees I saw the monument of Napoleon on which were the battles he fought. I went in the Leuve palace were there were some beautiful Italian pictures. Then I went home. I remain my dear Janet your afectionate friend

Arthur G. Meredith

[Added in the hand of GM:]

This is entirely as you would wish it to be—the small man's own, and bearing the stamp thereof. He will have a lot more of it to tell you when he has you by the ears.

*To Mrs. Janet Ross

MS.: Yale. Published: *Letters*, i. 41, with inaccuracies.

Tuesday, October 8, [1861]

My dear good Janet,

Forgive me. I have been lying by to write you an account of the Travels of self and son; but I am now so torn to pieces and hard at work that I can't sit down to any thing. Your letter was based on false intelligence, my dear. It was perfectly right of you to take up the case as you did. I am glad you like me well enough to do so. Be sure I would

---

* [Written on the back of Arthur's letter.]

3 Maximilian I (1459–1519), represented as kneeling on a marble sarcophagus, at the sides of which are 28 bronze statues of ancestors and contemporaries.

4 Andreas Hofer (1767–1810), Tyrolean patriot, subject of numerous ballads and at least two tragedies. He was captured by the Italians in 1810 and shot, allegedly on orders by Napoleon.

not miss your friendship for much; and would stoop my pride for it, even if that stood in the way. As it is there is no feeling of the sort. God bless you. I will write fully in a few days.—I saw your father two or three days back. He is looking as ever. In health I also am better. Arthur is now at Weybridge seeing his mother daily.[5]

Your faithful and affectionate
George M.

120. *To* SAMUEL LUCAS

MS.: Yale. Excerpts printed from a typed copy: *Altschul Catalogue,* p. 162.

Copsham Cottage, Esher
[October 1861]

My dear Lucas,

'Phantasy', if you read it attentively, will really stand as it is very well. I leave it to you, of course (to strike out—: not to alter), but I do think that the effect would be spoilt by the scissors.

Why haven't you sent proofs of the lines 'By the Rosanna'?[1] I insist upon it that they are good of their kind. If you don't think so, let me hear. Return them and reproachfully shall they face you in alien pages!

I want to bring little Swinburne to introduce him to you this week or next. I think you will find him valuable.

Your faithful
George Meredith

P.S. Please send duplicates of these proofs, if you are for incision and will imbrue.[2]

119. [5] Stevenson (pp. 95–96) says that Mary Ellen Meredith, after her flight with Wallis, returned to England in 1859 and was living at this time at Grotto Cottage, Oatlands Park, Weybridge. Seriously ill, she asked GM to come and see her upon his return from the Continent, but he refused. After some hesitation, however, he permitted Arthur to visit her. A month later she was dead.

The 'false intelligence' alluded to by GM probably had something to do with stories that Janet had heard about GM's refusal to permit Arthur to see his mother or about his break with his wife.

120. [1] Published in *OaW* on 19 Oct.

[2] Pistol: 'What! shall we have incision? shall we imbrew?' *2 Henry IV,* II. iv. 210.

121. *To* FREDERICK A. MAXSE

Text: typed copy, Maxse Papers. Published: *Letters*, i. 53–55, with substantial omissions.

Copsham, Esher, Surrey
October 19, [1861]

My dear Maxse,

Tannhäuser was in yesterday's *Post*, and exceedingly well done.[1] I read the extracts also. They produce on me the effect, after three lines, of too much sugar on the palate: something rich, certainly, but of a base richness. I don't agree with you that they have brought Venus sensibly to the reader at all, though it's fair to say that with Elizabeth it is less so than Venus. The former is a prim good miss, a shrew when in a passion; she quite justifies (to me) Tannhäuser's choice of the dear voluptuous Goddess whom they call such naughty names, and who, I begin to think, is the favourite daughter of Mother Earth.

This to you, who are in love, and well in love!—Do you know, I have seldom seen anything with so much pleasure as your honest, modest, manly, love for her. You don't tire me in telling me about it, and of your feelings, and your thoughts about her. The fonder and the deeper your emotions reach, the more I see and admire the large nature you are gifted with.

I trust it may be that Heaven brings the other half of her. She is, I am sure, a very sweet person: but how *strong* she is, or can be made, my instinct does not fathom. I am so miserably constituted now that I can't love a woman if I do not feel her soul, and that there is force therein to wrestle with the facts of life (called the Angel of the Lord). But I envy those who are attracted by what is given to the eye;—yes, even those who have a special taste for woman flesh, and this or that particular little tit-bit—I envy them! It lasts not beyond an hour with me.

Happy you with all the colour of life about you! Has she principle? has she any sense of responsibility? Has she courage? Enough that you love her. I believe that this plan of taking a woman on the faith of a mighty wish for her, is the best, and the safest way to find the jewel we are all in search of. As to love 'revealing' all the qualities in one great flash—do you believe it even in your present state? Still of so fair and exquisite a person it is just to augur hopefully; and when one comes to read her face, surely that is a book with plates of virgin silver. Well! of her face I will tell you, without trying to make you too happy, that I don't know any face the memory of which leaves with

---

121. [1] I infer from the context that Maxse had reviewed *Tannhäuser* in the *Morning Post*, where he later reviewed GM's *Modern Love*, etc. but I have not seen the review.

me the unique impression of *music* so completely. There is that softness in the curves, and purity of look, which move like music in my
mind.

As to her singing qualities, that is another matter, and really I had
forgotten. But on coming to consider this, there's something right in
one—a woman—who knows her capabilities to be not brilliant, sitting
down to do her duty at the piano to pass the evening properly. Some
fair ones would have declined resolutely. For my part I like simple,
gentle, unpretending songs, and shall be always glad of the privilege
of hearing them.

Health somewhat better. Working on pomes. By the way, I put
the 'Rosanna' in *Once a Week*. Do you mind? I ordered them to
send you a copy. You will find some alterations, much for the better,
I think. People say it goes well.

Rossetti admires your beloved, though she has not green eyes and
carrots; which, I tell him, astonishes me. He sent me a book of MSS
original poetry the other day, and very fine are some of the things in it.
He is a poet, without doubt. He would please you more than I do, or
can, for he deals with essential poetry, and is not wild, and bluff, and
coarse; but rich, refined, royal-robed! Swinburne read me the other
day his French novel 'La fille du Policeman':[2] the funniest rampingest
satire on French novelists dealing with English themes that you can
imagine. One chapter, 'Ce qui peut se passer dans un Cab Safety',
where Lord Whitestick, Bishop of Londres, ravishes the heroine, is
quite marvellous. But he is not subtle; and I don't see any internal
centre from which springs anything that he does. He will make a great
name, but whether he is to distinguish himself solidly as an Artist,
I would not willingly prognosticate.

I am much distressed about the domestic matters of which you
[? write], but I won't bruise you with them.—From Wyse I had
a letter of two lines, on his return from Caprera, saying he would
write 'to-morrow'—a month since, or more.—My darling boy is
quite well. He has cried a little, I am told. I am afraid his feelings have
been a trifle worked upon, though not by his mother so much as the
servants and friends in her house.[3] On the whole he flourishes.

Rossetti is going to illustrate my 'Cassandra', which pome has taken
his heart. I am obliged to make money as I can, to meet these new
claims on me, and so all my pieces must be published before they're
collected. Your name, you know, may be withheld from the Dedication then if you please.

What do you think if I offer to go down to Crystal Palace and call
on your Eve, and paint for you (with pen) her portrait, and send it?—

121. [2] A burlesque novel, still unpublished.   [3] See Note 5, Letter 119.

But don't know her address. I would do so if it would please you, and refresh you in your arid desert of distance from her.

Fred Chapman has met a young woman with £30,000 and is to marry her very shortly. Poor Kate[4] is acting at the St. James's. I say 'poor', for MacNamara[5] (though very anxious to marry her), is a horrible temper, it seems, something of a rogue too. Young Dormer and he have duels of jealousy in Kate's presence, and which, described by her, would kill you with laughter. I have heard of nothing more comic than the scenes between these three in her poor little room where she lives and 'does for herself', as they say. It might be put in the past tense?—God bless you dear friend. Write again soon, and know me ever

Your faithful and affectionate
George Meredith

Tell me more of Duke Ernst. I have a great admiration for him. Why, why didn't we make the Englishman of *him*!

Arthur being asked whether he sends any message to you, replies: '*Send him my love, and, when am I to see that little girl!*' Verbatim report.

122. *To* WILLIAM HARDMAN

MS. (written on black-bordered paper): Garrick Club. Published: *Letters*, i. 42, with variants.

Esher
Wednesday, [? October 30, 1861][1]

My dear Hardman,

How can I thank you for the trouble you take! Your friend Holroyd's[2] opinion is worth having and will be serviceable. I received the *cartes de visite* on the day I was quitting Copsham for Suffolk (the *Giles* of Counties,[3] I always think) where I lived in a dumpling state

---

[4] Kate Terry.   [5] Unidentified.

122. [1] GM's usual practice was to date letters with the day of the week only. Hardman, who kept GM's letters in bound volumes, almost invariably noted on them month, day, and year; but sometimes he must have added the date as an afterthought, for occasionally his dates are wrong. So with this one, which he dated 19 or 20 Oct. 1861. But the 19th and 20th were respectively Saturday and Sunday, and GM has dated the letter *Wednesday*. Further, the first paragraph shows that the letter was written after the death of Mary Ellen Meredith, which occurred on 22 Oct. (General Register Office, Somerset House). In 1861, 30 Oct. was a Wednesday and hence, I think, the most likely date.

[2] Edward D. Holroyd, to whom Hardman sent his journal as a monthly letter.

[3] 'Giles' is sometimes a mildly humorous generic name for a farmer (from Robert Bloomfield's poem, 'The Farmer's Boy', which enjoyed great popularity in the years following its publication in 1800).

for a week. When I entered the world again, I found that one had quitted it who bore my name:[4] and this filled my mind with old melancholy recollections which I rarely give way to. My dear boy fortunately will not feel the blow as he might have under different circumstances.

I tell you this to excuse myself for my silence. I will come to-morrow, if you please. I have an engagement in town to-night, which necessitates a tail coat. So don't be frightened when you see me: nor stand in awe: nor strive to emulate.

I hope for music, for which I have great longing.—I am engaged getting ready a volume of Poems. If I had a piano, and my rooms here were only a little bigger than yourself and Mrs. Hardman, I would have the audacity to ask you to come. The dread of my soul is the evening! How shall a poor guest be amused here? Yet is November fine: a great observer, old, shrewd, unerring, said to me once 'I always took my holidays in November, being sure of a greater number of clear fine days than in any other month.' I corroborate. Think over this and communicate with me. To Mrs. Hardman I would say that in November she 'being well wrapped up' might even enjoy the late autumn sunshine on the *Mole*.

[Signature cut away]

123. *To* SAMUEL LUCAS

MS.: Yale. Excerpts printed: *Altschul Catalogue*, p. 162.

Esher

Saturday, November 1861[1]

My dear Lucas,

I doubt if Rossetti will be back next week; I don't see any use in your having Swinburne to dinner; and, as I have had my turn, I am of opinion that you may as well, for the credit and honour of *Once a Week*, invite a new batch. You know me well enough to believe that I can in all sincerity back out of a dinner for the common good.

Lady Gordon has written a short and most vivid Diary of her *sail* to the Cape. It struck me at once it would do for you, and I proposed it to

122. [4] The cause of death is described as 'renal dropsy', the signature of the informant was that of 'Susan Keene, present at the death, Weybridge', and the occupation of deceased was stated as 'wife of George Meredith, solicitor'.

123. [1] This letter, so dated by GM, may have been written on 2 Nov. Rossetti was in Yorkshire, where he had gone to paint a portrait of Mrs. Heaton. He wrote to his mother on 4 Nov. that he expected to return on the 7th (Oswald Doughty and J. R. Wahl, *Letters of Dante Gabriel Rossetti*, 1966, ii. 424).

Gordon, who acquiesced, but wanted it printed immediately. For the printing, if you think the Diary won't suit you, I will pay.—

I know that you are really kind with regard to my poor work. I do my best always, and let it take its chance. I never publish anything that hasn't a meaning distinct to *me*, and not indistinct to fellows here and there. You will find by and by that when taken altogether I am clear. This 'Rosanna' was written to a friend, and was play, with scenery, and a background of design. I am sorry for your sake that it confuses people.

I will call on Thursday evening with Swinburne, and you shall criticize as you please.

Your faithful
George Meredith

124. *To* Augustus Jessopp[1]

MS.: Yale. Published: *Letters*, i. 44–46.

Copsham Cottage, Esher, Surrey
November 13, 1861

My dear Sir,

I have received your letter. Let me tell you at once that I feel it to be most generous, and I should be glad to think I deserved such hearty praise as fully as I do the censure. But on that point, I must be allowed to give you two or three words of explanation. Apropos of the 'Rosanna', it was written from the Tyrol, to a friend, and was simply a piece of friendly play. Which should not have been published, you add? Perhaps not, but it pleased my friend, and the short passage of description was a literal transcript of the scene. Moreover, though the style is open to blame, there is an idea running through the verses, which, while I was rallying my friend, I conceived to have some point for a larger audience.

It is true that I have fallen from what I once hoped to do. The fault is hardly mine. Do you know Vexation, the slayer? There is very little poetry to be done when one is severely and incessantly harassed. My nerves have given way under it, and it is only by great care and attention to the directions of my doctor, that I can work at all.—I have now more leisure and somewhat better health, and the result is, that I have gone back partially to my old mistress.

As to my love for the Muse, I really think that is earnest enough. I have all my life done battle in her behalf, and should, at one time,

---

124. [1] For a biographical sketch of Jessopp, see Biographical Section, p. 1718.

have felt no blessing to be equal to the liberty to serve her. Praise sings strangely in my ears. I have been virtually propelled into a practical turn, by the lack of encouragement for any other save practical work. I have no doubt that it has done me good, though the pleasure your letter gives me, and let me say also the impetus, is a proof that I should have flourished better under a less rigorous system.

If you do me the favour to look at *Once a Week* during the next two months, you will see some poems of mine that are of another cast. The 'Cassandra', you will see, is as severe in rhythm as you could wish. But one result of my hard education since the publication of my boy's book in '51 (those Poems were written before I was twenty) has been that I rarely write save from the suggestion of something actually observed. I mean, that I rarely write verse. Thus my Jugglers, Beggars, etc., I have met on the road, and have idealized but slightly. I desire to strike the poetic spark out of absolute human clay. And in doing so I have the fancy that I do solid work—better than a carol in mid air. Note the 'Old Chartist', and the 'Patriot Engineer', that will also appear in *Once a Week*. They may not please you; but I think you will admit that they have a truth condensed in them. They are flints perhaps, and not flowers. Well, I think of publishing a volume of Poems in the beginning of '62, and I will bring as many flowers to it as I can. It may be, that in a year or two I shall find time for a full sustained Song. Of course I do not think of binding down the Muse to the study of facts. That is but a part of her work. The worst is, that, having taken to prose delineations of character and life, one's affections are divided. I have now a prose damsel crying out to me to have her history completed;[2] and the creatures of a novel are bubbling up; and in truth, being a servant of the public, I must wait till my master commands before I take seriously to singing.

This is a long letter for a man to write about himself; and it is the first time I have been guilty of such a thing. It has not been possible for me to reply to you in any other way.

I will conclude by saying that, whenever you are in London, if you care to visit me, it will give me great pleasure to welcome you. I must warn you that my cottage has very much the appearance of a natural product of the common on which it stands, 'far from resort of men'.[3] But I can give you a bed and good cookery, of its kind. In the winter it will be difficult to tempt friends to meet you. In the summer they find the place pleasant, and believe me, I shall hold it an honour if you will take rank among them.

Very faithfully yours,
George Meredith

124. [2] *Emilia in England,* published in 1864.
   [3] 'Far from resort of people . . .' (*The Faerie Queene*, I. i. xxxiv, line 3).

125. *To* MRS. JANET ROSS

MS.: Yale. Published: *Letters*, i. 46–53; *The Fourth Generation*, pp. 113–18—both with substantial omissions and numerous variants.

Copsham, Esher
November 19, 1861

My very dear Janet,

I plead ill health: I plead vexation, occupation, general insufficiency: I plead absence from home, absence from my proper mind, and a multitude of things: and now I am going to pay my debts.[1] But are not my letters really three single gentlemen rolled into one? This shall count for ten. Now the truth is that my Janet is, by her poet at least, much more thought of when he doesn't write to her than when he does. Vulgar comparisons being always the most pungent, I will say, Lo, the Epicurean to whom his feast is still in prospect: he dreams of it: it rises before him in a thousand hues and salutes his nostril with scents heavenly. He dines. 'Tis gone. 'Tis in the past and with it go his rosy visions.—Your P[erfect] G[entleman], to wit Hawkins—I saw him the other day, and shall probably dine with him on Thursday; quoth I, at a period of our interview—Have you, O Hawkins! replied duly to the fair Alexandrienne? Then went he through much pantomime, during my just reproaches, and took your address—which may be an excellent P. G. performance, and no more. You will see. He is in new chambers full of pictures, Old Masters, we hear. For a fine putative Leonardo, he disbursed recently £400. And Sir Charles Eastlake[2] said —never mind what. Then, too, a Masaccio for which he gave £19/7/6¾, was exhibited at the British Institution and the papers took note of nothing else. And Sir Charles Eastlake said—as before. Hawkins is a good old boy. He has a pleasant way of being inquisitive, and has already informed me, quite agreeably, that I am a gentleman, though I may not have been born one.[3] Some men are always shooting about you like May flies in little quick darts, to see how near you they may come. The best thing is to smile and enjoy the fun of it. I confess a private preference for friends who are not thus afflicted, and get the secret by instinct. As my Janet does, for instance.—The dear indifferent Bart. I meet occasionally; in the train, or on lonely Celia;[4] looking as if

125. [1] Janet Ross (*The Fourth Generation*, p. 113) says: 'I had written several letters to my Poet without getting an answer, so at last I declared I would write no more unless he sent me a few words. This brought the following answer. . . .'

[2] Sir Charles Eastlake (1793–1865), Keeper of the National Gallery and an old friend of Janet.

[3] So much has been made of GM's reticence on the subject of his origin that it is worth observing that the Duff Gordons and their friends were obviously aware of it.

[4] Sir Alexander Duff Gordon's mare.

he bore with life, but had not the exact reason for his philosophy handy. He speaks out like a man concerning your husband, and I should wish every husband to have a father-in-law who appreciated him as heartily. —Your Mother's Diary[5] will not, I suppose, reach you before this letter. On the whole it is very hopeful. Secondly, it is immensely amusing, and shows her fine manly nature admirably. O what a gallant soul she is! and how very much I love her! I had only time during the passage of the train to read it, and couldn't get to the end. As yet the voyage has wrought no *cure*: but the change and the sea breeze and shaking have done good and produced favourable excitement. I have new friends whom I like, and don't object to call by the name. A Mr. and Mrs. Hardman I met in Esher this Autumn. She is very pleasant and is one of the rare women who don't find it necessary to fluster their sex under your nose eternally, in order to make you like them. I give her private's rank in Janet's Amazonian regiment, with chances of promotion. Also, he is a nice fellow: a barrister, who does photographs of his friends principally. On that head, let me say, that I went (thinking of you solely) and was *done* the other day, and will send a copy to you immediately. It looks absurd; but I must conclude it faithful.— My friend Maxse, for whom I have an affection, is in love and confides his delirium to me. His passion is returned, so I am spared the first impetuosity of the tide. She is a fair winning person, in some aspects and at certain moments beautiful. They are to be married in January. The poor fellow hardly sleeps—at all—like Chaucer's Squire 'a lover and a lusty bachelor'. His father thinks all marriages folly. Behold what he has done! His eldest son, Fitzhardinge Maxse,[6] who was in the Guards (the original of Digby Grand)[7] went to Germany, and in return for his father's refusal to 'come down' with anything, whenever he had previously proposed a 'parti', married an actress. So the family won't receive her (though she's a charming person and Duke Ernst, of Coburg, does all he can to smooth matters) and there's a split. Poor Maxse has a battle to fight for himself. Fortunately, his mother supports him. 'Can I leave a young wife?' he asks me, piteously; and wants to leave the Navy instead, and so forth. Which is nonsense: for he is the youngest of our port captains and a promising officer.—Your slippers and kind letter for the little man have just come. How good of

125. ⁵ Lady Duff Gordon had gone to South Africa for her health. The diary referred to here was later published as *Letters from Egypt* (1865).

⁶ (Sir) Henry Berkeley Fitzhardinge Maxse (1832–83) rose to the rank of lieutenant-colonel in the army by 1863, when he went to Heligoland as lieutenant-governor. He became governor the following year. In 1881 he was appointed governor of Newfoundland, where he died in 1883. The marriage mentioned here was to a daughter of Herr von Rudloff (*DNB*).

⁷ *Captain Digby Grand: an Autobiography* (*1853*) by G. J. Whyte-Melville, one of the C. & H. novelists.

you! He is staying for a week with some people in Oatlands Park, named Virtue, who are fond of him. He will reply on his return.—

You have had particulars of our travels; at least, items. Munich is a glorious city to pass through, and the Tyrol a wonderful country for the same. I had, the truth is, a miserable walking companion: to wit, Buonaparte Wyse (son of the Minister at Athens, who will hardly own him), and of Mde Bon[aparte] Wyse (Lucien's daughter), whom he will hardly own. This is a nice position for a son. Mon Dieu!— Well, he is half Prince, half Paddy; with little pluck, a great deal of desultory reading, a wretched stomach, and no control over his nerves. He couldn't walk in the sun: he wouldn't walk after its setting: the rain he shunned as if he had been dog-bitten—in fact, he was a double-knapsack on my back. Certainly, the heat was tremendous. The Tyrolese men are the handsomest I have seen: the women the ugliest. The Alps gave me shudderings of delight; but I didn't see enough of them, and I can't bear being coop'd long in those mountain-guarded valleys; so I shot through them in two weeks, and then saw Italy for the first time, emerging by the Adige, which the Austrians are fortifying continually. Verona lies just under the Alps, and is now less a city than a fortress. You see nothing but white coats—who form 2/3 of the inhabitants. The little man asked innumerable questions about the amphitheatres, and the gladiators, the shows, and the Roman customs. Thence to Venice, where he and I were alone—Wyse parting for Como and his mother. Our life in Venice was charming. Only I had to watch the dear boy like tutor, governess, courier, in one; and couldn't get much to the pictures; for there was no use in victimizing him by dragging him to see them, and I couldn't quit him at all. We hired a gondola and floated through the streets at night, or out to Malamocco[8] to get the fresh breeze. A fresh Levant wind favoured our visit. To the Lido we went every morning: Arthur and I bathing— behold us for a solid hour under enormous straw-hats floating and splashing in the delicious Adriatic. The difficulty of getting him out of it was great. 'Papa, what a dear old place this is! We won't go, will we?' I met and made acquaintance with some nice fellows (Austrians) in the water. The Italian fish are not to be found where they are: Venice looks *draped*, and wears her widow's weeds ostentatiously. Our Gondolier, Lorenzo, declared that he had seen 'Lor Birren', when a boy. 'Palazzo Mocenigo, Signor—Ecco.' On the Lido one thinks sadly of Byron and Shelley. I found the spot Shelley speaks of in 'Julian and Maddalo' where he saw the Vicenza hills in the sunset through the bell tower where the lunatics abide, on an island. Of the glories of St.

---

[8] On the Littorale di Malamocco.

Mark's who shall speak. It is poetry, my dear, and will be expressed in no other way. In Venice I learnt to love Giorgione, Titian, and Paul Veronese. I cannot rank Tintoret with them (Ruskin puts him highest) though his single work shows greater grasp and stretch of soul. Viennese crinoline and the tyrant Whitecoat do their best to destroy the beauties of St. Mark's. Charming are the Venetian women! They have a gracious walk and all the manner one dreams of as befitting them. Should one smile on a Whitecoat, she has the prospect of a patriotic dagger smiting her fair bosom, and so she does not; though the Austrians are fine men, and red-hot exclusiveness for an abstract idea sits not easy on any ladies of any land for longer than—say, a fortnight? Consequently Vienna sends Crinoline to her children. I made acquaintance with a tough Baronne, who had brought two daughters of immense circle! How quietly the pretty Venetians eyed them! The square of St. Mark's is the great parade.—The weather was fiery: but we had no mosquitos.—Milan is, for heat, next door to Pandemonium. The view from the Cathedral you have heard of. I went to Como to see Wyse, who was with Il Principessa. She received me affably at her Villa—Villa Ciani, *près* d'Este. She has a handsome daughter,[9] fair as a highborn English girl, engaged then, and since married to, General Türr. Madame la Princesse will be Mdme la Princesse, and desires that she should hear it too, as I quickly discovered. I grew in favour. She has no difficulty in swallowing a compliment. Quantity is all she asks for. This is *entre nous*, for she entertained me, and indeed I was vastly entertained. Look for it all in a future chapter. A good gross compliment, fluently delivered, I find to be best adapted to a Frenchwoman's taste. If you hesitate, the flavour evaporates for them. Be glib, and you may say what you please. Should you, in addition, be neat, and ready, they will fall in love with you. Mademoiselle, the fiancée, perceived that I was taken with her before I had felt it. Hence she distinguished me, till the General came. It's a real love match. She wouldn't sing then—couldn't. Nor did I press it: for Oh!—She sings in the rapid French style: all from the throat: and such a hard metallic Gordigiani rang over Como's water as sure our dear old muddy Mole never knew of! Young Captain Gyra, Türr's *aide-de-camp*, and I, then fell upon the Princess.

'Mdme la Princesse! but permit me that I tell you that never in my life, never, have I seen a bust—shoulders, so superbe!'

This is Gyra. The Princess smiles on him, and I am dark.

Myself. 'Ah, Mdme la Princesse! were such shoulders, a bust so

---

125. [9] Adeline, who married General Stephane Türr, one of Garibaldi's officers. She was one of the several children of Lady Wyse ('Il Principessa') whose paternity Sir Thomas publicly denied.

perfect, to be seen in England, our sculptors would not have a reputation so wretched!'

The Princess ruffles, and talks of it as pure matter of fact for quiet discussion. Her bust (which is little eclipsed by conventional attire) merely heaves under our admiring eyes. It has stood the battery 50 years and more.

'Mdme la Princesse! but were you, may I ask, always so beautiful, always so exquisite?' (Gyra)

Mdme la Princesse assures us that contemporaries were formerly as flattering as he now.

'If equalled, Mdme la Princesse is not eclipsed by her lovely daughter. England feels the loss of her' (Poet) for she has lived in England, as England knows.

A *carte de visite* is at once accorded to me, unsolicited, as conqueror. The miserable Hungarian subsequently gets one. Then up gets the Princess, tucks up her skirts, and runs to look after the betrothed couple. This last performance is frequent. The Princess tells us, it will not do to leave them together, and we gaze on the floor.

King Victor gave Türr some royal Tokay, which he brought to the villa, and we were merry over it. I like Gyra, a very gallant fellow: only 24, and served through the Hungarian revolt, and all the Garibaldian campaigns.

Before dinner we all bathed in Como, ladies and gentlemen ensemble. Really pleasant and pastoral! Mdlle swims capitally: rides and drives well; and will make a good hero's wife. She scorns the English for their bad manners, she told me. The Emperor allows her £1000 a year: her mother gets £2000. *Vive l'Empereur!* I heard a great deal of scandal of the Empress. Mdme la Princesse detests her. A son, Paul, is in the Navy. Wyse calls him his brother.[10] This fellow has a fine future and will be an admiral before he's thirty, if the Buonapartes last.

Thence over the Mount Cenis to Paris. The little man was in raptures at the thought of crossing the Alp[s]. He would barely close his eyes. I had him in my arms in the coupé of the diligence, and there he was starting up every instant, shouting, and crowing till dawn; when I had no chance of getting him to sleep. When we reached Mâcon at night I put him to bed and gave him a little weak coffee in bed. He slept like a top till morning: when to Paris, which you know. Arthur was impatient to be home; and cared little for Paris. I gave him a dinner at Véfours and at the Trois Frères. He appreciated it: but longed for his England. Paris is delightful! Under the circumstances, with a remonstrating little man, there was nothing for it but to return hastily.

---

[10] Paul was Lady Wyse's illegitimate son.

Thank Heaven! I got him home safe—a little worn: but he soon got over that and has improved his young mind considerably. The journey did me good. I am much stronger and am beginning to be able to work much better, but have to be careful. I have left Emilia Belloni untouched for months; and my novel is where it was. *En revanche*, I am busy on Poems. I think it possible I shall publish a small volume in the winter, after Christmas. I have had letters from strangers, begging me to do so. One man, head-master of a grammar-school,[11] writes a six-page letter of remonstrance and eulogy, concluding 'I have often said I wished to see 3 men before I died: Humboldt, who is gone: Bunsen, whom I had the fortune to meet: and——!' Guess, my dear! He says that the 'Enchantress' scene in *R[ichard] Feverel* made him ill for 24 hours: and that he and his friends (Cambridge men) rank me next to Tennyson in poetic power; and so forth. I tell Janet this, because I know she will like to hear it. I listen to it merely as a sign that I am beginning to be a little known. The man praises my first book of verse, which I would have forgotten. 'Grandfather Bridgeman'[12]—an idyll: true to English life, and containing a war episode, approved by friends who have heard it;—'The Old Chartist', 'The Patriot Engineer', 'Phantasy', 'A Love-Match', and 'Cassandra' (about to be illustrated by Rossetti), are among my later pieces. When these are out I shall set myself seriously to work on a long poem. For if I have the power to do it, why should I not? I am engaged on extra pot-boiling work, which enables me to do this; and besides I can *sell* my poems. What do you think? Speak on this point.—

My housekeeper, good Miss Grange, has just had an offer from Claremont to go and attend the Princess Françoise;[13] and I am afraid she'll go; which will be a complete upset here: for she's an invaluable person: excellent temper, spotless principles, indefatigable worker, no sex: thoughtful, prudent, and sensible. Where shall I get such another? Of course, I can't advise her to stay. It's a terrible bother.—They have been hunting a little; but the Prince de Joinville has not yet returned from America, so not much is done in that way. What do you think of the Comte de Paris' step?[14] I can excuse him better than his adviser. He was courteous and kind to me here (Maxse introduced me) and so

125. [11] Jessopp.

[12] Published in *Modern Love*, etc. (1862), with the other poems mentioned here. Except for 'Grandfather Bridgeman', 'Cassandra', and 'A Love-Match'—presumably a tentative title for 'Modern Love'—all appeared earlier in *OaW*.

[13] Wife of the Prince de Joinville, who, like the Comte de Paris, mentioned below, was a member of the exiled House of Orleans living at Claremont, just outside Esher.

[14] Possibly that he was joining his uncle, the Prince de Joinville, in the Union Army. General McClellan (*McClellan's Own Story*, N.Y., 1887, pp. 144–5) says that the Duc de Chartres and the Comte de Paris, accompanied by Joinville as mentor, served as aides on his staff, with the rank of captain, from 20 Sept. 1861.

I wish him well—and therefore well out of it.—Let me hear what you think of Buckle,[15] who has become a topic.

My dear! the well is not empty, but the bucket kicks. I have some things to do before I speak of them; but I dare say I shall see you before I offer you your wedding present. I hate offering mere jewelry. I have thought of half a dozen things; but your mother's illness and inability to go to London prevented the likeliest.[16] I have sent books etc. to Sir Alec to forward when he can. Be sure my heart is very faithfully with you. You know I approve of the man you have chosen so much that I pardon him his mortal offence.—Talking of that, Alice, who was Prinsep,[17] writes to her father from S[outh] of France, that she 'thinks marriage a fine institution and wonders who invented it'. I heard this repeated before some men, who thought it fast, and clever.

May all good be with you and yours!

Your faithful and loving
George M.

Frederic Chapman is just married.[18]—Your book[19] is being well reviewed. I hope Lewes will do it in the *Saturday* [*Review*].

126. *To* ROBERT ORRIDGE[1]

MS.: Yale.

[Copsham Cottage, Esher]
Wednesday, [? *ante* November 25, 1861]

My dear Orridge,

Be plucky and bring your wife . . . to meet Hardman and Izod—no more. Perhaps, as it's tempting fine to-day, Mrs. Hardman *may* come. I know *she* wouldn't mind sitting at this table with three mild men. I don't say more. Dinner 6 1/2 past p.m.

Your faithful
George Meredith

When ladies are here, there's no 'retiring'. Where she goes all follow. What we do she does. Sex is confounded.

---

[15] Henry Thomas Buckle (1821–62), author of *The History of Civilization in England*. Janet Ross (*The Fourth Generation*, p. 119) says that GM mentions him because she had written that Buckle had arrived in Alexandria with two little boys as travelling companions.
[16] i.e. an enlarged photograph of Lady Duff Gordon.
[17] If my conjecture that Alice was the daughter of H. Thoby Prinsep is correct, she had married Charles Gurney.
[18] Frederic Chapman married Clara Woodin on 21 Nov.
[19] i.e. *EH*, in which the heroine is Janet fictionalized.
126. [1] See Note 1, Letter 110.

127. *To* WILLIAM HARDMAN

MS. (written on black-bordered paper): Garrick Club. Published: *Letters*, i. 56, with minor variants.

Esher

Monday, [November 25, 1861][1]

My dear Hardman,

Stop! What do you mean by smoking 1/2 a dozen cigars of the Holy man in solitary enjoyment? Give unto thy brother a chance of conversion, even upon Friday evening next. And will you have my glove in Gordon Street?[2] 'Twill save me 2/- which is to a poet no mean sum. I suppose Mrs. Hardman has gone.[3] I hope she will not have trouble. When she returns, may Copsham hail you both! We have all weathers here. I am at my Pomes.

Your faithful

George Meredith

Don't the telegrams read as if the Northerners had got another licking?[4]

128. *To* AUGUSTUS JESSOPP

MS.: Yale. Published: *Letters*, i. 57–58, with omission of last two sentences and with minor variants.

Copsham Cottage, Esher

Wednesday, November 27, [1861]

My dear Sir,

I know Souvestre tolerably well, and have not hitherto cared much about him. Some of his Breton sketches I have found repulsive. But I thank you for your edition,[1] which has been forwarded to me in your name, and I will read the story you indicate.

As I said, my cottage here, is of the very humblest kind; so much so that I hesitate to ask ladies to come to it, though there are some who do me that honour. You will find me about as plain a man as you could meet. I do not know many literary men myself: those I do know are

127. [1] The bracketed date is Hardman's, as hereinafter are all bracketed dates in letters to Hardman unless otherwise specified.

[2] Hardman lived at 27 Gordon St., Bloomsbury.

[3] Mrs. Hardman left on 25 Nov. for Liverpool, where her father was ill.

[4] Curiously, GM, whose political liberalism gradually deepened into radicalism, sympathized with the South in the Civil War, as did his Conservative friend Hardman as a matter of course.

128. [1] E. Souvestre, *Contes* . . . Edited with Notes by Augustus Jessopp (1860).

among the best; they are not guilty of over-bearing brilliancy at all:—unless, haply, one should be conscious of a sucking Boswell at his elbow, which is a rare case, and is possibly seductive. The general feeling is, that it is best to let 'good things' come as they may, and thus the best point of breeding is attained: all have a chance, and one man does not draw a reputation at the expense of the others. Believe me, I have as great a respect for a good scholar, as you can have for a man who writes books. If you will let me know when I may have the pleasure of receiving you here, I will take care to have a bed disengaged, and will meet you at the station. Let me mention that Thursdays and Fridays are days when I am commonly in town.

Believe me, / My dear Sir, / Your very faithful

George Meredith

129. *To* W. C. Bonaparte Wyse

MS.: State University of New York at Buffalo. Excerpt published: Ellis, p. 160.

Copsham Cottage, Esher
December 1, 1861

My dear Wyse,

I received your last letter: but between that and the short note you sent from Como, on your return from Caprera, no word from you has reached me.—Now, this would not have caused my silence; but seeing that I had mentioned my circumstances to you, it seemed to me that another letter would possibly be misconstrued: and that you would think I was urgent about this trifle. I hope you understand this clearly. On matters where money is concerned (large sums or small) I never take offence. I can be offended only by other matters.—I should certainly fear that your letter has been lost. It would be as well to enquire about it instantly. Was it registered?—My wife is dead.—All is much the same here. Arthur flourishes.[1] We have the winter on us. I wish I had you here to read to you some of the Poems I have lately written. Fellows say that they are my best. I think it likely that in a couple of months I shall publish a volume.—I fancy, judging from what I hear, that they would sell. This, if there's no war with the Yankees, which at this moment looks too probable. You will see the cause for it in the Italian papers.[2] Maxse, though expecting to be married in a month, has resolved to ask for a ship;—so anxious is he to teach them manners,

---

129. [1] This and the two preceding sentences were extracted from this letter and printed separately by Ellis (p. 87).   [2] i.e. the Mason and Slidell incident.

if the chance offers. This feeling is universal, and one may be proud of seeing it:—so calm! so fixed! No shrieks of passion! Such steady facing of every difficulty, and serene strength! If I were abroad it would bring tears of love to my eyes.—Write and tell me what you are doing; what are your immediate prospects. I was terribly hurt at that letter from Athens to *Galignani*,[3] and only wish it had been a case where it would have been possible to take up arms for so innocent and sweet a person.

If Elaine is with you, give her my very kind regards and Arthur's. Believe me ever

Faithfully yours,
George Meredith

130. *To* FREDERICK A. MAXSE

Text: *Letters*, i. 56–57, with omissions. I have supplied the omissions from a typed copy inserted in W. M. Meredith's own copy of *Letters* in the Bodleian Library.

Copsham, Esher
[December 1861]

My dear Maxse,

You knew how glad it would make me to hear the good news,[1] and I thank you for making me feel that she does not take you away from those who love you. I don't think there will be a war. I don't even think that the withdrawal of our Ambassador would give the signal for one.[2] In any case there can be no reason why you should go. Dismiss the notion. A war with France would tax all the energies of this country. All would have to serve. With America we can fight quite comfortably—Why, those Yankees took a slap on the face from Spain![3] They are beastly bullies, and I shall be astonished if, the moment they find us in earnest, they don't growl and give in. So be married

---

129 [3] This is almost certainly a letter from Sir Thomas Wyse, in Athens, to Galignani's *Messenger*, denying paternity of Adeline Bonaparte Wyse, who was called a daughter of Sir Thomas in announcements of her marriage to General Türr.

130. [1] Probably that all the difficulties in the way of Maxse's marriage to Cecilia Steel had been smoothed away. Maxse's father was opposed to the match, but his mother supported him.

  [2] There was naturally an outburst of public indignation when news reached England on 27 Nov. that the Confederate Commissioners Mason and Slidell had been forcibly removed from an English vessel by a Federal gunboat on 8 Nov. There was talk of withdrawing the English Ambassador and of war if the prisoners were not yielded up. But GM was right: on 27 Dec. news arrived that the prisoners would be given up.

  [3] Presumably a reference to the landing of Spanish troops at Vera Cruz on 17 Dec., following conclusion of a Convention on 31 Oct. between Britain, France, and Spain, alleging Mexican mistreatment of their nationals.

quickly to that dear and sweet person who is to make you happy, I doubt not. I look at her and should envy you, if I did not feel for her through your heart.—I mean the photograph, which I prize.—De Stendhal I have had to send to Paris for. You will have *L'Amour*[4] in a week. I told them (Hachette) to send it to you, from me. Write as often as you can spare time. Give her my kindest salute and know me, your loving

George M.

I have done a great deal of the 'Love-Match'.[5] Rossetti says it's my best. I contrast it mentally with yours, which is so very much better!

131. *To* FREDERICK A. MAXSE

Text: typed copy, Maxse papers, Published: *Letters*, i. 57, with omission of a sentence.

193 Piccadilly, London, W.
Friday, [? December 13], 1861

My dear Maxse,

I will come.[1] So shall the little man. I hate wedding-breakfasts, which make one take wine and eat I don't know what at unholy seasons of the day, and are such a stupid exhibition of the couple.

Tell me when you think it may take place, that I may keep all clear for that day. I'm sure you're going to be happy, and I'm like Keats and the nightingale—'happy in your happiness'.—I wonder, now, whether any nice woman will ever look on me?—I certainly begin to feel new life. Also a power of work, which means money. There is evidently great folly kindling in me. All the effect of example!

I have matters in hand, which you will like, I think. They won't drag you down to the Roadside and the haunts of vagabonds!

How do you like de Stendhal? *L'Amour* ought not to be dissected, and indeed can't be. For when we've killed it with this object, the spirit flies, and then where is L'Amour? Still I think de Stendhal very subtle and observant. He goes over ground that I know. Let me hear. —I bow to your lovely bride. The photograph is not just to her.[2] Is she becoming appreciated in her new circle?

All blessings on you both!

Your loving
George M.

---

[4] Stendhal's *De l'amour* was first published in 1822, but there were editions of 1853 and 1857.   [5] i.e. 'Modern Love'.

131. [1] To Maxse's wedding. The date was set for 2 Jan. but had to be postponed twice because of a cold contracted first by the bride and then the groom.

[2] See preceding letter.

132. *To* WILLIAM HARDMAN

MS.: Garrick Club. Published: *Letters*, i. 58–59, with minor variants.

Copsham
Tuesday, [December 17, 1861]

My dear Hardman,

Rossetti talks of a meeting of good fellows on Thursday evening. Therefore, don't take stalls anywhere, or make engagements, till you're cock sure you would rather not go to the artists.[1]

It struck me last night that Schubert must have meant that words should be affixed to the introduction to the Addio.[2] A moment's reflection supplies them. E.g.

> (tūm tūm tūm tūm de dum-measure)
> 'Yōu wĭll bē spōonў, Sir!
> Yes, You'll be spoony, Sir!
> You must be spoony, Sir!
> Big tho' you be!

Don't you see it? With this warning, you and I and many a poor devil might have been on our guard. Perhaps saved! Which to contemplate is most wondrous. At any rate, I think our sex ought to demand to have it sung as a piece of preliminary fair-play.

Your faithful
George Meredith

133. *To* FREDERICK A. MAXSE

Text: typed copy, Maxse Papers.

Esher, Surrey
Monday, [? December 23, 1861]

My dear Maxse,

Hail! I want to know the hour when I am to see you in the Church.

---

132. [1] Mrs. Hardman was still away, and Hardman had been spending his week-ends at Copsham with GM (S. M. Ellis, *A Mid-Victorian Pepys*, 1923, p. 73). Hardman liked the kind of men he met there—literary men and publishers—and GM promised to take him to call on Rossetti. He did so, and Hardman said of Rossetti, 'He is a very jolly fellow, and we had a most amusing visit' (*MVP*, p. 77). No one else was present, but Hardman wrote to Holroyd that he was going to Rossetti's again on Friday [20 Dec.] 'to a social reunion of artists and literary men'. Later he wrote a three-page account of the party (*MVP*, pp. 78–80).

[2] i.e. 'Adieu'. Grove's *Dictionary of Music and Musicians* pronounces the work spurious, made up of phrases put together from Schubert's songs by A. H. von Weyrauch, who published it himself four years before Schubert's death.

If the weather is intensely inclement, I shall hardly be able to bring my little man. I hope she is well?

Send me one or two bundles of 'Last Words'.

I write to-day, not knowing the news from America. I still think peace will be kept. I hope so, if only for your sake.

Don't go to the St. James's by any chance! Unfortunate Kate[1] is *in tights.* Mon Dieu! a tape fitted round her forehead!—

I am writing, of course. But the poem's morbid, and all about Love. So I despise my work, and sneer secretly at those that flatter me about it.

Do you think Borthwick[2] would take one or two articles a week from me? Shall I call on him? I want to make some money.

Your loving
George M.

NOTE: I mean the hour when the ceremony is to take place. *Transmit* or [*sic*] immediately.

134. *To* WILLIAM HARDMAN

MS.: Garrick Club.

Copsham
Tuesday, [December 31, 1861]

My dear Hardman,

Fancy the wretched lover![1] His darling has a cold, and defers Bliss from the 2nd to the 6th, and that date not positive. Well, in consequence, I shall not bring the little man to town on Thursday, unless Demitroïa[2] shall have made very peculiar arrangements. But I am at her bidding. Only she is not to insist, saving in the case of arrangements being already made. I wish to see her and would call on Thursday, but I think I'll let her rest a week. Mind, if she has not come to you by Saturday next, you come to me, or I suspect the worst. Do come, for it's such a pleasure to me.

With my bow to her possible presence,

I am your faithful
George M.

A jolly new Year! and may we
Three spend much of it together!

133. [1] Kate Terry.   [2] Algernon Borthwick, editor of the *Morning Post.*
134. [1] Maxse.
  [2] A coinage of GM's, referring to Hardman's five-year courtship of Mary Anne— half the length of the siege of Troy; hence Demi-Troïa, Demitroïa, D. Troïa, or D.T., as he variously wrote it. As the context shows, he was uncertain whether she had returned from Liverpool or not.

135. *To* FREDERICK A. MAXSE

Text: typed copy, Maxse Papers. Published, with omissions: *Letters*, i. 41.

Esher
Thursday morning, [? December 1861–
January 1862]
My dear Maxse,

I shall most probably have Wyse with me on Saturday. May I bring him?—We will come, or not. Leave to me the divine uncertainty, and you will make the more sure of me.

As to the temptation, it was Eve's own doing, born of champagne and the promptings of her blood. It's a curious fact I have observed personally more than once, that when Eve begins with the R.N., she turns to Literature, and vice versa. But since you ally the two, who is to resist you? She is a well-meaning girl. Be kind to her. Do not grow ironical. Forbear from satire at tender intervals. Make her believe (she will so readily!) that she is never ridiculous, or that you never see it, which is a subtler flattery; for woman is cute, and would rather that you should have the bandage on your eyes than that she should. You will then more nearly resemble the son of Fortune that you are, Fortune beloved by Venus! My sincerest congratulations! But don't neglect Ben.[1] Prosper, and be the envy of your faithful

George Meredith

136. *To* W. C. BONAPARTE WYSE

Text (? fragment): Ellis, p. 91. (See Note 1, below.)

[Copsham Cottage, Esher]
[? January 1862][1]
I'm glad you take to *Shagpat*, and I still think the poems[2] rubbish.—As to the question of misogyny,[3] why can't you see that I'm on no side but the laughing side? Your view is the heroic, if not the right one, for it's against the world's experience, and smacks entirely of chivalrous youth. . . . Women, my dear fellow, can occasionally be fine creatures,

135. [1] A red retriever, later presented to GM.
136 [1] Among the Meredith papers is a clipping from an unidentified publication in which this and another Meredith letter were published and from which the initial sentence of this letter is taken. The sender said of this letter that it was written from Esher in 1862. Maxse's wedding and the echo of 'Modern Love' suggest Jan. 1862 as a reasonable date.
[2] No doubt *Poems* (1851).
[3] In the clipping this word is *misogamy*.

if they fall into good hands. Physically they neighbour the vegetable,[4] and morally the animal creation; and they are, therefore, chemically good for man, and to be away from them is bad for that strange being, who, because they serve his uses, calls them angels.

I respect many. I dislike none. I trust not to love one. For what if you do? Was there ever such a gambler's stake as that we fling for a woman in giving ourselves for her whom we know not, and haply shall not know when twenty years have run?[5] I do blame Nature for masking the bargain to us. The darlings ought all to be ticketed. Nevertheless, I envy your state of mind with regard to them immensely. I have seen infants fed with pap-spoons. They took all in faith, and they were nourished. If I thought myself superior, I who looked at them loftily, and drank more than was good for me that night, was I not an ass?

137. *To* EDWARD WALFORD

MS.: Yale. Printed: *Altschul Catalogue*, pp. 23–24.

Copsham
Sunday, January 5, 1862

Dear Walford,

All kind greetings to you in return!

I told Lucas he should not have 'Gr[andfather] Bridgeman',[1] which I read to him and really thought he did not cotton to, so made other arrangements.

As to the Jacobite young woman, I can't do the 'For Charlie!' business.[2] But I should like to see the sketch of Millais' and would then tell you.

Faithfully yours,
George Meredith

---

[4] Adrian, the Wise Youth of *Richard Feverel*, asked Sir Austin (in a letter): 'Has it never struck you that Woman is nearer the *vegetable* than Man?' (First edn. ii. 115; Modern Library ed n., p. 234).

[5] 'Great God! the maddest gambler throws his heart' (*Modern Love*, xix).

137. [1] First published in *Modern Love*, etc.

[2] The 22 Feb. 1862 issue of *OaW* included a drawing by Millais entitled *The Fair Jacobite*. No text accompanied it.

138. *To* SAMUEL LUCAS

MS.: Yale. Excerpt printed: *Altschul Catalogue*, p. 85.

Esher
Monday, [? January 1862]
My dear Lucas,

We will decide not to trouble Rossetti about 'Cassandra',[1] and then it will be decidedly better to withdraw it from *Once a Week*, for which I've always thought it unsuitable. I'm sorry to hear of your being laid prostrate. Evans postponed the meeting, so I thought it needless to write. Let me hear soon that you are better.

Your faithful
George Meredith

139. *To* FREDERICK A. MAXSE

MS.: Maxse Papers.

Copsham, Esher
January 5, 1862
My dear Maxse,

On Wednesday, then: at a quarter past 11 a.m.![1]—and God bless you! I have no doubt that she will do her part towards it.—Arthur's coming will depend on the weather. He wishes to be present. I need not rig him out specially, I suppose?

Let me hear where you are after a week. I want to send you proofs of 'A Tragedy of Modern Love', for inspection. You read the first few lines when you were here. The poem goes into the volume to be dedicated to you, and which I am now preparing to publish.

The Christmas number[2] you allude to is sufficiently despicable: but I fancy the writers know their level.

I met Browning the other day, and like him. He has plenty of animal fire.—Wouldn't you like Rossetti to do [a] sketch of your beloved? It may be managed some day, I hope: for it seems to me that he alone could render the poetry of that sweet face.

If you go to Hampshire, or anywhere in our island, for the Honeymoon, send me word, for I have a small wedding-gift for her, the which beg her to accept.

Your loving
George Meredith

138. [1] First published in *Modern Love*, etc.
139. [1] A reference to Maxse's wedding, which had to be postponed after all till 22 Jan.
     [2] Of *OaW*.

140. *To* WILLIAM HARDMAN

MS.: Garrick Club. Published: *Letters*, i. 60–61, with omissions and numerous inaccuracies.

Copsham
Wednesday, [January 8, 1862]

My dear Hardman,

Again cruel Fate has deferred the junction of our loving couple. He has caught her cold: 'from sympathy', he says. They communicate their tender impressions in sneezes. Morris, you may remember, sings of 'Two red Roses across the Moon'.[1] But Maxse seems to think that Two Red Noses across the Honeymoon, would spoil the lustre of the orb. He may be right. On purely material grounds, and apart from sentiment, I should say that where a sneeze is to be apprehended, it's better to hold back. Picture it to yourself! The Muse warleth[2] at the ugly contemplation thereof. 'Tis the very [illegible word][3] of Cupid!

I presume that you come on Saturday. I had arranged for the Virtues to lunch here, and for us to walk back with them and dine: [? but they are][4] engaged this Saturday. It may be managed a fortnight subsequently. For on Saturday week Maxse's to be married! At least, if we can defeat the malignity of the East wind. Full South-west it blows now, with a glorious coloured sky, very enjoyable after a ducking. Last night there was pure poetry in air. I bow to Demitroïa, and am,

[Signature cut away]

[marginal postscripts:] Sons[5] have been over to Oatlands. His love is sent to Nelly:[6] but just at present I think she must consent to share it with Miss V[irtue], who is in the ascendant. The poor boy was cut up about the Pantomime business.

I haven't been to the Post this morning. There may be news from you. In that case, you'll see that this is no reply.

My Jessopp comes next week. He has asked me whether I taboo tobacco? 'Fore Gad! This is of noble augury! What say you?—

140. [1] A ballad of the name by William Morris.
[2] *Warl* = to wail, whine, complain without shedding tears (*English Dialect Dictionary*).
[3] It is certainly not *butchering*, as transcribed in *Letters*.
[4] Words cut away.
[5] This is the first appearance of GM's curious plural designation of his son Arthur, who had been visiting the Virtues.
[6] Hardman's daughter, Helen.

141. *To* FREDERICK A. MAXSE

MS.: Maxse Papers. Envelope postmarked *Ja 8 62.*

Copsham

Wednesday, [January 8, 1862]

My dear Maxse,

I share your feelings. It's an awful bother.[1] But, you see, I'm right about the Yankees.[2] So you'll have a long Honeymoon.

The wind is South-west. Now, if you can leave your bed, and quit the sight of your beloved, for a day, change of air would just bring you round, and do you all the good in life. Or, if you're still on your back, shall I come and read to you?

I will call on Borthwick this week or next. Thanks, for writing to him.

Would you like to see proofs?[3]

Since your name is to decorate the book, I think you are bound to.

Your faithful

George Meredith

142. *To* FREDERICK A. MAXSE

Text: *Letters,* i. 60.

London

January [? 17], 1862

My dear Maxse,

I send you a portion of proofs of the 'Tragedy of Modern Love' There are wanting to complete it, 13 more sonnets.

Please read, and let me have the honest judgment. When done with, return. This poem will come in the middle of the book.

I called on Borthwick to-day, but could not see him. I shall call again to-day, if possible. If not, next week.

I say, you'll review my Poems in the *M[orning] Post?* You may flog me, too, if the prompting comes to do it.

I suppose the book will be out in six weeks.—Who was right about the Yankees?

141. [1] i.e. postponement of the wedding.

[2] News had just reached England that the Federal Government had informed Lord Lyons in Washington that Mason and Slidell would be released when and where he pleased. They were released on 1 Jan.

[3] Of *Modern Love,* etc.

How are you, my dear fellow? I feel rather anxious to know, and but that I'm in such a mess and might stumble across some of your people, I would call.

By the way, tell me, do army men—ensigns, fight in undress uniform? Did any at Inkermann? Or is the full dress *de rigueur?*—[1]

Your faithful
George Meredith

143. *To* FREDERICK A. MAXSE

MS.: Maxse Papers.

Copsham, Esher
Sunday, [January 19, 1862]

My dear Maxse,

I commence writing for *Morn[ing] Post* to-day, with an article on Roebuck's Salisbury speech.

'My children most they seem, when they least know me',[1] says Nature. That is, while you lovers are acting Nature you are ignorant of her; and she has to cure you of your idealistic mists, by running the sharp thorn of Reality into your quivering flesh. Romance is neither in nor out of nature. It is young blood heated by Love or the desire for Love. It's true while it lasts—no longer.—

I'm glad exceedingly to hear you're better; and very much wish the ceremony to be over, for your sake.

Thanks for the Guardsman's dictum.[2] What other people but Britons would fight in full dress?

I told Hachette to send the Dante, thinking there was hurry—for Saturday. I must subsequently get it bound etc.

I like Borthwick very much. He gave me wonderful stories of Kate's doings. Her battles with the Herbert[3] have been gallant. She has beaten that woman! I receive reproachful letters for not calling; but

---

142. [1] This inquiry no doubt relates to 'Grandfather Bridgeman', a poem about the Battle of Inkermann.

143. [1]
'But nature says: "My children most they seem
When they least know me: therefore I decree
That they shall suffer." '<br>'Modern Love', xxx.

[2] i.e. a reply to GM's question in the preceding letter about British battle dress.

[3] Louisa Herbert, the leading lady of Wigan's company. *Who's Who in the Theatre* (1922) gives 24 Mar. 1862 as the date when Kate Terry was suddenly called upon to substitute for her in *Friends or Foes* and enjoyed a smashing success. Tom Taylor, who was a friend of hers, praised her performance in *The Times*, and her reputation was established. Perhaps the victories she scored over Miss Herbert before 24 Mar. were dressing-room triumphs.

have really no time. And then—why? She is going in for the ninon business: which is ambitious, but only practicable where peculiar accomplishments exist. I like the ambition so much that I would not for the world breathe to her a doubt of her success. Only I never make one in a tail.

I bow to your beloved, and am

Your loving
George M.

144. *To* AUGUSTUS JESSOPP

MS.: Yale. Published: *Letters*, i. 59 (dated *Dec. 20, 1861*).

Copsham Cottage, Esher
Monday, December 20, 1862
[error for January 20, 1862]

My dear Sir,

How happy you that have a Pallas! I will not envy you. I will hope that she also will visit me in the flesh. She is not supposed to visit poets in the spirit.

Apropos of her poetical counsel, is she adapting her wisdom to the mind of the British matron, and of the snuffling moralist so powerful among us? Does she know that my literary reputation is tabooed as worse than libertine in certain virtuous Societies? . . . that there have been meetings to banish me from book-clubs? And that Pater familias has given Mr. Mudie a very large bit of his petticoated mind concerning me?—These are matters to be thought over. In the way of Art I never stop to consider what is admissible to the narrow minds of the drawing-room. But is it well to call up what is marked for oblivion? Isn't it a sort of challenge; and an unnecessary one?

I think I will not publish in *Macmillan*[*'s Magazine*], seeing that my volume is shortly to appear. I have had a suggestion to that effect, once or twice, from a brother-in-law of Macmillan's.[1]

I can only regret that the weather was so bad when you were with me, and trust it will be brighter when you next do me the favour to come.

Your faithful
George Meredith

144. [1] Doubtless Robert Orridge, whose sister Frances married Daniel Macmillan.

145. *To* SAMUEL LUCAS

MS.: Yale. Excerpts published: S. M. Ellis, *William Harrison Ainsworth and his Friends* (1911), ii. 238; Stevenson, p. 101.

Copsham, Esher
[*post* January 25, 1862]

My dear Lucas,
    Walford has all the particulars about me that your friend can require: but I should prefer to be 'dropped'.[1]
    I have told Rossetti to give up 'Cassandra'.
    I have read *East Lynne*,[2] and also your notice of it. I have read the latter with almost less pleasure than the novel. It is (the novel) in the worst style of the present taste. What a miserable colourless villain, Levison! The husband a respectable stick: the heroine a blotched fool: all the incidents forced—that is, not growing out of the characters: and the turning-point laughable in its improbability. Why do you foster this foul taste? There's action in the tale, and that's all. This manufacture is supplied by the *London Journal*. I don't deride it by any means.

Faithfully yours,
George Meredith

146. *To* WILLIAM HARDMAN

MS.: Garrick Club.

Copsham, Esher
Tuesday, [January 28, 1862]

My dear Hardman,
    I have been anxious to hear of your condition, since I saw you last.[1]
—I presume, and hope, I shall see you here on Saturday next. Last

145. [1] A reference to *Men of the Time* (a biographical dictionary), of which Walford was editor.
    [2] Much has been made of GM's refusal of *East Lynne* when it was submitted to C. & H. by William Harrison Ainsworth, who was running it serially in his *New Monthly Magazine*. It was turned over to GM, in his capacity of reader for the firm, and his judgement, recorded in the manuscript book, was, 'Opinion emphatically against it'. Ainsworth requested a second opinion, and Chapman is said to have asked GM to reconsider his judgement and to have got a refusal. The MS. was also refused by Smith, Elder & Co. before it was accepted by Bentley, who realized large profits from it. Chapman's daughter, however, later quoted her father as saying that the final decision to decline the novel had been his, that 'he considered the tone of the book was not good for the general public'. (The story is told in greater detail by Waugh, pp. 145–6, upon whom I have drawn for most of this information.)
    Lucas had reviewed the novel favourably in *The Times* for 25 Jan.
146. [1] Hardman had been suffering 'most acutely' from tooth-ache (*MVP*, pp. 91–92).

Sunday and Monday were glorious days. Let's trust the South-west will puff just another week, and we will soon bring you round and give bloom to Demitroïa, to whom all joy and greeting! Write to Chapman & Hall's, for I may have to come to town to-morrow.

Your faithful
George Meredith

147. *To* MRS. JANET ROSS

MS.: Yale. Published: *Letters*, i. 61–62, with omissions and inaccuracies; *The Fourth Generation*, pp. 120–2, with omissions.

Copsham Cottage, Esher
February 15, 1862

My dear Janet,

You come in April. You are even now packing and preparing, and your heart is bounding for England. So I will hope the best of you, my dear child, though your letters have saddened me and I see that your physical condition is lowered. I never liked the climate for you, though I perfectly approved of the husband. After all, it's merely a probation, not a settlement. There has been little hunting here this winter, owing to the absence of the Princes.[1] The weather is good for it; the frosts are short, and the ground soft and wet, and not too much so. —Haven't you heard from the P[erfect] G[entleman][2] yet? He said he would write, and abused his P. G. reputation, but I always have suspected him to have something of a woman's nature: *id est*; he must see a body to be with a body. Now, you can't say that of me! What do you think (as a proof the other way)? I was walking out with Hardman (the man being absent from his wife), and I commenced 'la-la—la-la—' and so on, ending 'la-la-lā-tē-to-te!' in my fine voice, when he cried 'Halloa!' and I meekly responded. 'That's my spooney song.' 'And it's mine!' quoth he. 'The song that always made me sentimental', said I. 'The song that bowled me over', said he. I told him, with a yawn (noble manhood's mask for a sigh) that I had written words to it. He and his wife petition for them. So, please, to spare me from having to write fresh ones, send me, if you have them, a copy of my lines to Schubert's Adieu.[3] If you have *any* objection, don't do it.

Maxse is not the man you saw with me in Esher. That was Fitz-Gerald.[4] Maxse is quite a different fellow. He performed the cele-

---

147. [1] Of the House of Orleans.   [2] Hawkins. See Note 3, Letter 77.
  [3] The verses are printed in *Letters*, i. 12–13. But see Note 2, Letter 132.
  [4] Maurice FitzGerald.

brated ride in the Crimea, as Lord Lyons' aide-de-camp. Arthur and
I attended his wedding, when the little man was much petted. The bride
was almost beautiful—very sweet and charming. Lady Maxse and the
daughters are pleasant people in their way, with aristocratic vices well
under control. The wedding was at St. Paul's, Knightsbridge,[5] and
there was a wedding-choir, and all that sort of thing. I went with
Borthwick, of the *Morning Post*, a very nice fellow indeed, whom
I will ask to meet you when we have you here. Maxse rests now for
a month in England. Then goes to Italy for six months, and finally,
I hope, settles near Weybridge, as he can't be happy unless he's on
water. By the way I write for the *Morning Post* now, at odd hours,
which pays your poet. And I've a volume of Poems coming out in
three weeks; but I won't send the volume. You shall have it when you
come. Jessopp, the man I spoke of as liking my works, has been here—
did I tell you? He begged to be allowed to educate Arthur at his own
expense, and under his own supervision. The kindness was great, but
I could not let him be at the charge while I have power to work, you
know. I like him very much and so would you. Can I meet you in
Paris? Nothing would please me better: But I fear I can't leave my
pen. Borthwick promises me introductions there. It would be pleasant.
I will see. There's yet time. I will write again shortly. Pray give my
salute to Miss Power[6] and your husband and hold me ever

Your faithful
George M.

148. *To* WILLIAM HARDMAN

MS.: Garrick Club.

Esher
Tuesday, [March 4, 1862]

Private

My dear Hardman,

On reading what you tell me of Demitroïa's suggestion concerning
Sandars[1] having lost his way, I went out to see whether he had really
moved (for, you know, he could hardly lose his way without doing so).

---

[5] Maxse and Cecilia Steel were married at St. Paul's Church, Wilton Place, Knightsbridge, on 22 Jan. Maxse is described in the register as a bachelor residing at 21 Eaton
Terrace and Cecilia Steel as a minor living at Cleveland Square, Hyde Park. Witnesses
were Lady Caroline Maxse, William McGeorge, and Robert Liddell.

[6] Marguerite Power, niece of Lady Blessington, had been spending the winter with
Janet and her husband.

148. [1] I find no Sandars listed in the *P.O.D.* as living at Esher.

But no; I found him fixed. It must have been somebody else you saw in the road.

Thanks for the suggestion about Emilia; wherein I see point.

I will come on Thursday, gladly.

Aux Câpres!²

In haste,

Your ever faithful
George M.

There is a proposition for foot-ball, this afternoon. I keep such religious observances, Mr. Hardman, though you may be above them in Gordon St. Hence my hurry.

149. *To* WILLIAM HARDMAN

MS.: Garrick Club. Published: *Letters*, i. 62–63, with omissions and inaccuracies.

Copsham
Sunday, [March 16, 1862]

My dear Hardman,

You are well out of this weather. Myself am in appearance much like the atmosphere: in sentiment I am due East. King Æolus holds his court within me. I feel as one who has run a gallant race half way to perdition, and thinks of returning as far as he can before the final trump shall sound to him.

Last night came off the raffle. I record it. Sons got the number 35. Yourself and Demitroïa respectively, 36 and 38. Walford 18. Morison¹ and spouse about 30, I think. I had two throws—1st 39, 2nd 41. The Granges 39. The Claremont people² 38. So GM is the winner of what he doesn't want at all.³ So it happens! If Demitroïa won't have the thing, it shall go to Miss Grange.

Please look for the story of 'Praxaspes'⁴ in Herodotus, and sketch

148. ² Presumably an anticipation of dinner.

149. ¹ James Cotter Morison (1832–88), son of the purveyor of Morison's Pills, wrote for the *Saturday Review* and other periodicals and in 1863 published a life of St. Bernard. He had married Frances Virtue, daughter of George Virtue of Oatlands Park in 1861.

² The Orleans princes.   ³ Some castors.

⁴ The mad King Cambyses of Persia dreamed that his brother Smerdis was seated on the throne and had him assassinated by Prexaspes, a trusted confidant. Even after Cambyses shot Prexaspes' son through the heart with an arrow, Prexaspes continued to serve him faithfully. In the absence of Cambyses two Magi took advantage of the fact that the death of Smerdis was not publicly known, and one of them—who was named Smerdis and bore a resemblance to the dead Smerdis—assumed the throne. In mounting his horse to ride to the attack, Cambyses was fatally impaled upon his own sword. The false Smerdis, with the connivance of Prexaspes, now seemed secure on the throne. Ironically, he turned

it in six lines, when next you go to the Museum. May I trouble you so far?

I hope to hear good news of Demitroïa. If not, you can no longer, as a man, decline to open a vein and supply her from your abundance. I confess I am astonished that you have not volunteered to do so. Why, you've blood enough for both of us!

Your faithful
George M.

150. *To* Mrs. William Hardman

MS.: Yale. Excerpts published: Ellis, p. 191.

Copsham
Wednesday, [March 19, 1862]

Dear Mrs. Hardman,

I have given the Castors to Miss Grange, since you reject them. How could I keep them? I should soon be ruined in trying to match myself with such fine things; and for 10/- I can get them quite as serviceable, when I'm a b[ritish]-h[ouseholder].—Thank the illustrious student for the trouble he took to get me the story of Praxaspes.

I wish to come on Thursday—but don't expect me.—We are all in confusion here; for the rat who troubled us in life, is vindictive in death, and there is a successive emigration from all the rooms of the house. We march out formally, and back again. I think that never did the classic maid[1] desire to give her brother's corpse rights of burial so much as I that rat!

You don't say that you are better—why is that?—*Can* you suppose I have given up our plan *à nous trois*? But a house founded on castors must fall. I prefer to make books my basis, and notably prose. When I write a verse, I say, 'So many lines—so many leagues from your cottage, my lad'.

Hoping I *may* see you on Thursday: and that a good genius will force me to be happy that day, I am

Your ever faithful
George Meredith

To the ruddy man, the future Cook's oracle, the sapient Rotundity,[2] kind greeting.

out to be a good and generous ruler; but powerful nobles aware of his deception conspired against him. In a counter-move, Smerdis assembled the people to hear from the lips of Prexaspes the statement that the true Smerdis was indeed alive. Prexaspes climbed a tower to address the people but unexpectedly told the whole story and then threw himself headlong from the tower.

GM's request was apropos of an allusion to Prexaspes in one of Jessopp's letters.
150. [1] Antigone.   [2] i.e. Hardman.

151. *To* WILLIAM HARDMAN

MS.: Garrick Club. Published: *Letters*, i. 64, with omissions and inaccuracies.

[Copsham Cottage, Esher]
[March 24, 1862]

——Anorribo!——

I take up and conclude the awful word.

Dear friend! Ifeel for you in your profound affliction.

Has she returned?[1]

Pardon my asking.

You break out beautifully into dishes and show a lovely and most becoming bravado, but, alas!—Taunton! Taunton! Such a fillet of British Householder, larded, as you present to me in imagination! It's the saddest thing I ever—

Demitroïa, too!

'And every dog shall have his day.'

Old Song

————

————

Morison didn't come. He was right. But oh, what a day this day! And how I wish you were here to wander about. The smell of the earth is Elysium. I'm really not tauntin' you.—On Wednesday I will come to your desolate household, if the S[outh] W[est] doesn't blow.— With what different feelings!

Your ever faithful
George Meredith

Bill for fly to Oatlands 5/- just come in. I promised to tell you, and I'm a man of my word.

152. *To* AUGUSTUS JESSOPP

MS.: Yale. Published: *Letters*, i. 63–64, with omission of the postscript and with minor variants.

Esher
Monday, March 24, [1862]

My dear Mr. Jessopp,

My boy thanks you heartily for the book of verse. He delays to write himself, he says, until he has read it through, and can speak

151. [1] The Hardmans' house was undergoing alterations, and Mrs. Hardman was staying with friends in West Drayton to escape the smell of paint. Though Hardman wrote a part of his monthly letter to Holroyd on 23 Mar., his letter throws no light on the obscurity of this letter. The reference to Taunton, which is continued in following letters, is baffling.

sagely on the subject. Of this you will approve.—He, let me tell you, is not a 'George', but is 'Arthur Gryffydh'.—I must say I think the selection very Patmorian, but it's a pleasant book for a boy, and this little man reads it with pleasure. The sentimental pieces, of course, affect him the least; for he is a natural fellow, and I never trouble the roots of him. Dibdin is almost his favourite: he recites the lines on Sir Sydney Smith gleefully.

Apropos of Praxaspes.[1] Shame on me! I had to hunt him up. My old impression of him, and my new, differ. Duty is a fine heroic business; but a man should be a slave to nothing. P. was a slave to his conception of this virtue. What! he serves the man who slaughters his son: he takes pride in being faithful to the dynasty of a madman!—I give my sympathies to the persecuted Magi.

Praxaspes might be cast in the form of a monologue. But, you see I am on the other side.

Does Mrs. Jessopp really mean to visit me? Does she know the sort of place she will be coming to? She will do me great honour and make me very happy, but I desire that she be distinctly aware of what she must undergo in a hut—for this roof that covers me is nothing more. Does she not travel in Switzerland? She can, then, rough hardship.—Let me know when I may expect you, if you hold by this good resolve.

My book hangs a little. I am sick of the sight of it. A council of friends say that the Rosanna poem must be published, as embodying something of *me*!—Of the old volume nothing will appear.

Your ever faithful
George Meredith

I remember with regret that you say you are somewhat involved in the persecution befalling Mr. Rowland Williams.[2] There are men *chosen* to make head against the multitude in these matters. I hope you do not feel that you are of this elect?

---

152. [1] See Letter 149.
   [2] Rowland Williams (1817–70), Anglican divine, who contributed a review of Bunsen's 'Biblical Researches' to *Essays and Reviews*. He was prosecuted for heterodoxy by his Bishop, and hearings before the arches court of Canterbury were held in Dec. 1861 and Jan. 1862. The verdict went against Williams, though the judgement virtually conceded his position in Biblical criticism and the relation of scripture to science. On appeal to the Privy Council, he was vindicated, though subsequently condemned by the synod. The case, in its various aspects, dragged out until 1864 (*DNB*). Meredith, as a Freethinker, strongly sympathized with Williams.

153. *To* WILLIAM HARDMAN

MS.: Garrick Club. Published: *Letters*, i. 65, with omissions and inaccuracies.

[Esher]
Tuesday, [March 25, 1862]

My dear Hardman:

Please don't expect me positively to-morrow. I may call on Thursday: but what I want to do is to go with you and Demitaunton[1] to the Monday popular concerts to hear Joachim,[2] and music, since your infernal alterations stop all chance of that at home. So, some Monday may I come? Ask Demi——(turn over) taunton.[3] And yet, suppose I am weak and come to-morrow! You may turn me back from the door without giving offence: for I shall know I've deserved it; and I shall have had the Imperial luxury of indecision; as one who from the couch of indolence surveys the realms of Bliss.

By the way a letter from Alexandria. My Janet *refuses* to give the verses,[4] unless I stringently insist; for, says she, they were compoged[5] for me, me alone, and I don't want to lose the sense of their being peculiar to myself. . . . Can I insist?—I must e'en write Demitaunton a new set of verses.

P.S. I really think I shall come. But *don't expect me.*

Your faithful
George M.

Good bye to Demitroïa! and How d'ye do to Ditto-taunton.

154. *To* FREDERICK A. MAXSE

Text: *Letters*, i. 66–68. Salutation supplied from the Maxse Papers.

Copsham, Esher
[*c*. April 1, 1862]

My well-beloved friend!

Is it the same sky over us? Mine is of the grimmest grey, with a fog-lining. The daffodil in the meadow has been nodding to this genial

153. [1] Mrs. Hardman. See Letter 151.
   [2] Joseph Joachim (1831–1907), Hungarian violinist and composer. From 1859 he was leader of a quartet that appeared in London concerts on Mondays and Fridays. *The Times* of 25 Mar. says that 'the quartet playing of Herr Joachim is attracting all musical London to these entertainments'.
   [3] Written *Demi* on one side of the paper and *taunton* on the other.
   [4] Written to Schubert's Adieu for Janet. See Letter 147.
   [5] A Sairey Gampism.

wind for the last two weeks: and now we have the pen-bird heralding the cuckoo, and I suppose summer is coming: but we are all in suspense to know whether we are to get a daily ducking or live the life of non-purgatorial beings through the months. Last Sunday there was a puff of sunshine. I walked with a couple of fellows to Box Hill. What changes since last year! I looked over the hilly Dorking road we traversed. It wound away for other footsteps. Well!—you at least have nothing to regret. I hope the sunshine will cling to you.

The Naples correspondent of the *Times* gives a horrible account of the state of the country,[1] and rather alarms one about you: but having so precious a charge to protect you won't be rash, I'm sure.—Of course, you have heard all about the *Monitor* and *Merrimac*.[2] A pretty business sea-fighting comes to! Was there ever so devilish an entertainment! Blood bursting from the eyes and ears of the men at the guns, who seemed to be under the obligation of knocking their own senses to atoms as a preliminary to sending the souls of their foes to perdition. If they want me to go on board such vessels, I plead with Charles Lamb, 'Lance, and a coward'.[3]—The whole business affects the imagination awfully: but in reality an old sea-fight was a far bloodier business. Science, I presume, will at last put it to our option whether we will improve one another from off the face of the globe, and we must decide by our common sense.

Read John Mill on 'Liberty' the other day; and recommend it to you. It's a splendid protest against the tyranny society is beginning to exercise; very noble and brave.

The book[4] will be out the Monday after Easter. I sent with Borthwick as many of the proofs as I could collect; thinking you would have no time to review in Rome. But, if you have not done it, let me beg you to be in no hurry. The book can wait. You will find one or two poems that you have not seen. The 'Ode to the Spirit of Earth in Autumn' may please you.

I heard from Borthwick of the Violet's charming adventure with the Emperor, and can picture it.

---

154. [1] *The Times* for 24 Mar. had carried a report from its Naples correspondent of rioting between students and townspeople. Several people were wounded by pistol shots, and later a bomb was exploded. Tension was so high that the national guard was called out.

[2] The *Monitor* and the *Merrimac* had fought the first battle between ironclads on 9 Mar. Though the engagement lasted four hours at close range, the duel was a draw. The news reached England only in time for the 27 Mar. newspapers.

[3] If Charles Lamb wrote this, I have been unable to trace it. And if so, was he remembering Xenophon (*Cyropaedia*, trans. Maurice Ashley, 1728, ii. 129): 'Whoever has learnt the Skill of polishing a Lance, it will be well for him not to forget a Polisher, and he will do well to carry a File. For he that sharpens his Spear, sharpens his Soul at the same time; for there is a sort of Shame in it that one who sharpens his Lance, should himself be cowardly and dull.'   [4] *Modern Love* etc.

What you say about Christianity arresting sensualism, is very well: but the Essenian parentage of Christianity was simply asceticism. Hitherto human nature has marched through the conflict of extremes. With the general growth of reason, it will be possible to choose a path mid-way. Paganism no doubt deserved the ascetic reproof; but Christianity failed to supply much that it destroyed. Pompeii, as being, artistically, a Grecian Colony merely, cannot represent the higher development of Paganism.

Alas! I fear I shall not join you in Venice.—By the way, take care to get an introduction to Rawdon Brown,[5] while there. He has lived and worked at the Archives in Venice for 20 years, and can tell you more of the place than any other man. I hear he is also a good fellow.

Pray, give my kindest regards to your Cecilia.[6] I am flattered to hear that Englishmen stand so high with her now that she can make comparisons.—Write soon; and know me ever

Your faithful
George M.

In Venice read 'Julian and Maddalo'. It is one of Shelley's best: admirable for simplicity of style, ease, beauty of description and local truth. The philosophy, of course, you may pass.

155. *To* WILLIAM HARDMAN

MS.: Garrick Club. Published: *Letters*, i. 64–65, with omissions and variants.

[Esher]
Tuesday, [April 22, 1862]

My dear Hardman,

Thanks for your services with the notable Smallfield.[1] I let the thing pass. Let the public drive me to a 2nd edition, if they want further alterations.

Friendliest Tuck![2] I dine with you at the hour you please to name on Thursday; you will decide about Chapman. It's a matter of policy

154. [5] An Englishman who loved Venice so much that he lived there for forty years. Browning in his poem 'Rawdon Brown' has him say, 'London's "Death the bony"/ Compared with Life—that's Venice!' [6] Mrs. Maxse.
155. [1] Frederick Smallfield (b. 1829), an artist who exhibited at the Royal Academy intermittently from 1849 to 1886. Hardman's journal throws no light on the services he performed, but he may have been suggesting that Smallfield illustrate a new edition of *Shagpat*. A second edn. appeared in 1865, illustrated by Frederick Sandys.
[2] By now the friendship of GM and Hardman, in which there was a great deal of jollity, had progressed to the point of calling one another Friar Tuck (suggested by Hardman's build and temperament) and Robin Hood or Robin of Copsham.

simply. Let me know. If we dissipate subsequently we should dine at 5.30.—If not, 6.

I say!—poor dear old Morison!—I suppose you have heard of his purl?[3] Horse went down with him on high road and precipitated the source of St. Bernard[4] in the dust, which was nearly stopping flow of same. All's well that ends well! but one feels one likes him warmly when there's a note of danger. He has been shaken considerably—had a slight fever, and is without his strength, though he managed to walk to me yesterday. I walked back with him. He had to take a fly at Walton Station.—I saw the old lady:[5] who, I think, cannot last much longer. Meantime, the fair Farouche is kicking up her heels, just about! as the boys say. You'll hear startling news of her soon, I trow.

Tuck!—in thine ear:—she wants to be married.—No more!—Henceforth, she is fair Humpty-Dumpty! Hulloa! here's bottom of page.

Salute! Your friend,
George M.

Letter from Jessopp. Desires to bring wife on Monday. I am perplexed. Must put off Tunbridge Wells.[6]

156. *To* WILLIAM HARDMAN

MS.: Garrick Club.

Piccadilly
Thursday, [April 24, 1862]

Dear Tuck!

I found Rossetti who will come, if you can possibly put the dinner hour at 1/2 past 6.[1] He is moving and is tied to a van. As B[ritish] H[ouseholder] Tuck will appreciate his position.

Faithfully ever,
George M.

[At the top of the letter:] No Fred: Chapman here.

---

³ Slang or colloquial for *spill* or *upset*.
⁴ Morison was writing a life of St. Bernard. GM's nickname for him was soon to be St. Bernard or St. B.
⁵ Mrs. Virtue, Morison's mother-in-law. The 'fair Farouche' is Morison's sister-in-law, whose love affair with Morley is mentioned in Letter 324.
⁶ i.e. a visit to Edward Chapman at Tunbridge Wells.
156. ¹ Hardman (*MVP*, pp. 114–16) sent Holroyd an account of the dinner, which he thought added 'fresh laurels' to his reputation as a gourmet—'an enviable notoriety, but expensive'. The guests included Rossetti, GM, and Dr. Liveing, a physician. 'We kept it up until 2:30,' wrote Hardman, 'and Meredith (whom I with difficulty piloted through the Haymarket, he was so very *rampant*) came home and staid all night with me.'

157. *To* WILLIAM HARDMAN

MS.: Garrick Club. Published: *Letters*, i. 68–69, with omissions and variants.

Piccadilly
Friday, [May 2, 1862]

Such weather!
And at Copsham no Tuck!——
　Anathema:
Spoken by the Poet on receiving
　　　　Tuck's
　　Card:[1] May 2nd 1862
'May his company find him utterly dull, and he his company!
May he hear good things and not comprehend them!
May he long in great anguish to laugh, and when the laugh comes,
may he forget the cause thereof, and go seeking it for the remainder
of his years, with the aspect of such a seeker!
May Demitroïa exclaim, "I am of a different opinion from
William!!!!" '——
　(Climax attained)
　(Close of anathema)

———

Went to Exhibition[2] on opening day, with Borthwick. Crush.
Saw everything. Had the Japanese ambassadors under my nose two
minutes. Ahem! Was told they were of high rank. Agreed. Dined
with Morison and Hicks,[3] and drank Hocks. Etc. Anticipated seeing
you, cock certain, to-morrow. Will never believe you're cock certain
again!——
　Book to be delivered this evening or to-morrow.[4] Has subscribed
wonderfully well.
　In spite of all,

Your loving
George M.

Profound salute to Demitroïa
[Marginal postscript:] A letter of explanation and an apology for this
conduct, are demanded.

157. [1] Postponing a visit to Esher.
　[2] The International Exhibition of 1862, which opened on 1 May. The Hardman family
visited it with Shirley Brooks and his son, and Hardman reported the Japanese 'a rum lot'
that he kept to windward of. Ellis (*MVP*, 119 n.) says that there were thirty-six of them
and that they 'were looked upon as a new variety of curious savages'.
　[3] Unlisted in local directories. J. Power Hicks, of 7 New Square, Lincoln's Inn, however, would have been a neighbour of GM's on his town days.
　[4] *Modern Love* etc.

158. *To* WILLIAM HARDMAN

MS.: Garrick Club. Published: *Letters*, i. 69, with omissions and inaccuracies.

Copsham
Monday, [May 5, 1862]

Madrigal

'Since Tuck is faithless found.'[1]

Since Tuck is faithless found, no more
  I'll trust to man or maid;
I'll sit me down, a hermit hoar,
  Alone in Copsham shade.
The sight of all I shun
  Far-spying from the mound:
I'll be at home to none
  Since Tuck
  Since Tu-a tua tua
taiaaia tuuuoa Tuck
  is faithless found.

Oh! what a glorious day. I've done lots of *Emilia*, and am now off to Ripley, or St. Demitroïa's Hill,[2] or Tuck's Height, carolling.

I snap my fingers at you.

And yet, dear Tuck, what would I give to have you here. The gorse is all ablaze: the meadows are golden-green, humming all day. Nightingales throng. Heaven, blessed blue amorous Heaven! is hard at work upon our fair wanton, darling old naughty Mother Earth. Come, dear Tuck, and quickly, or I must love a woman, and be ruined.

Answer me, grievous man! In thine ear!—Asparagus is ripe at Ripley.—

God bless you both! in haste

Your constantly loving but
wounded friend,
George M.

To
  Tuck: friar.

158. [1] Inspired by Hardman's cancellation of a visit on the preceding week-end.
  [2] St. George's Hill, west of Esher; elevation 250 feet. Here, GM once told Hardman, he wrote his 'Pastorals' (Ellis, p. 64).

159. *To* WILLIAM HARDMAN

MS.: Garrick Club. Published: *Letters*, i. 70–71, with minor variants.

Copsham Hermitage
Tuesday, [May 6, 1862]

I dare say! You know how badly you have behaved, and now you praise the Poet to cajole the Man!—[1]

Is it Tuck that sends me a letter of this kind?—Not a word of repentance for a promise *foully* broken. No appointment for—or let me say, expression of humble desire to receive pardon of, Copsham in the flesh next Saturday.—I won't come to you on Thursday. I will emit fresh Anathemas! Read next page or no; rhyme is more kindly.

(Tune: *Johnny's too late for the fair*)

Tuck! Tuck! once you would flatter me,
Saying that I in due season should fatter be.
Here is asparagus—what can the matter be?
    Why don't you join in the fare?

Ripley's a place with a jolly old Talbot Inn;
Once we two passed there, you know, and were all but in,
Rhyme now commands me to throw here a small 'but' in
    —Why don't you join in the fare?

I saw the Japanese at the Exhibition on Thursday last. This Thursday I dine with the *Once a Week* people and shall ask Hamilton[2] for a bed—I won't come down to you unless I can be more with you. Now, please come for *some days* in this magnificent weather. The nightingales are now at their best. I went to St. Demitroïa's Hill yesterday, saw the Great Irrational[3]—the Crystial[4]—Walford's domicile[5]—Harrow—Windsor—Berks—Bucks—Hants—Hog's back.

---

159. [1] Hardman, after cancelling his visit to GM, had written flatteringly of 'Modern Love' on 4 May. (Excerpt: 'No other man but yourself could have written it. No other man possesses that wondrous knowledge of the human heart, that weird power of analysis of feelings, that deep and pitiless probing of the soul. . . .') (*MVP*, p. 118.)

[2] Nicholas Esterhazy Stephen Hamilton had joined the staff of the British Museum as second-class assistant in 1852 and by 1871 had attained the rank of senior assistant. In 1860 he published *An Inquiry into the Genuineness of the MS. Corrections in Mr. J. Payne Collier's Annotated Shakespeare Folio, 1632.* Hardman speaks of Hamilton as a friend of his and says that Hamilton and Cotter Morison were joint authors of a review of *Modern Love* etc. in the *Parthenon* (*MVP*, p. 125). Mrs. Hamilton was a cousin of Marie Vulliamy, the future Mrs. George Meredith, and it was through the Hamiltons that GM met her in 1863.

[3] Shirley Brooks's name for the Exhibition of 1862.

[4] The Crystal Palace, presumably. In 1854 it was moved from Hyde Park to Sydenham.

[5] In 1866 (and I suppose in 1862) Walford lived at Hampstead.

Mon Dieu!—And no Tuck near.—To Demitroïa all kindness!—Still (through weakness of resolve)

> Your loving
> George M.

160. *To* AUGUSTUS JESSOPP

MS.: Yale. Printed: *Altschul Catalogue*, p. 39.

> Esher
> Wednesday, [? May 7 or 14, 1862]

My dear Jessopp,

(Since you encourage me to drop the formal prefix which your high magisterial function would have imposed on me much longer), I have to reply to you concerning Mrs. Jessopp's kind intention towards my little man.[1] I am not restrictive. I have no objection to his reading the Bible, though I confess that I am already baffled by his comparisons between the dogmas of Genesis and the mild facts of Geology: nor do I think the Old Testament—the Jew Creed and History—can do good to any young creature. He reads the New Testament willingly: the more so that nothing is forced on him.—It is not my principle to bring up a child in antagonism to any existing force. I try to make him feel compassionately towards the Devil, whenever the deeds of that Gentleman are broached: no more than that; and that should be essential Christianity, if it be not modern.

I scarcely expected that these new Poems of mine[2] could please you much. We will do better next time, I trust. I look to a severe drilling from the Reviewers, and fold my hands. It is worse to think that Mudie, (my old enemy, who quashed *R[ichard] Feverel*), has hoisted the banner of British Matrondom, and ejected me. If Novels and Poems are to be written for young women only, I suppose I must learn the art afresh, and make a new beginning. With kind regards to Mrs. Jessopp,

> Know me ever / Your faithful
> George Meredith

160. [1] Mrs. Jessopp wished to give Arthur Meredith a Bible on his birthday, 13 June.
   [2] *Modern Love*, etc. reviews of which began to appear on 14 May (dated 17 May).

161. *To* W. C. BONAPARTE WYSE

Text: Ellis, pp. 160–1.

[Copsham Cottage, Esher]
May 15, 1862

My dear Wyse,

I this day get your letter, and am glad to see it, and shall be glad to welcome you. This opening year I have thought of you much, from the contrast of last spring. I am better in health and strength. The little man blooms constantly. I have just published a volume of Poems, of which a copy is ready for you, when you arrive. Let me know the day you are likely to be in England: what are your immediate intentions, etc.: when I am likely to see you. I write in great haste, that this may not fail to reach you.

Know me ever your faithful
George Meredith

162. *To* WILLIAM HARDMAN

MS.: Garrick Club. Published: *Letters*, i. 71, with minor variants.

Copsham
[May 18, 1862]

Questions & Answers

Q. What's a continual Feast?
A. A day given up to Tuck.
Q. Why am I of a most vigorous capacity of Digestion?
A. Because I never can have too much of Tuck.
Q. Is it true that an Alderman before he finishes his day, must necessarily take a bracing walk?
A. Necessarily so; for he makes the CIRCUIT OF TUCK!

Confound the *Press* for its impudence in calling me a pupil of anybody![1] Never mind: if we do but get the public ear, O my dear old boy!—I rejoice to think I may soon have you, but grieve for Demitroïa. Come on Tuesday, if you can; 'cause Wednesday is the day before Black Thursday,[2] when George Pegasus Esquire goes into harness and [illegible word] what donkeys feel when they are driven.

162. [1] 'Mr. George Meredith', began the *Press* reviewer (17 May), 'is in some respects a pupil of Mr. Robert Browning.' (I am indebted to Professor L. T. Hergenhan for a copy of the review.)
[2] i.e. the day he spent in London preparing his copy for the *Ipswich Journal*.

Also, arrange, if it seemeth fit to you, for a walk with Hinchliff[3] or alone, from Saturday next: or arrange to come to me. As you will.

Gathering up my soul in its might, I say (and damn all consequences) My love to Demitroïa!

There!
George M.

163. *To* WILLIAM HARDMAN

MS.: Garrick Club.

[Esher]
Wednesday, [May 21, 1862]

Dear Tuck,

I come. I *had* an engagement! Eheu!—It was a last chance. Never mind. Here's a pelting day. Just finished article for *M[orning] Post*, and got to run down to Railway.

Yours ever,
George M.

164. *To* FREDERICK A. MAXSE

Text: typed copy, Maxse Papers. Published: *Letters*, i. 71–74, with substantial omissions.

Copsham, Esher
June 9, 1862

My dear Maxse,

I look about vainly for a long letter already written to you; but it's as good as nowhere. I must trust you to know yourself constantly in my thoughts. But I feel that you are quite at peace and as a river embayed, a deep quiet mirror to illimitable skies. Shall I stir my mind about the Elect? Let them walk in their Paradise! So, though I think of you, it is as one under seal; fixed, stamped, monotonously certain of his fate. This destroys all sequence of ideas in me. I revert inevitably to the original proposition—'He has aimed and hit the mark.' All around him now is empty babble. However, I will talk, for you may be beginning to sigh for a breath of England. Ah me! how I would wish to be with you, if wishing availed. But I must work on, and it is

---

[3] Thomas Woodbine Hinchliff, one of the founders of the Alpine Club; author of *Summer Months Among the Alps* (1857). Ellis (*MVP*, p. 113 n.) calls him 'a pleasant bachelor with many friends'.

just now imperative, or nothing would keep me from Venice and you at this season, or from Italy and you. I know we should feel together on so much there; and then sunshine means ten times more with sweet companionship.—I am working at *Emilia Belloni*. Health is so-so— it has been pretty good. What works I could throw off if I had the digestion of any of the creatures that hope to be saved! I am fretted with so much in my head that my hands can't accomplish. The other day I walked with a good fellow[1] whom you should know (his wife would make a charming companion for St. Cecilia) to Mickleham, after dinner. There we slept. Next morning early we took our old route—over Dorking to Wotton: round Evelyn's grounds on to Shere, then on the downs to St. Martha's: thence to Guildford, Godalming, Milford, to the little Inn where you heard the nightingales and were ravished by them. After that my friend limped, so we had to return the day following, by train.

I hope, by the way, your review won't be written before you see the book.[2] One poem, new to you ('Ode to the Spirit of Earth in Autumn'), will please you better than all—please you specially. It will suffice for me if you tell me what you think of it, and not the public. The notices that have appeared fix favourably on the Roadside poems, but discard 'Modern Love', which, I admit, requires thought, and discernment, and reading more than once. The *Saturday R[eview]* has not yet spoken. One paper calls me a genius—one, a meretricious clever bold man.[3] I find, to my annoyance, that I am susceptible to remarks on my poems, and criticisms from whipsters or women absolutely make me wince and flush. I saw Robert Browning the other day, and he expressed himself 'astounded at the originality, delighted with the naturalness and beauty'.—Pardon my egotism—I write to please you!—

I have not yet seen Gibson's Venus.[4] I went to the Int[ernational] Ex[hibition] on the opening day—have delayed to go since. It was a poor unimpressive show. Fancy the Poet Laureate in the line of march!—

June 13th. Your letter from Lucca:—You complain of sun. The S[outh] W[est] [wind] has been blowing since the middle of May, and this year has not yet known one day of sunshine.—Rossetti is beginning to ask about your Lady, to know when he may have a sitting.

---

164. [1] Hardman. The walking trip began late on 23 May and ended on 25 May. Hardman sent a detailed account of it to Holroyd (*MVP*, pp. 127–37).

[2] Maxse reviewed *Modern Love* etc. for the *Morning Post* (20 June), having seen only the proofs.

[3] It was the friendly *Parthenon* that hailed a 'new original genius' and the *Spectator* that pronounced the effect of the book 'that of clever, meretricious, turbid pictures'.

[4] John Gibson (1790–1866), sculptor, whose Venus was tinted.

He, dear fellow, is better—still somewhat shaken.[5] Mention it not—
he buried his MSS. poems in his wife's coffin, it is whispered. He, his
brother, and Swinburne, have taken a house (Sir T. More's)[6] at Chelsea: a strange, quaint, grand old place, with an immense garden,
magnificent panelled staircases and rooms,—a palace. I am to have
a bedroom for my once-a-week visits. We shall have nice evenings
there, and I hope you'll come. . . .—The Notices of my book are
scarce worth sending. The *Spectator* abuses me . . . the *Athenaeum*
mildly pats me on the back: the *Parthenon* blows a trumpet about me:
the *Sat[urday] R[eview]* makes no sign.—Whatever number of books
you may like to have, pray accept as your own. Is not mine yours, in
all things? I would prefer that you should not buy books of mine.
That is for the good public to do.

I wish particularly to be kept *au courant* of your change of abode:
there's no knowing what I might do, on the spur. Whither in Switzerland do you go, first? I presume, across the Italian Lakes, and over the
Splügen to Lucerne. Be careful of the waters of that lake: at some
points it is dangerous at any moment.—Tell me, don't you find that
great heat somewhat *narrows* and *sharpens* the reflective power? The
effect, in Southern climates, on Art, is to sacrifice all to outline, as
a rule, and murder detail. Even during the short time I was in Italy
I experienced this in a small degree. If the passions did but slumber,
Italy would be the very spot of earth for great work to be done. Here!
—I should like to try it.—I have a comedy germinating in the brain,
of the Classic order: *The Sentimentalists*.[7] I fancy it will turn out well.
Emilia Belloni goes slowly forward, for the reason that I have re-
written it: so, all will be new to you. I shall send you the *Cornhill
Mag[azine]* next month. Adam Bede has a new work in it.[8] I understand they have given her an enormous sum (£8000, or more! she
retaining ultimate copyright)—Bon Dieu! will aught like this ever
happen to me?—Shall you stay long at Turin?—Of all the horrible
cities! Two or three days at Milan will give you quite enough of the
pet Italian city: go to the Brera: and see Leonardo's wrecked Last
Supper. On Como stop at Bellagio—not at the Villa d'Este: the hotel
is good at the latter place, but the scenery is not so fine.

London is full to bursting—Of Kate I see little, or nothing. She

---

[5] Rossetti had returned on 11 Feb. to find his wife (Elizabeth Siddal) dead from an
overdose of laudanum.

[6] Ellis (p. 165) says that GM was mistaken in thinking the house More's.

[7] GM soon put aside *The Sentimentalists*, which he took up again in 1870, 1883, and
1898. It was completed by J. M. Barrie and produced, in compliment to GM, on 2 March
1910.

[8] The *Cornhill Magazine* paid George Eliot £7,000 for the serial rights to *Romola*—
an over-payment in the judgement of posterity.

writes that she is forgotten—she knows it—that she is jealous of all—
jealous of Fred Chap[man]'s wife, jealous of the servant who waits
on MacNamara,[9] of the harmless creature who does that duty by me!—
Say, is not this a fearful glimpse in to feminine gulfs?—

God bless you both! My darling boy says, 'Of course send my love
to Mrs. Maxse, and if she goes to Zurich, I was there, at the Hotel
Belle Vue.' Go there to the Hotel Baur, on the Lake. For beauty
Zürich is inferior to the other lakes.

Your constant loving
George Meredith

165. *To* WILLIAM HARDMAN

MS.: Garrick Club. Published: *Letters*, i. 77, with omissions and inaccuracies.

(New Square, Lincoln's Inn)[1]
[12 June 1862][2]

My dear First person plural![3]

I wish I could come to you. The rolling seasons seem to have gone
round thrice since I [words scratched out] (I forgot whom I was
addressing) shook your hands (Qy. hand). I remember one, Tuck,
a jovial soul, a man after my heart, whom I loved. I ask Nature for
him;—she draws a South-west veil across her eyes, weeping. Francatelli nods a cold and tasteless response! Tuck!——no answer! I explore
the woods of Copsham daily fruitlessly!

On Friday is the illustrious small man's birthday, and he *mustn't be
left*. Edward Peacock[4] and his boy are staying with me till Saturday.
Rossetti and Swinburne come on Saturday. Will you come the week
following?—

Aha!—as if I can't *see* that I'm cut, and that the gulf of a tail-coat is
forevermore twixt me and Tuck. Oh, what a dreadful evening, what
an appalling sight, when Tuck [breaks off illegibly].

Believe me still and ever, / My dear F. p. plural, /

Your loving
George M.

164. [9] Unidentified.
165. [1] The address of T. E. Foakes, a barrister whose wife had inherited the *Ipswich
Journal* from her deceased husband. It was there that GM went on Thursdays to prepare
his copy for the paper.

 [2] Hardman's date, *July 12, 1862* (reproduced in *Letters*), is clearly wrong, since
Arthur's birthday, mentioned below, was on 13 June. 12 June, in 1862, was a Thursday,
GM's day in New Square.

 [3] i.e. Mr. and Mrs. Hardman, elsewhere referred to as *We*.

 [4] Brother of GM's first wife.

166. *To* WILLIAM HARDMAN

MS.: Garrick Club. Published: *Letters*, i. 74–75, with minor variants.

[Esher]
Wednesday, [June 18, 1862]

Well-beloved Tuck!

(Though I know I'm cut). The ninth progressive station of Ginger-beer to eventful Pop, passed pleasantly.[1] Your kind recognition of it was received by him with loud exclamations of delight.

Come on Saturday, I prithee. But excuse my attendance on Friday. I'm obliged to be here. And indeed, notwithstanding your taunts, Copsham is worthy a visit, just now. The Roses and the Rumford ale are in their finest condition. In haste,

Your faithful
Robin Selkirk

Island of Juan Fernandez[2] Copsham.

My homage to Demitroïa, as ever.

Menu approved: But to send it now, when the feast is over![3]—Am I embracing a phantom?—does my mouth water for a corpse? Does not the favourite poet of 'We' say, 'Look not mournfully into the past?'[4] You make me.

167. *To* FREDERICK A. MAXSE

Text: typed copy, Maxse Papers. Published: *Letters*, i. 75–76, with omission.

[Copsham, Esher]
June 23, 1862

My dear Maxse,

I write in haste, a short note, on the chance of speaking to you before you leave Turin. Your article has appeared in the *Post*.[1] It is very good: but do you think it? You should have whipped me on the score of the absurdities, obscurities, and what not. I feel that you have been sparing me, and though I don't love the rod, I don't cry mercy. I'm

166. [1] i.e. Arthur's ninth birthday passed pleasantly.
  [2] Robinson Crusoe's island.
  [3] The Hardmans were giving a series of weekly dinners.
  [4] Longfellow, *Hyperion*, Book IV, chap. 8: 'Look not mournfully into the Past. It comes not back again. Wisely improve the Present. It is thine. Go forth to meet the shadowy Future, without fear, and with a manly heart.'
167. [1] Maxse's review of *Modern Love* etc. in the *Morning Post*.

exceedingly sorry that you did not review from *the book*. The 'Ode to the Spirit of Earth' will, if I mistake not, catch hold of you. I will see that notices of the Poems are forwarded to you. But let me know your route and resting-places.—Tell me when you write, whether your scenic faculty has been excited and by what.—I am at work on Emilia Belloni, and bringing her more to your taste. I have remodelled the whole—making the background more agreeable and richer comedy. I have an immense quantity of work in store. Prose, poetry: a comedy (*The Sentimentalists*) etc. Health is still weak and will never be much, I fear, unless I can purchase two years' perfect rest and travel.—B. Wyse came the other day: *acknollodged* his foregone errors, and hoped for forgive*miss*: 'Me deer Mardith,' etc.!—He hopes to get some property now. I fear he is in a prospective mess. His present one is without dispute.[2] I helped him to the best of my ability, and he departed, praising me, magnifying me.—Fred Chapman, you know is married to the daughter of a rich picture-dealer. He goes to Florence in September. Tom Trollope (who lives there) tells me that September is a delicious month for Florence, the best in the year.—What are your plans about the winter? Don't fail to let me know, because, if you are in Italy in early Spring next,—say, Feb.–March to June, I *will* come over, as I desire to breathe that air with you.—I have not yet been to the International [Exhibition] a second time.

Are you writing anything beyond impressions or voyages?—What you told me once on that head (that I have influenced you against your own compositions, acting so as to check you) weighs upon me sadly, now and then. I know you will be happier if you write, and I am convinced you will, if you choose, write a *good* book. Pray, don't put aside that old and excellent ambition of yours. You will miss a friend.

I begin to yearn to see you—just as I did when in Tyrol. You will get a sentimental poem this time.—

You hear all about the Yankees and politics, of course.

Read *Les Misérables*, if you can get it. Six volumes are out. It is conceived in pure black and white. It is, nevertheless, the master work of fiction of this century—as yet. There are things in it quite wonderful.

I bow my head to your dear Lady, praying that her health may be improved, and am,

> Your loving
> George Meredith

My dear boy is quite well, flourishes wonderfully.

167. [2] Wyse's father had died in Athens in April. Wyse inherited £5,000, but seven years of litigation to have the will declared invalid were beginning.

168. *To* EDWARD CHAPMAN

MS.: University of Texas.

Esher
June 30, [? 1862]

My dear Ed: Chapman,

Your letter has been delayed in the delivery, so that I had no time to answer it. I would have telegraphed, but don't know your exact address. I was in on Friday, and incapable of attending. I had no opinions to give to Marsh,[1] so deferred till this week. If I can come to-morrow, I will. But if you don't see me, let me know whether you can take the little man on *Friday* till the *Tuesday* following. I fear I shall not be able to come for him, though I should like it. Arthur is anxious to confab with Reggy.

Your faithful
George Meredith

169. *To* [? MRS. JAMES STANSFIELD][1]

MS.: University of Texas.

Copsham Cottage, Esher
July 2, [1862][2]

Dear Madam,

I received a letter from Mdme Venturi, dated June 22nd, this day. She speaks of leaving England on the Saturday following the date. I have written to her address in Brompton Road, but I fear that the letter will miss her, and as I am anxious to assure her of my willingness to be of any possible service to her, I take the liberty to write to you for her continental address. If you will oblige me by sending it to Chapman & Hall's, Piccadilly, I shall be there on Friday and shall be able to communicate with her, I trust to her satisfaction, without loss of time.

I have the honour to be, Dear Madam,

Your faithful Servant
George Meredith

168. [1] Unidentified.
169. [1] Sister of Emilia Ashurst Venturi, subject of the letter.
　[2] This date is added in pencil in another hand. As the Ashurst family papers for 1862–3 are incomplete, it is not clear whether this was the time of Emilia's dramatic journey to Italy, carrying funds for the insurgents, or not. (See E. F. Richards, *Mazzini's Letters to an English Family*, 1922, iii. 32.) There is no certainty indeed that the letter belongs to 1862.

170. *To* WILLIAM HARDMAN

MS.: Garrick Club. Published: *Letters*, i. 79, with omissions and minor variants.

193 Piccadilly, London W.
[August 7, 1862][1]

My dear Hardman,

Here's a precious liberty I'm going to take! Sana[2] has come, and I must stop in town, and so must Sons. Will you bed us (Sons and self) till Monday? I fancy Sana will be delighted to come on Sunday. He looks wild and rough, but who wouldn't after being herded with 397 men and *3* women? One of the latter wears a fine moustache. It struck me (I saw the whole boilin' of 'em) that one of the 397 left it on her lip by accident; or all the 397 contributed.

Might I bring Sana—but no.

Oh, Tuck! shall I tell it?—It's a fact: but in anguish I beg you to conceal it even from D[emitro]ïa. Sana came smack at my cheeks when we met. It was done before them all. Now I feel what Lucretia's emotions were: or those of the little girl with the sense of colour so strong, examined by Knox.—I dare say I shan't be able to arrive before 10 to-night.

Your loving
George M.

Sons invade you with this letter.

171. *To* WILLIAM HARDMAN

MS.: Garrick Club. Published: *Letters*, i. 77–79, with omissions and numerous inaccuracies.

Ryde [Isle of Wight], Pier Hotel
Saturday night, [August 16, 1862]

Beloved Tuck!

To-morrow we sail![1] We're off to the West, love!

170. [1] This was a hand note and was not dated by either GM or Hardman. I have supplied the date from internal evidence of the letter and from Hardman's August letter to Holroyd in *MVP*.

[2] Sana, a Doctor of Laws, had come with a party of 400 excursionists from Vienna to see the Exhibition of 1862 and London in general. GM had met him in Austria the preceding summer. Hardman (*MVP*, pp. 162–5) gives an amusing account of Sana's visit.

171. [1] In the absence of James Virtue, who had gone to New York on business, the Morisons had invited GM to go with them on a yachting excursion in Virtue's yacht.

> To-morrow I am going
> —I cannot tell you where
> The wind is stoutly blowing
> The ladies'—
> (word of 2 syllables à discretion)
>   bare

> ———————

> And now for a toast!
> (To Tuck the toast shall be)
> I'm off along the coast,
> I would he were with me.

(Popular London air, commonly chanted by Tuck and Robin.)

Here's Morison drunk with salt water. Mrs. M. ditto. GM ditto ditto. We swear we'll live on it till we come home pickled. I've got a pea-jacket, and such a nautical hat, and such a roll of the legs already.

Now, Tuck—will you do this for me?—Will you write for this week's *Ipswich Journal*, a Summary of the week's news: *and* an article —on America, if you like.[2] Follow the Press. Will you call and see Foakes? And if you don't see him, will you, nevertheless, send your work on Thursday, or *take* it, to Mr. *Gough*, at 1 New Square, Lincoln's Inn (where you sometimes call and see your Robin on Thursday); and if you, perchance, don't see Gough, will you post the aforesaid to *H. Knights, Esq., Ipswich Journal Office, Ipswich*. I shall write and post one article, but I shan't be up in the latest news.

> For I'll be in a cabin,
> Just 3 feet long, 4° square;
> Just ponder on your Robin,
> The figure of him there.
> I don't care a dam,
>   etc. etc.

You will immensely oblige me by doing this, and I shall then be able to run over to the Channel Islands. If not, I must up to London from Weymouth. Please write there immediately (Post Office), that I may hear from you on *Tuesday* morning. Adieu.

[Marginal postscripts:] Post Office *Weymouth*, if you write on
                                                              Monday,
              „   „   Torquay, if on Tuesday.

My (Neptune embolden me!) love to Demitroïa.

Your friend, penitent, loving, lastingly,

                                        George Meredith

[2] Hardman was glad of an opportunity to have a Tory medium in which to advocate recognition of the Confederacy and express his strong Tory views in general.

—By the way, why don't you go down to Copsham for a day or two, next week?—If you can write for me, I shan't be back till Tuesday or Wednesday week. The Cottage and all in it are yours. There can you invite R. Cook[e][3] to dine with you, in place of my doing so. And I wish you would! There's wine in the cellar. If you think well of this, drop Miss Grange a word of warning—I'm surprisingly *aux cieux* already. A dreadful hitch in *E[milia] Belloni* has been distressing me of late. This day tides me over the difficulty!— To-morrow I am moodily leaning on the bin (2 *n's*, I think)-nacle, thinking of Tuck! Au revoir!—Mind! the Weymouth Post Office! Torquay on Wednesday.

172. *To* WILLIAM HARDMAN

MS.: Garrick Club. Published: *Letters*, i. 79–80, with variants.

'George Inn'
Great Marlow
[September 7, 1862]

Dearest, and if possible, More Precious, Tuck, because absent! and yet not so, but more desired. And thereby hangs a philosophy.—

Johnson[1] hath me in an iron grip: saith, I shan't go, save as the arrowhead from the bow which himself twangeth. I say, that but for black Foakes'-day, known to no calendar save mine—alas! I would,

> Willy-nilly,
> be off with you a jolly dance
> To Falmouth, Torquay, Penzance,
> or Scilly.

But Johnson adds—'Will Hardman come down to me at Hoddesdon, on Monday week, and go and see Hatfield[2] (famous old garden and

171. [3] An employee of John Murray. He had introduced GM and the Hardmans.
172. [1] Andrew Johnson (1815–80)—usually called 'Bullion' Johnson by GM—became attached to the clerical staff of the Bank of England in 1832. In 1862 he held the position of Deputy to the Principal of the Bullion Office and later that of Principal. He retired on pension in 1873 because of ill health. (Information from the Chief of Establishments, the Bank of England.) Kelly's *P.O.D.* for 1862 lists him as a resident of High Street, Hoddesdon, Herts. Johnson was a friend of John Chapman, who had published his translation of F. W. J. Schelling's *The Philosophy of Art* in 1845 and whom GM would have known at the *Westminster Review*. Thus Chapman may have been the connecting link between Johnson and GM.
[2] Seat of the Marquis of Salisbury in Herts.

House), and Panshanger,[3] where are pictures of price . . . if so, let him say so, as a man and he's welcome.'

To this I add, from him and from me:—

Come down *here* for a day, or two. We are comfortable. The country is delicious. The walks are heavenly. The river is a dream of green herbage and reflected Heaven. The weather promises. May we expect you on Tuesday or Monday night, perchance—on a sudden: a great feat! You are free—and soon going to be melancholy, if without excitement. Do come. I would return with you on Wednesday, or, if you please, Thursday morning. Johnson is very desirous to make acquaintance with the grasp of your hand. I, when I am parted from it, pine. As you know!—Write. But should a true Tuckian inspiration seize you, outstrip the post, as alone you can. In all love,

Your faithful
Robin

173. *To* ARTHUR G. MEREDITH

Text: *Letters*, i. 124.

[? Great Marlow]
[? September 1862][1]

My Own dear Little Man!

We went on the water yesterday and fished; and I caught nothing; but Mr. Johnson hooked an enormous Jack of a quarter of a pound weight, which makes him very proud. I should like to have my darling boy with me. But you shall come here some day. There are beautiful meadows by the brink of the stream, on one side, and on the other, tall thick woods hanging close over the water. The Thames is very different from the river Inn or the Adige, or the Passeyr. It is quite smooth, and broad, and still; green with reflection of the trees and herbage, a capital place for you to bathe in.—Remember me to Tom, with whom I have no doubt you are getting on well. If you want

---

[3] Near Hertford, the seat of Lord Cowper. Among the pictures were a fine Tintoretto, five Reynoldses, four Knellers, three Lelys, a portrait of the poet Cowper, and several Dutch paintings, including a Van Dyck (*Victoria History of the County of Hertford*, iii. 471–72).

173. [1] W. M. Meredith dates this letter *Autumn 1863*, which can hardly be correct since Arthur would then have been in school at Norwich. The *Tom* to whom GM sends greetings ought to be Tom Peacock, Arthur's cousin, who had visited Arthur in June. I conjecture that Arthur was visiting the Peacocks a part of the time that GM was with Andrew Johnson and that he joined GM at Johnson's a short time later. The description in this letter tallies with that in Letter 172, and I know of no other time when GM was fishing on the Thames.

anything, write me word of it. But I should like to hear from you, in any case, so sit down the day that you receive this, and write me a few lines, that I may hear from my dear little man the best news that can come to me—that he is quite well and quite happy.

Your loving Papa,
George Meredith

174. *To* AUGUSTUS JESSOPP

MS.: Yale. Printed: *Altschul Catalogue*, p. 40.

[Hoddesdon, Herts.]
September 12, [1862]

My dear Jessopp,

I am now beginning to think seriously of sending my Arthur to school. So, if you are in harness once more, be so good as to send me word what may be the preliminary arrangements necessary before a small boy can be gathered to your flock: as to whether any special application is made, or introduction needed. That you personally would have him under you, gladly, I do not doubt. You are aware that I would trust him, who is my only blessing on earth, to you with full confidence.

I fancy that you have been on the Continent, or I should have heard from you.

Arthur has gone to bed or he would disburden himself of the abundant 'love' that every little boy finds ready within when called upon. Under the circumstances, Mrs. Jessopp will permit me, I trust, to act as proxy in the matter.

Know me / Your faithful
George Meredith

My address until next Thursday is 'Care of A. Johnson Esq. / Hoddesdon / Herts.' / After that day / 'Care of Edward Chapman Esq., / Camden House / Camden Park, Tunbridge Wells.'

175. *To* WILLIAM HARDMAN

MS.: Garrick Club. Published: *Letters*, i. 80–81, with substantial omissions and numerous inaccuracies.

Foakesden, after-Foakes-day
September 19, [1862]

My dear Tuck,

I rejoice to hear that the wandering atom 'I' is the happy and thrice blessed 'We' once more. Here's my news. Thursday last a letter from Copsham to say that Zillah has smallpox!—Luckily the little man was at Hoddesdon. I have written to Jessopp, who will take him immediately. Hard as it is, to let him go, he goes on Friday next—So I have been prompt, on this occasion. But conceive the horrible bore! The house won't be habitable for 2 months; and friends won't come under 4. I have notions of 'skedaddling'. I go this day down to Tunbridge Wells; return on Wednesday following. On Friday to Norwich. Then to Oxford with Morison, on Tuesday, for a short period. Then to Sussex. Then—perhaps to Tuck for two or three days, if he has returned to the Refectory. Health at Marlow excellent: at Hoddesdon poor. Result in London—megrims.—I heard of poor Hinchliff from Hamilton last night who spoke croakily. Pray convey to Hinchliff my word of sympathy and hope to see him recovered soon, etc.

Also, congratulations of the heartiest kind to that humble aspirant for woman's honours, the fair young Betsy![1] Amphitrite, we might have been sure, would do the business for her. Now for Cupidon.

Johnson is a really good fellow. His women are what he described. Not interesting but very kind, and very homely. They laugh more than the candlestick but scarcely accomplish more observations. They have a ready shine of their own, and they hold the light to Johnson— and in fact the simile would run on cheerfully, but I stop it. They have been thoroughly kind to Arthur. I am grateful with all my heart.

Went to Hatfield and to Panshanger. Hertfordshire is a pretty county. I would rather not dwell in it. Yet with Tuck (and when I say, with my WE Tuck, I don't mean to diminish him and make him small— the contrary: yea, I double him almost), with my WE Tuck I could dwell in many places and exchange friendly nods with Providence.

Pray, remember me to Mrs. Knowles[2] when you see her, and tell her that, if I should ever come to Lancashire, I shall pretend not to have seen her in London. This will be best, you know. Not that, between ourselves, there was anything more than what may be called giddy in her behaviour in the Metropolis. Still, we know what Lancashire gossips are.

My love to Potter and Nellie.[3] To Demitroïa all sweet things.

Write to 'Care of Edward Chapman Esq. / Camden Park / *Tunbridge Wells*.' And write soon. I leave the place on Wednesday, perhaps

Tuesday, and want a letter from Tuck.   [Unsigned]

P.S. At Hoddesdon facing Johnson's house, there's a butcher. His name is ——

---

175. [1] Hardman's children's nurse.   [2] Hardman's mother.
[3] Hardman's children, Ethel and Helen, called Potter and Nellie in the family.

By the way, you know I was engaged to Morison last Thursday?—Somehow I couldn't get him to write, and the smallpox news from Copsham upset me and silenced me.

176. *To* AUGUSTUS JESSOPP

MS.: Yale. Published: *Letters*, i. 156–7 (dated *Sept. 20, 1864*), with substantial omissions and minor variants. Omissions printed: *Altschul Catalogue*, p. 40.

Care of Edward Chapman, Esq.
Camden Park, Tunbridge Wells
Saturday, September 20, 1862

My dear Jessopp,

With regard to Arthur, I am in this position. At the end of two weeks' absence from Esher, my housekeeper writes to say that her niece is pronounced guilty of smallpox: so that I can't return there with the boy for two or three months. I had designed to send him to you at Christmas. If you can take him now, it will relieve me. And if you can do so, will Mrs. Jessopp let me know what clothes he should bring with him? etc. . . . I need not add that Arthur is a perfectly safe vessel. He had left the cottage about twelve days before the child showed symptoms of malady, and we have not been in communication with it, since. I am a wanderer.

Should you have any wish for him to come later in the year, pray don't hesitate to declare it.

As to the Poems: I don't think the age prosaic for not buying them. A man who hopes to be popular, must think *from* the mass, and as the *heart* of the mass. If he follows out vagaries of his own brain, he cannot hope for general esteem; and he does smaller work. 'Modern Love' as a dissection of the sentimental passion of these days, could only be apprehended by the few who would read it many times. I have not looked for it to succeed. Why did I write it?—Who can account for pressure? . . .

Between realism and idealism, there is no natural conflict. This completes that. Realism is the basis of good composition: it implies study, observation, artistic power, and (in those who can do more) humility. Little writers should be realistic. They would then at least do solid work. They afflict the world because they will attempt what is given to none but noble workmen to achieve. A great genius must necessarily employ ideal means, for, a vast conception cannot be placed bodily before the eye, and remains to be suggested. Idealism is as an atmosphere whose effects of grandeur are wrought out through a series of illusions, that are illusions to the sense within us only when divorced from the groundwork of the Real. Need there be exclusion, the one of the other? The artist is incomplete who does this. Men to whom I bow my head (Shakespeare, Göthe; and in their way, Molière, Cervantes), are Realists *au fond*. But they have the broad arms of Idealism at command. They give us Earth; but it is Earth with an atmosphere. One may find as much amusement in a Kaleidoscope, as in a merely idealistic writer: and, just as sound prose is of more worth than pretentious poetry, I hold the man who gives us a plain wall of fact higher in esteem than one who is constantly shuffling the clouds and dealing with airy delicate sentimentalities, headless and tailless imaginings, despising our good, plain, strength-giving Mother. Does not all Science (the Mammoth Balloon,[1] to-wit) tell us that when we forsake earth, we reach up to a frosty inimical Inane? For my part, I love and cling to earth, as the one piece of God's handiwork that we possess. I admit that we can re-fashion; but of earth must be the material.

And so, farewell! Let me hear from you by return of post, if possible. I purpose, you willing, to bring Arthur at the end of next week or the beginning of that which follows.

This is Arthur's character. It is based upon sensitiveness, I am sorry to say. He is healthy, and *therefore* not moody. His nature is chaste: his disposition at *present* passively good. He reflects: and he has real and just ideas. He will not learn readily. He is obedient: brave: sensible. His brain is fine and subtle, not capacious. His blood must move quickly to spur it, and also his heart.

Your faithful
George Meredith

176. [1] Balloons, though not exactly new in GM's day, must have exercised on his generation something like the fascination of the aeroplane for our own time. The first balloons date 1783, but their early development was largely by the French. In 1863 M. Nadar's *Géant*, with a capacity of 215,000 cu. feet, was displayed and attracted large crowds at the Crystal Palace. And in England the several ascents of Coxwell and Glaisher in 1864 were reported at length in the newspapers.

177. *To* ARTHUR MEREDITH

MS.: Berg Collection, New York Public Library.

Hollyshaw, Tunbridge Wells
Wednesday, [September 24, 1862]

My dear little Man!

Florry[1] says she has not forgotten her determination to have you for a husband, as she means honourably, and does not wish to hurt your feelings. Meta[2] laments that she was absent while you were here. Florry's heart is beating against the table, so that my writing is necessarily at sea. Meta's heart is beating on the other side. I saw the little girls who took to you, and they have by no means forgotten you. Little Wally[3] went to have his hair cut, the other day. Says he, 'I want my hair cut like Master Chapman's Arthur.'

Mrs. Chapman sends her love, and hopes to see you in your holidays. Also she has given me half a crown to put in your new trousers pocket. I shall see my own boy on Friday. I come to Hoddesdon by 5 m[inutes] past 4 train; so you can meet me, if you like. Cheer up poor Mr. Johnson as well as you can. Tell him I am getting statistics in the different counties I visit of all the people who have caught a fish, in their life-time, for his consolation and encouragement.

Your loving Papa,
George Meredith

Enclosed is a letter from Mrs. Hardman.

178. *To* FRANCIS BURNAND[1]

Text: *Letters*, i. 83 (undated, unsigned).

Tunbridge Wells
[*c.* September 24, 1862]

My dear Frank,

Your letter has been forwarded to me here. My house-keeper's niece at the Cottage has fever: fortunately Sons were absent. So we

177. [1] Florence Chapman, daughter of Edward Chapman, at whose house GM was staying.
　　[2] Daughter of Edward Chapman.　　　　　　　　[3] ? Son of one of the servants.
178. [1] (Sir) Francis Burnand (1836–1917) attended Eton and Cambridge (B.A., 1858) with the intention of becoming an Anglican minister. Conversion to Catholicism in 1858, however, diverted him from this course, and to please his father he qualified as a barrister (1862), though he was not attracted to the law profession. Following his natural bent, he helped found *Fun* in 1861 and subsequently joined the *Punch* staff shortly after his first

are all in exile: and consequently, I pronounce the dread word, and he is already breeched for school.

I shall be in town on Friday, and will order 'that' a copy of *Modern Love* 'be' sent you. The printers' errors are innumerable.

I am going to Norwich with Sons at the end of the week, to the King Edward's Grammar School, the Head Master of which is a friend, and very fond of the little man. Write to me, 'Care of Rev. A. Jessopp, The School House, Norwich', whether you can take me for a night, on my return. If the young Mauritius[2] is at Hurstpierpoint,[3] and will have me for 2 or 3 days, I shall then go to him. If you go too, all the better.

That you have been wearing the mask of 'Fun'[4] for some period, I have known.

> As often in a bun
>   The currants you surprise,
> Behind the mask of Fun
>   I catch my Franco's eyes.

179. *To* AUGUSTUS JESSOPP

MS.: Yale. Printed: *Altschul Catalogue*, p. 41.

193 Piccadilly, London, W.
September 26, 1862

My dear Jessopp,

I design to bring my darling boy to you to-morrow: but it is just possible that I may be disappointed in getting certain things that he will immediately require. In which case, I come with him on Monday. You see, I take you at your word, and impose myself upon you for two or three days.

In haste. My kind regards to Mrs. Jessopp, to whom I see a long vista of thankfulness for care of my dear little man.

Your faithful
George Meredith

contribution in 1863. He remained a member of its staff until his retirement in 1906, having served as editor from 1880. He was knighted in 1902. In addition to his work for *Punch*, he wrote more than a hundred burlesques and adaptations for the stage.

In *Records and Reminiscences* (i. 360 ff.) Burnand recounts his first meeting with GM (in 1859) while visiting his old Cambridge friend Maurice FitzGerald at Esher. He and GM had jollity in common, and they remained lifelong friends, although as time went on they saw less and less of one another. It was Burnand who, after GM had been talking with unusual 'vivacity and charm', demanded, 'Damn you, George, why won't you write as you talk?' (H. M. Hyndman, *The Record of an Adventurous Life*, N.Y., 1911, p. 71).
[2] Maurice FitzGerald.   [3] Near Brighton.
[4] i.e. 'have been writing for the magazine *Fun*'.

I hope we shall be quite out of the range of dinner-parties, and the respectability whose banner is a tail-coat;—for I, you should know, am cut off from my resources. I am in squalid plight.

180. *To* WILLIAM HARDMAN

MS.: Garrick Club. Published: *Letters*, i. 84–86, with omissions and inaccuracies; excerpts published: *MVP*, 187–8.

[Cambridge]¹
[October 4, 1862]

Tuck, sweet charmer, tell me why
I'm at ease when you are by?
Have you had a 'round' with Care,
Left him smoshen, stript him bare,
That he never more can try
Falls with me when you are by?

Ah, but when from me you're screen'd,
Atrabiliar glows the Fiend:
Fire is wet and water dry:
Candles burn cocked hats awry:
Hope her diamond portal shuts,
Grim Dyspepsia haunts my—ahem!

(Madrigal written in St. John's Col[lege]
Cambridge, Saturday, October 4, 1862)

Yes! I'm here. Meeting of British Ass[ociation]²—so, why not? And I've wandered up and down Trinity, thinking of Tuck, the radiant, and of others: mooning by Cam, into which classic flood drop numerous dead leaves. I've dined with Fellows and am to dine with them again: have been cordially received, and inhabit chambers of an absent graduate, whose slave is my slave. Jessopp brought me. We return to Norwich to-night. What a good fellow he is! And his wife takes high rank in Demitroïa's corps. She is quite charming: she unites worth, and sweetness of manner, and *capacity*. They have the same face for the school that they show to the world. I never conceived a place better managed. Jessopp has 25 boys in his house. They have studies where two sit together and are never intruded upon. He breakfasts and dines with them. We have a good deal of prayer. Oh, Tuck! have we

---

180. ¹ In a notebook preserved in the Altschul Collection GM jotted down an idea for a story under the heading 'Cambridge, Oct. 4, 1862'.
  ² The British Association for the Advancement of Science, founded 1831.

not led thoughtless lives and snuffed our own conceit? Tuck!—In the evening, Jessopp, his wife, a *pretty* niece, and myself, do music, read Molière, and are really happy. I feel so much so that I would gladly live near them, if it were possible. I particularly wish you to know them. Tuck! it would do thee good, for, an I be not deceived, thou art but a lost sheep and one of the ungodly.—The dormitories of the boys are thoroughly ventilated, cool as a twilight balcony: each boy is *partitioned* off from his neighbour, and the main punishment is for infringing this partition. Jessopp has sent up here [Cambridge] six scholarships lately.—Well, Sons are wonderfully *buoyant* in a jiffy. Mrs. Jessopp writes to say that she took the boys to Lowes-toft yesterday. Sons were so independent that they assured her they were *exactly like the other boys* and didn't want looking after. This is a fair prospect for my dear man. Mrs. Jessopp is the friend of every resident in the house, and the boys love her. In wit and in blood she is one of the brightest little women that you could meet. Jessopp may well praise her fine qualities. The Lord decreed to him a helpmate. I say, Tuck! does praying get us wives of this sort? If so—but it's clear that it doesn't, for Tuck never goes on's marrow-bones as I've been doing 24 times *per diem*, of late. Jessopp won't let me depart till *Monday week*. I'm very comfortable, so why not?—Then I go to Sussex: then to Richmond, then to Morison, then to Oxford, then to Glaisher and Coxwell,[3] then to Endymion's dear love (I will drop you some green cheese regularly at 6 p.m., while there). After that, Bedlam, I suppose, for I don't know of any other place for which I shall have been such an accomplished graduate. What's coming to me? I feel the sensations of some peculiarly scampish racket-ball. *Love* to—now, don't get in a passion, Tuck! human nature will out, sometimes—Potter. And Nellie. And Potter's mother, and Nellie's mother, and Tuck's wife. So, there, you see: your jealousy brings it on you 3 times instead of once.
    Adieu!

Your loving
George M.

[Marginal postscripts]: Address to me, and immediately, and a long letter, care of Rev. A. Jessopp, / The School House, / Norwich.
    That the Mother of the Pantagruelians[4] is well I frequently pray. Pray, thou, Tuck!—
    Yesterday Huxley had such a tussle with Owen! The thinking men all side with the former. You will read of it.

---

[3] English balloonists. This is chaff, of course.
[4] Mrs. Knowles, Hardman's mother.

181. *To* FREDERICK A. MAXSE

Text: typed copy, Maxse Papers.

The School House, Norwich
Monday, October 7 [6], 1862[1]
My dear Maxse,
I found the enclosed written in answer to your first letter, in my writing-book. I send it, not for any value in the remarks, but to prove to you that my mind communicated with you in reply, though I am indeed a 'bad correspondent'.—Nothing could please me better than this place for Arthur. He lives in Jessopp's house, whose wife is a most accomplished, bright kind and loveable person—quite beloved by the boys all. The boys are healthy, gentlemanly fellows, who work hard, and play all the games of their generation. So, are occupied. They have a fine river for rowing; a good cricket ground etc. They have in the school 8 Scholarships of £40 and £60: and two good Fellowships for Corpus, Cambridge (I went there the other day and was very kindly received at St. John's). All the rooms of the school are warmed with hot-water pipes for winter: and in summer the bed rooms are cool and fresh as a meadow. Each fellow is partitioned by a wall of 7 feet from his neighbour. Tell me whether I can see you this day week, and at what hour. If you want me to dine, know that I can only do so if you are absolutely *alone*, having no evening suit. I very much want to see you both. I leave here on Monday next. Write before Saturday.

Ever yours,
George M.

182. *To* WILLIAM HARDMAN

MS.: Garrick Club. Published: *Letters*, i. 86–87 (dated *Oct. 4, 1862*), with omissions and inaccuracies; excerpts published: *MVP*, pp. 189–90.

The School House, Norwich
Friday, [October 10, 1862]
To Wm. Hardman Esq.
Dear Sir,
I take the liberty to write to you, requesting a line of information concerning one, Tuck, a ruddy man and a lusty, with whom I suppose

181. [1] 7 Oct. was a Tuesday in 1862.

you to be acquainted, and about whom I have recently been feeling a considerable anxiety. He has relations at Hoddesdon, Tunbridge Wells, and Norwich; but they have no recent knowledge of his proceedings. I have written to him and can get no reply. You will acknowledge that I have cause for anxiety when I tell you that in a work I have lately been reading, it is said, with regard to fleshpots, that he who giveth his heart to them is on the highroad to perdition. Which was truly and sadly the case with this named Tuck. A dangerous man, Sir! for he tempted us to love this life, and esteem it a cherishable thing: yet withal one whom to know once is to desire ever. For indeed such a one is seldom seen. Pity that such roseate healthful bloom as that he wore upon the cheeks of him should be a banner of Repletion! Alas! and that the sunny perfection delighting us in him signified verily, that nature, though proud of him, struggled greatly, whereof came these hues of her desperation! Even so, the noble rotundity, the fine protuberance, was excess of Potatoe! Yea, and also the very frankness of him partook too largely of Francatelli. Hence my fear for the man: In that he, who was good himself as an egg fresh laid, had the love of things good, and did attract them to him profusely: which is against one of the decrees.

Dear Sir! should you see him and the faithful and loving spouse, Demitroïa by name, who is ever at his side and the pride of his soul, be so good as to make known to him these my inquiries; and that, should he be ill, I recommend any cure but the epicure: moreover (which he will understand) that I trust among the chief things in this life that 'WE' may never be split in two. Finally, that I am in Norwich till Tuesday next, after that, Chapman & Hall Piccadilly's my address ... if gout permit him use of pen. Gout alone can have kept him silent to his loving friend and admirer. I would wish him to know that Sons are well and happy—had a great fall at gymnastics last evening, being adventurous; but are none the worse.

Yours respectfully,
George Meredith

183. *To* WILLIAM HARDMAN

MS.: Garrick Club. Published: *Letters*, i. 88–89, with omissions and inaccuracies.

Norwich
Saturday, [October 11, 1862]

Embrace me once more, O Tuck! Thou liv'st!—

This is to chronicle the sudden and unexpected descent of a small man from a height of 17 feet to the ground. Poor Sons little intended the feat, and therefore performed it satisfactorily. In the crypt here, there is a gymnasium, fitted up under a regular professor, who is 5th master, one Reinecke. He did this and that, he went in and out and around and over, and his pupils did the like. Apparently Sons had their emulation violently excited, for while we were all engaged in other wonders, Sons must mount a ladder by himself, and from the top of it make a catch at a pole from whence to slip down naturally. Instead of which he came plump to the floor. I felt him tugging gently at my hand and couldn't make out what was the matter with him. He had come to tell me he felt queer, and 'what he had gone and done'. I took him up and his nerves gave way just a moment (not noisily). Then we rubbed him a bit and discovered him to be sound. He was jolly and ready for fresh adventures in a quarter of an hour: wiser Sons, as we trust. My parental heart beat fast under its mask.

Jessopp and his wife (who is one of *the* wives of this generation) do all that's possible to make me happy in my own way. They don't want me to go. They don't poetise me but honour me by treating me as simple flesh, so that one doesn't feel mounted on a pole and ultimately destined to come down, as Sons did. Yesterday I went to visit a splendid fellow, one of the most capable men of his time. Whereof when[1] we meet. I stay with Morison in town. Shall I dine with you on Wednesday? He's alone, if you can ask him too.—I wrote to Mr. Hardman for tidings of you; but anticipate no reply—a stuck up Cambridge swell! Tuck for me! My love to everybody.

George M.

[Marginal postscripts:]

The marrow-bones don't wear out. They *harden*. Think of the amount of practice to bring dear experience!

Sons wear the College Cap, and have commenced lessons.—

184. *To* FREDERICK A. MAXSE

Text: typed copy, Maxse Papers. Published: *Letters*, i. 87–88 with substantial omissions.

The School House, Norwich
Saturday, [October 11, 1862]

My dear Maxse,

I don't like to hear of your wife being so weak. Poor Mrs. Ross has just passed through the ordeal, and not at all satisfactorily. I hope she is commonly able to take exercise, of some sort. I hope, too, I may see her, when I come. I can't leave here till *Tuesday*. They provide all

---

183. ¹ GM wrote *we* twice instead of *when*.

kinds of amusement for me. By the way, Arthur had a tremendous fall, the night before last, at gymnastics in the crypt of the School House. While we were all engaged at a particular swing, this small man mounts up a ladder to catch hold of a pole—misses it and comes down about sixteen feet, not on his head, or arms, thank the Lord! I felt a slight tug at my hand, and the little fellow related his disaster, shaken and sick, but pluck as stout as ever. No harm done, and some experience gained. I will give you an account of the school when we meet. Yesterday I visited a model Englishman: primarily a gentleman and scholar: a Reverend, also, with full tolerance and zeal for his duties: a farmer, a gardener, and exhibitor of fruits and flowers, and winner of prizes: an innovator in all things, as a man who in all things thinks for himself. He is besides a profound geologist and correspondent of Lyell: a paleontologist, the friend of Owen: one of the Alpine climbers:—in short, the most capable human creature that I have ever met. Be sure I studied him. He did me the favour to invite me to stay with him, which, to my regret I can't do now.

Now, as you move to your new house on Wednesday, I won't name that day. Shall it be the next? Write to me care of

J. Cotter Morison, Esqre. / 7 Porchester Square / Bayswater

I shall be staying there during the week. I can dine on a chop, and *at your hour*, so there need be no preparation or putting out of fresh harnessed domestics.

Your faithful and loving
George Meredith

185. *To* MRS. CATHERINE COOPER HOPLEY[1]

MS.: University of Texas.

193 Piccadilly, London, W.
October 24, 1862

Dear Madam,

We believe that you will find the papers you mention, among the MSS. delivered by us to your messenger on Tuesday last, and which should be by this time in your possession.

We are / Dear Madam / Your very obedient Servants,
Chapman & Hall[2]

185. [1] Author of *Life in the South from the Commencement of the War*, by a Blockaded British Subject (1863). The letter is annotated thus: 'George Meredith, the novelist, was Chapman & Hall's Reader when I wrote *Life in the South* and his writings and annotations on the margins of the Proofs were most entertaining. [Signed] C. C. H.'
 [2] Though signed 'Chapman & Hall', the letter is in the hand of GM.

186. *To* MRS. AUGUSTUS JESSOPP[1]

MS.: Yale. Published: Ellis, p. 176; printed: *Altschul Catalogue*, pp. 41–42.

Copsham Cottage, Esher, Surrey
November 4, 1862

Tune: '*Lady Geraldine*'

Burden, '*Chatter chatter*' ad. inf.

Dear, my friend and honour'd Madam! of hard facts I'm not a hoarder,
And that you will quite forgive me my forgetfulness, I beg!
It had pass'd me what was requisite to stock the little boarder,
But dream we of its feathers when the chick has burst the egg?

Oh! the happy Close of Norwich, with its towering Cathedral!
Its boys that shout at Prisoners' Base, the envy of a man!
Oh, the happy 'harping' hours when at Confederate and Federal,
We talked, what time of Partridge full and eke of Parmesan!

Methinks, to let the days slip by, it was not noble, Madam,
While my infant was deficient in such necessary things;
Compell'd to rest on Charity, or else to sleep like Adam,
Without a tow'l to wipe his face, a spoon to oil his springs.

Ha! you scorn us? is it not so? I am led to think it, Certes;
But so terrible a poet's wrath, I pardon ere I blame.
I see the little fellow who so lovely in his shirt is,
And I swear an oath that this day week the sheets shall own his name.

The pillow-cases likewise, towels six, and silver fourchette;
The tea-spoon and dessert-spoon (for I have it all by rote):
I will send them in a jiffy. But, pray, tell me (with the door shut),
Do you find him such a darling 'tis no wonder that I dote?

Oh! had I but a passion now,[2] to tear it all to tatters,[3]
And storm as doth the limp young man who frightened Geraldine!
I have chatter'd as that weedy, woman's-tender-ruffian chatters—
May it give you satisfaction!—which remaineth to be seen.

186. [1] This amusing apology for GM's failure to outfit his son properly is written in the form of a burlesque of Mrs. Browning's 'The Lady Geraldine's Courtship'.
[2] Dubious reading.
[3] Hamlet: 'O, it offends me to the soul to hear a robustious periwig-pated fellow tear a passion to tatters . . .' (III. ii. 9–11).

Oh, Lady of the Three Black Cats! farewell, and let me hope a
Meeting we may compass, ere in effigy you stand,
In Norwich's Cathedral, our illustrious St. Jessopa,
A scroll to tell a Boarder's needs in Heaven, in your hand!

George M.

187. *To* WILLIAM HARDMAN

MS.: Garrick Club. Published: *Letters*, i. 89, with numerous variants.

193 Piccadilly, London, W.
November 7, 1862

Tuck, Carissimo!

The news being this: Jeffs[1] hasn't got R. Houdin.[2] If it's to be had
at Nutt's,[3] or at Dulau's,[3] it will be immediately forwarded to you.

Lucas we visited àpropos of that fellow Hardman's article.[4] It is to
be inserted soon. I told Lucas Hardman was not a fellow to be trifled
with: said, 'he was a GASTRONOME!'[5]

'Oh, Lord,' says Lucas, 'we mustn't offend him.'

I remarked that Hardman had invented NEW DISHES.

'God bless my soul,' says Lucas, 'I should like to know him.'

'But,' said I, 'the culinary comments of Tuck, delivered under
globular light, are in themselves meat, wine, and wisdom, and eclipse
Hardman as a Christmas flank of Beef lords it over the leaner seasons
of the year.'

'By jingo,' says Lucas, 'it's a privilege to know him!'

Steadily facing my Editor, I said: 'And Tuck is my pupil.'

He wrung my hand, speechless:

'All I exact,' said I, 'is, that you publish "Tar and Feathers" instanter,
or you experience the operation.'

He made sign that it should be done *within a month*.

Your loving
George M.

---

187. [1] William Jeffs, a bookseller in the Burlington Arcade who specialized in French
books.

[2] A reference to R. Houdin's *Les Tricheries des Grecs*, or *The Art of Winning at All
Games*. Hardman was revising an English translation for C. & H., published in 1863 as
The Sharper Detected and Exposed.

[3] Well-known booksellers.

[4] 'Tar and Feathers', published in *OaW* (15 Aug. 1863).

[5] Dickens had published an article by Hardman, 'The Roll of Cookery', in the 6
June 1857 issue of *HW*. But his reputation came mainly from the dinners he gave.

[Marginal note:]

The *Telegraph* of yesterday contains an article in *support* of Colenso.[6] I think this is the first editorial toe that Moses's Behind will have tasted, and it deserves to be bought.

188. *To* WILLIAM HARDMAN

MS.: Garrick Club. Excerpts published: *MVP*, p. 207.

[Copsham, Esher]
[November 10, 1862]

Oh! did you ne'er hear of a jolly young Carpenter,[1]
    Sawing his logs, with the song of the lark:
In tripping the lasses there ne'er was a *Sarpenter*
    Didn't they think his voice sweet after dark!

To give his opinions and thoughts in extenso,
    I can't, so, to say they were moral, will do:
His Bible he stuck to, in spite of Colenso,
    And taught the girls Genesis while the cock crew.
                    Ahem!——

Dear Tuck,

I'm glad to hear of Hardman's appointment.[2] Professor of Ology in the Gordon St. University, is a step for him. But his arrogance is almost insufferable. Does he never see a *French* Dictionary, or read a French political leader?—The word that so startles him would meet his astonished gaze often enough, if he did.

Damned Pedant!

If *you* (not Hardman) see the King of Bonny,[3] give my kind regards and good wishes to him. The time is now fast on him.

I say, Tuck, I'll wager you (we're sure to have an account subse-

187. [6] J. W. Colenso (1814–83) was Bishop of Natal when his work *The Pentateuch and the Book of Joshua Critically Examined* (7 parts, 1862–79) brought down the wrath of Episcopacy upon him. In his examination of the Pentateuch, he concluded that Numbers and Leviticus were written centuries after the events narrated and that Chronicles had been falsified to exalt the priests and Levites. The controversy that followed was long and bitter.

188. [1] 'Meredith has taken lately to felling trees and sawing up logs of wood, as a healthy exercise, to promote the circulation and improve his digestion. With the latter object in view he has also adopted a wet compress on his stomach, and has found great benefit from it' (*MVP*, pp. 206–7). The verses are in imitation of 'The Jolly Young Waterman', a popular song in *The Waterman*, a ballad opera first produced at the Haymarket in 1774. (I owe this note to Professor Phyllis Bartlett.)

[2] A reference to Hardman's difficulties in translating Houdin. Hardman lived in Gordon St.; hence Gordon St. University.

[3] N. E. S. A. Hamilton. Mrs. Hamilton, née Vulliamy, was of French origin, and in the verses in Letter 192 GM refers to her as 'first subject of Bonny' (Bonaparte).

quently) that, in spite of the king of B's pronounced respect for well-brought-up petticoats, they (i.e. King and Queen of Bonny) are on the *floor* by 3 o'clock a.m.— ?—

A tremendous South-Wester is wakening great woodland hymns. I'm out. My logs are sawed, my song is sung.

From the embrace of Compress,

Your loving
George M.

189. *To* WILLIAM HARDMAN

MS.: Garrick Club. Excerpt published: *Letters*, i. 89–90.

Copsham, Esher
Wednesday, [November 12, 1862]

Tuck, Great Heart!

I will come to you to-morrow, and dine, and hear music, and sleep, if you can take me. Dinner with O[nce] a W[eek] postponed.

Still we carpenter. It is great exercise. I have half cut my great toe off already. Axe went slap through my big plodding boots, and set me dancing over the meadow as if Demitroïa had struck up the Tarantella. In consequence of the sweating and action of Compress, the stomach, where Emilia resides, is becoming an agreeable tenement, and I'm glad to say her features are improving.

Sons say that they have addressed a letter to Gordon Street.

With salute to all of you,

Your loving
George Meredith

190. *To* ARTHUR G. MEREDITH

Text: *Letters*, i. 126–7 (dated *Nov. 12, 1863*).

Copsham Cottage, Esher
November 12, [1862][1]

My dear Little Man!

Island Pond is frozen over, and all the common looks as you saw it that Christmas morning when we walked over to Oatlands. Sandars[2]

---

190. [1] W. M. Meredith's date *1863* for this letter is surely incorrect. The tone of the letter is of one written to a newly enrolled schoolboy, with admonitions about study and a natural request to know the names of newly acquired friends. (Several of these GM mentions in letters *ante* 12 Nov. 1863.) Further, Arthur had visited the Chapmans in the summer of 1862 and would have owed Mrs. Chapman a belated bread-and-butter letter, whereas so far as is known he did not visit them in the summer of 1863.

[2] Possibly a son of the Sandars mentioned in Letters 148 and 246.

is seen sometimes, with brown gaiters and a green tunic. His legs continue to grow, but his body does not. All your playthings, your theatre, books, etc., are put away, but you can get at them easily when you return. You can imagine how glad I shall be to hear your voice again in this neighbourhood; and if I were not working very hard, I should find the place too dull to live in, without you. Shall I hear at Christmas, that you have been learning, and have got a little more friendly with your Latin Grammar? Mind you don't waste your time. If you do your best, I shall be satisfied. Tell me the names of the boys you play with most, and what fellows you think are the best. I suppose you see Mr. Sandys. Have you been to Mrs. Clabburn's?[3] Let me be sure that I shall have a letter from you every week. When you have written to Captain Maxse, you must write to Mrs. Edward Chapman, 'Camden Park, Tunbridge Wells'. The name of her house is 'Hollyshaw'. God bless my dear little man, prays his loving Papa,

George Meredith

191. *To* WILLIAM HARDMAN

MS.: Garrick Club.

[Copsham, Esher]
[December 3, 1862]

My belovëd Tuck!
> Absolution, O Friar!

> O shrive me Friar, my ghostly Friar!
>> Quick, shrive me now, he cried.
> For I have kiss'd a mortal maid,
>> And something more, beside.

> The Friar he frown'd, his belt he hitched,
>> In accents stern spake he.
> The thing that in my day I did,
>> Was never meant for thee!

Etc., etc.

Owing to a muddle there will be no O[nce] a W[eek] dinner this week. Most probably next Thursday, of which you shall have warning. Tuck will not see me this week.

Penitentially!
Robin

190. [3] The Clabburns, wealthy silk and poplin manufacturers of Norfolk, were friends of the artist Frederick Sandys, who also lived in Norfolk. William White, *History, Gazeteer and Directory of Norfolk* (1864), lists two families: Thomas Clabburn, of King St., and William Clabburn, of Thorpe, near Norwich. In 1869 William Houghton Clabburn was the owner of Sandys' *Medea* and is therefore perhaps the likelier of the two to be meant here.

192. *To* WILLIAM HARDMAN

MS.: Garrick Club. Published: *Letters*, i. 90, in scrambled order and with omissions.

[Copsham, Esher]
[December 10, 1862]

Tuck, my treasure! Tuck, my pleasure!
Lucas won't have a meet at the 'Cheshire
Cheese' till after Christmas—truly,
He's a bore and I'm yours, duly,

Robin!

P.S.

And if you love me, write and say so.
Quaequae cupit, sperat[1]—sings Ovidius Naso:
To-day, you know, I dine with Morison.
Is there a dinner with Tuck in the horizon?
I'm expecting, of course to behold Mrs. Hamilton,
First subject of Bonny[2] (which to mention were dam' ill ton).

193. *To* MRS. AUGUSTUS JESSOPP

MS.: Yale. Printed: *Altschul Catalogue*, p. 44 (dated *Saturday* [1863?]).

Esher
Saturday, [December 13, 1862]

My dear Mrs. Jessopp,

I comply. When you regard the Photograph[1] say to yourself 'This comes of wilfulness in woman.'

It may be a portrait. If so, that men should stand before me, is a marvel.

I call it, Photograph of a Boy and a creature who would disprove the great Darwinian theory by force of countenance. Add, 'and he fails'.

I jump with delight at the hope of having my darling in my arms.—I will be at Shoreditch station at 6.30 p.m. on Wednesday.

If Angove[2] remains in Town, I will look after him.

192. [1] 'Quodque cupit, sperat, suaque illum oracula fallunt' (Ovid, *Metam.* i. 491): And what he desires, he hopes. . . .
[2] See Note 3, Letter 188.
193. [1] A photograph of GM and Arthur, probably the one reproduced in Ellis, *George Meredith*, opposite p. 182. GM was unduly sensitive about pictures of himself and always disparaged them.
[2] A fellow student of Arthur's at Jessopp's school.

Ask Mr. Jessopp what time in January you are to do me the honour to visit me. (I say nothing more of the wretchedness of the place of Reception.) I wish to know, because, my friend of the yacht,[3] with a chosen band, takes his trial trip of about four days from the Isle of Wight, in that month; and I must make arrangements. I need not add that I would not miss you for anything, and that the thought of your coming pleases me thoroughly, for it *also* flatters me. After a certain age this is necessary to our pleasure—says a cynic (to-wit, Sir Austin A. Bearne Feverel, Bart.)—

Your ever faithful
George Meredith

194. *To* WILLIAM HARDMAN

MS.: Garrick Club. Published: *Letters*, i. 91, with substantial omissions and numerous variants.

Copsham, Esher
13
Saturday, December ~~11~~, [1862][1]

From 'Gentz's' Diary.[2]

(Tagebücher von Friedrich von Gentz:—ed. Varn[hagen] von Ense *'J'ai lu le soir les feuilles infernales de* COBBET(t) *du mois d'Avril*—' (He reads it on Friday 21st July, 1809—shortly upon *Wagram*, I think, or Lobau, on the Danube.)

'La crainte, que je nourrissais depuis quelque temps de quelque grande catastrophe, menaçant l'intérieur de l'Angleterre, a été prodigieusement augmentée par cette lecture, dont l'effet sur moi—je ne puis le dissimuler— a été presqu'aussi grand, que celui des plus épouvantables nouvelles, qui retentissait dans mon visinage [voisinage] direct.'

Gentz was, by birth, a Prussian, in Austrian diplomatic service, of high ability, much trusted, conversant with English politics and politicians, the friend of Metternich and others. He writes this cer-

193. [3] Cotter Morison had just bought a yacht of about 100 tons, which he named the *Irene* and which he wished to try out before embarking on a Mediterranean cruise (*MVP*, p. 238).
194. [1] Dated *Saturday, Dec. 11*, by GM. Hardman has corrected the date to *Dec. 13*. 11 Dec. was a Thursday in 1862.
[2] Friedrich von Gentz (1764–1832), German writer, statesman, and ardent anti-Bonapartist, was close to Metternich from 1812–22 and in intimate touch with all the important events of European history. In 1814–15 he was Secretary to the Congress of Vienna. His diaries, covering the years 1800–28 (ed. Varnhagen von Ense, 1861), are an invaluable source of authentic information about the people and events of the time (*Encyclopedia Britannica*).

tainly under excitement, but it is useful, as showing the dread Cobbett
could inspire abroad, the view taken on the continent of his writings
and their presumed results. Gentz evidently confounds him as utter
Radical. Perhaps you might look out in Cobbett's *Register*, of this
date, and see what's to be gathered. At any rate, what I have written
out, might make a good footnote illustration.[3]

To Tuck from Robin

Sons come on Wednesday!—Demitroïa will translate the French
for you, I'm sure, if you ask her humbly. In concord and with reverence,
adieu, my lusty Friar!—

> Adieu, adieu, my Friar, he cried;
> 　My lusty Friar, adieu!
> O, much I trust that they have lied,
> 　Who tell these things of you:
>
> That when you go forth to tell your beads,
> 　That waggling paunch behind,—
> You do but count the maidenheads
> 　You've ta'en from maids too kind:
>
> And therefore in a jealous fit,
> 　Damn every mother's son,
> Who fain would have a taste of it,
> 　By humbly taking *one*.

195. *To* WILLIAM HARDMAN

MS.: Garrick Club. Published: *Letters*, i. 90, with omissions and inaccuracies.

> [Copsham, Esher]
> [December 13, 1862]

Dear Tuck,
　In reply to your mandate,[1] this day received:—Sons come up on
Wednesday and sleep in Town that night: but how can I possibly
keep him from Copsham on Thursday? I fear me I must take him
down. It was his special request six weeks ago,

---

[3] Hardman was working on a life of Cobbett which he never completed.
195. [1] To bring Arthur to 27 Gordon Street instead of taking him to Copsham. In the end
Hardman had his way.

And tho' my friar's mandate is severe,
The wishes of the Son of Sons are dear.
I really fear
I must bring home my little man on Thursday;
(As you would rhyme) that he may in the furze play.

—Acknowledge that a friar cannot always be obeyed.
I shall regret not to see the King and Queen of B[onny]. I bitterly regret missing the account of his First. Should he relate his Second, the Charade will be complete, and we may easily guess his————
In saecula saeculorum, amen!

Thine, usque ad in aeternum,
Rob[in]

196. *To* F. M. EVANS

Text: typed copy furnished by Messrs. Bradbury & Agnew.

Esher
December 15, [1862]

My dear Evans,
I want £35., and I want you to send me that sum.[1] I cannot promise to be of immediate service, in return; but *Evan Harrington* may be sufficient surety for my good conduct. It may seem unfair that I should apply to you. Take my word, that I never ask for money without a sharp necessity.
Also, please send a copy of *E[van] H[arrington]*,[2] for correction, to Chapman & Hall, under cover for me.

Yours faithfully,
George Meredith

197. *To* ARTHUR G. MEREDITH

Text: *Letters,* i. 92.

[Copsham, Esher]
December 15, 1862

My darling Little Man,
I shall be at Shoreditch station, on Wednesday, to meet the Train at 6.30. But, you must not be disappointed, if I tell you that it will be

196. [1] The old ledgers of Bradbury & Evans record an entry of £35, marked 'advance', for 24 Dec. 1862.
    [2] The second edn. of *EH* was not published until 1866.

too late for you to go on to Esher that night; and you will sleep at Mrs. Morison's, in Porchester Square. Mr. Hardman wants me to dine with him on Thursday, but I have told him I am afraid you won't let me. Copsham will be delighted to see you. All the dear old woods are in their best winter dress. Mossy Gordon has come from Eton. Janet leaves England next week; but hopes to see her dear boy before she goes.—Be careful not to have any larks in the train. Only fools do that. As much fun as you like, but no folly. Look out for Ely Cathedral, just before you get to Ely station. At Cambridge you will see the four towers of 'King's' Chapel, built by Cardinal Wolsey. Tell Angove, that I will get a bed for him, if he wishes to sleep in Town on Wednesday night. And give Angove your address, written down; that he may let me know when he will come to London from Cornwall, and we will go to the theatre together, and then he will take you to school again.

> Your loving Papa,
> George Meredith

198. *To* WILLIAM HARDMAN

MS.: Garrick Club.

Copsham
Wednesday, [December 17, 1862]

Friendliest Tuck!

If you don't see me, or hear from me, know that I accept your noble offer for Friday morning. You must be at Foakes den by 10 o'clock a.m. and add any news of importance to the tail of the 'Week'.[1]

> Your loving
> Rob[in]

Thursday: I'm sure Sons won't let me come.

199. *To* WILLIAM HARDMAN

MS.: Garrick Club. Published: *Letters*, i. 95, with inaccuracies.

Esher
Tuesday, [December 23, 1862]

My Christmas Tuck!

I'm preparing for the pudding with tremendous exercise.

I had made up my mind to go with you to Boxing-night festivity, with Sons likewise. But, he will not like the Strand. He is ardent for

198. [1] i.e. Hardman was to complete Meredith's column of news for the *Ipswich Journal* in order that GM might be free to devote himself entirely to Arthur.

a jolly clown, a pantaloon of the most aged, the most hapless, a brilliant twirling Columbine, a harlequin with a wand on everybody's bottom. This does the small man seriously incline to. Can I say nay? And he vows he detests plays and burlesques. I remember his last visit to the Strand. He is too young for puns. So, if you have taken tickets, sad shall I be: but I am for Drury Lane, or Covent Garden: for uproar; a pit reeking with oranges; Gods that flourish pewter-pots and tricks that stick and show their mortality at starting. Would, would, would, that Tuck were then at my side![1] I declare that I have swung my beetle[2] and roared at the anticipated headlong fun with Tuck. I would go to both: but, you see, I have again *promised* the Son. I must go the following night, and there's a further loss of time, if I disappoint him. I understood you distinctly a *pantomime*, bully Tuck!

Do we quarrel? If so, I send Love to somebody and snap my fingers at you. If not, my regards of the warmest to both!

Your affectionate
George M.

200. *To* AUGUSTUS JESSOPP

MS.: Yale. Published: *Letters*, i. 92–95, with minor variants and inaccuracies.

Esher
Tuesday, December 23, [1862]

My dear Jessopp,

I found my little man looking marvellously brisk and clear of eye. All his friends exclaim that his School agrees with him. I am altogether pleased and satisfied, and (*quoique pauvre diable, comme vous savez*) should ungrudgingly pay double the annual sum, to have him with you and your wife: which I consider a privilege not to be measured by money.

I presume that if I send to Bankers at Norwich, according to direction, before the next session, it will do.

I am amused from morning to night by Arthur's account of the 'boys'. It is as I suspected: he knows their characters consummately.

---

199. [1] GM and Arthur spent Christmas Day with the Hardmans, who went with the Merediths to the pantomime at Drury Lane on Boxing Night (26 Dec.). Hardman records that there were showers of orange peel from the gallery into the pit and that he would have been inexpressibly bored with the pantomime had it not been for the raptures of Arthur (*MVP*, p. 229).

[2] A heavy iron weight of about nineteen pounds attached to a wooden shaft, used by GM for exercise. W. M. Meredith (*Letters*, i. 95 n.) believed that this violent exercise contributed to GM's later spinal weakness.

I had the same faculty when I was young. But, whether he gets it from deduction, or nervous feelers, or the conjunction of both, I can't guess. He hopes to get a prize next year: speaks of his success in 'dictation': not boastingly; but to assure him whom he suspects to be a sceptical Papa, that he is not lazy and not stupid. He is not, absolutely, either of the two. He is pre-eminently a growing boy, and has some characteristics to outgrow. He will never, I fancy, do credit to you by any display of acquired knowledge; but, after a period, I think you will find that his understanding is as sound as that of any fellow you have had to do with.

He says: 'Jerrard, minor, is the gentlemanly boy of the school.'

'Not Angove,' I asked.

'Yes, Angove, too; but he's not so *courteous* as Jerrard, minor. Jerrard minor always thinks of others, first. I like him.'

The one point he evidently a little chafes at (though not complainingly, and with Submission, poor martyr!) is the Sunday religious exercise, which you have dared to temper for the poor lambs, and which they must still think severe. I remember, at that age, how all love of the Apostles was belaboured out of me by three Sunday services of prodigious length and dreariness. Corinthians will forever be associated in my mind with rows of wax candles and a holy drone over-head, combined with the sensation that those who did not choose the road to Heaven, enjoyed by far the pleasantest way. I cannot hear of Genesis, or of the sins of amorous David, or of Hezekiah, without fidgetting in my chair, as if it had turned to the utterly unsympathetic Church-wood of yore. In despair, I used to begin a fresh chapter of the adventures of St. George (a serial story, continued from Sunday to Sunday), and carry it on till the preacher's voice fell. Sometimes he deceived me (I hope, not voluntarily) and his voice bade St. George go back into his box, and then ascended in renewed vigour once more; leaving me vacant of my comforting hero; who was not to be revived, after such treatment. I have known subsequent horrors of ennui: but nothing to be compared with those early ones. Your evening service is a noble relief, your evening discourse most sensible, healthy, and calculated to catch the wandering youthful mind. But, it is the third dose of the day. Is it, therefore, appreciated? I know you can't change the system, even though you should view the case as I view it. I am merely prattling. I think the drill an admirable idea for an assemblage of nascent anchorites. The future monk will be most grateful for it. I fear the future man will revenge himself.

I think my friend's yacht starts on the 7th January. It will be away about six days. I shall be back at Esher in time. But, at that period, keep me informed of your place of abode. I would not miss you for any number of yacht excursions. On this occasion (snow promising, or stiff gales) I go to please my friend, more than myself.

All that a thankful Papa can say, to the Lady of three Pussies Black!¹—Alack!—was not the omen a death?

The best thing I can wish you at this season, is, strength to conquer the Christmas pudding! I would that I dined at home! I would eat by the dictates of common sense and a discreet appetite. As it is I plunge with knowledge aforethought into a week's dyspepsia. I shall be ridden all night by a plum-pudding-headed hag: shall taste the horrors without the vacuity of Death! We will hope better things for our grandchildren. Or, are we simply degenerate stomachs? and ought we to eat the fearful dainty (the British Cook's one great conception) with gratulation?—Adieu!

Your faithful
George Meredith

201. *To* EDWARD WALFORD

MS.: Yale. Printed: *Altschul Catalogue*, p. 24.

[Esher]
Friday, [? 1862]

My dear Walford,

Take your choice. I think I must go on Sunday to Tom Taylor's; but I'll be back early—you'll be taken care of by my housekeeper. I can only say you are welcome. Come to-morrow, if possible, by the 2 1/2 train. There's another at 4.—5/4—6.10.—You know the road. Dinner at *6 1/2*. The weather is good, and delay is bad. Decide thou!

Yours faithfully,
George Meredith

202. *To* WILLIAM HARDMAN

MS.: Garrick Club. Published: *Letters*, i. 96–97.

Esher—Island of Copsham
[January 6, 1863]

Tuck, ahoy!

Messmate! This is the weather for yachting!¹ Yo—who—hoi!—

200. ¹ Mrs. Jessopp.
202. ¹ GM was about to go on a yachting trip with Cotter Morison, Hardman, and other friends. The verses that follow are anticipatory. Hardman, in *MVP*, pp. 239–43, gives a detailed account of the actual trip, which occurred during the week of 12–18 Jan.

The *Irene* ducks and runs amuck[2]
At all she meets on Ocean bobbin':
Hard to the taffrail clutches Tuck:
There's little of the 'cock' in 'Robin'!
Below, discussing pipes and beer,
And all that may and all that mayn't be,
St. Bernard[3] says that he feels queer,
And queerer still feels Mrs. St. B.
James Parthenon[4] of tempest tells,
Five jolly yachtsmen once were lost in:
Pales the red cheek of Tuck, as swells,
With Ocean's wrath, the gorge of Austin.[5]
'Now, do you think, you Argue-nots,'[6]
St. Bernard asks, 'sea-sick was Jason?'
The jolly yachtsmen eye their cots:
Austin cries, 'Oh!'—and Tuck, 'A bason!'
St. Bernard hurries on the deck:
Not long his chattering teeth have kept tune
At waves that threat the *Irene's* wreck,
When one bears off his pipe[7] to Neptune!
Then Tuck, half doubting he's afloat,
Rolls up, with eyes all greeny-sheeny:
Clutches St. Bernard by the throat:—
'Tell me! did Cubitt[8] build the *Irene?*'
—Five jolly yachtsmen! yachtsmen five!
And have you seen five jolly yachtsmen?
If they're not dead, why, they're alive:—
They're sprawling mid the pipes and pots, men!
A ghostly yacht at night you'll see
Come sailing up the British Channel.
A poet and a Friar there be

---

[2] Cf. Alexander Pope, *Imitations of Horace*, II. i. 69–72:

> Satire's my Weapon, but I'm too discreet
> To run a Muck, and tilt at all I meet;
> I only wear it in a Land of Hectors,
> Thieves, Supercargoes, Sharpers, and Directors.

[3] Morison.

[4] James Virtue, proprietor of the *Parthenon* magazine.

[5] Charles Austin, a contributor to the *Saturday Review* and the *Standard*, who was unable to go on the yacht trip because of illness.

[6] A dig at Morison, who was fond of arguing.

[7] Hardman's note: 'Morison is proud of a handsome pipe, carved in the similitude of a zouave's head' (*MVP*, p. 244 n.).

[8] Hardman's note: 'A hit at me, and my house in Gordon Street, built by Cubitt. Robin is very fond of chaffing me about the solidity of my house as compared with his tumble-down cottage at Copsham, Esher' (ibid.).

On board: the latter frock'd in flannel.
Like Lucifers with Lobsters dash'd,
The hue upon their cheeks and noses.
The Friar cries loud: 'Our fate we've hash'd.
'Why sail'd we not i' the time of Roses?
'There was a place call'd Gordon Street;
'A planet known as Francatelli:'[9]

****

(Here the Friar ventures upon familiar and non-admissable rhymes. He threatens this Island with strange foul winds, if he is not quickly landed. He is dismissed to seek companionship with the 'Flying Dutchman')—

—Tuck of the Earth! I can't come to you to-morrow, as I have to go to Chelsea. I think St. Bernard will ask me to him for Thursday. I doubt if we meet this week.

Have you heard bad news of James Virtue? Chapman is never to be credited, and yet he alarmed me on Sunday. Thinking over it, I hope the best. If you have aught pressing to communicate, address—16 Cheyne Walk, Chelsea S. W.[10] Adieu!

Your loving
George M.

A letter from Tasmania has reached me: 'Saved *from wreck* of *Colombo*.'[11]

203. *To* W. C. BONAPARTE WYSE

MS.: Yale. Published: Ellis, pp. 180–1, with omission of the final sentence and the post-script.

Copsham, Esher
January 7, 1863

My dear Wyse,
    Brief are the oracles! The talismanic phrase of Eastern fable, is of one syllable.

202. [9] Hardman's note: 'My supposed fondness of good-living is hit off' (*MVP*, p. 244 n.).
    [10] Address of the house taken by Rossetti (see Letter 164) in which GM had a bed-room for his once-a-week trips to town and shared the dining-room as a sitting-room with the two Rossettis and Swinburne. Afterwards W. M. Rossetti remembered that GM's tenancy lasted until about Apr. 1863 (*D. G. Rossetti: His Family Letters, with a Memoir*, 1895, i. 235.), but his memory was faulty (see Letter 231).
    [11] On 24 Jan. Hardman received a damp letter from Holroyd, stamped 'Saved from the Wreck of the Colombo.' GM's letter was probably from Mrs. Louisa Twamley Meredith, a C. & H. author with whom he occasionally corresponded and whom he persuaded with some difficulty that he was not her husband's long-lost brother (*MVP*, p. 56).

In answer to your stentorian summons, I reply, 'I have been busy.' How small it looks! and yet, O parturient mountain! Mr. Ridiculus Mus is eloquent enough if you will look into him. Busy, my good sir, so as to drive the pen as fast as Stonewall Jackson is driving the Federals: busy to get money for voracious creditors: battling in the hot whirlwind, with scarce a thought of your golden sward, where you recline, watching an ever sinking sun across a quivering sea; with fair eyes over you!—

Bref: I hope to finish this dreadful work[1] in six weeks. Then I shall be free to disport. Why don't you write to me, I may ask? My darling boy is home, much improved, likes school, thanks you for your inquiries after him; is flourishing, I thank the Disposer of things! or the stamped fact!

The day I had your letter I passed through Coram: with melancholy. Thence home and to your well known handwriting. Coram had whispered as much.

Maurice FitzG[erald] was here the other day. Goes to Ireland this month. I go to try a friend's yacht next week from Portsmouth to we know not where.

He starts for the Mediterranean in February. I have promised to be due to him at Nice, or Genoa, or Naples, in March. But, I know not!

My kindest regards to your Ellen!

Your faithful
George M.

I wish you success in your litigation.[2] Above all, a speedy settlement of some sort.

204. *To* AUGUSTUS JESSOPP

MS.: Yale. Published: *Letters*, i. 97–99, with minor variants.

Esher, Surrey
Wednesday, January [7], 1863

My dear Jessopp,

Will you come on Friday evening, at 6 p.m., next week? I hope you will stay the day following, at least. I am too modest to press the cottage strongly upon you, and bid you do as it seemeth best to you.

In the matter of Anchorites. Do you really believe them to have been men of thews and breadth of brow? Yes, if they have slaughtered their dozens and begin to think Heaven a pleasant resting-place.

---

203. [1] *Emilia in England.*   [2] Over the estate of his father.

As a rule, No. Endurance is not a test of the fact. The physically robust man would have wasted and succumbed. The bilious and the nervous man will last longer than the sanguine. Physiology will tell you so much. Then again, can I morally admire, or reverence, or see positive virtue in, St. Simeon?[1] Was he a hero, of his kind? Does the contemplation of him bring us nearer to God?—To what a God! I turn aching in all my flesh to adore the Pagan, in preference. He smites kind Nature in the face, to please his God!—St. Sim[eon] may be a very strong man. Granting it, I shall think more of Milo.[2] He tears up the groaning oak, which I hold better than to pluck with fanatic fingers at the roots of humanity.—Don't you see, that it is not adoration moves the stinking Saint, but, basest of prostrations, Terror. Terror, mighty to knit a man for endurance when allied to a cringing greed for a fair celestial seat.—The truth is, you sniff the Sublime in this creature. Your secret passion is for Sublimity. Beauty you love; but, by the way; under protest; and with the sense of being a sinner. Clerical training is to blame. But, change the system. Beauty is to be sought—let Sublimity come. Both are rare: but the former is our portion—belongs to us. To deface it, is not sublime—villanous, rather! To outrage reason as well as beauty, shows the organization of a ruffian. Be not misled by this dirty piece of picturesque Religiosity, animated! My gorge rises! Plunge them into the pit, O Lord! these worshippers of the pillar.—

'Cujus ad effigiem, non tantum meiere, fas est.'[3]

Your faithful
George Meredith

205. *To* MRS. AUGUSTUS JESSOPP

MS.: Yale. Printed: *Altschul Catalogue*, p. 45 (dated Monday [*1864?*]).

Copsham, Esher
Monday, [January 19, 1863]

Dear Mrs. Jessopp,

I have just returned and find the enclosed[1] waiting here for you.

Pray, write to me, and tell me I am forgiven.

I thought that, according to your latest letter, you were most likely to be here on Wednesday: and that Friday had ceased to be a distinc-

204. [1] St. Simeon Stylites, whose mortification of the flesh surpassed that of all his fellow monks.
[2] A celebrated athlete of Crotona, Italy, famed for his great strength.
[3] Juvenal I. i. 131: 'On whose likeness it is not only proper to urinate.'
205. [1] ? A note that he had left for Jessopp. But it is clear that Jessopp had called in his absence, and one would expect such a note to be delivered to him.

tive day. Still, I cannot defend myself. I stated my case to my friends on board the yacht. They said 'Write that you have flown.' But I knew not any address;—you were to leave Norwich, on Monday, and be anywhere. Once out in the yacht, we were dependent on the winds. I was borne away, and with a racking conscience, that would torture me worse by pleading for me and not consenting to be beaten down.

Here come asterisks, for language faileth.

Indeed my punishment is sufficient: for I miss you and am not yet clear that I deserve the mischance. Why, since the holidays are extended (an indescribable boon to me), don't you remain in London, or at least away from Norwich? I write 'immediate' on my letter that it may be forwarded, in case you are not at home; and may haply still bring you to me.

Angove writes that the day of return is Tuesday. Arthur says Monday. I hope the former as I have made arrangements to take them both to the theatre on Monday night.

I trust that Mr. Jessopp will himself write to me the handwriting of reconciliation.

Adieu!

In all humbleness of spirit and body, / Your most faithful and contrite

George Meredith

206. *To* MRS. WILLIAM HARDMAN

MS.: Yale.

Esher, Surrey
Tuesday, [January 20, 1863]

Dear Mrs. Hardman,

Sons have a respite until Monday next; so, I don't think I shall sleep in Town on Thursday. And besides, I must tell you that I desire not to encounter one Tuck, who is frequently at 27,[1] and has latterly, I hear, been spreading false reports of my behaviour on board the yacht *Irene*, to his own glorification. Well for him were he as reticent!—If arrangements can be made that Tuck be absent on Thursday week, and Mr. Hardman send me a letter of apology for him (indeed he's quite at my mercy, for I have *such* things to relate of *his* doings), why, then I may come, which it will give me great pleasure to do. Hoping you are all well, and are not blown to pieces by that dreadful robust creature, rude B[oreas] in person,

I am your most faithful
George Meredith

206. [1] 27 Gordon Street, the Hardmans' address. For similar double-talk see Letter 182.

207. *To* WILLIAM HARDMAN

MS.: Garrick Club. Published: *Letters*, i. 99–100, with omissions and minor variants.

[Copsham, Esher]
Wednesday, [January 28, 1863]

Dear (at any price) Tuck!

I come. Dinner you give me at 1/2 past 5, I presume? A note to Foakes-den, if earlier. *Let* us have five minutes for a pipe, before we go. You know we're always better tempered when this is the case. I come in *full* dress to do honour to the Duke's motto.[1] Morley[2] has been here for a night. I saw my little man off on Monday, after expedition over Bank with Angove, and to Tower. Thence to Pym's,[3] Poultry:— oysters consumed by dozings. Thence to Purcell's:[4]—great devastation of pastry. Thence to Shoreditch,[5] where Sons calmly said: 'Never mind, Papa; it's no use minding it. I shall soon be back to you', and so administered comfort to his forlorn dad. My salute to the Conquered One, and I am

Your loving, hard-druv, much be-bullied
Robin

208. *To* WILLIAM HARDMAN

MS.: Garrick Club. Published: *Letters*, i. 100–1, with substantial omissions and minor variants.

Copsham
Sunday, [February 1, 1863]

Dear Tuck!

Come, if you can tear yourself away, on Wednesday. Dinner at 6 1/2. Orridge and wife, Wyndowe.[1] Robin, most anxious.

> Friar uxorious!
> Ain't it notorious
> You have no joy a-
> -way from Detroïa?

207. [1] A popular melodrama of the 1862 season was *The Duke's Motto* ('I am here!'), by John Brougham (1810–80).
  [2] John Morley (1838–1923), later Viscount Morley of Blackburn, had been at Oxford with Cotter Morison, who introduced him to GM. He became one of GM's most intimate friends and was later one of his executors.
  [3] i.e. Pimm's, in the Poultry, an oyster shop.   [4] A coffee house.
  [5] The railway station from which Arthur left for Norwich.
208. [1] Captain W. Wyndowe lived at Claygate, Esher.

And if only to revive the memory of the place, come for an afternoon. I will return with you on Thursday morning.

The dinner will be tolerable: the wines are vouched for. We are likely to have a good fine blowing afternoon for the heath and woods: if you come by 12.20 train; or even 2.25. Remember, 2.25—not 2.30.

I say no more. Only,

> Write me no pretty note
> Puling excuses.
> Scorn'd by the Muses,
> Who's tied to a petticoat!

A new Receipt:—I try it at Orridge's tonight.

'Lark Pood'n'

'A bottom of stout juicy steak, Topped by 2 dozen and 1/2 bearded oysters: Topped by 1 dozen larks.'

General sentiment, by anticipation: 'Gollopschtious!'

I have an idea that 2 kidneys *might* be introduced.

I have hitherto refrained from touching a lark: not wishing that divine bird to sing reproaches to me from Heaven, and fill the foundations of my digestion with remorse. Do I degenerate? Is it recklessness? or the noble prosecution of Science? the wish to *know* all?— Alas! that were surely punishable! Nor have I that giant desire.

Adieu! 'Tis Friendship that says 'Come!'

What reply?

> No, he *wouldn't* leave his wife,
> And he *shouldn't* leave his wife,
> He didn't come to Copsham, cos,
> He COULDN'T leave his wife!
>
> Robin Laurelpate

209. *To* WILLIAM HARDMAN

MS.: Garrick Club.

[Copsham, Esher]
[February 3, 1863]

Right Excellent Turk!—I mean, Tuck!

I confess I did not expect this noble conduct. I am surprised, and think—Can the dinner I have to give him compensate for the dreadful privation—the division of 'We' once more into errant genders etc. etc.—

If you can put in your bag six penn'orth of Parmesan cheese you will oblige me *grately*.

Till we meet / Admiringly / Your

Robin

Menu

Modeste de Copsham
Feby   th 1863

pour le service de Tuck, de Rosygildas, Prieur

Poisson

Turbot—sauce aux Câpres

Entrées

Côtelettes de mouton à la Soubise

Poulet à la Vincent

Pâtés de mouton à la Windsor

Second Service

Les pluviers d'or————Les bécassines

Entremets

La Gelée de sago: Omelette de Friar Tuck
Blanc Mange: Tourtes.
Fromage;—*Fruits etc.*, Oranges, Poires;

Vins

Sauterne 1840:—Hock—Rüdesheimer:—
du Madère, Amontillado, de Bourgogne (Romanée)
Claret—Larose.

[Marginal note]: Hors d'œuvre:—

Canapées d'anchois.

210. *To* WILLIAM HARDMAN

MS.: Garrick Club.

16 Cheyne Walk, Chelsea
1 o'clock Saturday morning
[? February 7, 1863][1]

My dear Tuck,

Rossetti says he has a model coming to-morrow, and can't put said model off, and must finish picture immediately. So begs you and Maxse to come on Friday next. And will you write *here* and say so. And excuse him. It's not possible for him to arrange otherwise.

This is an official letter, written at the hour of midnight by Tuck's loving

Robin

211. *To* WILLIAM HARDMAN

MS.: Garrick Club.

Esher
[February 9, 1863]

Bully Tuck!

I have stated the case to Bullion Johnson![1]

Between you both I am a shred, an atom.

Nay, not that; for an atom belongs to itself.

I do not.

I am as one expecting every moment to feel a dividing tug and fly asunder. I am a young man of *parts*, most verily!

How much of me do you expect to see on Thursday? Pull hard, or you won't see much more than was born 35 years ago—Oh, Lord! It's an awful long time, Tuck!

I come in *Dress*. !!!!!!!! ————

Any thing less, would be indecent, on one's birth-day.

Menu for the same.
————

Soupe, à la sage femme.
Cabillaud de mère.

210. [1] The only clue to the date of this letter is that it is filed by Hardman between the letters of 1 Feb. and 3 Feb. 1863. 31 Jan. and 7 Feb. would be the nearest Saturdays to these dates.
211. [1] GM's birthday was 12 Feb. It seems likely that both Johnson and Hardman wished to have a birthday dinner for him. At any rate he went to the Hardmans'.

Filets de smack-botbot, sauce aux larmes.[2]
Boudin à l'anaconde et sans limite.
etc. etc.

Your loving
George M.

I sleep in Chelsea to-morrow and till I see you, on Thursday, address 16 Cheyne Walk, Chelsea, S. W.

212. *To* WILLIAM HARDMAN

MS.: Garrick Club.

16 Cheyne Walk, Chelsea
Monday, [February 16, 1863]

Mr. Tuck,
    Sir:
    The meanness which has induced you to impute to the unfortunate lady whom you have, from a person, transformed to the shadowy part of a plural number and mere feeble, pallid, compulsory echo of the word 'We', expressions of annoyance with me and contempt of me, which small exercise of the arts of divination teaches me to perceive are your own dictation, if not direct utterance:—the injustice of the same:—and the absence of any apology, I having waited for the same daily and hourly: these things now inspire me to say that, to one who can be guilty of them, I scorn to defend myself.[1]—Further, let me casually remark that
    Lucas / & / Evans /
have asked Mr. Hardman / to dine with them / on / FRIDAY.[2]
The hour halfpast six.
The place 11 Bouverie Street, Fleet.
    If Mr. Hardman will call at Piccadilly between 4 and 5 o'clock on Friday, he may see Mr. George Meredith. Robin will be out.
    To-morrow to Esher. B. Johnson there on Saturday.

Mr. Tuck, sir, / Yours truly,
Georgium Sidus

211. [2] Meredithian chaff, of course.
212. [1] See following letter.
    [2] Hardman had dinner with Evans, Lucas, GM, and Dr. Andrew Wynter, contributor to *OaW* and author of *Curiosities of Civilization*, in Bouverie St., where the famous *Punch* dinners were held, on 20 Feb. The purpose of the dinner was to arrange for future articles for *OaW*, and Hardman regarded his invitation as acceptance into the ranks of contributors.

213. *To* WILLIAM HARDMAN

MS.: Garrick Club.

> Foakes den [1 New Square,
> Lincoln's Inn, London]
> [February 19, 1863]

~~Tuck, Sweet!~~ [struck out]
Dear Sir,

I go to Bullion Johnson to-night. To-morrow at the hour of three
p.m. I meet Captain Maxse and wife at 16 Cheyne Walk, Chelsea. It is
unlikely therefore that I shall be in Piccadilly after two o'clock. The
dinner is in Bouverie Street, *Once a Week* office. You will find your
way there, I trust, safely. I shall be punctual to receive you.

> Yours obediently,
> George Meredith

The Head of Joan of Arc, at Chelsea, is worth seeing.[1] I remark this
incidentally. Also, that a *friend* would come and advise as to furniture,
etc. etc. of rooms; paint, style[2]. Enough. v. sap.—Perhaps you have
written to Esher? If so there lies the letter. And, I say, Old Tuck!
did you say in it you are sorry for your virulent offensive letter that
I received in Chelsea the other day? I don't doubt but that you did.
If so, a slap on the back and we're friends again—ha! ha!—

214. *To* MRS. AUGUSTUS JESSOPP

MS.: Yale. Published: *Letters*, i. 138–9 (dated *March 1864*), with minor variants.

> [Copsham Cottage, Esher]
> Monday, March [? 1863][1]

My dear Mrs. Jessopp,

May I beg you to give my little man, on my behalf, five shillings?
He writes for half-a-crown, but we double it.

I have been disturbed of late at not hearing from him. He now says,
that he has written. The letter did not arrive. Would it be as well to
question him on the point, and make inquiries of the housekeeper?

213. [1] Rossetti's oil painting of Joan of Arc kissing the sword of deliverance. Of it,
William Michael Rossetti says, 'Nothing that my brother produced was, to my mind,
more thoroughly satisfactory than the *Joan of Arc . . .*' (*D. G. Rossetti: His Family
Letters*, i. 239).
   [2] GM was planning to build and furnish a house but never did so. (See Letter 216.)
214. [1] The evidence that this letter belongs to 1863 rather than 1864, as dated by W. M.
Meredith, is strong enough to warrant redating. The discussion of Sunday services continues a subject begun in Letter 200 to Jessopp. Other evidence will be found in Letters
215, 216, and 270.

I am so busy and bothered with work (consequently doing it ill and
—wrathful and—utterly unworthy to hold pen to you) that I break
off without a reply to your remembered last letter. Though, with
regard to the Sunday arrangements of the Schol: Norv: let me assure
you, O fair advocate, that I think you make wonderful improvements
on a state of things rather hurtful to Nature in her untamed years.
Hurtful to her, and therefore she has her revenge: a not unholy thing
when we see it to be simply the action of violated laws. Young blood
will not sit so frequently, and so long, on the seventh day, without
a desire to stir, which becomes in the brain a remonstrance. I may
say of my dear little fellow that he was not at all complaining when
he spoke to me: but casually stated a fact common to boys. Another,
too, it seems, thinks even the 7th day in Norwich a hard day: 'as
hard or harder than any one of the other six.'—The truth is, that our
Puritanism is beginning to weary even the English world, and much
as you are disposed to lighten the claims of worship to poor little
fellows, your being in East Anglia must of a necessity keep you behind
us.

Do forgive me for this! I feel already that the wind is East on me!

I hope my little man continues to satisfy *you*? His master—it is as
I predicted. But, I am sure things will turn out better by and by: can
wait—content that he should be under your care. With kindest good
fellowship salute to your husband, I am your most faithful, contrite,

George Meredith

215. *To* AUGUSTUS JESSOPP

MS.: Yale. Printed: *Altschul Catalogue*, p. 42.

Esher
Tuesday, [? March 17 or 24, 1863]

My dear Jessopp,

I know you have many pardons in your wallet—because I need
them. Emilia has been bothering me. The gestation of this young
woman is laborious.

My little man comes to me at Easter.[1] He says, for three weeks. Is it
so? I hope, not less.—Do you really like him greatly? I have a fear
that Dewe (whom he designates 'that ass!') will make him a present of
his measles, and induce him to spend his holidays in bed.

At the end of next month, if possible, I start for Sicily. Morison has
by this time reached Gibraltar. I sent you his *St. Bernard*—?[2] How do

215. [1] Easter was 5 Apr. in 1863.
 [2] Cotter Morison's *Life and Times of St. Bernard, Abbot of Clairvaux*, published by

you like the work? The Duel between Criticism and Dogmatism is not so well done: but the rest is excellent. I anticipate dissatisfaction on your part.

Alas! I can conceive the heterodox object I am in the sight of Mrs. Jessopp, after my last letter to her. I am in the spirit like poor Dewe in the flesh: a spotted thing, that entertains opinions of his own. Assure her, notwithstanding, that I have not yet grown to be sentimental about the devil: nay, believe in him, and want to see him well thrashed: and dislike to hear him invoked by weary people sitting on hard seats listening to a sounding homily

> —while the worn-out clerk[3]
> Brow-beats his desk below

My friends! You at least will have charity for such an outcast. Commending myself to you most confidently, I am

Your loving
George Meredith

216. *To* WILLIAM HARDMAN

MS.: Garrick Club. Published: *Letters*, i. 103, with omissions and inaccuracies.

Picadil
[March 20, 1863]

Tuck, great Archer!
  Thrice thy shaft has hit me!
  On Thursday night we meet at Robert Cook[e]'s.
  On Wednesday shall I dine with thee?
  I am overwhelmed with disgust at Emilia. Am hurrying her on like ye deuce. She will do. But, ahem!—she must pay. I have taken some trouble with her and really shall begin to think her character weak in this respect, if she don't hand me what I think due, speedily.

  I'm *afraid*, considering hopes of cash, house to build, land to buy, that *Once a Week* will hold me from St. B. and the blue Medi T.

  A letter at last from Sons, of the sweetest! I have mooned and crooned in a rapture ever since.

C. & H. had appeared several weeks earlier. Writing of it to Holroyd in February, Hardman said, 'All the reviewers have remarked the traces of Carlylese language which are distinctly to be seen here and there throughout the book. Originally the work was strongly impregnated with this Carlylese element, but happily Morison had the good sense to be guided by Meredith, to whom he submitted it, and expunged the greater part of it. It is only by oversight that any of it remains to be found fault with' (*MVP*, p. 249).   [3] Tennyson, 'To J. M. K.'

Longing to see you, and with $\mathscr{L}$· to a person who will pardon the impudence and is not of the great host who care only to see two strokes put through the middle of that eloquent letter,

Your devoted

George M.

217. *To* WILLIAM HARDMAN

MS.: Garrick Club.

[Esher]

[March 25, 1863]

O have you seen my Tuck? my bonny bonny Tuck!
O have you seen my Tuck? my darling and my dear!
He carries of his paunch like a ship about to launch,
(Bis) With his body-guard of Bass's bitter beer!

(Chorus) He carries etc.

Tupperian Chorus. He carries a million times etc.

O I have seen your Tuck! your bonny bonny Tuck!
O I have seen your Tuck! your darling and your dear!
He followed of his paunch like a mighty avalanche,
(Bis) With his body-guard of Bass's bitter beer!

Little Martin Tupper[1]
Sang for his supper
In such pretty verses,
Praised the Northern Lass,[2]
Deep from Tuck the curses
Came from Beer of Bass.

[Unsigned]

217. [1] Martin Farquhar Tupper (1810–89), author of *Proverbial Philosophy* (1838) and a popular versifier held in scorn by serious students of poetry. In honour of Princess Alexandra's arrival in England to marry the Prince of Wales, Tupper had written an *Ode of Welcome*, two copies of which, printed on white satin, were sent by the Queen to Osborne, to be placed on the dressing-tables of the bridal pair. The ode, published by James Virtue, roused Hardman's ire, and he sent his friend Virtue an amusing parody, 'By Mighty Foolish Tupper, A.S.S., Author of *Proverbial Folly*', beginning—

A hundred thousand Curses!
A hundred thousand Curses!
And fifty millions more!
On him who printed verses
We ne'er heard like before.

(*MVP*, p. 284.)

[2] Princess Alexandra, whose name Tupper rhymed with 'Most Welcome Wand'rer'.

218. *To* WILLIAM HARDMAN

MS.: Garrick Club.

Copsham
Monday, [March 30, 1863]

Dearest Tuck; Loyal One!

The little man comes on Wednesday. Can you receive us for that night? He arrives at Shoreditch at 6.30, so I can't dine with you.

Mrs. Jessopp retires from the controversy ap: Religious exercises on Sunday: by begging that I will not impress Sons with my opinions. I reply that they are in his nature: if unaroused as yet will not be summoned forth by me.

Hearty worshipper of Princesses![1] Adieu! To the Great Mother,[2] my profound respects (since more is not permitted).

Trusting that We are well,

Your loving
George M.

Chorus. 'With his body-guard' etc.

219. *To* WILLIAM HARDMAN

MS.: Garrick Club.

Copsham
[April 6, 1863]

Dear Tuck,

Little man has got measles coming out.[1]

Now, may I trouble you to send me globule bottles of Puls: and any other medicine necessary; stating what to be given during the dort[2] of fever etc.

I know I may ask you to do this service.

If all goes well, I will pass the Thursday with you where you like.

Your loving
George M.

218. [1] See Note 1, preceding letter.
 [2] Hardman's mother, Mrs. Knowles.
219. [1] Arthur, home for the Easter holidays, had been made 'a present' of the measles by a schoolmate named Dewe (Letter 215).
 [2] 'A sulky or sullen mood or humor; the sulks. [Prov. Eng. & Scotch]' (*The Century Dictionary and Cyclopedia*).

220. *To* WILLIAM HARDMAN

MS.: Garrick Club. Published: *Letters*, i. 103–4, with omissions and variants.

Copsham
Wednesday, [April 8, 1863]

Dearest Tuck,

Your medicines and directions came opportunely, deciding me not to send for Izod. Sons are as a mulberry in the shade. They are spotted like the pard. They are hot as boiled cod in a napkin. They care for nothing but barley-water, which I find myself administering at all hours of the night, and think it tolerable bliss, and just worth living for, to suck an orange. I am sorry to say they have a rather troublesome cough. Otherwise all goes well.

Do you dine me on Thursday night? Even where you may please. A word to Lincoln's Inn, if anywhere but at Gordon Street.

Your loving
George M.

221. *To* FREDERICK A. MAXSE

MS.: Maxse Papers. Envelope postmarked *Ap 16 63* and addressed to Captain Maxse, R.N., Highwood, Romsey, Hants.

Copsham, Esher
Wednesday, [April 15, 1863]

My dear Maxse,

I hope you're comfortable in the new nest, and approve of the surroundings. I am very anxious to see you, if only for this reason, that I can cure you of you[r] dyspeptic ailment and wash rose into your cheeks instead of yellow. Let me briefly say, take exercise: but not much walking. Open the chest vigorously, to give play to the vital organs. Above all things, see that you *sweat* daily, and not to a small degree. This relieves the system and saves it from a clog: also keeps the blood sweet. I have a dozen recommendations to give, but will wait. Do not, I entreat you, take what they call strengthening medicines.

I shall send you proofs of *Emilia* shortly. Let me know your *first* impression, because that will be nearer to the public view. I can trust you to speak plainly.

I doubt whether I can manage to spare time for the Mediterranean after all. Perhaps I will come to you, an if you can receive me, in May for a day or two. Are you near the New Forest?

By the way, my darling little man came home at Easter, measly exceedingly. He has been carefully nursed and now runs at large with eyes like two agates (in crystal currents of clear morning seas!)

Swinburne has ready a volume of poems[1] of a kind to attract notice. My kindest regards to Mrs. Maxse. My love to boy.[2] Arthur will not go to school for another week or so. He is writing Tales and Dramas. Poland and Mdlle Pustovozdova?[3]

Your loving
George M.

222. *To* WILLIAM HARDMAN

MS.: Garrick Club.

Copsham, Esher
Friday, [April 17, 1863]

My dearest Tuck,

Just returned—letter from you!—A thousand pardons that I did not answer. The dear little man is perfectly sound again and chirping— Zillah on her back, and as one budding all over—budding slowly.[1]

Next week on Thursday I go to Bullion J[ohnson]. He comes on Saturday following if all favourable. When do you?

In haste for Oxshott post.

Your loving / (with the small amount to
[? due] you)
George M.

221. [1] ? *Poems and Ballads* (1866). T. Earle Welby, *A Study of Swinburne* (n.d.), p. 72, says that 'all but sixteen of the pieces seem to have been composed in 1862–1865'. *Atalanta in Calydon*, however, appeared in Apr. 1865.

[2] Frederick Ivor (later Gen. Sir Ivor), born 22 Dec. 1862.

[3] At the outbreak of a Polish insurrection Mlle Pustovoydova, daughter of a Russian father and a Polish mother, joined the insurrectionists, and when the Poles hesitated before infantry fire at Grochowiska, she rode up and led them forward. Later she took refuge in Austria and was imprisoned by the government, which, however, ordered her release shortly before GM's letter (information from a dispatch by *The Times'* Special Correspondent [14 Apr.], who makes a point of the spelling of her name which I have adopted).

222. [1] Arthur had, in turn, made her a present of the measles.

223. *To* AUGUSTUS JESSOPP

MS.: Yale. Published: *Letters*, i. 104–5 (dated *Sept. 1863*), with minor variants. In W. M. Meredith's copy of *Letters* (Bodleian Library) the date has been altered to *May*, and in the second edn. of *Letters* the letter appears on p. 105 with other letters of May. Excerpt published: Ellis, p. 182 (dated August).

Esher
Monday, [April 27, 1863]

My dear Jessopp,

There is a 10.57 train from London to your City—which snatches small boys from the hearts of their parents. On Tuesday next, my little recovered rosy man will journey down, alone, by that train, chewing the cud of anticipating fancy (I hope). The Guard will be bribed to keep eye on him. Will you send some person to meet him? He will be somewhat at sea, with his swoln bag, in the press of an arrival.

Thank Mrs. Jessopp, from me, for her last letter.

She will know, that, whatever Jerrard's inconsiderate relatives might do, *my* care for the sanatory condition of K[ing] Ed[ward] 6th's Grammar School is too great to permit me to allow a convalescent to return without performance of proper quarantine. I expect great praise from her. And indeed, my heart is heavy at parting. I let him go from me now under a high sense of duty. What strange dispensation is it which gives you my boy for the best portion of his young years?—

I am in alarm about his boating on your river before he can swim.

Is there always some responsible, careful, fellow in the boats with the youngsters? Pray, tell me.

And also, write to me, I beg, to let me know that he comes safe to you. Address, Chapman & Hall, for Wednesday morning.

As to your book,[1] those publishers will not do. I should certainly put my finger on Macmillan. If not, then Longman, who is a gentleman, as well as man of business.

I had the pleasure of exchanging salutes with Mr. Jessopp of Cheshunt[2] on Friday morning, as I was returning from Hoddesdon.

If you will take me in for a few days at the end of May or beginning of June, I will gladly come, and see some cricket, among other things.

Your ever faithful
George Meredith

223. [1] A book of Jessopp's sermons published in 1864.
[2] Between Waltham Cross and Hertford. It was the birth-place of Augustus Jessopp.

224. *To* FREDERICK A. MAXSE

Text: typed copy, Maxse Papers. Published: *Letters*, i. 101–3, with omissions.

Esher

Tuesday, [Early May 1863]

My dear Maxse,

The principle of health is this, to make good blood plentifully, and to distribute it properly. Exercise of the right sort, acting on seasonable diet, keeps the machine clear. Sweating saves us from *impurities*, at all events. The form of exercise must depend upon observation of our peculiar economy. As a *rule*, walking much is only good for people in health, any other exercise you can stop the moment you've had enough: but you can't exactly time your distances: and the instantaneous effect of fatigue, where there's one weak function, is to fall upon it bodily. A weak stomach is thus awfully oppressed by long walks. Then again, walking does not *force* the blood about, and there are exercises that specially suit a stomach demanding a quick flow of blood to help digestion. Avoid purgatives. If you think something wanted, take at night (an hour clear of eating and drinking) three globules of Nux Vomica (Homoeopathic). Don't fear that your system will hold out against them.

My best solitary exercise, is, throwing the beetle—a huge mallet weighing 18 or 19 pounds—and catching the handle, performing wondrous tricks therewith. The best in the world is *fencing*, which braces the nerves, tightens muscles, occupies brain, better than anything going: contains fit measure of excitement and is thorough exercise. Boxing is a little brutal, though good. Fencing brightens the eye without blackening it. Avoid beer, which is gaseous exceedingly. You see, very old ale is too strong for the head, if drunk as ale: and the young unseasoned beer we drink has to be digested with difficulty. Avoid new wines. A bottle of oldish claret might serve you four days. See that it's good and sound. That makes blood without heating. Your evenings—but what are an Englishman's evenings? Hotbeds of dyspepsia, as a rule. There should be liveliness, music, billiards, dancing, dialogue, sunless laughter—*choice* of all these. Instead of which—I ask you!

Don't *drive* your mind a step.

I hope I shall come to you soon, and then we'll see better what your condition is. We must hear the nightingales together. Last night I had them all round me on the heath. The woods were one orchestral semicircle. What priceless weather, O my friend! And how of your Ladye? Ah, happy you! At this season what a beggar am I, that hold out my hand and touch space at my fingers' ends! Back comes the blood to my heart, which says, 'Well! let's strike on like a hammer, then!' Ding-dong, is my tune.

I saw Borthwick the other day, and see that your brother has got Heligoland, where his wife will help to make him popular.[1] Altogether a good appointment, my Lord! Here the Princesse Françoise marries the Duc de Chartres.[2] First cousins! But necessity of state overbears the duties of flesh. They must marry something Royal, and what if their children howl, or hang limp, so long as the blood is kept pure?— The philosopher laughs sadly at these things. He inclines to say 'Down with Institutions!' They do much for us—do they not undo more? The truth is that everything that is would be right (according to the optimist, who sees half the truth) would be right, I say, if we were just wise enough to pluck the flower and not tie ourselves to the roots. So the age of an Institution (*quiconque*) becomes the slavery of its supporters. To know when a thing hath perished, or is vital, is one of the tests of wisdom. Figure to yourself a lover who hears a voice in his ghastly bosom, demanding answer to the question—'Was it all delusion?' And thus he bases his logic—'Impossible; it could not be delusion, for the dream was so immense, the rapture so heavenly.' We all cling to the days that were and won't be sons of Time. To be the sticks and stones of a glorified past day we think better.—Better be men, I say!

Alas! those visits of the meek and guileless clergy! Thou errant one, that art invited to archery Meetings!—'tis to the pew thou art being lured, or dragged perforce.

Love to boy. My kindest regards to your beloved, and know me ever

Your loving
George M.

225. *To* FREDERICK A. MAXSE

Text: typed copy, Maxse Papers. Published: *Letters*, i. 105–6, with omissions.

Esher
Monday, May [1863]

My dear Maxse,

I believe fully that the globules are efficacious. I have seen them produce the effects specifically intended. Never employ anopathic purgatives.

---

224. [1] *The Times* had announced on 4 May the appointment of 'Captain Maxse' to the governorship of Heligoland. But both the *DNB* and Boase state that he was appointed lieutenant-governor in 1863, governor in 1864. (He had been a major since 1855, was promoted to lieutenant-colonel on 6 July 1863.)
    [2] The wedding took place on 11 June.

Vegetable diet is generator of gases in a weak stomach. Moreover the pasturing on grass does not make a soul milder. My experience is this: that no healthy person ever takes to vegetable diet, excluding meat: but that some people may make themselves more clean and sound if they do so. For the reason that *weak* blood is apt to be irritated by the juices of flesh, which are too strong for it. All that I have ever known take to vegetable diet were scrofulous, in the second or third degree: not robust and pure. The best thing for you, now and then, is a chop and bread for dinner. If the stomach is quite down, eschew potatoes as well as beer. In exercise see mainly that you *open the chest.* Don't sit long at a time. Read out for a space. Rise quickly in the morning. Exercise after bath; and pray do not be more than half an hour without feeding, if you only take a crust of bread and water. Your Moulsey [Molesey][1] habit of long morning fasts, I remember. To bed early: but if you feel heavy take dumb-bell exercise. This must bring you round. Continue pepsine, with now and then a halt. Take no 'iron'. A wineglass of quinine half an hour before dinner for three or four days running might do good.

I feel that such a case must be serious, my dear fellow, and that I can give the right advice. So I fill my letter with the same, to the exclusion of pleasanter topics.

My love to boy and salute to his Mama.

Let me hear how you get on. I will do my best to come soon. (I have lately been slain by a pretty face and am outcast of my warm philosophy.)[2]

> Your faithful
> George M.

226. *To* WILLIAM HARDMAN

MS.: Garrick Club.

> 193 Piccadilly, London, W.
> Wednesday, May 27, 1863

Chèr Tück,

Lucas *is*, there is no doubt:—never was.

Yes. Let us even dine together on Thursday. I will comfort thee. O thou sorely-used Friar![1] Yesterday, I went out for a holiday. Did

225. [1] Where Maxse had lived earlier.
  [2] Unless the owner of the pretty face was one of the Misses Vulliamy—possibly Marie —I am without a suggestion. (See Letters 249 and 250.)
226. [1] Because Lucas had not yet published Hardman's 'Tar and Feathers'.

you? I got among people with chicken and ham and salads and trombones. Enjoyed it *very* much. Chèr Tuck! Hampton Court is a charming place. Whither whither whither whither am I whirling, 'cause I see a pretty girl who sets her hair a-curling! And that she is a darling is certain, as I tell ye. Her eyes are grey: she does her hair à la Sir Peter Lely. Of all the heads in Hampton Court she likest to the Grammont.² Not often will you find her match—I'd wager many a damn on't! And as for me, you won't find mine, search through the fools of History. God bless thee, Tuck, austere and stoutest! Woman is a mystery!—

Your loving
George M.

227. *To* MRS. AUGUSTUS JESSOPP

Text (? fragment): typed copy made by a bookseller, Pierpont Morgan Library.

Esher
[*c.* June 8, 1863]¹

My little man's birthday is on the 13th. If I possibly can contrive to run down for it, I will. But it would not be possible for me to come before Friday. I have been working so hard lately that I have had no time to write or come whither my heart would have carried me.

In haste, / Ever your faithful
George Meredith

228. *To* WILLIAM HARDMAN

MS.: Garrick Club.

Esher
Tuesday, [June 9, 1863]

Dearest Tuck,

I feel anxious about D. Troïa, and should like to have news.¹

The King and Queen² departed this morning.—Ahem! more when we meet. Dictum, on the whole, against a particular supposition. At least, no sign of full sail yet; or even 'half reef'.³

226. ² Sir Peter Lely's portrait of the Countess de Grammont in the Portrait or Communication Gallery at Hampton Court.
227. ¹ A note on the letter, presumably written by Mrs. Jessopp on the original, reads, 'June, probably '63 or '64'. In 1863 the 13th fell on a Saturday.
228. ¹ Mrs. Hardman had been called to Liverpool by the serious illness of her father.
    ² Mr. and Mrs. N. E. S. A. Hamilton. The allusion to them as 'Royal Society' at the end of the letter is facetious.
    ³ This sounds as though there had been talk of Mrs. Hamilton's being pregnant.

I think, if I can manage it, I shall go to Sons on Friday. His blessed 10th annual salute to the Sun of his creation, is for Saturday. Going, I shan't return till the holidays have commenced, and may stop two days midway with Bull[io]n Johnson. Then we will offer ourselves to Tuck's embrace for a day.

Ah, such radiant, blusterously-beautiful, darling capricious weather! —Fond as I am of Royal Society, I sighed for a fat friar whom I know. The Lord be merciful to him, and me for loving him!

George M.

229. *To* Mrs. Augustus Jessopp

MS.: Yale. Published: *Letters*, i. 82–83 (undated but placed with the letters of late 1862), with variants.

Copsham, Esher
Monday, [? June 15, 1863]

My dear Mrs. Jessopp,

I thought I might have come on Friday; but on that day—I have three masters; and this is not a figure of speech, but a fact in the flesh. I could not get out of harness till 3 p.m. and the 4 [o'clock] express would have brought me to you too late. I should have liked so much to see the boys and my boy among them. He has grown strange to me in the long absence. . . . Now this is my proposition:—You will see it is delivered under the perfect conviction that I am welcome, and even wanted:—as thus: I will come to you this quarter for a week and bring home my little man at its close:—or:—I will come to you the next quarter for 2–3 weeks, lighter of heart, less burdened on head. I will then write nothing but poetry (not of the hedges and ditches), and I will bloom my best.

There!—You shall decide. If I come now I shall certainly not be sad about it: I am certain to be pleased: I can make all arrangements with a week's warning: but I am under some pressure: for this reason, among others, that my fastidiousness has made me turn from my new work to cut to pieces four printed chapters of *Emilia* (who begins to dissatisfy me totally, as do all my offspring that have put on type).— If I come next quarter this gloom and uncertainty will have vanished.

You will flatter me by deciding. I state the case—act thou. You know I shall be happy under the roof that holds my dearest; and more, among my dearest friends: so let your mandate be what it may, hesitate not.—Have I fixed the onus upon you cleverly? I have simply put matters as they stand.

What an unpleasant thing for Holden[1] is that scarlet-fever case! The disease has been going the round of all the public schools. May Norwich be spared! Yes; I *trust*; but parental humanity is anxious.

I shall write to Mr. Jessopp in a few days. Pray, let me hear speedily.

Your ever faithful
George Meredith

230. *To* AUGUSTUS JESSOPP

MS.: Yale. Printed: *Altschul Catalogue*, p. 43 (dated ? *1863*).

Esher
Sunday, [? June 21, 1863]

My dear Jessopp,

How can I thank you both for the capital photograph of my dear little man!—It's of no use saying how sorry I am that I can't be present at this year's grand illumination and break-up, when you, great Fount of things to blossom in after time, bless your flock, dispersing!—The truth, as you divine, I doubt not, is, that I am in harness. I have partly bound myself to a fresh serial,[1] to begin in late Autumn. Tell me, can you come to me before you start for either of the Poles?—I shall be here till July 7th, and your coming would make me glad. I shall not expect to hear from you, till your grinding labours give you pause. Meantime I promise, if you can take me in sometime next quarter, to be under your roof for a short term, and go through the Controversy, haply to be beaten!

Your faithful
George Meredith

231. *To* WILLIAM MICHAEL ROSSETTI[1]

Text: *Letters from George Meredith to Various Correspondents*, p. 6.

[Copsham, Esher]
June 27, 1863

My dear William R.,

Owing to an absurd confusion of dates in my mind, I had fancied the day of debit was this following week.[1]

229. Presumably Hubert Ashton Holden, LL.D. (1822–96), editor of Aristophanes and headmaster of Queen Elizabeth's School, Ipswich (1858–83).
230. [1] The plans for the serial were later cancelled.
231. [1] William Michael Rossetti (1829–1919), art critic, editor, biographer; brother of Dante Gabriel. This letter relates to GM's rent for the room he maintained in D. G. Rossetti's house at 16 Cheyne Walk, Chelsea.

I will bring you the money on Monday, and pray say to Gabriel everything in my excuse. I can conceive now that my recent absence from the house must look odd to him.

Your faithful
G. M.

232. *To* AUGUSTUS JESSOPP

MS.: Yale. Printed: *Altschul Catalogue*, pp. 43–44.

Esher, Surrey
Sunday, [June 28, 1863]

My dear Jessopp,

You don't say whether you will come to me; or that you have a contrivance for a meeting. Will you come on Wednesday [July 1]? or on Friday afternoon [July 3]? We are here till Monday [July 6], when we go to Sussex, and so round among various counties. On Monday [June 29] I am in town, but engaged first, to see the match (Gentlemen and Players) at Lord's; and then at the St. James's Club. Tuesday [June 30]—what will you do on Tuesday? I presume you have your hours marked, as you have mentioned those two days. I shall hope to see you here on Wednesday.

What you say gives me great rest of spirit, àpropos of my boy: but a man bears his own burden while he can do so. I should always feel at peace in leaving my darling to your care, either in my going for a term or for good. So, you love him? He is a charming nature: wanting briskness, nevertheless. *Strength* may be infused. Example and teaching might marvellously develop his moral quality.

Enfin, I want to see you both, and shall think (I beg Mrs. Jessopp to note) *shall think*, if you don't come, that forgiveness may be Christian, but is not cultivated in a garden I wot of. *Argal*, that garden must prove itself not infidel.

Please, reply. If I have time, I will look in at the R[oyal] Academy on Monday; about 1 1/2 to 2. Visit the North room at that hour.

By the way, I am grieved to hear of Reineke's quitting the school. How and why? My Son turned his head with a twinkling eyelid when he told me. Reineke's farewell speech dwells with him yet.

Your loving
George Meredith

233. *To* WILLIAM HARDMAN

MS.: Garrick Club. Excerpt published: *Letters*, i. 106–7, with inaccuracies.

[Copsham, Esher]
[June 30, 1863]
The Record
of Robin's Sad Effort to
Fool
for the beguilement of his Sovereign Lord
Tuck[1]

'A lady, the other day, having cut half her acquaintance, cut her own finger!'

Nay, my Lord, spare the lash! I will yet better. 'Such is the severity of *rating* in St. Pancras parish that a tom-cat, while trying to get over Mr. William Hardman's garden defenses, was cast-*rated* in the effort.'

Ha? ha?—What! Still frowns my Lord? Yet again we try!

'Robin, on being told that he was imitating the jesting of Burnand, replied: "Didn't I tell you I was Robin' Burnand?"' My Lord! My Lord!—

On receiving your commands, I thought first of hunting up the King and Queen[2] for matter new and strange: but lots of calls on me keep me away from them. I dined yesterday with one Creyke,[3] Lord Carlisle's secretary, who met Swinburne at Milnes',[4] and got him to bring about a meeting: after which, to astonishment of Poet, said P. was dropped. We dined at St James's Club, after passing the afternoon at Lord's Cricket Ground, where we saw Gentlemen against Players—first-rate match, and I had a fine set of characters about me: old country squires; knights and lords; old cricketing hands hot for the honour of the game. Notably a Colonel Mundy[5] amused me, and shall see himself if he looks one day in a book of mine. Then in the evening talks Creyke of ME: of the effect of my work on him: and to the effect that in the circles he best knew, your Robin had made impression deep. That: that: and that!—He's a nice fellow; with good sense: handsome: of the world, and a little more. He succeeded Herbert Wilson,

233. [1] Hardman was in Liverpool, where Mrs. Hardman's father had died on 23 June, leaving Mrs. Hardman 'a very handsome fortune'. Hardman speaks of 'spending a mouldy fortnight at Liverpool' and of the amusing letters that GM wrote him while he was there (S. M. Ellis, *The Letters and Memoirs of Sir William Hardman*, 1925, pp. 45–48); cited hereinafter as *L. & M.*)

[2] Mr. and Mrs. N. E. S. A. Hamilton.

[3] Robert Gregory Creyke, called by Thackeray in a letter to Lady Stanley 'my disciple Mr. Creyke, who was with Lord Carlisle in Ireland' (Gordon N. Ray, *The Letters and Private Papers of William Makepeace Thackeray*, Cambridge, Mass., 1946, iv. 84).

[4] Richard Monckton Milnes (1st Baron Houghton), 1809–85.

[5] Doubtless Lt.-Col. Charles Fitzroy Miller Mundy, of the Bengal Staff Corps.

who succeeded Charles Sheridan, as Madame Doche's[6] lover. Gave me
lots of Parisian life, and English.

To-day I go to Jessopp, in town, and I send my Tuck a letter I've
had from him. Preserve it for me. On Monday I go to 'Seaford, Sussex',
for a week or ten days.[7]

Sons accompany me, of course. I shall probably be out of sight for
three weeks. By the way, Is there a fellow called Foakes extant?

O cruelty, super-refined! To tell your enamoured Robin of the
Great M[other] sending him 'keind remembrances'.

I'll write a real sort of letter to you in a day or two. This is done in
a ten-minutes' rush while the whistle of Esher's train calls me over the
common.

Now, I pray you Tuck, give my sincere love to Demitroïa; and tell
her that my heart is with her in good or ill. I hope to see her soon, and
to see her smiling the pleasant familiar smile that becomes half the
happiness of those who have the honour to be ranked her friends.

Among whom is—and if not it is the fault of a fat man, nameless—
is?—Let us say without question, in confident good heart is

Tuck's faithful (too fond)
George Meredith

I shall take another medium for conveying my sentiments to the
Lancashirian Dame.[8] I turn to my Homer.—Tuck! was the Great
M[other] born from the foam of the sea? And did she come up the
Mersey into Liverpool originally on a shell? And also—I was going to
ask, and also—you know Homer says Laughter and smiles distinguish
that famous Lady of the Apple. It has struck me—I am indeed slain
by the thought.

234. *To* WILLIAM HARDMAN

MS.: Garrick Club. Published: *Letters*, i. 107–8, with substantial omissions and numerous
inaccuracies; omitted verses and excerpts published: *L. & M.*, pp. 47–48.

[Copsham, Esher]
Saturday, [July 4, 1863]

The world is full of different fates,
Of good and evil luck:
Happy is he who at Love's gates,
May cross the T of Tuck!

[6] Marie-Charlotte-Eugénie de Plunkett Doche (1821–1900), French actress whose
youth and beauty made her début at the Vaudeville in 1838 a success.
[7] To visit Maurice FitzGerald.
[8] Hardman's mother, Mrs. Knowles, 'Great Mother of the Pantagruelians', who lived
in Lancs.

My friends in smiles of Fortune bask,
  The flowers of Fortune pluck:
I envy not: I only ask
  To cross the T of Tuck.

Survey man's race: the few in front,
  The many in the ruck!

A fit of sneezing arrests the Muse. Chime the rhyme, great friar! chime the rhyme; and cross the T!

Dropping out of Ch[apman] & Hall's the other day, I fell on the placid face of Poco.[1] Who, without the ruffle of his surface, received me, that would have sent a hundred million ripples coursing rosily over Tuck. The Signor Poco spoke of a 'fat man'—poor vulgarian that he is! and without reverence, or holiness. Not yet of the elect! Yet is this foreigner hopeful, and one, let us hope (as we may), of a right excelling future. He hath desire in him for companionship among the Pantag[ruelian]s: humble desire; and he taketh his occasional, most healthful, snubbing. He is going to send you the *Court Journal*. I may as well give you the last report of the H. R. H's.[2] The Prince took a ride: the Princess took a drive. *Verbum sap*:—By the way, Creyke told me that when the Prins[3] was at the Curragh, he came to the Viceregal Lodge and played cricket. Creyke warned all the opposition bowlers that the Royal patronage of the manly game depended on the Prins getting at least ONE RUN. Having missed, while fielding, two fine smack-into-the-hand catches, Wales goes in. And faced an unwarned, steady, determined Briton of a bowler: round; ruddy—an inevitable creature: one clearly selected by the Gods to do this black business with the utmost satisfaction and comfort. Down went the wicket of your Prins at the FIRST DELIVERY OF BALL!—To make the matter worse, some wretches (not knowing that the wicket was a Royal one, or not feeling that to knock it over was rank treason to the Throne and to Cricket) applauded lustily. Your Prins marched out with his bat amid the thunders. *He hasn't played from that day!*

At the first ball his wicket fell, and sins
No more has batted your illustrious Prins.

234. [1] Lionel G. Robinson (1839–1923), for many years a member of the Directing Branch of the Exchequer and Audit Department at Somerset House; editor of the *Annual Register*, 1879–1900. At the time of this letter he was living with his parents next door to the Hardmans. Hardman introduced him to GM, who promptly dubbed him Poco (*poco curante*).

  [2] The Prince and Princess of Wales. The Princess's pregnancy was already a matter of speculation.

  [3] A spelling borrowed from Thackeray's 'Diary of Jeames de la Pluche'.

There, Tuck! Now don't say I'm not out harvesting for your delight.
And I'll get more stories for you—don't fear!

[Unsigned]

235. *To* WILLIAM HARDMAN

MS.: Garrick Club. Published: *Letters*, i. 108, with scrambled order of pages (1, 3, 4, 2)
and omissions and inaccuracies.

[Copsham, Esher]
[? July 6, 1863][1]

Dearest Cupid—Tuck!

I thought it all along! I said: 'This—my friar whom I love—must
be the Rosy Boy well plumped on British fare', and now that the
G[reat] M[other] (Oh!—dost thou mark a similarity of initials, most
wondrous? Yea, is it not full of meaning?—) acknowledges that she
came up the Mersey in a cockleshell, Tuck cannot deny that he is
Cupidon. And 'tis he who has twanged his bow and done his Robin
this dreadful damage—alack! No more of this. But, seriously, I am
filled with a flame that must be quenched. Find thou the tank.—I am
amazed at the thought of thee in thy natural costume, most rubicund!
The wings!—The!—We will talk as mortals, not forfeiting what we
do know, ne'ertheless.

The other day, another man, a publisher, asked me to read for him.[2]
I have hesitated: am tempted. Anything for hard cash.—ha! ha! how it
must make you roar to see me picking up my miserable pennies.

You, leaning over the thigh of a fat Olympian cloud floating over
Copsham. I see you turn to Demitroïa-Psyche. 'Poor Robin', you say.
'Let's have him here', says she. 'He'll never get to Heaven', says you,
'till a woman brings him.' 'True', sighs D.-P.

(Damn that Tuck—he kisses her, pretending she wants [to] be
consoled!—Has Olympus no shades?—)

Write to me,
care of Maurice FitzGerald, Esq. / Seaford, / Sussex.

I shall be there perchance a week and yet a day more, unless they
gamble awfully.

Tuck! that I love thee thou knowest. Equally with thee, her who
seemeth as thy full half (spiritually, be it understood). May the Disposer of things continue to bless ye both. A special salute to one Potter,

235. [1] Not dated but filed by Hardman between the letters of 4 and 10 July.
[2] The publisher was C. Warren Adams, a friend of the Duff Gordons who had
acquired the firm of Saunders & Otley.

the emanation of Tuck, in whom he sees himself beginning again. Under slightly different conditions. Please remember me kindly to all who care for me. Why don't you tell me how your sisters are? They're married, you know. You're right to protect your mother, but your sisters have husbands. Good-bye. I hope to be able to spin livelier rubbish after I have taken rail and seen new men, fresh faces, other minds.

George M.

236. *To* WILLIAM HARDMAN

MS.: Garrick Club. Published: *Letters*, i. 109–10, with numerous omissions and inaccuracies.

Seaford, Hades[1]
Friday, [July 10, 1863]

Dear Tuck,

(A letter to the above address will find me.) Oh!—but rage and anguish stifle me. I tell thee, Tuck,—why should I tell thee who carest not—? Here am I become as an animal. Our life is monstrous. I see my Copsham stomach with all its (figurative) hair on end at the sight of its Seaford transformation. My breakfast would supply a work-house: my luncheons are equal to the refection of four fat friars: my dinner would satiate the soul of a ticket-of-leave man. I go to bed when Apollo lays his red nose over the eastern hill, and the light-foot hours carry it on their shoulders in triumph to 27 Gordon Street, what time Tuck, with a final snore, says 'Blow it!' and consents to rise. Up to three p.m. I loo,[2] and even Cupid-T[uck] will praise me for objecting to be lewd. Indeed there is much petticoat here, but I have ceased to be of the order of the sniffing man (*der Sniffirender*) and cry for soul—till a man with a fish-basket stops before me, remarking 'Werry fine ones to-day, sir; fresh!'—Not the vast sea can give me what I want!— Here is Frank Burnand that reeks a pun from every pore. Maurice and Gerald[3] FitzGerald: Signor Vignati,[4] Hyndman[5] (Cambridge),

236. [1] GM was on a visit to Maurice FitzGerald.
[2] Burnand (i. 360) says that FitzGerald was very fond of a quiet game of 'Cambridge loo'. [3] Elder brother of Maurice.
[4] Identified by H. M. Hyndman (*The Record of an Adventurous Life*, p. 69) as 'an Italian . . . some connection of Fitzgerald's . . .'.
[5] H. M. Hyndman (1842–1921), the Socialist leader, then a Cambridge undergraduate and a member of the Sussex County Cricket eleven. The meeting with GM at Seaford was the beginning of a fifty-year friendship, and in *The Record of an Adventurous Life* Hyndman devotes several pages to GM at Seaford. In spite of its unpleasant associations with Mary Ellen in earlier years, Hyndman says that GM 'was almost as jolly as Burnand, whose unfailing good spirits and happy humour have always been the wonder of his friends from his early days upwards' (pp. 69–70).

Laurence,[6] painter, and others coming. I suppose I shall stop through next week. I don't think it possible for me to *start* with you.[7] Of course I shall follow you:—don't fear! You have a little wounded and shot an arrow at your Robin for why couldn't you wait for me? or *consult* with me about going. Still, I do give you my word that there is great probability of my running over to join you during your *last two weeks*. Write and say, before you go, what you fancy will be your arrangements. And, O Tuck, write from among the mountains, astonied, that will look on you, and tell me of the hearts to whom YOUR COMPANION[8] shall have imparted swifter motion and a habit of breathing as if Mount Blank were on their breasts. Of Demitroïa tell me; of her health and spirits (put away vile I—see bottom of page).[9]—You always pass her out in a smudge. Divide the We for me. Tell me of yourself fully. Say where you are to be found in or about Thun; and instruct me of the means of getting to you. I do passionately desire to see great wonders of creation with my Tuck, so that in days to come, when Robin is as a rushlight, and Tuck one of Price's patent composite tallow-vats, we two may say—This we saw and that we saw—green Alpine lakes where the brides of the angels bathe; snows pure as the forehead of YOUR COMPANION; peaks, passes, and all the other p's:—until, my Tuck, the Sublime and Beautiful should forever stand by as witnesses of the marriage of our true affection—the same being registered in verse, immortal by reason of the subject.—In Thun you will see Jessopp: haply you may hear him out of tune (influence of Burnand). But, if you hear him you can't mistake him. Think of a cock-chafer informing the world that his wife has run away from him:—so deep, so desolate, the voice of Jessopp.[10] Take to thy mind Nature's bassest note: conceive a voice millions of fathoms below this crust of earth:— the incarnation of three minor canons, primed for their holy labours on port:—a cathedral voice: a voice that you shake to and curiously look to see whether one works his coat-tails as bellows to inflate and give inspiration to such a voice:—even such the voice of Jessopp. He desires very much to see and know you. Do your best to meet him. You know that Demitroïa has exchanged words with his wife.—Enough. Comfort me here with a letter or two. I'm rather knocked over by seeing

---

[6] Samuel Laurence (1812–84), the painter. GM always spelled his name with a *w*, but I have corrected the spelling throughout the letters.
[7] The Hardmans, Hardman's sister Sarah, and his cousin Alice Skirving were leaving on the 16th for five weeks on the Continent.
[8] Marginal note in the hand of GM: 'small caps'. The 'companion' was Hardman's sister Sarah.   [9] At bottom of page: ℔

[10] GM borrowed Jessopp's voice for the Revd. Mr. Barmby, who 'carries his musical instrument at the bottom of his trunk', in *One of Our Conquerors*.

you depart, and feeling rather bound. I have the consolation (poor! poor!) of knowing that you will long heartily for Gordon Street after a week's absence.—Well: Good-bye! I wish you all joy. Demitroïa, YOUR COMPANION, Hinchliff, and the three jolly good fellows rolled into the one Tuck whom I know and love.

George M.

237. *To* MRS. WILLIAM HARDMAN

MS.: Garrick Club. Published: *Letters*, i. 110–13, with numerous inaccuracies and omissions.

Seaford, Sussex
[July 12, 1863]

Most fair and dear Sceptic,

Now it was told of a man that an angel leanèd out of heaven and dropped to him a ring, of which, he said, Catch hold: and the man sought to catch hold: but ever the ring swayed, and its swaying was the promise of bliss and the baffling of desire. So the man thought, if I jump I catch it. And lo, he jumped. And at the first jump he touched the ring, which flew from him. At the second jump likewise, and in addition his falling was upon his nose. Even so it went at the third and the fourth essay, and on. Then thought he: this ring is cast so far from me because that the Angel droppèd it so near!—

Alas! what sadder thing is there to the full heart of great wishes than the word 'almost'. If the man, dear critic of my weakness, had seen said Ring distant, he had remarked, the birds of air may catch it!—but it hung within mortal grasp—almost! He could just touch it. The effort to seize sent it Heavenward—him to Earth.[1]

Yet, by Heaven! as Ocean collects her billows for one great plunge, I know not but that I will try. I see you are making a circuit and that the Wild Man of Gordon Street[2] is for pranks. So to be with you one must start with you. If you see me on *Tuesday*, it will be that I have come to Town to make immediate arrangements for joining you, for the reason partly that the W[il]d Man is not, in my opinion a fitting protector of ... of *you* of course he is (after a fashion), of, I was going to say ... and it's of no use his frowning at table d'hôtes: for they will openly admire a lovely woman, on the Continent:—where, let me add, Beauty if not zealously watched and guarded ... and a fresh English wild-rose without a disengaged hand and forecasting mind to pave its way and shield it from foul breathing, may be in danger of a moment's sensitive disquiet—at the contemplation of which possibility the hearts

237. [1] All of this is an allegory of GM's efforts to arrange to accompany the Hardman party on a trip to the Continent.   [2] Hardman.

within us do painfully pant and heave.... Protector of—But let us talk seriously. Is YOUR COMPANION[3] quite well? May I beg you to present her with my kind regards? Prompted by the fatherly feeling (which must exist, though the position be denied to me), pray assure that young lady that I am pervaded by the very warmest interest in her welfare, and claim, by right of my expressed admiration (that excessive daring might call affection) of Another and greater from whom she springs,[4] to declare that my sentiments on her behalf are parental in their depth.—All this means that if I can can can come, I will: that there is just a chance: that I'm going to make the spring and if the Ring don't swing I may cling like anything and just be caught up to a six weeks' Heaven among you, and nothing short of it, under your wing.

My state no weathercock with a thunderstorm on the South-east and the wind due North-west, would describe. Pierrot straightening hands and legs to dance facing the four corners alternately would look foolish beside me. The newly caged wild-cat might outwardly represent my condition. I boil to go. I am frozen. There comes a thaw. In a twinkling I am all rosily rippling like a summer sea in the calm confidence that I shall go. Then blight falls. I find myself stript like a gladiator fighting with the single sword against the three Women of the Net and the Thread. A voice whispers: 'If you cut the Net, the Thread will likewise be severed.' I swoon and the hideous spectators cry ''Tis done!' O my dear Madam! are *you* one of the Three? Why do you teach unhappy men to love you? For I love not that Tuck at all. He has taken to swearing of late. His letters come on me louder than Blatchington Battery hard by, which blew off a Volunteer artilleryman to Neptune's bosom some time ago. I say I love not that Tuck. He is profane: a puffed out insolent friar—who goes about saying that He is the better half of 'We'. If I come I shall take delight in the snubbing of him.

—My goodness! suppose, after all, I don't come!

—It's of no use looking into that enormous Black Pit. Daylight is with you, dear Mrs. Aurora! and I hope that in subscribing myself I may really prove as responsive to the ray of light received from you this morning, as did the Stony Harpist of old,[5] and so earn a right to be [to] you ever nothing other than

George Memnon

[3] Hardman's sister.
[4] i.e. Mrs. Knowles, mother of Hardman and Hardman's sister. GM always wrote of her with elaborate courtesy and gallantry.
[5] 'Ancient writers record that when the first rays of the rising sun fall upon [the statue of Memnon] a sound is heard to issue from it, which they compare to the snapping of a harp-string' (Bulfinch).

P.S. I send my love to the Household.

N.B. Tell me who has got most in the scramble. And Oh, please Somebody write that I may get a fillip of encouragement on Tuesday morning here, and so perhaps shut my eyes and let my heart steer me—which it doesn't always do badly, does it?—not falsely, I'm sure. And if, poor fellow, he goes wrong and meant right—why, he's certain to lead one to experience, which, taken properly, is wealth, wisdom!—Hurrah!

238. *To* WILLIAM HARDMAN

MS.: Garrick Club. Published: *Letters*, i. 113, with minor variants.

[Seaford, Lewes]
Tuesday, [July 14, 1863]

I find I can't get the reading and Foakes both done; and so collapse like a demnition bladder[1]—woe's me, Tuck!—Chapman must have some MSS. immediately read. On the whole, I do so [see] that it's the right thing for me to work straight on; this year I lose a great pleasure, dear Tuck! Think of me. If you can spare time, or are blessed with a rainy day, write to me. My warmest salute to Demitroïa. The same, properly clipped and cooled, to YOUR COMPANION. My love to you, all joy with you.

I had ordered a travelling suit and got half ready to go!

Yours lastingly,
George M.

239. *To* WILLIAM HARDMAN

MS.: Garrick Club. (This long and vexing letter, often barely legible, sometimes illegible, is a joint production of GM—R = Robin and Lionel Robinson—P = Poco. W. M. Meredith excerpted only half a dozen random sentences and some of the verses: *Letters*, i. 114.)

Copsham, Esher
Sunday, [July 19, 1863]

Tuck!

R. —I have returned from Seaford, having seen the dawn every morning of my recent life there, and presenting much of the green and yellow hue of the young Aurora; and here too is Poco, who—

238. [1] i.e. GM's plans to accompany the Hardman party to the Continent collapsed because of his duties as publishers' reader and writer for Foakes's *Ipswich Journal*. 'Demnition bladder': cf. Mr. Mantalini in *Nicholas Nickleby*.

P. —Salutes the obese man and thanks him for his letter; which was highly typical—though one or two remarks were somewhat superfluous—the feeding at Lisle, Calais etc. to wit—

R. —But we rejoice both at the 'commodious' establishments sacred to his ease, and erected specially (as we doubt not) for the occasion of his grand triumphal tour: and as Poco says—

P. —he trusts you followed out the instructions contained in his proposed tour—perhaps you did right after all in choosing the H[otel] de Flandre—but it is decidedly noisy—There is more dependence to be placed on Robin than you give him credit for—he did turn up on the day appointed, forsaking the fleshpots of Egypt and quitting the tents of Kedar—(N.B. his sentences are awfully long.)

R. —So, you have traduced me, Tuck, and have flown from my vengeance; knowing that I must pray Providence for YOU, absent! But there is question of my following YOU; and Poco (a strange mild man, of an ineffable dreadful composure, which fills me with a haunting fear that Fate is a Being personally known to him) says, speaking as an oracle, that this thing must be . . . I waver, I doubt, but this inexplicable creature says there is no doubt and there can be no wavering . . . where am I?

P. —*tout au contraire*, as an inexplicable desire of sneezing seized the strong man, even so has a longing to see Switzerland and follow in your footsteps taken hold of the 'waverer'—we therefore purpose leaving town on Friday or Saturday week at the latest and making for Grenoble and the Monte Viso[1] district—

R. —Good God! Listen to him, Tuck! I have not decided; can't decide, and he talks as if the thing were done. Already I feel whirled out of myself and scudding through thin upper air to a jolly British bouquet of faces, fresh and sweet: even

> Tuck, Demitroïa,
> Ariadne, and Froyja;
> The loveliest quartette
> To give a man joy-a!—

P. —It's hardly fair to write poetry on the spur of the moment— especially when the other collaborateur in this letter always [takes] five and twenty minutes to find a rhyme—I therefore continue in terrible prose—Did you have salmon at Strasbourg—and pâté de foie gras—it's not a good place for the latter—but the goose-house is worth a visit and you might moralize on the necessity of passing through a fiery furnace before attaining distinction.

239. [1] In the Cottian Alps.

R. —And the Paradise of being served up before some celestial rosy Tuck of the spheres we hope to visit together when our livers refuse to continue their mortal functions further.

> But, O my Tuck, go not before me!
> A lonely sun is shining o'er me.
> Think of your Robin, 'tis no joke, O,
> Left in the grasp of demon Poco![2]

P.   —Believe him not; no sun, nor moon
> Afford the faintest light—
> But only candles such as made
> Of patent composite.

The parrot is packed—there was some difficulty in inducing him to enter the ignominious hamper—but you had left no cage in which he could be sent—The bills are paid—the letters sent—excepting one which as it looks like a dun I don't forward.

R. —Lucas wants me to begin in *O[nce] a W[eek]* the end of October.[3] I don't think I can. And how can I possibly if this infernal Poco, who has got hold of me . . . and my last chapters of *Emilia* to retouch . . . and the proofs. And here's Poco meditating another costive poetic effort—

> Even as some little doggie
> Whom his mistress will not see,
> Quasi-squatted by the wayside
> One leg lifted; fixed on three.

P.   —My verses run (by rail at least)
> Though *some* may say they hobble
> What matter's that?—for well it's known:
>
> Two poets always squabble ⎫ utrum horum mavis
> We're starting for Grenoble[4] ⎭ accipe—[5]

And as we are determined on this tour it's useless to begin at once. Just point out to Robin how absurd it will be for him to begin a new work before his other is well off the stocks—he won't be able to do justice to himself. The *Once a Week must* not commence before

239. [2] Marginal note by Robinson opposite the verses: 'Incubation lengthy.'
   [3] Another reference to the serial that never materialized.
   [4] Marginal comment by GM:
> His verses run and that's a fact
> ('Twere better would they tarry)
> But where they ran was never track'd
> Nor what the sense they carry.
   [5] 'Take whichever of these you prefer.'

January at least. In the meantime if Lucas wants something to fill up with I will send him some poetry.

R. —*Le Pauvre* Lucas! It only wants Poco's poetry to sink *O. a W.* to the veriest Bottom.—Let me tell you that Poco has this day gained, after three astounding efforts, admission to the ranks of the Pantagruelians. Doubtless you heard the last, faintly. Copsham heard and trembled. Going through the woods subsequently, we found a portion in flames. A fact. Poco was 'hoist' with it. He is whole; but weak: yet as firm in his terrible grip of poor Robin as ever.—Of Sons, let me say that they are wonderfully browned by Seaford sun and breeze and very jolly. *If* I come, he will stay at Copsham. Tuck! I don't think.—*

*P.S. he seldom does to much purpose—P.

N.B. This is the comment resulting from the calm continual gestation of imperince.[6] R.

[P.] —The Hermits of Copsham to their brother *In partibus Infidelium*[7]

Health and Appetite—

Know that we be filled with a longing to salute thee again and to receive that spiritual consolation and advice, which thou, O golden mouthed, alone canst afford—Let thy prayers daily ascend that strength and resolution be given to our dear brother Robin to carry out those good intentions which are springing up in him—for if they bear no fruit, verily he is good for naught—and why when we have looked for grapes should we find thistles? Waft therefore the ἄνεμος[8] of thy inner self to this holy place—fructify all his efforts, that ere long we may meet in the valley of the blessed—Oh that will we [? be] joyful, joyful, joyful, etc. etc.

R. —For of a truth, of Robin, *quaeque cupit, sperat: suaque tuum oracula fallunt*[9]—too often! and it shall be said of him that, with his great master and spiritual chief by his side, he was as the Pagan Hercules; but severed from him and abandoned, a weakling lamb, yea, as the vine about a stricken elm. Thus much. And now to numbers.

> Tell me where he wanders,
> Gentle breezes, pray!
> If in peace he saunters (qy, spelling?)
> Regular each day.—

---

[6] A Sairey Gampism for *impudence.*
[7] 'Among the infidels.'
[8] i.e. 'spirit'.
[9] Quoted inaccurately from Ovid, *Metam.* i. 491: 'What he desires, he hopes for, and his own oracles deceive him.'

Here's Poco crying out for his turn, confound him! I was getting on to sentiment rapidly.

[P.] —Believe him not, my Tuck, I have tried to work on his sentiment all day and now stern justice asserts its sway—Have I not abandoned all further development of my Pyrenean tour? have I not thrown over a man who wanted to accompany me? and all for what? that Robin might have his mind refreshed by the air of the mountains, and rejoiced by the sight of his Tuck. *Fiat justitia, ruat caelum*,[10] since you must have Latin. Touch him to the quick when you write, scathe him with the lightning of your eloquence—and let him fly towards you on the wings of your own words (ἔπεα πτερόεντα)[11]

[R.]   —A poet by the wayside went.
           He met a monk, a holy man.
           'O shrive me, friar', he said and bent
           His head. 'Confess', the monk began.

           'O one of thine I've loved too well.
           Too well I've loved that friar so fat.
           The Muses blew into a shell
           Whene'er he laughed, and sweet his chat!'

           'No more', the dark Confessor said.
           'I know him: one of many, thou!
           He when thy heart is won, has fled:
           For ages he has done as now.

           'There is no hope: thou canst not rest:
           Obedient to his wanton whim,
           Yea, North and East and South and West,
           Forever must thou follow him.

           'Young Cupid was he call'd of old;
           With Will o'Wisp incorporate:—

Damn this Poco! He won't be quiet—Nor reverences he Castalia's fount, nor them that drink there, them that mount the fiery steed, and on the brink there, spur with speed, and drink the distance, killing space, folding existence in one embrace—

           'Tuck is he named, a reveler bold
           To follow him is ay thy fate.

239. [10] 'Let justice reign, let the heavens fall.'   [11] 'Winged words' (Homer).

> 'He hath thee in a golden mesh
> And thee will have forevermore.
> He is the Genius of the Flesh.'
> —Yet still, my Tuck, I thee adore.

[R.]   —Pity the sorrows of a *poor young man*[12]
         Who vainly seeks a rhyme

[P.]   Of rhythm he's not over much
         But compensates in *time.*

I assisted at the birth of Robin's last attempt, and never was I (since embracing the career of Mrs. Gamp to the Muses), present at so tedious a labour. The poor sufferer is quite exhausted—and is swaying himself in the anguish of suppressed pain.

By the bye we are most anxious to know how you managed with your foreign tongues—the *lingua francesca in bocca Gordoniana* was we hope a success—but are somewhat sceptical—however courage, *mon ami—paulo majora canamus*[13]—And now farewell. Kindest remembrances to Mrs. H—to whom I bring her repentant Robin—have I not done all to merit the title of her obedient slave—the proper thing to the rest of the dove-cot?

Ever yours most sincerely,
Lionel Robinson

If Robin doesn't come (which he *must*) I go to the Pyrenees.

[R.] —Adieu, also, for a time. I hope—much: but can't say. To fair Ariadne my humblest sheepish salute: to the golden haired Freyja[14] a modified London bow, to Demitroïa much that Cupid might say in company; to you my blessing.

George Meredith

240. *To* George P. Boyce[1]

MS.: University of Texas.

Copsham
July 25, [? 1863]

My dear Boyce,

I have been away, and now first hear of your sad case. I went at

---

[12] Marginal note by Robinson: 'Robin.'

[13] Virgil, *Eclogue* iv. i. 1: 'let us sing of somewhat greater' (matters.)

[14] Ariadne . . . Freyja: Hardman's sister and his cousin, who accompanied the Hardmans.

240. George P. Boyce (1826–97), the landscape artist, whom GM probably knew through Rossetti. I do not know what the 'sad case' referred to in the letter was.

once to the spot, but found no red blood there. I will peruse the heath continually: but why not come yourself? That seems best. In haste

Your faithful

George Meredith

241. *To* WILLIAM HARDMAN

MS.: Garrick Club. Published: *Letters*, i. 115–18, with omissions and inaccuracies.

Copsham

Saturday night,

August 1, [1863]

My beloved Tuck!

Poco is off: started on Friday for Havre; for Bordeaux; for Bayonne, the Pyrenees; and so round to Dauphiné. He is gone; but the hold of the terrible calm fellow is on me still. I am fast bound by my word, to meet him at Grenoble, and tread the Dauphiné Alps with him, and the ways that he pleases to take me. I couldn't resist him. He has a damnable calm way—and I couldn't start till Sons had gone. How I'm to do it at all, I can't imagine; but apparently it must be. The chances of our meeting on the continent this year, are small: and Oh, Tuck! I should have liked it so!—Lucas has just written to say that Tom Trollope follows *Eleanor's Vic[tory]*[1] in *O[nce] a W[eek]*,—so there's no immediate pressure for me, save to hand my proofs to friends.—Poor old Bullion! What do you think? I was awfully bothered, and somehow in request, and couldn't go and see him when he was recovering:—had he been relapsing I should undoubtedly have gone:—but I've now written, begging him to come to me. Reply: 'You have taught me a sharp lesson etc., etc.: I shall know in future etc.: don't let Arthur think me a humbug.' Tuck! I have hurt his sentiment!—Now I like Bullion and recognize his capital qualities: but, Heaven's my witness, never professed deep friendship. In fine, never felt towards him as I do to— some one. I think you have understood my side of the relations twixt Robin and Bullion. I am sad about it:—write to him now to say what I can. It will pass: but Bullion will never never feel what he felt in the days when Robin was masked.—I've been to Goodwood with the Fitz-Gerald Champagne-Loo party: saw much life, which I wanted: backed wrong horses: lost £5. Certain, therefore, of knowing my lesson. Wise grows the loser: merely happy the winner. A great pastime! The scene was glorious. We elbowed Dukes: jostled Lords: were in a flower

---

241. [1] *Eleanor's Victory*, by Mary E. Braddon (Maxwell), 1837–1915, ended in *OaW* on 3 Oct., and *Beppo, The Conscript*, by T. A. Trollope, began on 10 Oct.

garden of Countesses.—Another publisher has requested me to read for him:[2] discern and select. I never refuse work. Of this more by and by. For the present, MUM—Oh! how my mouth waters, my heart leaps, at the thought of Tuck planted, as 'twere, in the very eye of the Gods, the rosy crowing British cock! Store a thousand reminiscences for me. I can't bear to think of leaving England just about the period of your return, and missing Demitroïa's smiles and rapid recitation of adventure and fun. There's something dreadful about Poco. He's not as other men. He won't believe in my impossibilities. Tuck, I'm sorry we've admitted him amongst us. I am. It was your doing. Poco persists. He's never satisfied with my answers, if I don't assent. When once I do, or half do, he treats me as a man of honour, and I'm fixed. He has sailed, as secure of me, as if he had me at Grenoble already. (His mother came to the Station to see him off!—a good old lady: I quietly remonstrated with her upon the propriety of her having produced such a specimen. She said, 'Pray take care of my son.' The joke took away my breath.)—I shall send the *S[aturday] R[eview]* to Chamounix a day after this letter.—Sons are in good case. I hope your darlings are well: but of them you are at least well informed. If you hadn't thought proper to cut off communication between the Great Mother and me, I might have told you particulars of them. Well!—Parliament's up!—I think Morley will do my *Ips[wich] J[ournal]*.—You see the *Times*, of course: I spare you paper news. Old Copsham is pretty sound. The beetle[3] soars.

> The beetle soars, the beetle spins,
> The beetle is up in the air, Tuck;
> 'Twill crack Robin's crown as a stamp for his sins,
> Or make him defy old care, Tuck.

Pray, write and say, how (the route) and when (the week) you return. Poco says *I* must start on the 22nd.—I suppose you haven't come across Jessopp?—He has promised to journey here and I hope will take back Sons with him. My poor darling begins to see dimly again that holidays have a termination. 'If I hadn't such a kind master!' he remarks. 'I'm very happy down there, Papa, you know!'—You see, Tuck, he has his choice of different kinds of happiness. Blessed is he who can even *look* on such alternatives for a little human soul. I am twice blest, for that my friend is happy as well as my Son. Tuck, I'm going to bed. If I dream, sail thou across the vision, like a jolly monkish owl.

---

[2] See Note 2, Letter 235.   [3] See Note 2, Letter 199.

My jolly friar,
Now lift thy cowl,
And send me a laugh
Like a revelling owl.
Were I lying and groaning
In pits of fire,
Thy laughter like water
Would fall, my friar!

Good night, Tuck! Goodnight, dear Demitroïa! Good night to the 'two young ladies'. I say!—have they been much admired? 'Cause, we won't have our English wild roses stared at by 'mannikin' foreigners. Tuck, have you been a zealous guardian of those treasures? Alas! who would have done that duty like me? There's a song called 'Poor Robin'. Sing it.—Poco sailed under a big full moon.

I cry for a blessing upon you all, and sleep.

Your loving
George Meredith

242. *To* WILLIAM HARDMAN

MS.: Garrick Club. (This letter accompanied the one written on 1 Aug.) Published: *Letters*, i. 118, with several inaccuracies and with only the initial *W* for *Wyndowe*.

Monday, [August 3, 1863]

My dear Friends,

I reopen to tell you what might have been the saddest tale I should ever have to tell.

Yesterday, Wyndowe found Arthur out alone; put him on his horse, after shortening the stirrups—suddenly let go the reins, for some purpose unknown; my little darling was carried off, fell, dangled to the stirrup and was dragged headlong over the furze. Not killed! mercifully spared and no bones broken: but the shock has been tremendous. He lies upstairs, and was insensible till this morning. Had he been kicked, or dragged on the road, I should have had a shattered heap of all I love given to my arms. He was saved by his short length, and by his boot being pulled off: (he had elastic sides to them). Izod says he is *doing well*. He can't keep anything on his stomach, and complains of his head: but he sleeps soundly and *calmly*: breathes peacefully. My poor lamb!—'Oh! is it a dream?' he said, as I undressed him after the accident. He can now recount all that happened till he was dragged. I think I may hope that he will recover, and be as sound as he was. Of poor Wyndowe it is useless to speak. He is sorry, of course.—Don't be distressed, for you know I should not be quiet at heart if all did not look very hopefully. I have had a rude blow. I will write to you in three days. God bless you.

George Meredith

243. *To* WILLIAM HARDMAN

MS.: Garrick Club. Published: *Letters*, i. 118–19, with variants and with only the initial *W* for *Wyndowe*.

Copsham, Esher
Wednesday, [August 5, 1863]

My dear Tuck,

Sons are on their legs again!

The poor little fellow is very weak and somewhat shaky; covered with bruises: but vitally sound, bones all right: head uninjured, as far as human eye can reckon. This day he was allowed to get up. Yesterday he swallowed food without immediately rejecting it. He is not much the worse for his terrible mishap; quite cheerful—slightly damns himself for mounting such a big horse, but excuses Wyndowe. Poor Wyndowe has been in a great way. It's no comfort to me to make another miserable when I am struck; and it's of no use to examine a catastrophe which I am sure *he* will not help to repeat.

Well, Tuck, my darling is returned to me out of the jaws of death. Wyndowe says he's thankful I was spared the sight, which will haunt him till he dies. He feared to look at Arthur, making sure that he was killed. Had it been on the road, or had the little fellow's boot not been of elastic sides, the worst must have happened. The boot wrenched off, is somewhere on the common now—no one knows where. The distance Arthur was dragged is about fifty yards, as far as I can make out. There, Tuck!—We have put up our thank-song to the Supreme.

With this I forward the *Saturday* [*Review*].

How little poor Ethel knows the danger her betrothed has run.— Break it to her gently. And write a jolly long letter, if you can manage, saying whether you return before the 21st August: and by what route, when you do return. If things go well with Sons, I join Poco in Grenoble on the 24th leaving England [the] 22nd.—I should like to see you first. Jessopp is en route homeward. He wrote from Aachen, and will probably be at Copsham on Saturday, if the news concerning Arthur does not bring him before. Say sweet things to Demitroïa, or let as many pass your Douane as you consider for her good—and your own. Hoping the young ladies are not getting troublesome,

Your loving
George Meredith

244. *To* WILLIAM HARDMAN

MS.: Garrick Club. Published: *Letters*, i. 120–1, with omissions and inaccuracies.

Esher, Surrey
Tuesday, [August 11, 1863]

My dear Tuck,

This letter is a chance shot sent at you: for I doubt you'll have left Chamounix before it arrives.

My darling boy is going on all right. His head though bruised, and blue behind the ear, is sound: and his little innocent rump, which occasionally twitches him, is on the whole as well capable of taking what his conduct may earn him as yours, Tuck, or mine. The recovery is wonderful. I thought while I was by his side that first night of the accident that had befallen you, and thanked you for going through the performance for your Robin's comfort in future years. His boot (whose elastic sides saved him) still travels at a swift pace over our common, and will be discovered, tired, by a succeeding generation.— Jessopp and wife came on Friday. Arthur returns to them this day week. On the Thursday following I am off to join awful Poco; who has written to fix me irrevocably. He was at Bordeaux, at Claret as hard as he could tear. Impassively. Can you not see him?—Full of this wine, he was starting for the Pyrenean baths. I wrote to Luchon[1] on Sunday. He sent his love to Tuck. Pretty well for a youngster! I can't yet make him understand that, among the Sons of the Great Mother, we count our time from the hour we first saw Tuck. He says: 'Tell Tuck he is to go home by Grenoble: to be there (Hotel de l'Europe) on the 24th'—which is Robin's day of appointment—Lord how I wish you would do it!—Eh, Tuck? I would go on upon this theme but I have the ridiculous idea that I shall be bawling persuasion at Chamounix while you are a day distant across an Alp. My letter will catch you or be 24 hours too late. Still if you get this, think seriously of the possibility of your going home by Grenoble, for I want to see you, mightily.

I forgot to say, I wrote the second letter to you, telling of Arthur's recovery, as promised. Doubtless you have had it.

244. [1] The nearest town to the central Pyrenean range; famed for its baths.

I now desire to join Poco, for I feel as if I had been dragged by a horse, and were blue behind the ear, with stern-quarters creaking rather. I want restoration. Tuck being absent, I go to Nature, in her sublimest. Greet Demitroïa and her chickens from your loving

George Meredith

245. *To* WILLIAM HARDMAN

MS.: Garrick Club. Published: *Letters*, i. 121, with omission of two sentences.

Piccadilly
Thursday, [August 20, 1863]

Dear Tuck,

I am coming to you—shall be at Hotel Choiseul[1] on Friday or Saturday. For Heaven's sake, be there. Make [? sure] that we meet. I bring article in *OaW*, 'America'[2] etc. and *Vie de Jésus* by Renan[3]— one of the finest of the works of this generation. Yours in all love (with half to Demitroïa),

George Meredith

Sons are all right—at Norwich. No fresh letter from Poco. I start to-night: Newhaven–Dieppe.

246. *To* WILLIAM HARDMAN

MS.: Garrick Club. Published: *Letters*, i. 121–2, with omissions and variants.

Copsham, Esher
Wednesday, [September 16, 1863]

Tuck! I am of return.[1] I come to arrive on Sunday and amid such a press of work! I try to recover my native tongue. I must tell you of

245. [1] In Paris.
[2] 'America Seventy Years Ago: an Imaginary Tour', by Hardman, published in *OaW* (15 Aug. 1863).
[3] Ernest Renan (1823–92), French philosopher and Orientalist, whose *Vie de Jésus* (1863) made a profound impression on English intellectuals.
246. [1] GM had been on the Continent with Lionel Robinson (Poco) since 21 Aug. Before joining Robinson, he stopped at Rouen to confer with a writer who had submitted a MS. to C. & H. and then went on to Paris, where he spent two days sightseeing with the Hardmans. At the end of the day on 23 Aug. he took a train to meet Robinson at Grenoble, and next day the Hardmans returned to England. Hardman (*L. & M.*, pp. 69–71) gives an interesting account of the sightseeing and gourmandizing during GM's two days in Paris.

our travels by and by. Suffice, that Poco was at the Station (it is one of
his vanities to be coolly punctual—he meets you as though he said,
'You see, I promised to be striding the North Pole at 9 a.m. on the 27th
of August 1891.') He was there. We went to the Grande Chartreuse,
filling all the valleys of approach with the joint names of Tuck and
Demitroïa. We slept there. We walked away with 9 bottles of liqueur
and toiled over mountain passes. Through Dauphiné we walked. We
walked ourselves into prolonged silences. Our ordinary course was
ten hours per diem; sometimes it went to 13. We crossed Mont
Gènevre into Italy: to Turin: to Lago Maggiore then over Piedmon-
tese mountains and lovely valleys into Switzerland to Geneva: thence
to Dijon, where Poco reaching me the hand of friendship and shutting
up the tongue of seduction, parting in fact very prettily, set out for
Liège. I for Paris . . . remaining there four days of delight, save for the
absence of One. . . . Strange chapters in the Book of Sandars² have we
to narrate: a few little adventures: peculiarities of Poco (he has a right
proper feeling towards D'Troïa; the germs of reverence for Tuck), etc.
We went too fast. We trudged like packmen. Still I have much enjoyed the trip: am better, fresher. The weather was so-so: neither very
bad, nor Tucklike. Poco desires to say that, according to D'Troïa's
arrangement, he shall make his bow at 27 Gordon St., on the 4th of
October. Robin vows the same. Business calls him or much would he
write. To Pot[ter]-Ethel my love and to Nelly. To D[e]T[roïa] much
warmth of affection. I heard at Geneva that the blessed little man goes
on all well.

Your loving
George Meredith

247. *To* MRS. AUGUSTUS JESSOPP

Text (excerpts): composite of excerpts from Sotheby Catalogues (27 Nov. –4 Dec. 1911,
p. 23, and 19–21 Dec.1921, p. 93).

Esher
Monday, [?October 1863]¹

[An omission expressing his distress at not hearing from Arthur.]
   . . . My time is quite bitten through by the glutton world. In a week
I shall be setting to proofs. . . . Do write, and request Mr. Jessopp to
do likewise. Surely he is pregnant with some fresh scheme? either for
the overthrow of Governors or mighty uplifting of the school?

246. ² I suppose this to be the same Sandars mentioned in Letter 148, but am unable to
identify him.
247. The only clue to the date of this letter is the reference to proofs of *Emilia*. (See
following letter.) It probably belongs to mid-October.

248. *To* WILLIAM HARDMAN

MS.: Garrick Club. Published: *Letters*, i. 122–3, with substantial omissions and editing.

Copsham
Wednesday, [October 21, 1863]

Dear and Sweet Tuck!

Your aid I rejoice in: your suggestions I for the most part follow, bowing the head of acquiescence to almost all your emendations.— I believe you too, when you say you like the work,[1] and the thought comforts me.

The night of the day you read this, we dine at Poco's Papa's table.

You don't mention having heard from Chapman? I suppose they delay that they may consult me as to *sum*.[2]

I must see you before I speak as to my own SUM—which by the way I shan't get from *them*. Do you think that, as novels go now, I may fix something huge? or content me with a modicum, and, sniffling a beastly low content, say, 'Such is the world'? Or—if I can't get my price, take all the risk?—

My use of 'stress' is arbitrary—wrong. Her 'flanks' seemed to strike me on the temples out of the printed page.

On the whole nothing could be neater than your criticism. Maxse's is amusing. Objects to her conduct in going with Gambier to booth 'Because every girl is conscious that she should never trust herself alone with a man' etc.[3]

So the sentimental worshipper *will* always make them animals— with the finger of a fixed thought, from their birth upwards (and pressing more and more consciously), directed upon * * * * Eh, Tuck? But we know otherwise, we libertines; coarse boys that we are! God bless you, Tuck.

Your loving
Robin

---

248. [1] *Emilia in England* (published Apr. 1864), to which most of the remarks of this letter refer.

[2] Chapman, who was exasperatingly slow about payments at times, had not yet paid Hardman for 'America Seventy Years Ago', published in *OaW* on 15 Aug.

[3] *Emilia*, Chapter XI.

249. *To* MRS. N. E. S. A. HAMILTON

Text: typed copy furnished by Simon Nowell-Smith, Esq.: The London Library.

Copsham, Esher
Thursday, October [1863]

My dear Mrs. Hamilton,

I will come on the Thursday that follows. I don't think it can be your cousin 'Kitty'[1] whose casual passing by me the other day impressed me: but if it was—or let me say, in any case, your grave, most simple and natural, remark that she walked truly in the Oxshott direction, but commonly 'with her fiancé':—let me assure you that no experienced matron, adept in the art of flinging cold water, could have done it more admirably. I take the towel of Philosophy and compliment you heartily while I rub myself dry. The person whom I saw was fair, on the borders of twenty, and swung her left hand slightly as she walked (a little in the manner of young governesses who begin to feel that they must walk for health). If *she* was walking to or from a fiancé, it is only another proof that every desirable woman in the world is engaged. At any rate I have seen this 'she', whoever she is, and can feel it to be something even when the little that it is appears dolorously to shake its head at me. Is not that Resignation? Pray, accord me your most matronly approbation, and believe me, your faithful, continually improving,

George Meredith

250. *To* KATHERINE [?] VULLIAMY[1]

MS.: University of Texas. Published: *Letters*, i. 123, with minor variants.

Esher, Surrey
Wednesday night, October 28, 1863

Dear Miss Vulliamy,

Thursday is unhappily my one day in the week when I am in harness

249. [1] Katherine Vulliamy, sister of Marie whom GM was to marry a year later. If it was not Kitty that GM saw, it may well have been Marie—and the beginning of the romance. Mrs. Hamilton, it may be remembered, was a cousin of the Vulliamy girls.

250. [1] There is nothing about this letter, the envelope of which has not been preserved, to indicate which of the several Misses Vulliamy is being addressed. W. M. Meredith assigns it to Katherine, and he may be right. In any event this is an interesting letter because it marks GM's first contact with the family into which he was to marry.

It is curious that GM had not met the Vulliamy family earlier. In Letter 288, in which he gives the family history, he says that they have lived in the Vale of Mickleham for about five years, approximately the same time GM had lived at Esher, only seven miles away. At the time of this letter Mr. Vulliamy was a retired French manufacturer, with three unmarried daughters, who had moved to England seven years earlier at the instance of his English wife, now dead. GM was introduced to the family by the Hamiltons.

and have to do Press-duty in London. On Monday, too, my engagement to go on a yachting-expedition to the Channel-islands, holds me
bound, I fear. But if this can be put off, I shall come to you gladly.
I would much rather be in Mickleham. If the fates drag me away,
notwithstanding, I may hope to be permitted to call on you when I return? And, since it pains you that I should take 'long walks' to no purpose, I will also take the liberty of consulting you, *d'avance*; though,
let me assure you again, the length of my journey is not to be deplored.
As to my walking back at night;—I am an associate with owls and
night-jars, tramps and tinkers, who teach me nature and talk human
nature to me. If I stay in Mickleham, do I not lose those privileges of
a neighbour, who bows himself out to his own bed, and is therefore
welcomed without formality? But, during my first visit I should be
ungracious not to accept Mr. Vulliamy's invitation in all its particulars. I beg that you will thank him in my name.

On consideration, I thought that *The Ordeal* could not do you harm:
I can only trust that it will not offend. It deals with certain problems of
life, and is therefore not of a milky quality. I am afraid that it requires
stout reading. If you weather it, unshocked, you will find my other
works less trying.

I am, / Dear Miss Vulliamy, / Most faithfully yours,

George Meredith

251. *To* AUGUSTUS JESSOPP

MS.: Yale. Published: *Letters*, i. 124–5.

Esher

Sunday night, [October or November 1863]

My dear Jessopp,

You say that you are anxious about my little man. You take the
wind out of all my sails. Pardon me, but I shall have no peace till
I hear whether I have dwelt on the word too strongly. If you are only
anxious as to his mental briskness, I am not alarmed; and I know also
that he 'potters' and plays after his own fashion and is not a boisterous
fellow. But I am always open to fear for his physical health. His
circulation is not rapid, his stomach is weak. He requires to be watched.
And the medicines of the old system do not suit him. Even for a trifling
illness, I wish him to have the attendance of a homoeopathic physician.
—I should imagine that, if you see languor, it arises from indigestion—
constitutional weakness of digestion. I should like him to have a course
of cod-liver oil. If Mrs. Jessopp thinks good, I will send some down
from Savory and Moore's. And as a drink at dinner, some light claret

mixed with Brighton seltzer water, might inspirit him. Would you allow of this? Any other wine, or beer, he must not take. I don't want to give trouble, but my heart broods over him, and I am unmanned at a breath of doubt concerning him.—I told you that his powers of acquisition would not be marked. But you will find by and by that he has sucked in much and made use of it in his own way. He will never be a gladiator; but he may be a thinker: I expect him to be a man of sense. If only—and here my sails flap the mast miserably. I would come down at once but my fresh work detains me. I have my hands full. Mrs. Jessopp will be moved to give me the state of the case. Will you tell her that a hamper will come for Arthur this week, containing, among things more precious to him, the necessaries she wrote for. I had much to discourse on to you.

This, doubtless very silly, perturbation of the parental mind, chases the gabble from my tongue. God bless you. I have perhaps scarcely recovered from the shock of the Accident during Arthur's holidays. The tone of a word relating to him makes me melancholy. For myself it takes much to make me hang out that yellow flag for an hour even.

Your loving
George Meredith

N.B. My wine-merchant shall send down the claret, if Mrs. Jessopp thinks it will suit the boy, and approves generally.

252. *To* WILLIAM HARDMAN

MS.: Garrick Club. Published: *Letters*, i. 126, with omission of one sentence and with minor variants.

Esher, Surrey
Saturday, [November 3 (error for October 31), 1863][1]

My dear Tuck,

I am under extraordinary press of work: must also rewrite two 'frolic' chapters:[2]—but I believe I shall see you on Thursday—at least, even if you go into the heart of the gale, instead of dancing diabolus on vexed waters—for time enough to squeeze your hand. God bless you. If the wind rages I shall yet more wish myself by your side. I am whelmed in MSS; full of envy of you free men, dejected as regards this novel, full of confidence for the future.

Ever, forever, / Your loving
George M.

252. [1] Hardman's date (in brackets) is obviously wrong; the correct date must have been 31 Oct. Hardman was going on a duck-shooting expedition with Morison and Virtue in the *Irene* and left London on 5 Nov. for Southampton. The party sailed on the 7th, ran into a gale, and returned to Portsmouth empty-handed (*L. & M.*, pp. 92–95).
[2] Of *Emilia*.

253. *To* WILLIAM HARDMAN

MS.: Garrick Club. Published: *Letters*, i. 127, with gross inaccuracy.

193 Piccadilly, London
Friday, [November 13, 1863]

Dearest Tuck! my bonny wild duck! whom I might have addressed to off Flushing, but for the fact that in 17 hours and 1/2 you came homeward rushing (turning a tail of such a marvellous breadth, I believe it still darkens the Dutchmen!)[1] I've written to Maxse: and now let me ax ye—if Chapman & Hall are *such* men, what wonderful powers must your Robin possess to be able to run with them fairly? 'Tis Frederic's fault that no answer you've had;—his letters he writes but rarely.[2] Old Edward tells me this, and remarks, you shall quickly a cheque get, commensurate. As for the conduct of 'Firm' he admits with a shrug that I properly censure it. The thing would be settled at once but Fred is 'taking a little holiday' (the 6th this week)—Adieu! When we meet next time will be *my* jolly day.

Signed: Robin

254. *To* WILLIAM HARDMAN

MS.: Garrick Club.

[Copsham Cottage, Esher]
[November 23, 1863]

Dearest Tuck,

　　Dog Sailor[1] arrived duly, very much astonished at the change in his fortunes. I am very well pleased with him. He has a capital head and good habits. On Thursday, Tuck! And I won't join you any longer in that bage[2] conspiracy against Demitroïa. If she has the execrable taste to prefer *Bel Demonia* to the Haymarket,[3] we will, we *will* do as she pleases. Or we might get her consent to let us go to the Haymarket *after* the Lyceum performance?—!—? In haste,

Your loving / Rob[in] / of Copsham

253. [1] See preceding letter.
　　[2] i.e. Frederic Chapman had still not paid Hardman for his article published in *OaW* on 15 Aug.
254. [1] Man or beast? I am unable to explain.
　　[2] A Sairey Gampism for *base*.
　　[3] *Bel Demonia*, 'a love story in twelve tableaux', adapted from Stendhal, was currently running at the Royal Lyceum, with Fechter and Kate Terry. Concurrently the Theatre Royal was offering Mr. and Mrs. Charles Mathews, after an absence of two years, in *Silken Fetters*, an adaptation of Scribe's *Une Chaîne*.

255. *To* MESSRS. HARPER & BROTHERS

Text: J. Henry Harper, *The House of Harper* (N.Y., 1912), p. 165. (One sentence supplied from the sales catalogue of the Jerome Kern Library, sold at Anderson Galleries, 21–24 Jan. 1929.)

Copsham Cottage, Esher
Surrey, England
[? October–November 1863][1]

Gentlemen,—

I send you proof-sheets of the first volume of a new novel of mine, now being printed (to be published by Messrs. Chapman and Hall).

This, as you will see, is called *Emilia in England* and will be complete in three volumes. *Emilia in Italy* will follow next year.

You have done me the honour to publish my *Evan Harrington* in New York. I wish consequently that you should have the early sheets of all my works. My friend Mr. James Virtue tells me that *Evan Harrington* made no mark among you. The present volume is of a different texture, and will not moreover offend as *The Ordeal of Richard Feverel* is said to have done. I think you refused to publish that; and though I have received testimony from certain of your countrymen that it was not distasteful to them, I must allow you to be the best judges of the saleable quality of a book.

Will you let me know whether you would like to have an arrangement made to publish *Emilia in England* simultaneously in New York and London? I am aware that in the present unhappy posture of affairs you cannot treat so liberally as of old. As far as that matter goes, I place myself in your hands. I have had offers previously from Mr. Fields, of Boston, but prefer, if possible, to have my books republished by the gentlemen who first made my name known in America. May I ask you whether you have seen the *Shaving of Shagpat*? If not, I will endeavour to get a copy and have it sent to you. Those who like it like it greatly; though I am bound to admit it is a little caviare to our multitude. The taste, I am told, is growing to it gradually.

Oblige me by replying without delay to the above address.

I am, Gentlemen, / Yours very faithfully,
George Meredith

---

255. [1] Hardman had the proofs of volume two of *Emilia* in November and wrote Holroyd that GM was coming on 18 Nov. to argue over his criticisms and suggestions (*L. & M.*, p. 98). He had the first sheets of volume three on 13 Jan.
Nothing came of the proposal to Messrs. Harper.

256. *To* MRS. JANET ROSS

MS.: Yale. Published: *Letters*, i. 127–30, with inaccuracies; *The Fourth Generation*, pp. 148–51, with omissions.

Esher
December 1, 1863

My dearest Janet,

I have put back my letter, thinking I might get some book to offer you.[1] You know that I recommended you for Renan's *Vie de Jésus*? Chapman had the offer of it, and would have done it, with pressure. But our worthy and most discreet Bart[2] declined to have your name mixed up with it. As things go, perhaps he was right. So the book went to Trübner.—You remember Adams,[3] whom your mother sent to the altar first and subsequently to me? He is now flourishing, if the being able to buy a business comes under that term. He consulted me after taking that step, or I think he would not have purchased Saunders & Otley's. But so it is. He is now Saunders & O. At his earnest request, I advise him. Of course, this is a secret. The position will put books for translation in my way, now and then. I had one the other day, but the translator's name was requisite. 'Une bouchée de pain.' Mrs. Gatty[4] does it. Murray called at Jeffs' to get the copyright two days after Adams had secured it.—

Now of myself a little. Can I ever forget my dearest and best woman-friend? And I must be cold of heart not to be touched by your faithfulness to your friendships. I, who let grief eat into me and never speak of it (partly because I despise the sympathy of fools and will not trouble my friends), am thereby rendered rather weak of expression at times. The battle is tough when one fights it all alone, and it is only at times that I awake from living in a darker world. But I am getting better, both in health and spirit. It is my punishment that I have to tell you what I never prove, that I love you and shall do so constantly. For I hold nothing dearer than your esteem, my dear! Writing letters seems a poor way of showing it, and yet even that I don't do! But you never vary. If you were like me, our lights would soon pass out of sight of one another, leaving me many regrets, certainly; but I acknowledge you to be the fixed star of this union, as you will be one of mine forever. So, pardon this sentimentalism. As I said, it's my punishment to have to put my case in such a tone.—I fancy, too, that your instinct believes me true to the memory of our old kindness, careless of it though I appear?—

256. [1] i.e. to translate.   [2] Janet's father.   [3] See Note 2, Letter 235.
[4] Mrs. Alfred Gatty (1807–73), writer of children's books. Her translation of Jean Macé's *Une Bouchée de pain*, under the title of *The History of a Bit of Bread*, appeared in 1864.

The noble Bart gave me capital accounts of you and my lost lady.[5] The accident occurred to Arthur while she was at Poole.[6] When he went to Norwich, I started at once for Italy to get fresh scenery and extraneous excitement. I hoped to see her on my return; but I heard that she was not alone and in the end as I was making up my mind to write for an audience, the news came that she had just reached Calais. I smote my undecided head. I am vexed beyond measure at having missed her. The news of her is so good that it tastes like fresh life to me. On this head, please give me particulars. And if she could be persuaded to write, how glad I should be!

I am here at Copsham still. Next year I shall have the place to myself, to buy or lease. I hope to be able to buy it, and then it may be made agreeable for friends. At present none but men can come. Some are usually here from Saturday to Monday. Of the Esherians I see next to nothing.—By the way, Izod behaved very nicely in his attendance on Arthur—just as you said would be the case. He was cheerful from the first. You can conceive my condition. From six in the evening to half past four in the morning my darling was insensible, only saying, once: 'Oh! is it a dream!' and staring wildly. He had on elastic boots and this fact saved him. If the boot had not come off, he would have been dragged till—I have looked over into the pit. I don't think I misbehaved myself and I certainly did not reproach poor Wyndowe—of whose folly we need not speak, seeing that he won't renew it. There is every reason to feel sure that Arthur has taken no damage whatever: nor, I think, is his pluck at all lessened.

Your Holbeins![7] I went to get them done, and was told that the Kensington Museum had been remonstrated with by photographers generally, and had abandoned the work. I tried to get Dante Rossetti to give me his. I have thought of numerous things to supplant them, but jewels seem the only resource, though I can't bear to see them either on arm, or neck, or fingers. You will receive something or other (overlooking my bad taste) with my novel in January. It is called *Emilia in England* antiposed to *Emilia in Italy* which is to follow— both in 3 volumes. The first is a contrast between a girl of simplicity and passion and our English sentimental, socially-aspiring damsels. The second (In Italy) is vivid narrative (or should be). I hope you will like it:—I can't guess whether you will. You saw, I suppose, that the *Saturday Review* has gently whipped me for *Modern Love*.[8] I am not

---

256. [5] Janet's mother.   [6] In Dorset.

[7] This and the several sentences that follow relate to the belated wedding present that GM had not yet selected—or at least obtained—for Janet.

[8] The *Saturday Review* had at last reviewed *Modern Love* etc. on 24 Oct. 1863. It conceded GM a place among living poets and novelists 'who may be said to unite real originality of thought and aim with conspicuous cleverness in workmanship', praised

the worse. And doubtless the writer meant well. I regret to say that I can't give up writing poetry, which keeps your poet poor.

You were charmed with Kinglake's book?[9] In style it beats anything going, but in judgment it is bad, and it cannot take place as a piece of artistic history. Here is Maxse writing hard against it, he being a reverent admirer of Lord Raglan and a just man. Kinglake's treatment of the French is simply mean.—And mean too is the position England assumes as critic everywhere—as actor nowhere, if it can be helped. We are certainly in a mess about this Congress,[10] and the French alliance is a matter of the past.

I read the *Times* Alexandrine correspondent[11] diligently to catch the friend's hand behind the official pen.

How good of you to look forward to my little man's future! Who knows? He might be found fit to be a merchant and what offer could be better than yours? But I must first get at his inclinations and try his strength.

Now, my dearest good Janet, adieu for a space—till I repeat it. Write to me. Give my warm regards to your husband, and know me ever

Your loving
George Meredith

Arthur comes home on the 23rd. He will write to you before the month closes.

257. *To* WILLIAM HARDMAN

MS.: Garrick Club. Published: *Letters*, i. 131, with inaccuracies and omission of the postscript.

[Copsham Cottage, Esher]
Tuesday, [December 1, 1863]

Dearest Lovely Tuck,

I dine with Maxse at the 'Garrick' to-morrow and, as I want to converse with you on the matter of your objections to points in *Emilia*, I should like to know whether you can give me a bed, 'cause if you can you will: which is established in my mind. And if you can, will you

---

'The Old Chartist' and the roadside poems, but said that GM 'indulges in an elaborate analysis of a loathsome series of phenomena which he is pleased to call "modern love"'.

[9] The first two volumes of Kinglake's *Invasion of the Crimea* appeared in 1863, the seventh and eighth in 1887.

[10] Presumably the one proposed by Napoleon III on 4 Nov. 'for the settlement of various international difficulties'. The invitation to participate was declined for England by Earl Russell on 25 Nov. (Joseph Irving, *The Annals of Our Time*, 1890).

[11] Janet herself.

send a line to Chapman & Hall's; or better, to Maxse, at the Garrick containing the wishèd word for me. Yes, say to Maxse at the Garrick (with my initials in the corner of address) and then I'll come to Tuck and fight him; but with full acknowledgment of the soundness of some of his criticism and value of his advice. I'm glad Tuck likes it, on the whole. It's impossible to tell him what a difficulty I got myself into, by altering my original conception and scheme.

With fiery love, / Your own
Robin

—I presume you have by this time heard from Fred C[hapman] for I received by the morning's post a refutation of the Virtue report of calling for St. B's account;[1] hot, indignant, anxious; ('pray communicate with Morison' etc.). So he may have decided to conciliate Hardman's opinion. It has been simple carelessness combined with a bashful reluctance: which coyness must now be melted, and I trust Tuck has taken the Vy. [or Vq.?] of a cheque.

    Adams sends back map.[2] I enclose. Has he written approval to you? He says, 'dear little map—forward to H[ardman].' I obey.—

258. *To* WILLIAM HARDMAN

MS.: Garrick Club.

Esher
Christmas Day, [1863]

A Thousand to Tuck! and not one more than that to Demitroïa!—

    Sons desire of Tuck that he go, and for five Bob procure or book, or toy, or what he and his she think good, and present it on Sunday to Nelly in Arthur's name.[1] For which Sons will refund on their approaching visit.—

    Out walking yesterday, Sons found their lost boot![2]—We enshrine it, damp with a thousand rains—the doer of a priceless service.

    FitzGerald can't come. His wife's state is serious. I am alone with the little man. Health, digestion, and all blessings to you both.

Your loving
George M.

257. [1] St. B. = St. Bernard = Cotter Morison, whose brother-in-law, James Virtue, was apparently the source of a report, denied by Chapman, that pressure had to be exercised before Morison's account was properly balanced.

    [2] The map to accompany *Explorations in Australia: The Journals of John McDouall Stuart during the Years 1858–1862*, which Hardman was editing for Adams's firm, Saunders & Otley.

258. [1] Helen Hardman's birthday, 27 Dec., was celebrated by the Hardmans instead of Christmas.

    [2] i.e. the one lost in his riding accident of the previous summer. (See Letters 242 and 243.)

259. *To* Mrs. Augustus Jessopp

MS.: Yale. Published: *Letters*, i. 131–2, with minor variants.

Esher
Tuesday night, [December 29, 1863]

My dear Mrs. Jessopp,

The Son blooms in the air of home. How could I have stopped envy[1] from my living heart so long? But I have him and won't moan that it's only for six weeks. More than ever do I thank the blessed chance that inspired you to make yourselves known to me and render me the most deeply indebted of men. For, I see not only that every care is taken of my darling under your roof, but that Happiness is his vital air there. He breathes it. Shall he not be robust in spirit? At least I have faith in the experiment.

Now, I have an engagement to go to my friend Maxse with Arthur next month—a visit long delayed by me and not to be put off. But, you must come to me this time . . . will you not? I should be grieved to miss you! I wish to know when you are to be in London . . . the date! And I will conform to it. Please, reply; so that I may write to my now impatient sea captain, who will not believe that I mean to be with him at all. And tell me of Gordon,[2] and of your Christmas. Thackeray's death startled and grieved me.[3] And I, who think I should be capable of eyeing the pitch-black King if he knocked for me in the night!— Alas for those who do not throw the beetle!—Of Emilia I cannot speak. She grieves me. I have never so cut about created thing. There's good work in her: but *the* work? That note of interrogation is in person

Your faithful
George Meredith

260. *To* William Hardman

MS.: Garrick Club. Published: *Letters*, i. 133–4, with numerous omissions and inaccuracies.

Copsham
Tuesday, [January 12, 1864]

My bones, dear Tuck, are more eloquent to me of the Ball on Friday night than I shall be to you. Old Parsimony[1] must be right.

259. [1] Doubtful reading.   [2] Unidentified.
  [3] Thackeray had died suddenly in the night of 23 Dec.
260. [1] His housekeeper, Miss Grange.

'You changed thick breeches for thin, thick socks and boots for them capering patents, and out in that ther' frost, and then wonders you feels pains in your bones, and calls it Indigestion and Izod's wine—' (For I dined there on Sunday, accepting the invitation only *after* hearing that they were to give also a dinner party on the day before—alas! Soup with the meat floating in shreds and telling of twice boiling: woolly cod, sausage cutlets! spareribs of pork: mince pies baked for the twentieth time!— Enough. Wine called margaux.—Well! Yesterday I walked to Mickleham with Sons, taking him on my back returning, and then two miles in a fly, so that he wasn't tired. It didn't cure me. I shiver and feel like an ancient frame. Grenobbbble[2] was not at home.—The Ball? I try to remove the mists of jaundice, but I can't get a view of it without some yellow. It was frightful to me. The young women (saving the Clarke girls) were hideous. The old ones talked of the weather and shivered, as I do now at the recollection of my suffering. My dear Tuck, if you want a sight of the room, open your piano's lid; strike all the notes and see the little bobbing heads in the interior. They bob to some purpose; but Oh! this sight! Esher's young men were hardly better than its females—I use the word in all its offensiveness. At 12 midnight, supper. Champagne-cup (small beer, sweetened, with a fizz) to wash down blocks of incarnate dyspepsia in a room half frost, half fire. The women who had danced would sit in the draughts, and those who hadn't, chattered they knew not what with imbecile chins. All partook of Champagne-cup. I have the satisfaction of knowing that I pressed it upon two; filling my own glass at the same time and speeding it down the table with admirable dexterity. I left at two a.m. I am told that some young men, called upon by Izod to cheer the ladies, hostesses of the evening, did so until they were drunk. I pardon their frail stomachs.—Wyndowe, after the bottle of Moselle, gave a sniff, and lit a cigar, and refused to go. But that your Robin always keeps his appointment he would have followed the Captain's[3] example. I walked to Esher and walked home, and precious cowowowowowold it was, Tuck.— Yes, a *short* article on W[ester]n Australia would help me.[4] I don't *think* I can come to you on Thursday. On Friday to Maxse. My Love to that changeful creature, Demitroïa. I send you proofs of *Emilia*. Forward them to Johnson, Bullion Office, Bank.

Your loving
Robin

---

260. [2] Justin Theodore Vulliamy, GM's future father-in-law. Though Mr. Vulliamy was of French extraction, I know of no association with Grenoble.
[3] Captain = Wyndowe.
[4] Hardman wrote an article on 'The Australian Protest' for the *Ipswich Journal*, substituting for GM (*L. & M.*, pp. 124–5).

[Marginal postscripts] Jeames's leaders of joy in the *Times* on the 7 months' Royal Baby have been magnificent and should procure for the family La Plûche a patent of nobility.⁵ My Prins!

The Prince of Hesse, through the Princess Alice, does more to move the Queen than the Prussian.⁶

Remember me to Poco.

261. *To* AUGUSTUS JESSOPP

MS.: Yale. Published: *Letters*, i. 132–3 (dated *Jan. 1864*), slightly edited.

Esher
Wednesday, [January 13, 1864]

My dear Jessopp,

Shall you be in Town and visible to me, on Wednesday, on Thursday, on Friday week?

Do, write and tell me you are well: for, all my friends are croaking; fog is about: blue mould sits on the fair aspect of Companionship, and I want to know that somebody's all right. My son is all right. I am not all right. Emilia Belloni is not all right. She has worried me beyond measure and couldn't expect to be all right. She will be, when she's in Italy. As to character, I think you will have no doubt of her flesh and blood. How you will like the soul of the damsel, I can't guess. Out in February.—

Are you rejoicing at a seven months' Heir to England's Throne? Have you not admired the loyal leaders of Jeames de la Plûche in the *Times*? My Prins! It is of course matter for quiet hearty congratulation, but I confess that this excited flunkeyism of our Press makes one even look at the other extreme and see a manliness in the American.¹

Your words on Norwich School Prize-Day appeared in *I*[*pswich*] *J*[*ournal*].²

⁵ A son was born to the Prince and Princess of Wales on 8 Jan. As the Princess had been on the ice at Frogmore at four o'clock in the afternoon, the birth of the child at 8.58 was the cause of great surprise and comment. The confinement had not been expected until March. Leaders apropos of the event appeared in *The Times* on 9 and 11 Jan.

Thackeray had published in *Punch* (1845–6) *The Diary of C. Jeames de la Pluche, Esq.*, in which Jeames, a footman, acts as commentator on current events. For GM's earlier designation of the Prince of Wales as 'the Prins', see Letter 234.

⁶ Princess Alice, second daughter of Queen Victoria, had married the Grand Duke of Hesse in 1862. Her older sister Victoria had married Frederick ('the Prussian'), heir to the throne of Prussia, in 1858. GM's remark refers to the trouble over Schleswig and Holstein, which came to a head four days later with Bismarck's ultimatum to Denmark, followed by an Austro-Prussian invasion. Though English sympathies were overwhelmingly with Denmark, the Royal family was divided—the Queen being pro-German and the Prince of Wales pro-Dane.

261. ¹ See preceding letter.

² As one of GM's weekly contributions to the *Ipswich Journal*.

Arthur sends his love to Mrs. Jessopp, and I ask you, what privileges are these of his years that enable him to send that pretty wheedling word, while I have to content myself with 'regards'! I am almost tempted to say with exclamatory, dramatic, cockney bards, 'forsooth', after it. And I mean so much more, don't you see! But these are things one endures with one's acceptance into practical life—collars likewise. When collars and tail-coats are abolished,—well! I shouldn't like to be photographed then. However, till I wear that broad grin, I am your loving

George M.

262. *To* WILLIAM HARDMAN

MS.: Garrick Club.

Copsham Cottage, Esher
Wednesday, [January 13, 1864]

Dear Tuck,

Still queer, though not enough to pull the spirit down and prevent exercise for medicine. Ye galley slaves! (Pardon the use of apostrophe —I know it's French.) Ah!—hem!—I send more proofs. Forward to Bullion Johnson, and your opinion, and remarks, to me. Poor Maxse! a letter from his wife to say he's suddenly prostrate with bronchitis. Our visit postponed. I wonder whether I shall see Tuck to-morrow? I'm damned if I think I *could* see him to-day, if the fog's anything with you as with us. I can't more than see across garden.

A letter from Grrrenobbl',[1] inviting Sons and Pa to-day: but the moist fog supervenes.

How is that fickle Demitroïa?

Does she want any French books?

Et, vous, mon Tuck, comment vous etc. etc.

Your befogged
Robin

262. [1] See Note 2, Letter 260.

263. *To* WILLIAM HARDMAN

MS.: Garrick Club. Published: *Letters*, i. 136.

66 Brook Street
Hanover Square, London[1]
Thursday, [January 21, 1864]

Sweet Tuck,

I bring Sons to go to Rossetti to have his face taken. If I can I will get away and sleep at Gordon Street. Haply he mayn't be at home. I shall not be later than half past ten.

Your loving and grateful
Robin

Love to the fickle ONE.

264. *To* FREDERICK A. MAXSE

MS: Maxse Papers. Envelope postmarked *London, Fe 4 64*.

[London]
[February 4, 1864]

My dear Maxse,

I muddled my time on Monday, missed the train that should have brought me to you before dinner, and becoming but a fizzing vessel after, I lost all count of time and rushed to you at an unearthly hour. I need not say how much I regretted not seeing you.—But shortly we must meet, even if I go house-hunting with you. My time will soon be my own.—I can't bear the notion of your going to sea, but as little do I like your giving up a profession in which you have made a name and would gather laurels. You will, if you do give it up, feel the blank time grievously as you get older. You renounce what you have vowed. My personal feelings would counsel you like a loving (or *too* loving) woman, and say 'Offend not the Deities of Mischance by daring them.' I desire my friend to be safe and breathing the air that gives me life, peacefully: but I do not wish him to defeat the promise of his youth.—England's position at present is painful to a man who loves her.[1] Snubbed by small Germans on all sides; quietly sneered at by France—Peace! Peace! but at how sad a price! Yet, for *us* war is very serious. We have become a Peace-machine.

263. [1] A printed address on paper borrowed at the office of Saunders & Otley.
264. [1] A reference to the Austro-Prussian invasion of Denmark (see Note 6, Letter 260). Palmerston had refused to intervene despite strong English sympathy, not shared by the Queen, for Denmark.

Much as I should delight to have you near me, I must tell you that, though the houses you mention are high in station to a healthy air, they *are* cockney—a plot of eight, with *towers*, without a tree, to my mind detestable. Write soon, dear friend, tell me minutest things of yourself and know me ever your loving

George M.

Boy,[2] I presume to be well, and his Mama—at whose photograph there is a constant gathering of all visitors here.

265. *To* WILLIAM HARDMAN

MS.: Garrick Club.

Copsham
Wednesday, [February 17, 1864]

Dearest Tuck!

Tuck ever! though reduced. The same thought was striking my heart while it passed through yours—what a time since I saw Tuck! But it ain't you know, for I've been living in Gordon Street of late.

To-night to Morison. To-morrow to Mdme Venturi[1] just from Genoa for particulars in relation to *Emilia in Italy*. The week following engaged unless I come on Wednesday?

I write in a horrid hurry. Pardon and love me ever. Tell D.T. I eat with good appetite off my 'piece of plate'.[2] Ever to both of you

Your loving
Robin

266. *To* WILLIAM HARDMAN

MS.: Garrick Club. Published: *Letters*, i. 137–8, with omission of two sentences.

Esher
Wednesday, [February 24, 1864]

My dear Tuck,

I have been away from the cot. I am direly disturbed at my enforced absence from you and Demitroïa and—and the G.M.![1] Take G.M. from

264. [2] Maxse's son Ivor, now two years old.

265. [1] Emilia Venturi, sister-in-law of James Stansfield, M.P., Junior Lord of the Admiralty, and a close friend of Mazzini.

   [2] No doubt a birthday present, as GM's birthday was 12 Feb.

266. [1] G.M. = Great Mother = Hardman's mother, Mrs. Knowles. The first G.M. in the following sentence is of course Meredith.

the G.M. what remains? Nothing. I feel as nothing. There's an extraordinary fatality about Bullion. He crosses our star, Tuck. Not
satisfied with robbing you of me, he must now take Morison.—What
a Thursday evening I shall pass under the strong light of Fancy's contrast. Oh! Lord! the women! *and*—Though, I must not be ungrateful
to poor Bullion, who is a good fellow:—only he is so unlucky in his
plans. All pleasure attend you! Success wait on you! Smooth flow the
Sauces!—may the filets tender be! Nor aught to ruffle the Olympian
brow of Tuck the host!

being the prayer of
his loving Robin

267. *To* WILLIAM HARDMAN

MS.: Garrick Club. Published: *Letters*, i. 138, with inaccuracies.

[Esher]
Tuesday, [March 1, 1864]

My dearest Tuck,

Your invitation is a mockery. You have combined with Circum-
stance to keep me from a sight of the Gr[ea]t M[other]. On Wednesday
to Morison: on Thursday to the 'Wandering Minstrels'[1] at Lord
Ed[ward] Fitzgerald's, after dining with Arthur Lewis:[2] on Friday to
a dinner here: on Saturday, Copsham reception. Sunday—guests.
Monday—Mickleham:[3] and so on. Damn you, Tuck! What do you
mean by it? And, Oh Lord! I must retrench, for I'm going to publish
on my own account. I give no more to crossing-sweepers and drink
small beer, if Emilia fail to hit her mark. Give my respectful compliments to your Mama. And I hope your tum-tum is stronger, old boy?
I still improve. Since I can't see you,—write like a dear fellow, and tell
me of yourself, Demitroïa and the chicks. Arthur flourishes.

Your loving
George M.

267. [1] A famous amateur band, of which Lord Edward Fitzgerald was a member.
   [2] Arthur Lewis, a member of the firm of Lewis & Allenby, theatrical agents, cultivated
the society of artists, writers, and musicians. He was conductor of a choir first called 'the
Jermyn Band', because it met in Jermyn St. (1858–62), and later 'the Moray Minstrels'
when Lewis bought Moray Lodge. In 1867 he married GM's friend Kate Terry, the
actress.
   [3] Though he does not say so, GM was going to Mickleham to see Marie Vulliamy, his
future wife.

268. *To* WILLIAM HARDMAN

MS.: Garrick Club.

Copsham
Friday night, [March 4, 1864]

Dearest Tuck,

Can't I dine with you on *Sunday*: by which means I secure a better
chance of seeing Mrs. Knowles. If this gets to you in time let me hear
by Sunday morning's post. Miss Grange is only now recovering from
a cough that has knocked her down, and no one is here. I have made
arrangements to be free on Sunday, and *may*, even if I don't hear from
you, run up to Town in the afternoon. How about a telegram: only
don't send it after six p.m., or it will go to Richmond.

Ever, in spite of your intense coldness and beastly injustice,
the Robin who loves you

269. *To* ARTHUR LEWIS

Text: Maggs Brothers Catalogue 346 (1916), p. 90.

Esher
March 6, 1864

Dear Lewis,

Will this do? I think it beats t'other.[1]

270. *To* AUGUSTUS JESSOPP

MS.: Yale. Published: *Letters*, i. 136–7 (dated only *1864*), with omissions and minor
variants.

Esher
Monday night, [March 7, 1864]

My dear Jessopp,

As to the book, [illegible]!—one of Chapman & Hall's men put
a paper on it, with your name, and returned it. He has written to
Mudie to that effect; but stupidly delayed doing so. The matter must
be set right in a few days, and I'm sorry exceedingly that your
kindness should have given you such bother.—I met Clabburn and
Sandys the other night at Arthur Lewis's. Sandys has some fine conceptions for pictures. Altogether, he is one of the most remarkable of

269. [1] Said to have accompanied a poem entitled 'Hatton's "God of War" ' and support-
ing Denmark in its war with Prussia. Forman (*Bibliography* p. 222) prints a dozen lines
of the poem from the Maggs Catalogue. Hatton was presumably D. L. Hattan, the
composer, who had written 't'other'.

the 'brushes' of our day, with the quaintest stolid Briton way of looking at general things. But artists see their square of canvas and little more—add the gilt frame. Sandys has a romantic turn that lets me feed on him.—What you say of Arthur requiring to *make blood* to be lively in body and mind, is my view and shows me that we strike one note. Let men make good blood, I constantly cry. I hold that to be rightly materialist—to understand and take Nature as she is—is to get on the true divine highroad. That we should attain to a healthy humanity, is surely the most pleasing thing in God's sight. Now, of another matter. The book is to be published at my risk and for my profit.[1] It will be out in a fortnight. In a month from that date I can draw something. Meantime, if any pressure should be perchance on you, you, my friend, will let me know, and I will get what is wanted and forward it. Nothing but my carelessness puts me behind in my money accounts. I make, apart from novels, enough for Arthur and myself. It comes and goes. If this novel does not pay well, I shall retrench rigidly, book my bills, deny friends, and have no purse, and look above the head of the crossing-sweeper. I know that you understand how the delay has been superinduced. It will hardly occur again. I have trusted to your good heart in full faith, as doubtless you feel. That I should at all inconvenience you, is not necessary, and you will always speak openly on that head—as I am now acting—will you not? —The novel has good points, and some of my worst ones. It has no plot, albeit a current series of events: but being based on character and continuous development, it is not unlikely to miss a striking success.

But, hail to the Beetle! verily I have made new blood by its aid, of the pure crimson, from which great Poesies and stern conceptions should flow! I am growing fuller of hope and thirst for work. I begin to believe again that I may do 'something'. Judge me not by this present performance!—I think I may say that I will be with you, Heaven consenting, the middle of this month. Is Arthur correct when he talks of holidays commencing the 23rd of March?—We shall have much to talk over; and by the way Alys[2] has not arrived, O man whose energy did win the admiration of Sandys and myself jointly! I want to see it; I want to see you. Give Mrs. Jessopp my warmest greeting. My heart is with her who watches over my boy, more than with the others of this world, except perhaps for a weak leaning towards whomsoever it may be. Write, and know me ever

Your loving
George Meredith

270. [1] A reference to *Emilia in England*.
     [2] Unidentified: apparently some literary work.

271. *To* FREDERICK A. MAXSE

Text: *Letters*, i. 134–5, dated 1864 and placed among the letters of January. Collated with the typed copy in the Maxse Papers, from which the lower-case italics have been adopted.

Esher
Friday night, [? March 11 or 18, 1864]

My dear Maxse,

I had thought of 'Hamble Ridge', and also of 'Hamble Mount', which latter, though more common, is perhaps preferable.[1] Either one would do very well. Is there any characteristic of the *river* to give it christening? as a *reach*, a *bluff*—'Hamble Reach' would not sound ill. We should sit together and give it a title over a cup of claret. Any *trees* to distinguish it?—'Hamble Willows', 'Hamble Elms', etc.—The site of the House impresses me favourably. I must have for *my* daily meal a good *plateful* of sky; and the sun must drop into it, or I'm not satisfied. I feed on him and the field he traverses. This, apparently, you will get.—How is health with you? I progress excellently, but only to get into a higher circle of desires and hopes, despairs and dreams. And if a fair face touches me, what is there for me but to moan at my loss of philosophy?[2] Can I go to her and say, 'Love me'? She sucks my comfort from my life, and that's all. Or, not all! It's experience!—for this were we born. My philosophy distils again to just that bitter drop.— *Emilia* in a fortnight *positively*.[3] Poor little woman! What will the British P[ublic] say to a Finis that holds aloft no nuptial torch? All she does, at the conclusion, is to leave England. Perhaps you, too, will be disappointed. I trust not.

Say to Mrs. Maxse that I shall be very anxious to be, if not the first, one of the first of her guests at Hamble the, as yet, unnamed. And we will go and hear the nightingales, as you and I did, my dear fellow, when they chuckled a love-snatch and your heart had not found a home. Note 'Frost on the May-night' close at the end of *Emilia*.— You will receive your copy the day she appears. Shall you haply review the production? It's my undertaking—the risk mine and the uncounted profits. I told Chapman I should want a good sum, and did not object to publish the book myself. He thought the closing alternative best, and it may be for me.—What are you reading? What

271. [1] Maxse, who had been house-hunting in February, had found a place in Hampshire. The name eventually chosen for the house was Ploverfield.

[2] An oblique reference to GM's feelings for Marie Vulliamy.

[3] The references to the publication date of *Emilia* and to GM's growing love for Marie provide the main clues to the date of this letter. Although in Letter 270 GM also says that *Emilia* is to be out in a fortnight, the italicized adverb *positively* here seems to warrant a slightly later date than for Letter 270. The novel appeared some time within the first week in April.

meditating? The Fates are stirring with a mighty spoon at this hour.—
May Heaven bless you and yours through it all and soon give me sight
of you!

Your loving
George M.

272. *To* AUGUSTUS JESSOPP

MS.: Yale. Published: *Letters*, i. 140 (dated only *1864*), with variants.

Esher
[? c. March 16, 1864]

My dear Jessopp,

Morley's *Writers before Chaucer*[1] is not worth buying, seeing that
I am about to bring the book to you.

Your cheery letter gave me particular peace of mind on a matter
that worried me.[2] I trust all will go tolerably well with the book,
though, what the public will make of 3 volumes without a climax of
incident (Finis waving no nuptial torch)—the climax being all in
a development of character—I am at a loss to imagine; and so wait
patiently, hoping for here and there a critic to interpret me to the
multitude.

As to your proposal (for the Whist I'll be one, notwithstanding that
I am led to suppose Mrs. Jessopp plays *comme quatre*!)—I *must* let the
boy decide; and think he'll be for Copsome, in the county of Surrey.
I expect to be able to come to you next Saturday. Or, if Arthur comes
to me, shall I bring him back, and stay for a longer term? I know what
sharp feminine eyes will discern in this. It really isn't base treason—
indeed! I am at her mercy. Write by return of post, that I may get
the letter before I leave here.

Yours ever,
George Meredith

272. [1] The first volume of a projected history of English literature by Henry Morley
(1822–94), who became Professor of English Language and Literature at University
College, London, in 1865. The book was published by C. & H.
[2] Arthur's fees.

273. *To* FREDERICK A. MAXSE

Text: typed copy, Maxse Papers. Published: *Letters*, i. 114–15, with omissions.

Esher

Saturday, [March 26, 1864]

Dear Maxse,

I could not answer your letter in time on Thursday, and much as I wished to come to you, could not, seeing that I had to meet the Son at Shoreditch station that evening.[1] He is, I thank the Lord! well and brisk. Have you decided anent the title of the house? I could only help you with criticism. No really taking name struck me. I go to Norwich with Arthur in about two weeks, and have multitudinous engagements, but will keep myself pledged to you for a week in May.—Now that Emilia's off my mind, alas! Poetry presses for speech! I fear I am, unless I make great effort, chained to this unremunerative business for a month or so. I am getting material for the battle-scenes in *Emilia in Italy*.[2] But, I have an English novel, of the real story-telling order that must roll off soon and precede it.[3] Minor tales, too, and also an Autobiography.[4] Which to be at first, is the point, and while I hesitate comes a 'Wayside piece', a sonnet, a song—Ambition says—'Write this grand Poem.' I smile idiotic and should act with all due imbecility but for baker's bills and Boy.

I hope yours is well. Tell me of your health and Mrs. Maxse's, to whom my kindest salute, and know me ever

Your loving

George Meredith

273. [1] Arthur was home for the Easter holidays. Easter was 27 Mar. in 1864.

[2] The sequel to *Emilia in England*. It was first published under the title *Vittoria* in the *Fortnightly Review* (hereinafter cited as *FR*), 15 Jan.–1 Dec. 1866.

[3] *Rhoda Fleming*, published in Oct. 1865.

[4] W. M. Meredith (*Letters*, i. 115 n.) says that the autobiography was never written. But Richard B. Hudson ('Meredith's Autobiography and *The Adventures of Harry Richmond*', *Nineteenth Century Fiction*, ix. 38–49) demonstrated that it was the novel finally entitled *The Adventures of Harry Richmond* and that W. M. Meredith's inaccuracy in transcribing Letter 279 was responsible for his erroneous statement. (See also Note 3, Letter 113.)

274. *To* MRS. EDWARD CHAPMAN

MS.: Yale.

Copsome, Esher
[Late March 1864][1]

Dear Mrs. Edward,

We have trusted too long to One, whose skill in keeping me from the Wells[2] is only equalled by his treason to you. He has told me again and again, that you really don't care much to see me; and I, in deep sadness, have felt bound to believe him. But, I do so no more. I have determined for the future to communicate personally with you. I will match the fire of a young heart against the infamous cunning of Old Ed:!—I . . . much.[3] Will you name your week in April when sage Meta and flighty Florry are at home? I shall then have shipped the Son back to Norwich—say, after the tenth? Please, let me hear. A letter addressed to Piccadilly will be best (*not* entrusted to the Traitor). . . .[3] Make an engagement and I will solemnly append my signature to it.

I am, with kind regards to my fair friends, Dear Mrs. Edward,

Your faithful
George Meredith

275. *To* WILLIAM HARDMAN

MS.: Garrick Club. Published: *Letters*, i. 140–1 with omission of a sentence and with numerous inaccuracies.

The School House, Norwich[1]
Care of Rev. A. Jessopp
[April 6, 1864]

My dear Tuck,

You will have received a copy of *Emilia* before this. Though the letter of yours sent to Chapman & Hall's was a week old, the laughter in it was fresh; and the picture of Tuck, with a Champer in his hand, stalking majestic about his new domain,[2] will not speedily pass into

---

274. [1] The internal evidence supports this date, and on the evidence of Letter 278 GM did visit the Chapmans in Apr. 1864.

   [2] Tunbridge Wells, where the Chapmans lived.

   [3] Part of a line cut away.

275. [1] GM had returned with Arthur to pay the Jessopps a visit, and though he does not say so, Marie Vulliamy was also in Norwich at the same time. I think it unlikely that they travelled up together, but it is clear from Letter 279 that they travelled back together.

   [2] Hardman had rented Thames Cottage, Hampton, which he was busy furnishing toward the end of March (*L. & M.*, p. 166). His London house was undergoing alterations.

spectral tints. I am very busy. To save myself from poetry (which I haven't done), I am writing a few stories, but shall soon be at the regular jog-trot and in a new style. Health becoming really good; conception's blooming. I foresee that I shall get knocks on the head from the reviews, and should like to be out of hearing for 3 months, but courage!—I am here with the Son, who is in good condition. Jessopp as cheery as ever: his wife a little more matronly in appearance though not in tone.—I have a work on my hands to correct; while the boys are in school—*Mazzini's Works*³—there's a Red cloak for you, Sir John!—With this, a tale, sketch of novel etc., my hours are occupied. Write, and give me Demitroïa's comments—they'll be cruel! Assure me of your love, old boy! and know me

[Signature cut away]

276. *To* SAMUEL LAURENCE¹

MS.: Yale.

Copsham Cottage, Esher
Friday, [? April 29, 1864]

My dear Laurence,
   Maurice Fitz-Gerald tells me you are willing to come to my small home. Do, and let it be the first of many times. I have to speak to you about a matter:² but no more of it till we meet. On Sunday morning there's a train at a little past nine.* Come by that, for the next is at 2 p.m., and I should like to show you a bit of our country here, and how we defeat winter. Maurice will doubtless communicate with you to-morrow (Saturday).

Ever faithfully yours,
George Meredith

   *A quarter after nine.

275. ³ Smith, Elder & Co. published Madame Venturi's translation of Mazzini's works in six volumes, 1864–70. GM was not only a friend of Madame Venturi but also an ardent champion of Mazzini, who is depicted at the beginning of *Vittoria* as a heroic leader called 'the Chief'.
276. ¹ See Letter 236 and Note 6.
   ² A portrait of Katherine Vulliamy which GM commissioned Laurence to paint as his wedding present to her. She was married on 11 June to Francis George Wheatcroft, described in the Mickleham Registry as a clerk living at Caen, France, but said by Robert Esmonde Sencourt (*The Life of George Meredith*, 1929, p. 133) to be a clergyman.

277. *To* SAMUEL LAURENCE

MS.: Yale.

Copsome Cottage
Esher, Surrey
May 4, [1864]

My dear Laurence,
  The lady[1] is to be married in June. There is no time to lose. Can you come to Leatherhead (S. Western line), by 9.45 train on Monday morning next? I will meet you there and we will walk on [to] the house. Do, if only you can; for she will then be ready. Look at train book to verify time. A later train would make you rather late in the day. There may be one about 12, if you cannot come before. I will try and call on Thursday or Friday, but pray write, in the event of your not seeing me.

Your faithful
George Meredith

Appoint Tuesday, if Monday's unsuitable.

278. *To* WILLIAM HARDMAN

MS.: Garrick Club. Published: *Letters*, i. 141–2, with omissions and inaccuracies.

Copsham, Esher
Wednesday, [May (? 4), 1864]

Respected Sir!
  Indeed if you are that same Tuck whom I knew;—which is possible, albeit you no longer, as is told to me, wear a waistcoat boasting the power to embrace two sacks of potatoes:—if you are the same, I know positively that your heart at least will not have diminished and that I am not ejected from it during its daily operations. I have been that busy—but more, I have besides had engagements so numerous—and besides, here's a man staying with me (Sandys, the artist) painting a great picture of Spring. *He came down here when I came.*[1] He will remain probably two weeks longer. Dear Sir, might I bring him over on Sunday?—

277. [1] Katherine Vulliamy.
278. [1] Sandys lived off and on in Norwich and seems to have come down on the same train as GM and Marie, but in a different compartment, I infer. (See following letter.) The *Athenaeum* (11 Mar. 1865) in its 'Fine-Art Gossip' says that Sandys is reported to have been engaged on the picture for two years and that the subject is represented by a young girl dressed in white, with spring flowers in her lap.

My dear Old Boy (for it must be you, though you do talk so strange) I am very anxious to see you. I have been to Norwich, to the Isle of Wight, to Tunbridge Wells:—I think I shall have to go to Italy, for everybody says *Emilia in Italy* should be forthcoming as speedily as may be: and I want a little local colour. I wish to hear your plans, and had intended in any case to try you for Sunday. You will like Sandys (if it is not objectionable to you to receive him: in which affirmative case, Robin alone). He is a fine painter and a good fellow. As regards myself, and that's what you like to hear of, I know, I am working at divers things: 'Wayside pieces', Odes (to Garibaldi and Beethoven), Sonnets—*Emilia in Italy*—An Autobiographic tale:— Heaps of MSS.²—Are not my hands full? So's my heart; but there's always a comfortable chamber there for you both.

I was at Cambridge during Newmarket Week with certain Under-graduates.³ The Cook of Trinity distinguished himself nightly. I rode on the Beacon turf, but didn't bet. I wanted to study the scene, and have done so. I saw my Prins.

I am not in the best of spirits, as perhaps you divine. Health is good and so is power to work, and one daren't pray for more.— They've elected me for the Garrick, my Tuck. To whom the honour?— How is Poco? There's no room for him here or I should have made a request for his society. Does he prosper in his suit? Write to your much-tried friend and never judge him harshly. I have an instinct that Demitroïa has found more excuses for him than you have.

Your loving
George Meredith

Ethel and Nelly must be well, of course, since they are barely men-tioned. My love to them.

279. *To* AUGUSTUS JESSOPP

MS.: Yale. Published: *Letters*, i. 142–4, with variants and inaccuracies.

Esher
Wednesday, May 18, 1864

My dear Jessopp,

The [*Ipswich*] *Journal* is so full of advertisements that I am post-

278. ² For the various compositions mentioned here, see Notes 2, 3, 4, Letter 273. The MSS. were not his own but those that he was reading for C. & H. and Saunders & Otley

³ This was the occasion of GM's visit to H. M. Hyndman, whom he had met at Maurice FitzGerald's in Seaford the preceding year. Hyndman (*The Record of an Ad-venturous Life*, pp. 71–73) describes the visit, which he says lasted a fortnight and included exhausting walks, sight-seeing about the University, and expeditions to Ely and New-market. It seems unlikely, however, that the visit could have lasted so long.

poned, anent the notice of Sermons,¹ weekly, and can't predicate when
it will appear. Meantime, send a volume to C. Warren Adams, Esq.,
66 Brook St., Hanover Square.² He will review it, (and at least without
hostility), in the *Church and State Review*: I hope this month: but am
not certain. I shall try to get a fellow to notice them in a general discussion of the subject of school sermons. I am vexed and irritated at the
treatment you receive: but it is of this world!—I get slaps for having
written *Emilia*. I am 'eminently' this or that, unpleasant, in Review
style.³ Have you ever met a Reviewer? It's curious to see how small
this thing that stings can be.—She moves, which is good. A favourable
touch to her in the *Saturday* or *Times* would launch her into more than
the middle of a 2nd Edition. I am hard at work on *Emilia in Italy*:—
all story, tell Mrs. Jessopp: no Philosopher present: action: excitement: holding of your breath, chilling horror: classic sensation. I hope
to get finished in the Autumn.—I have also in hand an Autobiography.⁴
*The Adventures of Richmond Roy, and his friend Contrivance Jack:
Being the History of Two Rising Men*:—and to be a spanking bid for
popularity on the part of this writer.

I say! what a charming line of Rail from Norwich to London by way
of Ipswich. But apparently little known, for those who took the
Journey from Norwich on a day last month were alone in the carriage
the entire length of the route;⁵ and really it is hard, for a young lady
demands all your resources to amuse her: and I wonder whether I did?
She wants a photograph of the little man. Could one be got for her?
She is well, practising music daily, and I still wonder why both of you
won't think her very handsome. The will is clearly manifested in your
refusal to do so. I mean, handsome, of that style. Some vitality being
wanted; but the lack of it partially compensated by so very much
sweetness. Thus may a cold but friendly spectator speak of her!—

Sandys will have been with me next Friday just three weeks. He is
painting country for background of a picture of the maiden Spring[:]

'Then came fair May, the fairest maid on earth'⁶

279. ¹ GM's notice of Jessopp's *Norwich School Sermons*, recently published.
² The address of Saunders & Otley, of which Adams was proprietor.
³ The *London Review*: 'Yet the work before us is . . . for several reasons eminently
unsatisfactory . . .'. Read: (Hergenhan, p. 48).
⁴ W. M. Meredith's substitution of *and* for the period at the end of this sentence
confused scholars about the 'Autobiography' for almost half a century. See Note 4,
Letter 273.
⁵ GM and Marie Vulliamy.
⁶ Spenser, 'Mutabilitie', Canto VII. xxxiv: 'Then came faire May, the fayrest mayd on
ground.'

with heaps of flowers at her feet and immense rosy periwigs of apple blossom about her poll: She with a look of unconsciousness and a rainbow over her head and such larks in the sky: a nice girl. We walk hard, though Sandys is not much of a leg at it and develops groaning feet etc. At 7 1/2 we dine and are uproarious, and I wish and he wishes you were with us. Tom Taylor speaks well of his work in the Academy. I suppose he will be here about a month longer, he has so much to do. He is going to give me a drawing of Arthur, and also of—what's the name? I've forgotten the name of the person,[7] but am not the less grateful for his kindness. This latter in the time to come.—I ask him whether he has a message for you, and he says (or tries to say) that one never knows what message to send to those one cares for, except that he'd be glad if you were here.

Since we parted I've been to Tunbridge Wells, to Ventnor, to Cambridge, and half over Surrey; I came here first with Sandys so you may imagine that I haven't had much time to spare. All kind things to Mrs. Jessopp! The young lady[8] who made her acquaintance in Norwich says innumerable kind things of her. (I don't mention what is the Norwich return for this ingenuous heartiness.)

Addio, dear friend; I am your loving
George Meredith

280. *To* MRS. [? RICHARD] COLE[1]

MS.: Yale.

Esher, Surrey
Saturday, May 21, [1864][2]

Dear Mrs. Cole,

I wished to have sent you my last novel that it might reach you in time to make a bow to you on your birthday morning. Owing to my carelessness this idea has failed. I beg you, when you receive the books to accept them as testimony of my earnest wishes for your happiness and my hope that you may live long to look after that very difficult and stormy boy, Charles. I am

Your most faithful
George Meredith

---

279. [7] Meredithian playfulness: the person was of course Marie, and Sandys did make a drawing of her.   [1] Again, Marie.
280. [1] I can only guess that this is the wife of the Richard Cole of earlier days (see Letter 41) whom I was unable to identify.
  [2] The only year during the time GM lived at Esher when 21 May fell on Saturday. The books being sent, then, would have been *Emilia*, published in April.

281. *To* WILLIAM HARDMAN

MS.: Garrick Club. Published: *Letters*, i. 144–5, with minor omissions and variants.

Esher
Sunday, [May 29, 1864]

My dearest Tuck,

I dare say you have thought that something was going on to make my love for you seem less faithful and constant than it was. I have an immense deal to tell you and something to ask you to do.[1] But you must remain mystified till we meet. I would come to-day, but Leth-bridge[2] (Smith's partner) is here and I can't leave him. Try and hold yourself disengaged to go on a mission with me next Wednesday. You will be away all night, but Demitroïa will excuse it, seeing that it is to make of me a new man. I will come on Monday evening or Tuesday afternoon.

I hope to get *Emilia in Italy* into the *Cornhill*. Tell my dearest D[emitroïa] that she will be launched on a sea of adventure and excite-ment. And, by the way, thank her for the pretty notice I see to-day in the *Saturday* [*Review*].[3] She gives her criticism very gently—con-scientiously, of course. But (tell her this) there's an end now to my working with puppets. I enter active life with my people, and am resolved to merit money—which should mean, to make it. Health sound and brain in fine working order.

I must stop or I shall be rushing into betraying exclamations. It will not be a severe task for you, this service I require of my friend. D[emitroïa] at your elbow starts one brilliant guess, and is right. Good bye.

Your loving
George M.

281. [1] It is clear that behind the deliberate but not very deep mystification of this letter lies some important development. What had happened was that GM had proposed to Marie Vulliamy and had been accepted, subject to her father's approval. The favour that GM wishes to ask of Hardman is that he hold himself in readiness to accompany GM on the following Wednesday to interview Mr. Vulliamy.

[2] William Lethbridge (1825–1901) took B.A. and M.A. degrees at Cambridge (1850 and 1853). After serving as schoolmaster for some years, he was admitted to Lincoln's Inn in 1859 and called to the bar in 1861 (Venn). He had been W. H. Smith's coach and friend in college, and William Tinsley (i. 122) says that Smith 'enticed' him into the firm despite his never having seen the inside working of a business house before and that afterwards he 'had a good deal of the control of the Smith and Son business'.

[3] Mrs. Hardman's review of *Emilia* in the 28 May issue (pp. 660–1).

282. *To* FREDERICK A. MAXSE

MS.: Maxse Papers. Envelope postmarked *My 30, 64.*

Mickleham[1]
Monday, [May 30, 1864]

My dear Maxse,

I am too happy. When can you come and see her?[2] I tread on air, and work as from a furnace.

Emilia in Italy goes on most rapidly: not simply because money is a necessity, but I have a double force in me. I hope to get her into the *Cornhill*, Smith willing. Such adventures and romantic scenes, my dear fellow! They shan't say this isn't a novel, or amusing. I am here with her, and have heaps to tell you, but no time, hardly the will, and perhaps not the power. But that I love you with just as full a heart, be sure, my dear friend. She wishes to see and know you. I am

Your loving
George Meredith

283. *To* SAMUEL LAURENCE

MS.: Yale.

Esher
Tuesday, [May 31, 1864]

My dear Laurence,

If I possibly can call this week I will. I have a prodigious deal to tell you—matter most sweet to me, but filling me with a great responsibility. I don't know whether you half guess it. If you do, believing me also to be an earnest man, you will understand that my head and heart are full.—If you don't see me, it will be as well to get the portrait[1] framed in the ordinary fashion and sent down to Mickleham so that it may be there by Friday week. It should be hung before the guests on Saturday (the bridal day). I am sure I shall like it. When you know me better you will know that I speak out any objections in criticism loudly, and can take as well as give. I believe you have the face, and the lady tells me it is improved, though saddish. That is, she admits, the characteristic. Come down here, on Saturday fortnight—will you? It's just possible you may not see me, otherwise. I am thoroughly occupied for full two weeks during my days in town.

282. [1] Where, at The Old House (built in 1636), lived Justin Theodore Vulliamy and his three unmarried daughters.   [2] Marie.
283. [1] See Note 2, Letter 276.

Are you aware that you are a particular favourite with your own favourite[2] over there? She says very pretty things of you. Adieu, my dear Laurence. Divine me as best you may.

> Your faithful
> George Meredith

284. *To* WILLIAM HARDMAN

MS.: Garrick Club. Published: *Letters*, i. 145, with minor variants.

> Mickleham
> Wednesday afternoon, [June 1, 1864]

My dear Hardman,

Here the word is that Saturday will do better.[1] Also will that suit you? Please send word to Ch[apman] & H[all]'s.—I shall go to Mickleham on Friday, and my M[arie] says *we* will meet you at the Leatherhead station on Saturday, if you will assure us of the train you will come by. She adds that you are to speak your full conviction of me, seeing that her Papa can't bear to lose her, though he always lets his daughters have their way in this matter, *sauf* the guarantee of moral character and sufficient pecuniary resources. Those are the points. God bless you, and take all my thanks for your good heart (and D[emitroïa]'s) to me in this the closest business that ever hugged my heart.

> Your own
> George M.

285. *To* FREDERICK A. MAXSE

MS.: Maxse Papers. Envelope postmarked *Ju 2 64*. Excerpts published: C. L. Cline, 'The Betrothal of George Meredith to Marie Vulliamy', *Nineteenth Century Fiction*, xvi. 231–43.

> Esher
> Wednesday night, [June 1, 1864]

My dearest Friend,

To deal with gross matter first:—of course, you feel the proceeding to have been rash: but you are one who can forgive, because you can comprehend, love's adorable folly. It happened—who knows how? She has done me the honour to love me for some time. Her sisters perceived that a snake moved in the grass. One thought my Marie merely

[2] Marie.
284. [1] For the interview with Mr. Vulliamy. See Note 1, Letter **281**.

trying her wings; and one that I was haply studying matter for a fresh novel. Between them I led a singularly excited life; acting outwardly with a composure that roused their astonishment. Not a change of feature, while my heart thumped and drummed up to my ears. But she could not act. 'When you returned from Norwich, and shook her hand in the garden, I saw her arm shuddering for half an hour afterwards', says her sister Kitty (a bride next Saturday week, my beloved being first bridesmaid, and myself not distant—how to bear the sight of her near the altar!)—Well, the Papa was spoken to, and he immediately set about making enquiries concerning your friend—satisfactory on the moral side. At last, my darling wrote, being shy in speech, and said 'I am yours, and have been long.' She told me I might ask for her, albeit nothing, as she knew, but a poor poet. She felt keenly the coldness of my welcome at the house, and the manner in which I was being misjudged. So, I met her in Norbury Park, and we decided that I should take the great plunge in the little parlour with her Papa. He listened gravely, agreed that the pecuniary look-out was not bright, but admitted that, from what he had heard, my literary status was not contemptible and that I might possibly make a sufficient income:— must see and talk to a friend or two of mine.[1] There's a reversion of a few thousands coming to me; that's all I have.[2] Marie is to have money bringing two hundred a year, settled on her. This at her father's death may perhaps be doubled. I can make by my novels doubtless five hundred annually. My other work gives me four hundred and fifty, or five hundred.[3] My health is splendid, and my beloved fills me with energy and brightness; so I think I may say that I understate what may be counted on for the novels. *Emilia in Italy* goes on swimmingly; and I am just engaging to do a serial for *Once a Week*.[4] I am

---

285. [1] GM was quite right in telling Hardman (Letter 284) that the points at issue before Mr. Vulliamy's consent could be obtained were 'the guarantee of moral character and sufficient pecuniary means'. On the evidence of this letter to Maxse it is clear that GM had come away from the interview with Mr. Vulliamy without apprehension: the usual formalities must be undergone, nothing more. Then all would be clear sailing. If this was his assumption, he had mistaken both the character of Mr. Vulliamy and the situation. 'Justin Vulliamy', says Stevenson (p. 139), 'was not only a successful businessman who despised improvidence; he was also a devout Christian of strict moral principles. The shadow overhanging Meredith's first marriage implied all sorts of impropriety.' More than six weeks were to elapse before the consent was obtained, and meanwhile the lover was subjected to a harrowing experience that he later termed 'a passage through fire'. (I have recounted the story in detail in the article listed above.)

[2] Under the will of W. J. Meredith of Gosport, his great-uncle. Mr. Meredith left one daughter, a mentally deranged woman between fifty and sixty, who stood between half a dozen reversionary heirs and an estate of £12,000–£14,000.

[3] Apparently an exaggeration: on 2 July 1864 GM wrote to Mr. Vulliamy (Letter 298) that in return for additional work for C. & H. his income was to be increased by £125, making a total of £550, in addition to his earnings from novels.

[4] The intended serial was *The Adventures of Harry Richmond*, but it was not published in *OaW*.

surcharged with stout material.—By the way, Mazzini is going to give
me an interview next week, to help me in *Emilia*.⁵ In Italy, she moves
like a fire of the skies: and they shall say of her, there, that she does
animate a novel. I long to read you some of the chapters. My Marie
pleads to be allowed to copy them, so that you can peruse them in her
handwriting, if you like. I cannot tell you how sweet she is. She is one
of the most naturally well-bred young women whom I have ever seen.
This, without any shadow of an affectation of manner. And certainly
no mind could be purer, no heart more simply devoted. Did I tell you
I engaged Laurence to make a drawing of her sister Kitty—the bride?
He saw Marie during the days when I was acting my part of 'friend and
no more', and said that he thought her the most charming creature he
had ever beheld, and *the* one whom he could go on his knees to, were
he a man disengaged. It may be that he smelt my sentiments, notwithstanding the fine mask I wore; but he was sincere, and is an earnest
man. Oddly, too, her sisters now begin to see that she is fair. Enclosed
is a libellous photograph of her. We shall soon get a better one done.
Sandys has promised to give me a drawing of her, as his offering for the
occasion. He will do it next week, I hope. Return the photograph immediately, for at present I have nothing else. Much of her beauty is in
the exquisite colouring. The hair is perfect:—fair, with a golden line
just over the forehead: the eyes blue, the lips red, soft, and full. Her
figure is ample, but plastic, and the carriage of the bust full of grace and
ease. She plays the piano divinely, and indeed it is in music (and now in
letters to her lover) that she *speaks*.

Well?—is the prospect bad? Are we both very big fools? My
dearest friend, we love. You know love and how it enlarges the heart,
spurs the vital powers, and speeds the intellectual. My life is doubled
by her. My burden of responsibility is faced and I have no fear.—We
shall have to wait some months. I must get a house (where?) and
furnish it, and arrange, and arrange, and then we two are launched,
and may the Heavens bless us!—As to the 'cousin'—he was a lad five
years her junior, who looked entirely to her for sympathy, and so
drew her to think that she was all to him, and that therefore possibly he
must be so to her. She wished me to know her better and also to make
bare to me the real facts, when I first spoke.—Write, write instantly.
I thirst for words from you. And don't forget to return the photo.

Your ever loving
George M.

Tell me in your letter when it will be that you think you can walk to
Mickleham vale to be introduced to her. She wishes to know you.

---

⁵ The interview was postponed and never took place (Stevenson, p. 131).

Were it permissible, and you thinking well of the prospect of our union, I should like you to write to her what you feel about it. . . . You see I'm almost delirious. Addio.

286. *To* WILLIAM HARDMAN

MS.: Garrick Club. Excerpt published: Cline, op. cit., pp. 235–6.

[Copsham Cottage, Esher]
Friday, [June 3, 1864]

Dearest Tuck,

We will get a copy of the will next week.[1] It will not be a special matter at the first interview.

As to Arthur's[2] report: there is, or was a child[3]—not mine, who was taken by the father, and of whom I hear and shall hear nothing. You can say the truth that incompatibility of temper separated two people of whom the man was eight years the junior,[4] the woman very clever:—her qualities we may leave where they lie. To say that she approached near madness without being quite mad is to express her mental and moral character. She dallied with responsibility, played with passions; rose suddenly to a height of exaltation, sank to a terrible level. And was very clever.—I think Mr. V[ulliamy] will wish to hear little more, if anything, on this subject than he has heard from Hamilton.[5] The *money*, he thinks of:—you may tell him I can insure my life for £2000 and settle that on Marie likewise. We shall not get more than five minutes together on Saturday. They will all be horribly disappointed if you can't stay. Lucas appoints a meeting to make immediate arrangements for a serial story.—Tell Mr. V[ulliamy] my habits: that I have principle (if you think this): that I have been after a manner careless

286. [1] See Note 2, preceding letter.
[2] Arthur F. Vulliamy, a lawyer, who was Mr. Vulliamy's nephew and who was consulted by him throughout the protracted negotiations. It is probable, though not certain, that GM learned of this report through Marie between the time of his own interview with Mr. Vulliamy and the writing of this letter. The information about GM's first marriage conveyed here is all that was furnished Hardman for the interview, and as I have pointed out in the article cited it was not nearly enough to satisfy Mr. Vulliamy.
[3] Ellis (*L. & M.*, p. 196 n.) says that Mary died 'leaving one son by Meredith, named Arthur. Her illegitimate child, by Wallis, was also a boy, named Harold, but later called "Felix" '. Stevenson (p. 58) says that the child was born at Clifton, near Bristol, on 18 Apr. 1858, that Mary was looked after by a foster-sister, and that the registration gave the father's name as 'George Meredith, author'.
[4] In the Register of Burials in the Parish of Weybridge and in her death certificate, the age of Mary was given as 41 at the time of her death in Oct. 1861. Edith Nicolls, however, in a biographical notice of T. L. Peacock in his *Works* (ed. Sir Henry Cole, 1875), gives her mother's birthdate as July 1821.   [5] N. E. S. A. Hamilton.

both of making and saving money but shall be so no more. We will meet you at train, if no rain.

Your loving
George M.

287. *To* AUGUSTUS JESSOPP

MS.: Yale. Published: *Letters*, i. 146–7, with the omission of two sentences and with errors in transcription.

Esher
June 6, [1864]

My dear Jessopp,

It is time that your friend should show you a clean breast.—He loves a woman as he has never yet loved, and she for the first time has let her heart escape her. She is not unknown to you, as you both immediately divine. She is the sweetest person I have ever known, and is of the family which above all others I respect and esteem. Her father is a just and good man; her sisters are pure gentlewomen: she is of a most affectionate and loving nature. May I be worthy of the love she gives me!

Your surprise over, you will possibly think me rash. My friends, who know of this, think me fortunate, on reflection. They see that I shall now first live; that I shall work as I have never yet done; and that, to speak materially, marriage will not increase the expenses of a man hitherto very careless. My hope stands like a fixed lamp in my brain. I know that I can work in an altogether different fashion, and that with a wife and such a wife by my side, I shall taste some of the holiness of this mortal world and be new-risen in it. Already the spur is acting, and health comes, energy comes. I feel that I can do things well, and not hap-hazard, as heretofore.—A little money will be settled on her. She is to have two hundred a year, the income of money sunk in her name; and at her father's death more. I can hardly make less than eight hundred, reckoning modestly. And I shall now hold the purse-strings warily.

I shall not speak to Arthur till he is with me. She is very fond of him, and will be his friend. He will find a home where I have found one.

I cannot play at life. I loved her when we were in Norwich. 'Cathedralizing' would not otherwise have been my occupation. I believe that I do her good: I know that she feels it. Me she fills with such deep and reverent emotion that I can hardly think it the action of a human creature merely. I seem to trace a fable thus far developed by blessed angels in the skies. She has been reserved for me, my friend. It was seen that I could love a woman, and one has been given me to love. Her love for me is certain. I hold her strongly in my hand. Write —I thirst to hear words from you. Address to Piccadilly. And if Mrs. Jessopp can feel that she can congratulate my beloved and thank her for loving me,—Ah! will she let her know this?—Her address is

> Miss Marie Vulliamy, / Mickleham, / near Dorking, / *Surrey.*

Also, tell Mrs. Jessopp that *Emilia* is running very fast in Italy, and that we may hope to see the damsel of the fiery South (no longer tripped and dogged by Philosopher or analyst) by late Autumn. I have an arrangement to do a serial for *Once a Week*, and a series of wayside pieces for the *Cornhill*, Sandys illustrating, is on the tapis.[1] These will ultimately form a volume special and I hope popular. Adieu to you both! Will two be welcome some day to the School House? She has venture[d] to say that she hopes so.

Your loving
George Meredith

288. *To* FREDERICK A. MAXSE

Text: typed copy, Maxse Papers. Published: *Letters*, i. 147–50, with omissions.

[Copsham Cottage, Esher]
June 6, 1864

Esher, is the address, and your letter to Mickleham astonished us all. I read it and handed it to my beloved, who said—'How heartily he writes! he must be one of your true friends.' I think, dear Maxse, I might almost call you my dearest. Pray, write to her at once, if you have the kindly impulse. It will please her, for I have talked much of you and my feeling for you: of your happiness with *your* beloved, which she would rival. And she wishes to feel that my friends are to be hers. Address,

> Miss Marie Vulliamy, / Mickleham, / Near Dorking, / Surrey.

The letter will be a charming surprise to her. An assurance also that I am cared for, here and there, and by worthy men. Your wife is sure to love her. If God gives her to me, I may certainly say that our wives will be as much heart in heart as we are. We shall see one another more.

---

287. [1] For the serial see Note 4, Letter 285. The wayside pieces apparently never materialized.

Ah! when you speak of Ploverfield[1] for us during the first sweet days
of our union, you touch me deeply and breathe fair auspices. I shall
accept, if it can be arranged. I could not choose another place while
that door stood open. My friend, I have written of love and never felt
it till now.—I have much to pass through in raking up my history
with the first woman that held me.[2] But I would pass through fire for
my darling, and all that I have to endure seems little for the immense
gain I hope to get. When her hand rests in mine, the world seems to
hold its breath, and the sun is moveless. I take hold of Eternity. I love
her.—She is intensely emotional, but without expression for it, save in
music. I call her my dumb poet. But when she is at the piano, she is not
dumb. She has a divine touch on the notes.—Yes, she is very fond of
the boy. Not at all in a gushing way, but fond of him as a good little
fellow, whom she trusts to make her friend. As to her family: the old
man is a good and just old man, who displays the qualities by which
he made what fortune he has. There are three sons, four daughters.
The sons are all in business in France—wool manufacturers, or something. They and the girls were strictly brought up at home at Nonancourt in Normandy. Marie was seventeen when seven years ago they
came to England. They have been about five years in Mickleham Vale.
On Saturday next, Kitty, the third—the one preceding my beloved—
is to be married at the little church: Marie being first bridesmaid, and
I shall see her. The eldest sister is married to a French officer, who has
an estate in Dauphiné, and is a good working soldier—'a rough
diamond', says Marie. The eldest unmarried sister, Betty, is a person of
remarkable accomplishments and very clear intellect, vivacious and
actively religious: therefore tolerant, charitable, and of a most pure
heart. Kitty, the present bride, takes her Christianity with more
emotion: she teaches the children of the parish, while Betty every
Sunday evening has a congregation of the men and women in a barn.
Do you smile? Much good has been done by these two women. I saw
last Sunday a man rescued by Betty from inveterate drunkenness, and
happy. They—indeed all of them, are thoroughly loved by the poor
throughout the district, and respected by all but the party clergyman,
who declares that their behaviour (Betty chief culprit) has been a
scandal and that he will countenance none of them—neither marry
them, bury them, nor in any way bless them. I heard him preach last
Sunday morning, and Oh! alas for Orthodoxy! Marie, however (she
has strong common sense, my darling, as have all *real* emotional

288. [1] The Maxses were going away and had offered their house, Ploverfield, near
Bursledon, Hants, for the honeymoon.
[2] This was now clear to GM: on 5 June Mr. Vulliamy had addressed a formal letter to
him, requesting personal information about himself, Mary, and their marriage.

natures) takes her own view, and says she thinks Betty wrong in taking the clergyman's work out of his hands. 'But if he doesn't do it?' 'Yes, but his curate is anxious to try, and Betty has such influence, and speaks so closely to the hearts of the poor, that they will listen to no one else.'—The controversy is at that point. Marie does not go to the barn: but, to please her sister, is willing, now that Kitty goes, to do her best among the children, until she likewise is led away.—To Ploverfield? I sound the echoes of the future. Oh! is it to be? There could not be a fairer, sweeter companion, or one who would more perfectly wed with me. She tries to make me understand her faults. I spell at them like a small boy with his fingers upon words of one syllable. Of course some faults exist. But she has a growing mind and a developing nature. Love is doing wonders with her.—I could write on for hours, but I have letters and work calling loudly stop. We shall live, I fancy, about my present distance from London. But where to find a cottage of the kind I require, is the problem. What you say of income is sensible and has not been unthought of by me. If I did not feel courage in my heart and a strong light in my brain, I should not dare to advance in this path; but in those vital points I have full promise. I shall now write in a different manner. We will speak further on the subject when we meet. Let me know what day you think I may select to present you. The week after this will exactly do. And the Monday or Tuesday of it would be the best days, if possible; or add, the Wednesday. Try to give her the *whole* day, so that you may hear her play in the evening, and see her in all her lights and shades, and know the family—the best specimen of the middle-class that I have ever seen—pure gentlewomen, to call one of whom wife and the rest sisters is a great honour and blessing. God bless you, dear fellow. This letter and all the tenderness of my heart is for Mrs. Maxse as well as for yourself. My kindest wishes for Boy. I am ever

Your loving
George Meredith

289. *To* WILLIAM HARDMAN

MS.: Garrick Club. Published: *Letters*, i. 150–1, with several sentences omitted.

Esher
Tuesday, [June 7, 1864][1]

My dearest Tuck,

   She wishes to see Esher and a friend drives her over to-morrow. It has

289. [1] Hardman's meeting with Mr. Vulliamy had taken place, as scheduled, on 4 June.

been postponed once or twice, and I have consented to meet her. I shall be with you—I had better say Monday next. I may sleep at Mickleham on Saturday.—What do you think of her? Is she not worth anything, or all this world? And she likes you so much—thinks I believe better of me for having such a friend, and hopes that Mrs. Hardman will take to her. I never touched so pure and so conscience-clear a heart. My own is almost abased to think itself beloved by such a creature. The day when she is to be mine blinds me. Will it come? It flickers like a lightening in my brain. It will not burn steadily—I can't grasp it. What does this mean?—I am troubled, but can work. God bless you both.

Your loving
George M.

Send a word to Piccadilly with regard to Monday, and a word as to what you think of her.

[Hardman wrote at the end of the letter: 'I and M(ary) A(nne) drove over to Copsham at once on receipt of this—and G. M. came to us the same afternoon and made a full exposition of all his affairs.[2] W. H. June 8th.']

290. *To* JUSTIN T. VULLIAMY

MS.: University of Texas.

Esher
June 8, 1864

Dear Mr. Vulliamy,

I have been unaware that there was an understanding between yourself and Mr. Hardman, that he was to see you again this week. I have not yet obtained a copy of the Will.[1] This document will be in Mr. Hardman's hands on Monday. He proposes to bring it over to you the same day, and is of opinion that it will be better for him to

---

With the meagre information at his disposal he was quite unsuccessful in satisfying Mr. Vulliamy on the subject of GM's first marriage, and a second meeting was appointed for 9 June. Hardman for some reason failed to tell GM of the arrangement, so that GM was in ignorance of it at the time of this letter.

[2] This disclosure, which Hardman treated as confidential and did not record in his journal, was of course necessitated by the second meeting between Hardman and Mr. Vulliamy, which GM first learned of when the Hardmans drove over to Esher on 8 June. As GM had dawdled about getting a copy of the will of his great-uncle (see Note 2, Letter 285), which Mr. Vulliamy must have requested at the interview 'in the little parlour' (*ante* 1 June), the second meeting had to be postponed.

290. [1] See Note 2, preceding letter, and Note 2, Letter 285.

come to you then, when he will be fully armed, than to-morrow. Will, therefore, Monday be a day suitable to you for such a conference?

I trust you will not blame me very severely for the delay. My fault was to have depended upon others for doing what I might have done myself. My difficulty is that if I go to London I lose a day's work; and when I am compelled to attend to business there, every minute of my time is occupied. Also, let me plead again that I had no knowledge of an appointment between yourself and Mr. Hardman this week.

The Replies shall be forwarded.[2]

Mr. Hardman's address is 'Thames Cottage,/ Hampton, Middlesex'. But, I can write to him from Mickleham on Saturday, if it is your pleasure. I am

Very faithfully yours,
George Meredith

291. *To* FREDERICK A. MAXSE

Text: typed copy, Maxse Papers. Published: *Letters*, i. 151, dated only *1864*.

London
Thursday, [June 9, 1864]

My dear Maxse,

I have told my darling girl that you will come and inspect her on Monday. She, having a great heart, stands prepared, and a hope is expressed that you will consent to dine there. We will sleep at the Inn or walk home to Esher, just as you think fit. And how will you arrange to come? Will you come to Esher in the morning and walk to Mickleham in the afternoon? In that case she will march to meet us. Or will you get out of the train at Guildford and take another that will (see train book) put you down at Dorking or Box-hill station. In that case, *we* should march to meet you. I confess I should like to see you first; for I am told by a lady[1] that she would not be considered handsome though she is perfectly charming in manner and in face. I tell you this with a rueful drop of the chin and a yearning strain of the eye. You are to suppose that I have not called her handsome.[2]

290. [2] Mr. Vulliamy, dissatisfied with his first meeting with Hardman, did not depend upon the second to provide him with the information he desired. On the day following the meeting with Hardman (i.e. on 5 June), he addressed a formal letter to GM containing eleven questions which he requested GM to answer in writing (see following letter). It is these replies to which GM refers here.

291. [1] Mrs. Jessopp.

[2] In Letter 300, GM does call Marie handsome, and I should expect him to have written here 'You are not to suppose . . .'. Both *Letters* and the typed copy in the Maxse Papers, however, omit the *not*.

Give my dearest regards, my thanks, my kindest wishes, to Mrs. Maxse, who speaks so tenderly of her and me. Write by return post. I am ever

Your loving
George Meredith

292. *To* JUSTIN T. VULLIAMY

MS.: University of Texas. The questions and answers in Note 1 are published in my article previously cited (*NCF*, xvi. 237–8).

Esher
June 10, 1864

My dear Mr. Vulliamy,

I trust you will pardon my delay in forwarding these replies.[1] I had to verify certain of the dates, and my time is valuable. I find your letter here, and fear that you will blame me for not replying previously.

Believe me that no anxiety which you may show for Marie's future welfare, is considered by me to be excessive, and that no questions which you may think it proper to put to me, will be considered impertinent.

I have the honour to be / Your faithful servant,
George Meredith

292. [1] The replies to Mr. Vulliamy's questions, submitted in a letter of 5 June. They were as follows, with GM's replies in italics and Mr. Vulliamy's annotations of them in square brackets:

1. The date of your birth: *1828.*
2. The date of your marriage: *1849.*
3. The date of the birth of your son: *1853.*
4. The date of your separation from your wife: *1857.*
5. The date & place of her death: *Nov.* ⟨error for Oct.⟩ *1861. Weybridge.*

[We must suppose they had lived happily together the first 4 yrs. of their cohabitation. What was it which so embittered the remaining 4 years?]

6. The place of her interment: *Weybridge.*
7. The mode of your separation: *Mr. Hardman will better explain this. The separation was her own doing, though not regretted by me, save for my boy's sake. It was not a formal separation, and was not considered to be final, until I had reason for knowing that it must be so.*

[They must.]

[Wallace or Wallis in Scotland.]

8. Whether after the separation you both continued to reside in the same Village, Town, or place: *We resided apart. I saw her once, but for the space of two minutes, on a matter concerning the boy.*

[At whose cost was she maintained during the interval between the separation in 1857 & her death in 1861?]

9. Whether after the separation she continued to be known and called by your name: *I believe she went by the name of Mrs. Meredith.*
10. What name to the best of your knowledge and belief she was known by at the time and place of her death: *She lived partly with her father, and under my name.*
11. What was the name of her first husband: *Lieutenant Nicolls.*

[When did Mr. Meredith meet with Mrs. Nicolls?]

293. *To* WILLIAM HARDMAN

MS.: Garrick Club.

[Copsham Cottage, Esher]
[Saturday, June 11, 1864][1]

Dearest friend,

I find that the will was proved not in London but at Gosport, where John Meredith, my Great Uncle, a clerk, I think, under Government, died.—I have written to a lawyer to send it to Mickleham by post or Rail (copy) instantly. I dare say I shall not be there on Monday. If a packet comes addressed to me, as I trust, open it.

In haste

Your ever loving
George M.

Marie is *very* anxious to see Mrs. Hardman.

294. *To* SAMUEL LAURENCE

MS.: Yale.

Esher
Monday, [June 13, 1864]

My dear Laurence,

Please, pardon me.[1] My publisher is my banker. On receipt of your letter, I wrote for money: but found him, when I went to town, absent and my request not attended to. I half expected you on Saturday, but see that perhaps you did not like to come, having mentioned what makes men tremulous. I will bring or transmit this week. Let me hear that I am excused. I feel that I have no time for anything, hardly a conscience save for one. I am

Most faithfully yours,
George Meredith

293. [1] Hardman has dated the letter 'Saturday—June 12, 1864,' but 12 June was a Sunday in 1864.
294. [1] For his inability to pay upon request for Laurence's drawing of Katherine Vulliamy.

295. *To* JUSTIN T. VULLIAMY

MS.: University of Texas.

193 Piccadilly, London, W.
June 17, 1864

My dear Sir,

Mr. Edward Chapman, head of the firm of Chapman & Hall, a friend of mine of between ten and eleven years' standing, and for whom I have done work nearly seven years; a father, and a man universally respected, will be happy to see you and give you his opinion of me.[1] His days in town are Monday, Wednesday, and Friday: the hours when he may be found in Piccadilly, being between 12 and 4 p.m. But he thinks it best that you should favour him by appointing a day and an hour, and then he would certainly be at the above address to receive you.

Sir Alexander Gordon is at Dover, and will not return to town before Tuesday,—not in time for office hours that day, I should presume.

I am, My dear Sir, / Most faithfully yours,
George Meredith

296. *To* SAMUEL LAURENCE

MS.: Yale.

Esher
Monday, [June 20, 1864]

My dear Laurence,

In haste; for the *Alabama*'s sunk and my heart's down with her;[1] and I'm off to Mickleham. A thousand pardons for my heedlessness.[2]

295. [1] At his own interview with Mr. Vulliamy, GM was requested to submit a list of personal references. A list was drawn up at the time, partly in the hand of Mr. Vulliamy, partly in the hand of GM, which contained the names of Dr. John Chapman, proprietor of the *Westminster Review*, Edward Peacock, T. E. Foakes, Andrew Johnson, and Sir Alexander Duff Gordon. The name of Dr. Jessopp was later added, and in this letter that of Edward Chapman.

296. [1] Readers of these letters will remember GM's curious sympathy for the South, contrary to what we should expect. The history of the *Alabama* is well known: here it will suffice to say that for nearly two years she had cruised the high seas and had captured 69 Federal merchantmen, most of which were burned at sea, and that she was brought to battle outside Cherbourg and sunk by the *Kearsarge* on 19 June. *The Times* on 20 June gave a brief running account of the battle which it received by telegraph on the preceding day. Further, Adams, GM's employer at Saunders & Otley, had heard of the *Alabama*'s putting into Cherbourg, rushed over, managed to interview Captain Semmes on the eve of the battle, and received from him his journals and log. With record speed he produced a book, *The Career of the Alabama*, 'No. 290.' *From July 29, 1862, to June 19, 1864*, for which GM wrote the first and last chapters.

[2] About payment for the portrait of Katherine Vulliamy. Payment was enclosed with this letter.

I have (as you shall hear) had much to distract me. When are you coming? Sandys is still here; and next Saturday the cottage is full. Arthur will be here the Saturday following. Say, will you come then and walk over on Sunday and see my Marie? She wishes to hear a word or two from you.—Write. My time is too busy to make it certain that I can call when in London.

> Your ever faithful
> George M.

297. *To* JUSTIN T. VULLIAMY

MS.: University of Texas.

> Esher
> June 25, 1864

My dear Sir,
   I have to write to a lawyer, to obtain definite answers to the enquiries you do me the honour to submit to me.[1] This will necessitate a certain delay, which I must beg you not to attribute to any dilatoriness of mine. I am

> Most faithfully yours,
> George Meredith

298. *To* JUSTIN T. VULLIAMY

MS.: University of Texas.

> Esher
> Saturday, July 2, 1864

My dear Sir,
   The person to whom I applied to obtain the special information you require, has, for some reason, taken offence at the Questions, and declines to answer them. I do so herewith to the best of my ability.[1]

297. [1] On 23 June Mr. Vulliamy had sent GM a list of eight questions relating to the estate of W. J. Meredith. (See following letter.)

298. [1] The 'special information' consisted of eight questions, submitted by Mr. Vulliamy on 23 June, relating to the estate of W. J. Meredith. The person to whom GM applied for information about the family was his own father, recently returned from South Africa. Mr. Vulliamy's questions and GM's replies (in italics) were:

1. The actual age of W. J. Meredith's only Child, Elizabeth Jane Meredith? *The actual age, I do not know: but I believe it to be a little above sixty.*
2. Are the two Ex[ecut]ors and the Ex[ecu]trix still living and where do they severally reside? *The Ex[ecu]trix alone is living.*

But I have seen my lawyer and old friend, Mr. Lambert, who expresses himself willing to give you any information both personal and legal, concerning me, my condition, and this present Will, as far as he knows or may acquire the same. The history of my married life is not known to him, seeing that I never distress people unnecessarily, or care to make a party for myself; and I have been silent thereon to him as to others, though I believe he has an affection for me.

Allow me to add that, owing to representations made by me to Messrs. Chapman & Hall, and my offer to do additional work that will not stand in the way of my writing, or take my morning hours, the sum I receive from them yearly will be immediately increased: that is, from Midsummer: and to the extent of £125 per ann.[2] This will give me an income of £550, apart from the works of fiction etc. which I may produce. I think that within six or nine months, there will be an increase in another quarter.

Mr. Lambert's address is Edward Lambert Esq. of the firm of 'Lambert, Hampton & Burgin' / 8 John Street / Bedford Row. He has gone to Cornwall, but will be prepared to receive you next Saturday, or Monday week.

I am, my dear Sir, / Most faithfully yours,
George Meredith

3. In what did the Tes[ta]tor's Freehold property consist? Has it been converted into money?—If so in what security have the Net proceeds been invested? If not what is the estimated value of such freehold property and where is it situated? *The Testator's 'Freehold Property' consisted, as I believe, in Houses in and about Gosport. He left an injunction, if I recollect rightly, that there should be no attempt to convert it into money until after his daughter's death. I must leave it to Mr. Lambert to obtain an answer to this that shall be full and satisfactory; as also to the Question succeeding. I have heard it estimated that the total amount of the Property, Personalty and Realty, bequeathed, would be about £14000.*
4. Total amount of the Net proceeds of the Personal Estate and in which of the British funds is it invested?
5. How many Nephews and nieces ('not of the half blood') are actually living? *Six: [sic] myself in addition, as Grandnephew.*
6. Your Father's age? *Should be about 72 or 73.*
7. Has he any child besides yourself? *Not any.*
8. The age of his present wife? *About 47; not less.*

P.S. These can scarcely be called Replies. They are given to the best of my ability. Mr. Lambert will supply the deficiency.

GM

[2] Waugh (p. 153) says: 'There is no note, however, of any eventual change; and the salary paid was certainly never "commensurate" with the work done.'

299. *To* WILLIAM HARDMAN

MS.: Garrick Club. Published: *Letters*, i. 152–4 (dated *July 12, 1864*), with numerous omissions and inaccuracies; excerpts published: *L. & M.*, pp. 214–15; Cline, op. cit., p. 231.

Mickleham
At the Sign of the 'Angel'
[July 13, 1864]

Beloved Family Hardman:

And here is Marie writing a race with me, by my side: and difficulties have been smoothed; we have indeed plunged through powerful conflicts; and verily, by Shadrack, Meshack and Abednego! we likewise have passed through fire, and by miracle we bear out our Rose from it, fresh, fragrant—did ever man have such a reward? And behold her, lashing her dear wits for the next word, and pretending all the while to be looking at her sister-in-law! She has got it!—No. Yes, she is off!—Well, Tuck, I trust our fight is nearly over. The present design is, that we be married on the 20th September: engage a furnished house for a year, and meantime look about for a house that will suit us.—I—your Robin, emboldened by his new and most lovely prospects—have done this:—I said to the Chapmans—lo, I have done much, will do more:—will be in Piccadilly three afternoons in the week:—will write *all* your letters, anent MSS;—will occasionally, when imperative, see the authors (my name not being given) and so forth: thus, as Tuck sees, becoming a chief person, and at no great cost, and with considerable additions to pay. It should be £300. It shall not be less than £250. The matter will be settled in a week.[1] Both Edward and Fred[eric] are glad of the work I have undertaken to do—Don't my Tuck approve? I know that Demitroïa does. Indeed the family Hardman does, I know. It will be a proper addition to our income. And the economical talk of my blessed Marie is such delicious music! 'Our towels will cost so much: our sheets so much: and you mustn't mind its being so dear etc.' Tuck, you talk of wisdom and you talk of poetry: but beat that, if you can!—Adams, do you know, is doing the 'Career of the *Alabama*'.[2] He heard of Semmes putting into Cherbourg: started: reached him, after marvelous difficulties with port admirals and *gens d'armes*, on the very eve of his fight with the *Kearsarge*. Semmes hailed him with joy: he 'wanted some one to whom to confide his papers, and was despairing of finding one':—gave the papers (Journals etc., Log) to Adams, to do as he pleased with them. I have done the 1st and last chapter—offered to do the whole, but Adams could only wait five days to get the book out; so I declined this

299. [1] Note 2, preceding letter.   [2] See Note 1, Letter 296.

fiery proximity to the printer's devil. Adams has been in a dressing-gown ever since, is blue about the chin, as if blown up in a recent naval engagement, and has generally the appearance of an elongated Manta-lini returned to his wife, but reckless. He grows taller, and hurries on. Jessopp has just left for Lucerne—will perform as executioner in September.[3] Odd that he is always following you on the Continent![4] He proceeds to Stresa on Lago Maggiore. By the way, there is a highly appreciative summary of my literary deeds in a lengthy article of the *Westminster Review*.[5] The New Novel (*Vittoria*)[6] is going on swimmingly. Sandys has heard the first 150 pages, and says it's extremely interesting and likely to be by far the best thing I have done. Lucas is charmed with the sketch of the autobiography; but owing to certain changes going on in relation to O[*nce*] *a* W[*eek*] he has not yet sent word for me to start away.[7] Thus we are in a little uncertainty. Poco has greatly pleased people here. There is talk of his acting a chief part in the ceremony at hand; and Oh, Lord! Tuck, here's my heart swelling and sinking like night waves pressing to a beacon-light. Oh, that it were over!

My compliments to Albrecht,[8] with whom I hope to make acquaintance. Poco and myself intend to compose an essay on the 'Concurrences'—illustrated by the meeting in this world of Albrecht and Tuck.

I had determined to walk over to Hampton[9] and see your darlings before writing; but this is Wednesday, and I shall have no afternoon to myself before Saturday, the day you name as the last for Bellagio. More letters, dear old Boy! God bless you both and keep you jolly! WE rejoice in your happiness!—Aha! WE! Give me address speedily. I will write. Marie will write. We are

Your loving
George M.

[3] i.e. will perform the marriage ceremony.
[4] In company with two friends, Captain and Miss Blake, the Hardmans (without their children) had gone abroad at the end of June for two months.
[5] In the July 1864 number (pp. 24–49), under *Novels with a Purpose*, by Justin McCarthy. Calling GM a novelist of the philosophical school who writes without regard to popularity, the reviewer points the moral: 'Men without a tithe of his intellect have found a far wider celebrity. He is, indeed, but little known to the novel-reading public in general.' *The Ordeal of Richard Feverel* and *Emilia* are examined at some length; then the review concludes with high praise of GM's mind, sensitive nature, and rich fancy but adds that his books can hardly be called successful because he has 'not as yet developed in himself the faculty of the storyteller'. [6] The new title of *Emilia in Italy*.
[7] The 'autobiography' was *The Adventures of Harry Richmond*, and the word never came from Lucas 'to start away'.
[8] A Swiss guide mentioned a number of times in Hardman's letters. According to Hardman (*L. & M.*, p. 62), he was educated at a Jesuit college, spoke English, French, German, Italian, and Latin, and knew every nook and corner of Switzerland. In May 1865 he visited the Hardmans in England.
[9] i.e. Thames Cottage, where Hardman's daughters were living.

N.B. Notice a few names of streets in *Milan*: in *Bellagio*: in *Camerlata*: any shrines, or wayside Madonnas that strike you, as good or comical.[10] Get a few of the milder Italian oaths now actually in use in north Italy: the interjections you hear, pray note.

300. *To* W. C. BONAPARTE WYSE

MS.: Yale. Printed: *Altschul Catalogue*, pp. 55–56; excerpt reproduced in facsimile in Maggs Brothers Catalogue No. 309 (May–June, 1913), pp. 94–95; excerpt published: Ellis, pp. 197–8.

Esher
July 23, [1864]
My dear Wyse,

Coming home last night I found your letter. I thank you for the cheque, but no thought of any claim on you had remained with me. I am rejoiced to hear that you have now some chance of settling down quietly; though, as you mention nothing of the good and true Elaine, I can hardly guess at your position,—I tried to see her (and you, I presumed) by calling at the house in Craven Street. She was out, and the impossibility of keeping any appointment subsequently withheld me from suggesting one. Hear the fact!—I have been for months, and I am now, desperately in love. You know that I am not subject to be smitten. The wound is all the deeper when it comes. I am beloved in return. She is a very handsome person, fair, with a noble pose, and full figure, and a naturally high bred style and manner such as one meets but rarely. Her father made a fortune in France. She is the youngest of the family. At seventeen she came to England. Her dwelling place is in the sweet little valley of Mickleham, nearby me. We are to be married in September and I am thrice a man in the prospect of it—admitting at the same time that some nervous excitement will keep me low till the marriage is complete. When I do love I love hotly and give the heart clean out of me. She does likewise. Her age, I may add, is four and twenty. She is an accomplished musician, and a very gentle nature—full of promise for one's home. I trust I may have strength, as I have honest will, to make her happy. She has money enough to make her independent of me, so she will not be leaning on a literary reed. At this moment we speculate profoundly as to where we are to live. I think we shall take a furnished house for a year till a friend has built us a house of our own in my neighbourhood.—I am hard upon a new novel *Vittoria* and it would do me no harm if you were by to help me as to some

299. [10] In his notebook (*L. & M.*, p. 204 n.) Hardman wrote: 'Walked about the little town of Bellagio to take down names of streets for George Meredith.'

Italian 'local-colourism'. Could you come to me for a week? Or how is Bradford on Avon to be reached, and could it be taken on the way to North Devon? Reply! I am ever

Your faithful
George Meredith

Arthur is here, and well. Were he in he would be for sending his love to Elaine.

301. *To* WILLIAM HARDMAN

MS.: Garrick Club.

Copsham
Sunday, [August 21, 1864]

Dearest Tuck,

God bless you both! and I thank him if you are back safe.

To-day I must go to Mickleham (where I am now almost located) to excuse Morison for not coming. To-morrow St. B. and wife are as saintly patrons of Wedlock v. Celibacy presented to Marie. They leave on *Tuesday*: and I'm engaged then to give Mickleham a little feast on St. George's Hill. Oh, Tuck!—Could you take the chicks and D[emi]troïa there to be there about $1\frac{1}{2}$—punctual feed at $2\frac{1}{2}$—? Tuck! Then we might all meet—The Son as well. He goes to Norwich on Wednesday. I propose to dine with you Wednesday evening. Send a letter to Ch[apman] & H[all] to say whether and where. If I don't hear, I take a shot at Hampton. But try St. George's Hill on Tuesday: With love to D[emitroïa]—in mighty haste

Your loving
George M.

We flow smoothly at Mickleham; but the fretting and the exercise have reduced me a little—I work well.

302. *To* WILLIAM HARDMAN

MS.: Garrick Club.

Copsham
Tuesday, [August 23, 1864]

Dearest Tuck,

Of course the rain has said veto to our pic-nic. Our plans are deranged. I can't come to you to-morrow, as I must be at Mickleham to take my Marie to town on Thursday to lunch with Mrs. Ross and Sir Alec. Back to Mickleham that night: but if possible I shall come to you then in the evening.—However, *Certainly* on Friday to dinner, if you are then at home. Please, drop a line to Piccadilly. I long to catch your hands and hear about your travels. Marie, too, wants to see you both. The Morisons are *charmed* with her. Who would not be?—I am glad to tell you that I am now treated very cordially by her father. *Vittoria* progresses capitally. Look at the last number of the *Westminster*.[1] In haste, with love to D[emitroïa],

Your affectionate
George M.

303. *To* WILLIAM HARDMAN

MS.: Garrick Club.

[Copsham Cottage, Esher]
Thursday, [August 25, 1864]

My darling Tuck!

You lay on the lash and I caper.[1]

I am incensed at myself when I think of your having put off Hawker to accommodate me. I beg you to believe that I am exceedingly grieved, and that it is a lesson to me.

But, Tuck, you generalize, and then it is not you but your wrath speaking, and then too I am made to defend myself a little. It is not a common thing for me to be guilty of these offences. You say that Morison has complained. My memory does not accuse me in his instance: but I can remember when he has asked me to his house and I have found him absent.

Again let me assure you that I cannot bear the thought of having upset an arrangement of one so kind to me. It would have disturbed me to have done so in any case to any body.

And Tuck! Was it with a little return of gentleness that you spoke of 'my wife'?—I hug the letter just for that one expression, and would bear the lashing twice. Yes, Tuck, *when* I have her! At present our

302. [1] See Note 5, Letter 299.
303. [1] GM had cancelled plans for the picnic on Tuesday and dinner with the Hardmans on Wednesday. (See preceding two letters.) Hardman had apparently complained of this sudden shift of plans after the Hardmans had put off their friend the Revd. W. H. Hawker to fit into them. It is unclear how the inconvenience arose, for Hardman, writing on 24 Aug. (*L. & M.*, pp. 203–4), says that Hawker 'arrived from London somewhat unexpectedly and dined with us . . .'.

separation causes me to behave irregularly—shamefully. God bless
you. You were justly wroth, but it's over, I know.

Most lovingly yours,
George M.

Of course, I don't expect (because I don't *deserve*) to find you
to-morrow (Friday) but I shall come, bow my head thrice, and go.

304. *To* FREDERICK A. MAXSE

Text: typed copy, Maxse Papers. Published: *Letters*, i. 154–6 with omissions.

Mickleham, Dorking
Monday, August 29, [1864]

My dear Fred,

I write with my beloved beside me; my thrice darling—of my body,
my soul, my song! I have never loved a woman and felt love grow in
me. This clear and lovely nature doubles mine. And she has humour,
my friend. She is a charming companion, as well as the staunchest
heart and fairest mistress. You will not fail us on our marriage day!—
A goodly host of friends will be here. Janet and Sir Alec come—and
Oh! I would that the day were over. The day, mind you!—Will it be
possible to get a cottage near the New Forest, or in it? or near Ploverfield, for two weeks, until my friend's house is open to us? I shall
come to you in about a week on my way to Normandy, to fetch hither
Marie's married sister who wishes to be present on the great occasion.
You will see the three together and what charming creatures they are.
I am quite fixed in this place, and all are kind. The old man is changed,
and makes the best of the bad business for him. He proposes to buy
Copsham, or any likely spot and build a house there for us, with
a portion of the money he settles on Marie. Meantime we take a
furnished house for six months, in or near Kingston. You and your
wife, my friend, will visit us. I know that your wife will find a large-
hearted friend in mine. You, too, will find that your friend is another
man. I think my work must prosper under such noble influence.—
Vittoria does not proceed fast, but the matter is of a good sort. I've
half a mind to bring you half a dozen chapters to read to you. My Marie
copies them regularly.—There's a chance of my getting an under
Editorship of a new Review:[1] a fellow who is merely to be titular
chief, acting as head. I presume I shall be paid well. It is decided in
a couple of months. More when we meet, on this subject. I fancy it

<hr>

304. [1] Presumably the *FR*. See Letter 313.

may be a good thing.—When I come to you I must expend a day at Lyndhurst in search for the furnished cottage,[2] but, could you mean-time make enquiries? I wish it to be tolerably near Ploverfield.—How of your health? You are silent upon that. Were I with you a week I would bring you into a better state. Now that I am no longer fretted, and running twice a day between Mickleham and Copsham, I begin to feel my strength again.—Marie says at my elbow—'The worst of being at Ploverfield is that Captain Maxse and his wife will be away when we are there.' This is not to be always the case. Adieu. My kind regards (we must sit together and invent new phrases) to Mrs. Maxse. Write, saying whether you can receive me next week—Friday week?

Your loving
George M.

305. *To* W. C. BONAPARTE WYSE

Text: Ellis, pp. 198–9.

Copsham, Esher
September 6, 1864

My dear Wyse,

You will, I know, pardon the silence of a man in love. My bride has the wish that you should come to our wedding. Can you? Will you? Write and say 'yes' at once. The day is the 20th September: a fortnight from this. The place is Mickleham, three miles beyond Leatherhead, and seven from old Copsham, where you may find quarters the pre-vious evening, and a friend will call for you and bring you on in the morning. It will give me great pleasure to see your face and shake your hand on that day. My darling also will remember the friends that day surrounding us. So, do come. I want you to see my Marie blooming. She is a full and perfect rose. You know the Gloire de Dijon?—of that kind, my friend, with the sweet flush and delicious odour—all the richness of the flower! Write to me 'care of Justin Vulliamy, Esq., Mickleham, near Dorking, Surrey'. I shall hardly be able to welcome you here before the noble day (would 'twere over!). You have thought of coming to London—contrive the visit to suit the 20th. Jessopp marries the pair. Maxse gives me his house near Southampton for a month or so. We live in an Esher house for six months, and then build or buy a place suitable for modest married lovers. I wish I could read you some of my new novel *Vittoria*. You must come to me in the winter and help me anent certain Italian matter. I am surcharged with work, with but little time at present to accomplish it.

304. [2] i.e. for the two weeks' interval until Maxse's house was available.

Your fine Epicurean contempt for the passing show of this life charms me. But, to be rightly and lastingly content, you must work, work! Set yourself to a task. Uncertainty has been your storm at sea, but now you are in haven, don't rot.

My kindest regards to your wife, and believe me ever your loving

George Meredith

306. *To* WILLIAM HARDMAN

MS.: Garrick Club.

[? London][1]

[September 9 or 10, 1864]

Dearest Tuck,

Wyndowe says, he tried Norbiton *Lodge*, next to Norbiton Hall,[2] and his report is that the place is *under water* in winter. I send you word on the spot.

I have dared to mention you as one of my references in the matter of an Insurance. I presume you can state all that's asked: but I would have forwarned and requested and desired and petitioned you if I had but had time. Board sits only Friday. Insurance must be effected before marriage.

Off to Maxse.

I must take the Cedars[3] for six months. More on this head. In haste

Your loving

George M.

307. *To* WILLIAM HARDMAN

MS.: Garrick Club.

Ploverfield, Bursledon,

Southampton

[September 14, 1864]

My dearest Tuck,

Didn't I give you my address?—Mr. Vulliamy expressed a strong preference for my taking the 'Cedars': and my letter written to the proprietor of the house before I met you, decided me, as under obligation to take the house. Otherwise I see that the Cottage[1] would have suited best.

306. [1] Written on a *Morning Post* letter-head.
　　[2] A warning to Hardman, who was at the moment negotiating for Norbiton Hall (Kingston).
　　[3] In Esher, described by Ellis (p. 201) as 'a pleasant house near the river Mole'.
307. [1] Thames Cottage, which Hardman was shortly to vacate.

Address to Garrick Club; and say what you think of Wyndowe's warning concerning Norbiton Hall in Winter.

I am whirled in a vortex. Some one bawls 'Tuesday'! There's a ring dropped halfway out of a swirl of vapour, while I roll along endless billows. Your coming to Mickleham is unutterably friendly, but doesn't astonish me. I know that I have your hand and D[emitroïa's] tight and always true.—Can you call at Copsham on your way on Tuesday morning? Jessopp and Sons will be there. If you come from *London*, I will see that a carriage is ordered to bring them over.

Your loving
George Meredith

Maxse's place here is quite delightful.

308. *To* AUGUSTUS JESSOPP

MS.: Yale. Published: *Letters* i. 154 (dated *July 1864*), with substantial omissions.

Ploverfield, Bursledon,
Southampton
[c. September 14, 1864]

My dear and good friend!

I know that you are excusing my singular way of treating you.

There will be provision and beds at Copsham on Monday for you and Arthur; a carriage shall be provided to bring you on to Mickleham, or my friend Hardman will call for you and take you up. The ceremony will have to be performed early, for Hardman has to make a rush to be in Liverpool at a brother-in-law's marriage the day following.[1]

You have perfect faith in me—I feel it. Let me just explain that the buying of a hundred things, paying an Insurance premium, and I know not what besides, keeps my hands for the moment empty. It is very unfair to you: but I shall behave better towards you presently.[2] I have a new arrangement to settle with Ch[apman] & Hall: I expect to get the conductorship of a new magazine,[3] well supported. I have laid lines right and left: engaged to do a 1 volume story[4] within a certain term:

308. [1] As it turned out, Hardman was unable to be present at GM's wedding after all. The ceremony, for which GM had procured a special licence, was duly performed by Jessopp on 20 Sept. Through error the licence was issued in the names of George Meredith and *Mary* Vulliamy, and Marie had to sign the register accordingly (Mickleham Church Records).

[2] Another reference to his inability to pay Arthur's school fees.

[3] See Note 5, Letter 313.

[4] *Rhoda Fleming*, which was expanded into the conventional three volumes and published in 1865.

and in short spread traps for money everywhere. Pardon me, meantime, for two or three weeks further. I shall soon get straight.

Your loving
George M.

Arthur's clothes will be ready. Let Norwich hat my little man.
Address Esher. I doubt whether I shall sleep at Copsham on Monday:
at Mickleham Hall, I expect.

309. *To* WILLIAM HARDMAN

MS.: Garrick Club.

Esher, *in haste*
[September 18, 1864]

My dear Tuck,

There's no letter from Foakes (who is apparently of them that
carry their tails twixt their legs).[1] Of course the money is safe: but
I *may* want it, so I ask you to send me (to *Mickleham*: or, if you think
you will be too late for Tuesday morning there, to Ploverfield) a
portion—say £15. It shall be returned in two or three weeks. Address
care of Captain Maxse, R.N., Ploverfield / Bursledon / Southampton.
I have the cheque sent to the Garrick.

I am not in much fear that I shall want money but I wish the hinges
to have a certain supply of oil so that our vehicle may not creak harshly
for one month under the happy moon.

Ever your affectionate
George M.

310. *To* MISS [(?)BESSY] M'HINCH[1]

Text: *Letters*, i, 157–8 (dated only *1864*).

Southampton
[End of September 1864]

My dear Bridesmaid No. 1,

I am quite well. Are you quite well? We are quite well.—The
conjugation being thus concluded, I proceed to tell you that we have

---

309. [1] GM had requested Foakes to remit the money due him for his *Ipswich Journal*
contributions and had had no reply.
310. [1] Niece of Captain and Mrs. John Smith of Mickleham Hall and good friend of
Marie's. W. M. Meredith does not give her first name, but I assume that she is the same
Bessy McHinch to whom GM wrote more than forty years later (Letter 2384). Mrs. Smith
had signed the register as one of the witnesses at the wedding of GM and Marie.

set our hearts (strike out the 's') upon your coming down here. Not that we are in need of even you, but we want to show you a picture of perfect felicity, and think it will do you good. Perhaps we may not mind talking to you, but we do not promise that we shall. Now, you good friend of my beloved, understand me clearly that we both wish to see you very much, and to have you with us when we are at Ploverfield, for the reason that you are dear to us in the first place, and in the second that we think we can amuse you here and give you pleasant yachting. We go to Ploverfield the first week next month. It will be a shame to take you from your Aunt. I must confess I should do so without compunction. Having taken Marie, I am capable of anything; and if I could discern a really deserving fellow—but Mrs. Smith need not fear: they are not too numerous and we have none at hand. We are on the point of going for a sail. Marie is at work terminating her letter opposite to me. She says that she is happy, and I believe the woman. Whither has the philosopher in me fled? Possibly you may have keener eyes. Come and use them. You see, I am not afraid of you. Do persuade Mrs. Smith to part with you for a short term. I promise to take every care of my Bridesmaid. I beg you to present my most respectful compliments to Mrs. Smith and to kiss Evelyn[2] for me mightily. Marie shall repay you for the outlay.

I am your most faithful

George Meredith

311. *To* WILLIAM HARDMAN

MS.: Garrick Club.

At Mr. Prince's
Pear-tree Green, Southampton
Monday evening, [October 3, 1864]

My dearest Tuck,

Marie writes to D[emitroïa], I to you. *We* to both. I have the sweetest bride in the world. I have never tasted happiness before. *Verbum sap.* But, Oh, Tuck! What a new life is this! I fancy I may say for my beloved that she finds her days with me pleasant. She is like music folding through every minute of my existence. We are a gormandizing, sleepy couple, most poetic; mankind being far beneath us, struggling and unquiet. You have had an explosion, I hear.[1] Well,

310. [2] Daughter of the Smiths. The correct spelling of her name was *Eveleen*, and the Merediths named their only daughter for her in 1871.
311. [1] On 1 Oct. the explosion of 1,040 barrels (104,000 lb.) of gunpowder at the government magazine near Erith, on the Thames, killed thirteen persons and was heard fifty miles away (*Annual Register*). Hardman (*L. & M.*, pp. 233–4) gives an account of it.

since Tuck is safe, what matters?—The air here is marvellous fine.
This here green used to be called the Montpellier of England. Five
minutes' walk on it restores Dan Cupid and bids him flap his lusty
wings and away like a sea-gull. The country around, and all around
Southampton, is astonishingly nice. I walked with Maxse on Sunday
to a house five miles from the town, commanding views of the New
Forest, Southampton water and the Isle of Wight; great rolling woods
and distant sea; on sandy soil near a ferny common, surrounded by
roaring pines; with a garden and lawn full of rare trees (the Deodora,
Wellingtonia Gigantia, planted by Pam[2]); the house roomy and comfortable, and twenty-three acres of ground: leasehold for 999 years;
and all to be had for £2000!—Your poet's mouth has watered. But
for the distance from town!—Maxse goes Tuesday week. We sail in
his little yacht and steam in a tiny vessel belonging to a friend of his.
Marie is a capital sailor, rejoicing in the bounding deep. We manage
the charming vessel beautifully and all is now plain sailing.—Ah! why
weren't you at the wedding? Poco's speech was first-rate. But, I can't
forgive the wretch for that 'of Copsham' in the advertisement. It made
me dance as on a red hot coal. Why 'of' anything? However, 'tis
a minor matter. I have my love. Already I'm at work. The fruits you
shall soon behold. Your article in the *I[pswich] J[ournal]* was good.[3]
Write to me, dear old boy! My address as above for the ensuing week.
A word as to your Liverpool Hymeneals[4]—the bride, the toasts,
Tuck's doings. Poco tells you of ours. We arrived here from London
comfortably, losing Marie's little maid by the way. She arrived at
midnight, and proves to be a good little body. Marie will tell D[emi-
troïa] of our want of a cook. If you could have seen Bonaparte Wyse
at the wedding and heard his brogue! The bare hint of it sets Marie
off laughing. My little man behaved in a lovely way and took to the
mother Heaven gives, sweet as milk. Tuck, I am running dry! I have
a dismal idea that next Sunday is Sacrament Sunday. These lodgings
are agreeable, airy, cleanly, and Mrs. Prince can cook, with the exception of making soup, or omelettes, or frying potatoes, or roasting
grouse, or being punctual. But, she is attentive. Mr. Prince reads
family prayers on Saturday to his household, of half an hour's duration.
He registers Births and Deaths. The air is such that the Births pre-
ponderate hugely. Marie has the ex-maiden habit of disliking babies.
Babies in Magenta and Blue; Babies in Green; Babies in brown;
Babies in satin; Babies in serge;—they besiege the gate all day long.

---

[2] Lord Palmerston.
[3] Hardman was writing GM's weekly articles for the *Ipswich Journal*.
[4] The Hardmans had missed GM's wedding because they had to go to Liverpool for
the wedding of Mrs. Hardman's brother.

It's like the apparition of Babies to the murderous Clown in a pantomime. Poor Marie turns faintly to the window. 'Another Baby!' she
moans. What's the signification? If she annoys me, I say—you be
babied! Next to them (not unlike them) and more welcome, come
Prawns. It may be the air, or our having eaten so many, but we go
about red as a pair of Prawns. In such trim we visited Salisbury
Cathedral the other day and sat among the intoning canons as if we
had been served up in white dishes. We go to Winchester this week.
Now and then we run over to the Isle of Wight or the New Forest.
I am prepared to call this one of the healthiest spots in England. Tuck,
good night. I can't afford to talk to you any more. Stay, let me thank
you for the cheque. Of my Foakes I have not heard.[5] I dare say I shall
not require to use the cheque; but it's a relief to have it handy in case
of need. Adieu, dear friend! Let us hear about Norbiton Hall, among
other things.[6] My love to D[emitroïa] and kisses for the little ones.
I am ever

Your loving
George M.

312. *To* WILLIAM HARDMAN

MS.: Garrick Club.

[Pear-tree Green, Southampton]
Saturday, [October 8, 1864]

Dearest Lord Tuck!

(Lord Abbot of Norbiton,[1] whose crest from friendship was the
Hooded Robin, the which he did stamp with a great seal.)

It astounds me not that you should be even host to the Finances.[2]
There is, as you prove, a grander than they, as there is a higher than
fortune. I try to hang on to their skirts: and Mrs. at times pretends to
be willing to permit it, but Mr. gets into a passion, and as a rule when
we meet I am cut. So I plant my harpoon in the noble Leviathan back
of him who embrances the Finances. I need not enquire concerning
them. They must flourish. Are they not yours?

How sweet is delicate Pantagruelism! How rare! How divinely
a woman converses in privacy whose soul possesses the gift! Marie and
D[emitroïa] are sisters. Were it not for thy ghostly character, Tuck,
I'd say—and we are brothers.

---

311. [5] See Note 1, letter 309.   [6] See Note 2, Letter 306.
312. [1] Actually the title to Norbiton Hall, Kingston, did not pass to Hardman till 12 Oct.
   [2] Hardman's monthly letter to Holroyd sheds no light on the identity of 'the Finances'.

To-morrow's Sunday. I think I am in for it to-morrow. It's nice to see my darling take her bit of bread. I'm sure I would give her mine too, if she'd take it. Bless thee, Tuck! Would it be well to ask for an aerated morsel? I get my mind into a singular plastic train till I feel as a comfortable partaker. The period of the 2nd Century of the Church (not Anglican) holds my spirit, and I eat and drink defying Pagans and objects of false worship. It is a merciful Heaven, I devoutly believe. But why did the Lord of it concern himself so greatly about the foreskin of little Jewish Babies? And why did Zipporah say she had a bloody husband when at last she gave in and shore small Moses with a flint?[3] And why?—But Questions are of a propagating kind.

And this brings me again to our tribulation here. I have spoken to Mr. Prince. It raineth not but it poureth Babies. Prince tells me to my horror that the old ones don't die to make room for them! We, Tuck, of intermediate age will be jammed to death between the two if this goes on. It's shocking. And the Babies are all so horribly healthy. They squall themselves red and straighten their backs till they look so like their instrumental progenitor that I modestly turn aside. 'What's to be done?' I ask of Prince, whose 'Well, Sir', seconded by a deliberate smile, causes me to snigger feebly and smooth my chin with a glance at the firmament. 'The Spacious firmament on high and all the blue ethereal sky.' Which reminds me that Dr. Watts[4] was born in Southampton and has a statue here, and ever since I [have] been here I've seen nothing but blue firmament. Doctor, I thank thee! But, if Babies were cherubs, by Jingo, shouldn't we have clouds!—Write to your Robin yet again. He is happy, and hard at work: but the morning letter is pleasant. Marie cries out—'A letter from Mr. Tuck? May it be seen?' I reply—'When you are promoted,' and read her bits—which she calls 'the decent part of the Ri[gh]t Rev[eren]d epistle.'—Oh, Tuck! she says that we be sinful men! Is it so? She's a sweet woman, at any rate. We are going to Winchester soon—afternoon service. I date my letter from the Pair-tree, for we grow together and are one in heart. So will I continue to date them. Joke not of fruits.

With Love to D[emitroïa], I am, Tuck,
> Your servant and soul's friend,
> George M.

To the Gr[ea]t Mother, likewise my salute.

[3] Exodus iv. 25.
[4] Isaac Watts (1674–1748), the hymn writer. The quoted lines which reminded GM of him were not by Addison, as once thought, but by Marvell (*Athenaeum*, 19 Sept. 1868, p. 370).

313. *To* FREDERIC CHAPMAN[1]

MS.: Yale.

Ploverfield, Bursledon,
Southampton
October 10, 1864

My dear Fred,

I enclose in a parcel letters to Mr. Bailey (Platt's Novel—*Angelo Lyons*): to Ollier (*All the Year Round* articles) and to A. Leigh Hunt (*Spiritual Manifestations*).[2] Send me note paper and envelopes for official letters—omitted in the last packet. We have a capital time, yachting and running from place to place. I am at work on a 1 volume novel for Christmas.[3] Write of anything new. Have you heard more of Danby Seymour?[4] He is a friend of Maxse's, who thinks the Magazine will have a fair chance and hopes that I shall have the working management of it. I have not mentioned a word of your design to run Buckland from the *Field* and supplant the same: but let me hear what is doing.[5] I should be rather nervous, the outlay being excessive: but Buckland, if a reliable, is a good man, and a host. Are there really strong grounds

---

313. [1] Although Chapman's name has appeared in GM's letters from time to time, this is the first letter that I have found addressed to him. As GM appeared weekly at the offices of the firm, he would have had no occasion to write to Chapman previous to his honeymoon. (For a biographical sketch of Chapman, see Biographical Section, pp. 1718–19.)

[2] Letters written on behalf of C. & H. to authors who had submitted MSS. I am unable to connect 'Mr. Bailey' with William Platt, minor novelist, whose *Angelo Lyons* was published by Saunders & Otley in 1866. Edmund Ollier might logically have offered his *All the Year Round* articles to C. & H., as publishers of the magazine, but I find no record of their publication. The *British Museum Catalogue* (hereinafter *BMC*) lists two books (1868, 1870) on the ancient borough of Thetford by A. Leigh Hunt, but I find no record of *Spiritual Manifestations*.

[3] See Note 4, Letter 308.

[4] Henry Danby Seymour (1820–77), M.P. for Poole, 1850–68; one of the founders of the Cosmopolitan Club.

[5] The one thing clear in all this puzzling business is that GM still hoped to be *de facto* editor of a new magazine. But what magazine—the *Fortnightly Review?* In 1865 Frederic Chapman, Anthony Trollope, Cotter Morison, and probably several others (Edwin M. Everett, *The Party of Humanity: 'The Fortnightly Review' and its Contributors, 1865–1874*, Chapel Hill, 1939, p. 17) founded the *FR*, modelled upon the *Revue des Deux Mondes*, and G. H. Lewes, its first editor, mentions Danby Seymour as being present at a conference about it on 30 Dec. 1864 (Haight, *The George Eliot Letters*, iv. 172–3). The *Field*, to which Francis Trevelyan Buckland, a well-known naturalist, contributed articles on pisciculture, was chiefly concerned with field sports and other interests of country gentlemen and was in no sense a competitor of the *FR*. Surely nothing could have been further from the intentions of the founders of the *FR* than to supplant the *Field*. Could Chapman have been contemplating still another new magazine, such as *Land and Water*, which Buckland himself founded in 1866 after breaking with the *Field*? It seems unlikely; but granted the contemplation of such a rival, how does a competitor 'run' a staff member from his position? (*Luring* Buckland away would doubtless have been easy since he broke with the *Field* a short time later.)

for his leaving the *Field*?—not going by his own account of it, I mean.
—My wife sends her regards to you. Believe me

Yours ever,
George Meredith

A parcel of MS. is forwarded by to-morrow's train. Get the letters addressed and despatched with MS. at once. The Book on the Sutton-Dudleys: *Amy Robsart* may be published, *if paid for*.[6] We can risk nothing on it. Look to date of my letters, and have them copied if not sent on *Wednesday* from Piccadilly.

314. *To* WILLIAM HARDMAN

MS.: Garrick Club. Excerpt published: *Letters*, i. 158–9 (dated *October 12, 1864*).

Ploverfield, Bursledon, Southampton
Tuesday, October 18, 1864

My dear Lord Abbott,

We have parted from the prolific parent, Prince. The sound of the multitudinous baby waxes thinner as though the roar of a sea had diminished to the song of a gnat—yea! as though great ocean now played upon a thread of sound. Poor Marie is in a state of horror lest a simple residence on Pear-tree Green should have—and, as I say, if anything comes, it must perforce be a pair! Otherwise, how account for the population of the Green? She hangs her head.[1]

I am working mightily. Last night I awoke, and at 3 a.m., struck a light and wrote a poem on 'Cleopatra' for the *Cornhill*, to suit Sandys' illustration.[2] Also an 'Ode to the Napiers' (part of it) and part of 'The Ex-Champion's Lament'.[3]—I say, young Copperfield!—I never had such a fit on me since the age of twenty-one; and my good love, waking too, joyfully assisted by lending note-paper and soothing me for having disturbed her slumber. She *is* a darling.—The air here, the views from the house, and proximity to salt water, make the place glorious: and the house is as comfortable as could be desired. Here would I fix, were it possible! Write, most venerable father!—Marie writes about cooks to D[emitroïa] to-day or to-morrow.

[6] Of the several books on this subject published within the decade, none is identifiable with this MS., which may never have been published.

314. [1] The jesting of this paragraph is explained by Letters 311 and 312.

[2] Sandys' 'Cleopatra' appeared in the *Cornhill* for Sept. 1866, but the accompanying poem was by Swinburne. GM's 'Cleopatra' was apparently found unsuitable and was lost sight of for almost a century. It was published by Phyllis Bartlett, 'George Meredith's Lost *Cleopatra*' (*Yale University Library Gazette*, Oct. 1958, pp. 57–62).

[3] I have found no trace of these two poems.

I really trust to have a 1 volume novel for January, ripe and ready. *Rhoda Fleming—a plain story.*

Your loving
George M.

315. *To* WILLIAM HARDMAN

MS.: Garrick Club. Excerpts published: *Letters*, i. 159–60, with inaccuracies.

Ploverfield, Bursledon, Southampton
Monday midnight, [October 24, 1864]

My dear Lord Abbott,

You frisk not in your letters to me. I pay you due respect, but an you continue this tone of formality, by God, I will unfrock you!—Know that Marie is the wife of Pantagruel. She is sublime in laughter. We sit on the humourous Olympus, and roll over the follies of mortals. Your letters are seen, forsooth! Your letters, O my father, are reverently handled: and if therein talk of the Secret Chamber of the three seats honourably filled by the fumigating trio, Poco, Tuck, and Robin, that portion is put under a veil. This is so. The reverence for our spiritual father, entertained by me, is shared by Marie.—Life here is jolly. I rise, bathe, run, and come blooming to breakfast, having tied up Sam, the vagabond dog, who breaks Maxse's heart, who in return does his best to break Sam's back. I treat the dog differently, and being a Celt myself, the Irishman comprehends and loves me and won't leave me. To-day we went out fishing in the boat, and Sam would follow, swimming a mile. Whereupon, we summoned Hiram, our cowardly boy in an accompanying boat, and bade him take in Sam and row him home. Sam was haled into the boat, which is small. Sam was tied down in the bows and Hiram had to turn his bottom to him to row. He sat gingerly, gave a pull and a howl. We fancied one cheek clean gone. I nearly fell overboard with laughing. Hiram tried again, and to see him pull, start, pull, start, tremble, shriek, and finally stand up and scull back'ards to face his enemy, was right good pastoral fun. His condition upon reaching home must be like his cowardice, bottomless.—The house is most pleasant. We can't accustom ourselves to anything smaller. And yet, Tuck, tell me of Thames Cottage, for I haven't heard from the faithless Dame Douglass, who swore she would write and send agreement.[1] I still hold to the idea of Thames Cottage, if we can do it with your consent, and Douglass fail. Vulliamy père was against it: why,

315. [1] i.e. for The Cedars.

I know not: but in some things he lacks true sense. Marie is guided by me, though she does hate small residences. So do I: but I'm a man, a patient man. Tell me, if Thames Cottage is really in sight, what amount of furniture would be wanted for it, and of what kind. Also, what accommodation for servants: and whether I could have a room for writing, in which too I could dress (with a fireplace that my pen may not shiver) etc. A man who would in old time have taken the Cot, says to Marie that the servants are badly bedded there. How of this?—

Poco's articles for the *I[pswich] J[ournal]* are good. His 'Week' is weakly.[2]

I receive telegrams from Adams.[3]

Rhoda Fleming is a right excellent story. If I can compress it into one volume I shall bring it back complete. In any case, it will be out in the winter.—I won't forget the Sonnet: but, O Tuck! when so many are to be critical on a theme so mighty—think! And I a bridegroom.— I see that George Meredith is dead. That is he who had the child born to him—killed by his own stroke! Ye Gods!—I shall rejoice to see the Hall. But, my father, in your future letters, date them from the Refectory, as of yore. The Oratory delights me not.—We talk of cooks and stare aghast. There are none to be had. Marie will have to tuck up her apron and I to don the paper cap.

I give myself seven years, and then, an I be not a pallid ghost, I will fix here my abode. By the nine Gods! Fancy a salt river, crystal clear, winding under full-bosomed woods to a Clovelly-like[4] village, house upon house, with ships, and trawlers, and yachts moored under the windows, and away the flat stream shining to the Southern sun till it reaches Southampton water with the New Forest over it shadowy, and beyond, to the left, the Solent, and the Island. This is visible from our bed-room window. The air makes athletes. All round are rolling woods, or healthy hills. The roads are hard; but one can't have everything.—I am a man of Bursledon, mark you.

Adieu! I must to work. The clock's on twelve. My darling sleeps. I fondle Rhoda for an hour, and then retire. Out with the lights!— Tell me much news. We like to know that the world lives. There's trouble ahead:—a cook, I cry! If Nature really abhors a vacuum, she'll come. Once more Adieu! Good night, old boy! A kiss to Demitroïa.

Your loving
George M.

2 i.e. his summary of the week's events.
3 Presumably about MSS. that GM was reading for Saunders & Otley.
4 Clovelly was a picturesque fishing village in Devon in GM's day.

316. *To* WILLIAM HARDMAN

MS.: Garrick Club.

[Ploverfield, Bursledon]
[October 25, 1864]

Dearest Tuck,
　Dame Douglass sends agreement, fixing me.
　I foresee the possible botherations.
　Decision is one part of wisdom.
　If I had followed my own sense of prudence, instead of appealing to others (from a spirit of justice) I shouldn't have had this to think of, or the expense of moving and whether?—in May.

Ever yours,
GM

in haste in the dark after 7 hours of compoging.[1]

317. *To* MRS. ANNE WAUGH[1]

MS.: Yale. Published: *Letters*, i. 160–1, repunctuated.

Ploverfield
October 1864

My dear Mrs. Waugh,
　I don't forget the good heart you showed us during our days of trouble and uncertainty. Here is Marie writing to you and I rise up spontaneously to speak for myself and tell you how happy I am and what a capital wife I have got. I like the women who discerned her when yet undiscovered because I know that such women must be attracted by common sense, simple goodness of heart, and similar if noble qualities, dear to me as well. So I take a blunt way of complimenting you, do you see?—We should be glad to hear from you tidings of the student Frank; and are indeed glad to hear from the valley. You heard that the wedding passed like smooth music? And I had to make a speech, owing to the man who carried my hat!—the wretch had basely strung together some neat little illustrations wherewith to return thanks for the bridesmaids. He couldn't give them up and I was compelled to stand before all and make the perfect sacrifice of myself.

316. ¹ A Sairey Gampism.
317. ¹ A friend of Marie's, possibly the wife of Alexander Waugh of Leatherhead, the only person of the name listed in directories of the vicinity. Her son Francis Gledstanes ('Frank'), 1846–1902, attended Rugby and Oxford and became a clergyman. He was author of *The Athenaeum Club and Its Associations* (privately printed, 1897).

The whole business now presents itself to me as if I had been blown through a tube and landed in Matrimony by Pneumatic Despatch. I am, my dear Mrs. Waugh,

> Your most faithful
> George Meredith

318. *To* FREDERIC CHAPMAN

MS. (fragment): Yale.

> [Ploverfield, Bursledon]
> November 9, 1864

My dear Fred,

Mrs. Stowell Wilson[1] is a novel of some mark. It is very clever, not very interesting, but sufficiently vivid to keep readers up to the mark. It is not likely to create a deep impression: but my idea is it would pay, though I can't advise you to give much for it. I think it is a Mr. Wilson who negotiates for the authoress. See in the MSS. book,—forward to him the enclosed letter.—I shall soon be returning. Meantime send another parcel of MSS., that I may not be behind hand.

Mrs. Louisa Meredith's[2] *Ebbs* in three days.

I wish you would write and [the letter breaks off here].

319. *To* WILLIAM HARDMAN

MS.: Garrick Club. Envelope addressed to *Mister Abbot Hardman, Norbiton Hall, near Kingston, Surrey*; postmarked *London, No 21 64.*

> Ploverfield. We leave it
> tomorrow (Tues[day]).
> [November 21, 1864]

Dearest Tuck,

'Tis not impossible I may demand of your hospitality a bed (bachelor's) on Wednesday night. How if a word were sent to Mickleham? For man knoweth not the dinner hour of Norbiton; neither that he may come, if alone; nor what shelter there is in that abode for him.—

I have good things to tell you.

I have worked at my NOVEL.

---

318. [1] Apparently never published.
  [2] Louisa Anne Twamley (Meredith), authoress of *My Home in Tasmania* (1852), *Loved and Lost!* (1860), *Our Island Home* (1879), etc. *Ebbs* is not listed in the *BMC* or the *English Catalogue* (hereinafter *EC*).

Marie, alas! had to go out of Church during Psalms last Sunday. Her husband by chance was absent from the service. It was Communion day, and his old [?]¹ shyness had come upon him. My love to D[emitroïa]. *If you are the man I knew*, the same to you.

Ever heart and soul
Your own George M.

Look at the last *Revue des Deux Mondes*, 15th November.²
Foakes sent a melancholic epistle àpropos of the excellent scoundrel Poco.

320. *To* AUGUSTUS JESSOPP

MS.: Yale. Published: *Letters*, i. 161–2 (dated *October 1864*), with minor variants.

Ploverfield, Bursledon,
Southampton
[November 21, 1864]

My dear Jessopp,

Now, on the last evening of my stay here, I write to you, having been intending the thing from the day of my arrival. The truth is, I write little to you because I love you so well: which is a paradox on the surface only. When I think of writing my bosom swells to its fullest and I shrink in dismay from the thought of emptying it, I that write for money money money!—Do you see that? I grasp the pen frenziedly now: more I fear from a feeling of duty, or because I'm ashamed not to have written. We return to Mickleham to-morrow. To Esher in about a week. Marie is a capital wife, and my little man will now have a mother.—I say! Do you know that you made an impression on Miss Vulliamy¹—It's too true. As a consequence she will not, I think, write the review of your volume of Sermons, as she once promised. I will press it. But why are you handsome? and why is your manner charming?—Thus the women pronounce: and I'm dreading that it will go against the plan I had of getting Miss V[ulliamy] to do the Review. 'She would not dare.' O Rev. Apollo! to these things shouldst thou look: nor frizz the lock, nor modulate the tones. For if you carry about the battery it is useless to plead that you shot not, neither did you aim.

319. ¹ Blotted word.
  ² Émile Forgues (1813–83), well-known French man-of-letters who specialized in English subjects, translated a condensed version of *Emilia in England*, under the title of *Sandra Belloni*, in the 15 Nov., 1 Dec., and 15 Dec. issues of *Revue des Deux Mondes*.
320. ¹ Betty Vulliamy. The book to be reviewed, mentioned below, was Jessopp's *Norwich School Sermons*, published some months earlier.

Forgues, in the *Revue des Deux Mondes*, is translating *Emilia*.

A publisher with whom I have an appointment this week proposes to give me four figures (with no dot between) for a novel.[2] Am I rising? The market speaks!

I have, during the last month of my stay here, written 250 pages of 'A plain Story'[3] of 600 pages (2 vols). *Vittoria* lags: but will be good, I see. I have had to resist awful temptation in the matter of verse: and succumbed once or twice. Smith (of the *Cornhill*) while 'personally admiring "Martin's Puzzle",[4] is compelled to say he thinks it would offend many of his readers, and must therefore beg to etc.' The 'Cleopatra' to Sandys' illustration is done. 'Lines' merely! Not of much value, but containing fire as well as wind.—When shall we meet? —I shall be a MILLIONAIRE next year. My 'plain story' is first to right me and then the 3 volumer will play trumpets. Write to me—perhaps the Garrick Club is the best address for two or three weeks about Wednesday and Friday time. Give my love to your wife whose dear hearty face I long to see. Will you will you will you come to us at Christmas?—Adieu. Here I am and could go on now almost to the verge of the soup, beyond the dinner bell. Take my heart and my name at the bottom of it.

George Meredith

321. *To* MISS JENNETT HUMPHREYS[1]

Text: *Letters*, i. 162–3, with the addressee identified only by her initials; published also: Ellis, p. 240, with the name of the addressee.

193 Piccadilly, London, W.
November 22, 1864

The chief fault in your stories is the redundancy of words which overlays them; and the chief hope visible in them is the copious youthful feeling running throughout. Your characters do not speak the language of nature, and this is specially to be charged against them when they are under strong excitement and should most do so. Nor are the characters very originally conceived, though there is good

---

[2] Is this *The Adventures of Harry Richmond*, published 1871 by Smith, Elder & Co.? GM had mentioned the novel to Jessopp in Letter 279. In any event the figure is surely inflated.

[3] *Rhoda Fleming*, planned as a single volume, now grown to two and soon to expand into three.

[4] Published in the *FR* (1 June 1865, pp. 239–41).

321. [1] Author of children's books and of many articles in the *DNB*; a frequent contributor to various magazines.

matter in the Old Welshman C. Rees. Your defect at present lies in your raw feeling. Time will cure this, if you will get the habit of looking resolutely at the thing you would portray, instead of exclaiming about it and repeating yourself without assisting the reader on in any degree. We certainly think that you are a hopeful writer, and possibly we have been enough outspoken to encourage you to believe us sincere in saying so.

322. *To* MISS JENNETT HUMPHREYS

Text: *Letters*, i. 163–4 (undated), with only the addressee's initials given; published also: Ellis, 240–1, with the name of the addressee.

193 Piccadilly, London, W.
[? End of November 1864]

Madam,

You speak of the exclamatory style as being, you think, essentially and naturally feminine. If you will look at the works of the writer of *Adam Bede*, you will see that she, the greatest of female writers, manifests nothing of the sort. It is simply a quality of youth, and you by undertaking to study will soon tame your style. Interjections are commonly a sign of raw thought, and of vagrant emotion:—a literary hysteria to which women may be more subject than men; but they can talk in another tongue, let us hope. We are anxious that you should not be chagrined by any remarks that we have made. There is real promise in your work: but remember that the best fiction is fruit of a well-trained mind. If hard study should kill your creative effort, it will be no loss to the world or to you. And if, on the contrary, the genius you possess should survive the process of mental labour, it will be enriched and worthy of a good rank. But do not be discouraged by what we say; and do not listen to the encomiums of friends. Read the English of the Essayists; read de Stendhal (Henri Beyle) in French; Heinrich Zschokke[1] in German (minor tales). Learn to destroy your literary offspring remorselessly until you produce one that satisfies your artistic feeling.

322. [1] Johann Heinrich Daniel Zschokke (1771–1848), author of *Der Flüchtling im Jura, Der Creole, Alamontade*, etc.

323. *To* AUGUSTUS JESSOPP

MS.: Yale. Published: *Letters*, i. 164–5, with omissions and variants. Omissions printed in *Altschul Catalogue*, p. 46.

[The Old House, Mickleham]
Friday, [? December 2, 1864]

My dear Jessopp,

We go to Mickleham Hall¹ to-day: till the end of January: the Son residing with Mr. Vulliamy, close by. Do make arrangements to come to us subsequently. It is specially desired by both of us that you will do so, and not disappoint me again. The *Fine Arts* and *Laurence Sterne* await you, just unpacked.² Classical books have no chance with Chapman & Hall—and Oh, the Catullus! which is in another box and which I want to put my hand to before you print it.³

—Have you heard that the Countess Guiccioli has two continuation cantos of *Don Juan* and means to publish them?⁴ Likewise more of Byron!—He's abused, so I take to him; and I'm a little sick of Tennysonian green Tea. I don't think Byron wholesome exactly, but a drop or so—eh? And he doesn't give limp lackadaisical fishermen, and pander to the depraved Sentimentalism of our drawing-rooms. I tell you that *Enoch Arden* is ill done, and that in twenty years' time it will be denounced as villanous weak, in spite of the fine (but too conscious) verse, and the rich insertion of Tropical scenery.⁵ Now, then!—are we face to face, foot to foot?—Forgues is translating *Emilia* (somewhat condensed) very well in the *R[evue] des Deux Mondes*. I write to my little man to-day. Let me hear speedily the period you fix on to come to us. Give my love to your wife, and believe me ever

Your faithful
George Meredith

323. ¹ The residence of Captain and Mrs. John Smith, friends of the Vulliamy family.
² Books published by C. & H. which GM received free of charge: one was certainly Percy Fitzgerald's *The Life of Laurence Sterne* (reviewed in the *Examiner*, 18 June); the other was probably Ralph Nicholson Wornum's *The Epochs of Painting* (reviewed in the *Examiner*, 18 June).
³ I find no record of a book on Catullus published by Jessopp.
⁴ An inaccurate rumour. The last complete canto was published in 1824; a fragment of Canto XVII did not appear until the edition of E. H. Coleridge in 1898. But the Countess did publish in 1868 a book translated in England in 1869 as *My Recollections of Lord Byron and Those of Eye Witnesses of His Life*, comprised mainly of borrowings from the 'eye witnesses'. A much more original work, her *Vie de Lord Byron en Italie*, still remains unpublished except for excerpts.
⁵ Tennyson's *Enoch Arden* was published in the preceding July.

324. *To* WILLIAM HARDMAN

MS.: Garrick Club.

[Mickleham Hall]
[Wednesday morning, December 7, 1864]
Dearest T.,

(In haste) ALL RIGHT. It was not Marie's fault—but mine. I said:
Let's be at Tuck's so that I may go over house and grounds and see
the morning at Norbiton and the great Lord of Norbiton swell as he
tries to point the limits of his premises. And we can roll hoops, I said,
and have all kinds of fun—of course, never calculating your being
among the Aristocracy now, and out every other night of your life.

Morley and Virtue are (as) one.¹ 'Tis so, and may they be happy! He
has gone through the dread interview with Papa. And it went well.
James² (grown dyspeptic and savage) is, it is expected, the *bête noire* of
the sweet dream. I'm glad the little woman found her mind at last, and
somewhere, Tuck, this earth will be peopled—never fear. God bless
you, noble abbot. Goodbye!

Your loving
George M.

325. *To* WILLIAM HARDMAN

MS.: Garrick Club. Excerpt published: *Letters*, i. 164, with inaccuracies.

Mickleham Hall
Sunday, [December 18, 1864]
Beloved Tuck!

For Love insists, despite your high office, O great Lord Abbot,
rotund, rubicund! upon this old familiar address, now and then, as to
water the drouthy present with the frisky past:—nor should a man
when he enters a new state (short of Beatitude) cast off his byegone
self utterly:—and albeit we do perceive a rueful droop of thy mouth's
left corner, the name of quaint endearment being pronounced before

324. ¹ This refers to a love affair between John Morley (I suppose) and a daughter of
George Virtue, though there is no reference to it in biographies of Morley, whose own
Recollections and letters leave the impression of a cold intellectual and political machine.
All that can be said for certain is that John Morley was acquainted with the Virtue family
through his friend Cotter Morison and that the affair came to an end a couple of months
later.
² James Virtue, the girl's brother.

thee, and there is manifested much inward cogitation as to whether it shall be permitted, this liberty we take: still we take it, amiable Tuck: trusting thy bowels to be lively, even if thou be stiff in brain.

The Christmas season causes that contemplation should make you specially its object. Marie went in the afternoon for a second edition of the Reverend Burmie[1] and a strange moustached clergyman who calls his God—'Gaed' and his Paul—'Pell,' and says that a 'Cherrrestion quuuawlity' should be shown at this period, but excites it little. I aloft to Mickleham downs, where the great herded yews stand on a pure snowfield. I thought to have fallen on the very throne of Silence. In a few paces I became a Druid. Time withered from the ends and all his late writings were smudged out till I lived but in the earlier days of Britain when he with difficulty made his mark. It was a sublime scene, that long roll of the unfooted snow with the funeral black plumes of the yews spreading in a dumb air, as if all had ceased, or nothing was begun. Impressed by it, my spirit conjured up a passionate desire to snowball Tuck till he cried himself a sinner. I moaned that the man was not there, that I might snowball him till fainting he dropped to earth. By God! I would have snowballed Tuck with a gallant and an eager heart in that glorious solitude! But he was absent and I passed on. Eh! what a changing of the cards of our fortunes, Tuck! I am married, and thou art Lord of Norbiton! and of these things we dreamed not a year back. Wherefore must I think truly there is a Spirit and a peculiar Spirit to the New Year. And I greet you and wish well to you and yours (who are mine) in the Year to come. And let this practice be established between us: for verily I marvel at what has happened to us; and if the years advancing are to surpass themselves, I shall haply be shot into Venus within the next five, while thou (the planet, Tuck, the planet) danglest among the Pleiades—the lost one found!—My walk was interrupted by none. The harmless rabbit tripped before me, aware that I despise his flesh. Once I was accosted sheepishly by two sheep, ashamed of their coats, in which I could see plainly they knew not themselves upon the snowfield. Such are among the lessons taught by contrast. Even so, Tuck, shall we be among the Angel quires when I thrum the cymbal, and you, bottomless, endeavour with large-puffed cheeks—endeavour, by the aid of the trumpet, to produce the sonorous, incomparable note of religious praise which in honour to Nature you, when otherwise endowed, accomplish below. The pair of sheep took, as their fashion is, to staring, and then turned their inexpressive tails on me and once more I was alone. The day sank. An I could have snowballed thee for one minute, Tuck! But it was not to be. My fervent love to D[emitroïa] and may Heaven bless your house!

325. [1] The Revd. Alfred Burmester, the Mickleham rector (1813–67).

(You would have been sent to me here to-day if the best had been in store for you.) This is Robin's Christmas blessing. Adieu! Write in reply. I may say as much as our joint love to you, though Marie is dressing and away from her husband's pen.

[Signature missing]

326. *To* MRS. WILLIAM HARDMAN

MS.: Garrick Club.

Cedars, Esher
[*c.* January 24, 1865]

Dearest Mrs. Hardman,

The enclosed[1] refers to our projected furnishing of the Lodge; and it's what Marie wants, that she may know whether the costly articles which catch her eye will *pack* in our abode. Will Mr. Mason[2] make the sketch 'as per inches', at a small cost, do you think? And if you have time will you go to him and inquire? I personally know nothing, and I can't do anything and I won't. At the same time, I'm ashamed of myself, and my dear girl offers to supply all my deficiences, rather loftily. So I say to her, my friends will back me to be equal to you at all points! 'Will they!' says she and immediately I declare that I will put Mrs. Hardman to the proof.

—Give my regards to your husband, whose recent coldness I don't understand: but must, I presume, accustom myself to it. Between the Squire of Kingston Lodge and the Lord Abbot of Norbiton Hall the old familiarity will not be possible. Probably you have heard that 'all is up' between Morley and the fair F[arouche]?[3]—Don't blame him hastily. It's not his fault: by no means hers. Mysterious Fate has struck division.—Inform Mr. Hardman that, were we together, I could talk. It has pleased him to have it otherwise. On Thursday I dine again with Maxse's mother[4] and on Friday Marie and he and I and his wife and

---

326. [1] See accompanying sketch (of the rooms of Kingston Lodge, which the Merediths had taken).

   [2] Samuel Mason, builder and contractor, of Eden St., Kingston-on-Thames.

   [3] See Note 1, Letter 324.

   [4] Lady Caroline Maxse, who lived at Effingham Hill, three or four miles west of Box Hill, was a daughter of the famous 5th Earl of Berkeley who had neglected to marry his wife until after the birth of their first son. Later attempts to establish the legitimacy of the son failed. Viscountess Milner (*My Picture Gallery: 1886–1901*, 1951, p. 8) describes her grandmother as a woman of brains who had 'a keen appreciation of cleverness in others'. GM learned from her the story of Caroline Norton which formed the basis of *Diana* and depicted her as Lady Charlotte Eglett in *Lord Ormont*.

sister go to see Miss Bateman.[5] When do you return from Morison's?[6]
—It was a good Christian motion to have such a sponsor! At any rate,
I hope *you* will write a word; and I am

Your ever loving
George Meredith

[In the writing of Marie Meredith:]

A rough sketch of each room with the dimensions thereof as '8ft—
4inch feet by 5ft—3in feet.'* (or Width by length.) Also number of feet
and inches in each space from chimney to door, door to door, door to
window, & window to door, thus:

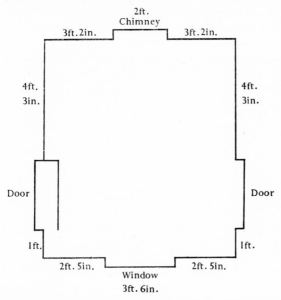

*For size of carpet.

[5] Kate Bateman (1843–1917), American-born actress, had first appeared on the stage in
1852 as an 'infant phenomenon', but her real début was made at the Adelphi in 1863,
when her emotional performance as the Jewess in *Leah* became the talk of London. The
Merediths and the Maxses saw her in a return engagement.

[6] The Hardmans were going on 1 Feb. to Abingdon, near Oxford, to stand as god-
parents to the Morisons' daughter Margaret.

327. *To* AUGUSTUS JESSOPP

MS.: Yale. Printed: *Altschul Catalogue*, p. 47.

Cedars, Esher
[*c.* January 24, 1865]

My dear Jessopp,

I send a cheque within two or three weeks on behalf of small man. If things don't go better (in this respect) he will have to go to Switzerland.—Why have you treated us so badly in promising to come and never coming? Long talks I proposed to myself, and that you should meet those whom you have shamefully charmed. I trust you no more. —We go to Kingston Lodge, Kingston, in about six weeks:—no country around—brick, brick, brick; but a middling pretty little house and Marie likes it, so I submit. I will write fully in a short time. The weather is deadly and fits an iron cap on my brain.[1] Let me hear how you are and give your wife my love.

Your affectionate
George Meredith

[At top of letter:] *Arthur pays his fine.*

328. *To* AUGUSTUS JESSOPP

MS.: Yale. Published: *Letters*, i. 166–7, with omissions and variants.

The Cedars
January 30, [1865] night

No my dear Jessopp: for this there is no necessity.[1] But, hear! the man went and got married: it was well for him: he bought linen, he bought plate, disbursed early and eke late: the fat end of his purse did set flowing towards his fireside, and the lean was to them that did accredit him. So. And meantime, in prospect of the needful, he put aside *Vittoria* (which contains points of grandeur and epical interest), to 'finish off' *Rhoda Fleming* in one volume, now swollen to two—and Oh, will it be three?—But this is my D^d. D^d. D^d. uncertain workmanship. You see, I am three days in town, and I am hustled with moving and can't get my shoulders into a place, but the toe of Fate takes me somewhat lower and away I go; and this is not favourable to composi-

327. [1] Clara Middleton thinks in terms of the same metaphor about the mental atmosphere of Sir Willoughby's household (*The Egoist*, 1879, i. 105).
328. [1] Jessopp had probably offered to waive Arthur's fees, as in the beginning he had offered to educate him without cost.

tion, though my dear wife does all that she can for me, and would hush the elements, bidding them know me pen in hand. However I hope in six weeks to be clear of Miss Rhoda, into whose history I have put more work than she deserves. Ere that time, I will remit to you a portion of the due. I wrote in saddish spirits, rare with me. Stomach, my friend. I am not in the bracing air which befits me. But, in future I will be punctual. By degrees I will reduce the portentous OO's. And I thank you with all my heart for the friendly peace-breathing letter. It's precious balm to read.—*Vittoria* is one third towards completion. Did you see the translation of *Emilia*, by Forgues, condensed, in the *R[evu]e des Deux Mondes*? He has apparently taken to me; he has sent for *R[ichar]d Feverel* to review.[2] A New Edition of *Shagpat* with an illustration to 'Bhanavar' by Sandys, comes out in a month.[3]—Marie has, I believe, written fully anent the Son. He threatens—appalling thought!—to be knock-kneed. We mourn and howl over him.—When are we four to meet again? You see, there is a new witch now, and she's a darling.—Adieu, for a space! I am

> Your loving
> George Meredith

329. *To* FREDERIC CHAPMAN

MS.: University of Texas.

> Cedars, Esher
> [Early 1865]

Dear Fred,

The novel of Miss Thomas.[1]—I have read it with some interest; the story, as far as I have here seen of it, is distinct, and it *runs* well. She has studied Trollope with advantage, and throws in her hunting-bits very cleverly. It is written for the market and will suit the market. There is no fire or genius in the book, and no pretension. There is a certain atmosphere of impropriety, here and there, from the point of view of the British Public—not from mine:—Richmond Dinners, with a slight flavour of the demi-monde; and her men lay about with oaths, without compunction of parentage. But they speak like men;

---

[2] A condensed version of *Richard Feverel*, translated by Forgues, appeared in the *Revue des Deux Mondes* (15 Apr., 1 May, 15 May 1865).

[3] The second edn. of *Shagpat*, 'affectionately inscribed to William Hardman of Norbiton Hall', was published by C. & H. as part of the series Standard Edition of Popular Authors.

329. [1] Annie Thomas (Mrs. P. H. Cudlip, 1838–1918), a prolific novelist. The MS. under consideration was doubtless *On Guard*, published by C. & H. in 1865, but I have not seen the novel.

throughout, the dialogue is singularly smooth and natural. The cast of the story is not new. I do not guess how she continues it in the two succeeding volumes; for I have only had one sent to me: but I can't help thinking she has too early exhausted her material for creating excitement, unless she has a fine scheme to develop. Question her on this point. The chapters she relies on for intense interest in the batch given to me, are not the best written, and do not excite me. They represent the two chief men in the book,—one half dead in a ditch with his horse on top of him; and one (from finishing a novel) tumbled in a heap, the victim of a false girl combined with angina pectoris. But two men thus bowled down do not produce amazement and curiosity. —I would not decide to take the book until the whole is seen. It seems good and marketable, offends a little, is not original, and is by no means a bad book to publish; though I rather fancied better of the authoress and presume that she will not increase her reputation by it. As to her sustaining the weight of a serial story, she must develop stronger quality for that than I have yet seen. She is certainly very clever, and quite shallow enough for common readers. I would not, remember, *buy* the book at the price named: not engage for it absolutely till more is seen of it: but the authoress has vigour and power of narration, and she *must not be lost* to us.

Yours ever,
GM

330. *To* [? ROBERT GREGORY] CREYKE[1]

MS.: Berg Collection, New York Public Library.

The Cedars, Esher
Monday, [February 6, 1865]

My dear Creyke,

I find that my wife's birthday falls on this very Friday. Let our meeting at the Garrick be Thursday—? Or, if this does not suit you, name your own day. The Wednesday of next week, if this Thursday does not do. Send word to the Garrick. I am in confusion lest I should thus derange any plans of yours; but one can't settle the day upon which one's wife is to be born, and a proper observation of it befits the lowly mind.

I am ever / Your faithful
George Meredith

330. [1] See Note 3, Letter 233.

331. *To* FREDERICK A. MAXSE

Text: typed copy, Maxse Papers. Published: *Letters*, i. 99 (placed with the letters of January 1863), with omissions.

Garrick Club
Wednesday, [February 1865]

My dear Fred,

I want to write a long letter: but the receipt of the cheque requires acknowledgment. You know that you put me under no obligation: or better, that I should be quite happy to owe you everything. The expenses of furniture are awful. What must it have been in your case?—

Rhoda now rushes to an end. I don't at all know what to think of the work. I am confused by this frost. It nips and impoverishes me.

By the way:—What of the dog? If you haven't heard of him, it is by no means improbable that he has left the neighbourhood, the County, the south-west, in fact, and trotted back to Yorkshire. The Colley is famous for his 'sagacity' as the Natural History books say, in this respect; and will find his way back to a point in Scotland out of England.

Please write. You haven't my excuse. I see you in that dear little room, warm, with one eye on a winter prospect, snow and black river between the banks.—Tell me, how the frost takes you; kindly or not. —Gilmore[1] àpropos of acting and art, is powerful. He as a thorough 'Gallery' critic—hates, adores, flings his orange-peel and empties his brandy-flask, and is quite satisfied with himself at the conclusion.

Miss Bateman is said to have failed as 'Julia'.[2] I can see that to be possible, though I bow to her Leah.

Let me have a letter speedily.

Yours lovingly,
George Meredith

331. [1] This friend in common reappears several times in the letters. The only Gilmore that I have found in Surrey at this period is A. Gilmore of Upper Richmond Road, Putney, about whom I know nothing, and I have been unable to find anyone of the name in Hampshire. There are various Gilmours, however, and GM's spelling of proper names is always unreliable.

[2] Kate Bateman had appeared as Julia in *The Hunchback*, by Sheridan Knowles, on 30 and 31 Jan., and then the play was suspended until 7 Mar. because of her illness. Suspension of the play at the beginning of her assumption of her second major role gave rise to the rumour that she was a one-role actress who had failed when she tried another. The rumour proved unfounded: *The Times* (31 Jan., 1 Feb.) praised her performance highly and said that she had 'more than surpassed all expectations'.

Give my warmest regards to your wife. I am curious to know whether she takes exercise and of what kind, in this cold-baked condition of earth and air. Marie walks but protests like ancient Posloe [Pistol].

332. *To* WILLIAM HARDMAN[1]

MS.: C. L. Cline.

[? Kingston Lodge, Norbiton]
[? *c.* March 1865][2]

My Australian critic has a fine crashing hand. He doesn't think enough of Emilia herself, but that's from lack of sympathy, and he doesn't consequently allow for the influence of such a character on such a fellow as Wilfrid, who, as I am ready to contend but can't possibly prove, would not in real life of necessity have cut short the dialogue to put his 'Hippogriff' (as my bluff boxer phrases it) to hers. An author musn't ask for a poetic appreciation of his work when he gets such solid criticism as this of the Antipodes. The remarks upon Wilfrid please me, because few men understand what difficulty there is in representing the absolute character of my youth, or believe one of them an actual being when they see him painted before them, and none have done me justice for this study. The combination of sensualism and sentimentalism—of a tyrannous delicacy of imagination with the grossness of developing appetites, has not yet, as far as I know, been attempted; and no one in England has given me credit for it.

As regards Sir Purcell Barrett's[3] remarks on the French and English languages, I have nothing to do with them. I would contend that the French are richer in stereotyped social phrases, and admit them to be poor in the language of passion. Concerning myself, when I have to use this latter tongue, I never coin or hazard a word.

I must thank my critic in conclusion for his good open hitting and rejoice to get such a thorough shake of the hand from him.

[George Meredith]

332. [1] This letter was found among some miscellaneous pages of William Hardman's journal. Since it was written on the same thin paper as Hardman used to send to his Australian friend E. D. Holroyd the monthly letter that comprised the journal, it was obviously written for enclosure and should therefore perhaps be regarded as addressed to Holroyd.

[2] In his October letter Hardman says, 'I think I will send [*Emilia in England*] you by next mail' (*L. & M.*, p. 232). There were monthly mails to Australia, but there is no mention in *L. & M.* of Holroyd's criticism or of GM's reply. The only clue to the date is the numbering of the pages of the MS. journal, which suggests February or March.

[3] Purcell Barrett is a character in *Emilia*. The allusion is to Chapter VIII.

333. *To* WILLIAM HARDMAN

MS.: Garrick Club. Published: *Letters*, i. 167, with minor variants; S. M. Ellis, *The Hardman Papers* (hereinafter *HP*), 1930, p. 152.

[Kingston Lodge, Norbiton]
[April 18 or 19, 1865]
To W. Hardman, Esq., J.P.[1]

Dear Sir,

Am I to be damned to all eternity because I curse at a vile organ now afflicting me with the tune of Jack Robinson, presently to be followed by the Hundredth Psalm, in a simulation of the groans of [a] sinner.

Perhaps you will put this before your Reverend friend.[2]

But are not you to be damned in the present, for permitting the infliction, and not, at least, commanding a fresh importation of organ into Kingston, and the exit of the old?

This is a matter for you to reflect upon.

I am, Dear Sir, even as a chestnut on the hob,

Your bursting
Author

334. *To* AUGUSTUS JESSOPP

MS.: Parrish Collection, Princeton. Excerpt published: Ellis, p. 218.

Kingston Lodge, Norbiton
Kingston-on-Thames
Monday, April 24, [1865]

My dear Jessopp,

I received the letter in the well-known hand, and return the son to you;[1] only too glad at heart to think that you are in working order with your gallant helpmate.

Rhoda Fleming is just completed (all but the last two chapters). It is a 3 volumes six months' work, minus a week or so. Tinsley offers (won't look at the MS.) Four hundred for it. But, I fear me he is not a safe man. And I don't quite like to sell it for that sum. Chapman bids

333. [1] Hardman was sworn in as Justice of the Peace, to his great satisfaction, on 23 Mar.
[2] The Revd. Robert Holberton, incumbent of St. Peter's, Norbiton, whose organ was being complained of by GM. In the following year he was one of Hardman's adversaries in a controversy over the bells of St. Peter's, which Hardman tried unsuccessfully to have silenced.
334. [1] Arthur had been home for the Easter holidays. Easter fell on 16 Apr. in 1865.

me wait till November—by which time I hope to have another novel done. I'd rather, if he'll advance. I shall see in a week. Meantime, it's cheerful to think that I can work tolerably quick. The last chapters commonly disturb my gastric juices. But, I am here near Richmond Park, and Hampton Court, where I can go play tennis, and the river: so, I think I can right myself. It's probable I may write in the *Fortnightly Review*.[2] *Not*, I fancy in the *Shilling Magazine*,[3] in the disgusting Advertisement of which, I see that they have blazed out my name. *Forgues*, in the *Revue des Deux Mondes*, is now translating *Richard Feverel*, and doing it, after his fashion, well.

When shall we meet? The time, as far as I can indicate, is remote, for Marie won't be a traveller.[4]—When I can afford it, I must have a special drill-sergeant for Arthur who threatens to be as knock-kneed as any John Thomas in the Kingdom. And also a man to grind him in rudimentary Latin, hard, over and over. He ought to have a thirst for history, by this time; but the appetite in him seems to be for sensation novels. My son does not promise. I am not impatient; but he potters at everything—play and work. He's a good fellow—which must content me.

Give my love, and Marie's, to your wife. Let me hear from you soon. I wish I could help you at all in your classical books, but they are not in the way of the firm which takes my Counsel.—Alas for Lee![5] And, Oh! for the newspapers of my native land. Did you ever see such weathercocks to the wind? We are all now due *North*. I am ever

Your loving
George Meredith

335. *To* F. M. EVANS

MS.: Parrish Collection, Princeton.

Kingston Lodge, Norbiton
Kingston-on-Thames
Tuesday, May 2, 1865

My dear Evans,

Two things I have to ask:—*Will you sell your share of Evan Harrington, that I may have it at my disposal?*[1]

334. [2] For an account of the founding of the *FR*, see Note 5, Letter 313.
   [3] Samuel Lucas, having made a failure of *OaW*, was founder and editor of the *Shilling Magazine*, of which he was also to make a failure.
   [4] She was in her sixth month of pregnancy.
   [5] Gen. Robert E. Lee had surrendered on 9 Apr. GM, it will be remembered, was a Southern sympathizer.
335. [1] On 19 Dec. 1865 Bradbury & Evans credited GM's account with £100 as payment for his share of the copyright

And secondly:—are you looking for an Editor for *Once a Week*?[2]— I believe I could manage to make it swim satisfactorily. I should not increase the present costs. I can bring good, cheerful and not cormorant workers to my aid. In fine, I'm willing to try. This is between us, and need not be mentioned, if nothing is to come of it.

Oblige me by replying to this letter. I am

Your faithful
George Meredith

Once a Week continues to be sent to Esher. Let it be changed to the above address.

336. *To* ?GEORGE SMITH OR H. S. KING[1]

MS.: Yale.

Kingston Lodge, Norbiton, S.W.
June 12, 1865

Dear Sir,

Like many others, as I hope, I am anxious to see the *Pall Mall Gazette* succeed as it deserves. During a recent visit to the S[outh] Western counties I have been astonished to find that my friends were quite ignorant of the existence of such a paper. When they saw it, they became subscribers to it. I can't but think that it would be worth while to advertize the *Gazette* largely among the landed and country families. I am told that you have an interest in it, and so I apply to you, and merely because I want to see vitality put into a good journal, of the health of which I have not heard favourable tidings. I have no doubt you will pardon me, and I am

Yours faithfully,
George Meredith

[2] Extant records indicate that *OaW* lost money during most of its existence. In attempting to bolster sagging sales, Lucas—or the publishers—had given up experimenting with relatively unknown authors and had turned almost exclusively to established authors. The result was an increase in cost which was not balanced by increased circulation. On the departure of Lucas, Edward Walford, who had been sub-editor, succeeded to the editorship.

336. [1] The first issue of the *PMG* appeared on 7 Feb. 1865 with Smith, Elder & Company as publishers and Frederick Greenwood as editor. J. W. Robertson Scott (*The Story of the 'Pall Mall Gazette'*, Oxford, 1950, p. 133) says that Smith's partner, H. S. King, had an option to sell his interest if the paper did not satisfy him and that when King withdrew, an interest was offered to Greenwood. Presumably it was accepted. I think it unlikely that the letter was addressed to Greenwood: it was not published by W. M. Meredith, who had access to GM's letters to Greenwood. Anthony Trollope remains a possibility, but GM knew Trollope and the tone of this letter suggests someone that he did not know.

337. *To* WILLIAM HARDMAN

MS.: Garrick Club.

[Kingston Lodge, Norbiton]
[Sunday, July 2, 1865]

Tuck, thou graceless sinner!—
Not till thou'st done thy dinner,—
But having done it, then go
And pass th' abode of Bengo!—[1]

'Tis the terrible stench of slain horses decaying,
On whose carcases myriads of blue flies are preying.
The little boys run with their noses clutch'd tightly.
Your Robin goes groaning and retching unsightly;
           Yawns whitely;
Reels, and is haunted by whinnyings and neighing.

The stoutest man 'twould flummox:
It sounds the gong in our stomachs.
To Hades, say, shall men go
Because of Tuck and Bengo?

'Levius fit patientia
Quidquid corrigere est nefas—'[2]

is a good saying, but does not apply in this case. It is a rage to smell Bengo this day. In truth I am taken hold of by the nose and led into regions of vast distraction. There is the mother of pestilence (Bengo's spouse) in Combe Lane.[3]

Affectionately as thou abidest by this,

Robin

---

337. [1] John Bengo, Jr., of Combe Lane, Norbiton, was charged in Borough Court with using a shed on his premises as a slaughter-house without licence, and shortly later his father was charged with maintaining on his premises a heap of manure containing a quantity of offal which gave off an unbearable stench. Bengo Senior deposed that the manure was not on his premises but offered to clean it up if given time. This he apparently did, for the case against him was dismissed later upon payment of costs of 15s. 6d. Bengo Junior requested six weeks in which to clean up a refuse heap amounting to not less than 500 loads, and the case against him was dismissed with costs of 9s. 6d. after testimony was offered that the heap had been nearly all removed (*Surrey Comet*, various dates, Aug.–Oct. 1865).
  [2] Horace, Ode I. 24. 19–20, to Quintillius: 'that which cannot be changed will be made lighter by submission'.
  [3] GM lived at the corner of Combe Lane and London Road.

338. *To* FREDERIC CHAPMAN

MS.: Yale.

193 Piccadilly, London, W.[1]
July 21, 1865

Dear Fred,

Foakes, in some strange fit of absence of mind, has forgotten the bill. I've seen him, and he says, his banker has received instructions to pay it forthwith. There is no reason to fear that this will not be done.

Please, pay in to my bankers' £20 . . . of which sum I have to give you a cheque for £7 . . . and £3.17, which I will do on Monday or Tuesday.

Ever yours,
George Meredith

339. *To* EDWARD WALFORD

MS.: Fales Collection, New York University.

[Kingston Lodge, Norbiton]
July 27, 1865

My dear Walford,

Lucas has been promising to send me the *Dyke Farm* for months. I am of opinion that a good thing (of that *class* of thing) may be made of it. Can you call on me at the Garrick to-morrow? If you can, send word at what hour of the afternoon, and I will be there. If not, tell me your views by letter. Address:

Kingston Lodge, Norbiton
Kingston-on-Thames.

I have been in some trepidation about the birth of a boy. It's happily over, and this new son proves to be a very lusty fellow.[1] Arthur is over at Caen in Normandy for two or three weeks.

Yours ever faithfully,
George Meredith

338. [1] Printed address.
339. [1] William Maxse Meredith, named for GM's friends Hardman and Maxse, was born on 26 July.

340. *To* W. C. BONAPARTE WYSE

MS.: Parrish Collection, Princeton. Published: Ellis, p. 217, with omission of two concluding sentences.

Kingston Lodge, Norbiton
Kingston-on-Thames, Surrey
July 27, 1865

My dearest Corsican and right good friend and brother of Parnassus!

I delayed to reply, having had to visit Maxse and await the result of my wife's confinement.[1] It's over and here's a new Boy in the world of uncertainty. And now, mother and child going on as well as at present, I shall be free about a fortnight hence, and may perhaps drop down and spend a few days with you, if you can receive me. I have lots to talk about. Just now I haven't time for a word. There are letters to be written and dispersed among all my wife's relations, that they may know of this marvel. Write to me by return and tell me whether you will be at home and can give me housing in the middle of August. I shall walk on to Lynmouth and Ilfracombe.[2] Perhaps subsequently run over to Brescia and the subalpine cities, to see to my colouring in the novel *Vittoria*, which is to appear in the *Fortnightly Review*. I have just completed a novel called *Rhoda Fleming.—Emilia* I will cause to be sent to you from Chapman & Hall's. Adieu. With love to your good Ellen, whom as well as yourself, I am anxious to see, I am

Your loving
George Meredith

Arthur is well.

341. *To* FREDERICK A. MAXSE

Text: typed copy, Maxse Papers.

Kingston
August 3, 1865

My dear Fred,

Marie and I wish you to be Godfather to the Baby Boy, if you will. There will be no necessity to attend the ceremony, and only a little feeling of alliance to him if his father should make the dark journey first. So would he travel with a less loaded heart into the greatly-

---

340. [1] See preceding letter and Note 1.
[2] In Devon.

peopled, solitary kingdom, O my friend! There would be all good arrangements made for Boy, and nothing wanted from those concerned in this relationship, save the kindly supervision which it would require no relationship or bond thereof to induce you to give to my son.

If you have insuperable objections, name the fact, and be satisfied that I trust you too well in all things to be hurt in any way.

If I am at Ploverfield on the 11th, will it be in time?—I will come. The prospect is glorious.

Tell your Cecilia that our son here is a prodigy. He is pronounced just as big as a baby of three months, of the common sort: and this by experienced persons. He is fair, with a fine quantity of silver hair, dark blue eyes, a very gentle look, a full chest, broad back, lusty limbs, and sonorous yell. His mother comes more to her way of thinking about babies (as she prophesied). Adieu; write immediately. I would call the new man 'William Maxse Meredith', or if you prefer not to give the surname, then 'Fred M.': but the first suits in sound:—I might, instead of 'William' give a Welsh name for prefix.—

Your loving
George M.

342. *To* FREDERICK A. MAXSE

Text: typed copy, Maxse Papers. Published: *Letters*, i. 174–5, with omissions.

Garrick Club
Tuesday, [August 8, 1865]

My dearest Fred,

I now remember your having told me that you refused to stand godfather to your brother's child, and am vexed with myself for reducing you to make this reply again.[1]—Let him be your lay godson. As regards the ceremony, it is a piece of the old secondary barbaric system of teaching men to be humane; and is of the same class as Freemasonry, in which you bind yourself to help a man, because he knows how to press your knuckles in a particular manner. I can't bear asking men to do this;—but I do wish the boy to have some little link with you, such as your name will give him.

We differ in our spirit of objection to the dominant creed: but I suppose that twenty years hence we shall not differ. When the Ministers of Religion press on for an open rupture by attempts at persecution, it will be time to take rank under colours: until when I hold myself in reserve. I don't want the day to be advanced. I think you altogether

---

342. [1] See preceding letter.

too impetuous: 500 years too fast for the human race: I think that where the Christian Ministers are guilty of little more than boredom, you have got them in a state of perfection and at least owe them your tolerance for theirs:—And so I shall continue to think until next I go to Church. Adieu. I have no notion whether I am to see your Cecilia when I come. I come on Saturday:—by some afternoon train from Kingston, if I can manage it.

Your loving
George M.

343. *To* EDWARD TINSLEY

MS.: University of Texas.

Catherine Street, Strand
August 11, 1865

Dear Sir,

I place my novel *Rhoda Fleming* in your hands to publish for me; you to receive one fourth of the profits in return for your expenditure of labour etc:—the profits accruing from American and foreign issues and sales to belong to me solely.[1]

Yours faithfully,
George Meredith

344. *To* EDWARD WALFORD

MS.: University of Texas.

193 Piccadilly, London, W.[1]
August 11, 1865

Dear Walford,

The author of *Goldbourne*[2] brings his own volume to you, and I think it would suit you, in the serial form, for *Once a Week*—running to just the length you require. It is objected to by Chapman & Hall because they do not care to publish one volume novels, or two, if they can help it.—

Yours faithfully,
George Meredith

343. [1] *Rhoda Fleming* was published by Tinsley Bros. in Oct. 1865. Edward Tinsley died in 1866 and his brother William (i. 135) says that the novel 'had a very poor sale'.
344. [1] Printed address.
  [2] William Duthie, author of *The Pearl of the Rhone and Other Poems* (1864), *Counting the Cost* (a 3-vol. novel, 1867), *Proved in the Fire: A Story of the Burning of Hamburg* (3 vols., 1867), etc.

345. *To* FREDERICK A. MAXSE

Text: typed copy, Maxse Papers.

Kingston Lodge
Friday night, [August 11, 1865]

My dear Fred,
There's a train from Guildtord at 2.18 p.m.

I start from Mickleham to meet that train on Monday. It reaches Botley at 4., and if you can't send, I'll get a fly, or walk. I forward my portmanteau from Kingston to-morrow, so that the impedimentum is discharged and my mind is free, and vive la liberté!—not that I like being away from my good Marie: but it's good to sniff the air of fresh regions and draw nourishment from other minds.

I fear that you are crumpled up with this accursed dyspepsia. Will you put aside your vile British prejudice and try a system of medicine? —the only one which *may* do good and *can't* hurt? Even the thrice insular Sir Alec Gordon said to me, this day—but you sneer already! And it is you who perceive a goddess in Nature! and I offer you Nature's medicine!—as I repeat, the only *system* in existence.

How's Gilmore?[1] I feel like a boy at the thought of that rosy-gilled riddle-propounder. Consider my state, when Gilmore makes me leap! And Purcell![2]—And the fair face, the Lady of our companionship! I desire greatly to look on her. May the S.West blow showerless while we toss with the foam! I hope you have nightingales about you. Adieu, my dear Fred! Perhaps you've forgotten what a holiday is.

Ever your loving
George Meredith

346. *To* N. E. S. A. HAMILTON

MS.: University of Texas.

Ploverfield, Bursledon,
Southampton
Tuesday, [August 22, 1865]

My dear Stephen,
I don't know a man on the *Pall Mall Gazette*, save Anth[ony] Trollope. If Dr. Ingleby[1] has special matter of importance, I believe

345. [1] See Note 1, Letter 331.　　　　　　　[2] Skipper of Maxse's yacht.
346. [1] Clement Mansfield Ingleby (1823–86), LL.D., a Shakespearian scholar who shared Hamilton's interest in Shakespeare forgeries; author of *The Shakespeare Fabrications* (1859).

the editing to be good enough to ensure him a fair reading of his paper and a probable trial of its merits. If he merely wishes to serve as a clever scribe, the *Pall Mall* has that article in excess. I wish I could help him or any friend of yours. In this case I am powerless.

At Mickleham all were disappointed by your failing them last Monday. I in the morning turned my back on the deep bower of Green, and walked to Guildford on my way hither, where Maxse gives me yachting as a restorative, and a very good one too. Much should I rejoice, O Stephano! an thou wert among us, pouring forth gratulation with an eloquence most distinguishing!—I have finished my novel, and put salt water between that and the one to follow.[2] Adieu.

Your ever faithful
George Meredith

347. *To* WILLIAM HARDMAN

MS.: Garrick Club.

Mickleham
[September 1865]

The cause for my silence, dearest Tuck!—Imprimis, my wits were fairly bounced out of me by the great seas over on the way to Cherbourg:[1] so that, though I had much, most friarly, to communicate, I could only just manage to send a letter to the [*Morning*] *Post*, as promised. (If you have seen that paper, don't confound me with the 'Special.')—Next, and later, I've had to get off proofs of *Rhoda*; and with Trollope and Lewes[2] at me to get up steam for *Vittoria* I have been hardly capable of a word to my ghostly adviser.—Also—I,—*we* have been bothered about the Christening.[3] All was arranged and Mrs. Smith had postponed her visit to Scarborough on purpose to meet you, when, *Soudain*, on a Saturday night, Edward Vulliamy[4] appears!—must return on Sunday evening:—came over solely for the ceremony; and it had to be done. I sent in your name and his. I am deprived of a rare gratification. To have seen Tuck at the baptismal Font would indeed have comforted me!

346. [2] On 15 Aug. he had sailed on Maxse's yacht to Cherbourg, where the English and French fleets were meeting.
347. [1] See Note 2, preceding letter.
    [2] G. H. Lewes, editor of the *FR*, in which *Vittoria* appeared serially (15 Jan.–1 Dec. 1866).
    [3] William Maxse Meredith was christened on 27 Aug. by the Revd. John H. Smart, curate. His father's occupation was listed as 'Gentleman' (Mickleham Church Register).
    [4] Marie's eldest brother.

Marie wants you to come over to us on the 20th—our Wedding-Day. You may remember you were shamefully absent on the chief occasion of which this will be the Anniversary. So, come! Your Godson is growing charmingly: eats, sleeps, bellows—a perfect Triad for Babies. I'm sure you won't feel that you were neglected àpropos of the Christening. It could not be helped. In fact, I was compunctious about asking you to come up from the Island:⁵—Lord! how I thought of you at Niton when I was mid-Channel. Never did Tuck tighten on me as such a favourite of the Gods!—

A letter! and tell me all about yourself and dear D[emitroïa]; to whom my love. I hope she's thoroughly set up. I know the Sandrock Hotel (the situation and neighbourhood). With pleasant company, it must have been capital.

Ever affectionately yours,
George Meredith

[Marginal note:] A thousand thanks, dear friend, for your thought of the small man. Out of the beaker may we drink good and hearty wine. —On the 20th?

348. *To* WILLIAM HARDMAN

MS. (written on black-bordered paper):¹ Garrick Club.

Mickleham, Dorking
[September 24, 1865]

Dearest Tuck,

Of course you [are] engaged to dine with ye Cotterills:² There was no engagement of any kind with me. I wish we could have done something to amuse you when you were here³—suddenly discharged Mr. Vulliamy through a doorway upon you; or engaged Mr. Smart to dance the more decent half of the 'Curate's Caper'. I will most probably write an admonitory word of my coming—or I will take ye consequences. I dined at one of the Houses here last night, and I don't—no, I don't think Kingston could get *so* stupid a set of people together; all rich and all damned, I should say; if the wits have anything to do with

---

⁵ The Hardmans were spending several weeks at the Royal Sandrock Hotel, Niton, Isle of Wight, with their friends, the Bellews.

348. ¹ I know of no deaths in the Meredith or Vulliamy family at this time.

² William H. Cotterill, who lived at Norbiton Park, had been one of the witnesses against Bengo. (See Note 1, Letter 337.)

³ For the Merediths' wedding anniversary on the 20th.

saving of souls. Otherwise, you and I, Tuck, will look for the agreeable society and let the Blest go hang. I hope D. T. will continue to look as well as on Wednesday.

Your loving
George M.

Willie is well—looking as if he had drained a bumper off the beaker.

Do you see it stated that the Queen would hardly permit Lord Russell's Gastein[4] letter to go.—!

349. *To* WILLIAM HARDMAN

MS.: Garrick Club.

Mickleham
Wednesday, [October 18, 1865]

Yes, Tuck, on the 23rd.—But not to Bengoland; to the land of the Hero—Archangelic Tuck who slew the Foul One![1] Mary Anne Moore[2] brings this to Kingston. Also a copy of *Rh*[*oda*] *Fl*[*eming*]: long kept by for you. Adieu. Marie sends her love to you both. A kiss from me to D. T.—In haste

Your ever affectionate
George M.

350. *To* FREDERICK A. MAXSE

Text: typed copy, Maxse Papers. Published: *Letters*, i. 168–9, with omissions.

Kingston
Friday night, [? December 8, 1865]

My dear Fred,

Great thanks for the game decorating our larder.—I was very anxious to see you when I called at Lillieman's, if only to hear of the

348. [4] At the Treaty of Gastein, signed 14 Aug. 1865, Austria and Prussia divided the spoils (Holstein and Schleswig) won from Denmark in 1864. Earl Russell, Foreign Minister, then addressed a confidential note to British ambassadors, complaining 'that the European system of law was set at naught' (R. B. Mowat, *A History of European Diplomacy, 1815–1914*, 1922, pp. 187–8). *The Times* on 18 Sept. printed an accurate summary of the note as published in *Indépendance Belge* the previous day, and English newspapers had the full text a few days later. GM's allusion is of course to the Queen's well-known German sympathies.

349. [1] For Bengo, see Note 1, Letter 337.
[2] Possibly the daughter or other relative of Frederick Moore, grocer, of Cambridge Road, Kingston.

dear little man's condition. I hope my poor Freddy's[1] bad symptoms will wear off under sound dieting. Have you heard anything of the merits of Vichy water in such cases? I have heard men say that it is useful, though much of it drags down the system. There is an agency in London.—Miss Longworth[2] has something to complain of, and I think Dr. Hunter[3] an effronté Yankee. But surely you admit that British Juries are commonly sentimental to an infinite degree in favour of the protesting female? The late verdicts are merely a reaction.—I must tell you that I am becoming an admirer of President Johnson.[4] And have you seen the Book called Sherman's great March?[5] If you get it, examine the heads of his Generals. They are of a peculiarly fine cast and show the qualities of energy and skill, and also *race*. They are by no means vulgar. Place our best men (headed by the Duke of Cam-[bridge])[6] alongside them, and start. The contrast will not be flattering to us.—Hawthorne has just the pen to fascinate you. His deliberate analysis, his undramatic representations, the sentience rather than the drawings which he gives you of his characters, and the luscious morbid tone, are all effective. But I think his delineations untrue: their power lies in the intensity of his egotistical perceptions, and are not the perfect view of men and women.—Goethe's elective Affinities—the *Wahlver-*

350. [1] Maxse's older son, Frederick Ivor, later called Ivor. A second son, Leopold James (Leo) was born on 11 Dec. 1864.

[2] Maria Theresa Longworth (?1832–81), authoress, better known as plaintiff in the Yelverton case. In 1855 she accepted a proposal of marriage from William Charles Yelverton (afterwards Viscount Avonmore), and on 12 Apr. 1857, Yelverton read aloud the Anglican marriage ceremony at her lodgings in Edinburgh. On 26 June 1858, however, Yelverton married a Mrs. Forbes, and on 31 Oct. 1859, Miss Longworth sued him for restitution of conjugal rights. The validity of her marriage was upheld in Ireland in 1861, only to be nullified by the Scottish court of session the following year. This judgement was affirmed by the House of Lords in 1864. Miss Longworth's attempt to reopen the case at Edinburgh in Mar. 1865 failed, as did a final attempt in Oct. 1867 (*DNB*). At the time of this letter her suit for libel against the *Saturday Review* was pending, but the verdict on 9 Dec. was against her.

[3] An American physician of dubious qualifications, Dr. Robert Hunter had come to England in 1854 and established a large medical practice by means of extensive advertising of a cure for consumption. Following a disputed bill for attendance on a Mrs. Merrick, Hunter was attacked in his office on 2 Nov. 1865 by the husband and brother of Mrs. Merrick. His assailants were arrested and committed for trial. Hunter himself was arrested on 24 Nov., charged with the rape of Mrs. Merrick, but was found not guilty. On 10 Nov., however, the *PMG* had attacked the advertising practices of a certain class of medical impostors, among whom was Hunter, and cited the Merrick–Hunter case as an illustration of the consequences. Hunter then sued the *PMG* for libel and was awarded damages in the sum of one farthing. (The verdict was reported on 3 Dec.)

[4] No doubt it was President Johnson's moderation toward the South and his resistance to extremists that won GM's admiration. But Johnson's message to Congress (4 Dec.) did not reach England until two weeks later.

[5] *The Story of the Great March*, by Brevet-Major George Ward Nichols (Sherman's aide-de-camp); reviewed in the *Saturday Review* for 4 Nov.

[6] The Duke of Cambridge (1819–1904), a cousin of the Queen, was Commander-in-Chief from 1856–95 despite the Queen's disapproval of his personal life and of frequent criticism of his competence.

wandtschaften—would delight you, as they have nourished Hawthorne.
—I wish I were going to meet you at Lord Hardwicke's.[7] I like my
Lord.—I am very hot upon *Vittoria*. Lewes says it must be a success;
and it has my best writing. I fancy I begin in the *Fortnightly* in February. Perhaps I have given it too historical a character to please the
brooding mind of Fred. But, we shall see. I think one must almost love
Italy to care for it and the heroine. There are scenes that will hold you;
much adventure to entertain you; delicate bits and fiery handling. But
there is no tender dissection, and the softer emotions are not kept at
half gasp upon slowly-moving telescopic objects, with their hearts
seen beating in their frames.—Marie thanks you warmly for the mono-
grams[8] which are doubtless very pretty jugglery and show how one M
can stand on the head of another and have W interlacing his legs—like
a basketful of lampreys or [   ].—Give my love to the boys and
make Freddy remember me. I kiss your Cecilia's fingers, and am ever
Your loving friend,
George Meredith

We go to a house in town on Friday for a week. To Mickleham on the
21st for a week.
    Mortality has never flourished better than does the new sprig of it,
Willie Maxse. He is a very fine little fellow.

351. *To* G. H. LEWES

Text: *Letters*, i. 175–6.

Kingston Lodge
December 9, 1865

My dear Lewes,
    I shall be glad to make over to you the use of the copyright of my
novel *Vittoria* for issue in the *Fortnightly Review*, in consideration of
the sum of £250: all subsequent rights to the use of it being reserved by
myself. Your saying 'write to me' did not seem to imply 'write immediately or there will be no contract'. In fact, I supposed you were
careless about any stipulation until more of my work had been submitted to you. I am hard at it, and as carefully as possible. Pardon me,
if my apparent negligence shall have put you out. I thank you very
much for your foregoing letter, which quite solves my difficulty, and
settles the matter justly.—If my progress seems to you slow, remember

---

350. [7] The 4th Earl (1799–1873), a Navy man; Lord Privy Seal 1858–9.
    [8] ? A Christmas present to William Maxse Meredith.

that I am on foreign ground and have to walk warily. I read a good deal of the novel to Mdme Venturi the other day, who says that the Italian colouring is correct.

352. *To* WILLIAM HARDMAN

MS.: Garrick Club.

[Kingston] Lodge
[December 11, 1865]

My dearest J. Peace,

Maturely weighing your admirable suggestion, *We* have arrived at the conclusion that the original proposition should hold. We say, Such as we are let us be taken. If there's a mishap, lo, have we not additional Laughter in the house wherewith to greet it?—Marie fully believes that D.Troïa is prepared to encounter and overcome even Swiss difficulties and disasters to-night. Hurrah for the New Housemaid. I say, Tuck! You rascal! None o' that, Sir!—An thou lov'st me, Tuck, no winking. God help us all, inspire the cook, nerve the maid, and aid digestion. The prayer of your loving George M. on Monday morning.

353. *To* FREDERICK A. MAXSE

Text: typed copy, Maxse Papers. Published: *Letters*, i. 169–71, with omissions.

Mickleham
Thursday evening, [December 28, 1865]

My dear Fred,

It will annoy and astound you to hear that I consider Bixio[1] brave and constant, though I question whether much is gained by any individual action before there is cause for general discontent. Merely to deny, is not to show a love for truth. It shows fanaticism—which is evidently what delights you so much. The fanatical worship of truth will always be fruitless: it is nothing better than the embracing of

---

353. [1] Not General Nino Bixio, as W. M. Meredith thought, but his brother, Jacques-Alexandre. A native of Chiavari, Italy, he was educated in France as a doctor of medicine but practised little and turned to journalism and politics, serving in the Assembly. His opposition to Louis Napoleon's *coup d'état* in 1851 caused his arrest and imprisonment for a short time and his retirement from politics. In accordance with his wishes, as an avowed unbeliever, he was buried on 18 Dec. 1865 without religious services. His death and riteless funeral, reported in English newspapers on 20 Dec., led to a discussion between GM and Maxse of the proper attitude for enlightened men to take toward such matters.

a phantom. For, what is Truth? Bixio could state nothing. He fires a sounding shot while there is peace, and against a superstition which, in the present day, rather averts intolerance than invokes it. What I venture to say is, Live on and be placable under some trifling irritation, till men are near a majority (or nearer to one) in contempt of imposture; or till the apprehension of priests prompt them to commence their old game. At that hour is time enough for us to think of action. A tyro in conspiracy will tell you that these isolated protests never exist. Some (miserable philosophers) have said that they owe their origin to vanity. I am not quite of that opinion. It is worthy of your school to rush at once on a presumption that, as I differ from you, I must be a time-server. The Faggot-and-Torture priests said likewise —'If not for, against us.' You appear to me to want to raise up an extreme party that shall rouse the other party to extremes, and so do battle-fight for a shade; gain what Time would have given you without waste of blood, temper, and divine meditation. Between you Philosophy would have no home on our planet. You presume moreover to declare yourself as if, perceiving a system to be faulty, it was an imperative duty to explode every shred of it to the winds. You must bear in mind that Christianity will always be one of the great chapters in the History of Humanity: that it fought down brutishness: that it has been the mother of our civilization: that it is tender to the poor, maternal to the suffering, and has supplied for most, still supplies for many, nourishment that in a certain state of the intelligence is instinctively demanded. St. Bernard checked Abelard, it is true. But he also stood against the French Barons, rebuked and controlled them. The Church was then a Light. Since it did such a service to men, men I think should not stand out against it without provocation.—You speak, my dear Fred, of 'the deepest questions of life'. They are to be thought over very long and very carefully before they are fought over. I cannot think that men's minds are strong enough, or their sense of virtue secure, to escape from the tutelage of superstition in one form or another, just yet. From the Pagan divinity to the Christian, I see an advanced conception, and the nearer we get to a general belief in the abstract Deity—i.e. the more and more abstract, the nearer are men to a comprehension of the principles (morality, virtue etc.) than which we require nothing further to govern us.—I write expecting dinner bell.—As regards Hawthorne, little Meredith admits that your strokes have truth. I strive by study of humanity to represent it:— not its morbid action. I have a tendency to do that, which I repress: for, in delineating it, there is no gain. In all my, truly, very faulty works, there is this aim. Much of my strength lies in painting morbid emotion and exceptional positions; but my conscience will not let me

so waste my time. Hitherto consequently I have done nothing of mark.
But I shall, and *Vittoria* will be the first indication (if not fruit) of it.
My love is for epical subjects—not for cobwebs in a putrid corner;
though I know the fascination of unravelling them. *Vittoria* begins in
the *Fortnightly* on February 1st, if not Jan[uar]y 15th.

I am at Mickleham until the 8th or 9th. Then Kingston Lodge.
Say March for Ploverfield, if you can. I'm not certain.

Your loving
George M.

Willie Maxse flourishes exceedingly. I rejoice that both your boys
are well. I salute your Cecilia affectionately.

354. *To* WILLIAM HARDMAN

MS.: Garrick Club.

Mickleham
January 1, 1866

My dear Tuck,

It was kind of you to write. We return full heartily to you both the
fair wishes for the years to come;—in the words of Rip van Winkle,
'Here's your health and your family's, and may you live long and
prosper.'[1]—Shirley Brooks must have done capital service at the Nelly
feast.[2] His news concerning poor Orridge[3] has shocked without
greatly surprising me: but I did not expect the catastrophe so soon.
It's hard; for Orridge loved his life. If you (or I) don't attend to a few
plain rules, Tuck, we go over a precipice. That's the lesson for all
ages of men and mules after early youth, when Nature wipes out
scores and is a prodigal in favour of prodigals. Thou, vast son of
prosperity! Abbot of Rosygildas! and I,—we shall likewise in our
turn join the majority: we shall be ashes, white or black! May Fate
remove the day until our work is done!—Call on General Hopkins[4]
and reflect with him on Human Life.—Yesterday the Rev. Burmey

354. [1] Quoted from Dion Boucicault's play of the name, which opened at the New
Theatre Royal, Adelphi, on 4 Sept. and ran for 170 nights. Hardman saw it in December,
but I don't know when GM saw it.

[2] Helen Hardman's birthday, 27 Dec.

[3] Orridge had died on 28 Dec. It was his house at Esher that the Hardmans had
occupied for some weeks during the summer of 1861, when Hardman and GM first met.

[4] A retired army officer who lived at Norbiton. An eccentric neighbour, Lady Eleanor
Cathcart, sent him unflattering caricatures of himself, goaded him into filing suit against
her, and provided GM and Hardman with a great deal of fun. GM later used the story as
the basis for 'The Case of General Ople and Lady Camper', published in the *New
Quarterly Magazine* (July 1877), pp. 428–78. See Stevenson, p. 214.

gave out 'To-morrow Monday being Circumcision Day, it will be observed in this Church at 11 o'clock, and the congregation are requested to attend.' On going out, I passed among groups of ladies and set them quivering with a torpedo-stroke, saying mildly: 'Shall you attend the service in the Church to-morrow?'

Lewes writes to say that he thinks of beginning *Vittoria* on the 15th of this month. Conceive me profoundly occupied: the devil is behind me; I shall feel the very wind of my necessary forward march with Time until *Vitt[oria]* is full born.—Adieu. Our love to you both and to the children. Your Godson is immensely admired here, and is a charmer. I am ever

Your friend
George M.

We really don't know when we return. It's fun being paid for and no weekly cheques.—Did you see about Bixio's death?

355. *To* FREDERICK A. MAXSE

Text: *Letters*, i. 176–7. Collated with the typed copy in the Maxse Papers.

Kingston Lodge
Kingston-on-Thames, S.W.
January 8, [1866]

My dear Fred,

We have returned,[1] and if this S[outh] W[est] holds, I shall rejoice to see Ploverfield on Saturday. But if it freezes again? Well, you shall write and command. I want to come.—I certainly think that prayer is good for children. It is good even after the period when blind reverence ceases to be fruitful—it is good for men. It is at once an acknowledgment of some higher power: it rouses up and cleanses the nature, and searches us through to find what we are. Only, the praying for gifts, and thanking for gifts, is really damnable. It's like treating the Lord as an old uncle. A child should pray in verse—don't you think so? I have thought of trying to write a morning and evening song for Freddy. Say if you care to have them.[2] Arthur used to repeat some lines.

Oh! I quite acknowledge that I am conquered by you. But then, I never attempted to get the better of you. The more you flourish the prouder I am of my work, and if you prefer to give your gratitude in due form to a medical man, I don't complain; you choose the least humiliating alternative, as you may think. There was a report in

---

355. [1] i.e. from Mickleham.   [2] The lines, if written, are not extant.

London yesterday that you had given up Meat. I hope this is not true, though I know I used to tell you that we consume too much meat, and you (I remember) appeared to reflect on my words. The determination which you hinted, that you would by and by abstain from clothing yourself, will not I trust be carried into effect. It would please none but Monboddo's ghost.[3] I have in fact said that we wear too much clothing —still, Fred, it is surely an excess to forswear a single garment, and rely upon hair to cover your body, as you look to impudence to protect your shivering arguments!

I long intensely to see you and walk with you: and I shall correct you very gently. Don't forget that mental arrogance is as a fiery wine to the spirit—a little of it gives a proper pride: but you carry too much. Adieu. I bow to your Cecilia, and am your loving

George M.

356. *To* FREDERICK A. MAXSE

Text: typed copy, Maxse Papers. Published: *Letters*, i. 165–6 (dated 1865), with omission of the first paragraph.

Garrick Club
January 14, [1866]

My dear Fred,

Marie wrote for a Cousin to come to her, but a begging-off letter disarranged the plan, which would have left me free of conscience to run down to you; and though my good girl urged me to start in spite of your letter, I thought it kind and right to take your advice. I am sure you understand rightly how the case stands. I shall see you in February, so I should not be selfish. We hope also that you will take the opportunity to see your blooming Godson, who is the sweetest freshest little fellow possible, a marvel of strength and intelligence.

It was my intention to write the Verses[1] at Ploverfield. I will write and send them—that is, if you agree with my view.

Verses, because they fix a child's memory and remain with him, and become a part of his child's understanding of reverence, perforce of the music, and necessitate simplicity of expression.

---

[3] James Burnett, Lord Monboddo (1714–99), lord of session in the Scottish courts for thirty-two years. Prominent in his six-volume *Antient Metaphysics* (1779–99) is the contention that houses and clothes are unnatural developments of civilization that are injurious to man. Later GM has Diana (of the Crossways) remember reading a wonderful old quarto book in her father's library, written by an eccentric Scottish nobleman, in which clothes and houses are regarded as the cause of human degeneracy.

356. [1] See preceding letter.

I hold to the word 'Father'. No young child can take the meaning of 'Spirit'. You must give him a concrete form, or he will not put an idea in what he is uttering. He must address some *body*. Later, when he throws off his childishness, he will, if you are watching and assisting him, learn to see that he has prayed to no false impersonation in addressing an invisible 'Father'. If you do otherwise than this you are in danger (as I think) of feeding his mouth with empty words.

Of Creed not a syllable.

Now let me ask you for a piece of advice. Marie and I, following your example, are abjuring (we follow it tentatively) alcoholic liquor. We find the water dreadfully cold, though one pledges Purcell! and the other Fred! We suppose that we shall get used to it, as you and your Water-God have done. But now our water-pipes are frozen. We have *nothing* to drink. Please what are we to do? Answer before we choke.

Ever your loving
George Meredith

357. *To* FREDERICK A. MAXSE

Text: typed copy, Maxse Papers. Published: *Letters*, i. 172–4 (dated 1865), with omissions.

Kingston
Monday night, [January 15, 1866]

Dearest Fred,

In re Bixio.[1]

There is no such thing as a *sum* of successive protests in favour of Truth, when those protests are not directed by wisdom. Will bawlings in the street avail, save to disturb and annoy the lieges? They irritate the slumbering dominant party, without strengthening the insurgent. What is being done in the *Fortnightly*, for instance, and elsewhere, is efficacious, and does strengthen, while it increases, the silent band.[2] Let Philosophy sap the structure and work its way. What we have to anticipate is this: There is, and will further be, a falling off of the educated young men in seeking an establishment as Churchmen. These are highly educated, and in their nature tolerant. They are beginning to think for themselves and they give their lives to other matters. The Church will have to be recruited from a lower, a more illiterate, necessarily a more intolerant, class. These will find themselves at variance

357. [1] For the context of this letter, see Letter 353.
[2] From the beginning the *FR* had published articles on dogma and religion that GM approved of.

with their intellectual superiors and in self-defence will attempt to
wield the Dogma and knock us down with a club. In about twenty
years' time we may expect a conflict to come. If in the meantime we
alarm such placid fellows as we see in the clerical robes, we are really
doing Truth no service. Objectless (that is, indistinct, blind) protests,
are like all unseasonable things, useless, and are shelved as mother
nature shovels away the dust which does not serve her. Let Bixio do as
pleases him; I don't complain; I say, that he is not an example—except
for a constitutional rebel, and he is a curiosity and will never get
followers.

In reading Carlyle, bear in mind that he is a humourist. The insolence offensive to you, is part of his humour. He means what he
says, but only as far as a humourist can mean what he says. See the
difference between him and Emerson, who is on the contrary a philosopher. The humourist, notwithstanding, has much truth to back him.
Swim on his pages, take his poetry and fine grisly laughter, his manliness, together with some splendid teaching. It is a good set-off to the
doctrines of what is called the 'Empirical school'. I don't agree with
Carlyle a bit, but I do enjoy him.

We returned from Mickleham on Friday last. I waited, expecting for
the last week a summons to Town to meet you at the Garrick. Nothing
was written . . . are not you to blame?

We will meet in town in February.

You should read Lewes' article on Comte in the *Fortnightly* before
this:—also Harrison's on 'Co-operative labour'.[3]

Tell me what you think of *Vittoria*.[4] Lewes is enamoured of her,
I know the workmanship is good. Further I am unable to judge.

As regards Gilmore's house, I should like to take it. But I have
determined to save up and put by and endure this place (if possible)
for the three years' term. And when I move I will move to a fixed
place. Rich men may be houseless rovers: it upsets poor ones. Besides,
wives don't like foreign houses and won't let their heart's fibres cling
to any place not their own—don't you know that?

Willie Maxse is the sweetest blooming little man in all the world—
(Yes, Mrs. Fred, in *all* the world!) His ready smile is lovely. He
develops splendidly, and on mere mother's milk. Yet, though he is
flourishing so well and acts like clockwork, we have a throng of
people saying, 'Oh! he must be fed by hand as well: no mother can
stand it, no child can thrive etc.'; and their own children, thus according to their system, bottle and biscuit fed, wheeze and cough and wake

---

[3] G. H. Lewes's 'Auguste Comte' and Frederic Harrison's 'Industrial Co-operation'
appeared in the 1 Jan. issue of the *FR*.
[4] It began in the 15 Jan. issue of the *FR*.

of nights and have convulsions—God knows what. With such parents we may expect fools at least in the next generation.

Marie joins with me in tender greetings to your Cecilia. Adieu, my dear Fred, and write frequently. I trust the two dear lads will go on well. Salute Freddy from me.

Your affectionate
George M.

358. *To* FREDERICK A. MAXSE

Text: typed copy, Maxse Papers. Published: *Letters*, i. 187–8 (dated 1867), with omissions.

Kingston
January 17, [1866][1]

My dear Fred,

Pardon me—just one moment; you see, I turn to you from my work and give you a sheet that should have formed part of my magnum opus:—*ice-water* is not wholesome. Farmers will not give frozen water to their cattle, and melted ice, to be drinkable, must be clean—a thing difficult to obtain. But when taken it should be, as all civilized people will tell you, partly in solution. Ice, but not ice-water, is a specific for indigestion, though one to be rarely used. Compelled to set you right!

I think that you take a philosophically false estimate of a child's intelligence and nature. He retains what he learns just as much and no more than he remains what he is. Certain mental, and physical, food is necessary for him. Beware of training him to scepticism! I can't bear to think of Freddy as being *educated* in *opposition* to the opinion prevailing.—The title 'Father' really does not suggest the aspect of a man to a child's imagination, if you associate it with prayer to an Unseen One. Neither does the jingle of Nursery Rhymes destroy his sense for the pure flow of good verse. The prayer you sketch is not objectionable; but it is not enough to my mind. I will in a few days send you a version. I would not say 'God,' but 'Father of all Good.' The title 'God' is bestowed by a child (in obedience to the enquiries he has made) on him who rolls the thunder and sends the currants that form the pudding. He may always retain this notion. I am sure your excellent Mrs. Lewis[2] does, perhaps her estimable husband likewise. But the

---

358. [1] This letter was found in an envelope dated 1867; hence the date in *Letters*.

[2] Possibly Mrs. George H. Lewis, wife of a solicitor employed on one side or the other of almost every *cause célèbre* in London for thirty-five years (*DNB*). Later the Lewises lived at Ashley Cottage, Oatlands Drive, Walton-on-Thames, and GM saw them at frequent intervals. Lewis was knighted in 1892, created baronet in 1902.

'Father of all Good' soon grows to mean the utmost in the *regulated* mind of a child. I am afraid I can't see how a child is to pray to Jesus Christ as Man: but one may teach him to pray to be likened to him as when he walked the earth.

Ever yours,
George M.

N.B. If you can help us with another suggestion (practicable and sound, of course) concerning the water in this frost, we shall be very thankful. If I find (when I can get it) that it rather *bakes* my inside [sentence *sic*].

359. *To* ALGERNON SWINBURNE

MS.: Ashley Library, British Museum. Published: *Letters*, i. 182–3, undated but placed between letters of September and December 1866; excerpt published: Stevenson, p. 151.

Kingston Lodge
Kingston-on-Thames
[? End of February–early
March 1866]

My dear Swinburne,

Vittoria, as I am told by Chapman and others, is not liked; so you may guess what pleasure your letter has given me. For I have the feeling that if I get your praise, I hit the mark. It seems that I am never to touch the public's purse. Why will you content yourself with only writing generously? Why will you not come and see me? My wife has constantly asked me how it is that you do not come. Must I make confession to her that I have offended you?[1] It is difficult for me to arrange for spare evenings in town; I can't leave her here alone. If we meet, I must quit you only too early. I wonder whether Sandys would invite us to dine with him;—when we might have one of our old evenings together and come to an understanding about future evenings at Kingston. I will speak to him on that head.—I am very eager for the Poems.[2] The promise of the essay on Byron[3] makes me extremely curious, for though I don't distrust your estimation of the manliness of his verse, he is the last man of whom I would venture to foretell your opinion.—As to the Poems—if they are not yet in the press,

---

359. [1] Stevenson (p. 151) says that a coolness had sprung up between GM and Swinburne, attributed by Sandys to the portrait of Swinburne as Tracy Runningbrook in *Emilia in England* but more likely caused by GM's unflattering opinion of Swinburne's 'Cleopatra'.
  [2] Swinburne's *Poems and Ballads*, then in press.
  [3] Swinburne's preface to *A Selection from the Works of Lord Byron*, published by Moxon in March.

do be careful of getting your reputation firmly grounded; for I have heard 'low mutterings' already from the Lion of British prudery; and I, who love your verse, would play savagely with a knife among the proofs for the sake of your fame; and because I want to see you take the first place, as you may if you will.—Apropos, what do you think of Buchanan's poetry? Lewes sends him up I don't know how high.[4] My feeling is that he is always on the strain for pathos and would be a poetic Dickens. But I can't judge him fairly, I have not read his book. Adieu. Remind Moxon of the Byron, and write to me again. I am ever

Your faithful
George Meredith

360. *To* ALGERNON C. SWINBURNE

MS.: Yale. Printed: *Letters from George Meredith to Algernon Charles Swinburne and Theodore Watts-Dunton* (privately printed, Pretoria, 1922), pp. 5–6.

Kingston Lodge, Kingston-on-Thames
Monday, March 12, [1866]

My dear Swinburne,

I have just taken the 'Essay on Byron' in at a gulp and give you my first impression. In one word, it defines for me my own idea of him. I delight in his manliness (of verse and imagination); I am torn by his ruggedness; I adore his humour, which is about the highest we possess; I now and then bow to his descriptive splendour, wherein, if it does not convey, there is the touch [of] the sublime—(beastly phrase! and you wisely avoid it). On the whole, I think the Essay to be the justest summary of poetic Byron ever written; and it is charmingly written. I enjoy the tone of it throughout. It comes from a man who has the right to judge his fellow. How true is what you say of his power of overleaping idyllic details and striking the pure elements! This fairly accounts for your admiration of Hugo, who can do the same, when he will not insist on being French. Our *accepted* poets appear fettered by their eyesight and their oxen laurels. I trust the hit will reach them. Will it? Will anything shrink the skin which our existing public soaps? I believe the Essay will do much towards restoring a great name to its proper rank, even in a day when the drawing-room and the tea-table are Imperial in Britain.

359. [4] Lewes, in reviewing Robert Buchanan's *Idyls and Legends of Inverburn* in the *FR* (1 July 1865), had concluded with the sentence: 'Such as he is, I believe him to be a genuine poet who may one day become a distinguished poet.'

I am very anxious to meet you and talk matters of this sort over.
If Sandys should nobly offer to join us at his table, let him make it
known to me. On Wednesday and Friday I am engaged.—You speak
of coming here. My wife will give you the best of welcomes; so, decide
upon it when I see you. Arthur is at school. Your message will gladden
him. There is now little Willie-Maxse, a darling little man, for you to
make acquaintance with. I respect and love you for the impulse which
prompts you [to] subscribe to the Mazzini testimonial. He is one of the
chiefs of our age of the Tame Ox.¹ I gave my subscription to Madame
Venturi; but she is at present away from home. I will let her know your
wishes, and she will communicate with you. Have you by chance read
her translation of the Collected works of Mazzini? If you have not,
get them at once. Smith & Elder publish them. Three volumes are out.
By the way, Mazzini would appreciate the Essay thoroughly. Good
night. Know me ever

Your affectionate
George Meredith

361. *To* AUGUSTUS JESSOPP

MS.: Yale. Printed: *Altschul Catalogue*, pp. 46–47.

[Written on Garrick Club paper]
March 27, [1866]

Dearest Jessopp,

I send you herein cheque for £25:—the rest next month. Pray,
forgive delay.

I go to Lord Houghton's¹ for the Easter, in Yorkshire and shall see
but little of my Arthur. You *must* ask me to spend some days with you
at the end of April or in May. Busy in a thousand ways. *Vittoria* not
yet done. *M[ornin]g Post.*—And I think I shall give up the *Ip[swich]
J[ournal]* which doesn't (really) pay me. I am behind with you simply
because Foakes owes me twice the amount and pleads 'expenses' here
and there. Adieu. Mrs. Jessopp frightened me a little about Arthur.
Give her my warmest love and, I say, *can* you, *will* you come to us *as*

360. ¹ When *Poems and Ballads* was withdrawn by Moxon in August, Swinburne
quoted the last phrase approvingly in a letter to George Powell (Lang, i. 171).
361. ¹ Richard Monckton Milnes, 1st Lord Houghton, lived at Fryston, Yorks. Stevenson
(p. 152) says that GM went with Swinburne and that other guests were Samuel Baker,
explorer of the source of the Nile; Henry J. Selwyn, M.P.; Connop Thirlwall, Bishop of
St. David's and historian; Revd. Charles John Vaughan, preacher and former Head-
master of Harrow, and Dr. John Henry Bridges, exponent of Comte's Positivism.

you return to Norwich? I shall leave my Lord's place after five or six days. And then you can behold little Willie-Maxse, who is delightful. Adieu.

Your loving
George Meredith

362. *To* MRS. MARIE MEREDITH[1]

MS. (inserted in W. M. Meredith's personal copy of *Letters*): Bodleian Library.

[Written on Garrick Club paper]
Thursday, March 29, 1866

My dearest girl,

I am just about to start. I found it impossible to get away yesterday and I have had two maniacal midnights in the lonely lodge. God bless you and my darling. I will write from Yorkshire. Adieu my best heart. I am your husband and lover,

George Meredith

363. *To* FREDERICK A. MAXSE

Text: typed copy, Maxse Papers. Published: *Letters*, i. 177–8, with omissions.

Kingston Lodge
Midnight, April 25, [1866]

My dearest Fred,

It is lucky that I advised myself not to come.

Marie had a friend staying with her and I half decided to take a holiday and share it with you.

The article on the *Travailleurs de la Mer* is Morley's;[1] I think it scarcely does justice to the miraculous descriptive power. The Storm is amazing: I have never read anything like it. It is *next* to Nature in force and vividness. Hugo rolls the sea and sweeps the heavens; the elements are in his hands. He is the largest son of his mother earth in this time present. Magnificent in conception, unsurpassed—leagues beyond us all—in execution. *Not* (nur Schade!) a philosopher. There's

362. [1] Letters of GM to Marie are extraordinarily rare. I think it likely that he destroyed as many as he could find at her death, but, if so, this and a few others—principally a series of about a dozen, written when he was on the Continent in 1869—somehow escaped.
363. [1] Morley's review of *Toilers of the Sea*, a translation of Hugo's *Travailleurs de la mer*, appeared anonymously in the *Saturday Review* for 7 Apr. and elicited from Hugo a letter of thanks for 'une page de haute et profonde critique' (F. W. Hirst, *Early Life and Letters of John Morley*, 1927, i. 53–55).

the pity. With a philosophic brain, as well as his marvellous poetic energy, he would stand in the front rank of glorious men forever.

His occasionally dirty speech is just a part of his grotesque greatness. It costs me nothing to overlook it—especially in this age of satin.

Fryston[2] is the dullest house with the dryest company in the dismallest country I have ever visited. Houghton of course was pleasant, but I think I could never travel two miles to go there again.

I will send your 'lost' letter back to-morrow. I fancy an article might be concocted on it.

What you tell me of my little Freddy grieves me deeply. How is his brother?—Willie Maxse blooms still on pure mother's milk. In May he is to taste Cow with 'tops and bottoms'—foretaste of our common fate! We go to Shere, and let our house for three or four months. Do you remember 'Combe Bottom'? with the juniper and yew-trees, the aspens and the beeches. We shall be just under it.

Have the articles in the *Pall Mall G[azette]* on coal and England's prosperity made you a trifle uncomfortable?—

Gladstone's behaviour has been wretched.[3]

Doubtless a combative Berkeley[4] *would* have supported him in spite of conscience. I can hear you making a short speech in condemnation of the Government while you promise to record your vote in its favour. Next to fighting the world, fighting oneself is the prime luxury; and to put yourself in such a position that you will have to do the latter, because you have done the former, is genius. It must be an intense grief to you to be out of Parliament now.—I take no interest in Reform. I see no desire for it below. If there were, I would give it; I have no fear of Radicals. Democracy must come and the sooner it overflows rulers who are *cowardly*, the better for all. We say— Democracy, as if it were some deadly evil; whereas it is almost synonymous with Change. Democracy never rests. The worst of it is that it *can* be violent in its motion. To you, who prefer the Allopathic system of medicine, it will come as a natural matter. Good night, dear Friend. Write to me, and often. Give me better news of your wife. I am   Your affectionate
                                                                 George M.

---

[2] Lord Houghton's house in Yorks., where GM had spent Easter.
[3] When in 1866, Earl Russell's government brought forward a proposal to liberalize the franchise, the main responsibility fell upon Gladstone, as leader of the House of Commons. Attempting to be moderate and conciliatory, he sometimes appeared weak and evasive, and even to staunch reformists he often seemed less interested in reform than in his own version of it. Government was defeated on one of the issues and subsequently resigned. Looking back on the session, the *Herald* said that Gladstone 'spared no opportunity of misstatement and invective, and resented all opposition as a kind of high treason . . .' (quoted by the *Globe*, 26 Oct.).   [4] Maxse's maternal family.

364. *To* FREDERICK A. MAXSE

MS.: Maxse Papers. Envelope postmarked *Kingston-on-Thames, My 1 66.*

Kingston
[April 30 or May 1, 1866]

My dear Fred,

Instead of coming, I sent to you yesterday a dozen of the light claret of which I spoke. Express your opinion thereupon (not the act but the claret). And this weather is beastly. I am better away from my friend while it rages.—Are we to have war in Italy? If so, I mourn for the Italians. Their army is not yet fit to cope with the Austrian; not a single arm of the Service is up to the mark, though great things have been done with the artillery. I am told that the infantry is as bad as London militia—with the exception of Bersaglieri,[1] Guards, and a Tuscan and Brescian regiment or so.—

Your letter[2] wants correction here and there:—'*figures* innocent of ambush'.—You mean to say '*charms*': otherwise the phrase means nothing. It is careless to write: 'Two ladies *were stated*' etc.—Consider it. 'We are told that two ladies appeared at a ball' etc. *The* fashion does not ebb. The corsage may; and it ebbs in *obedience* to the fashion; or *prevailing taste.* 'The too intrusive *glare*'—of eyes? If so, you must simply put 'glance'. It is otherwise too downright a statement of facts. The *maternal result* of Juno—?? You must alter this. I can but suggest: —'The qualifications attendant on Latona, and the severe figure of the divine Huntress—it would be invidious of the "lily maid" to attempt, if she dared, to mask her distinction.'—'*Mistresses*' is not excusable where it stands. In this case you must consult the general ear, which would give it but one meaning. The word in itself is good; and we won't let it be lost; but here it won't do, and in this letter a false word is like a false step elsewhere. The simpler the more forcible.

—Write that I may know how you all are. Personally, how fares it with you? I long to be with you on a fine day and for an evening.

Ever yours,
George M.

---

364. [1] Rifle battalions, the most famous and most popular Italian army corps.

[2] I am unable to identify Maxse's 'letter' with any of his printed pamphlets. It may have been intended for the *Morning Post*, where some of his letters appeared.

365. *To* FREDERICK A. MAXSE

MS.: Maxse Papers. Envelope postmarked *Kingston-on-Thames, My 5 66.*

Kingston
May 5, [1866]

My dear Fred,

Some such phrase as 'the sumptuous Rubens-like proportions'—
'the brimming superabundance of charms'—
(I should have put 'Lucina' not 'Latona'.)
'the matronly perfections'—
'the full-blown developments'—
'the overflowing beauties—too-generous . . .' or some such.—But,
if you like, I will try my hand at the letter and you shall perfect yours
from a criticism of mine. I think however yours will do well, if you will
consent to correct risky phrases. A letter must be colloquial and simple
—just what *you* think a novel should be.

I will most probably pen an article on the letter. I saw Borthwick on
Friday; very softly blooming: beardless, which does not become him.
Once he was not unlike the Indian Bacchus dressed as modern gentleman. He looks now like a debauched Apollo; or Silenus aping society.
We are nearly ruined, in England, you see. I shall go to France.
Borthwick tells me of the Ladies' Clubs. Mon dieu!—I prefer a downright sinful to a vulgar aristocracy that is nothing if not simious. B. is
quite tender to this sort of silly halting folly. I tell him they are bump-
kins and Audreys at bottom—all! They can't move freely.—Is it true
that Mr. John Brown?[1]—but, by and by. The 'Nemesis of Virtue'
should come sooner or later.

Ever yours,
George M.

365. [1] John Brown (1826–83), the Highland gillie who entered the Queen's service in
1849 and was promoted upper servant and the Queen's personal attendant in Dec. 1865.
The freedom of his manner toward the Queen and her unconcealed partiality for him
were not unnaturally resented by the public. When she conferred the title of esquire
upon him, *Punch* issued a special Court Circular:
Balmoral. Tuesday. Mr. John Brown walked on the Slopes. He frequently partook of
a haggis. In the evening Mr. John Brown was pleased to listen to the bagpipes. Mr. John
Brown retired early.
The Tomahawk even ran a cartoon entitled 'The Empty Chair', in which Brown is
shown about to occupy the Prince Consort's royal chair. (See Ellis, *The Hardman Papers*,
1930, pp. 178–83, for other interesting details of the Queen's favouritism and the public
resentment of it.)

366. *To* FREDERICK A. MAXSE

Text: typed copy, Maxse Papers. Published: *Letters*, i. 171–2 (dated 1865), with omissions.

Kingston

Friday, [? May 11, 1866]

My dear Fred,

I look over your recent letters (your pertinacious defence of your untenable position and ingenuous affectation of a triumph being amusing to me) and find questions I have not answered.

A man named Greenwood, newly elected [to the] Garrick,[1] is the Editor of *Pall Mall*.—The 'bar of Michael Angelo'[2] has puzzled hundreds. I can't attempt to explain it. I have been foolish enough to think that it must mean a peculiar girder-like hanging brow that one sees on Buonarotti's face. Great poets attain a superior lustre by these obscurities. If *I* had written such a line, what vehement reprobation of me from Ploverfield! what cunning efforts to construe! and finally what a lecture on my wilfulness! In Tennyson it is interesting. In Browning you are accustomed to gnaw a bone and would be surprised to find him simple. But G.M. who is not known, not acknowledged, he shall be trounced if he offers us a difficulty—we insist upon his thinking in our style. Very well, Fred. I am used to it.—No, I hate the black East, and I don't like the frost; I like nothing in Kingston. But I envy you the fine S.W. now showing soft white and blue, and taking you in its arms. Adieu; mark two or three points (a few will serve) in my advice to you from time to time, and note and communicate your sensations when at last you appreciate and adopt them—for scientific purposes; not for my satisfaction at all.

Ever your friend,

George M.

Last night I saw C. . . . just returned from Malta and awfully done up by 'change of climate'—and some light foam taken to relieve it, I fancy.

366. [1] Commander E. S. Satterthwaite, R.N., Hon. Secretary of the Garrick Club, kindly informs me that Frederick Greenwood was elected to the Garrick Club on 21 Apr. 1866. So much for W. M. Meredith's date of 1865 for this letter. My own date is conjectural but, I think, reasonable.

[2] Tennyson, *In Memoriam*, 87, ll. 39–40:

And over those ethereal eyes

The bar of Michael Angelo?

GM was right. According to G. B. Woods (*Poetry of the Victorian Period*, N.Y., 1932, p. 78 n.), 'It is said that Michelangelo . . . the great Italian artist, had a distinct ridge above the eyes. Hallam once said to Tennyson: "Alfred, look over my eyes; surely I have the bar of Michael-Angelo"' (*Memoir*, i. 38 n.).

367. *To* AUGUSTUS JESSOPP

MS.: Yale. Printed: *Altschul Catalogue*, p. 24.

[Written on Garrick Club paper]¹
May 18, [1866]

My dear Jessopp,

We are at 'Shere, near Dorking' for a month. I am rapidly finishing *Vittoria*: The *Morning Post* makes me war correspondent in case of war,² for money I must have somehow. Of course all's politically undecided; but I think war must be and that I shall soon be in Italy, where Phibus' car doth shine afar and make and mar the foolish fates.³ I trust my darling boy is doing well.—I am nursing a thought that he should go to Switzerland and learn languages. I doubt his power to acquire a scientific knowledge of Greek and Latin. Is not our country old and worn and all in the background, greedily devouring its (coaly) heart? —I wish I could have come to your school gymnastics. The pleasure would have been great. My wife and little Willie I left journeying to our new—really country—residence, sniffly with influenza. I am working my fingers blunt. Adieu for a while.

Your loving
George Meredith

368. *To* FREDERIC CHAPMAN

MS.: University of Texas.

Shere, near Guildford
May 22, [1866]

Dear Fred,

Played Out,¹ as far as the MS. goes, is interesting—decidedly better than *Walter Goring*.¹ But bear in mind that the MS. in hand scarcely covers more than one third of a 3 volume novel, and *On Guard*¹ was

367. ¹ Written in London, where GM stopped off, leaving Marie and Willie to go on to Shere alone.
² The Treaty of Gastein had not settled the Schleswig-Holstein question. When Prince Frederick of Augustenburg proposed to incorporate them into a new German state, with himself as ruler, he was supported by Austria. Bismarck saw that there could be no unification of Germany without a war with Austria first, and while von Moltke prepared the Prussian army for the conflict, Bismarck by diplomatic manœuvres led Austria on to the point of no return. On 14 June 1866 the Diet of the German Confederation, under the leadership of Austria, ordered mobilization against Prussia, but for a month Austrian troops had been steadily dispatched to the north, and war had appeared inevitable.
³ *A Midsummer Night's Dream*, I. ii. 37–40.
368. ¹ Novels by Annie Thomas, published by C. & H. in 1866, 1866, and 1865 respectively.

a failure after the 1st volume.—You may advance money, but don't fix a price for the book until you have seen more of it, or the whole.

The style is exactly the same as in her foregoing books, and I wish she would go over it carefully and avoid iterations and slang. There is much that will give offence and do her discredit.

Such a word as 'unquestionably', occurs I don't know how often. Young men are constantly soliloquizing 'What the devil' etc. And a young lady 'would have preferred Satan eloquent to a Saint who was stupid'. Which, if powerful, has been expressed before.

I am almost prostrate with Influenza.

Yours ever,
George Meredith

369. *To* WILLIAM HARDMAN

MS.: Garrick Club.

Shere
Monday night, [? June 4, 1866][1]

Dearest Tuck,

We have all been floored with Influenza. I have been down, absolutely, in a sneezing slimy ditch, for a fortnight, unable to work or do more than convey a horrible handkerchief to a nose that I would willingly have given to the first fool who asked for it. The damned suffer as I did. Bismarck, I find, has profited by the interval, and we are to have war. I am now finishing *Vittoria*. Verily the Sofa *is* abandoned, for in two weeks or less I am off to Italy. I have only to wait for the last chapter—*fatto questo*, I start. There is also just a chance of my getting a good and permanent post abroad, but of that we won't speak till things are clearer.[2]

The family quit this lovely place on Saturday. I understand that the design of Mickleham is to invite you and poor D-troïa to see us there. How? Can you come? Or are you sending souls to Hades in such flocks that you yourself have to surrender all other pleasure?[3] I must contrive to see you somehow.—The beauty of the walks about Shere are [*sic*] not to be surpassed. Addio. Willie's just cutting his first tooth—an operation which is accompanied by his firing continuously into his napkin. And all's well.

Your loving
George M.

369. [1] The evidence for dating this letter is conflicting, but on balance I think 4 June the most likely date. 28 May is, however, a possibility.
[2] He hoped to get a post as correspondent for *The Times* on the Continent.
[3] A reference to Hardman's duties as magistrate.

370. *To* EDWARD WALFORD

MS.: Yale.

[Written on Garrick Club paper]
Friday, June 8, [1866]

My dear Walford,

I send you a piece of fun, that has also some meaning in it. You will see that the character of a *dream* is preserved throughout. If it suits you, put my initials to it.[1] Address to the 'Garrick Club'—for I shall be a wanderer some weeks; and be speedy in your decision;—I may be off to Italy in a couple of weeks.

Ever yours,
George Meredith

371. *To* FREDERICK A. MAXSE

Text: *Letters*, i. 178–9.

Mickleham
June 8, 1866

My dear Fred,

Don't think I desert you. The truth is, that to write politics satisfactorily, one must give up one's time to the study of politics—one must be in the thick of the fight. And only in such cases can you exact from Editors a proper respect for you. You must prove that your political opinions are worth having in type, or be so useful to them that they can't refuse to insert them. Now Greenwood, and doubtless our B[orthwick] as well, don't regard me as a political writer, so I am always in danger of slipping into the waste-paper basket, unless I write review or essay. They rely on a sufficient number of handy men to supply the wants of their journals. And the truth is, I can only now and then afford time to write an experimental article on politics. When my last debts are paid, and I have finished my next novel, I shall have a free hand. I'm sure you don't suppose that I willingly abandon you to your fight. I could have no wish but to stick by you, and the more so as your views are mine.

Moreover, Editors object to articles upon subjects which are not immediately prominent. I tried the *Pall Mall* with your pamphlet,[1]

370. [1] Apparently the 'piece of fun' did not suit *OaW*; all trace of it has been lost.
371. [1] Whether this pamphlet is identical with the 'letter' of Letters 364 and 365 is impossible to say.

but Greenwood was indifferent in tone. The subject will revive speedily, but the moment it lay down it was temporarily dead for Editors.—I have not meant to say I will not write unless I see my pay —but that it's heart-breaking to feel that I have given up my time, with some amount of ardour in a theme, all to no purpose save to see my manuscript as the froth tossed up from the wheel of an Editorial mill.—But surely, even though you should feel some disappointment with me, you accuse my circumstances more than me.—Adieu. Your sketch of the *Grebe*[2] flying to Havre drives me mad. I hope Mrs. Fred will enjoy the week at Ascot and have the long, blooming holiday thoroughly due to her.

Your loving
George Meredith

372. *To* MISS JENNETT HUMPHREYS

Text: *Letters*, i. 179–81, with the addressee identified only by her initials; published also: Ellis, pp. 241–2, with the name of the addressee.

193 Piccadilly, London, W.
June 15, 1866[1]

The Reader of Miss Jennett Humphreys' tale of *Anwyl Anwyl* presents his compliments to her, feeling profoundly guilty—for the blame of this long delay rests entirely upon him. He put the MS aside, after he had read it; his intention was to write a long chapter on what to write, blot and avoid. He can say in personal extenuation that Miss Humphreys could not possibly have made any 'commercial' use of the tale; and that if she had published it, it would have done harm to her reputation.

The Reader is in town on Thursday next, and, if it shall please Miss Humphreys to listen to a few of his critical objections to her style, perhaps he may be enabled to do her more good in that direction than if he attempted to write them down. Therefore, should she be willing to call at 193 Piccadilly on Thursday at four p.m., he will endeavour penitently to repair his shameful behaviour. The truth is, he did nothing at all, because of his having intended to do so much.

371. [2] Maxse's cutter yacht.
372. [1] Although I copy W. M. Meredith's date for this letter, it is very dubious. In the letter GM offers to interview Miss Humphreys on 'Thursday next' (21 June). The interview, as we know (see following note), took place. Yet GM's first dispatch from the seat of war was dated from Ferrara on 22 June.

If Miss Humphreys should prefer to avoid vocal criticism it shall be written down, but it will possibly not be so effective, and it may seem more severe.

In making this proposal, the Reader has taken an unusual course by which he trusts to be able to show his desire to expiate his previous carelessness. It needs hardly to be said that obscurity is his most comfortable cloak, whenever he undertakes the thankless duty of looking at a MS.[2]

373. *To* WILLIAM HARDMAN

MS.: Garrick Club.

[? London]
[? *c.* June 17, 1866]

Dearest Tuck,

One word of adieu. I have been and am so busy that I've no time for more than to wish you health and D:troïa strength and the children how-dye-do and good-bye.

I shall be in Munich on Wednesday: in Vienna on Friday.[1] Peace will send me on to Venice. I shan't get much to write about in Vienna; but I get change for myself and shall be able to do something, I doubt not. Ring out wild bells to the wild sky!—Poco has been doing the *Ipswich* the last two weeks. He started for the Glarus range to-day to drink liver-water—he looks pea-green, poor fellow. How are the merry bells of Norbiton?[2] Marie, Willie, and Arthur are in Normandie.

---

[2] Miss Humphreys replied that she was willing 'to throw aside her own cloak and receive a face-to-face castigation' and duly appeared for the interview. She later gave Ellis an account of the interview. For it, see Ellis, *W. H. Ainsworth*, ii. 270 n.

373. [1] GM was going to Italy to report the progress of the Austro-Prussian War for the *Morning Post*. His dispatches, later reprinted in the Memorial and de luxe editions of his works, were dated from Ferrara (22 June), Cremona (30 June), Bozzolo and Marcaria (3 July), Torre Malimberti (7 July), Piadena (8 July), Gonzaga (9 and 12 July), Noale, near Treviso (17 July), Dolo, near Venice (20 July), Civita Vecchia (22 July), and Marseilles (24 July). The war lasted only seven weeks, so great was the superiority of the Prussian army, with its needle gun which could fire three times as rapidly as the old muzzle-loaders.

[2] A jesting allusion, as is the quotation from *In Memoriam* ('Ring out wild bells . . .'), to Hardman's annoyance at the installation of quarter chimes in the Norbiton Church, about 100 yards from Norbiton Hall, in May. Hardman succeeded in having the bells muffled for a time, alleging that Mrs. Hardman was unwell and that the bells kept her awake at night. But when it was observed that Mrs. Hardman was well enough to attend a flower show and go away to the seaside, they were unmuffled. At the end of June Hardman obtained an injunction against the Revd. Robert Holberton and the churchwardens. The case was first heard on 19 July, with a string of witnesses on both sides, including Frederic Chapman, who was occupying Kingston Lodge in GM's absence. After a continuance the judge dissolved the injunction on 16 Nov., with costs against Hardman (*Surrey Comet*, 2 and 9 June, 7 and 21 July, 25 Aug., 1 Sept., 17 and 25 Nov.).

The divine Williams is developing splendidly. Swinburne's poems[3] are out. Oh, bawdry! Oh, nakedness! Oh, naughtiness. Tuck, I know where you would put the volume. But it holds some fine stuff. I embrace you and am

> Your loving
> George M.
> (Someone else being involved
> with you)

374. *To* FREDERIC CHAPMAN

MS.: University of Texas.

Wednesday, [1866][1]

Dear Fred,

I do not agree with the author of *Won by a Head*[2] that the last part of his book is the best. It is written hurriedly, elucidates the foregoing but does not make much of it. The novel is very well written. I doubt whether it it [*sic*] be thought remarkable. You must be careful to publish it upon *safe* terms. Publish it by all means, for Mr. Austin can and will do good work, and you had better secure him.

> Yours ever,
> George Meredith

375. *To* TOM TAYLOR

MS.: University of Texas. Envelope addressed *Tom Taylor, Esqre, Board of Health, Whitehall, London, England*; postmarked *Milano, 10 Sep. 66.* Published: *Letters*, i. 181–2, with inaccuracies.

Milan
September 10, [1866]

My dearest Tom,

Bird[1] had left for Ischl when your letter reached me in Vienna.— I write, in case you should see Mowbray Morris[2] and have favourable

---

373. ³ *Poems and Ballads*, subsequently withdrawn by Moxon as a result of harsh criticism and reissued by Hotten. But Lang (i. 167 n.) says the publication date was about 16 July.
374. ¹ Almost certainly written before GM left England.
    ² A novel, by Alfred Austin, published by C. & H. (1866).
375. ¹ T. O'M. Bird, *The Times* correspondent in Austria from 1848 to Aug. 1866, when his health compelled him to retire (*The History of 'The Times'*, 1939, ii. 456).
    ² Mowbray Morris, manager of *The Times* from 1847–73. No doubt GM's hopes of a place on *The Times* depended mainly on the influence of his friend Tom Taylor, who was in effect, but not officially, art critic of *The Times* from 1857–60 (ibid., p. 439).

news to communicate, to say that my address will be for the next six weeks: 'aux soins de M. Théodore Vulliamy, | à Nonancourt | (Eure), | France.' I came over the Semmering to Venice, remained there ten days and worked my way through Padua and Vicenza hitherwards, where, from the upper windows of the Hotel Cavour I see white Alps. Italy is where I would live, if I had the choice. Here I am so happy that I only want my wife and little ones with me to wish for nothing further. In all probability I shall go back to Venice for the fêtes—if the delay is not great. The M[ornin]g Post should have an account of them. Perhaps Borthwick will insist on my doing the work, and I shall not be sorry; for what a correspondent wants is something to describe, and not to continue writing about nothing.

Do you remember the Carpaccios in Venice? Surely justice is not done to his extraordinary sweetness and richness. If I did not love Giorgione and Titian so much, I should rank him my favourite. His faces are as sweet as Fra Angelico's, with variety and humanity super-added. The Baptism of Christ in the Church of San Lorenzo, Vicenza, by Giov. Bellini is the only Christian head of the Saviour that I have ever seen. I dare say you know it.—Curious to see the ebbing of the Austrians out of all this district! I have sent the *Post* some letters, but I must reduce my impressions to an article. I hope very much that the *Times* will take me on. In a settled position (I wish it were in Italy), and with command of news, or the sources of it, I believe I should show the requisite judgment. Adieu, my dear Tom. If there is anything I can do for you in North Italy, write immediately to the 'Hotel Cavour, Milan'. If you won't like *Vittoria* (pure obstinacy, or base siding with the majority), I promise you quite another sort of next novel. Kiss your little girl from me and give her a stranger's love, and God bless you all. I am

Your affectionate
George Meredith

376. *To* FREDERIC CHAPMAN

MS.: University of Texas.

Hotel Cavour, Milan
September 17, [1866]

My dear Fred,

Will you pay £15.5 in my name in to Drummond's Bank to the account of Admiral Sir George Lambert—?[1] And will you take the

376. [1] The owner of Kingston Lodge, which Chapman was occupying in GM's absence.

lodge for another month? If not, try and dispose of it for that term. You shall command a 'reduction'. I have been a month in Vienna, two weeks in Venice, a week here; what I am next going to do I can't say. Italy is in bad condition; Venice is starving, and if there is further delay and any irritation of the bad feeling, a row is probable. The Austrians, officers and soldiers, are as conciliating as men can be. Write a line, to say what is doing, to the 'Hotel Choiseul, Rue St. Honoré, Paris'. I have heard from Morley and Tom Taylor; from none others. I suppose *Vittoria* is hopelessly damned by you all. I met Sala[2] in Venice, and Layard at Vicenza. They and hundreds troop to see the Italian occupation of Venice, for which I don't think I can wait. Correspondent's work when there is something expected and nothing happening is heavy, and worse to him than to his readers, if you'll believe it. I hope your boy is well. I have the best accounts of my young one in Normandie. Good-bye. I am ever

Your faithful
George Meredith

377. *To* WILLIAM HARDMAN

MS.: Garrick Club.

Mickleham Hall
Thursday, [? November 22, 1866][1]

Dearest Tuck,

I regret horribly to have caused bother to you.

I have earned enough to pay my debts, and will satisfy Burton[2] next week.

Scirocco in Venice, business in Vienna, prevented me from writing to you, as I desired to do and again and again meditated the act; but I knew the awfully full letter it would be and frightened myself.

We return on Monday, I late, I think. I want excessively to see you and talk. Your godson blooms finely. In great haste.

Your ever affectionate
George Meredith

376. [2] George Augustus Sala (1828–95), war correspondent for the *Daily Telegraph*. GM does not allude to an unpleasant scene between himself and Sala which is mentioned by H. M. Hyndman (*The Record of an Adventurous Life*, p. 75).

377. [1] Janet Ross (*The Fourth Generation*, p. 161) says that she encountered GM in Venice at the time of the entry of King Victor Emmanuel on 7 Nov. and that the two made several excursions together and talked much of old days at Esher. Exactly when GM returned to England I do not know, but it must have been after the middle of November. This letter seems to be the first, except possibly for a telegram or note on business, which GM wrote to Hardman after his return.

[2] I am unable to identify this creditor of GM. Or, conceivably the reference is to John Burton, a solicitor of Serjeant's Inn, his representative.

Give my love to your wife when you write to her.[3] I've got such stories! and Sana sends the most amorous messages to you both; *not* of Swinburne's kind.

378. *To* FREDERICK A. MAXSE

Text: typed copy, Maxse Papers. Published: *Letters*, i. 183–5, with omissions.

Kingston–on–Thames
Tuesday, [? November 27, 1866]

My dearest Fred,

I was too late for the post yesterday, but you know how such good news will have gladdened me.[1] I hope the girl will have the mother's looks. Marie congratulates you both—chiefly the mother.

Our Willie Maxse is quite charming; he is healthy and spirited, and very intelligent. You should see his face when he is laughed at. His sense of humour, with a momentary disgust at finding himself the mark for it in others, produces the most comical expression possible. Marie says she can understand some delight in welcoming a boy; but a girl! who would care for a girl! Experience, I suppose; I hope it's to be distant.

The system by which you are correcting your troubled physical condition is I am sure sound. To a strong stomach occasional draughts of wine do good rather than harm. Our fault is to eat in excess while we drink wine as well. One dish and one pint of wine, old and sound, go harmoniously, but wine should be treated as a luxury.—I agree with your practical deductions, at the same time, I note with dismay your tendency to extremes. You are right just now. Nevertheless you must needs lay down positive principles as if your existing state were the key of things. You will become a fanatical Retired Admiral advocating Maine Liquor laws for every natural appetite on earth, and dogmatically refusing to hear an opinion.[2] I foresee it,—unless you can be humble while there's yet time, and admit that I am right, who preach moderation, and you are wrong, who raise the banner of Abstinence with all its tissue in tatters.—I dare say you will continue to deny that it was *I* who gave you the good advice months—years back. And then probably when we are old men you will consent to my saying it was *me* who did it. Dogmatism confounded in the last crisis

---

[3] *The HP* does not mention Mrs. Hardman's absence.
378. [1] The birth of Olive Hermione on 24 Nov.
[2] See Letter 382, dated Christmas 1870 but written a few weeks after this one. (The State of Maine had prohibited the manufacture and sale of intoxicating liquors in 1851.)

escapes by a quibble! How much better to take a manly modest view of a friend's deserts:—I do congratulate you with all my heart on your prospect of recovery, which I think clear. *Only*, I am amused at the physiological lecture. Why, I have said as much a hundred times! But you now turn round, and with supernatural force hurl my own wisdom at me, and say, Read that! Surely the argumentative virus was never more wonderfully displayed. If the trick is old, it is at any rate uncommonly well managed: and no doubt almost unconsciously. Confess to my value in one bright instance, and even you would hardly be able to stand against me in other matters, so, to maintain your antagonism, you affect an air of total independence. Such tactics will serve you well in the House of Commons.—What do you think of Lieutenant Brand?[3] He seems to be the victim of a poor education and a superfluity of red pepper. Still, I don't like to see all the English Press down on him, for he's a boy, and isn't it rather hard to *break* him for writing insolent letters to a M.P.—? Wouldn't it be sufficient to degrade him in rank, as he is already in reputation?—But when our Press is unanimous, I am always against it. Our Press was unanimous in favour of Lieutenant Perry[4] till he showed too unmistakeably as a low dog.—Borthwick starts to-day for Marseilles, thence with Sir Henry Storks[5] to Malta, to Tunis, to Spezzia, to Rome, to Nice—*et vogue les papillons*!—Adieu, dear friend; I don't like to leave off talking to you.

Your ever loving
George M.

378. [3] A commission sent out to ascertain the facts in Gov. Eyre's actions in the Jamaican insurrection of 1865 reported in Apr. 1866 that the severity had been excessive, and two officers responsible for the court-martial proceedings which condemned a mulatto to death were committed for trial on a charge of murder. One of them, Lt. Herbert C. Brand, had been President of the court. The case was later thrown out by a grand jury.

The Times (22 Nov. 1866) printed an exchange of letters between Brand and C. Buxton, M.P., who was active on behalf of the Committee formed to prosecute Gov. Eyre. Having seen in the *Standard* a letter of Buxton's, Brand wrote a virulent reply, charging that the letter was filled with 'many wicked and malicious lies', and added: 'You may be a very fine buckra amongst the polished gentlemen at Exeter-Hall who wanted Mr. Eyre suspended "with a rope," and the old ladies of Clapham, but when you come with your peculiar little assertions in print, and such barefaced lies, too, I think it is time for the trampled worm to turn. . . . England and the Admiralty are my judges, not Buxton and company.' Buxton replied on 2 Sept., and Brand answered with another offensive letter on 23 Oct.

[4] Untraced.

[5] Sir Henry Storks (1811–74) had been Governor of Malta in 1864 but had been sent to Jamaica as a member of the investigating commission; he then served as Governor of Jamaica, 12 Dec. 1865 to 16 July 1866.

379. *To* FREDERICK A. MAXSE

MS.: Maxse Papers.

[Written on Garrick Club paper]
December 14, [1866]

My dear Fred,

Your letter came on a day when I was a prisoner at home; we had arranged to send *all* our servants out to a play of Kingston Amateur Theatricals, and I could not leave Marie alone. You gave no London address. Next morning at the Garrick I could get no news of you. Confess that you *meant* to perform a cruel joke on me. *Any* other night but that Tuesday I could have come.

If you can answer me on this point satisfactorily, I will try and come to you for two days after Christmas—after the first week of January, for I much desire to have evening talks, and now that I have, as I hope, partially effected a cure of your Dyspepsia, you will, if you still argue, not wrangle, and instead of seeking to confound an adversary with quibbles, will attempt an aim at truth, as I do. I can't believe you are better unless I hear from you more frequently. Or the alternative is that I charge you with neglect. Let me hear of your new babe and the mother; and of what you've been reading and doing. I will, if I can get it in time, bring down a book illustrative of Comte's philosophy. Meantime possess yourself of Lewes' *Biographical History of Philosophy*:[1] and this subject shall be our theme. I will divert your attacks—if possible. You shall thunder at established Sages.—We leave Kingston on Thursday next for Mickleham, a ten days' absence.

I am your loving
George M.

380. *To* FREDERICK A. MAXSE

MS.: Maxse Papers.

Kingston-on-Thames, S.W.
Monday, December 17, [1866]

My dear Fred,

I see what you mean. You are right and I was wrong. Pardon me for assuming to have directed you to a step that I should be the last to advise. I was unwise—I gave you only moderate counsels. I did not say—Fred, you're hot; strip at once, plunge head-long into the

---

379. [1] G. H. Lewes, *The Biographical History of Philosophy* (1845–6), of which the *Cambridge History of English Literature* speaks slightingly but says that 'later editions . . . not only greatly increased its extent and removed many blemishes but showed the author's ability to appreciate other points of view than that from which he started' (xiv. 35–36).

embrace of the North Pole; get the Frigid Zone about your loins! To one whose every motion is for extremes, I addressed the language of a philosopher. I see how offensive it must have been to you at the time, by the scorn you are now casting on its fruitlessness. Did you come to London to take the oaths,[1] and funk the trusting my discretion when you got there? I must conclude it to be the case, since you have prudently twice shunned the topic. But, believe me, I should no more have laughed at you than I would deride the action of a pendulum behind the door of a calm-faced clock. I know by this time that it is your way of moving; and apparently it suits you best. Then why not break your last bottle of dry champagne on Neptune's head and fly to the central office of the Teetotal Society to become enrolled as a High Priest of the Element? Though I did not counsel, I can approve of it, I assure you. I repeat that I could never advise it. My precept is ever Moderation. You hold Moderation in contempt. So consequently my wisdom is foolishness to you. I have no longer an idea of charging you with ingratitude. If the post brings me good long letters from you, I shall perfectly rejoice in your teetotal change of system, character, habits, nature and principles, and your moral independence.

You feel of course that you can't stop where you are. You must have the world moving in your own fashion. Drench the political world with pure water. Attack us all from your new point of view. Combative as you are, for you to see a truth and not insist on it universally, will be impossible. I, meantime, will stand by and mark.

'Olive Hermione'[2] is very musical. I prefer 'Olivia' to 'Olive', but it won't go so well with sweet Hermione. 'Hermione Maxse' is not so pretty as 'Cecilia Maxse', but never mind—the mother can't be equalled by her children. I like the thought of that charming Mrs. Sartoris[3] being godmother.

Remember, you're bound to prove the virtue of your position by giving me a letter at Mickleham. I hope to see you soon.

Ever your loving
George M.

P.S. When your spirit shall become as discomposed as your body has been, do not forget that there are a great many naval Captains among the Plymouth Bretheren.[4] I can get you a Manual of their Doctrines, and shall be quite prepared for your application for it.

---

380. [1] The teetotaller's pledge.

[2] The name the Maxses had settled upon for the child born on 24 Nov.

[3] Presumably Adelaide Kemble, who married Edward John Sartoris in 1842 and lived at Warnford Park, Hampshire, in 1866. Viscountess Milner (p. 6) says that she used to play with the Gordon children, grandchildren of Adelaide Kemble.

[4] A religious sect that arose at Plymouth about 1830. They believe in Christ but have no formal creed or official order of ministers (*Oxford Companion to English Literature*).

381. *To* FREDERICK A. MAXSE

Text: typed copy, Maxse Papers. Published: *Letters*, i. 185–7, with omissions.

The Old House, Mickleham, Dorking
December 22, [1866]

My dear Fred,

I cannot accept the illustration of the mackerel. It is ingenious, and no more; though it may be praised for throwing a side light on the mental characteristics of the discoverer. If you had always turned sick at the smell of wine, to force you to drink any wine would be cruel and wrong. If half a mackerel were daily plumped down the throat of a man who had never in his life taken 10 lb. of mackerel per diem, it would be monstrous to subject him to the meal. But if he has eaten much mackerel—too much—there is (supposing virtues to exist in mackerel as in wine) no harm in asking him to take a little, from time to time. I, for instance, should say to him—'The 10 lb. a day were a poison to you; but that is no reason why the occasional half mackerel should be the same.' You fancy it, because one excess begets the conception of another: you have become the victim of a kind of mental elephantiasis—you fancy all things as immensities; you cannot understand the value of an intermediate measure. I warned you again and again that *10 lb.* of mackerel per diem was *excessive* etc., but *mackerel* is *nourishing*. Really, Fred, I have driven you hard to make you fall back on the mackerel argument—Mackerel is poison to some, ergo, wine, which is likewise poison to some, should be similarly avoided. But I tell you that Mackerel, if hurtful to any constitution, shows itself noxious from the first and won't be taken. And if wine is really *bad* for you, a glass would originally have inspired you with all the wisdom you insist on having gained for yourself in contempt of your best advisers now. On the contrary, wine has never poisoned you, but a wilful resolve to take as much as you pleased of it (do you remember Cherbourg, where you *would*, despite an agony of protestation from me, order and drink a bottle of Burgundy at a third-rate Norman provincial hotel)—*that* has done the work of poisoning your health. At this festive season, my dear Fred, one reflects on your fearful relapse from clear and eminent sense, with a melancholy deeper than wrath. I know what is coming next. I have anticipated it and written it down.[1] I will mention it another time.

What I dread most is that you are by these still degrees, as it were, boiling, or simmering, yourself down to a sort of human type, and engine. When you think you think suddenly, vehemently—with the

---

381. [1] No doubt Letter 382, the date of which is a hoax and the text of which is a spoof.

force and swiftness of a meteor, and perhaps with the result, but in any case your apparent incapacity to listen to the *wisdom* thrust in your way, is fraught with incalculable evils, and more and more I feel Fred going and an eccentric Force usurping his place. I will allude to this further by and by. Do you feel for the Pope yet? The Holy Father is unfortunately situated, surely.[2]

> I am ever yours,
> George M.

N.B. I confess I have written without consideration as to whether it is kind to knock over the theories by which you assure yourself that your wildest changes of system are sound and admirable. On my honour, I am careless about gratitude, though the sight of ingratitude naturally pains.

382. *To* FREDERICK A. MAXSE

Text: typed copy, Maxse Papers. Published: *Letters*, i. 218–20 (dated Christmas 1870), with omissions.

> Kingston-on-Thames [actually Mickleham]
> Christmas 1870 [actually 1866][1]

Yes, Fred, what you say of the beautiful picture presented by an Ascetic priesthood which shall be allowed marriage that one child of the union may reproduce the cultivated virtues of the parents, is very true. Something of this I have said before (though you will not remember it); but I objected and still object to the priesthood. Why any *priesthood?* Surely when I see you walk from Holly Hill[2] to Bursledon

381. [2] The withdrawal of French soldiers from Rome on 11 Dec., in accordance with Napoleon's pledge two years earlier, left the Pope undefended in possession of Rome. When the War of 1870 removed fears of further French interference, the King of Italy took over Rome and the Pope became the prisoner of the Vatican.
382. [1] This letter is no doubt GM's anticipation of Maxse's 'fearful relapse from clear and eminent sense' and GM's prophecy of 'what is coming next', as mentioned in the preceding letter. It is actually a clever hit at Maxse's eccentricities, especially his tendency to adopt extreme measures and take up extreme positions from which he stubbornly refused to budge. The post-dating of the letter, called for by the fictional prophecy, was of course not intended as a hoax, but W. M. Meredith took it at face value and printed it among the letters of 1870. René Galland (*George Meredith: les cinquante premières années*, Paris, 1923, p. 314), so far as I have ascertained, was the first to perceive that the date was spurious, but he incorrectly ascribed it to 1867. Professor Stevenson (p. 162) has set the matter straight.
[2] Maxse was purchasing the Holly Hill Estate (Hants) from Lord Henry Cholmondeley. He retained it until 1879 (*The Maxse Papers: a Catalogue*, pp. 11–12).

in stole and cope and beretta I cannot but feel at times that you undoubtedly have what I confess I have thought once or twice before—
a tendency towards extremes; though the demure look you assume is
very becoming and eclipses all the curates ever dreamed of by a pulpit-
stricken virgin. But I object to your taking on a sacerdotal garb. It is
true that you should have a distinctive dress, and I think it right that
Purcell[3] should have one likewise. The Basin of Miraculous Water
which he carries about that you may rub it upon the stomachs of this
generation would, I perceive clearly, not impress mankind with a
proper sense of its holiness, if you and he were not *peculiarly* attired,
and in our climate you would not (at least not yet) go about like
a couple of St. Johns. Still I demur to a priestly garb—the more
especially when I bear in mind your late extraordinary oration against
One who turned the Water into Wine—in which you so violently
denounced Him for having done so. Let me remark parenthetically
that I do *not* deem Him unwise or misguided in this matter: but you
will declare that I wish to force an argument, and I let the subject pass.
That the parents should be separated *immediately* after the birth of one
child, is, I am prepared to say, a mistake in your doctrine. It is not
human. You state that you have become superhuman. All are not as
you, however. I have read in the *Pall Mall Gazette* of your appalling
invasion of the banquet given by the Mayor of Southampton to the
American Plenipotentiaries come to treat for the admission of Great
Britain among the States of the Union. It appears that you approve the
policy of our becoming one Star in the spangled Banner. I have myself
previously advocated the measure. But, as I never can go so far as you,
I cannot countenance you in exclaiming that you are the Water God of
Hamble Point, and then at a given signal to Purcell, making cockshies
of all the wine-bottles on the Mayor's hospitable board, and drenching
the guests with water from an enormous hose in connection with the
main-pipes. Here I decidedly join in the condemnation of you pronounced by the newspapers. Your behaviour was essentially tyrannical.
That I was prepared for. But it was also indiscreet, for it will raise the
masses not only against you but against the element you adore. If every
one of these American envoys had come from the State of Maine,[4] you
would but have given them their evening dose. As it is, you have
disgusted the majority. You will have seen my defence of you in the
M[orning] P[os]t. It is weak, because I really could not say much.
I have restrained Morley's hand both in the *Saturday [Review]* and the

---

[3] Purcell, the skipper of Maxse's cutter yacht, had died in 1868. Letter 406, in which
GM laments his death, should have tipped W. M. Meredith off to the nature of this
letter.

[4] Another allusion to the prohibition of alcoholic beverages in the State of Maine.

Fortnightly. The joke in the *Times*—'that the notorious Naval Captain who walked over Hampshire with his Neptune behind him, drew the water which he dashed at the people's bellies from his brain, and had apparently an inexhaustible supply'—is neither witty nor laughable. But that it *is* thought wit, and *is* laughed at, should make you reflect. There is evidently the *will* to laugh. I consider this a damnatory sign.

I know your rejoinder perfectly.—Extremes are the chief teachers:— One excess corrects another; Truth must out in any shape. Very well. In December of 1866 I was finally convinced that you would on all subjects take your own course; or at least imagine you were doing it by going further than any one else would or dared go. Voilà! The poet has said, *Ire necesse est*—we must go on: and each in his own way, I suppose. Kiss little Olive Hermione's new sister from me (she has come in spite of the priesthood—bravo the piccolo!)—I have just finished the History of the inextinguishable Sir Harry Firebrand of the Beacon,[5] Knight Errant of the 19th century, in which mirror you may look and see—My dear Fred and his loving friend

George Meredith

383. *To* FREDERIC CHAPMAN

MS.: University of Texas.

Kingston
January 7, 1867

Dear Fred,

I have just returned from Mickleham. Sydney Whiting's book[1] is in its present form impossible. I shall see you within two days and will tell you why; and bring the MS; and all remaining with me.

Yours ever,
George Meredith

384. *To* MRS. EDWARD PEACOCK

MS.: Yale.

Garrick Club
January 14, [1867]

My dear Mrs. Edward,

I have been kept back from calling on you, as I have wished to do.

382. [5] Perhaps needless to say, a fictitious work. But Ellis and other writers, taken in by this letter, have regarded it as either a lost work or *Beauchamp's Career*.
383. [1] Probably *The Romance of Garret: a Tale of London Life*, published by C. & H. in 1867.

The fatal news[1] in your letter was utterly unexpected, and to me and to my boy it was a shock that comes rarely to us in life. Arthur cried bitterly, poor lad, and the loss of him whom he knew and loved best of all his relatives, was heavy on his young heart. Tom is left to you. He will, I feel sure, be true to his duties. Tell him never to forget that he has a relative and friend in me, and that if I can aid him while I live, I will. Tell him that Arthur will be glad to be in communication with him and keep to cousinship and friendship—I hope, through life. Arthur will write before he goes to school.[2] I will endeavour to bring him to you before he goes. God help and comfort you. All words are weak in the presence of your deep grief. I am ever

Affectionately yours,
George Meredith

385. *To* ALGERNON C. SWINBURNE

MS.: Ashley Library, British Museum. Published: *Letters*, i. 188–90, with omission of the sentence about 'little Willie Maxse' and with minor variants; excerpt published: Stevenson, p. 164.

Kingston Lodge, Kingston-on-
Thames
March 2, 1867

My dear Swinburne,

I have waited to read the Ode,[1] and also to ship off my Arthur for Switzerland.[2] The Ode is the most nobly sustained lyric in our language, worthy of its theme. Broader fuller verse I do not know. I had a glance at the proofs, and my chief sentiment was envy. Now I can read without that affliction. For me there will never be time given even to try the rising to such a song. I am passionately anxious to see the *Italy*,[3] and have a thousand spirits of fancy about it. Let me know when you return to town and when you will come and pay us a visit.

---

384. [1] Of the death of Edward Peacock, brother of GM's first wife. According to the records of the General Register Office, Somerset House, Edward Griffydh Peacock, solicitor, age 42, died at 45 Hunter Street, London, on 4 January 1867.

[2] Arthur, for reasons of economy and dissatisfaction with his progress at Norwich, was going to Hofwyl School, near Berne, Switzerland. In the Sotheby Catalogue for 19–21 Dec. 1921 there is a brief summary of a letter dated 30 Jan. [1867] in which GM announced his intention to Jessopp.

385. [1] Swinburne's 'Ode on the Insurrection in Candia', written at the request of some Greek friends, was published in the *FR* (Mar. 1867).

[2] See Note 2, preceding letter.

[3] *A Song of Italy*, published in 1867 by Hotten. It did not sell and was reviewed unfavourably.

I need not say that my wife will be glad to see you. Has she not fought your battles? I was in Austria when the heat of the storm was raging:[4] I returned from Italy in the winter after all was over. It would not have been my advice to you to notice the reviewers: but it's certainly better never to keep red-hot shot in store, and perhaps one broadside in reply does no harm.[5] I wish rather that it had been done in verse. As for the hubbub, it will do you no harm, and you have partly deserved it; and it has done the critical world good by making men look boldly at the restrictions imposed upon art by our dominating damnable bourgeoisie.—*Vittoria* passes to the limbo where the rest of my works repose. You alone have hit on the episode of the Guidascarpi. I have not heard or seen another mention of it. I would have carried it into fulness but the vast machinery pressed on me. My object was not to write the Epic of the Revolt—for that the time is yet too new: but to represent the revolt itself, with the passions animating *both* sides, the revival of the fervid Italian blood; and the character of the people:— Luigi Saracco, Barto Rizzo etc. Agostino Balderini is purposely made sententious and humourously conscious of it: Carlo Ammiani is the personification of the youth of Italy of the nobler sort. Laura Piaveni and Violetta d'Isorella are existing contrasts.—I am afraid it must be true that the style is stiff; but a less condensed would not have compassed the great amount of matter.—I see the illustrious Hutton[6] of the *Spectator* laughs insanely at my futile effort to produce an impression on his public. I suppose I shall have to give up and take to journalism, as I am now partly doing.—Yes! if you could get a place to say something of *Vittoria*! Morley stated your suggestion to me, and appeared willing that it should be done in the *Fortnightly*, if your or some such good name fathered the article.[7] But his opinion is that it should be a general review of me: the writer could dwell on the work pleasing him best. There is some doubt about giving a special review of a novel that has appeared in the *Fortnightly* pages. Adieu, my friend. I beg you to write to me, as I have requested. Arthur is away, by this time in Berne. The little Willie Maxie is a flower of promise. What is the address of Sandys? I do not see him at the Garrick.—I want you to bring Baudelaire when you come; and anything you may think of besides, in the way of verse. I am being carried off from the Singing.

---

385. [4] Over *Poems and Ballads*, withdrawn by Moxon as a result of the critical 'storm' and transferred to Hotten. Hardman (*HP*, p. 209), writing in Jan. 1867, says that Swinburne had been GM's guest recently, but the several sentences including this one, and the final sentence, do not sound as though the two had met in recent months.

[5] Swinburne had replied to his critics in a pamphlet, *Notes on Poems and Reviews*, which appeared in Oct. 1866.

[6] Richard Holt Hutton (1826–97), literary editor of the *Spectator*, which had reviewed *Vittoria* on 3 Feb. 1866, and again on 9 Feb. 1867.

[7] John Morley had succeeded Lewes as editor of the *FR* on 1 Jan.

I stand on an inexorable current. I shall look forward to meeting you with great pleasure.

Your faithful and affectionate
George Meredith

386. *To* LORD HOUGHTON

MS.: Trinity College, Cambridge.

Norbiton, Kingston-on-Thames,
S.W.[1]

March 2, 1867

Dear Lord Houghton,

A lady who, among other things, has written the tale of *Mdlle Mori*,[2] is advised by a publisher to collect a volume of poems illustrating History: a Templar poem of yours has struck her fancy, and she makes use of me to apply for permission to print it. She has I believe found it difficult to awaken attention to her petitions in other directions. Will you give her your formal sanction? I am Dear Lord Houghton,

Your most faithful
George Meredith

387. *To* ? MRS. ANNA C. STEELE[1]

MS.: University of Texas.

Kingston Lodge, Kingston-on-
Thames

March 21, [1867]

Madam,

My volumes of poems are at Lady Wood's disposal for the selections she may please to make. Printers' errors are scattered thickly over them, which I beg may not be reproduced. It is entirely my loss that I do not hear you speak the request. I have the honour to be

Your most faithful servant,
George Meredith

386. [1] Embossed address.
 [2] Listed by the *BMC* as by Miss Roberts (1860).
387. [1] This letter refers to *Leaves from the Poets' Laurels*, Selected, Edited, and Prefaced by Emma, Lady Wood (1869). GM had been requested by Mrs. Steele—or possibly Lady Wood—to permit inclusion of some of his poems in the book. Two were included: 'The Meeting' and a sonnet from 'Modern Love'. In the preface, dated Nov. 1868, Lady Wood says that she is much indebted to Mr. George Meredith. (As GM no longer lived at Kingston in 1868, 1867 is the most likely year for this letter.)
 For Mrs. Steele and Lady Wood, see Biographical Section, pp. 1719–20.

388. *From* Mrs. MARIE MEREDITH
To JUSTIN T. VULLIAMY

MS.: Meredith Papers.

[Kingston Lodge,
Kingston-on-Thames]
March 21, [1867]

My dear Papa,

We received the enclosed only last night.[1] I send it to you immediately. On the day appointed, Clutton[2] was ill and deputed his brother to see George. So all G. could do was to state the case. The brother however was not discouraging, nor I think is this letter. If between now and Mrs. Hope's[3] return any one could speak to Mr. Rickards,[4] and make love to him for us, call us 'desirable neighbours' etc., etc., he might influence Mrs. Hope in our favour. If he is a trustee, as well as her solicitor, his word and advice may have some weight. You see George kept the Bow windows in the background so as to fall back on them if they can't afford to grant us the two rooms. Tell Bettie perhaps if she mentioned the matter to the Knights[5] or the Chapmans,[6] it might do something for us,—or the Budds.[7] We are all well and have good accounts of Arthur. George is very hard at work, morning, noon and night. Money is horribly scarce. We can't get any from any body. Foakes is in great trouble, having lost a great deal of money and now puts himself at the mercy of his tradesmen and friends (so he says, he has certainly put down his carriage and sold his dogs). What chiefly affects us is that what he owes us (£76 and upwards*) he cannot pay at present, so that a bill he gave George some time back has been dishonoured at the L[ondon] and W[estminster] B[ank] and it must (if it can) come out of my April dividend. So much for seemingly good business men, and the state of things generally in this country. George is writing in the *Owl* and the *Morning Post*, which pays him well, but it is uphill work just at present.

My love to Betty and George's and mine to you.

Ever your affectionate daughter,
Polly

*At the end of this month £48 more are due.

388. [1] Some communication relating to Flint House, Box Hill, which the Merediths were attempting to buy or lease and succeeded in buying later in the year.

[2] Probably of the firm of Robert, John, Henry, and Robert George Clutton, surveyors, of 9 Whitehall Place, in their capacity of house agents. A solicitor and an architect of the name are also listed, but neither had a brother associated with him.

[3] The owner of Flint House. The Hope family, originally of nearby Deepdene, Dorking, were extensive property owners.

[4] ? E. Henry Rickards, of the firm of Rickards and S. Walker, solicitors of 29 Lincoln Inn Fields. [5] Unidentified.

[6] ? The Frederic Chapmans or the parents of 'Gina'. (See following letter.)

[7] The Edward Budds, of The Grange, Lingfield (Surrey).

389. *From* Mrs. MARIE MEREDITH
To JUSTIN T. VULLIAMY

MS.: Meredith Papers.

Norbiton, Kingston-on-Thames
April 12, [1867]

My dear Papa,

I have every day delayed writing until I should have heard about Flint House.[1] The enclosed came last evening and has greatly disappointed us. I suppose there is no help for it and I must now recommence the uphill work of looking for houses in the paper.

George went to the City last week and saw Mr. Rickards who was very civil—etc., etc.: chiefly anxious that you should not have thought him uncourteous in his reply to your letter to him, he having only intended not to inconvenience you as he is only home very early and very late.[2] Of course he could say nothing one way or the other about the house until he had seen Mrs. Hope when he promised to write the result of his interview. He has not written and you see the enclosed is from Clutton so we suppose he did not like the disagreeable task of refusing us and so put it on Clutton to do. It is most provoking.

I see Bermie's cottage and Cowslip[3] are both in the *Times* today.

I think Gina Chapman[4] deserves well of her country. Strangely enough I saw the happy Joe Roberts[5] here with her the second day they met and fancied something might be in the wind. Everybody seems much pleased about it. George is hard at work. He has just had a nasty influenza cold which he cannot shake off. It has hindered him a great deal lately; that and *bother* of various sorts. Little Willie has been quite ill (for him) with a feverish cold and his eyeteeth together. He was miserable all this week until today when he is himself again. The servants and I have quite escaped so I conclude it was not influenza.

I have no news of any sort nor have I been anywhere or seen anything. I hear from different sources that the Hardmans are trying to sell their place for £15000, a price which they indignantly refused for it at this time last year; *now* it is feared they will certainly not get it. *Ce qui donne à penser* that their bell controversy[6] placed them in such an

---

389. [1] For the context of the first half of this letter, see the preceding letter.

[2] E. H. Rickards had residences at Connaught Place and West Drayton, but why Mr. Vulliamy did not call on him in the City, as did GM, is not apparent.

[3] i.e. Burmester House and Cowslip Cottage, in Mickleham, were both advertised in *The Times* to let.

[4] Possibly a niece of Edward Chapman, who had five brothers. The family originally lived in Richmond, Surrey.

[5] *Boyle's Court Guide* lists a Joseph Roberts, of 52 Upper Seymour St., but he may not be identical with the one mentioned here.

[6] See Note 2, Letter 373.

unfavourable light with the neighbourhood and they find themselves so unpopular that they want to go. To us they have not mentioned the matter. An obnoxious neighbour has lately put up a doorbell so loud and incessant (it is fastened to the door so it rings twice for each person who enters) that there is no escape from it and it drives even our cook wild, how much more George! It renders his writing nearly impossible and makes me more than ever regret Flint House. Thank you very much for the hints about it contained in your last letter; had not the luck been against us they would have been more useful.

Our kind love to Bettie and with much from us both for yourself. Believe that I am ever

Your very dutiful and affectionate daughter,
Polly

390. *To* J. COTTER MORISON

MS.: University of Texas.

Kingston
May 26, [1867]

My dear Morison,

Morley tells me you are promoted from pencil to ink. This looks like the fresh flow of blood. How I long for one of those old evenings in the upper loft of Porchester Square! I remember that the recollection and the prospect of them used to be equally pleasant, as it is with all good things. Oh! the talk about nothing for hours, which was Chiosso and Maclaren[1] for the wits, after all. Say, that there, here, or somewhere, we are to have them again.—My wife is off with Willie to the Old House, Mickleham, for a week. I take a knapsack for a couple of days to roam over heaths. I am hard-worked and want the pasture, and I have such a longing to write poetry that I fear I shall break the bonds of the butcher, the baker, and candlestick-maker, and be at it. I hope not, for I mustn't. I have one novel nearly finished and another advancing; but *Vittoria* has made the publishers' faces cold. I knock at many doors.—We had a good night at the Garrick: Morley and his brother, the doctor, Greenwood, and two Lancastrians. Fair give-and-take conversation all round, with a wind-up of politics, which gives the

---

390. [1] Captain James Chiosso (1789–1864) operated gymnasia and schools of arms in London for many years and was the author of several books on gymnastics. Archibald Maclaren (1819–84) was the proprietor of the Gymnasium, Alfred Street, Oxford, to his death. He was the author of several books on gymnastics, physical education, and fencing, and Boase says that the British army was trained on his principles and in gymnasia which he invented.

bloated table a sense of importance for a conclusion. This is the effect of example—while Parliament speaks, political dialogues descend in circles down to the pot-house. But (unless in the form of Chiosso on the brain, as aforesaid) I don't see the use of it, though it's funny to hear men uplift their arms and voices, and glance at one another contemptuously, and fight the dusty questions over in a stew. They 'don't think this'; and, 'What! do you really mean that you justify Disraeli in—' and such like; extremely provocative of calls for brandy and soda-water. So it must be an instinct of nature, and excites the system that refreshment may be enjoyed.—I fancy I go to Morley's for two or three days on Thursday, but it's uncertain.

Adieu. My love to the babes and salute to your wife.

Your affectionate
George Meredith

391. *To* H. Dufton[1]

MS. (signed 'Chapman & Hall' but in the handwriting of GM): University of Texas.

193 Piccadilly, London, W.
September 13, 1867

Dear Sir,

Will it be convenient to you to call here on Monday at 2 p.m., that we may speak upon certain matters connected with the book?

Yours very obediently,
Chapman & Hall

392. *To* H. Dufton

MS.: University of Texas.

193 Piccadilly, London, W.
September 18, 1867

Dear Sir,

Have you—or can you find—a few remarks to make on the *iteghe Toroneche*—the wife of Theodore who is pretty and impudent and high born———?[1] Just to show that you are acquainted with the

391. [1] Henry Dufton, author of *Narrative of a Journey through Abyssinia in 1862–63* (the *book* of this letter), published by C. & H. on GM's recommendation in 1867. The first edn. sold out and a second was called for.
392. [1] Dufton says (p. 178) that he once saw 'the fair Toronetch, Iteghe (or Sultana) to the Abyssinian monarch', who was named Kassa but assumed the name Theodore.

circumstances etc. even if you have not seen her. Your proofs are here and forwarded with this post.

Very faithfully yours,
George Meredith

Please return proofs *here.*

393. *To* H. DUFTON

MS. (signed 'Chapman & Hall' but in the handwriting of GM): University of Texas.

193 Piccadilly, London, W.
September 23, 1867

Dear Sir,

Will you call here to-morrow early?—Say, at 12. m? The Appendix will then be ready: the map will not be completed before Thursday. The 5 Chapters are sent herewith, but we beg you not to think of delaying the book by publishing them—delay of any kind will be fatal.[1] A preface explains all, and the preface can be written here to-morrow.

Yours very obediently,
Chapman & Hall

394. *To* JAMES PAYN[1]

MS.: Yale.

Kingston Lodge, Norbiton
October 24, [1867]

Dear Massingberd,

If found, will you come here on Sunday or Saturday. I would rather the two. Do. Perhaps nobody else will be here. Tell me the train you

393. [1] The subject of Abyssinia was indeed timely. King Theodore, fancying that the English Consul was interfering in the affairs of the country and offended that a personal letter from himself to Queen Victoria had been ignored, had imprisoned all Europeans that he could lay hands on. Normal diplomatic efforts to secure their release had failed, and Parliament had debated the means of securing their release without agreement before proroguing at the end of August. Subsequently, however, Government had decided upon a liberating expedition, which was known at the time of this letter to be *en route* and which landed on the coast of Abyssinia in October.

The book was produced with record speed: it was being reviewed on 19 Oct. The five suppressed chapters, according to the preface, related to a journey through Dongola and the Bahiouda desert to Khartoum.

394. [1] James Payn (1830–98) had succeeded Leitch Ritchie as editor of *Chambers's Edinburgh Journal* in 1858. Serial publication of his *Lost Sir Massingberd* (2 Jan.–16 Apr. 1864) is said to have increased circulation of the magazine by 20,000. GM always called him *Massingberd.*

select, and I'll meet you at station. My wife says she likes the names of your novels, and very much wishes to meet the composer. Carlyon's ear,[2] she says, must have heard a lot. I'm thinking (it's imitation) of issuing the 'Confidences of Dionysius's'. Come. It's the last week we shall be at Kingston, and I want you to come here while we are here. Afterwards you will with the smoother spirit come to us at Mickleham. If Ladbrok[3] comes he shall behave, but I have not yet consulted him.

Ever yours,
George Meredith

N.B. No hollow trees in the garden.

395. *To* MRS. ANNA C. STEELE

MS.: University of Texas.

Kingston
October 26, [1867]

Dear Mrs. Steele,

I am not daily in town, my visits to my club are irregular. So when I had your letter, I had but time to direct my steps to Thomas's Hotel, collecting all imaginable answers on the road. I think I remembered that Thomas was a Questioner and would not believe until he had put his finger into the wounds.[1] Mine were ready to prove what amount of divinity there may be in the poem.[2]—I deserved my ill luck in missing you. It was said that you had gone, not to return that day.—I will in future make a point of calling at the Garrick every day that I am in London;—merely to save myself a repetition of the chagrin. To be a perfect Epicurean, one must take some pains, you see.—How could you turn from the road to Italy? Companion of mine that did, I would condemn to eternal steamboat on the Channel among *commis voyageurs* and their wives. I passed the remainder of the day on Friday with a Venetian friend and his bride, an Albrizzi, whom our climate has turned green. Can there be a greater folly than in hurrying young brides from the altar over Europe? This poor creature was cast on our shores tired but human. She might now be labelled medicine. Since she

---

[2] A reference to Payn's *Carlyon's Year*, which ran serially in *OaW*, 6 July–26 Oct. 1867.

[3] *Boyle's Court Guide* for 1866 lists Felix Ladbroke of 21 Belgrave Road, S.W., about whom I know nothing more. There were also the brothers Henry and John Ladbrooke, landscape painters, whom GM might have known through Sandys, Laurence, G. F. Watts, or Thoby Prinsep.

395. [1] John xx. 24–28.

[2] I find no poem of this time attributed to Mrs. Steele; perhaps GM found no divinity in it.

left the Canal Grande she has been sighing for it. Instead of novels, will you; or shall I, or shall we by means of novels, interest young people to learn to know what it is they like, before they shall waste years, health, hope, in finding it out . . .? But perhaps nothing will teach. Wisdom is more than half of it force of *feeling*. Who has that? I find it rare. Moderately shrewd 'intelligent' young men and women abound, who walk the plank of life just steadily enough, and joylessly; but of those who feel deeply enough to take their lives in their hands and perish or gain wisdom—this appears to be àpropos of Bradshaw,[3] so I go no farther—the page prohibits it. I am

Your most faithful

George Meredith

396. *To* MRS. ANNA C. STEELE

MS.: University of Texas.

[Written on Garrick Club paper]

October 30, 1867

Dear Mrs. Steele,

I write with a dismal fear that I am about to address my letter to a place that will miss you. It happens most unfortunately for me that I have asked Swinburne to come to me on Thursday: so, I am a prisoner. Next week I change house (or it is done for me) to Mickleham, and then I take flight in all directions,—wherever there is a hand beckoning at the window. I think too that next week Mr. Morley is disengaged for a day. But at any future time, dating from Tuesday, I shall be very happy to come, leaving that be-Burked[1] editor to do as he will. By the way, your remark on 'that politician' is (you are being largely criticized and will enjoy the phrase) exquisitely feminine. I am

Your most faithful

George Meredith

397. *To* MRS. ANNA C. STEELE

MS.: University of Texas.

[Written on Garrick Club paper]

November 6, [1867]

Dear Mrs. Steele,

Unhappily your letter has performed a circuit in coming to me;

395. [3] The railway guide.
396. [1] Morley's *Edmund Burke: an Historical Study* was published in 1867.

I am in London and disengaged, but I don't know whether I am to visit Belhus or Rivenhall.[1] I suppose the former, yet I may be wrong. I will call at Thomas's Hotel to-morrow for the chance of seeing you. Or if you receive this, will you telegraph to the Garrick? Pray pardon my stupidity. In the case of my not hearing from you, will you appoint another day?—one *after* the following week.—Mr. Morley starts for America on the 15th.[2] He can't or won't relieve my perplexed mind—and merely says 'go', which is oracular and editorial without being comforting. Believe me, I very much regret to give you this trouble, and know that I (in all probability) miss a great pleasure to-morrow, unless my good fortune brings you to town and you take me out of it. I am

Your most faithful
George Meredith

398. *To* HENRY MORLEY[1]

MS.: Yale.

193, Piccadilly, London, W.[2]
November 21, 1867
Fortnightly Review

Dear Mr. Morley,

In the absence of the present editor, I have charge of this Review. I write to ask you if you will write a notice (three or three and a half pages) for the January number on Mätzner's 1st volume of *Altenglische Sprachproben*,[3] a remarkable work that no one could better do justice to than you. This first volume treats of poetry entirely. The next will be prose.

My address is 'Flinthouse, Mickleham, Dorking'. If you will intimate to me that you are willing to do it, I will direct that the book shall be forwarded to you. I am

Very faithfully yours,
George Meredith

397. [1] Belhus (Essex) was the country seat of Sir Thomas Barrett-Lennard, husband of Mrs. Steele's sister Emma. Rivenhall Place (Essex) was the home of Lady Wood, her mother. The proposed visit probably did not come off, I infer from letters to GM written by Mrs. Steele and Sir Thomas Barrett-Lennard (Altschul Collection).
[2] GM's 'Lines to a Friend Visiting America', addressed to Morley, is dated 15 Nov. 1867, and appeared in the *FR* (1 Dec. 1867). In Morley's absence GM edited the *FR*.
398. [1] See Note 1, Letter 272.
[2] Printed address.
[3] Eduard Mätzner's *Alt-Englische Sprachproben*, vol. i, was duly reviewed by Morley in the Jan. 1868 issue of *FR* (pp. 110–15).

399. *To* LORD HOUGHTON

MS.: Trinity College, Cambridge.

Flint House, Mickleham, Dorking[1]
December 2, 1867

Dear Lord Houghton,

Will you write a Review of Robert Lytton's Poems?[2] The new book *Chronicles and Characters* has, I believe, been sent to you.—I have the management of the *Fortnightly* while the Editor is absent in America; and I am anxious to give some variety to the tough grain of the articles. Pray, assist me. I think Lytton's book will interest you. Crown him with bays or execute him, as you think fit; but write on him for the January number of the Review. Or, will not men say that after launching your last and biggest favourite, you have become careless of what is done in literature? There is real matter in the *Chronicles and Characters*. The mimetic stuff does not so much abound, or it has become part of the soil, and the writer's real quality is more distinct. I am,

Dear Lord Houghton,
Your most faithful
George Meredith

400. *To* HENRY MORLEY

MS.: Yale.

Flinthouse, Mickleham, Dorking
December 13, 1867

Dear Mr. Morley,

Will you send your copy to the printers early next week?[1]— 'Messrs. Virtue & Co., 294 City Road, E.C.' We have to get all the printing done before Christmas.—I hope you will be able to think of an article for the Feb[ruar]y or March number. We carry big but immoveable guns, and the work you can supply will be heartily acceptable to me.

Has there ever been an examination in English of the legends— Norse and alt-Deutsch—which were shaped into the Nibelungen-lied? German literature is surcharged with new publications on this theme.

399. [1] This is the first of GM's letters that I have found written from Flint House, located at the foot of Box Hill, near Dorking, and hence presently called simply 'Box Hill'. It was to be his home for the rest of his life.
    [2] *Chronicles and Characters* of the next sentence. Lytton, of course, was better known as Owen Meredith. Houghton evidently declined to write the review. (See Letter 407).
400. [1] A reference to Morley's review of Mätzner. (See Letter 398.)

It would make a delightful article.—Then, too, for you who can do it, and have not exhausted the subject, might I suggest a *poetical* comparison of the chief works of Cymric and Saxon Bards—say, the 'Gododin' and 'Beowulf' as indicative also incidentally of characteristics of race.[2] M. Arnold has only touched the ground: 'Irish and British Ballads' etc.[3]

But I do not pretend to suggest articles to you. I shall be too glad if I can excite your fancy to select one wherever you will. I am

Very faithfully yours,
George Meredith

401. *To* FREDERIC CHAPMAN

MS.: University of Texas.

Flinthouse, Mickleham, Dorking
[December 1867]

My dear Fred,

Please send the remaining £40 for the monthly expenditure of *Fortnightly* to my bank, L[ondon] & Westminster, St. James's Branch, by *Monday's* post; so that I may hear of no complaints, and work in ease of mind. I deserve to get the little that comes to me, for I am writing letters or correcting proofs or reading MS. every day, and I am hampered for want of money.

From what I see of the *Fortnightly* there is a chance of its making a permanent stand. But contributors must feel that what money they are to get is sure to be paid punctually to the day. This is the case with *Fraser*, with *Blackwood*, and the *Cornhill*.

I'm sorry to say that until the *Fortnightly* is rid of the *White Rose*[1] the number of pages will have to be 124: that is up to February. After Feb[ruar]y the arrangement shall be for 104. The men who contribute to the Feb[ruar]y number are Morison,[2] Bagehot,[3] Harrison,[4] Cliffe Leslie,[5] Godkin[6] (Fenianism, its Cause and cure) and Clayden,[7] all good men,

[2] Morley's 'Three Old Yorkshire Poems' (*FR*, Feb. 1868, pp. 121–30) was written in response to this suggestion.
[3] Arnold's *On the Study of Celtic Literature* (1867), a publication of four lectures delivered at Oxford and subsequently published in the *Cornhill* (Mar., Apr., May, July 1866). Allusion is made to it in Morley's 'Three Old Yorkshire Poems'.
401. [1] A novel, by G. Whyte-Melville, running serially in the *FR*.
[2] Cotter Morison's 'Ireland for the British' appeared in the January issue; thereafter for a while he contributed nothing except reviews in the May and October issues.
[3] Walter Bagehot's second article on 'Physics and Politics' was delayed until April by his illness.
[4] Frederic Harrison's 'The Transit of Power' did not appear until April.
[5] T. E. Cliffe Leslie, 'Ireland in 1868'.
[6] James Godkin, 'Fenianism and the Irish Church'.
[7] P. W. Clayden's 'The Ecclesiastical Organisation of English Dissent' did not appear until the May issue.

and I can't put off one of them. The *White Rose* (conclusion) occupies upwards of thirty pages. You see, there is no help for it; considering that the articles deal with pressing subjects. Do let me hear from you that you have sent to my Bank, as requested, and believe that my interests are yours as well as yours mine. I dare not overdraw. Yet I have to pay nearly all that I ask you for, according to Morley's instructions.

Yours ever faithfully,
George Meredith

My wife is at work on a pretty cushion. She and I join in salutes to your bride. Good cheer to you through the Christmas.

402. *To* MONCURE D. CONWAY[1]

Text (excerpt): The American Art Association Catalogue of the Collection of William F. Gable [n.d.].

193 Piccadilly, London, W.
January 14, 1868

I am responsible for the omission to send you the enclosed cheque last month, and I beg your excuse. I had lost your address. Mr. Chapman has done me the favour to show me your letter from Jonathan to John.[2] If the style had been something less familiar and had embraced a statement of politics as well as feelings, I should have regretted its not having been sent to the *Fortnightly Review*. . . . I conduct the *Review* in Mr. Morley's absence.

403. *To* ALGERNON C. SWINBURNE

MS.: University of Texas. Published: *Letters*, i. 190; Lang, i. 287–8.

[Written on Garrick Club paper]
January 27, [1868]

My dear Swinburne,

The *Fortnightly* is no longer in the hands of a company, but of a publisher, who tries to diminish the expenses as much as he can; the

---

402. [1] Moncure D. Conway (1832–1907), a liberal American preacher, author, and lecturer who had accepted the pastorate of South Place Chapel, Finsbury, London, in 1864. The cheque was in payment of Conway's review of Heinrich Ewald's *The History of Israel to the Death of Moses* (*FR*, Dec. 1867, pp. 732–4).

[2] If this was ever published, I have not found it.

editor being the chief sufferer. I had to pay for the two poems.¹ 'The Halt before Rome' has evidently been omitted from the list of what is due to you. When I see Morley I will state your complaints to him; but from the sum he gets it's scarcely possible to pay more, without doing so out of his own pocket. It will grieve him as it does me to hear that you are dissatisfied.—I received for my 'Phaëthon' (about 150 lines) £5.—²

Do—if it's not possible, as I suppose—to buy a copy of Hugo's poem,³ lend it to me for a day or two. They say that Garibaldi has replied to it—in verse.

I propose to come and lunch with you some afternoon. Will you have me? I will stay from two or three to six, and if we are alone, we will give and take, though I shall take ten times the worth of what I give. I have just got your *Blake*. M. Conway's notice of it in the *Fortnightly* is eulogistic, but whether sufficient and closely and warmly critical I can't yet say.⁴ My wife and Willie hope to greet you in the warm spring days.

Yours ever faithfully,
George Meredith

404. *To* FREDERICK A. MAXSE

Text: typed copy, Maxse Papers. Published: *Letters*, i. 191, with substantial omissions.

Mickleham
January 28, [1868]

My dearest Fred,
Historicus (on board his Thames wherry) completely smashes Seward (in his Leviathan *Monitor*).¹

403. ¹ During GM's editorship of the *FR*, Swinburne's 'A Lost Vigil' (Dec.) and 'Ave atque Vale: In Memory of Charles Baudelaire' (Jan.) had been published. 'The Halt before Rome' (Nov.) had been published before Morley left for America but on the evidence of this letter had not been paid for.

C. & H. had taken over management of the magazine from its founders, and Chapman was never a liberal paymaster. Because of Swinburne's dissatisfaction with payment for his poems, a meeting was arranged between him and GM at which the subject was discussed. An argument is said to have ensued, and there followed a period of coolness between the two for several years. (See Stevenson, pp. 166–7, and E. R. and J. Pennell, *The Whistler Journal*, Phila., 1921, p. 24. Letters 450 and 491, however, cast doubt upon the accuracy of these accounts.)

² Published in the 1 Sept. 1867 issue.

³ A reference to Hugo's poem on Garibaldi's defeat at Mentana. Originally entitled *La Voix de Guernsey*, the title was changed to *Mentana*. An English translation by an 'Oxford Graduate' (Edwin Arnold) appeared in 1868 (Kenneth Ward Hooker, *The Fortunes of Victor Hugo in England*, N.Y., 1938, note 1, p. 287).

⁴ Swinburne's *William Blake* was the subject of a review by Moncure D. Conway in the February *FR*.

404. ¹ American claims to reparations for damage done by the *Alabama* were undisputed ,

I am one of those who think the *Monitor* would sink the wherry in an engagement, and wish to silence the conquering sound of noisy writers.

If the spirit of the nation were of your temper, I should counsel Historicus's show of independence for the nation at large. Fred, it's clear there's no such spirit now in this pot-bellied country—none of it.[2] Bend, while you can do so with a pretence of dignity. I declare to you, I have watched the changes of mood in the Government, the Journals —say, the people: and I have seen them moved by apprehension and by panic, and by nothing else in their foreign relations; by little else in their dealings at home. The aristocracy has long since sold itself to the middle class; that has done its best to corrupt the class under it. I see no hope but in a big convulsion to bring a worthy people forth. The monied class sees the same, and reads it—will do anything to avoid it— will eat Historicus's words and him rather than accept the challenge he provokes. You are misled by your natural hot chivalry, and don't perceive the humiliations you are bringing on.

As to Ben.[3] I want him *immediately*. Only, I delayed to reply, in the hope of seeing you, to ask you whether it is all clear concerning him; and none of you feel grief at losing him. If there is a shadow of that, I cannot take him. Let me know. Willie Maxse is well and a most flourishing sapling, full of song and chatter—hearty without a varia- tion—I was on the point of writing when your letters came this after- noon. I shall be too glad to hear of your relief. Let me hear from you soon—as to Ben. And don't fail to write how things go on. We are both anxious for good news. Can I send books to your wife? I have some that might amuse her. Sartoris[4] was at the Club the other day. Little B. came in, perplexed by his Turk brother and a sort of hymeneal debate going on in his mind.[5]—When will you ask me to come and

and in 1867 Lord Stanley, Foreign Minister, had suggested arbitration. Seward, the American Secretary of State, declined the proposal unless England conceded that her recognition of the belligerent status of the South and its consequences should form a part of the case for arbitration. In effect Seward was arguing that there would have been no civil war except for England's intervention, only a mere domestic insurrection. In a series of letters published in *The Times* in Jan. 1868, 'Historicus' (Sir William V. Harcourt) showed that if this argument were allowed, England would be responsible not simply for the damage done by the *Alabama* but for all of the damage done by the war. But he re- futed such a theory from Seward's own dispatches. (All of this is discussed in some detail by A. G. Gardiner, *The Life of Sir William Harcourt*, N.Y., n.d., i. 195 ff., from which my information is derived.)

404. [2] The growing softness of the English people is a recurring theme in GM's letters.
   [3] A red retriever.
   [4] Edward Sartoris was elected to the Garrick Club on 5 July 1851, but whether GM is writing of the husband of Adelaide Kemble or his son is uncertain. He later mentions 'young Sartoris'.
   [5] Probably Borthwick, whose brother George had entered the service of the Sultan of Turkey, rising to the rank of Major-General in the army (Reginald Lucas, *Lord Glenesk and the 'Morning Post'*, 1910, p. 45.)

see you? In March?—Did you go to Knaphill⁵ after all? I know the
place well, and the garden of American plants. Heaven bless your boys.
I am

Your loving
George Meredith

405. *To* WILLIAM HARDMAN

MS.: Yale. Published: *HP*, pp. 303–5; excerpts published: *Letters*, i. 192–3; Stevenson, p. 168.

Box Hill¹
January 31, 1868

Dearest Tuck,

I have been, so please your Worship, hard at work, old boy, or
I should have written to your honourable Bench.—Confound this
reminiscence of your greatness, under which I lived three whole years!
May it please—no, it doesn't please you nor me neither. Sooner or
Later,² as Shirley Brook[s] says, I was going to write, but I had to
manage the *Fortnightly* for Morley during his absence in America, and
that with incessant composition and pot boilers kept my hands tied.
But I am training my toes (first and second of right foot) to indite
epistles and *Ips*[*wich*] *Journal*, while I pursue my course complacently
above. So no one will be complaining, unless it be Her Majesty; for
there's a chance that in a fit of distraction I may stick a corn plaster on
the envelope instead of a Queen's Head—a horrible thought and an
abominable. Right so, Tuck. And have you read England's Book?³ It
sent me up Box Hill dancing a Tupper-jig.⁴ I swear by Gosh the God of
the Loyal, it is a Book. And I like the Book better than the people who
go retching in praise of it. Yet they also are interesting to the studious,
and well trained in the matter of belching might let off their loyalty in
regiments with applause. I asked Woodward,⁵ Queen's Librarian, to
write a critical notice for the *Fortnightly*. He began 'At this moment
Europe is threatened with convulsion. Turkey, we see' etc. (6 lines)
Austria etc. (7 lines) Russia etc. Prussia etc. France etc., then England
—Fenianism of course—ending his paragraph 'it is at such a moment

---

⁵ In Surrey, where Waterer's American Nursery is located.
405. ¹ In the early days of his occupancy of his new residence GM designated it
variously as Flinthouse, Mickleham, and Box Hill before settling upon Box Hill.
    ² The title of a novel by Shirley Brooks; reviewed in the *Athenaeum* on 18 Jan.
    ³ *Leaves from the Journal of Our Life in the Highlands*, by Queen Victoria, published
in January.
    ⁴ Martin Tupper, whose platitudinous poetry was often the subject of ridicule by GM
and Hardman, was said by Hardman to be a favourite of the Queen (*MVP*, p. 285).
    ⁵ Benjamin Bolingbroke Woodward (1816–69), appointed librarian at Windsor Castle
in 1860 (*HP*, p. 304 n.).

as this that the Queen of England publishes her book!'—Real honest anti-climax. I've never seen the like. Yet I believe that if I had printed it, the retchers and belchers, the lechers and welchers, the bigwigs and piggiwigs,—none of them would have perceived but that the writer had expressed one way or another, with more or less of ventral energy their emotions. Shall such a people live? And Holroyd[6] has been at it over in Australia! 'Tis well. We are only putting human nature back another million years or so. May thine and mine live in the Age of the final Eradication of Humbug. But then wilt thou and I be flying particles on the breath of the South-West. Ah, Tuck! What is mortal splendour after all? There may be Purgatory for thee after thou hast ceased to plant a forefoot on the necks of criminals—sniffing the incense of Kingstonian praise. Well; pass we to lighter themes. Thine ideas are those of the Crowned. I am, I was, I always shall be, a vagabond. And Heaven must love such to take me in. This is veritably as I state it.

Willie-Maxse has, months back, had you once pointed out to him (cap on, cigar in mouth, cock in th' eye—generally likerous expression) in our book of photographs. He was looking at it yesterday, and coming to you, cried: 'That's dear Godpapa.' He flourishes. Who could help doing so here? I am every morning on the top of Box Hill—as its flower, its bird, its prophet. I drop down the moon on one side, I draw up the sun on t'other. I breathe fine air. I shout ha ha to the gates of this world. Then I descend and know myself a donkey for doing it. For sooth Tuck I have to remain in harness an unconscionable time. (See poems in *Macmillan, Fortnightly, Cornhill* (to come),[7] and articles in *M[orning] Post* etc. etc., and my desk bursting with MSS.) Now as to your invitation. I'll come if I can, and I think I can. I have to put off a pre-engagement if possible. You will see me (an I do come, as I hope) about 3 p.m. Sunday. I can't sleep away from home, as it appears to upset Marie, and we have not yet a dog, and do on the left side lean on the wilds, where there are rabbits, and maybe weasels. So to soften a wife's uneasiness, I leave Surbiton 9.10 that night; catch Wimbledon 10.1, home about 11.5 p.m.—Norbiton, I salute thee. Tuck, I love thee. To thy wife my amiablest salutation, and as affable a bow as Briton on his guard dare be guilty of to thy fair guest.[8]

Thine

R[obin] of Box Hill

405. [6] Hardman's friend, Edward Dundas Holroyd, whose letters of reply to Hardman's monthly letters were being published in the *Standard* under the heading 'From our own Correspondent'.

[7] 'The Orchard and the Heath' appeared in *Macmillan's Magazine* (Feb.) and 'Aneurin's Harp' in the *FR* (1 Sept.), but GM had nothing in the *Cornhill* until 'The Song of Theodolinda' (Sept. 1872). [8] Mrs. Holroyd.

406. *To* FREDERICK A. MAXSE

Text: *Letters,* i. 195–6.

Mickleham
February 17, 1868

Our old friend! It chokes me to think that we have lost him.[1]
I have Purcell's dear old wind-blown brown gleam of a face, the
manner of him, the voice and walk, more firmly stamped in my mind
than most living men are. He comes up to meet me now—I see him
dashed with spray—parrying a thrust from me—I can't believe he's
gone. His voice is alive in my ears. Only, I know that when I come to
Holly Hill I shall feel the truth sadly enough. Poor, dear old man! This
will change Summer and the yacht to you and your wife. He was so
true a gentleman, with a pardonable old dog's growl now and then—
after all, very rarely. I reproach myself that I should have let him ever
sink a trifle in my esteem. And I am always on my guard against the
influence of these sectional impressions, and try so much to get and
keep possession of a man's character, so that I may never fall into these
silly errors. It seems to me that the old man has gone carrying my debt
to him away for good. The little history revealed to you by his death
is wretched.—What will be done for the children? That's the most
lamentable thought of all.

Marie is in grief for the loss of Purcell. He belonged to our early
marriage days. On my soul I think I shall never smell salt water or
look on a grey ridge of sea or sea haze without thinking of him.

The typhus probably followed gastric fever, which one gets from
fretting; it speedily sends us on.

Alas! my dear Fred, I didn't expect sad news from you.

Our Willie Maxse will be three years old in July.

Then let me have Ben.[2] I delight (so does Marie) to think of him
coming. But I'm bothered, I'll write about him to-morrow.[3]

Your loving
George Meredith

406. [1] Purcell, the skipper of Maxse's cutter yacht, who had died.
[2] See Note 3, Letter 404.
[3] The letter, if written, has not survived.

407. *To* FREDERIC CHAPMAN

MS.: University of Texas.

Mickleham
April 28, [1868]

Dear Fred,

I am completely knocked up with Influenza.—

You will have arranged according to your pleasure as to Lytton's Poems. I wrote the Review because I could find no other man who would consent to do it, and thought that there should be one in the *Fortnightly.*[1] But I could not write a puff. You may depend on it that he is too sensible to care for such notices as those in *Macmillan* and the *Times*. They do him harm with the public. One purpose of my review was to show by the contrast of the poems of old and new date that he no longer deserves those hard terms which one often hears applied to him. I make every allowance for your position. The old poems have been cut out, and the review may go to the waste-paper basket if you like.

Ask Tracy whether the Poems sent in the last MSS. parcel are the Hon. Roden Noel's?[2]—I don't think they can be. They are very bad.—

Pray, decide upon *nothing* as to Thornbury's collection[3] until we have talked together. You are under some delusion in this respect. If he is hurrying you to decide postpone him. The sum he asks for seems to me monstrous high—but there are other considerations.

I can't go on.

Yours ever,
George Meredith

408. *To* MRS. ANNA C. STEELE

MS.: University of Texas.

Mickleham, Dorking
October 6, 1868

Dear Mrs. Steele,

Is it possible for you to lend me a copy of the book? Let me see it

---

407. [1] Lord Houghton evidently declined to review Lytton's *Chronicles and Characters* (see Letter 399), whereupon GM wrote the review himself. Chapman, as Lytton's publisher, objected to critical elements in it and in the end a modified version appeared in the June issue of *FR*. In point of fact GM was temperate in criticism and generous in praise, as well as erudite and just: the review is surely one of his finest.

[2] The Hon. Roden Noel's *Beatrice and Other Poems* appeared in 1868, but whether the book and the MS. are identical is impossible to say.

[3] Possibly *Old Stories Retold*, by George Walter Thornbury, published by C. & H. in 1869.

and I will write a letter of which you may make what use you please. I am grieved beyond measure at the thought that there should have been criticisms on your mother's book of this base old sort I know so well. I do not see the *Athenaeum*, but I know how that and other Journals fall upon plain speaking.[1] No other charge, I am certain, could honestly be brought against Lady Wood.—Yesterday in town I tried to get the book. An acquaintance pounced on a quotation to satisfy me. I perceived at once how the case went. There may of course be an enemy at work, but such a person is not wanted to fly at passages which are a transcript of actual villainies and a villain's nature.

—I wish to see the novel that I may the more conscientiously speak on these points.

If you can lend it, the address to reach me for the next six or seven weeks is 'Holly Hill, Southampton'—care of Captain Maxse, R.N. There I shall be hard at work electioneering. Pleasant for a lover of peace! This is what it is to have friends—that one can't see them in a contest without joining it.—Adieu. I need not tell you that I feel with you deeply about this annoyance, and I may assure you that when you choose to exercise a claim on such poor services as I may offer, you will have them. I will write to Lady Wood as soon as I have seen the book. Believe me, Dear Mrs. Steele,

Your very faithful
George Meredith

408. [1] What had happened was that the *Athenaeum* had administered a stinging slap in the face to Lady Wood in reviewing her novel *Sorrow on the Sea* (published by Tinsley Bros.) and that Mrs. Steele had appealed to GM. The only mystery is why it took so long for the slap to be felt. Perhaps some 'kind friend' called Lady Wood's attention to the review in the 2 May issue. '*Sorrow on the Sea* is a very bad novel', begins the review. 'No such work has proceeded directly or indirectly from an Englishwoman of title since Smollett was induced by the notorious Lady Fane to insert in *Peregrine Pickle* those "Memoirs of a Lady of Quality" which are at the same time the record of the woman's shame and the novelist's dishonour; but which the author of *Sorrow on the Sea* goes out of her way to commend for truthfulness and interest. . . .' Then follows a summary of Lady Wood's novel: two brothers are in love with the same girl, one with the intention of marrying her, the other with the intention of making her his mistress. When the chambermaid produces fabricated evidence of the girl's falsity, the decent brother confronts the other with it. The review quotes a part of the dialogue that follows: ' "What the devil is it to you if [we cannot quote the rest of this sentence]? She prefers being my mistress to being your wife; very kind of her, and very good taste, too, I think." ' 'The details of these volumes', concludes the review, 'are literally unfit for presentation in any language.' I have found no trace of any letter that GM may have written.

409. *To* EMMA, LADY WOOD[1]

MS.: University of Texas.

Mickleham, Dorking
October 6, 1868

Dear Lady Wood,

You will not accuse me of discourtesy in taking a few days to deliberate on the purport of your letter, in which I fancy I have discovered a spring of personal kindness, and I will reply to it. I am of all the 'intelligent gentlemen' of my acquaintance the poorest just now, and perhaps I might be acceptable. I would propose another if I knew of one. The task seems to me a privilege. It can scarcely be less if your sister resembles you. Only in that case how is one to feel that this is money fairly earned?—I would beg permission to run down to visit you but I have to go off immediately to help a friend through his election struggle, and with him I must remain until the middle of November.[2] Can the matter be deferred for my return to consult with you? By no means let the matter be deferred if you can light on a suitable person. My address will be to the care of 'Captain Maxse, R.N., Holly Hill, Southampton'.

I have sent by this post a letter to Mrs. Steele touching a subject of greater moment.[3] I am, Dear Lady Wood,

Your most faithful
George Meredith

410. *To* LADY WOOD[1]

Text (excerpt): American Art Association, Anderson Galleries, Inc. Catalogue (1 Apr. 1931), p. 25.

Holly Hill
October 15, 1865 [error for 1868]

The literary policemen rarely forgive that [plain language]; the prudish magistracy of the libraries are in the habit of fining it summarily. . . . They will never learn that a woman of pure mind is often prompted by her anger at vice to speak of it in plain words. . . .

409. [1] It is evident that Lady Wood had written to GM requesting him to suggest the name of some 'intelligent gentleman' who would be willing to read to her wealthy sister, Mrs. Benjamin Wood, one afternoon a week. (For Mrs. Wood, see Biographical Section, p. 1719–20.)

[2] Captain Maxse was standing for the House of Commons as a candidate of the Radical party at Southampton, and GM had promised to go down and canvass for him.

[3] The offensive review of Lady Wood's novel. (See Note 2, preceding letter.)

410. [1] For the context of this letter, see Note 1, Letter 408.

411. *To* AUGUSTUS JESSOPP

MS.: Yale. Printed: *Altschul Catalogue*, pp. 47–48; excerpt published: Stevenson, p. 170.

Holly Hill, Southampton
October 23, 1868

My dear Jessopp,

If I don't write at once I shall sink into my old quagmire. Your letter has come round to me here where I am staying with my friend Captain Maxse to see him through his election; a dismal business, but I take to it as to whatever comes. You may well imagine that you have touched remorse in me. Not to have written at all was *lèse amitié*, scarcely pardonable. But the case when you, like the best of fellows which you are, wrote to Kingston, stood thus. My wife's sister and brother-in-law with babe were about to pay us a visit of uncertain length. We supposed they would leave in time to make room for you, but waited for their decision. They came, the little baby fell sick and died in our house.[1] This quite shattered us and we went to Mickleham for a couple of months. After that I had to buckle to newspaper work to pay debts. And this has gone on ever since, with now and then a dash at verse. But I've not had heart to write to friends, my way being to go up in a corner when I don't flourish and trouble none that I can't help. Of any but constantly tender feelings towards you and your best of wives I am unconscious. Marie, I am sure, shares them.—I still hope for that leisure which will let me do the work I can do. At present I am tied to the pecuniary pen, and I am not a bright galley-slave. Arthur is well. I have excellent reports of his conduct and studies from his Master. He has taught himself Spanish and reads Cervantes. Italian I believe he is mastering; German moderately proficient in, and French. He seems to be much the same style of boy, plodding over-much in the book line when he should be at play; very quaint, very thoughtful, not brilliant. Little Willie is in good condition, and so is his mother. They have been staying at Southsea with Mrs. Maxse, but are to be at Holly Hill to-morrow.—I hope the paper you sent was put in the *Ips[wich] J[ournal]*. I sent a recommendation to that effect.—I write almost every week in the *Pall Mall Gazette*. Do you see it? And did you perchance see the poem of 'Phaëthon' done in Galliambics in the *Fortnightly Review* of last September a year back? To my mind they are near on the mark, but as the public is not near it I might as well have missed. Two or three lines want a correcting touch.

411. [1] The child was that of Katherine Wheatcroft. According to the gravestone in Mickleham Churchyard, it was born in 1866 and died in 1867.

—Our home is now at Mickleham, in a little cottage on the side of Box hill, charming as to scenery, small, but open ever to you two. We return there the end of November when these curst elections are over. Give my remorseful love to your wife. Take as much of it as you care to have to yourself.

I am ever your faithful friend,

George Meredith

412. *To* WILLIAM HARDMAN

Text: Ellis, pp. 169–70.

October 1868

Poor Dante Rossetti seems to be losing his eyesight, owing entirely to bad habits—a matter I foretold long ago: Eleven a.m.plates of small-shop ham, thick cut, grisly with brine: four smashed eggs on it: work till dusk: dead tired on sofa till 10 p.m.[1] Then to Evans' to dine off raw meat and stout. So on for years. Can Nature endure these things? The poor fellow never sleeps at night. His nervous system is knocked to pieces. It's melancholy.

413. *To* MRS. ANNA C. STEELE

MS.: University of Texas.

[Box Hill]
November 25, 1868

Dear Mrs. Steele,

I wrote yesterday to Lady Wood;[1] but forgot to put 'Mickleham, Dorking' for my address.—When shall I see you? I am in town on Tuesday, or earlier if an appointment is made. If I see you I will take you into my inmost mercenary mind and own that with a good pot-boiler I may finish a novel and a poem I have in hand, and which are hanging back while I stagger in the columns of the Journals.—We were badly beaten in Southampton. I had measured, but poor Maxse had not, the far striking deep root of Toryism in the soil of the country. So it has amazed him and merely distressed me for his sake. But I have

---

412. [1] Years later GM told Witter Bynner this story of DGR's habits ('A Young Visit with George Meredith', *Virginia Quarterly Review*, Spring 1956, xxxii. 244). See also Letter 2512.
413. [1] No letter of this date has been found.

the machinery for a very good story. Are you writing? And have you ever read Omar Khayyám? He refreshed me after defeat. If you'll forgive his praising wine, he will do the same for you and take a place in your heart to nerve it for similar moments. Is it your Hozier who has married a Miss Lyon?[2] I met the bride's sister at Maxse's: a cold, blue-eyed, pleasant person vowed to spinsterhood and horses.—I have passed the dreariest time in the business of canvassing—and it's all lost! We could have bought the pure elector freely had we willed. The gentle Conservative had no such faint heart as we. He thought it a principle of the Constitutional party that Wealth should be represented . . . Adieu.

Your very faithful
George Meredith

414. *To* WILLIAM HARDMAN

MS.: Yale. Excerpts published: Ellis, pp. 256–7.

Box Hill
[December 16, 1868]

Dear Baron Tuck,

I find this, O my Lord!—that I must work like Cerberus and the man who invented umbrellas—who was it, Tuck? it was not Danaë, you know (forgive me for mentioning her if you think her improper; she was a king's daughter)—I say I must work with three heads to keep off the drenching shower of Christmas ripe fruits. Art unacquaint with 'em?—Sweet William! now then dost thou toweringly prove thy superior sweetness. For between thee and a bill there is, Lord God! so great a difference that one may justifiably presume the latter to be of the composition of the vindictive old squat harlot who hangs like a web on her bones, and flutters about herself like a bat (so loose is her putrid puckered black flesh!), the devil's mother! In very truth, Tuck, I do hate these bills. They are, I protest, the obscene artillery of the stinking pit. I am no sooner touched by one than I have sensations of the damned. It is a proof whence they come.

In January rather late, if you'll let me (is it to be both of us?) come on a *Friday night* and stay till Sunday it will exactly suit me, and be agreeable. My days in town are now Friday and I am detained till half past eight there. If I come to you this month I lose valuable time. Next month I am not so shackled—especially the last week of it.—

---

[2] Henry Montague Hozier, lieutenant in the 2nd Life Guards, was married to Eleanor Elizabeth Lyon on 6 Aug.

A word from you, friend!—Poor dear Poco seems to have had a complete floorer. I could well have taken him in and nursed him here, but he preferred going to his brother *ganz natürlich.*—Old Mr. Virtue went suddenly.[1] By the way, I hear that little Ellen Terry's death is matter of comment now rather widely.[2] John Smith of Mickleham Hall lies in a doubtful state.[3] The Allopaths gave him up. A Homoeopath came and is bringing him round. But the heart is diseased. There has been a paralytic stroke. Let's think of youth and health. How's Ethel? How's Nellie? Hail to the daughters of the Conservative! And by Jingo, Tuck, it's the paying side.

I have no more to say. I love thee. Give an obole or so of that to thy wife an thou dar'st, and believe me

Yours the Vagabond and Harper,
George Meredith

Nursery chronicle. Or call it 'The Standard' with the venom extracted.
Willie Maxse Willikins is well. He sings many songs. He works the wheelbarrow merrily. Ben yesterday cut his hind paw on a bit of some cockney's glass bottle on Box hill. Our cat is growing the handsomest in the world.

415. *To* MRS. BENJAMIN WOOD

MS.: University of Texas.

[Written on Garrick Club paper]
January 28, 1869
Dear Mrs. Wood,

I hold myself bound to you to-morrow at the usual hour.[1]

Most faithfully yours,
George Meredith

414. [1] George Virtue died at the home of his daughter, Mrs. Cotter Morison, on 8 Dec.
[2] An inaccurate report: she left the stage in 1868 and lived in retirement with the architect and theatrical designer E. W. Godwin for the next six years. She died in 1928.
[3] He died in the following year.
415. [1] For his weekly reading to her.

416. *To* ARTHUR G. MEREDITH

Text: *Letters*, i. 193–5 (dated 8 Feb. *1868*).

[Written on Garrick Club paper]
February 8, 1868 [error for 1869][1]

My dearest Boy,

I have carried about this piece of Club paper for a fortnight, having been intending to commence a letter to you there, and unable either to do that or to go on with it since. My time is occupied with work, and I am, or rather, have been, much distracted by affairs. My two months down with Captain Maxse was a dead loss of time to me. I never regret anything I am able to help him in, as you will believe, but that's another matter. We were badly beaten at Southampton, but I think it will be proved that bribery was done there. We on our side were not guilty of it, I know. It is a very corrupt place. It has been found by experience of the enlarged franchise that where there are large labouring populations depending upon hire (especially in a corrupt and languishing town like Southampton) they will be thrown into the hands of the unscrupulous rich. At all events this is one of the evils we have to contend against until the poor fellows know by enlightenment where their own interests lie and the necessity for their acting in unison and making sacrifices. Old Toryism has still a long spell of life in this country where the vitality has need to be strong in the centre of thick decay that won't be shovelled out.—I fancy Captain Maxse had to pay about £2000 for the attempt. He acted simply in a spirit of duty, that he might enter Parliament to plead the cause of the poor.—Our commercial failures of two years back still press on us. Artists and authors suffer particularly. But the strain will be over with me very soon. My novels have been kept back by having had to write on newspapers—the only things that paid.—So take this as a moral: don't think of literature as a profession. I believe you to have too much good sense.— Who are the kind people of the name of Nicolls whom you visit in Berne?—Mr. Burnand asked after you the other day, and sent his love to you. He still writes regularly on *Punch* and puts plays on the stage. He is a distant relative—is he not?—of M. Émile Burnand your master.[2]—I calculate that I shall be free in June, about the middle of the month, and may be with you then or later for a tour together. But would you prefer to go with the other fellows, and spend some days with me afterwards? I think it quite as well that you should not return

---

416. [1] GM had canvassed for Maxse in Oct.–Nov. 1868; hence this letter belongs to the year 1869, not 1868, as W. M. Meredith thought.
[2] Quite possibly: Burnand, in *Records and Reminiscences*, alludes to various French-Swiss relatives, though not Émile.

to England until you do so finally to begin your apprenticeship to some business—I don't mean trade, unless you like it, nor do I suppose that you much desire to come home at present. One of the nicest arrangements would be for Mama and Willie to go to some pleasant Norman or Biscayan sea-coast and welcome you there, and I could take you back to Berne. Tell me what your views are.—Perhaps if you are found to be getting too old for Dr. Müller's school,[3] you might remove to Dresden. Spain and Spanish, I fear, would be of no use to you in the future. How much I long to meet you! Keep pure in mind, unselfish of heart, and diligent in study. This is the right way of worshipping God, and is better than hymns and sermons and incense. We find it doubtful whether God blesses the latter, but cultivate the former, and you are sure of Him. Heed me well when I say this. And may God forever bless you, I pray it nightly.

417. *To* AN UNIDENTIFIED CORRESPONDENT[1]

Text: *The Autograph*, 1 Oct. 1912.

Mickleham, Dorking
April 5, 1869

I have received a letter from Fräulein von Hof, in which she asks me, on behalf of a friend doing some work of translation, for the copy of a novel of mine, called *Vittoria*. It failed to touch the English public, and may, though the deduction is not immediate, fail with the German. If you would care to look at it, to decide whether the sending of it over is worth the trouble, I will send it to you [etc.].

418. *To* FREDERICK SANDYS

MS.: Yale.

Mickleham
May 25, 1869

My dear old boy,
I called in Leicester Square[1] to know what was being done; found, with thanks to the God of the Jews, you were off; and the sample of

416. [3] Dr. Eduard L. G. Müller had become head of the school at Hofwyl in 1855.
417. [1] Possibly Baron Tauchnitz or Herr Asher.
418. [1] i.e. at the Garrick Club (Garrick St., Leicester Square).

His favoured ones as well. This comforted me.—I am myself so bothered I can barely work a bit.

Well, what do you think? I have drawn a capital horse in the Garrick Sweepstakes.[2] The Alderman. He cost me a sovereign. But I might have given fifty on a library that would not have occupied my thoughts more seriously and severely. The Alderman! Nobody has ever heard of him. So I have him all to myself. Now your Pretender (a good horse enough) is in comparison with my fellow worthy of his name. Why, you can't get more odds than 2 to 1 on Pretender. On The Alderman you can get 50,000 to 1. So if I stake 1, and win, I make a fortune on the spot, whereas you have only a few pounds to boast of. Dear old Sandys, don't let this chagrin you excessively. My luck always has been, always will be. My prayer was for a dark horse. I have the very darkest. Not a soul has ever seen him. Now your Pretender is in every body's mouth. The notion of the Alderman's running at all fills me with laughter. He is mine—my Audrey, 'a poor thing but mine own'.[3] To enjoy without creating envy is the philosopher's eternal aspiration. None envy me the Alderman: all the Garrick are grinding teeth at your possession of Pretender. (You have besides Dumpling, Whack-straw, Nova Zembla, and Pipkin—or some such names). A truce to the subject. I have broken your bad luck gently to you. If Pretender should—that's to say if The Alderman should let (I don't guarantee it) Pretender win, why—*in case* he should—communicate your address to Mr. George Farman, Steward of the Garrick, and he will send you a cheque for a poor £200. But, mind, my stake is so high that I can't give you any favour. I stand to win £50,000 on the Alderman.—In haste. I will write again on hearing from you, and more news. I have little, and no time for that amount. With all good wishes for you, and somewhat livelier as to your prospects (I hear nothing but high praises by the public of your Medea as being the noblest and best in the Academy).[4]

Yours affectionately,
George Meredith

[2] What follows is Meredithian chaff. Of the 22 horses that ran in the Derby next day, only Pretender (the favourite and winner), among the horses named by GM, had existence.

[3] Touchstone: 'A poor virgin, sir, an ill-favoured thing, sir, but mine own; a poor humour of mine, sir, to take that that no man else will' (*As You Like It*, v. iv. 60 ff.).

[4] 'Mr. Sandys exhibits two pictures this year, of which one, the "Medea", a dark woman of tragic aspect, surrounded by her "charms and spells", possesses an unusual interest; the other, the portrait of a lady holding hearts'-ease to her bosom—a painting careful and laborious in its handling, yet preserving the highest qualities' (*Annual Register*).

419. *To* J. HOLDEN[1]

Text (excerpt): Sotheby Catalogue (27 Nov.–6 Dec. 1889), p. 22.

[? Box Hill, Dorking]
June 25, 1869

... As to Edgar Poe's 'Raven', if it requires a Persian traveller to discover flaws in the claim for originality for the poem, I should think that Poe is pretty well defended by the accusation. ... Who is it pleads for originality of poetic ideas or conceptions? In lyrics the originality lies in the fervour of the execution. ... He gave the idea shape in a fine roll of organ music. ... You may be sure that it is no translation. ... Who makes so poor an attack on a piece of excellent, almost first-rate workmanship, is not worth a hearing for he does not know the nature of poetry. ... Read again Poe's life, of which the 'Raven' seems a direct expression. ...

420. *To* WILLIAM HARDMAN

MS.: Yale.

Box Hill, Dorking
Thursday, [July 15, 1869][1]

Honoured Friend!

I hope that next week on [blank]
The Right Hon: Lord William Field Marshal Potentissimus Baron Tuck, holder of the Privy Seals, *vis à vis* of Jones[2] etc. etc. etc. any day you may please to name, for two days in the week, I may come to you;—if you can take me? Marie is suddenly summoned to keep house for her Pa, owing to Betty Vulliamy's running away to Germany. She has been urging me to take her over to you all along, but I had my work. Now it's off my hands for a time. We want to let our house. I vacate it and start in about ten days, I hope, for Berne and Arthur, who is to go to a gymnasium at Stuttgart—*Euge, puer, sapias!*—Well, I being just free think first of coming to you on the chance too of seeing the Grand Mother.—

419. [1] Possibly James Holden, author of *Poetic Zephyrs* (privately printed, Bury, 1866).
420. [1] The visit promised in this letter for 'next week' had to be postponed and did not occur until 24–25 July. The dating of this letter is derived from a reconstruction of events mentioned in Letters 421, 422, and 423.
[2] i.e. Hardman's neighbour, Frederick Jones, who had taken over GM's lease on Kingston Lodge. Jones is referred to by biographers as a London solicitor, but I have found him listed in none of the directories. When his daughter Ethel married in 1890, she described herself as daughter of Frederick Augustus Jones (deceased), merchant.

Miss Holroyd's MS. I have reserved to give you some remarks which you may repeat to her.[3] Dallas[4] is so queer a fellow and hard to be caught that—and *Once a Week* so poor a place of exhibition—it had better not solicit admission there. This I say after hunting Dallas for the purpose. He is hiding, poor fellow! The Club is no longer a home for him.—I say! that last about the Prince of Wales![5]—Never mind. Oh! Give my love to D. T. and to her who BARE you, to the children thence resulting, and write hither, my Tuck.

Your loving
George Meredith

421. *To* WILLIAM HARDMAN

MS.: Yale. Published: *HP*, pp. 302–3, with inaccuracies.

Box Hill
Thursday, [July 22, 1869]

Dearest Tuck,

Here ends my store of note paper, to say I wish I could have come on Monday, but will come to-morrow Friday *night* at TEN for Saturday and Sunday. If you can't take me in, I must go to Jones all night! Adieu; we meet soon, so hang the quill—which has in fact ever begoosed me. I am bothered by a concatenation of circumstances.

Your loving (with love to all of you)

George Meredith

[3] In Apr. 1868 (*HP*, pp. 346–7) Hardman wrote to Holroyd that he was trying to get some manuscripts of Holroyd's sister Caroline published in the *Quarterly Review* and *OaW*. (This is the last month of Hardman's journal printed by Ellis, who says that it was continued to Aug. 1871 but that the pages toward the end are faded and indecipherable.)

[4] E. S. Dallas (1828–79), journalist and editor. Both Boase and the *DNB* say that he edited *OaW* in 1868, but William E. Buckler ('E. S. Dallas's Appointment as Editor of *Once a Week*', *Notes & Queries*, 24 June 1950, pp. 279–80), establishes the dates as from 1 Jan. 1868 to 31 July 1869.

[5] Gossip, no doubt. In Nov. 1866 Hardman (*HP*, pp. 175–6) had written that 'all sorts of stories are current about Albert Edward. It is said that he has frequent intercourse with various ladies, noble and gentle'. Currently the Prince's name was being linked with that of the Countess of Sefton.

422. *To* MRS. MARIE MEREDITH[1]

MS.: University of Texas.

[Written on Garrick Club paper]
Friday, [July 23,] 1869

My dearest love,

I kiss you and tell you what news I have briefly:—

Foakes all right.

Sir Alec gone down to Economic[2] to state the case.

Greenwood advises me to send the MS.[3] to him and he will forward it with a strong recommendation to George Smith, and he recommends me to rely on him as a fair dealing man, who is sure to make a liberal offer for what he likes. He says that I am likely to get more in this way. I am to name the day when the book will be ready and ask for what I want now. He thinks George Smith will probably send it at once.

So this appears favourable again.

I send the MS. next week.

Poco quite well. Greenwood fagged. Have not seen Morley. Janet[4] in town.

Mrs. Norton[5] will write of Lady Duff in the *Times* and *Pall Mall*, also in *Macmillan's Mag[azine]*:—I told Sir Alec I would have offered but could not suppose he or anybody would care to have a funeral flourish before such a public as ours. I would certainly avert it from myself. Oddly enough he seems rather to like it. I rarely meet a man who has the ghost of a notion of true pride. God bless you. Embrace our Willie for me.

Your loving husband,
George Meredith

422. [1] Marie was keeping house for her father during the temporary absence of Betty Vulliamy and was to remain with him during GM's holiday on the Continent or to join him at Nonancourt toward the end of it.

[2] The Economic Life Assurance Society, in which GM had insured his life in favour of Marie in the sum of £2,000 in 1864. The 'case' had to do with the marriage settlement and the payment of a possible bonus. (See following letter.)

[3] Of *The Adventures of Harry Richmond*, published serially in the *Cornhill* (Sept. 1870–Nov. 1871) and by Smith, Elder & Co. in book form, 1871.

[4] Janet Ross was in England and was on the point of leaving with her father for Egypt, where Lady Duff Gordon was, when a telegram came announcing her death on 14 July (*The Fourth Generation*, p. 181).

[5] Caroline Norton (1808–77), whose article on Lady Duff Gordon appeared in *Macmillan's Magazine* (Sept. 1869) and who was no doubt the author of a column about her in *The Times* (26 July). GM had met Mrs. Norton earlier at the Duff Gordons and was to remember her later when he was writing *Diana of the Crossways*.

Salute your Papa (after Mrs. Hopkins)[6] and uncle Frederick,[7] from me.

423. *To* MRS. MARIE MEREDITH

MS.: University of Texas.

Hall of Norbiton
Saturday morning, [July 24, 1869]

My dear love,

I yearn to be back with you. Unless I move on I regret what I have left.—All are well here, children improved in everything but appearance. Lord and mistress looking well, the garden greatly superior for the change. We have to dine to-night with Tuck's tenants. I have no dress clothes here! They have a pic-nic in Copsham woods on Monday and want me to stay. But I am, you know, engaged. My natural wildness comes on me furiously here; I find it impossible to remain longer than a couple of days. The thought of to-morrow is a burden, except that I hope to hear of you and Willie.—Mrs. Knowles sends her love and kisses to you. I call on the Jones' in the afternoon.— Tremendous yells of the pic-nickians. 'The bells go a ringing for Sarah—for Sarah etc.' beery cheering and salutations to the neighbourhood. I listen and look on with melancholy. The Conservatism of this house is blatant. Tuck 'would like to sign the warrant to incarcerate Gladstone in a lunatic asylum'.[1] The amateur of fiendish sport might enjoy introducing Fred Maxse to him, and shutting up the pair for an hour. Extremes are the revelling of senselessness in politics.—I hope that the letter I sent you yesterday relieved your mind to some degree. It appears possible that you may go to Nonancourt without thought of the morrow.[2] There I will join you soon, my love and dear heart.— Remember me to the household. I am ever your own

George Meredith

---

[6] Mrs. Hopkins was not one of the listed Mickleham residents. As Mrs. John Smith, of Mickleham Hall, was Annie Hopkins before her marriage, I should guess that this was her mother (or possibly sister-in-law), summoned from Londonderry by the death of Captain Smith, who died in this year.

[7] 'Uncle Frederick' is not mentioned elsewhere. He must have been an uncle on Marie's mother's side, in which case his last name was Bull.

423. [1] Hardman's attitude toward Gladstone may have been more vehement than usual because Gladstone had introduced at the end of March a resolution to disestablish the Church of England in Ireland. A compromise was reached on 22 July providing for disestablishment in May 1871.

[2] This statement is, I feel sure, tied to the marginal note at the end of this letter and to the sentence, 'Sir Alec has gone down . . . to state the case', of the preceding letter. Its connotation is almost certainly financial.

[Marginal note:]
Sir Alec has written to say that the policy and marriage settlement are in hands of lawyers to see whether bonus may be paid. According to Poco there is no doubt. So the Office *did* have my letter.

424. *To* MRS. MARIE MEREDITH

MS.: University of Texas.

[Written on Garrick Club paper]
Tuesday, [? July 27 or August 3, 1869]

Dear love,
    Nothing new—no harm.
    In haste

Your loving
George M.

425. *To* MRS. MARIE MEREDITH

MS.: University of Texas.

[Written on Garrick Club paper]
[? August 10, 1869]

My dear love,
    Only one word of adieu. I have no news. When Willie brings this to you I shall be running between Dieppe and Rouen and thinking of you both most heartily.[1] How glad I shall be to find you in Normandy on my return! Kiss my little lad. Give my love all round.
        I am
        Your own
        George Meredith

425. [1] GM was going abroad with Lionel Robinson (Poco), partly to see Arthur and partly to have a change of scene. Marie and Willie were staying with Mr. Vulliamy, and GM planned to meet them later at Nonancourt. Instead, however, she and her father went to Wales. As nearly as I can calculate, GM must have left England on 11 Aug.

426. *To* MRS. MARIE MEREDITH

MS.: University of Texas. Excerpts published: Sencourt, pp. 168–9.

Thun[1]
Friday night, August 14, 1869[2]

My dearest love,

I find the boy well in all general aspects.—The voyage from Newhaven to Dieppe was pleasant; the view of the Seine all the way to Paris delightful. Paris tempted me, but I left it at 3 in the afternoon by slow train—a trial of patience—to Dijon. A young Marsellais, pupil at St. Cyr, two Parisians, a *libre penseur* and his echo, a Poitevin,[3] an Irishman guiltless of any tongue but Irish, a bridal couple, and myself in the middle, but they were capital fellows. We talked incessantly, I translating for the Irishman. At Dijon I had to wait three hours dismally. The number of children in the pens for travelling cattle were amazing; not less than a dozen of these little ones at that hour of the night! and none of them fretful. The route by Pontarlier is decidedly the best which can be chosen for entering Switzerland, and how I sighed to have you with me going through the Jura! Even in a train the mountain air had such an effect on me that I forgot Sleep though it had been due to me two nights, and Dirt, which was thick on my face. Cool air, hot sun, high Alpine meadows, grey peaks, fir forest, and glimpses of valleys—think of this! So down by the lake of Neuchâtel, lovely; the Alps from the Oberland down to Mount Blanc exquisitely but not too fatally distinct. You know the lake; it is a good introduction to nobler ones. At Berne soon after twelve, where I had my first wash after leaving Mickleham; then to Hofwyl[4] at once. The school stands high on central ground with a great part of the Jura chain to the left, the Jungfrau, Breithorn, Eiger, Mönch, and others to the right and immediately in front wooded mountains and hills covered with beech[5] and fir, a good lake in the middle ground, and flax fields, clover meadows, and corn and pasture up to the gardens; water flowing everywhere. Dr. Müller was absent, Arthur out wandering. I talked with Miss Müller till the boy burst into the room, pale from excitement and crying with the adolescent's voice 'Oh! I am so glad; so

426. [1] About 20 miles SE. of Berne.
[2] The 14th was a Saturday in 1869. From the reference to 'Friday evening' in the body of the letter and from the chronology of later letters, I think the error was in the day of the week rather than month.
[3] i.e. native of Poitou or its capital, Poitiers.
[4] About 6 miles north of Berne.
[5] GM wrote *breech*.

glad! Come at last! You are come at last.!'—He tops Poco by half a head—(Poco is here.) He is still flat in the chest and carries his feet badly, bends his knee horribly. It seems that he bears fatigue very well. He has never any symptoms of weak health, and his eye is clear and honest. The fits of shyness have not quite left him. His common sense is all that we could wish. To-day I had a chat with some of his fellows who were bathing. They appeared to regret his going:[6] they say he has plenty of fun in him, and is one of their best swimmers and the one whose wind is best; he can keep longer under the water than any of them. Returning with him from the Hofwyl station, I found Poco in the train according to his programme. He did not anticipate seeing me until he reached Berne (if there at all) and betrayed more agitation than was perfectly dignified in him.—I have not seen Dr. Müller yet. I may come back through Berne on the way to Stuttgart. He has fully done his duty by the boy, and I want to thank him. The fellows I saw are gentlemenly lads, very fresh and merry; Italians, English (of a good sort), Brazilian, French. Their tour this year was over the Jura and round by Geneva and Vevey by Thun. Arthur went to meet them. Pursued by his ill luck he climbed the Niesen in a mist of drenching rain. They had shunned it. He had to sleep at the inn and return by himself.—Tell Betty[7] that on Friday evening, sitting on the Terrace at Berne eating an ice I had a view of the Jungfrau all blushing from foot to summit in the Alpenglow—a sight of the upper Heavens! After the Jungfrau had paled the Eiger took the glow and held it long.—Now here I am in Thun just over the Aare: it rushes out of the lake and by my windows. I write in Poco's room, Arthur just gone to bed. We start to-morrow for An der Lenk.[8] Thence after two days to Brieg and the Rieder Alp. May I find a letter in your dear hand at Brieg! If the news is good I know you share it; if not, I know you would soften it for me. In any case I am getting stronger and heartier for work. I want to hear of your movements. Kiss my darling Willie from his Papa. I write from An der Lenk next. God bless you, my love. I would write more of scenery etc. but the boy starts if one enters his room after he's asleep: we have a *chambre à deux lits*; so I won't disturb his rest. Remember me to all.

Your loving husband,
George Meredith

426. [6] Arthur was transferring to a school at Stuttgart.
  [7] Marie's sister, who had returned from her visit in Germany.
  [8] i.e. Lenk.

427. *To* MRS. MARIE MEREDITH

MS.: University of Texas. Excerpt published: Sencourt, p. 169.

> An der Lenk, Obersimmenthal
> Canton Berne
> August 16, 1869

My dearest Marie,

From Thun to this head of the valley by diligence yesterday, rain all day. To-day rain. Promise of it to-morrow. The mountain air is invigorating, but as yet I have had no exercise. And I see glaciers in front! The great high rock is veined with sinuous cascades. Now and then I see the Old Man of the Glaciers with one claw close to his cheek in the descent. Vapour comes boiling up to him. Imagine a broadish valley, green where an overflowing glacier stream has left it green, innumerable chalets on beautiful ascending pastures, pinewoods intervening; here and there a peak lifting out of the vapour to right and left, and in face the tremendous precipice of the Räzli and Wildstrubel glaciers, about three thousand feet of it visible, the sources of the stream pouring down volumes. I shall push through the rain presently and get at something.—Arthur condescends to be a little laughed out of his grimness. He was touched by Betty's remembrance of him and speaks of the kindness of your letters. He has muscle and good wind. His chest is rather flat but long. His appetite is always good, intelligence sound though in appearance slow. He has the art of making the least of himself. One must not ask too much of a cub, and he certainly is one. I don't worry him, and I find the abstention a luxury. His feet point East and West. His eyes are honest and sagacious.

I wonder whether you are having clear weather. Poco marks the time by Mickleham hours; you are about three quarters of an hour behind us. 'Now, Robin, the people at the Old House are on the point of breakfasting' etc. We look down on you from three thousand feet, and really look down on you contemptuously, but, alas, with umbrellas up! I can barely feel that I triumph over Betty. I shall as soon as the sun comes out—if he comes at all. He is trying.—Old Poco roars to me to give over writing. Adieu, my love, for the moment. In better times you will be with me. I long to be at Brieg that I may see your handwriting, and know what has happened, what I may hope for and you are doing and feeling.—Evening. After a fine walk to the Siebenbrunnen (seven springs), a fall of several cascades right under the glacier on a green alp. Poco and Slouch[1] strolled behind but say

427. [1] Arthur.

they saw as much as I. It was magnificent. The rain held off. There has been a great inundation that swept half the valley and made the mountain paths torrents. The delight of pattering in wet feet! I lost my way returning and had a scramble over rocks in a wilderness for an hour, enough to revive any fainting man. Tell Betty I think of her whenever a sunbeam lights a green summit jewel emerald. Here the chalets are exactly of the pattern of the toy Swiss houses seen in England. Under the glaciers are falls of water of vast length, and again lower falls, and still lower. As I mounted I had them in view from every aspect. I heard them thundering through the gorges one minute. The next they were foaming beside me, and presently shaking the harebell of the meadows above. The East Lyn[2] magnified fifty fold and multiplied by twenty would resemble it, with the addition of glaciers overhead and mountains all about.—A month of this every year would always keep me right. I felt the change as soon as I set foot on the springy Turf.—Now we have heavy rain again, a wet cloak over all.—Poco bids me tell you he had an offer (*à la mode Française*) of marriage in Tours. The person proposed by the *douairière* young and with money. He chose to evade it, but at my suggestion consents to place the affair in your hands. *Chose extraordinaire!* I discover in his room the History of Joseph and his Bretheren in six pictorial compartments, *et plus extraordinaire encore!* just above Poco's pillow is the Scene—*Mdme. Potiphar en deshabille et Joseph qui se retire honteux.* These things are predestinated.

Will you ask Mrs. Benecke[3] to give me a letter of introduction to her friend's husband or brother in Stuttgart, and will you enclose it to the Poste Restante, Stuttgart . . .? That is, if you get this before you (as I trust) start for France. After Brieg, Valais, I have no doubt that Stuttgart will be my next address. The weather is a dismal look out. This valley will soon be a swamp, and I fear I shan't get much walking anywhere in Switzerland. If not, I might as well be on the plains.

Have you written to Smithers?[4] Some informality in the cheque must have stopped it.

My own dear girl: how often I wish you were with me. At the Curhaus[5] here you would have plenty to entertain you, piano, dancing, toilettes.—We are at the inn but go up to drink the decayed egg liquified under the name of *eau sulfureuse.* I expect that the Riederalp

427. [2] East Lyn (Devon).
    [3] The Beneckes, who were of German extraction, had lived at Cleveland Lodge, near Box Hill, since 1868.
    [4] Unidentified. He may have been a banker or an officer of the Economic Life Assurance Society and had something to do with the expected bonus mentioned in Letter 423.
    [5] i.e. Kurhaus, the Pump Room.

whither we go next (Wednesday or Thursday) would suit you better. But in such weather as this what would suit you? I? It's hard to be away from you when I'm shut up fast, as I expect will be the case to-morrow. Adieu, my love, for the night. Give Betty my warm greetings and Sarah[6] and your father and a smother of kisses for Willie.

Your own
George Meredith

Arthur says he has nothing particular to say. I may thank Aunt Betty for the pencil. That's all. (I regret that it seems to be all, though he must mean more, I suppose).

Poco sends you his kindest regards. He can 'so far report favourably of my behaviour'. He has discovered in Arthur one whose capabilities in walking are only equalled by his own, the result of which is that any conversation between him and me has to be carried on with three ravines intervening. He bids me present his respects to Mr. Vulliamy and inform Mdme Pous[siel]que that he builds high hopes of a visit to her next year. He has met an adorable Nun 'sweetly pretty', she would not look at him.

428. *To* MRS. MARIE MEREDITH

MS.: University of Texas.

Brieg
Friday, August 20, 1869

My dearest Marie,

Arrived here to-day; found your two letters. And first, though not foremost, be careful to stamp your good letters sufficiently: via *France* is 5 pence; without a direction of the route, it is 3 pence: you put 4 stamps on one letter and I had to pay 1 fr. 50 cents. Your Thun letters were not at the Poste when I called before leaving. I have telegraphed for them. All over Switzerland the cost of a telegram is simply 50 cents. I shall get them at the Rieder Alp. Meanwhile I know only that George Smith meets my views.[1] You can therefore, using your own judgment, go to Nonancourt,[2] and pass two or three days with me in Paris. Do as you think best. I can't bear your having no outing this year. I presume that the house is not let, and probably will not be. The sole annoyance to me is the effect this will have on you.

---

[6] Marie's oldest sister, married to Commandant Henri Poussielque of Pont de Beau Voisin, Savoy, who was visiting her father.

428. [1] On the matter of payment for *The Adventures of Harry Richmond*.

[2] Marie's holiday at Nonancourt had always been dependant in part on the state of the family exchequer. As it turned out, she accompanied her father to Wales instead.

I am always wishing you were with me—especially (I am ashamed to say) when it rains. But don't accept this literally. The truth is, we have had hardly anything but rain since we left Thun. All day in a diligence, drenched in spirit, up the beautiful, dripping Simmenthal from Thun to Lenk, whence I wrote to you. Rain every day. Impossible to attempt the Rawyl pass. We returned on Wednesday to Zweisimmen (see Murray),[3] had a faint burst of sunshine, on foot, up the Sarine valley; rain again. By diligence next day (Thursday) to Château d'Oex, where Edward Chapman is staying *en pension*; at which one, I could not discover until the diligence was cracking whip and M'sieur-ing vociferously. The damp in the Lenk valley (I have told you of its glimpses of grandeur) must have seized me. I had a shivering fit and a great sweating all night on the way to Château d'Oex, at Saannen (Gessenay). Next day I was fit for nothing but a diligence—a low pitch. The descent from the heights to Aigle in the Rhone valley is superb in mountain beauty. Aigle is a place for the grape cure. We had rooms gorgeously furnished. Poco (this to mark his sagacity) would not ask the price, would not stipulate for a *chambre à deux francs* or more. We expected to have to pay four; behold the bill—1 fr. et demi! Cheap entertainment. To-day I am well. We came up the Rhone valley by rail and diligence. To-morrow we mount the Rieder Alp, after which I hope to have excursions on foot. I look on Snow Alps that look on Italy, like the mountains on Marathon.[4] It's hard to be so near and not to go. The Simplon road winds up under my eyes. If I resist, it will be manful, and pertain to the nature of your abstinence, my poor dear love. That's the bitter in the cup. The rain is no more than one of Nature's vagaries. By the way, to-day was fine; blue sky and very light clouds curled thin about the necks of the peaks, almost intolerable to see when being dragged at the jog-trot to bell-music. To-night the moon rests bright on the snowy Monte Leone—beckons me, I would say, but that the heart is such a wicked and mischievous interpreter. Why, just on the other side is the Lago Maggiore, my dear! I might go to sleep with the diligence flea (a feat I can now accomplish) and wake to look on it! However, we shall see what the Rieder Alp does for us. *Notre hostelerie c'est l'hôtel de l'aventure de Joseph and Mdme Potiphar.*[5] We travelled from Aigle with a Provençal bride and bridegroom; the latter with no manners, the former of the handsome Southern type. Adventures of our own, none whatever! Arthur stirs a little in his stiff chrysalis; a little. On essential points he is sound. His style is

<hr>

428. [3] Murray's guidebooks were the standard ones of the day.
[4] *Don Juan*, Canto III:
> The mountains look on Marathon—
> And Marathon looks on the sea;
[5] See preceding letter.

merely backward. I think your Papa will like him. He wants energizing and being pushed and polished. His eye is too conscious, his feet not enough so, and his neck rather like the goose's. He is astonished that these things should be seen. I don't bother him. He declares he is happy, and I must accept his statement. Thank Mrs. Benecke for her great kindness in sending the letters of introduction. I don't doubt that they will be of service. And kiss my Willie and bless him for his nice picture of a foreign railway train; tell him I know it well and can judge of its truth to nature; but I want him in his next picture to draw a man with a horse beside it, and Papa looking out.— Calculate that I stop a *week* in this neighbourhood, then over the Furca (by the Rhone glacier) down the St. Gothard to Flüelen, across the Lake of Lucerne; thence to Zürich, Lake Constance and Stuttgart. So, write, my love, to Lucerne, Poste Restante, *three* days after receipt of this; and afterwards as soon as you like to Stuttgart, with the latest news. Give my love to all at the Old House. Tell Betty imagination has not been stirred, so I cannot write to her yet. I am anxious to know where you will go, if you do not go to Nonancourt. If to our cottage, Gilbert[6] *must* sleep there. I will make it good to him. I suppose the Thun letters will tell me whether you have been able to send the cheque to Clutton.[7] I send my acceptance of the bill, according to George Smith's directions, to Mr. Enoch,[8] and he will stamp it, and pay the money into my bankers.

Your lover and husband,
George Meredith

[Marginal notes:]

Arthur is in bed. 'Give her my love and thank her for sending me hers. You can give Willie my love also.' He has written to the Chapmans at Château d'Oex.

An idea!—Could not Poco with his sagacity, his noble connections, his vast experience and skill in managing affairs, cut out D ... W ...h?[9] —Poco, receiving the hint delicately, is willing. I think it would be the best thing possible. Meditate. Kind to young ones, scrupulously honest, an excellent supervisor!—surely a good suggestion.

---

[6] Unidentified; possibly one of the servants at the Old House.
[7] See Note 3, Letter 388.
[8] Identified by Booth, op. cit., p. 181 n. as manager of Smith, Elder & Co.
[9] This 'cryptogram'—at a guess—refers to one of the Waughs, probably a brother of Frank. I regret my inability to identify the object of this little plot.

429. *To* MRS. MARIE MEREDITH

MS.: University of Texas. Excerpt published: Sencourt, p. 170.

Rieder Alp
August 24, 1869

My dearest love,

We have been up here since I last wrote to you. On Saturday we mounted the Alp, about seven thousand feet above the sea's level, a long pull but amazingly pleasant, from meadow to fir copse, stony desert to meadow, and everywhere brooks descending with a carol of the mountain. The Weisshorn, the Matterhorn, the Monte Leone, Ofenhorn and others, soon became visible, such a sight! The clear thin air revived me exquisitely. I thought of you all the while. Would you be willing to make a three or four hours' ascent? If you would, this is the place for you. We look fronting Italy, but for the curtain of mountains. The rare cloud I see hangs above the Lago Maggiore. It is an Italian sky. Daily noble weather. The scene is one of the grandest on earth, delightful to every sense, perfectly sublime. From my window in the morning I gaze on the Monte Leone, the Fletschhorn and the Mischabel, peaks, bastions and slopes of snow, with the glacier crawling below. The Monte Leone is just in face, a pure snow line rolling to Italy, and dropping sheer to the North, as we observe it. What wonders of beauty are done between the light of heaven and mountain Alps! Now they are ghostly white; a little previously they were warm grey; just before of the colour of the Alpine rose (I send a sprig, the last of the season); at midday they have a shadowy richness, velvet, faint, half melting; they come trembling into view at dawn, the cloud round their necks, the impalpable whiteness scarce to be realized, until the sun rises and throws them out in air firm and majestic. We climb the Riederhorn hard by and have the whole panorama as far as the lower ridges of the beautiful and loftiest Weisshorn, a clear point of snow. Lying there on dwarf juniper, and harebell and smaller gentian, beside us innumerable herbs breathing sweet scents in the great heat, but fanned by freshest air, we have the feast of Alps. Behind is the Aletsch horn, underneath the great Aletsch glacier fifteen miles in length. We were on it yesterday. Fortunately we had the landlord's son, young de Seppibus, who came armed with cord and hatchet—otherwise we should not have fared well. As it was we were for three hours at fault in the midst of enormous crevasses which we had to leap at some peril thrice magnified by the depths, occasionally *en califourchon* along *arêtes* narrow as a poodle's nose, hideous—no lovely green chasms on both sides. The Sagacious one[1] led us into it.

429. [1] Poco.

'He knew the glacier.' But the glacier of one year is not that of another. Among these enormous seracs[2] you have no outlook. You are in the midst of the ice-world, hear nothing but the glacier rivulets and the chance fall of an ice-block into the abyss. Lunched on our dilemma. The idea of returning and having to do over again what we had done was detestable, the question being whether we really could do it. By the aid of the axe and rope we scaled half a dozen serac ridges and finally reached an unexpected ice-valley where all was open to the moraine near the mountain shore. The adventure was pleasant when over. Alpine men avoid these seracs scrupulously. Altogether it was five hours of very hard work, pretty nearly as much as is given to one of the lesser Alps. Arthur behaved excellently. In my anxiety for him I lost my own nerve, but he was quite cool and took everything as it came. He has crossed glaciers twice on his expeditions, and has a sure foot and perfect self-command in danger.—The Sagacious was right in bringing us to the Rieder Alp. The host is a gentleman, his wife a portly kindly woman. We live *en pension* at five francs a day, taking simply breakfast and dinner, both good. Tea as good as at F̶l̶i̶n̶t̶ [marked out] Mickleham, coffee, chocolate, French omelette, eggs, meat, and mountain strawberries in profusion. At dinner fish from a translucent lake, where I bathe morning or afternoon, soup, ham, cutlets, mutton, marmot, cream with fruit. So, my darling, once up here this vigorous air which would make you fall up[on] anything would prepare you for relishable feeding. We are on a plateau of meadows. The climb on either side is over heath and juniper, the descent through firwood and meadows.—My hand is still so scorched from the day on the glacier that it aches, and we have no glycerine. I knocked the nails all out of one side of my boots.—Arthur swims powerfully. On the whole he would be a very good fellow if he were somewhat more expressive of himself. He goes to his room every evening to write alone. He prefers to walk alone, find out his own way and rarely cares to converse with people unless there is a joke or a story current, or the subject is philology. Touch on that and he is immediately attracted. His voice is thick and deep, appetite always prodigious, and at dinner he likes his wine. He has asked several times about Fred Patton.[3] So long as he does not feel that he shows to disadvantage he shows to advantage, or moderately. As soon as he gets shamefaced nothing goes right with him.—Placed here between the Bel Alp and the Œggischhorn,[4] the Rieder Alp is almost unknown to tourists. We have the house to ourselves, and are infinitely better off

---

[2] Irregular pinnacles of ice on a glacier, formed by the intersection of crevasses (*Oxford Universal Dictionary*).
[3] A son of Mrs. John Smith by her first husband, Joseph Patton. [4] Or Eggishorn.

than if we were at the favoured haunts. Our view is as good, our situation superior, our host and feeding much to be preferred.—Give my love to Betty, your Papa and all at the Old House.—As to George Smith, he simply demands the security of my name.[5] If he paid down the money without it, he would bind me equally, but would not secure himself. Should we not come to terms, I refund the money just as I should have to do if there were no acceptance given. Don't you see? As a man of business he could not act otherwise. We leave the dear Rieder Alp on Monday, Poco to Lausanne, I to the glacier du Rhône, Andermatt, Lucerne (where I hope for a letter—I fear it's vain to expect another up from Brieg!), Zürich, Friederichshafen on Lake Constance, and Stuttgart.

The moment I have settled Arthur I start for home, treating myself to a day in Paris. I shall write from here before I start. Tell Betty I have her with me constantly in spirit and would chronicle the fact to her personally—will, when I am at the proper pitch to make her acutely sensible of it—shed the Alps on her and breathe some of the keen sweet air of our region. You write most freshly and nicely to give me comfort.

The Sagacious desires to be remembered to you and all at the Old House. He marks the time morning and evening. Our eight o'clock is your 1/4 past 7. Says he, 'Pierpoint[6] is now handing round potatoes'. At half past nine we are abed. You have at that period just finished dinner. The nights are cold, but bracing; not the cold of the underworld. Kiss and hug my Willie. How he would run and laugh up here! What feasting of milk and wild strawberries and raspberries for the little lad! God bless him. Arthur enjoys stories about him.

Now good-bye, my dearest. It is nine p.m. Adieu.

Your loving husband,
George Meredith

430. *To* Mrs. Marie Meredith

MS.: University of Texas.

Rieder Alp
Saturday, August 28, 1869

My dearest Marie,

I have been here a week, a week of Italian skies on the green Alp, with much climbing and descending, the sweetest air in life to breathe, and very pleasant quarters. We leave for Lausanne, Lucerne, Zürich,

---

429. [5] In return for advance payment for *Richmond*. In the preceding letter GM says that 'George Smith meets my views', but two sentences later in this letter he implies that the terms were not definite. In any event, the MS. was incomplete. (See Letter 431.)

[6] Butler at The Old House.

Friederichshafen, Stuttgart, on Monday, halting perforce a day at each place—a night, I mean. At Lucerne I shall hear from you. You will write also to Stuttgart, I hope.—Yesterday we walked to the Merjelen See,[1] a lake under the Œggischhorn, about 13 miles distant; up rocks and down, and over the glacier to where the great Aletsch breaks abruptly in cliffs of ice and a beautiful blue water carries little bergs of ice on it. Four glaciers are visible around it and an infinite number of crags and snowy peaks. There is winter, summer on the rocks. Arthur walked remarkably well. Poco, behind us as usual, knocked over a grouse with a sagacious fling of a stone. We were anxious about him until he was observed from the inn-doors waving his trophy. We have had the inn almost entirely to ourselves, so sheepishly do the English go in flocks. The Œggischhorn hotel is not half so well situated, yet they insist upon herding there, while the Rieder Alp is open to them, and they have to sleep two, three and four in a room. In the morning I walk out to one of the falling brooks, strip and get a cascade over my shoulders. Then after breakfast comes the expedition. Returning home I bathe in a delightful clear lake, always in view of the great Alps I have named to you, and whose beauty is transcendant, inexhaustible. We dine at five, and pace up and down till bed-time under Italian stars, unimaginably bright and large. Unlike the Riffel, the Rieder Alp enjoys a perpetually balmy air. The sun is on it from 5 a.m. to 5 1/2 p.m. For shade you descend half a mile to the fir forest. My morning bath is quite warm, and at night I can watch the stars for a while in my night-gown without the slightest warning of cold. Once up here how happy you and Willie and Betty would be.

———Sunday, Aug. 29th—I shall probably post this from Lausanne. The clouds have come.

Tuesday

Arrived at Lausanne.

To-morrow to Lucerne.

In great haste,

Your loving
George Meredith

P. S. Disaster with the ink-bottle!—

430. [1] Märjelen- or Mærjelen-See.

431. *To* MRS. MARIE MEREDITH

MS.: University of Texas.

[Stuttgart]
Friday, September 3, 1869

My darling Marie,

Arrived in Stuttgart late last night. But I find only one letter from you here—an old one, and I am chagrined.—I kept away from Lucerne, to save money, telegraphed for the letter to be sent to Zürich, on the line of my route, where I received it very gladly. Here I have a letter from Morley, kind and cheerful. I go to see Professor Zeller to-day at 6 p.m.[1]—I will date my next letters to the Post Office, Tenby.[2] Of course I could not but desire you to have the pleasure offered, though I think you should petition to pay the cost of journey. If it is rigidly disallowed, as that royal traveller and indulgent Papa will probably make it, then devote the expense to some personal outfit . . . a silk dress or so, and let me see you in it when I arrive, my sweet! —We quitted Poco at Lausanne, where he is in *pays de connaissance,* anxious to hear your opinion of his marital prospects . . . exceedingly anxious.[3] Our departure from the Rieder Alp was mournful. I will talk to you of that noble height when we meet. When? How I wish for it! My poor Arthur is not a particle of a companion. And besides I want my half-myself. I miss my Willie, long to hear him. The Alp did me good; a week more of it would have embellished the work, but I was impatient to settle the boy, and see your handwriting. To be out of the world is delightful, so long as the world continues to show itself attached. Otherwise it is uncomfortable coquetry.—I am much better and begin to feel vigour of brain.—I think I shall walk through the Neckarthal to Heidelberg, drop by rail on Homburg, walk a day on the Rhine, then to Paris (Hotel Choiseul, Rue St. Honoré) when I will make an expedition to Jouy, and home by Southampton to Fred,[4] if he will take me in. If not, Morley will.—The weather broke up after our descent to the valley. Lake Leman seemed to have resolved to a liquid for the sour scribes of Geneva to dip their quills in. On Lake Constance it was beautiful. Touch the German shores, and you feel that adieu to Switzerland has been said for you. A spirit of beer broods all along them; a heavy, good-natured, lumbering spirit lifting half an eyelid on

---

431. [1] Arthur was to lodge at the house of Professor Zeller while attending the local gymnasium.

[2] In Wales, where Marie was going with her father and other members of the family on holiday.

[3] Presumably a reference to the cryptogram in Letter 428.

[4] Maxse.

Alp and Heaven.—This little city of Stuttgart is really laudable, so civilized that ladies can go to the Opera alone. The streets are open and wide, the houses well built, monotonously modern, the ecstasy of architects, Hausmannish.[5] Park, public gardens, bands playing daily, or drumming like harmonious draymen rolling beer-barrels. Opera from 6 to 9 1/2 p.m. Theatre from 5 to 7 1/2. To bed early, up with daylight. They dine at 12 1/2. What could be better for Arthur? I hope he likes it, but he is inexpressive.—Write to me 'Poste Restante, Mainz am Rhein, Deutschland'. Afterwards to Paris. Coming for you to Tenby suggests the cost of travelling by English railways. I think I will hold out. What do you say? Isn't it best?—I am very anxious to finish *Richmond* and be at fresh work, which threatens to boil in me. I find I *must* have occasional movement, to be fecund.—I trust Clutton has received cheque, with excuses. Use your own cheques, as you require them, and if more, your Papa will advance, doubtless. Give my love to Betty. The letter I owe her leaps like a porpoise (say) in the Ocean of my bosom. Unhappily it is as yet not much more acceptable than a porpoise would be. So I withhold it.—Hark you! The man at the post office here denied that he had any letter for me except Morley's. Streaming tears and knocking knees on ground, I begged him to look again and again. He consented grimly. 'Why, mein Herr, who could tell that *that* was your name', said the wretch, holding up my wife's clear print of her husband's identification. Hug, kiss, and bless my Willie boy. Tell him I am always thinking of him, and love him. The Gordons[6] shall be thanked by me if I see them the day I am at Homburg. I shall simply *avoid* Eva. A girl who goes on the Continent *directly* to a gambling place, is not one that I care to recognise.

Supposing that your plans change, write to Tenby Post Office for your letters. I shall not, I think, be here beyond Monday next (6th) when this will reach you. I would it were I doing so. God bless you and give you to my arms very soon.

Your own

George Meredith

---

[5] i.e. after the manner of Baron Georges Eugene Haussmann, Prefect of the Seine (1853–70), who was responsible for much of the transformation of Paris into a magnificent capital.

[6] Dr. James Alexander Gordon and his family, who lived at Pixholme, half a mile away from the Merediths. Lady Butcher (*Memories of George Meredith*, N.Y., 1919, p. 6) says that Dr. Gordon had lived at Weimar in his youth, had known Goethe personally, and had served in the Austrian army. He had been physician to the London Hospital (1828–44) and was now living in retirement. Eva, mentioned in the following sentence, was his daughter, and in spite of what GM says of her here, she was invited to be god-mother to his daughter less than a couple of years later.

432. *To* MRS. MARIE MEREDITH

MS.: University of Texas.

Baden (with the dregs of my ink-
bottle)
Thursday, [September 9, 1869]

My own love,

I have left Arthur at Stuttgart in very good hands, I am sure. Professor Zeller is a straightforward man, pleasing; his wife, with a quaint mask of an almost noseless face, simple, good-humoured, heartily devout. She was a Fräulein Pichler, known as a writer of minor pieces of verse and prose. Three other boys are under their charge, apparently well-conducted lads, younger than Arthur. He has a capital room *au quatrième*, airy, with a fine view over the city, the hills and the open country. What could be better for him? We went together to the Director of the Gymnasium, who examined Arthur in Latin, and vehemently condemned the private school system of tuition, in which he is right, as we must bear in mind regarding our Willie. Boys of eleven here do Latin Composition of very good quality. It is not Arthur's fault that he is behind in it. He was the head at Hofwyl, and promises, and really wishes to study. If I had removed him to Stuttgart earlier it would have been better for him. The Zellers take long walks together; both come of a line of *pasteurs* and do no shame to the kind. I dined with them just before leaving on Tuesday. In Stuttgart is much eating and drinking of a good sort, no excesses; a fat, well-to-do, kindly, well-mannered, decorous, moral people. The morality is, I believe, actual. Military bands enliven the streets by day. At eight in the evening the inhabitants all shut themselves up to eat their suppers, and are no more seen. I am told that in winter there is evening visiting among the aristocracy. Ladies may at all times walk alone, take their dinner or coffee alone at the restaurants. They are but shyly looked at, never stared at:—The people are too thoroughly bent upon replenishing. I have fancied that in several respects Stuttgart would suit the Vulliamys. It reminded me of the dear Old House, minus Pierpoint, who might be supplied by reflection on the state of one's purse.— Here at Baden, the French world has ceased to reign. I met young Sartoris,[1] the gentle singer; he rides in the steeple-chases yearly and on this occasion came down a cropper with his horse, also with his money. A most lovely place for the Deuce to make his nest in! A little water traverses the valley, great swelling hills of fir and beech all about,

---

432. [1] ? The son of Adelaide Kemble and Edward Sartoris. (See Note 4, Letter, 404.)

beautiful meadows, every variety of green colour—especially in the forms of humanity playing at roulette. Last night the Grand Duke's birthday was celebrated by fireworks. The peasantry flocked in by thousands to gaze, and then they had an edifying peep at the Tables, where money made as big a blaze for as short a period from this and that poor devil's pocket. Perhaps the Grand Duke will be instructed by Prussia as to the advisability of regaling his subjects in future with this last exhibition. The towns under Prussian rule are happily doomed to close Hell-gates. I am encouraged to walk here, as the weather is lovely, the scenery enchanting. To-morrow I go to Homburg for a couple of days, to get a letter from you and money from the bank to take me home. I hope I shall see the Gordons.—These towns without you beside me are not enjoyable, nor is travelling at all so apart from you unless I have my pack on my back and pass uninterruptedly through fresh scenes. As soon as I stop I look for my wife and love.— I think I shall remain in Paris two days, and then to Fred, from whom I shall probably hear at the Hotel Choiseul. Will you write to me there? Your idea of putting my dress clothes in 'Borthwick'[2] was excellent. I will write word, if they are wanted.—The sweetest sight in the world must be our Willie pattering in the sea-water. Don't envy me, or if ever you do, think how much I am envying you, and him. My outing has freshened me, otherwise I should groan over time lost. The jewel of the time—its pure flower, rather, was the Rieder Alp. Baden grows so bedevilled in one's mind by the play of the gold pieces that it's impossible to think of it pleasurably. But my object in coming was to observe certain points that will be of use.—It won't be long before we are settled on our Box hill slope, which I have quitted for a while to appreciate it. I trust that your Papa made the long journey without much sense of fatigue. Give my warm love to Betty and to him, and kiss my Willie and say I am always wishing to hear his voice. I would pay the 'organ man' largely to play at my door in the morning. Your second letter to Stuttgart was sunshine. God bless and keep you, my own darling. Let me have a letter awaiting me in Paris.—I go out for a walk, then dine under green leaves, whereof a yellow in my soup tureen to a certainty, then a glance at the shabby *beau monde* and demireps round the *Conversationshaus*, to bed and early away in the morning.

Your husband and lover,
George Meredith

No more blue ink!

[2] ? In the luggage of Algernon Borthwick, editor of the *Morning Post*.

433. *To* MRS. ANNA C. STEELE

MS.: University of Texas.

Mickleham, Dorking
November 4, 1869

My dear Mrs. Steele,

I will read the novel[1] to an end: and you shall pay for your pleasant flattery by hearing me speak out.—It was the only portion of *Once a Week* that I could fix attention on.

I was startled by the bold cleverness, taken by the power here and there, pained by seeing the novelist's incontestible art run off to a torn fringe when the business was to weave an entire framework.—This may have partly been an effect of the appearance of the work in numbers. But it seemed to me you must be writing for numbers—a weekly issue for the *Once a Week*. My judgment was that if you had the whole story in your mind, you had not, previous to the conception, laid out your mind for the story. The writing struck me as better than the theme, and the novel seemed to me to be composed too much of detached sketches,—exquisitely true, whether descriptive of Belhus or Brighton, a coquette, or a frank and fiery girl, or an aristocratic gamin —but they lay in lumps, and the story was told in tableaux.—I fancied you had not waited for the mastering emotion to carry you off on a tide.—But *en revanche* I read diligently so long as the story appeared, and sufficiently to be sure that you want nothing but training to be among the first of our novelists.

Now, if you have faith of any durable sort in the virtue of my judgment, confide to me the scheme of your next story. I may then really be able to help you. Meanwhile I will finish the 3rd volume of *So Runs*, and apologize, or renew the blows. Please present my warm regards and respects to Lady Wood. I would ask permission to come to you for a day but am too busy to stir—preparing matter for your criticism.

Your most faithful
George Meredith

433. [1] *So Runs the World Away*, published in 1869 by C. & H. after its serialization in *OaW*.

434. *To* MRS. ANNA C. STEELE

MS.: University of Texas.

Mickleham, Dorking
[*c.* November 11, 1869]

My dear Mrs. Steele,

My wife cannot come; she bids me say she regrets it. I have the option, but I let Eltham[1] claim my spare time, justly as well as pleasantly. —I find that I had read your novel[2] nearly to a close—and what a close! The writer's voice grows hushed, the solemn sentences follow one another like—Oh! too too like the melancholy hired men of lugubrious drapery and pendent nose, the offspring and flower of sad ceremonials in our good England, without whom where would be the moral of the close? You have indeed pounded it on the head of your public. Dear Me! the moral may be said to have been forced into one's system. 'The Creator, Preserver, Destroyer, Regenerator, God, the wind, the sky, the grave'—all these tremendous agents lead off a lay figure husband and an ingrained coquette.—However, Douglas forgives without preaching anything like a sermon as long as Mr. Tennyson's blameless King over his prostrate Queen;[3] that's a gain. Now you pretend to say your coquette is repentant. The funereal strain necessitated some such show of a bowed head and so forth, but you know as well as I do that nothing but decayed teeth, poverty, baldness and similar trials would affect the woman you sketched.—Write for the public, you reflect the public taste. And don't make points; it's the same as the cocking of the eye in an actor. Lord Orme alludes to the pair of greys when the bridal couple start;—quite possible, and sufficient without Lady Diana's— 'Do you mean—?'—Several instances of this. They catch the military groundlings—whom else?

Azalea, good at the commencement, thins away in sentiment.— The opening chapters are the best; you had warm stuff about your heart there. But no clear view in the head, I opine. Lady Diana you have thoroughly well in hand, and show 'her paces' capitally. She is too much in the foreground because you have really nothing but a short tale to tell, and the unhappy reader who may never never hope for that reserve of kisses which is the perceptible centre of her attractiveness, does—pardon him—tire of her.—Cleverness, literary faculty, glimpses of a power of humour, at present rather hard, and the capacity for simple pathos, as well as a trained observation superior to that of many

---

434. [1] Where Mrs. Benjamin Wood lived.
  [2] *So Runs the World Away,* to which much of the remainder of the letter relates. The various names mentioned are those of characters in the novel.
   Tennyson's 'Guinevere' had first been published in 1859.

reputed good writers, your novel shows throughout.—I could discourse of it more to your satisfaction, but the misuse of your ability in producing *ad captandum* effects has irritated my pen, and I have allowed it to run its way because I believe in your talents as well as your generosity. Those who have the honour to know you at all can have no doubt about both.

If you know not De Stendhal's *Chartreuse de Parme* and *Le Rouge et le Noir*, get them and study them. They are the models of a clear style and the intelligent manipulation of character. The public may go hang for him—even the *French public*. His machinery is just a trifle intrusive perhaps, but it is a running analysis, the men and women move on— Here is the end of my paper sheet—'So runs' and I feel as mournfully verbal, or verbally mournful. Do pardon me! or don't, and attack me for I have a residue of hostility to the enchantress who *could* be of the true sort and preferred to attire herself in the conventional garb to tickle the English ear and captivate the English eye to the sacrifice of her art. Do thou use the quill's nibbed end and not the feather!—And there ends my impudence.

Your most faithful
George Meredith

435. *To* MRS. ANNA C. STEELE

MS.: University of Texas.

Mickleham, Dorking
November 18, 1869

My dear Mrs. Steele,

You treat Horace's *vir bonus* so much as he deserves to be treated, that he tries to be intelligible further on the points you contest.

Lady Di[1] may very well bow her head. The fault of the scene is that the author's tone grows so very overwhelming on the occasion. The scene should have been dramatized. You played a flageolet over it. Had it been Azalea and Thurston, the critical reader would have felt it to be proper. The poetical tone does not harmonize with the hard coquette and the vague figure of a husband. There is a tone that would have done—such as Göthe sometimes assumes towards humanity, or such, say, as a handsome clever woman might feel towards guardsmen who have been admiring and have amused her. The tragedy of Dolls can be supremely touched, but it must be handled with a mixture of

435. [1] See preceding letter.

irony and tenderness in which neither irony nor tenderness is perceptible.—

'The wind and the sky' are often in harmony with human desolation; but this painting of them just at the right time has become an author's trick. It should never be done but with the utmost lightness of touch, and again it was incongruous, I say, to wave the Heavens in their solemnity over Lady Di. Here two lines might have been allowed, just for a poetical suggestion to the reader's mind if you felt it in your own. —You will certainly do good things with the open soul you have to aid your shrewd head, and diligence.

Your most faithful
George Meredith

436. *To* MRS. ANNA C. STEELE

MS.: University of Texas.

Garrick Club
[? October–December 1869][1]

My dear Mrs. Steele,

If I can escape from Piccadilly for ten minutes I will come gladly; but I have to go out of town to-night:—and this week I cannot be with you at Rivenhall to pay my respects to Lady Wood. You will I am sure excuse a man heavily burdened with work. I am

Most faithfully yours,
George Meredith

P.S. I recommend an aluminium waistcoat. The Emperor wears one.— Also a line from Shakespeare. Nothing would arrest the dramatic hand so effectually.[2]

436. [1] Of the years possible for this letter—1867–70—I regard the suggested date as the most likely.
[2] Whether this postscript concerns Mrs. Steele's translation of Hugo's *L'Homme qui rit*, about half of which had appeared serially in the *Gentleman's Magazine* by Oct. 1869, or another of Mrs. Steele's works, I am unable to say.

437. *To* WILLIAM HARDMAN

MS.: Yale. Excerpts published: Ellis, p. 257.

Box Hill
December 19, 1869

Your letter, my dear Tuck, reached me in London and smelt of the old time like moss of the woods, with here and there a lurking violet; likewise I caught in it glimpses of wood nymphs, and of a Faun that did wantonly trip and give between whiles a smack to his hinder chaps. Needs not to say how refreshed I was. A breath from those coverts is eternally reviving. We live, we battle, but there grow our medical herbs.—Art yet a Knight? For me is no distinction. As for the world it has wagged till it waggles. Opposite the Memorial to the Great and Good,[1] I have meditated on Princes, Peoples, and Widows. We were lodged at Prince's Gate.[2] Anon—anon.—Marie proposed to come on (by proposition) to you. But I said, not till my work is off my hands. Will you take us for a couple of days towards the close of February? You should see Willie Godson in his sailor's suit. He is a most flourishing fellow. Of Arthur I have good news to tell you. I had him with me (old Poco a third) on the Rieder Alp: then away to Stuttgart, where I left him housed with a Professor to attend the Gymnasium. He writes quaintly of the Suabian folk, is marching well forward in Latin and Greek, I believe really working. He is bold on the ice and endures fatigue well; projects his head and chin, and turns out's feet too much, but that will mend. The lad is evidently a shrewd observer. His idea of a profession is, he says modestly, that of Philologer.—Alack, the *Holy Grail*.[3] Did you ever read such lines? The Poet rolls them out like half yards of satin. They look and taste cud-chewn. The figures are Dresden China. If he has hit the mind of his age, as it seems, the age too has hit him and knocked spontaneity out of him. But both are worthier than they show. Gold, the go-between, the abominable Sir Pandarus, has corrupted them.

I do gravely desire to exchange talk with you, Tuck, and long for the moment to lay down pen and frisk a space. Kiss your family all round, I beg you, in my name—but none else. Willie greets you reverently. Marie sends a kind word to you all, and I salute you according to your three characters,—the Justice with round capon

437. [1] i.e. Prince Albert.
    [2] The address of Lady Lawrence. (For the Lawrence family, see Biographical Section, pp. 1720–21.)
    [3] Tennyson's *The Holy Grail and Other Poems* was published late in 1869 (reviewed in the *Saturday Review*, 25 Dec.).

lined, the host of an exceeding warm embrace, and (between them, seen by few) the florescent son of Pan. Adieu.

Your loving
George Meredith

438. *To* FREDERICK A. MAXSE

Text: *Letters*, i. 197–8.

Mickleham
December 19, 1869

My dear Fred,

Morison will take notice of your pamphlet:[1] he says he cannot do so more than incidentally, as he would have done if you had written a book. . . . Greenwood has been (as one can conceive possible) too busy to read anything.—The *Holy Grail* is wonderful, isn't it? The lines are satin lengths, the figures Sèvres china. I have not the courage to offer to review it, I should say such things. To think!—it's in these days that the foremost poet of the country goes on fluting of creatures that have not a breath of vital humanity in them, and doles us out his regular five-feet with the old trick of the vowel endings—The Euphuist's tongue, the Exquisite's leg, the Curate's moral sentiments, the British matron and her daughter's purity of tone:—so he talks, so he walks, so he snuffles, so he appears divine.—I repeat with my Grannam,—to think!—and to hear the chorus of praise too! Why, this stuff is not the Muse, it's Musery. The man has got hold of the Muses' clothes-line and hung it with jewelry.

But the 'Lucretius'[2] is grand. I can't say how much I admire it and hate the Sir Pandarus public which has corrupted this fine (natural) singer. In his degraded state I really believe he is useful, for he reflects as much as our Society chooses to show of itself. The English notion of passion, virtue, valour, is in his pages: and the air and the dress we assume are seen there.—I turn to Rabelais and Montaigne with relief. See what a gentleman Boccaccio is in his narration! and always manly, always fresh.—Do you care to find the Holy Grail, Fred? Twenty years ago it would have excited me. This your foremost Poet is twenty years behind his time. Of course I expect a contrary opinion from you. But answer me—isn't there a scent of damned hypocrisy in all this

---

438. [1] *The Education of The Agricultural Poor*, a printing of a speech delivered at Southampton by Maxse.
[2] Tennyson's 'Lucretius' was first published in *Macmillan's Magazine*, May 1868.

lisping and vowelled purity of the Idylls? Well! just as you like. It's fashionable; it pleases the rose-pink[3] ladies, it sells. Enough.

I am your loving
George M.

I spoke strongly to Greenwood of Bradlaugh;[4] impressed him, I trust.

439. *To* FREDERICK A. MAXSE

Text: *Letters*, i. 198–9.

Box Hill
December 27, 1869

My dear Fred,

I return Ruskin's letter, a characteristic one.[1] I am chiefly glad that you should be in correspondence with a man who will appreciate and stimulate you; glad too that you seem to see where he falls short, or, rather, aims blindly. It is the spirituality of Carlyle that charms him.[2] What he says of Tennyson I too thought in my boy's days, that is, before I began to think. Tennyson has many spiritual indications, but no philosophy, and philosophy is the palace of thought. Mill is essentially a critic: it is his heart, not his mind, which sends him feeling ahead. But he really does not touch the soul and springs of the Universe as Carlyle does. Only, when the latter attempts practical dealings he is irritable as a woman, impetuous as a tyrant. He seeks the short road to his ends; and the short road is, we know, a bloody one. He is not wise; Mill is; but Carlyle has most light when he burns calmly. Much of

438. [3] A colour associated by GM with sentimentality. See Chapter I of *Diana*.

[4] Charles Bradlaugh (1833–91), as a persecuted atheist, enlisted GM's sympathies. One of the numerous lawsuits in which he was involved—the De Rin case, with Bradlaugh as plaintiff—dragged through the courts from 1867–70. In Dec. 1869 it was called before a referee, and Bradlaugh, unable to take the orthodox oath, was not permitted to testify. Though he won the verdict in the end, the case cost him £1,500 and was indirectly the cause of his ruin in business. His daughter, Hypatia Bradlaugh Bonner (*Charles Bradlaugh: A Record of his Life and Work*, 1898), says that, having been ruined in business, he turned to lecturing and later to politics. At the time of this letter he was delivering Sunday lectures in the New Hall of Science, and a couple of weeks later GM and Maxse went to hear him speak.

439. [1] Maxse had evidently sent Ruskin a copy of his pamphlet on *The Education of the Agricultural Poor* (see Note 1, preceding letter). In Lecture IV on 'The Future of England' (published as part of *The Crown of Wild Olive*), delivered at the Royal Agricultural Institution, Woolwich, on 14 Dec. 1869, Ruskin made a complimentary reference to Maxse's pamphlet. This is no doubt the origin of Ruskin's letter.

[2] Ruskin's published works are full of praise of Carlyle and Tennyson and condemnation of John Stuart Mill.

Ruskin's Political Economy will, I suspect, be stamped as good by posterity. He brings humanity into it. This therefore is not the Political Economy of our day.—I have turned Wendell Phillips³ like a drenching fireman's hose on a parson, and made him sputter and gutter and go to his wife to trim his wick. The Oration is very noble. Adieu. Write some day next year.

Your loving
George Meredith

440. *To* FREDERICK A. MAXSE

Text: typed copy, Maxse Papers. Published: *Letters*, i. 199–200, with omissions.

Mickleham
Tuesday, [? December 1869]¹

My dear Fred,

If you can fix Monday instead of Friday I shall prefer it, for I have been in town once this week, am very busy, and there are no late trains down here on Friday. But if there's a doubt about your having an engagement on Monday, and Friday should be by far the most suitable day, say so, and I will come gladly.

Will is in the garden on a rocking horse, new gift from his Aunt. His seat is as Cardigan's entering Balaclava guns.—Of course you've read Kinglake,² very deliberate, very conscientious. He has done all the work of the History of the Crim[ean] War except to write it. His writing is so fine—so fine (in both senses) that to say it is penmanship seems best to express it.—One sees the whole Balaclava business, as he saw it (and you) from the heights, through Kinglake's slowly-moving, dioramic, opera-glass, with the fifty degree magnifying power of patient imagination, full study and testimony, superadded. It deserves praise and thanks. Contemporaneous history should thus be written: but it is not an artistic piece of history. How glorious Scarlett at the head of his 300 Greys and Inniskillens! Yet one can't help feeling

---

³ Wendell Phillips (1811–84), the American abolitionist who became a famous orator. From the context I judge the Oration mentioned to be *Christianity a Battle, not a Dream*, published in London in 1869.

440. ¹ W. M. Meredith prints this as the last letter for 1869, and I have no better suggestion. The fact that the Merediths were at Mickleham points to the Christmas holidays, as does the rocking-horse given little Will by his aunt.

² The publication of vols. 3 and 4 of Kinglake's *Invasion of the Crimea* in the preceding year possibly made all of what follows fresh in GM's memory. He may have read them during the holidays.

that Kinglake makes them go astonishingly like the horsemen in a peepshow. Scarlett enters:—pause; now Shegogg:—pause; Aide de camp:—pause: now the Greys, presently the Inniskillens:—So on. Very good, very bad.

Adieu.

Your loving
George Meredith

441. *To* JOHN MORLEY[1]

Text: *Letters*, i. 201–2.

Mickleham
January 2, 1870

My dear Morley,

Very glad to hear from you—I called on Morison. He told me of your passage to Glasgow and lecture on Condorcet,[2] a capital subject for a philosopher. I shall read it in the *Fortnightly*.—Some fear struck me that you would not find things well at Lytham.[3]

I should have written to ask leave to review Tennyson's Arthurian Cycles; but I could not summon heart even to get the opening for speaking my mind on it.—I can hardly say I think he deserves well of us; he is a real singer, and he sings this mild fluency to this great length. Malory's Morte Arthur is preferable. Fancy one affecting the great poet and giving himself up (in our days!—he must have lost the key of them) to such dandiacal fluting.—Yet there was stuff here for a poet of genius to animate the figures and make them reflect us, and on us. I read the successive mannered lines with pain—yards of linen—drapery for the delight of ladies who would be in the fashion.—The praises of the book shut me away from my fellows. To be sure, there's the magnificent 'Lucretius'.

Fred Maxse has been corresponding with Ruskin.—Anon, anon. I am not at liberty to write of the latter's monstrous assumption of wisdom.

441. [1] This is the first extant letter from GM to John Morley (1838–1923), journalist and statesman, whose career is too well known to need summary here. Morison had introduced the two men in 1862, and in time Morley became, save for a three-year interruption (see Letter 473), the third of GM's closest male friends.

[2] *Letters* reads *Count d'Orsay*, a patent error since Morley's *Condorcet* appeared in the *FR* for Jan. and Feb. 1870. (The error is corrected in W. M. Meredith's hand in his own copy of *Letters*, now in the Bodleian Library.)

[3] In Lancashire; where Morley's mother and sister lived.

Ah! the Hindhead[4] and a Southwester on it in March or April!—
Yes! and then to Florence.

Let me hear when you are in London. I shall not be up till about the
11th or 12th. We will dine at the Garrick, an you please. Good luck
speed the *Pall Mall*.[5]—I rejoice to hear that your head is teeming. Did
I tell you that Fred and I went to sit under Bradlaugh one evening?
The man is neither to be laughed nor sneered down, nor trampled. He
will be a powerful speaker. I did my best to make Greenwood understand that. It was really pleasant to hear those things spoken which the
parsonry provoke. Here, at a party where our Willie entertained company of his own age, the hostess feared to see the children standing in
a ring because (she said—and she is by way of being independent) the
little—(parson's children—he begets annually—the children die decen-
nially—and he is 'chastened' but sees no natural curse—!) the little
——might think it was meant for dancing!

442. *To* FREDERICK A. MAXSE

Text: *Letters*, i. 200–1.

Mickleham
January 2, 1870

My dear Fred,

It's difficult to speak mildly of a man who calls John Mill blockhead,
and dares to assume Carlyle's mantle of Infallibility on the plea that it
is his 'master's'.[1] Still I agree with much that he says of Carlyle. I hold
that he is the nearest to being an inspired writer of any man in our
times; he does proclaim inviolable law: he speaks from the deep
springs of life. All this. But when he descends to our common pave-
ment, when he would apply his eminent spiritual wisdom to the course

---

[4] Morley took a house a few miles north of Hindhead in 1870 (Hirst, i. 163).

[5] The *PMG* had begun as a one-penny evening newspaper. On 1 Jan. 1870, it was
transformed into a morning newspaper, with an evening edition, each priced twopence.
The experiment lasted only four months ([Leonard Huxley], *The House of Smith, Elder*,
1923, p. 177). Morley was only a contributor at this time; he did not become editor until
1880.

442. [1] A continuation of the discussion of Ruskin begun in Letter 439. In *Time and Tide*,
among the passages later deleted (Cook and Wedderburn, *The Works of Ruskin*, 1903–12,
vol. xvii, Appendix VIII), Ruskin says of Carlyle, 'I only speak of myself together with
him as a son might speak of his father and himself' (p. 476) and two pages later calls him
'my master', and turning to Mill, says (pp. 478–9), 'He has never . . . fathomed the first
principles even of his own subject of Mercantile Economy; and his Essay on Liberty
I believe to be the foolishest book yet extant in literature, written by a man of disciplined
power.'

of legislation, he is no more sagacious nor useful nor temperate than a flash of lightning in a grocer's shop. 'I purify the atmosphere', says this agent. 'You knock me down, spoil my goods and frighten my family', says the grocer.—Philosophy, while rendering his dues to a man like Carlyle and acknowledging itself inferior in activity, despises his hideous blustering impatience in the presence of progressive facts.

Read the *French Revolution* and you listen to a seer: the recent pamphlets,² and he is a drunken country squire of superordinary ability.

Carlyle preaches work for all to all. Good. But his method of applying his sermon to his 'nigger' is intolerable.—Spiritual light he has to illuminate a nation. Of practical little or none, and he beats his own brains out with emphasis.

As to what R[uskin] says of John Mill I have not the *Pol[itical] Ec[onomy]*³ handy. I am inclined to think the present generation of P[olitical] Economists wrong—that they don't see that the obligations of Wealth pertain to its sources, and that R. has some vague truth for a backbone to his preposterous priestly attitude and inebriate conceit as against adversaries.

The Parsonry are irritating me fearfully, but a non-celibate clergy are a terrific power. They are interwound with the whole of the Middle class like the poisonous ivy. Oh! for independence, that I might write my mind of these sappers of our strength.

Your loving
George M.

443. *To* AUGUSTUS JESSOPP

MS.: Yale.

Mickleham, Dorking
January 7, 1869 [error for 1870]

My dear Jessopp,

Daily I postpone writing to you, that the lot I have to say may have comfortable space and time for delivery, but work over, I shun the pen; so take these few words of thanks to you for being mindful of me, and presently I will perform my whole epistolary duty. I am busy

442. ² Carlyle's anti-democratic writings range from *The Nigger Question* (1849) and *Latter-Day Pamphlets* (1850) to 'Shooting Niagara: and After?' (*Macmillan's Magazine*, Aug. 1867). GM was not the only man of his time appalled by them.
    ³ *Unto this Last: Four Essays on the First Principles of Political Economy* (1862).

finishing a novel for the *Cornhill Magazine*,[1] one of three or four that are carved out, and waiting. My stomach keeps me from writing rapidly and renders writing of any kind distasteful after the morning's work is done. I shall not bring it round to serve me like a Christian until I have had six months of rest—and they are remote, I fancy. Whether you will or won't like this novel coming out (I believe) when Charles Reade's story is finished,[2] I cannot guess. The general public will not let me probe deeply into humanity. You must not paint either woman or man: a surface view of the species flat as a wafer is acceptable. I have not plucked at any of the highest or deepest chords. (Hence possibly) those who have heard some of the chapters say it must be the best novel I have written. In the summer I removed Arthur from Berne to the Stuttgart Gymnasium. He is in the house of a Professor (should kind Mrs. Jessopp care to write to the boy, here's the address— 'Professor Zeller, 64 Reinsburgstrasse, Stuttgart') who sends me word this Christmas that he has made astonishing strides and is both a diligent and comprehensive student, besides being a most polite, mannerly fellow. This is comforting. With me he was scarcely civil though I believe he had no ill feeling. I have got introductions for him in Stuttgart; he has therefore friends to visit. His letters are quaint; I enclose you one. Latin and Greek are the chief points of his study. Do you know Stuttgart? It's a pretty little city, full of heavy eating and drinking, decorum and dulness, surrounded by vine-hills;—not much to the boy's taste in winter. On the whole he is satisfied. The Professors keep him in sharp exercise. His German is good, French middling. Italian and Spanish he reads. Latin composition he is growing proficient in.—

Have you read Tennyson's last volume?[3] Are you delighted with it?—Curious that one pretending to the title of great poet should have given so much of his time to such a composition, which is to poetry what Vestments are to Religion:—and he who writes the grand 'Lucretius'!—If you have not read Browning's *Ring and Book*,[4] I recommend the 'Caponsacchi'—'Pompilia', 'the Pope' and the two 'Guidos'. Browning has his faults, but at least they are not those of a mannered trickster airing a leg with love-knots.—

My kindest regards to Mrs. Jessopp. Are we never to see her here? You leave cards in Piccadilly!

Your affectionate
George Meredith

443. [1] *The Adventures of Harry Richmond*, published serially in the *Cornhill* (Sept. 1870–Nov. 1871). [2] Reade's *Put Yourself in His Place* ended in the July 1870 number.
[3] See Letters 437 and 438.
[4] *The Ring and the Book* was originally published in four volumes successively in Nov., Dec. 1868, Jan., Feb. 1869.

444. *To* JOHN MORLEY

Text: *Letters*, i. 202–3.

Box Hill
January 13, 1870

My dear friend M.,

You will write and let me know if there is anything I can do for you.[1] My hands are altogether at your service.

A copy of H. Rochefort's *Marseillaise* may interest you; it is the Republican (Red) shriek (the Irish word escapes me) over Victor Noir.[2] It's a good study of the French period.—Well, after reading it and repressing my gorge at this undignified fury and savage friendship, I turned to a leading article in the *Morning Post* in which the assassinated youngster is supremely sneered at as a linendraper's apprentice who caught an appetite for literature from the *Petit Journal*. (It seems that no less a man than Weiss had some hopes of him). On the whole, I was, critically speaking, most disgusted with our high-noted friend.

This number of the *Fortnightly* is excellent: your *Condorcet* to my mind an example of your best judicial style, minus the judicial excess of precision (occasionally as from an old maid to an errand boy—so like!) These studies which you put into so noble a shape and impregnate with your full mind, will help to bear good fruit in all directions. Meanwhile they are fine reading. Take to history. Preserve this style in historical narrative, and your name will not take a second rank. My dear M.! I don't know how it may be with you. I trust that you may have all your strength about you. If it ever comforts you to think of my affection, be sure that you have it.

Yours,
George Meredith

444. [1] This and the concluding sentences of the letter probably refer to the illness of Morley's mother, who died two months later.

[2] At the conclusion of a newspaper war between Prince Pierre–Napoleon Bonaparte and the *Marseillaise*, the Prince issued a challenge to Rochefort, the proprietor. Noir, with two other members of the staff, called on the Prince. According to the *Marseillaise* (quoted by the *Globe*, 11 Jan.), the Prince asked if, as seconds, they 'undertook the responsibility of M. Rochefort's acts'. They replied: 'We are responsible for our friends.' Thereupon the Prince struck Noir in the face with his left hand, drew from his pocket a ten-chambered revolver with his right, and shot Noir at arm's length. The Prince was tried in March and acquitted, though in a civil action Noir's family recovered 25,000f. and costs.

445. *To* JOHN MORLEY

Text: *Letters*, i. 203–5.

Mickleham, Dorking
January 27, 1870

My dearest M.,

The drama of a household burnt out under my eye here, has given me some excitement. Irish Mr. Sewell, six feet five, haired like Erebus, brawny as Vulcan's first forgeman, with a sniffling English wife, whose shawl is, like her nose, always thawing off her shoulder, and a family of four, a good honest lot for that matter, lived in a hut in the corner of a field abutting on our acres, to watch potatoes grow. Sewell was away at work, his wife sniffling somewhere, when out flaps the big girl with a whinny, Fire! Fire!—and I giving a touch to *Richmond*. I was soon in a gentle rain of thatch. The girl tumbled, and I assure you I saw the vision of Danaë in a jiffy. She lived (like woman's virtue) under a thatched roof. I saved the nuptial bed of these rash and un-wearied propagators; my gardener arriving later attached himself to the pigs. There would have been, as I told him later, a chance of roast pig—! I repeated Charles Lamb's story to him. He is without imagina-tion and 'hoped I was joking'.

... I'm afraid the *Pall Mall* can't be doing well, though when I went to Greenwood he insisted on the cheerfulness of its condition.—All speak with regret of it and of what they hear of it.—The tone—eh? of the leaders doesn't seem to me so good, though it's above the newspaper type. You see they have dealt with Bradlaugh. I spoke to Greenwood about him, insisting that he was a man of power, and was not to be sneered down; and that on the whole he said certain things comforting to hear by one suffering from Simon Peter.—As to *Harry Richmond*, I fear I am evolving his personality too closely for the public, but a man must work by the light of his conscience if he's to do anything worth reading.—I see the *Quarterly* deals rather firmly with the 'Holy Grail'—something in these days. It is hard on the 'Lucretius' —compares the flow of the English lines with the Latin Hexameters of the poet. No one but Milton has the roll of the English line. The French Alexandrine, which I have been studying of late, is (though far off) nearer to ancient poetical music than anything we have out of Milton. When I have leisure I hope to write some papers on poetry and versification.—I hear good things said of your *Condorcet*, and am con-vinced you are getting the right historical tone. Young Trollope[1]

445. [1] Henry Merivale ('Harry') Trollope (1846–1926), eldest son of Anthony Trollope, who had paid £10,000 for a one-third interest in the publishing firm of C. & H. for his son in Aug. 1869 (Booth, op. cit., p. 245).

complains that you employ hyphens too largely. I quote the criticism *pour votre gouverne*. Now goodnight, my dear friend; I do but chat to amuse you, if things permit of it. Doubtless you have your eye on the news, and I need not discuss politics. Adieu.

446. *To* AUGUSTUS JESSOPP

Text (excerpt): Sotheby Catalogue, (27 Nov.–4 Dec. 1911), p. 22.

Box Hill, Dorking
February 4, 1870

. . . He is one of the best of fellows—but an Editor, and from an Editor you must always be willing to take advice, and never no.[1]

447. *To* JOHN MORLEY

Text: *Letters*, i. 205.

Box Hill
March 5, 1870

My dearest M.,
We are both with you in heart. When your heart is bowed to the black metal gates, words of the best of friends can be but poorly helpful; but think of us and our love for you when you look up and around you once again.—I had this shock when I was a little boy, and merely wondered. . . .[1]

Your affectionate
George Meredith

448. *To* W. C. BONAPARTE WYSE

MS.: Yale. Published: Ellis, p. 258.

Mickleham, Dorking
April 20, 1870

My dearest of dear fellows,
The Mickleham nightingales believing in your vows of affection,

446. [1] A note in the catalogue states that this refers to an article submitted by Jessopp to Morley, as editor of the *FR*, who had rejected it as 'too late'.
447. [1] Morley's mother had died on 2 Mar. Meredith's mother had died when GM was five.

invite you to a concert here as early as you can come. If you bring your wife, whom mine will joyfully welcome and I greet irradiated, we will quarter you for the nights at an adorable inn, framed to figure in the annals of co-respondency. Come you alone, perhaps you will condescend to the old hammock-cot I used to sleep in at Copsham. Let me know the day you are to arrive in town. I can't tell you how glad I shall be to grasp your hand. You and I awaken from a Winter like that in the planet Jupiter, so let the thaw smite the rocks to torrents.

I've no photograph of myself, and shall not have one. Take instead my thanks for yours and *Li Parpaioun Blu*,[1] which I have been spelling over with astonishment at your facility, and delight in its effects. More of it by and by. I am trying to get a copy of my review of *Mirèio*[2] for you.

I wrote in the *Pall Mall Gazette* of the great meeting of the Félibres, little imagining that you were one of them and much their host!

Adieu for the moment, and to our meeting! My compliments and affectionate regards to your wife. I am

Your loving
George Meredith

449. *To* W. C. Bonaparte Wyse

MS.: University of California, Berkeley. Published: Ellis, pp. 258–9 (dated *May 13, 1870*), with omission of two sentences.

Box Hill
May 16, 1870

My dearest B[onapar]te,

A word to say how much I regret that we shall not have you here on your return.—The Reverend[1] received his copy of the *Parp[aioun] Blu* and sends you enclosed acknowledgment. I shall give the other copy to Swinburne, I think.—Am reading *Bread of Sin*;[2] moderately interesting, but not so exciting as an ordinary adultery case in the newspapers, and without the dignity of the tragic drama. Phædre was excusable, but Panette's longings are beneath expression in verse. You see, she has no character, no quality of mind. It is an attempt to make a dramatic poem out of the irritation of this female's gender. A strong young man and a middle aged wonton are not enough to compose a poem. Fanette is the Provençal Mdme Bovary, conceived provincially.—You should not make the elisions in words. Printing

448. [1] Lyrics in Provençal, with a French translation and an introduction by Mistral.
  [2] By Mistral. For GM's review, see Note 2, Letter 101.
449. [1] Jessopp.
  [2] An English translation by Wyse of Aubanel's Provençal drama, *Lou Pan de pécat*.

'to'rds' for 'towards' won't do, nor will 'meand'ring' and 'philand'ring';
do print the words entire—ungelded. Readers accept the run of short
syllables now.—No, we do not allow your wife to make such a stretch
of generosity as to part with the *Moans*.[3] We read it and shall return it.
As to her fear that we see nothing but the ludicrous in them, let her be
aisy. Only laughter is precious and is for company: the rest sinks deep.
None can fail to feel the awful tragedy of the situation, and the triumph
of fetching poetry of any kind out of it. Adieu. I am very busy. Shall
be glad to hear from you, and with very kind regards to your wife and
three kiss[es] to the little Lucien, I am

Your affectionate
George Meredith

450. *To* DANTE GABRIEL ROSSETTI

Text: Helen Rossetti Angeli, *Dante Gabriel Rossetti: His Friends and Enemies* (1949),
p. 125.

Box Hill, Dorking
June 8, 1870

My dear Gabriel,

I have not had such a delight for years. We never meet now, and
my regret is that I cannot talk to you of the pleasure and pride I feel
in your volume.[1]

You are our Master, of all of us. Some of the Sonnets and lines
throughout the poems, hang about me like bells. But to begin to praise
them is to lose the sense of the depth and subtle richness. Some I knew,
the whole I love; and that the book is out is to my mind a great piece
of good fortune.

The flux of critics poured over it rapidly. I had nowhere a place.
But I shall have much to say of it by and by. Will you come and hear?
Will you come to me this month? My wife will be as glad as I to welcome you. In such a case—almost too good to be hoped for—forewarn me should you choose a Saturday. Swinburne was coming, we
expected; but penned a line from bed, which gives me the old uneasiness
about him. He threw flowers on you in the *Fortnightly*:[2] not one was
undeserved. After first finishing the book my voice would have been
as unrestrained, less eloquent.

I am ever, my dear Gabriel,

Your loving
George Meredith

449. [3] *Moans of a Moribund*, sonnets by Wyse, privately printed.
450. [1] *Poems*, 1870.   [2] In a review of *Poems*, *FR* (May 1870).

451. *To* WILLIAM HARDMAN

MS.: Yale. Published: *Letters*, i. 205–6, with omissions and inaccuracies.

Box Hill
June 15, [1870]
Dearest T.,

It must have been as you say: I was thinking of twenty.—I send now cheque dated *24th* (which is a liberty on my part).¹ The truth is I have sent in my work and am waiting for payment, which I don't want to press for: and it is just possible I may have to ask you to hold on till the end of the month, when I come upon other resources sufficient for the time.—You can either return the old cheque, or tell me it is torn up. Next week we are engaged up to (save Tuesday) Saturday morning. You say nothing *der picknicker—warum dann nicht? Ich bin erstaunt ganz und gar.* Remember too that the dry days are going.—This next Saturday we dine out, Friday is my town day. Monday also. What do you say to Tuesday? On Wednesday and Thursday we are at Effingham Hill.² I mean, if you are at home, to be invited to you, solus, in early July,—when you *haven't* trumpets in your gardens and are not entertaining the wealth and beauty of the district. You will see Poco. He has told me things of our Bishops and Peers which have left me prone on Box Hill with sick dismay. Can such (O Tuck!) things (Good Lord!) be (Saints!) and an apron cover those holy men?—Dickens gone!³ The *Spectator* says he beats Shakespeare at his best; and instances Mrs. Gamp as superior to Juliet's nurse. This is a critical newspaper, you remember? My love to all at home and hope that they will be footing our brown hill soon.

Your loving
George Meredith

451. ¹ At age 42, despite publication of half a dozen novels and earnings derived from the *Ipswich Journal*, the reading of MSS. for C. & H., and the weekly readings to Mrs. Wood, GM had difficulty keeping financially afloat. He had borrowed £15 from Hardman (as shown by the following letter), had forgotten the amount, and now proposed to repay the loan with a post-dated cheque.
² At Lady Caroline Maxse's.
³ Dickens had died on 9 June.

452. *To* WILLIAM HARDMAN

MS.: Berg Collection, New York Public Library. Published: *Letters*, i. 206–7, with inaccuracy; Ellis, p. 216.

Box Hill
July 6, 1870

Sweet Justice of Norbiton, neighbour of Jones,
Have you paid in the £15 cheque?
The account at my bankers' has recently grown's
Fat as the Princess of Teck.[1]

But 'tis sweating already, it dwindles apace:
So I pray you (and here's to your luck),
Don't give to the matter a minute more grace,
And adieu, Serenissimo Tuck!

Halloa! you are off to the Isle of Wight?—Do you remember the 'race' off Sandown?—Perhaps I may run down for two or three days. —Thus our affairs: Marie waits to let her house, when she will convoy Wilkins[2] to Nonancourt. I remain working somewhere for three weeks, pouncing on friends: then I go to fetch her back. We return in September. Arturus has received an invitation from Marie's Sister to go to Joubasseau in Dauphiné for his holidays (Basle, Geneva, Chambéry); so he will be comfortable. I shan't be able to meet him. I wish you could see some of the letters he has written lately. They speak promisingly.[3]—My novel *Harry Richmond* is out of my hands, and appears in the *Cornhill* the 1st October.[4] By that time I hope to have another ready.

Wilkins in very fine condition. Ourself middling—in want of outing. Marie well.—I hope the illustrious Editor of *Punch* has got round again and rounder.[5] Adieu to you all.—

Your loving
George Meredith

The last of dear old St. Bernard was that he was down on his back.— We are off for a couple of days to Lady Caroline Maxse's, Effingham Hill. She has taken to Marie.

452. [1] Princess Mary Adelaide, daughter of the Duke of Cambridge, who married the Prince and Duke of Teck in 1866. She was the mother of Queen Mary.
[2] i.e. Willie.
[3] Several of Arthur's letters of this period are among the Maxse papers. One is struck by the formality of the tone and the humourlessness of the letters.
[4] Actually it began in September.
[5] Hardman's friend Shirley Brooks.

453. *To* ARTHUR G. MEREDITH

Text: *Letters*, i. 207–8.

England, Box Hill
July 14, 1870

My dear Arthur,

Write to Madame Poussielque when you know the day Professor Zeller starts, and go yourself that day. The later, the better, for your Aunt Betty does not leave here till the first days of August, and I should like you to see her, and to have her report of your condition. Besides she is charming society. Do not fail at one time or other of your visit to make the expedition to the Grande Chartreuse. I am sure it will delight you. Whatever money you may be in need of you shall have. Send me (clearly written) a detail of the value of your florins in francs, and how much the journey to Joubasseau costs you. When there, use what money you have remaining for pocket-money, and more shall be forwarded to you, according to the necessity of the case. I wish you to be careful, but to feel tolerably independent, and in all things to enjoy your holiday.

It has looked recently as if we should have war between France and Prussia, and I fear it must come on; but I think not immediately.[1] When men's brains are insufficient to meet the exigencies of affairs, they fight. If the war should burst out, I shall be grieved, for I like France, and yet see the good for Europe of having a strong central State composed of a solid people. There is no need at present to consider the course that you should take in the event of war encircling little Würtemberg. You will like the Commandant[2] (equal in military rank to our major) very much. He has seen a great deal of campaigning both in the Crimea and in Algeria. He is a Frenchman of the best kind. You will not find him an admirer of Prussia, but keep your judgment in balance on all questions upon which you have no personal experience, and have had no opportunities for reflection. . . . I have passed Chambéry and been at Grenoble. All the Dauphiné country is beautiful, so you are sure to be pleased. I trust with all my heart you will be happy, and am your loving father,

George Meredith

453. [1] A bad prediction: on the following day it was known that French reserves had been called up and that war was only a matter of hours away.
[2] Commandant Poussielque.

454. *To* JOHN MORLEY

Text: *Letters*, i. 209–10.

Box Hill
[*c.* July 19, 1870]

My dear M.,

I found the boy still troubled yesterday, and to-day the doctor says he will have to rest for two or three days: meanwhile he goes on well. Very doubtful whether Marie will be able to bring him over this week. The next I must give to Fred Maxse. Afterwards, you willing, we may come. That is, if I am on the spot. It's possible that I may start to French quarters for Borthwick.—If you like I will run to you on Thursday. This war agitates me; gazing on an old tree, or talking with you, are my febrifuges. I have just had the *Book of Orm*[1] sent to me from the author. It may be a settling, it's not a composing draught. The newspapers are mere chips of dry biscuit to my devouring appetite for telegrams and details. Yesterday and to-day, thank heaven, they haven't (I don't see the *Times*) sermonized. England hasn't screamed and scolded and clacked and nodded her cap, and sniffled to her clergyman for comfort.—I wrote some verse to you this morning, but as it isn't finished can't send it. Taste the beginning, perhaps never to end—never to have tail—like scornèd pigs.

> Friend, when the thundercloud is low,
> And in the expectancy and throe,
> Field, hill, and wave of forest grow
>   The hue that edges black on fair,
>   No voice is heard, and not a sound,
>   Though listen all the hollow ground;
> But swift I have known a white dove thread the air.
>
> So now these lines to you, between
> The loaded darkness and dead green,

Etc., etc. no more space.

May our hearts be stout, and we prove our begetting honest!

Ever yours,
George M.

---

454. [1] Robert Buchanan (1841–1901), *The Book of Orm*: a *Prelude to the Epic.*

455. *To* JOHN MORLEY

Text: *Letters*, i. 208–9.

Box Hill
July 21, 1870

My dear Morley,

... What news!—this of Prévost Paradol![1] Why talk of the horrors of war when we are fronting artillery at every second of our lives.— My *Pall Mall* comes to me this morning with the most ludicruous blunder about a name of a place ever printed. Forbach[2] is treated of as being in the Black Forest (where there is a little village of the name), and the *Pall Mall* speculates upon why hostilities should have commenced there!—Our friend can afford such errors less than any other journal.—On the whole, I side with France, or so incline. The instinct of the people in seizing an opportunity to dispute the aggrandisement of Prussia is right: it is not a Vanity war nor a King's, but a people's war—war of Germans and Frenchmen; a trial of actual strength for supremacy: and it was nonsense to think of postponing it, ruinous to delay.—The tone of our Press is sickening.—No correspondents allowed, so my chance is gone.

456. *To* JOHN MORLEY

Text: *Letters*, i. 210–12.

Box Hill
July 25, 1870

My dearest M.,

I am glad you like the verses. The next batch you will find plunge deeper. Mind, I swore them as to you, and you (though you blinked at the time, as much as to tell me I was intimidating you) consented to take them.—I am in poor mood for writing: an attack of stomach keeps me singular in ideas, and, like the contemplative dervish, with a fixed eye on the centre of my being, whence does not issue song at present.

455. [1] Lucien Anatole Prévost-Paradol (1829–70), professor at age twenty-five and member of the Academy at age thirty-six, had been appointed Minister Plenipotentiary to the United States. On landing, he was met with the stunning announcement of war, and refusing to be an accomplice in imperial policy, he shot himself. (See J. H. Fyfe, 'M. Prévost-Paradol', *Macmillan's Magazine*, Aug. 1870, pp. 316–19. Albert D. Vandam, however, in *An Englishman in Paris*, 1892, ii. 206, hints at other reasons for the suicide.)
[2] The doubt of the accuracy of the date of this letter expressed by Mona Mackay (*Meredith et la France*, 1937, pp. 150–1) is without basis. Although no battle was fought at Forbach until 6 Aug., *The Times* reported on 20 July a rumour of the beginning of hostilities there and on 21 July exchanges of shots between patrols and Customs guards.

The war of '70 is direct issue of '66. Just as we abused the Prussians then we howl at the French now, but the tremendous armaments on both sides were meant for this duel, and it mattered very little what was the pretext for the outbreak. Surely it's a case of Arcades Ambo.[1] The French felt themselves perpetually menaced by distended Prussia, irritated by her tone, even alarmed by the rumour and dread of projects the existence of which her antecedents might seem to warrant. At any rate it was a fight to come on; and here we have it; and if we are energetic and wise it may be the last of the great fights of Europe. The two foremost States in war and intellect may well be committed to cut the bloody tangle. I feel deeply for the Germans; I quite understand the ardour of the French. I think their cause, from their point of view, thoroughly good, and not likely to succeed. Armies can't do it: they can't check the tide of a great nation. As to the Emperor,[2] he appears to have thought the season for a trial of the new breech-loader field-pieces and Mitrailleuse had come, just as Bismarck could not afford to delay in trying his needle-gun on the Austrians. The Emperor had note of warning that his routed Prussians were also busy perfecting mysterious instruments. Poor devilry! All devilry is poor in the contemplation. But it is still the chief engine of history. You and I are forced into our channels by it. Friend, in the woods, you and I may challenge the world to match us in happiness. Out of them I feel myself pulled back a century or so.—And into a splash of shuddering matter.

By the way, you must remember that the Emperor did not make the grief against Prussia. It came to his hand. It was deep in the French heart. I turn to the *Book of Orm* and find a refrain—

> Grow, Seed, blossom, Brain
> Deepen, deepen, into pain.

Title of piece 'The Devil's Mystics'. There!
    Again—

> God feared the thing He fashioned
> And fled into a cloud!

Public of Britain! Here he is—your poet!

> Since that day, with cloudy face,
>   Of His own handiwork afraid,
> God from His Heavenly hiding-place
>   Peered at the thing He made.

456. [1] 'Arcadians both': applied by Virgil (Ecl. vii. 4) to Corydon and Thyrsis, young shepherds and poets.
    [2] Napoleon III of France.

Aha! If He made Bismarck and Napoleon according to the view of the Stock Exchange, the British Spinster, Clericus and Press (siding for once with their betters), then no wonder!—I would not mind our language if it came from an unselfish people: but a people notoriously craving peace for comfort's sake, and commerce's—they do but scold, they provoke contempt.—I regret bitterly that I am not out on a post of observation. I may still go for a month.

Your loving
George Meredith

457. *To* FREDERICK A. MAXSE

MS.: Maxse Papers.

[Box Hill]
Tuesday, July 26, 1870

Fred,

I shall rejoice with all my heart to receive you at home.

You wrong me damnably in saying I favour War.

The idea of England with an army at her disposal somewhat less than that of Würtemberg, not half so well drilled to the tasks of modern warfare, besotted on drugged beer, incapable of marching, badly officered, brainless from the drummer to the Chief—Lord in Heaven! What an idea! Yet people are saying calmly we may be involved. Our fleet is good. The anticipation is that the fleet is to do everything for us.

Ever yours,
George Meredith

458. *To* WILLIAM HARDMAN

MS.: Yale. Published: *Letters*, i. 215–16, with omissions and inaccuracies; omitted portions published: Ellis, p. 260.

21 Cavendish Place
Eastbourne, Sussex
[? September 1870][1]

My dearest Tuck,

Motives of Economy decided us to come here, much to my regret.

458. [1] This letter must have been written between 9 Sept., when Sir Richard Baggallay delivered his first address to the electors of Mid-Surrey at Kingston-on-Thames, with Hardman presiding, and 9 Oct., when GM wrote to Mrs. Steele from Box Hill.

We were at Tongswood, at the Cotterills,[2] and it was cheap to run to the Sussex, dear to the Isle of Wight, Coast. But, O You! had you written to Holly Hill you would have fetched me over to Sandown, and I should have fixed the bargain with a lodgement-letter. I remained for a fortnight at Maxse's, yachting when the gales permitted it: then joined Marie at Tongswood, good air, good hostess and host. Eastbourne is on the whole pleasant. The bathing is delightful, especially for those who enjoy a sight of bottoms. We have a flat sandy shore, and you see half a dozen fat men at a time scampering out of the machines a mile away to hide their middle nakedness posterior. Then they dive, they rise, there is a glistening on the right cheek and the left—too distant to offend the most gingerly. I opine so, for I have beheld antique virgins spyglass in hand towards the roguish spot. This salt-water fetches me round, Tuck. It's the next best to mountain air.

Marie and I thanked you for your thorough kind letter. I know how you would both feel on hearing of the dear good old man's death.[3] A just man; not lost forever to his family, for the example of such a man is a constant presence. But a dead loss to the poor.

So you do both care of [for] *H. Richmond.* I hoped it.—I wish some one like Shirley Brooks would let it be known it's mine. Lethbridge tells me he has seen it attributed to Lever![4] A word from you, Tuck, in the august Ear of Punch[5]—anon, anon, sir.—Mind and tell me how you like it as you go on. I shall have another to follow when *Richmond* ceases, and so by drumming may make the public hear me at last.— Oh! this war. I burst with pity for the French, but can't say they have not deserved defeat. Was ever a nation so shattered?[6] In nothing have they done well since Napoleon gave the wink to Gramont to roar in the Chambers.[7] My love to you all, with the children—kisses to you and them from Willie Godson. You should see him in his paddle boots in the low tide pools.—Tuck, you didn't reply to my letter because you were working for Lee Steere and Baggallay![8] Marie will write to

458. [2] The Cotterills lived at Tongswood, Hawkhurst, Kent. They were the same Cotterills who were Hardman's and GM's neighbours of Norbiton Park in earlier days.

[3] Marie's father, Mr. Vulliamy, who had died on 29 Aug.

[4] Charles Lever (1806–72), Irish novelist.

[5] i.e. Hardman's good friend Shirley Brooks, the editor.

[6] By early September France had suffered a crushing defeat at Sedan, where Napoleon III himself was among the 100,000 captives, 300,000 French soldiers were shut up in Metz, which was to capitulate on 27 Oct., and Paris was in the hands of Republicans within and was besieged by German armies without.

[7] The Duc de Gramont, Foreign Minister, had told a cheering Chamber of Deputies on 6 July that respect for the rights of others did not oblige France 'to suffer a foreign Power . . . to imperil the interests and honour of France' (*Annals of Our Time*, i. 925).

[8] Lee Steere was elected on 9 Sept. and Sir Richard Baggallay on 17 Oct. as Conservatives in separate by-elections. Neither was opposed.

D'Troïa on her return to Box. She did not at once, owing to hesitation as to the course to take, which ultimately Economy, our damned old friend, decided for us, and not badly, except for the loss of you two, and a certain poetical quality (I fancy it) haunting your district.— Have I made it plain to you that the feelingness of your letter to Mickleham was much felt there? I've no more space. Tuck, dear heart, I could chatter to you like a summer brook. Adieu. Imagine me talking on; as I do from hour to hour.

Your loving
George Meredith

459. *To* Mrs. Anna C. Steele

MS.: University of Texas.

Box Hill
October 9, 1870

My dear Mrs. Steele,

Both the blooming lady of the photographs and the fair dark *dédaigneuse* are charming; we cannot surrender either one. In truth the two have to be together to make a correct likeness. You look inclined to be kind when coloured. As the sun paints you you appear to be reviewing your regiment, all sighing loud as street paviours and provoking just that amount of compassion from their mistress.

I have heard several names for the author of *Harry Richmond* in the *Cornhill*. Some say Lever. I think I know him, but am warned that I can't be sure. Perhaps he knows you, though it is much more probable (a consultation of the photos tells me) that he does not.—Are you at work yourself? I trust you are. You greatmindedly took my criticism, and I long for the *revanche* of giving praise.

Present my respects to Lady Wood, of whom I hear generally at Eltham, though not the best of news. But I have learnt to put almost unlimited faith in the vital power of your family. I am

Your most faithful and
devoted
George Meredith

460. *To* WILLIAM HARDMAN

MS.: Yale. Excerpt published: Ellis, pp. 271–2.

Box Hill, Dorking
October 13, 1870

Time-honoured Tuck!

Here's a state of things! We shall have Queens marrying Commoners next. No wonder they've made the Pr[ince] of Wales a Scotch Freemason. A poor return of the compliment for our giving one of their Scotch Deuces an English Princess.[1] I write as a true Briton.—

Really, Tuck, I feel pleasure in my work when I hear you like it. I have an audience of about a dozen, but if they're satisfied I am too. And no man speaks so heartily as you do.

Some single night in the month of November (sweet season!) I propose to come to you and have a long chatter—you and I alone.

—Ha! ha! ha! he! he!—

—Yang! yang! yang! yang!

Great accumulations of gossip are already evaporating.

I grieve for your friends the De Finances and poor Dagobert.[2] As to the Vulliamys at Nonancourt, I fear they have the Uhlans quartered on them by this time. Relatives of their wives at Jouy (near Versailles) have housefuls of officers. But I bear in mind, as a corrective to wrath at the conquerors, that the brutallest invader in the world has always been the Frenchman. The Germans are going beyond the mark in their stipulations,—for which they also must suffer.

—Ha! ha! he! hi! hi!

—Yang! yang! yang! yang!

I know you don't like the Germans. They are not amusing, but they have their good side. You will say—the backside. I wish that were being shown to France. Lord, what a change of circumstances!

—He! he! he!

—Yang! yang! yang!

For the moment adieu, my friend, and my love to all your household and many recommendations of myself to a place in the memory of the Great Mother when you write to her. It's hard that you and I can't meet oftener.

Your ever affectionate
George Meredith

460. [1] A reference to the announcement of the impending marriage of the Princess Louise to the Marquess of Lorne, eldest son of the Duke of Argyll—the first marriage of a member of the Royal family to a subject since the Duke of York (James II) married Anne Hyde. Simultaneously newspapers announced the installation of the Prince of Wales as a patron of the Freemasons of Scotland.   [2] I am baffled.

461. *To* ARTHUR G. MEREDITH

Text: *Letters*, i. 212–15.

Box Hill, Dorking, England
October 25, 1870

My dear Arthur,

... I am not very rich at present, but I don't want you to be without pocket-money and minor comforts.—See that you have warm clothing for the winter—all that is really needful I gladly pay for. I leave it to your good sense to take measures to avoid chills, and to take daily reasonable exercise, and not to walk to excess. Your gastric attack last year will serve for a warning. Don't ever sit in clothes you have sweated in: the trouble of going upstairs and 'grooming' yourself saves trouble, and worse, in the end. Fellows who contract illnesses are usually guilty (I don't say always) of indolence—carelessness is only one form of indolence.—You will note that I lay stress on the physical condition. I do so for the reason that it is the index to the moral condition in young men. It is ten to one that a healthy lad is of good general worth. If not physically healthy he will not be of much value. The day comes when we are put to the test, and it is for this day we should prepare with cheerful heart. Don't imagine me to be lecturing you. I have favourable reports of you, and I merely repeat simple words of advice that it will be well for you to keep in mind.—Tell Professor Zeller, with my compliments, that if there is a fund for the wounded soldiers in Stuttgart, I shall be glad if he will put my name down for the subscription of £1, which he can charge to the next account. I cannot afford more just now. The French peasantry around Sedan claim everything of us that we can give. They are barely held up in life by the bread we are able to furnish; and a third of France will be demanding succour in the winter. Horrible to think of!—But do not let compassion or personal sympathy make your judgment swerve. This war is chargeable upon France, and the Emperor is the Knave of the pack.[1] Two generations of Frenchmen have been reared on the traditions of Napoleonism, and these meant the infliction of wrongs and outrages on other nations for the glory and increase of their own. They elected a Napoleon for chief because of his name, and in spite of his known character. It is said, the French peasantry did not want war; that their ignorance offended in electing this man; but who can deny that it was the Napoleonic prestige which gave him his first

---

461. [1] GM was writing, of course, without our later knowledge of the knavery of Bismarck in editing the Ems dispatch with the purpose of provoking France into a declaration of war.

step to the throne by overwhelming votes? This man was the expression of their ignorance, or folly, or vanity; he appealed to the Napoleonism in them, and had a prompt response. A more ignoble spectacle than the recriminations of Emperor and people upon one another as to the origin of the war, after defeat, history does not show. The Germans, on the contrary, reap the reward of a persistently honourable career in civic virtue. Consider what the meaning of civic virtue may be. It comprises a multitude of other virtues. As to German boasting, why the English also are great boasters. See the best in those about you. I say this, and I admire and respect the Germans, and God knows my heart bleeds for the French. But my aim, and I trust it will be yours, is never to take counsel of my sensations, but of my intelligence. I let the former have free play, but deny them the right to bring me to a decision. You are younger, have a harder task in doing that; you have indeed a task in discerning the difference between what your senses suggest and what your mind. However, try not to be let into some degree of injustice to your host, the German people, out of pity for France.— We had a capital time at Eastbourne, good bathing, Willie paddling up to his knees in salt water half the day. Now we have the autumnal gales and Box Hill looking on the last colours of the year. I saw your Grandpapa Meredith[2] on my way to Captain Maxse's; he had been unwell, but was better; he asked after you and so did Mrs. M. They were anxious as to your situation in the territory of war. Captain Maxse is out and out French; Mr. Morison intensely German; Mr. Morley and I do our utmost to preserve an even balance. There is talk of an armistice, but Paris must fall before the French will seriously treat for peace.[3] Count Bismarck gives audience to-day to that deleterious little Frenchman Thiers, who has been poisoning his countrymen for half a century, and now runs from Court to Court, from minister to minister, to get help to undo his own direct work. Count Bismarck will be amused, for he has a keen appreciation of comedy. Philosophers would laugh aloud at the exhibition of the author of the *Consulate and the Empire*[4] in the camp at Versailles. Modern France has been nourished on this lying book.—Here in Mickleham we are naturally anxious about the Nonancourt people. The latest telegrams say that the Germans are moving on Dreux—no great distance from the colony. You can fancy how sad the Old House looks now the

---

461. [2] GM's father was now living at Southsea in a house that belonged to his second wife.
    [3] Paris did not capitulate until 28 Jan. 1871, after a siege of 127 days, but Strassburg, one of the two 'gates' to Paris, had fallen on 28 Sept. and the other, Metz, was to fall two days after this letter was written.
    [4] Colburn had issued a translation of Louis Adolphe Thiers's *History of the Consulate and the Empire of France under Napoleon* in 20 volumes (1845–52). The Paris edition was in 21 volumes (1845–69).

good old man has gone.⁵—God bless you, my dear boy. If you have anything to narrate of the war, the wounded, the prisoners, etc., it might be useful to me. Train your eyes to observe, and while they are at that work keep the action of your mind in abeyance. Young eyes can observe shrewdly, but the opinions of young men are not quite so important.

I am your loving father,
George Meredith

462. *To* JOHN MORLEY

Text: *Letters*, i. 232–3 (dated *Dec. 7, 1871*).

Box Hill
December 7, [1870]¹

My dearest M.

... Oh Heavens! what treachery, I heard of it on Sunday at Effingham Hill.² And without consulting me! One comfort is, you haven't a tree on the Estate—not a shrub. Why, I know the house. I inspected it—I rejected it long before you had an idea of it! But I confess I'm jealous now you have really gone and made it your own.

Now to business—I have a Grand Ode to France—called simply 'France 1870': from my point of view of sympathy and philosophy; which I think is ours. Latterly I have felt poetically weakened by the pressure of philosophical reflection, but this is going, and a fuller strength comes of it, for I believe I am within the shadow of the Truth, and as it's my nature to sing I may now do well. The amount of space will possibly be 4 or 4 1/2 pages. Do not print it too close. I will send it on Monday or Tuesday next; and I should wish you to forward a proof to Harrison³ as well as to me, that I may have his opinion on it, if he will be so condescending as to give it, with possible suggestions, before the hour for returning to printer.—Let me hear from you that you will take it. I can say that it's worth a place, but there should not be delay in outing with it. If you won't I must, and O my poor purse!

⁵ Mr. Vulliamy.

462. ¹ Several pieces of evidence prove that this letter belongs to the year 1870, the most obvious being the ode, 'France, 1870', which GM is offering to Morley in this letter and which was published in the *FR* for Jan. 1871.

² At Lady Caroline Maxse's. The 'treachery' was Morley's purchase of the lease of Pitfield House, on the Hog's Back, half-way between Guildford and Farnham, without consulting GM. Hirst (i. 193) says that Morley bought the lease of it in the spring of 1871, which may be accurate for the consummation of legal formalities.

³ Frederic Harrison (1831–1923), barrister, writer, and positivist philosopher; founder of the *Positivist Review* (1893). He was a regular contributor to the *FR.*

Fred as usual. He declares he knows a lady—a great novel-reader—
who finds *Harry Richmond* quite unintelligible in parts. He advises me
in these serious times 'to take to political writing'. I reply that it
demands special study. He insists that I have only to give my genuine
convictions. I admit the novelty in newspaper writing but urge its
insufficiency. 'Not at all', says he. I am to be allowed to produce one
volume novels on Questions of the Day. Morley is quoted as being
utterly of his opinion. I propose to him an Opera libretto to popularise
the Democratic movement and bring our chief personages before the
eyes of the nobility. O[dger?] in love with the Princess L[ouise?]
meditates the *enlèvement* of the lady that he may breed Radicals from
Royalty: delivers idea in ballad. B[right?], impressionable to poetry
and music, is half won, but checked by religious sentiment:—Ballad—
The Waverer.[4]

Fred savagely: 'Good God! How you can spout buffoonery in
times like these!'

Pathetic ballad by M[axse] 'In times like these'.

The poor fellow danced with disgust. He is fast *assombrissant tout
entier.*

Your article on Byron admirable: nothing so good yet written of
him and from the highest view.[5] I confessed to Fred that if I could
write like that I would write more prose. He groaned. He has a private
chamber of groans.

George Meredith

P.S.—I sent Greenwood a review of an imaginary volume of poems,
'Armageddon, etc.', dedicated to Dr. Cumming[6] of Scotland. The
wretch posted proofs, but his courage seems to have failed him.

463. *To* WILLIAM HARDMAN

MS.: Yale. Excerpt published: Ellis, p. 260.

Box Hill

December 11, 1870

My dearest Tuck,

I would not write until I had thoroughly mastered the state of

462. [4] W. M. Meredith understandably prints only the initials of the actors in this Opera.
George Odger, a trade unionist who became President of the General Council of the
International Association of Working Men in 1870, Princess Louise, whose approaching
marriage to Lord Lorne was formally announced on 24 Oct., and John Bright, Quaker
and Radical politician, seem to me the most likely persons to have been named by GM.

[5] Morley's essay on Byron appeared in the *FR* (Dec. 1870); in it he treats Byron as
'the poet of the Revolution'.

[6] The Revd. John Cumming, D.D., expounder of prophecy and minister of the
Scottish Church, Covent Garden.

amazement I was thrown into by your last communication—used as I am to see you swell like a balloon and away to the empyrean![1] The vision of you in the robes obfuscates me still. Gods! what a sight. But we shall have it in a picture. Of all the list of dignities I have conceived for you as sure to fall to your lot, that of Mayor of the town of your adoption was alone beyond my prophetic ken. And I dare say you walk as composedly as a common man! For the moment I am not quite equal to meeting you on the terms of ancient friendship I know you will, sated with earthly grandeurs, insist upon. I must first go through a preparatory course of some sort, and I mean to write to a Committee of the New Educational Board for the receipt. I love to enter my friend's house, but should the appalling reflection come on me, without my being prepared for it that I am in a Mayor's nest, I am certain I shall give way.

You are rapidly destroying the sense of wonder in me, Tuck. Where will you stop? Are there bounds to you? I might vision you ultimately taking flight as one of the cherubic host, discarding the robes of blue and yellow, but that imagination never could deprive you of what you are so largely endowed with.——

You speak regarding Vaux.[2] Ahem. According to his spouse's report, he, poor fellow, is Vaux et praeterea nihil. She, they say, fierily postulated or -trated her case *links und rechts*. There are some lines of Catullus will describe said 'case'. May I quote them to you out of the dialogue between Janus and Catullus?—

> —non qui illam vir prior attigerit
> Languidior tenera cui *pendens sicula beta*
> NUNQUAM se MEDIAM sustulit *ad* tunicam.——[3]

(!)

Alas! Tuck, not even half way—a melancholy peruser of mother earth! To employ the German idiom—he had no amatory standpoint, so say the informed: . . . and that the lady has sofa'd her dozens, even as pancakes on the pan . . . Close we those curtains.—I long to spend a couple of evenings with you. I will write and propose myself

---

463. [1] Hardman had just been elected Mayor of Kingston-on-Thames.

[2] Two persons of this name are mentioned in Hardman's monthly letters, but I think it would be unfair to speculate on which, if either, is referred to here.

[3] Catullus, *Veronensis Liber*, lxvii. 20–22 Oct.:

> Non illam vir prior attigerit,
> Languidior tenera cui pendens sicula beta
> Nunquam se mediam sustulit ad tunicam:

An obscene (and disputed) passage which may be rendered, 'Her previous husband could not have touched her, since his organ, hanging flabbier than a soft beet, could never raise itself halfway up its tunic'.

shortly. Give my love to D: Troïa and the Miss Hardmans. Wilkins well, and Marie.

I am ever your affectionate
George Meredith

Norbiton Hall for sale! Whither whither whither, whither do you wander? Write me a line soon. How do you like the last of *Richmond*?

464. *To* AUGUSTUS JESSOPP

MS.: Yale. Printed: *Altschul Catalogue*, p. 48.

Box Hill
December 22, 1870

My dearest Jessopp,

I thank you a thousand times for your suggestion about the scholarship; and I have written word to Arthur thereanent.[1] I might be able to support him at Oxford for a couple of years; I don't quite know, but my wife and I would make a strain for the lad. I am writing in haste. Letters sent to Ch[apman] & Hall's are late in reaching me. O Jessopp! my address is still Box Hill, Dorking, and then, if you and the best of wifes and comrades would visit us, and consent to be quartered for the nights at the neighbouring inn, how glad we should be to have you! I promise on my honour I would listen decorously to your criticisms on my over-critical quality as a writer of fiction. I would, in default of evidence try to believe that you have a meaning in the said remarks. I would take your estimate of the fourth of a serial work as if it were based on a summary of the unpublished whole.[2] Indeed I would be thoroughly satisfied, though you are not. Look in the January number of the *Fortnightly Review* for an Ode.[3] Reprehend me in a gentle encomium. Have you seen Sandys? He will not answer my letters. But do you, and let me know where I can next address you and whether there is a chance of our seeing you.

Your loving (and your wife's)
George Meredith

464. [1] Arthur, who had been discouraged by his father in his desire to become a writer, was considering a career in philology. Nothing came of Jessopp's suggestion that he try for a Taylorian Scholarship in modern languages at Oxford.
[2] *The Adventures of Harry Richmond*, running serially in the *Cornhill Magazine*.
[3] 'France, 1870.'

465. *To* ARTHUR G. MEREDITH

Text: *Letters*, i. 216–18.

> Box Hill, Dorking, England
> December 23, 1870

My dearest Arthur,

I hope you will get this letter on the morning of Christmas Day to greet you and wish you happiness, strength, and fortune, which results from the two former gifts.—There will be money for you. Meantime if you are in want of funds, you can apply to the Professor for assistance with my sanction. I know I can rely on you to be moderate, and you in turn will feel that I desire you to have sufficient for your needs. Supposing you should go to Heidelberg for a few days you must have the wherewithal. Be careful to be warmly clad. And when on a tour have a care of your tongue and your company. The Professor says you do not consort with Germans at all. I am grieved at this. I am sure you do not altogether underrate the fine qualities of German youth; but perhaps your immediate sympathies, and a somewhat exaggerated sensitiveness, stand in your way. It will be a pity, if this is so, and for more reasons than one. If you do not cultivate the people you are living amongst in your youth, you will fail in having pleasant places to look back on—landmarks of your young days. And besides, the Germans are your hosts, and you owe them at least a guest's thankfulness. I esteem them deeply for their fine moral qualities. Just now they are abusing us roundly, but that will pass away. I know they have the capacity for friendship, and that as a rule English friendships are not so lasting. Look around you, and try to be accessible to your German associates. Consider whether you are not yielding to luxurious pre-dispositions in your marked preference for English ones. You will see enough of the latter when you return here.—I have had a letter from Mr. Jessopp, in which he suggests that you might when you come back go to Oxford and try for the Taylour[1] Scholarship in modern languages. Your knowledge of German might give you a chance. Are you sure that you are thoroughly grounded in German to stand a sharp competitive examination?—that is, to write good scholarly German prose; and perhaps translate into German verse. Set to your mind this task. Let me hear what you think of it. By winning the Scholarship you might be on your way to a fellowship. I will do my best to support you; that you may be sure of. But you will have to fall to work rigorously. Of course I like you to indulge in composition, but now is the time to store facts, to sharpen your weapon, to make

---

465. [1] See Note 1, preceding letter.

yourself capable by serving your apprenticeship. This is what the Germans do—they serve their apprenticeship thoroughly; and as they are not critics before their time, they are competent critics when the time comes.

Don't think I preach too much. I am naturally anxious about you. I have passed through the wood, and know which are the paths to take, which to avoid. By following my directions you will spare yourself many troubles, many a heartache.—Mr. Morley, who is an Oxford man, says that you would have a fair chance of the Taylour Scholarship, if you have a grammatical and literary mastery of German. You would have to choose two languages. Absolute excellence in one would land you victor. Mr. Swinburne gained the Scholarship through his knowledge of French, which is consummate. Probably Professor Max Müller[2] would be one of the examiners.

We have now the winter on us. Let me hear what you are doing, and how it fares with you. You never speak of the other fellows living with the Professor. Can you make nothing of them?—Have you had your interview with Marshal Canrobert?[3] Major Poussielque is commanding, I believe, at Langres, which is now invested. Good-bye, my dear boy, and God be with you.

Your loving father,
George Meredith

Do not forget to present my warmest compliments and my Christmas greetings to Professor Zeller and his wife.

466. *To* WILLIAM HARDMAN

MS.: Yale. Excerpt published: *Letters*, i. 221.

[Box Hill, Dorking]
December 26, 1870

My dear Lord Mayor,

All Christmas honours and delights to you! Yesterday we were made safe forever only by believing, every man Jack of us! My Lord, it is my hope that I shall follow you into the Kingdom of Heaven. By Gad, Tuck, I'll clutch a tight hold of the skirts of your Corporation and if you go in St. Peter must do more than flourish his celestial keys to keep me out.

465. [2] Friedrich Max Müller (1823–1900), formerly Taylorian Professor of Modern Languages and currently Professor of Comparative Philology at Oxford.
[3] François Certain Canrobert (1809–95), Marshal of France, had been captured at Metz and was a prisoner in Germany.

The other day I quietly informed Morley of your elevation. Looking at him (about one minute subsequently) I saw him collecting his Editorial fragments with a hand pressed hard on his fore midriff. He faintly expressed his amazement, but, as became a hero, his first thought was for his friend. Morison, he said, must not swallow this unheard-of pill[1] without due preparation: it would be too much for him in his sad state. We agreed to concoct a rigmarole, and write an account of a Kingston Pantomime—'Tuck Transformed'—telling him at the end of it that all was true. (The Pantomime closes with procession in State to Holberton's[2] Home.) Morley and I have determined, at the first intimation of success of the French arms, to get up a subscription for an altar piece:—

Apotheosis of T[uck]

A Christmas table of Wild Boar's Head, Ribs of Beef. Plum P[udding] —with honest hands grasping below—Blessedness above—in the centre the Great one rising.

Morison, I fear, is in a very bad way. I don't speak of it.—

At Nonancourt they have the Uhlans. Theodore Vulliamy, a sweet Protestant heart, admires the Grace they say over his meat and wine. He is tenderly paternal too. They nursed a baby they found in a cottage. He wept at the sight.—Henry Poussielque is at Langres now in the thick of it, a good soldier, and I trust he may be spared. Once more, Tuck, and for the fortieth time, I tell you to look at my 'Ode to France' in the forthcoming number of the *Fortnightly Rev[ie]w*. And now may all legitimate pleasures be yours, may your wife still see you scaling eminences (*Vide* altar piece pictures) and accept my love and esteem, and your children flourish, as I am happy to state that Willie Godson does, and Arturus of Stuttgart.

Your cordial
George Meredith

467. *To* FREDERICK A. MAXSE

Text: *Letters*, i. 222.

Box Hill, Dorking
January 3, 1871

My dear Fred,

Your last letter from Effingham Hill reached me (with the date on

466. [1] Morison, it may be remembered, was the son of the vendor of a well-known vegetable pill.
[2] Vicar of Norbiton, Hardman's old opponent in the bells affair. See Note 2, Letter 333.

the envelope Dec. 9) on Sunday morning, open. I have written to the Postmaster-General about it.—According to appointment I walked up to Ranmore, hailed for you in dense fog, and had, like the just man, nothing but the sound of my own voice for answer.

Good health to you and all dear to you this New Year! It begins lamentably. We need to be braced.

The French seem upon their final errand, as far as Paris is concerned. —Tell me how you take to my Ode now that you have it.—Karl Blind's article[1] is good: Von Sybel's[2] a professorial diversion—one smells the cognac of victory. Still I like him and note in him curiously where the German mind, broad though it is, flattens. The French points up. That the two should not be in harmony is our desperate look out. Adieu, my dear Fred.

Your loving
George Meredith

468. *To* WILLIAM HARDMAN

MS.: Yale. Excerpts published: Ellis, p. 261.

Box Hill
February 15, [1871]

Dear Son of Greatness, Tuck!

I wonder whether you can take me in on Saturday or Sunday? I am free to roam for three or four days and have visits to pay,—the pleasantest to my Tuck.—I read of you at the recent Kingston festival.

> Cool you proceed at speed
>   From station unto station,
> While I but in giving heed
>   Shed drops of perspiration!

For the 9000th time, have you read my ode to France in her agony— in [the] January number of *Fortnightly*?—

Please send me word in reply to question of my visiting you—to the Garrick Club.—I suppose the French are for peace now.[1] They rage and foam at us like the devil. I am in sorrow about them, but I fear they have too many of the devil's passions to float, though they have

---

467. [1] 'Results of French Designs upon Germany', *FR* (Jan. 1871).
    [2] 'The German Empire', ibid.
468. [1] Paris had fallen on 28 Jan., with the signing of an armistice, and a National Assembly overwhelmingly in favour of peace assembled at Bordeaux on 12 Feb. The Treaty of Frankfurt, officially concluding the war, was signed on 10 May.

many a noble turning, and are always a picture, good for study.—
Willie Godson has had bad Influenza, which he bequeathed to his
father, flooring me completely. I am still a little nosey.

But I say, tell me you're not going to wear the robes—I can't
stand it.—The fate of Semele warns me.[2] Adieu. My love to D'Troïa
and the fair fruit of the siege, now stately tall as pines on Ida!—Put me
off, if you have engagements. I *ought* to spend a day with Jones.

Your loving
George Meredith

469. *To* AUGUSTUS JESSOPP

Text: Sotheby Catalogue, (27 Nov.–4 Dec. 1911), p. 23.

[Written on Garrick Club paper]
February 18, [1871]

... I have been blockaded by influenza, with none but a nasal communication with the outer world; just recovering some manly use of
my senses now.... Your praise is always 'generous and refreshing' in
the actual sense. And apart from its noble bouncing quality I rarely
get any.

['(After alluding to two misprints in his poem on France—"France,
December, 1870", printed in the *Fortnightly Review*—he says that he
has been to see a picture by Sandys, as well as the Exhibition of Old
Masters, which)']

contains things to dream of. Such Moronis![1]—one, an ecclesiastic and
scholar, will live as long as the canvas. I go again to-day, having a post
influenza holiday, and saying, *Really* life is worth the burden of it,
after all. I am hoping to filch a Grand Drama from Time, if the old
villain does not screw his pocket awry and turn and tweak me in the act.

[2] Semele was destroyed by lightning when she asked to see Zeus in all his glory. GM
is speaking of Hardman's Mayor's robes.
469. [1] Giambattista Moroni (?1525–78), Italian painter.

470. *To* TOM TAYLOR

MS.: University of Texas.

Box Hill, Dorking
February 24, 1871

My dear Tom,

Will you and your Laura choose which you would like to have of these two enclosed.[1] Both resemble the little man as he was a year back: but if both take your heart you may keep them.

Ever yours,
George Meredith

471. *To* FREDERICK A. MAXSE

Text: typed copy, Maxse Papers. Published: *Letters*, i. 222–4, with omissions.

February 27, 1871

My dear Fred,

So you have returned to Holly Hill! I have been waiting to hear from you that you were there. Unfortunately for me, you write a week too late. I had a holiday last week, and was in want of change of air after a racking Influenza.—If I have another chance before Easter, I will ask you for three days' shelter.

Your speech reads capitally. I heard from Harrison at a dinner some time back that you spoke well at the London meeting; but some one told me that you obeyed a voice bidding you 'cut it short'. Is it the fact?—Falvey alive again![1]

Things are saddening enough in France. But do I not remember the gloomy forecasts following the Wars of Napoleon I? The Germans have retaliated in coin. They too must pay for it. These developments only prove that our speculations were more advanced than realities. Through such a course of teaching men must go. Can you pretend to believe that France was not in need of the bitterest of lessons? Her philosophers said one thing, but military glory stuck to the passions of her people. And many of her philosophers allowed themselves to be

470. [1] Pictures of little Will Meredith.
471. [1] So late as Jan. 1871 Maxse was among those who believed that France could be saved by English intervention. Frederic Harrison (*Autobiographic Memoirs*, 1911, ii. 15) says that he and others held a meeting of trade unionists at St. James's Hall on 10 Jan. and that Maxse and Sir William Marriott, 'both then looking out for Radical seats', and Bradlaugh spoke. Maxse's speech was afterwards printed with a pamphlet entitled *The German Yoke* (1871). (Falvey eludes me.)

hoodwinked by the idea that France should be dominant 'for the good of mankind', instead of seeking to make her dominant by virtue and a bright example. She trusted to the sword without even testing her steel. She is down. I grieve for her; I detest the severities practised upon her. But I cannot forget that she appealed to the *droit du plus fort*. Nor can I forget that she has always been the perturbation of Europe. The Germans may be. That is to be seen. They at least are what they pretend to be. A considerable number of cheap prophets have followed their triumphant march howling. I prefer to wait without prophesying. Let France train a virtuous democracy, and she will spring a mine in Germany amply to be revenged on the Hohenzollerns. Her cries of vengeance now are after the pattern—too shockingly similar!—of Ancient Pistol. She 'eats and ene she swears'.[2]

What I wish is that you and I should look to the good future of men with some faith in it, and capacity to regard current phases of history without letting our sensations blind and bewilder us. I am neither German nor French, nor, unless the nation is attacked, English. I am European and Cosmopolitan—for humanity! The nation which shows most worth, is the nation I love and reverence.

Confess that the French have conducted themselves like mere children throughout. The probation may accelerate their growth and bring their practice up to their best professions. The Germans have behaved as the very sternest of men, caring more for their Fatherland than for the well-being of men in the mass. I am susceptible of admiration of their sterling qualities, holding nevertheless that they will repent of the present selfish restriction of their views.—Rage at me, Fred! It is better to bend the knee to Wisdom than march in the chorussing ranks of the partizans.—I think with pain that the Germans enter Paris this very day![3] But the City is not a 'holy City' for me. The astonishing delusion which makes Frenchmen think it so is one proof of rudderless brains. Morley is not 'German'. He agrees with me that it would have been a silly madness to create a terrible and a justly wrathful enemy for ourselves (looking to the origin of this war), on the chance of securing a frenzied fantastical ally. So will you in time. Generous sympathies hold you spell-bound.

Your ever loving
George Meredith

[2] *Henry V*, v. i. 49–50:
> By this leek, I will most horribly revenge:
> I eat and eat, I swear—

[3] Actually the entry was made on 1 Mar.

472. *To* FREDERICK A. MAXSE

Text: typed copy inserted in W. M. Meredith's copy of *Letters* (Bodleian Library).

Box Hill
March 23, 1871

Exquisite loyalty, Fred! Consider that our 'Liberal' papers were all snuffing and giving tongue in the same track.

But the worst feature is, the mean perfidiousness of all this middle-class homage. Are you not sure, from previous hints and grumblings of this *Times*, that its flunkey readers would, were disaster to strike the island, be the first to howl at the Princes for bleeding them, and decry their large propagation.

Could there be a fiercer revolutionist than an English middle class man ruined?

Still these people of all classes have patience. Think of the Parisians! The assassination of Thomas and Lecomte[1] has ruined the Republic. Impatient fury is their curse. I am immensely downcast by the news from France.

Is young Cremer[2] going to carve a way to the upper front with his sword?

By the way, the marriage ceremony report in the *Times*, speaking of the Duke of Argyll in the kilt, as 'having every essential to that garb', was comforting.[3] On the whole Borthwick[4] took the noblest plunge into our national mire.

In future don't send me columns of print without a word in your handwriting.

Yours,
George Meredith

472. [1] Generals Thomas and Lecomte were seized by the Central Republican Committee of Montmartre, tried, and executed. Lecomte was accused of having ordered troops to fire on crowds in the Place de Pigalle, and Thomas was allegedly arrested with a plan of the barricades of Montmartre in his possession (*The Times*, 21 Mar.).

[2] The *Globe* (22 Mar.) reported that General Cremer had accepted the superior command of the forts and *enceinte* about Paris.

[3] The ceremony was the marriage of the Princess Louise to the Marquess of Lorne, eldest son of the Duke of Argyll, on 21 Mar.

[4] i.e. the *Morning Post*.

473. *To* JOHN MORLEY[1]

Text: *Letters*, i. 224–6, with the name of the addressee blank.

Box Hill
March 23, 1871

My dear Morley,

I will answer as plainly as you have written. I cannot but be shocked and grieved to think of the effect my manner of speaking has had in clashing with your 'opinions, ideas, and likings'. But that this should prompt you to tell me that it makes my society seem baneful to you; and that only with me do you suffer the consciousness that you fail to get new strength, and that your complaint of me is not captious because I am the only friend who has ever caused you to complain— these are accusations which point in one direction, that is, to the end of our intimacy. You consent to say that upon the larger matters we are one. I have thought so, and have considered the minor differences too small to dwell on, the possible expression of them by one or the other of us too mean a subject for the preciousness of friendship in our short life to brood on. For I am sensitive, and I likewise have thought myself here and there roughly used by you. But I pardoned the offend- ing minute when the hour had struck, and never thought of identifying the offence with my friend. I chose to blame myself, as the safer way of closing a slight wound. It seems that I have been roughening you for six months. When I last came over to you I was bright with the happiness of being with you, and I remember I denounced (as I sup- posed I might do to a friend) a poem that struck me as worthless. I spoke

473. [1] GM had received a letter from Morley in which Morley spoke of the pain inflicted upon him over a period of six months by GM's rough treatment of his 'opinions, ideas, and likings'. Little more is known of the episode. In Letters 454 and 456 of the preceding July GM had condemned Buchanan's *Book of Orm*, which Morley apparently admired, and in Letter 462 of 7 Dec. had alluded playfully to Morley's taking of a treeless house without consulting him as treachery, but the causes of the breach are more likely to have sprung from personal meetings and from GM's manner of urging his own opinions. Stevenson is right in speaking (pp. 186–7) of a certain insensitiveness in GM's compre- hension of the feelings of his friends and in pointing to similar breaks with Swinburne and Rossetti and frequent bickering with Wyse. In 1874, as a result of the friendly intervention of Greenwood and Maxse, Morley accepted *Beauchamp's Career* for serialization in the *FR*, and the friendship between the two was resumed.

Morley, in his *Recollections* (i. 42), says of GM: 'He was considerate, benevolent, and just, but the strong-hearted Pity, that was a glorious and visible note of Victor Hugo even at his most grandiose, was hardly a gift of Meredith's.' In alluding to GM's break with a friend, without revealing that the friend was himself, he continues: 'He was tender enough to feel the wound of even temporary alienations. A friend to whom he was much attached, troubled by something or another in his demeanour or too down- right and imperious speech, had written in foolish offence that they might perhaps not unwisely part company for a time. His reply was a model of magnanimous solicitude. . . . We may be quite sure that the breach, though its causes were not wholly superficial, quickly vanished in loyal oblivion.'

like a man coming off a country-road fasting. It may be too often my manner. I might well think my friend would not let it live with him, and that he knew my mind better than to allow a sense of variance to spring from such differences in open talk. Possibly a nature that I am proud to know never ceases in its growth, is passing now through some delicate stage which finds me importunate; or you feel that you have outstripped me, and are tempted to rank me with the vulgar. I can bring a thousand excuses for a letter that I have read often to assure myself it is among the things which are, but arrive only at the conclusion I have named. We will see one another as little as we can for two or three years, and by and by may come together again naturally. And if not, you will know I am glad of the old time, am always proud of you, always heart in heart with you on all the great issues of our life, and in all that concerns your health and fortunes. I suffer too much to-day to desire that any explanation should restore us to our past footing. Almost I am tempted to hope that I am quite valueless to you, for as I am not a man to send such a letter as you have just written to me, without deeply weighing every word in it and probable signification of its burden to the reader, or without weighing my feelings well against my friend's, so I am not the man to receive one without determining to abandon a position that has exposed me to be wounded. What you have permitted yourself to write, and I to quote from you, cuts friendship to the ground. That I should be the only one of your friends ever to have done you harm, is not a nice distinction to reflect on. But I think I have said enough. I have answered you plainly and fully, and as to a sane man master of the meaning of his words and meaning exactly what they commonly convey.

I am ever yours faithfully and
warmly,
George Meredith

474. ? *To* FREDERICK GREENWOOD

MS.: Yale.

Box Hill
April 25, [1871]

My dear [name effaced: ? Greenwood][1]
  You will have heard of the wrath of all the fools at your 'Note' with

---

474. [1] This letter must have been written to Greenwood, who was editor of the *PMG* until 1880. It is difficult to account for the effacing of the name on any other score than the letter having got into the hands of someone who had no legal right to it.

the quotations from Reynolds's putrid paper,[2] and that it conveyed a stench to the nose of her M[a]j[e]sty, which caused her to declare the *Pall Mall* interdicted at her table. But, if you haven't heard the same, still it's true, and, for the sake of the journal, would it not be as well for you to pen a Note on Misconceptions, hinting at the burdens imposed upon a journal that is expected to supply its readers with intelligence; the dangers incident to the not writing everything in full etc.— You see what I mean; *cite the Note.*

The article 'Prestige'[3] should have touched on Carlyle's definition in the 'Niagara' pamphlet.

Ever yours,
George Meredith

475. *To* ARTHUR G. MEREDITH

Text: *Letters*, i. 226–7.

Garrick Club
June 12, 1871

My dear Arthur,

The enclosed letter will introduce you to a lady who is the mother of (I met him at Mr. Benecke's at Mickleham, three days before the declaration of war last year) a Lieutenant von Schweizerbarth, a very gallant young officer. I have the letter from his brother, and I wish you to know him; from what I saw of him he is a gentleman, and I shall be glad to hear that you have made his acquaintance. He was, I believe, in all the chief actions and battles of the Würtemberg army, and before Paris, and fought at Le Bourget. He constantly sent communications to his mother during the progress of the war, and these were forwarded to Mickleham and were singularly modest and very interesting. Let me know whether you have seen him when you next write.

To-morrow is your birthday, my dear boy, and we all wish you happiness. I put down £2 as a tip to you, and you will receive £10 out of my money order to Professor Zeller for your journey either on the Danube or where you will. Out of this £12 I suppose you will find enough. I know that when I was a lad it would have made me jump

---

[2] On 11 Apr. the *PMG* in 'Occasional Notes' quoted the bulletin in *Reynolds' Newspaper* announcing the birth of a prince at Sandringham under the large-type heading 'Another Inauspicious Event'. The death of the child, under the heading 'A Happy Release', read: 'We have much satisfaction in announcing that the newly-born child of the Prince and Princess of Wales died shortly after its birth, thus relieving the working classes of England from having to support hereafter another addition to the long roll of State beggars they at present maintain.'

[3] In the 24 Apr. 1871 issue of the *PMG*.

like the French statue of Freedom on the column of the Bastille. The trip you propose looks promising. As to Vienna, you are quite aware of my objections to your going there. Still if you give me your word to behave honourably I shall not oppose your going.[1] Dr. Sana's last address in Vienna was No. 5 Kleeblattgasse near the Graben. I am sure he would be delighted to see you, but whether he is in Vienna now I cannot tell. Captain Brackenbury[2] lives in England. He was *Times* Correspondent with the army of Prince Frederick-Charles from Orleans to Le Mans. If you see Dr. Sana, perhaps he will take you round the beautiful Hollenthal and up the Schneeberg, as he did me, and it would be capital fun for you. The Schneeberg is about eight hours from Vienna (that is, you will be near the Chalets in that time). Go to the Belvedere at Vienna; the pictures are notable; there are superb Titians. The hotel Stadt Frankfort has good cookery, and if you mount to the third floor is not dear. It is close to the Graben, and is therefore the most central place you could find, though a little dearer than some of the suburb hotels, which are, however, dirty, I am told.— But here is your Aunt Sarah[3] inviting you to Dauphiné again. What do you say? It rests with you to decide upon your course. At any rate, write to her.—On the 10th your Mama presented us with a little girl; so besides a brother you have now a sister,[4] and I hope no more. Mother and babe are in excellent condition. I think I shall be at Stuttgart some time in August. This is not certain; it depends on supplies, but I want very much to see you and shall do my utmost to come.

Your loving father,
George Meredith

475. [1] In a reply of 20 June (now among the Maxse Papers) Arthur wrote: 'You may rely on my not doing anything in Vienna which I would think would displease you.'

[2] Captain (later Col. and Temporary Maj.-Gen.) Charles Booth Brackenbury (1831–90) served in the Crimea and subsequently filled various positions at the Royal Military Academy, including the directorship of the Artillery College (1887). He was military correspondent of *The Times* in the Austro-Prussian, the Franco-Prussian, and the Russo-Turkish wars and was author of a number of books and articles on military subjects. As the years went on, GM became increasingly attached to him.

[3] Madame Poussielque.

[4] The child was christened Marie Eveleen (after Mrs. Meredith and Eveleen Mary Smith, daughter of Captain and Mrs. John Smith of Mickleham Hall) but was usually called Mariette. Of the news of her birth Arthur wrote formally (letter of 20 June, Maxse Papers): 'Nothing could cause me more pleasure than the news you give me of the birth of a little sister. . . . I warmly congratulate Mamma and you and hope that we may all three grow up dutifully to you remembering when we are of age the good that you have done to us in our youth.'

476. *To* WILLIAM TINSLEY[1]

MS.: Yale.

> Flint House
> Mickleham, Dorking
> June 23, [1871][2]

Dear Sir,

I am so hard at work both here and on the rare days when I am in town that I cannot be certain of calling on you within a week. Can you come here?—We can then make an arrangement to your satisfaction and I can show you some work. I dine at seven and can give you a bed. A train leaves Victoria or London bridge a little after 4 and after 5 p.m. to *West Humble*. A train will take you back in the morning in time for business. It will be a great favour to me if you can decide to come:—say Monday or Tuesday next week. Be sure I do not allow debts to be unpaid for a longer term than I can help.

Write by return post.

> Yours very faithfully,
> George Meredith

477. *To* WILLIAM TINSLEY

Text: typed transcript furnished by Professor Lionel Stevenson, from the original letter in the Duke University Library.

> Mickleham, Dorking
> July 3, [1871]

Dear Sir,

I will save you from any possible inconvenience by making a point of calling next week, if you can't resolve to have a day in the country. My arrangement was to spare you the loss of a day at your business; and I wanted you to come that I might show you MSS. in progress to completion. It is still open to you to come if you like in the morning, but I can't let you go off at night. Decide therefore so as to please yourself. On Monday and Tuesday I am here. On Wednesday most probably in town but my hand is too full of work for me to appoint it positively. Understand that I wish to give you no trouble of any sort.

476. [1] William Tinsley (1831–1902) had published *Rhoda Fleming* in 1865.
[2] The year is established by other letters in the series to Tinsley. Apparently the obligation with which the letters are concerned was incurred in connexion with *Rhoda Fleming*, which Tinsley had published in 1865 in return for one-fourth share of the profits. The book sold poorly and, I infer, did not repay costs. GM hoped to discharge his debt by publication of further work through Tinsley.

The debt has been left unsettled owing to my having kept back my work to perfect it more. It was honourably incurred by me out of consideration for your house, because I doubted the chances of the novel attaining popularity: but it must not the less be paid; and it strikes me still that in a conference here we might arrive at a better understanding than under your skylight.

Yours very truly,
George Meredith

478. *To* ARTHUR CECIL BLUNT[1]

MS.: University of Texas. Published: *Letters*, i. 228.

Box Hill, Dorking
July 4, 1871

My dear Blunt,

Would it suit you as well to come on Saturday week? Some one makes a point of asking me to leave home on Sunday, and it strikes me that wet weather in this small and (except in babies) barren crib would act evilly on your nervous system. But, as I want you to come to walk you over these hills, decide *positively* for this Saturday if you are engaged for the following Saturday. Now this is plain. In any case prepare to tramp, fair or foul.

And write to me.

Your faithful
George Meredith

479. *To* FREDERICK SANDYS

MS.: University of Texas.

Box Hill
July 4, [1871]

My dear Sandys,

If I can come up to-morrow I will, and with a glad mind to see you again, and we'll dine at the Garrick—rather early; but it's a little uncertain, owing to work I have on hand. I did not get your letter till

478. [1] Well known as an actor under the name Arthur Cecil (1843–96). He joined the German Reed company in 1869, and was later joint-manager of the Court Theatre.

late last night on my return from town.—I am very anxious to hear
that you are weathering the cape, are out of the shallows.[1] Let me hear
from you, a good cheerful letter, if you don't see me. I have had so
many botherations of all sorts that I can't see a fellow fighting for free
breath without a bit of myself in him. Tell me it's over—

My wife thanks you for your good welcome of her little lass and
message to herself. She is up and well, and the babe is one of those
miracles of healthy machinery which dispose of milk in gallons *per
diem et noctem*, and when not operating sleep to prepare for further.
Willie is superb in strength, good looks, and lazyness. Arthur starts
to the Danube, Styria, Vienna, for a month's tour, about the 15th—
from Stuttgart. I hope to be over to see him on his return. Adieu—to
shake your hand soon, I trust.

Ever your faithful
George Meredith

480. *To* FREDERICK SANDYS

MS.: University of Texas.

Box Hill
Thursday, [? July 6, 1871]

My dear Sandys,
    There are trains from London Bridge L.B. and S.C. line at 4.20—
and 5.10—If you are off to-morrow, we implore you to come to-day.
It will be a great delight to us. As for me I am tied. I can't well leave
the house at night with none but women in it, and I am busy busy busy.
So you're the one to move, and do.

Yours ever,
George Meredith

Willie is a sight and the female babe a beauty.

481. *To* FREDERICK A. MAXSE

Text: *Letters*, i. 228–9. Collated with typed copy in the Maxse Papers.

Box Hill, Dorking
July 11, 1871

My dear Fred,
    Willie is delighted with his toy,[1] and all day long we hear shots and

479. [1] A metaphorical allusion, no doubt, to Sandys's constantly recurring financial
crises.
481. [1] An early birthday present? Willie's birthday was 26 July.

may see men transformed into women in a jiffy—to the mockery of the actual!—Will your poet's dreams ever bring us to the happy state of toys, that one crack in the eye may turn a hairy beast into a lovely beauty? You quote your poets, Fred, and expect them to perform just similar prodigies. Not what *should* be, but what *can*, as a step thereunto, is the reasonable aim. Nor will any of your pop-guns pelleted with uncompromising decisions affect much the existing state of things, though they will, I often fear, wear you out before your time. You do well, and even nobly, but you are one half wrong, for you go against nature, and nature says that to work soundly the creature must be in that state of contentment to which philosophy points you and poetry elevates you. You deny to man the right to be in this state while there is one miserable upon the earth, and you deny to the little ones peace in their infancy because of the existence of error. To put it in one word, the character of your opposition is *impatience*. Adieu.

I love you, and am yours,

George M.

482. *To* WILLIAM TINSLEY

MS.: Dartmouth College. Excerpt Published: American Art Association Catalogue (8 Feb., n.y.).

[Written on Garrick Club paper]

August 8, 1871

Dear Mr. Tinsley,

Your letter hit me in midflight to the Continent. I shall be back in about five weeks and will make an arrangement to pay the money if you cannot wait for the novel. Your patience I do not dispute; but before a novel is out of my hands I like it to be as good as I can make it.

Yours very truly,

George Meredith

483. *To* AUGUSTUS JESSOPP

MS.: Yale. Printed: *Altschul Catalogue*, pp. 48–49 (dated *October 11, 1871*); excerpts published: Stevenson, pp. 188–9.

Box Hill, Dorking
October 4, 1871

Dear and most Reverend Doctor of D.[1]—and of L. too, I trust, and may'st thou be ever a charm against him who so begins and ends the letters of his name, without whom thy craft is nothing!—I have returned from a six weeks on the continent and eight days with Arthur. He is a short man, slightly moustached, having a tuft of whisker; a good walker, a middling clear thinker, sensible, brilliant in nothing, tending in no direction, very near to what I predicted of him as a combatant in life, but with certain reserve qualities of mental vigour which may develop; and though he seems never likely to be intellectually an athlete, one may hope he will be manful. His manner of earning his bread in the earlier stages threatens to be that of the mass of us. In a competitive examination of fifty he would be about the twenty fifth; but in an aside conversation the penetrative professor would haply discover stores in his mind. An encouraging whip might still get him to go. I have half a mind to send him to Berlin, where study is matter of earnest, and beer and gallivanting denounced with the fury of a Saint's retro S . . .[2] Not that he is tempted at Stuttgart; but he soon takes colour of the heavy mind, and Suabia has not been maligned by the laughter directed at it—the PAUNCH of Germany!—He is always grateful to you.

Don't speak of *Richmond* till you have read the whole. When you have done that, say what you like. I shall be glad of criticism. Consider first my scheme as a workman. It is to show you the action of minds as well as of fortunes—of here and there men and women vitally animated by their brains at different periods of their lives—and of men and women with something of a look-out upon the world and its destinies:—the mortal ones: the divine I leave to Doctors of D. Let those far-sighted gentlemen speak on such subjects.—I dare say the novel won't be liked, but I know my plan, I do my work, and if I am kept very poor I hope to pay all in time. As for recognition of the stuff in my writing and the system it goes on, I care little for it now, and when I thrust myself into the pillory by publishing, the smack in the face and the pat on the shoulder are things in the day's order.

483. [1] Oxford had conferred an honorary D.D. degree upon Jessopp in 1870.
[2] 'Retro, Sathanas' ('Get thee behind me, Satan'): Matt. xvi. 23.

I wish I could come down to meet Palgrave,[3] who is one of the men I could learn from. I wish still more that I could have two or three days with you and your wife. But I have taken my holiday and must buckle to all sorts of work. For the moment the pen is a sprightly courser—is all for Mount Parnassus. Soon it will be jogging the gibbing cab horse. And I have hosts of work in well-defined partitions if only Necessity with a grocer's howl, a butcher's dirk, did not hound me into a daily trot for the bread department. My boy Willie flourishes, and is charming to look at, quick of eye and intelligence, lazy as a sunflower. The babe is a fine one, unmatched for cooing and roaring. My wife would delight in seeing you here. *When* will you two deign to come? You are not real, you are false; you are a mere epistle, a postage stamp! —Adieu. Will you write and tell me Sandys' address and all about yourself.

Your loving
George Meredith

484. *To* WILLIAM TINSLEY

MS.: Yale.

Box Hill
October 18, 1871

Dear Mr. Tinsley,

I meant to call on you yesterday when I was in town, but I was delayed.[1] I will appoint Friday about 12 noon if that should suit you, or the Monday following. It is my wish to settle this matter distinctly, to your satisfaction.

Yours truly,
George Meredith

483. [3] Probably one of the sons of Sir Francis Palgrave (1788–1861), the most likely being (Sir) Robert Harry Inglis Palgrave (1827–1919), banker and economist, who lived at Great Yarmouth, near Norwich. The other sons were Francis (1824–97), editor of *The Golden Treasury*; William Gifford (1826–88), traveller, diplomat, and author of travel narratives; and (Sir) Reginald Francis Douce (1829–1904).
484. [1] For context, see Note 2, Letter 476.

485. *To* WILLIAM TINSLEY

MS.: Yale. Excerpt from typed copy printed: *Altschul Catalogue*, p. 163 (dated *Friday* [1865?]).

Box Hill

Friday, [? October 20, 1871]

Dear Mr. Tinsley,

Do for heaven's sake hold over the bill till the 27th. The Dividends I rely on are not paid before the 26th.—I have been going to call on you daily to ask this and beg you to take £40 and give me a couple of months for the remainder. Surely it would not inconvenience you![1]

I will call on you on Monday. Meantime do me the service I ask of you. I cannot draw before the date I mention.

Ever yours truly,

George Meredith

I have been absent from home;[2] and I really supposed the date of the bill was later or I would not have delayed to call on you.

486. *To* WILLIAM HARDMAN

MS.: Yale. Published: *Letters*, i. 229–30, with minor variants; excerpt published: Stevenson, p. 189.

Box Hill

November 2, [1871]

Dearest Tuck,

Our letters have crossed. Yours has given me great pleasure.[1] The hand of the workman is inspirited by praise, and I know that you and the unpurchaseable D.Troïa never give it but honestly. It struck me that a perusal of the book without enforced pauses might lead you to see that the conception was full and good, and was honestly worked out. I resisted every temptation to produce great and startling effects (after the scene of the Statue, which was permissible in art, as coming from a boy and coloured by a boy's wonder).[2] Note as you read, the gradual changes of the growing Harry, in his manner of regarding his father and the world. I have carried it so far as to make him perhaps dull towards adolescence and young manhood, except to one *studying* the narrative—as in the scenes with Dr. Julius.[3] Such effects are deadly

---

485. [1] Possibly not, but Tinsley failed in 1878 to the extent of £33,000.
   [2] i.e. on the Continent for six weeks.
486. [1] A letter praising *The Adventures of Harry Richmond*, published in book form on 26 Oct.
   [2] In Chapter XVI.   [3] In Chapter XXIX.

when appearing in a serial issue. I was here and there hand-tied, too, by gentlemanly feeling in relation to the royal reigning House, sweet, Tory Tuck! or I should (and did on paper) have launched out. The Speech at the City banquet would have satisfied a Communist Red, originally.[4] And I had planned startling doings for the season of the Grand Parade.[5] But I constrained myself. I suppose I am unlucky, for I hear that the novel does not move. It is confounded by Mudie with the quantity coming out.—Let me hear of your address at Hersham.[6] Shall you have your Gold Barge on the Mole to float down to Kingston in? If so, I should like to accompany you. I have often desired to eat swan on board, and see my countrymen kneeling on the tow-path as the procession goes by.—We have decided to enlarge our cottage, if the walls will stand it; and then we shall have a spare bedroom for friends, and you will visit us. Even now—we have hardly the courage to suggest it—you could have our room at the Burford Inn, and pass a day or two in this region, walking about as in the period when you mooned musically over the tantalizing Siege.[7] Reply to this hint at your leisure.—Do you think that Shirley Brooks would care to read *Richmond*? I don't know his address up in Regent's Park.

—The babes are well. Willie Godson has arrived at the stage of Younker, and in him our little dwelling has to rejoice that it possesses, all in one, a perpetually rolling barrel, an incessant trumpet, a fife indifferently performed upon, a door creaking to every wind, a questioning machine, a hive of bees gone mad in the solstice and mistaking our ears for honey-bells—add on a cat, or its gut, striving after melody untaught. When haply I want to finish a last volume by sending a troublesome old gentleman into Bedlam, I shall bring the Younker on the scene, who will finish him quickly.

Marie Eveleen has shown a taste for dancing. I gave her inadvertently a first lesson and am now her marked victim. She *will* have me, and I have to dance her and sing her, and trot about the room, until, I assure you, half an hour of it is equal to as much of dumb bells or beetel.[8] She was Jennerated[9] last week and has taken well, is a new woman. Adieu. My love to you all, and I am

Ever your affectionate
George Meredith

486. [4] Reduced to a single sentence (Chapter XLI).
   [5] In Chapter XLI.
   [6] About a mile SW. of Esher on the Mole.
   [7] A reference to Hardman's five-year courtship ('siege') of Mary Anne Radley.
   [8] Or beetle, as GM usually spells it.
   [9] i.e. vaccinated.

487. *To* RICHARD H. HORNE

MS.: Ashley Library, British Museum. Printed: *Letters from GM to RHH*, pp. 8–9.

Box Hill, Dorking
November 9, 1871

My dear Horne,

It was kind of you to order your splendid sketch of the *Tragedy of Marlowe* to be sent to me.[1] The work is one of those I have forced my friends to read: and they have repaid me, I hope, by doing the same upon others, for it has long been out of my library, together with *Orion* and the towering figure of Pope Gregory; an image that I see always through your illumination of him.[2] I trust we shall soon have a library edition of your poems and tragedies. In that shape there will be a chance of preserving them about one.—Your letter and photograph from Australia came to me after a great delay;—too late, I assumed, for me to reply to the Australian address.[3] I have no photograph of myself to give in return, and I have not a single copy of poems or novels. They are borrowed and appropriated, and the English world does not think them such plums for its pudding as to call for second editions. I publish and find my head in the pillory, am battered with bad eggs, and am suffered to withdraw promptly. So the task of forgetting the world is not so difficult. I have ceased to care what it thinks in the matter of my contributions to light literature, and aim only at satisfying my own taste. It is the happiest of all states of mind for an author, and the best for inspiring good work in time to come. Let me anticipate that your creative fruits are still as abundant as your mind and heart are strong. No one will be gladder to hear that a new work of yours is in the press than I: few readier to do justice to its merits.

Believe me, / My dear Horne, /
Ever sincerely yours,
George Meredith

487. [1] Horne's *Marlowe* was originally published in 1837, but there was another edition in 1870.

[2] The *BMC* lists a ninth edn. of *Orion*, published in 1872 [1871]. *Gregory VII* had appeared in 1840; there was a third edn. in 1849.

[3] Horne had lived in Australia, where he was commissioner for Crown lands, among other things, between 1852 and 1869.

488. *To* GEORGE SMITH

MS.: Yale.

Box Hill, Dorking
November 14, 1871

Dear Mr. Smith,

I am told that W. H. Smith's Library gives the bound-up copies of the *Cornhill* containing *Richmond* in the place of the 3 volumes.[1] You are the principal party concerned in it. Are you aware of the fact, and is it worth a remonstrance?

Ever yours faithfully,
George Meredith

489. *To* TOM TAYLOR

MS.: University of Texas. Published: *Letters*, i. 231–2, with inaccuracies.

Box Hill, Dorking
November 18, 1871

My dear Tom,

How I envy you the new subject you have chosen![1] It has been ringing through me all the morning. I feel like a man who has been introduced to the beautiful betrothed woman of a friend, and found her incomparable, made for him himself; and all he can do is to cry out in honesty—take warning, if you don't espouse her within a fortnight, and further, if even then you don't do justice to her, positive and spiritual, I feel myself released from the obligation to respect your claims, I will challenge your reputation, and I will be at her forthwith, in contempt of you.

Why not first write the story, and then dramatize it? It would make as lovely a story as striking a drama. For the latter it has every splendid and noble quality. Oh! you happy fellow. But be worthy of your luck. Let nothing delay you.—I repeat my first warning.

What I just fear is, that you will make the brother a villain. Give him some higher ground of action, drop villany. There is here a chance of lending the theme a touch of old tragedy of the classic idea. For this

---

488. [1] *The Adventures of Harry Richmond* was published by Smith, Elder & Company, which was not connected with W. H. Smith & Son.
489. [1] W. M. Meredith says that this refers to Taylor's play, *Lady Clancarty, or Wedded and Wooed*, first produced at the Royal Olympic Theatre, 9 Mar. 1874.

purpose of course you must heighten the hero's character and have him to be more than a simple captain of horse. Jacobitism could hardly inspire him: the sense of fealty might, and it might give occasion to put stress on the ancient notion of loyal sentiment to a race in a young man's heart—inherited. The brother then, standing for law, order, and the like, might think the State had reason to dread this youth. The sister would take the woman's view. Then you have the three in a perfect triangle—fit for your best powers—or mine.

The above only to throw you a modest hint from your hasty outline.

> Ever lovingly yours,
> George Meredith

490. *To* George Smith

MS.: Yale.

> Box Hill, Dorking
> November 19, 1871

Dear Mr. Smith,

This is good news,[1] and it is very good of you to be so prompt in sending the cheque.

As to a preface, I can hardly bring myself to write one.

Will it not be enough to say 'Revised, corrected'?—

What I did was to rewrite a large portion of the work before it appeared in the *Cornhill*: so as to make it an almost entirely different thing from what you read in MS. It has been touched subsequently, but not enough to make mention of it and trip the practice of the library people.

As there has been little reviewing upon it hitherto, will it not be as well to keep the press open if you only print an extra 250 copies?— You will know best as to this point.

I have had six. I want three more, and one to run my pen on. After this I trust I shall not have to beg for further. One I want to be sent by post immediately to—

The / Lady Caroline Maxse, / Effingham Hill, / Dorking.
another to

D. G. Rossetti Esq., / Cheyne Walk, / Chelsea.

I will pay the postage when I call to-morrow for the two other copies.—

490. [1] That a second edition of *Harry Richmond* was called for. See Forman, *Bibliography*.

When I hailed you in an opposition Hansom the other day, I had my boy with me and wanted to show him.

Ever yours faithfully,
George Meredith

Did you send a copy to *The Academy?* I don't know the people, but something like criticism is done there.

491. *To* DANTE GABRIEL ROSSETTI[1]

MS.: University of Texas.

Box Hill, Dorking
November 19, 1871

My dear Gabriel,

I don't think you will care to read a modern novel, but I have ordered my last[2] to be sent to you, so that you may not forget me. I wish it were poetry. My chances of giving myself to such composition as you would care for get more and more into the background, and I am afraid that the impulse to do it bedevils my prose and will always keep me unpopular.—Have you not another **volume** coming out?—There is but one way of overthrowing the Philistines, and that is by hurling a succession of volumes at them. They can despise the quality of books, but quantity persuades them.—I have sent to Swinburne *H[arr]y R[ichmon]d*, written to him, and asked him to come to me; but I have no answer. Can you give me any news of him? If you see him, tell him that if I have offended him I regret it very much. I haven't an idea how it can have occurred.—Here, whenever you have a chance fit of *désœuvrement*, you know you will be always welcome. The cottage is small, but we have quarters for friends at the inn hard by, in a lovely district, under a sheer high descent of box, juniper, beech and yew. And how delightful it would be to me to stroll and have talks with you. It's too good to be hoped for. I am ever

Your loving
George Meredith

And I would read you the first half of a Comedy Play in verse.[3]

---

491. [1] The perfect friendliness of this letter must cast some doubt upon the stories of GM's overt breaks with both Rossetti and Swinburne. See also letter 450.

[2] *Harry Richmond.* See preceding letter.

[3] *The Sentimentalists.*

492. *To* ARTHUR G. MEREDITH

Text: *Letters*, i. 233–4.

Box Hill, Dorking, England
December 16, 1871

My dear Arthur,

Give my warmest regards to Florrie[1] when you arrive at Heidelberg. I think it remarkably kind of her to invite you—though I am sure you make your companionship worth having. I shall be delighted to have a letter from Heidelberg. The Odenwald in winter must be fine: not so suggestive of Ossian as a land of crag and mist, but with a grandeur of its own. As to Ossian and Homer, your choice represents a phase of thoughtful youth. Ossian's imagery is intangible. Homer's is all concrete. Homer's comes up from the heart of Nature. Ossian's is somewhat forced, and seems due to a sentimental habit and the imperiousness of sentiment in colouring all of its own hue. The Homeric battles, Councils and speeches are still as fresh as ever owing to the naturalness of the imagery, the vigour of the flow, the manly music of the lines. The death of Patroclus, the grieving of Achilles, are imperishable things; the parting of Hector and Andromache, the elderly Troy looking at Helen and other scenes:—and observe, that all the characters are distinct, painted without effort, but with the sharp outline of life.—Of course you must make allowance for the ancient spirit: and the truth is, the modern tone (under the guise of a weird, primeval, mystical melody and system of verse) is what catches you. I am not at all sorry, and you have good examples—Napoleon was once in love with Ossian. It has the same effect on the young as ruins of castles and abbeys seen by moonlight. The more imaginative and the sensitive are sure to like him best, but there is not a doubt as to which is the greater poet. In fact you are of an age to like the minor song, and not quite to appreciate the great organ-notes. I have known a period when I would rather have been reading Tennyson than Shakespeare: so you see you have an example. I wish I had time to write on.

Your loving father,
George Meredith

492. [1] Florrie or Florry (Florence) Chapman, daughter of Edward Chapman.

493. *To* MRS. ANNA C. STEELE

MS.: University of Texas.

The Lodge, Eltham
February 7, [? 1872]

My dear Mrs. Steele,

I am commissioned by Mrs. Wood to tell you (as clearly as this pen will allow) that she has had a relapse to her recent malady, and suffers also from catarrhal ophthalmia, and consequently will not be able to receive you this week. But she hopes that if you can make it convenient to come in the following week she may be in a fit condition to give you welcome.

She is decidedly opposed to the claims of 'Hervé Riel'[1] to be poetry or rhetoric or other than spoiled prose. And if you please, I, who am not quite so severe, would just ask you what there is in a fellow's doing what he knows he is perfectly able to do. Why does the poet make much of the 'Surprise in the frank blue Breton eyes'—? even to the extent of dwelling on it twice? Riel thought them all fools for praising him mast-high for doing no more than his business. Now Browning's ballad metre, and the lot he spins the story into, insist on Riel's being a hero, otherwise it's a noise and a tale nearly about nothing.

Dr. Bader[2] prohibits Mrs. Wood from writing and from reading. Thus it is that she appeals to me. She has lost her voice. Believe me

Ever your most faithful
George Meredith

494. *To* [? GEORGE SMITH][1]

Text (excerpt): American Art Association Catalogue (17 Nov., [n.y.]).

Box Hill
February 29, 1872

The strange sensations of an Author positively praying to know the amount of his indebtedness are over, and, whether pleasing or not,

493. [1] First published in the *Cornhill Magazine*, Mar. 1871; with *Pacchiarotto, with Other Poems*, 1876. I do not know how the subject arose.

[2] Dr. Charles Bader, of the staff of Ophthalmology, Guy's Hospital; Mrs. Wood's oculist.

494. [1] I can think of no one else to whom this letter might have been addressed, assuming that GM's debt to Tinsley had been paid. In Letter 490, GM thanks Smith for 'the cheque', which must have been in payment of what was due him on conclusion of *Harry Richmond* in the *Cornhill* or else an advance against the sales of the novel in book form. The remittance mentioned in the letter may have been to cover over-payments.

my thanks to you, and the sum herewith. The Prince is fatigued.² At any rate, you and I were not guilty of seducing him to uncover his pathetic premature baldness, after a frightful illness, on a raw February morning. Loyalty, you see, is a destructive passion in modern times. It feeds on that which it affects to worship. They say the Prince is suffering, and I am sorry for it. But if his sufferings forewarn him of the nature of the brass-throated crowd, they will do him a service.

495. *To* GEORGE SMITH

MS.: Yale.

London
March 4, 1872

Dear Mr. Smith,

No letter has come to me:—no enclosure from you! I cannot wait to see you to-day, for I have to leave town at 3.35. It's I who am in doubt now whether *your* letter may not have miscarried.—I will on any other occasion make a point of writing by return of post.

Yours very faithfully,
George Meredith

496. *To* MRS. ANNA C. STEELE

MS.: University of Texas.

Box Hill
March 13, [? 1872]

My dear Mrs. Steele,

Only a word or two to defend myself, and so modestly! I like Camp[b]ell's 'Battle of the Baltic',¹ but if it had celebrated the pugilistic encounter of a pair of Jack Tars:—or again, I like military music, but supposing that it were heading the display of an Albino woman:—

---

² On 23 Nov. of the previous year it had been announced that the Prince of Wales had contracted typhoid. A relapse occurred on 8 Dec., and his life hung in the balance until the 14th, when a slow improvement set in. Upon his recovery 27 Feb. was declared a day of national thanksgiving, and the Prince himself rode in a carriage from Buckingham Palace to St. Paul's and back. All of this is the background for GM's comments.

496. ¹ By Thomas Campbell (1777–1844), of whom *CHEL* says that he was 'nearer than any other poet among many to being a perfect master of the great note of battle-poetry'. For the context of all this, see Letter 493.

well, in these cases, I should say that I was unjustifiably excited by the method to swallow the matter without inquiry. The gallant spirited verse of 'Hervé Riel' is disproportionately stirring when one comes to reflect upon what it is about. Supposing Hervé, not knowing the channel, to have thought it worth while to risk his neck in a trial to elude the English, rather than see the fleet tamely captured, we should then have had the element of audacious heroism suitable to this grand South Western gale of sweeping verse; but Hervé (who also talks and talks) was simply doing his business: not to have done it would have been abominable in the fellow. True, he makes light of it. The poet flourishes him forward as 'Just the same man as before', with an afflicting stress on his simplicity, as though in a brave man it were much. But the thing done is the point; and I still think, with the utmost deference to you and a sailor family, that Hervé's performance would have gone better in a Dibdin ballad, or a plain (minus trumpets) narrative of a fact worthy to be remembered.—I love Browning and claim my right to criticize him. Moreover, will you believe it? the artistic creature that I am rejoices in shaggy realism enough to read 'The Luck of Roaring Camp'[2] with envy of the writer's power.— Mrs. Wood was better on Saturday. I was anxious and went to see. Adieu.

I am your devoted
George Meredith

497. *To* FREDERICK A. MAXSE

Text: typed copy, Maxse Papers. Published: *Letters*, i. 235–6, with omissions.

Box Hill, Dorking
March 21, [1872]

My dear Fred,

All thanks to you for your thoughtfulness about Arthur, into whose future I wish to see a path. But it would be impossible to get him over to compete, with a fair chance, within a couple of months, and I confess I shrink from the idea of his going to China.[1] He is having a good

---

496. [2] By Bret Harte, published in the second number of the *Overland Monthly*, founded 1868, with Harte as editor. GM probably read it in the collection to which it gave title, published in 1870.
497. [1] Maxse had suggested that Arthur take a Foreign Office examination and, if successful, go out to China as an interpreter. Apparently the interpreter was to learn Chinese after his arrival. (See Letter 500.)

thorough education, and is observant and interested in European affairs, and to him the East would seem banishment; and for what? There would be little chance of his rising, I apprehend. Don't think me hard to please. I am very anxious about him. Should you have further information in praise of this service, I should like to hear it, but I shudder at the thought of losing sight of the boy altogether.

The behaviour of the House of Commons was filthy. They are at red heat of loyalty, and I am persuaded that men anxious to serve the public would be wiser-minded in timing their motions. Think of it!— after the English have just seen a Republic overthrown by a Monarchy, they are expected to listen with decency to a pair of avowed Republicans!—and their Prince only lately well out of a typhoid bed![2] It is asking too much of them.

I should have liked to [go] up to the lecture,[3] but it involved leaving home for a night, and work for a morning, and I am hurrying a new performance. When it is printed send me a copy. I like the headings.

Millicent Maxse![4]

Hark at it!

> Miss Millicent Maxse was fond of her Ma,
> And chanted her aristocratic tra-la
> In contempt of her stern democratic Papa,
> And to spite him she married a Markis—ha! ha!

It won't do. It's horrid. It dances on the *m's* hoydenly.

Marie suggests Violet, since you have an Olive. . . . Geraldine is charming. Leila, Gwendolen. Maxse will take anything but Millicent.— Emilia Maxse gets a better accent. Millicent avaunt! It's a proper parson's wife's name; it overflows with female priggery. You have to lift the nose to enounce it.

I am glad you take to Davis. We have a great regard for her, and know her to be a single-minded brave old woman.

Yours ever,
George Meredith

[2] The avowed Republicans were Sir Charles Dilke, who was to become Political Secretary for Foreign Affairs in Gladstone's 1880 ministry, and Auberon Herbert. Dilke's motion to inquire into Civil List expenditures and the Queen's personal income aroused a storm of patriotic indignation; it got only two votes. The Prince of Wales, whose health had been a matter of concern for several months, was well enough to travel from Sandringham to London on 26 Feb.

[3] Doubtless on *The Causes of Social Revolt*, as the *BMC* lists a pamphlet of that title by Maxse under date of 1872.

[4] The Maxses were searching for a name for their recently born daughter, and GM seems to have laughed them out of Millicent in favour of Marie's suggestion of Violet. Violet Maxse did not marry a 'Markis', but her first husband (Lord Edward Cecil) was the son of a marquess (Salisbury) and her second a viscount (Milner).

498. *To* AUGUSTUS JESSOPP

MS.: Yale. Printed: *Altschul Catalogue*, pp. 49–50.

Box Hill, Dorking
March 25, 1872

My dear Jessopp,

Your proposal suits us perfectly. But Oh bring gentler winds from your terrific East, and then I will show you fine walks. Marie is very happy at the thought of your coming. The boy will welcome you like a man—(and wish you were Mrs. Jessopp if he knew you both better).
—I shall have a holiday at last—most desirable for me.

Afternoon trains from *London Bridge* to 'Box Hill and Burford Bridge Station' on the LONDON BRIGHTON & SOUTH COAST line.

After three o'clock p.m.

3 something.
4.15-or twenty.
5.10 or 15.
6.0—

We dine at 7.

Later, if you will let us know that you must come late, owing to your Norwich train or anything that hinders. I fear I can't get any men worthy of you to meet you.

Send word of what train you think you may hit at London Bridge on Thursday, and I will meet you at our station.

This is a most manful proceeding on your part and acts like wine on me.

Give my love to your wife. I can't dare to wish that she were with you here to go out into the cold at 11 at night; but we shall have a *mansion* in time.

Yours ever warmly,
George Meredith

499. *To* LORD HOUGHTON

MS.: Trinity College, Cambridge.

Box Hill, Dorking
April 2, 1872

Dear Lord Houghton,

It is very kind of you to think of me. Easter at Fryston is better spent than elsewhere, but unfortunately I am detained here, and though I should be as nothing among the great political men you have

gathered this time, I regret that I shall never be able to say I have heard
them all at once. I will seek an indemnity for the loss by calling on you
when you have returned to Town and hearing what remains are left
of them. Believe me, / Dear Lord Houghton,

Your very faithful
George Meredith

500. *To* ARTHUR G. MEREDITH

Text: *Letters*, i. 236–8. Excerpt published: Stevenson, p. 192.

Box Hill, Dorking, Surrey, England
April 25, 1872

My dear Arthur,

. . . Strong friendships and intercommunications with foreigners
will refresh your life in this island, and the Germans are solid. Stick
to a people not at the mercy of their impulses, and besides a people
with so fine a literature must be worthy of love.—Captain Maxse wrote
to me the other day about an examination in the Foreign Office for
the post of Chinese interpreter—for you: if successful to go out to
China with a salary of £200 per annum and learn the Chinese tongue
of li-ro and fo-ki. I declined it: I hope I was right. I felt sure that it
would be repugnant to you to spend your life in China, where the
climate is hard, society horrid, life scarcely (to my thought) endurable.
Perhaps you might have chosen Japan. But it would have been for
very many years perpetual banishment. Let me hear what you think of
it.—Study Cicero carefully. He is a fine moralist, a friend of scholars,
a splendid trainer for a public life of any serious and exalted ambition.
—What you say of our religion is what thoughtful men feel: and
that you at the same time can recognise its moral value, is matter of
rejoicing to me. The Christian teaching is sound and good: the
ecclesiastical dogma is an instance of the poverty of humanity's mind
hitherto, and has often in its hideous fangs and claws shown whence
we draw our descent.—Don't think that the obscenities mentioned in
the Bible do harm to children. The Bible is outspoken upon facts, and
rightly. It is because the world is pruriently and stupidly shamefaced
that it cannot come in contact with the Bible without convulsions.
I agree with the Frommen[1] that the book should be read out, for

500. [1] I suppose this to be a reference to the bookseller family of Frommann, whose
house specialized in philosophical and ecclesiastical works and had published an edition of
the Bible.

Society is a wanton hypocrite, and I would accommodate her in nothing: though for the principle of Society I hold that men should be ready to lay down their lives. Belief in the religion has done and does this good to the young; it floats them through the perilous sensual period when the animal appetites most need control and transmutation. If you have not the belief, set yourself to love virtue by understanding that it is your best guide both as to what is due to others and what is for your positive personal good. If your mind honestly rejects it, you must call on your mind to supply its place from your own resources. Otherwise you will have only half done your work, and that is always mischievous. Pray attend to my words on this subject. You know how Socrates loved Truth. Virtue and Truth are one. Look for the truth in everything, and follow it, and you will then be living justly before God. Let nothing flout your sense of a Supreme Being, and be certain that your understanding wavers whenever you chance to doubt that he leads to good. We grow to good as surely as the plant grows to the light. The school has only to look through history for a scientific assurance of it. And do not lose the habit of praying to the unseen Divinity. Prayer for worldly goods is worse than fruitless, but prayer for strength of soul is that passion of the soul which catches the gift it seeks.

Your loving father,
George Meredith

501. *To* FREDERICK A. MAXSE

Text: typed copy, Maxse Papers. Published: *Letters*, i. 238, with omissions.

Box Hill
July 2, 1872

My dear Fred,

Your account of Leo makes my head spin. I had myself a shock of your kind, and worse, once. All's right now, thank the Gods! but have him examined to see whether an injury has come to the *head*. It may, and may not show much, and you can provide against it if you discover it in time.

As to the Century Club supper, I thank you.[1] I return you the paper. The Club should not sup until it has deliberated a century before the

---

501. [1] Maxse had invited GM to a supper at the Century Club, of which Frederic Harrison (*Autobiographic Memoirs*, ii. 83) says: 'It was an evening talking Club, dealing with all the "most advanced" questions in politics, literature, or theology. On its winding up it became the nucleus of the "National Liberal" and "Eighty" Clubs.'

act. Supping on any occasion is doubtful wisdom, but when you do, it should be like sinning, profuse—a good go in at it, not 'inexpensive'. Really Fred, what are you coming to! I supped once with a damsel on ale, cheese and onions; not bad, and she saved it from being inexpensive. And what are you going to commemorate? You are going to make speeches! If there is one thing to make any meal indigestible, it's spouting. My neighbour retches crudities which I'm to bolt, good Lord!—The lighting of the Aquarium, where one may see the fish that won't come to the plate, is simply barbarous. I am *certain* it was at your suggestion that wines were excluded. I'm persuaded too that you're in error in supposing you belong to this Century, and it's only by courtesy the fellows of it don't tell you so; it's the next you belong to, and you will find it out; and you were not made for a Club, but for mankind, so you see you're wrong all round, and you will be like a member of the Aquarium out of water there. Don't go. Come to me that day.

Your unrefreshed
George M.

P.S. Does this 'Supper' mean 'Dinner' at a reasonable hour?—say. And is there a chance of no Speechification? And might I have time to inspect the Aquarium quietly by coming? And dress anyhow?—

502. *To* Mrs. Anna C. Steele

MS.: University of Texas.

Box Hill, Dorking
July 30, 1872

Dear Mrs. Steele,

I had to abandon Zincke[1] to the Lady of Eltham after a short fight for him. I had seen a tempting review of him, and I preserved my enthusiasm through some chapters as devotedly as a maid with her first hero; but the Zincke strut, the Zincke tone of 'I condescend to amuse you', and air of wearing 'all that weight of learning lightly like a flower', overcame me at last. After the chapter of the rehabilitation of the Mummy, I could make no further stand for Zincke. I read it with shouts of laughter. This cleric affecting the French dramatic style, is too funny.—Take a page of *Eothen*[2] and mark the contrast between

---

502. [1] The Revd. Foster Barham Zincke, whose *Egypt of the Pharaohs and of the Khedivé* (1871) is the book under discussion. The Lady of Eltham is of course Mrs. Wood.
   [2] By A. W. Kinglake (first published anonymously, 1844).

a man of natural verve and shades of style, and a barefaced pretender—a most 'assumptious' writer! I did not read all, though I would have done so, for Egypt is so suggestive a theme that a Zincke aping stylist can make himself readable, anent the Pyramids and the Hieroglyphs. The one thing pleasant about Zincke is that he seems to be, or would have us think him, superior to his profession. But for Egyptian *matter*, it is better to go to the Fountain heads—Sir Gardner Wilkinson[3] and a German or two.

The Lady of Eltham and I are at direct issue upon another book: 'Mankind and Their Destiny', by an Oxford M.A. of Balliol; a masterly work of great learning.[4] Here there is a grounded knowledge of the Egyptian system of worship. By all means get it to read. But you must not object to see Matthew, Mark, Luke, and John shuffled unceremoniously, and the Divine Origin of anything traced in a straight line from Darwin's forefinger.—Over all this I see the phantom of a huge battle to come. The champions of THE BOOK will soon be out in arms.—Where is the Tragedy comparable to the action of Belief in a large and honest mind?—Tending whithersoever human interests are strongest, I find myself drawn to the subject, without the slightest personal concern in it. I have a tragedy sketched, called the 'Infidel':—Conceive a poor curate, married, and feeling his innocent fe[rvour (? page torn)] first nipped by doubt! Married with a 'numerous progeny', *ce qui va sans dire*; and doubting, and in the end courageous enough to take his stand on it. Imagine the temporizing counsels of his clerical friends. His exile from his Paradise of a vicarage. His utter solitariness in a world where hitherto he has leaned on a palpable directing Lord. I think of doing it with Choruses. Be good enough to read 'Theodolinda' in the *Cornhill* in a month or two[5]—showing the perils of religious ecstasy.—I am busy on a novel, like all my others, an experiment.[6] The lady to speculate on is this time French.—How could I possibly give a full drawing of Ottilia in a book of the Adventures of a Son and Father![7] An autobiography is not a 3 volume novel of plot. But you are exceptionally good in thinking of it at all.—We transport our family to Normandy, to my wife's brothers, for four or five weeks next Monday—that is, if Miss Potts[8] can come to Eltham next week.

---

502 .[3] Author of *Manners and Customs of the Ancient Egyptians* and other works on Egypt.

[4] *On Mankind: Their Origin and Destiny*. By an M.A. of Balliol College, Oxford (1872). The book caused a sensation in its day. In GM's library at his death was a copy inscribed 'George Meredith from Caroline Maxse'.

[5] 'The Song of Theodolinda', *Cornhill Magazine* (Sept. 1872).

[6] *Beauchamp's Career*, published in Nov. 1875.

[7] A reference to *The Adventures of Harry Richmond*.

[8] Probably a friend. In a letter of 22 Feb. 1870, Mrs. Wood wrote to GM that Miss Potts had called the afternoon before 'and says she will stay with me till Mar. 7'. She may have been one of the two old ladies, friends of her youth, mentioned by Katharine O'Shea

Otherwise I shall follow the family a week later, for Mr. Phillips[9] goes to Tyrol next week, and I do not like the idea of the Lady of Eltham being left altogether alone.—I return Lord Hatherley's[10] letter. Warburton's notions of theological controversy are certainly out of date.[11] —I had almost forgotten 'Kenspeckle'.[12] My handy Scotchman is off to the Highlands. I never use these braw words myself, and am therefore ignorant of the meaning of Kenspeckle. A Glossary of Scott or Burns should say.—

Let me tell you how heartily glad I was to hear of your recovery; but in your blood all of you carry big sails and sink the gunwale perilously to all appearance under the water at times; you have a surprising and comforting habit of righting yourselves again. Present my warmest respects to Lady Wood. Will you invite me to call on you when you are in London in the Autumn? I am

Your most faithful
George Meredith

503. *To* WILLIAM MICHAEL ROSSETTI

MS.: Ashley Library, British Museum. Excerpt published: Oswald Doughty, *A Victorian Romantic: Dante Gabriel Rossetti* (1949), p. 507.

Box Hill, Dorking
October 6, 1872

My dear Rossetti,

I have but just returned from the Continent or I would have applied to Chapman & Hall for the MS.—or to you, if you had not sent it. I am sure that anything you recommend must have real value. Only, as you know, it would still have to be the question whether publishers would be paid by undertaking it; and whether I might venture to underline my report.—Send the MS. to Chapman & Hall addressed to my care. I will read it at once, and wrangle with you if I am not of your mind about it.

(*Charles Stewart Parnell: His Love Story and Political Life*, 1914, i. 103) as among the few callers permitted by Mrs. Wood. *Boyle's Court Guide* (1866) lists a Miss Potts at 31 Harrington Square, N.W.

⁹ Probably a member of Mrs. Wood's household staff.

¹⁰ William Page Wood, Baron Hatherley (1801–81), uncle of Mrs. Steele, was appointed Lord Chancellor in Gladstone's first ministry (1868). He resigned in 1872 because of failing eyesight.

¹¹ Presumably William Warburton (1698–1779), Bishop of Gloucester, a noted controversialist. But if there is any connexion with Lord Hatherley, it has escaped me.

¹² Scots for 'easily recognizable; conspicuous' (*Oxford Universal Dictionary*).

How is Gabriel? I was distressed by hearing a bad report of him in the summer a little time before I left England. Spare me two minutes to write word how he is. I hope also that you were none of you worried by that Buchanan attack.[1] Criticisms in England are usually an expression of the writer's personal likes and dislikes—what do they matter? It would certainly have been entertaining to me to read the opinion formed by the North of the South—by Scotch mists of Southern Sunshine—if the onslaught had not been made on my friend. But the victim in such a case might really enjoy it. Our sweet English and Scotch are always very suspicious of colour. Warmth of colour makes them huddle together and take a common oath that they will be virtuous. Eccentricity they have a general instinct to lapidate—as boys have a bird. I am ever

Your most faithful

George Meredith

504. *To* WILLIAM HARDMAN

MS.: Yale. Excerpt published: Ellis, p. 261.

Garrick Club

October 17, [1872]

My dear lord Tuck!

Coward[1] capsized me before I left London for France with intelligence of another of your transformations.[2] I went back on my heels. What do you say to the Presidency of Honduras next?—I had but a day or two in London—occupied to the tips of every minute. Thrice in one day I called at your Club—left my card—devil a word of notice of it. Of course I long to see you.—I think I shall be in town for an hour or so with you. Drop me a line *here*[3] by return, so that

<hr>

503. [1] A virulent attack, entitled 'The Fleshly School of Poetry: Mr. D. G. Rossetti', had appeared in the *Contemporary Review* (Oct. 1871, pp. 334–50) under the signature of Thomas Maitland. It was soon known that this was a pseudonym for Robert Buchanan. Gabriel, who was at first contemptuous and then very angry, replied in 'The Stealthy School of Criticism', published over his own signature in the *Athenaeum* in mid-Dec. 1871 (Oswald Doughty, *A Victorian Romantic: Dante Gabriel Rossetti*, 1960, pp. 494–6).
  winburne, also attacked by Buchanan, came to the support of Rossetti in a pamphlet entitled *Under the Microscope*, published in July 1872.
504. [1] T. L. Coward, manager of the *Morning Post*.
  [2] Hardman had become editor of the *Morning Post*, a position that he held for the remaining eighteen years of his life. 'He won for himself a foremost place in the catalogue of editors', says Reginald Lucas (*Lord Glenesk and the 'Morning Post'*, 1910, p. 246), 'but it must be understood that Borthwick never surrendered the powers of direction and control.'
  [3] i.e. Garrick Club.

I may have a chance. You have a house somewhere—Montague Place or Terrace.[4] I hope that D'Troïa and the young ladies are well. Willie Godson grows tall and good. Our Babbler is in her present stage the awfullest roarer! We had a nice time in France, *but* that we were upset (Theodore, Ned, Betty, Rose Vulliamy and your friend), Ned V. nearly killed, and I with a crack on my funny-bone, which sang and wouldn't heal for a fortnight exactly. Marie and Will were in a coach behind. We hurled out of a waggonette.

Illustrious and astonishing one!

I am, Tuck! the admirer of the former, fast friend of the latter.

[No signature]

505. *To* AUGUSTUS JESSOPP

MS.: Yale. Printed: *Altschul Catalogue*, p. 50.

Box Hill
November 15, 1872

My dear Jessopp,

Enclosed is a paper carefully put by by my wife after you left and just found. I have looked at the MS. of Mr. Cotesworth's at last.[1] The fact is I have been condemned to work in town for a couple of weeks to help a man staggering with his pen, and divert him from his course—which was into the fields of blazing ridicule. It was a task of whole days and half nights. Following that an Influenza seized me and has been leading me by the nose up to this day, when, like a man and horse bogged, I cease to squelch and drip because I have ceased to make further efforts—am one with mire, slime, and all the sunless inconsistencies of life.—The MS. is good, but it is simply a series of rapid notes;—which I like, because it is opposed to bookmaking, but the public will not. And Palmyra is not a new bourne for the publishing traveller, that would excuse this system of merely noting to the public. When ground has been gone over by others, *writing* is required. Still it should go to some Magazine. Shall I offer it to *Macmillan*? You must be prepared for rejection, for the reasons I have given. The suspicion that Burton[2] did not do what he said he had done is unworthy, considering the things he has undoubtedly accomplished, and which place

---

[4] Hardman had sold Norbiton Hall and now lived in Montague Street, Bloomsbury.
505. [1] Mr. Cotesworth was doubtless a relative of Mrs. Jessopp, who was Mary Ann Cotesworth before her marriage. The MS. probably was never published; I find no record of it.
[2] (Sir) Richard F. Burton, explorer and Orientalist; consul at Damascus (1869–71). His translation of *The Arabian Nights* was published between 1885 and 1888.

him in the front rank of adventurous travellers. I am astonished that you should seem to second it. Can you really imagine that our Consul at Damascus shrank from the few days run to Palmyra after toiling through Central Africa?

—Our stay in France was pleasant but for an upset I had in a carriage that split my elbow, raked my head, and gave me the sight of my brother-in-law insensible for several days. He is now recovering. Betty Vulliamy was with me, mildly bruised. Happily my wife and the children followed in a more composed conveyance. Our horse broke the shaft and bolted, or we should have been dragged like inglorious Hectors to the Shades. I went to Salzburg, and had sunsets and sunrises on mountains, and some fun. Adieu, and to your wife my love.

Your ever affectionate

George Meredith

I could not have recommended Hofwyl as a place for *learning*. Arthur was well when I saw him.

506. *To* ANTHONY TROLLOPE[1]

MS.: University of Texas.

Box Hill

December 3, 1872

My dear Trollope,

I said of the author of the *Last of the Lythams* that he was clever, and it was consequently implied that there were touches of cleverness in his book, but I did not praise the book. As to the state of it at present, it presents exactly the same faults that it did before; I cannot see where the alterations are, except perhaps in one or two phrases. There is no story—nothing that runs currently; nothing whatever to interest the reader: not one of the characters is concrete—you can believe in none of them, for you can neither feel nor see them. When a 'situation' is arrived at: as where Vivia goes to Ireland and comes under Sir Everard's protection it is sunk in a tableau of a dirty night for a yacht

---

506. [1] This letter refers to a MS., which I am unable to identify, offered to C. & H. for publication. Trollope's son Harry was a partner in the firm at this time, but even after he withdrew from it Trollope wrote to Miss Mary Holmes that 'I still have much to do with it, and am there almost daily' (Booth, p. 322).

at sea.—Another situation—Vivia left by her villain surrounded by the tide, ends in asterisks.—Read the first chapter for a specimen of modern rose-pink.—It is an impossible MS: but as you fancy that I am in a mist concerning it, you will do well to offer it to Orr, Etheridge or Marshall,[2] of your house, before you decide to reject it. I could rely on them to fortify my verdict, the three together:—just as John Forster[3] would, or any trained or untrained judgment. And let me assure you that I never require to see a MS. twice. What comes to me I read carefully.

Ever yours,
George Meredith

507. *To* WILLIAM HARDMAN

MS.: Yale. Excerpt published: Ellis, p. 280.

Box Hill
Tuesday night, [? December 17,
1872][1]

My Tuck!

The weather doesn't look promising, but if it should flatter you on Sunday morning next, there is a train from Victoria, or better, from London Bridge at 9.30 (but look in Bradshaw)—I have just looked and find it is *9.20* a.m., will bring you to us at 10.30—or so, and we can have a walk and dine at 6.30, sending you to the sublime couch overlooking Russell Square[2]—to the *Post*, I mean, not more than an hour behind the usual time. And between you and me and the *Post*, I have to tell you that if you chance to see the commencement of a set of Dialogues in the *Graphic*,[3] you will know that your Robin, ex of

---

[2] Orr . . . Marshall: William Somerville Orr is identified by Boase as a publisher who was in the employ of C. & H. at the time of his death (1873). The other two must have been employees as well. None are mentioned by Waugh.
[3] Dickens's friend and biographer; GM's predecessor as reader of MSS. for C. & H.
507. [1] Brackets and date mine.
[2] i.e. Montague St., where Hardman now lived.
[3] GM published five dialogues on topical subjects, entitled 'Up to Midnight' in the *Graphic* for 21 Dec. and 28 Dec., 1872, and 4 Jan., 11 Jan., and 18 Jan. 1873.

Copsham forest, has been taken on board that prosperous ship as one of the Stewards. And should you like any part of it, *quote it*, for that will fortify me. I never ask favour for novel or poem, but my pot-boiler I long to see praised, seeing that it is written for nothing else than the yellow flood that bursts through the Gates of Praise. I have sent copy for this next week. Encourage me, if you can, to think it will do, and also advise me. In no way better than by coming and administering the same with the live voice. Of course D'Troïa too, if she will honour us.—Alack! our cook is a lame 'un, but will we not put up prayers for her works on Sunday? I cannot at present often say that I am at home on Sunday and so I fix on this next day of rest —if you'll only come. Love to Borthwick.

I am ever your friendliest
George Meredith

508. *To* FREDERICK GREENWOOD

Text: *Letters*, i. 239–40. Excerpt published: Stevenson, p. 194.

Box Hill
January 1, 1873

My dear Greenwood,

Open your heart a minute to receive a greeting of the New Year from me. May you fight as victoriously—bravely you always will— this year as last! May suppressed gout go limping on the other side of the river! May you be touched with the wand of wisdom to throw off your one blindness and see the virtues of my pen as with a flash of revelation!

By the way, I am having some fun in the *Graphic*,[1] and might by and by turn the Dialogues to good purpose, but I fear the grave commercial men sitting on it won't stand me long. Glance at next number, if it should come under your eye. Do let us meet for an evening this month? Fitzjames Stephen's articles are fine outhitting and have judicial good sense.[2] They are the prose of Carlyle's doctrines, valuable, profitable, but to me, though I take their smashing force, just not conclusive enough to make me anxious to hear the rejoinder. It is of great importance that what he says should be said. His side of the case has hitherto been woefully dumb—unable to supply an athlete.

508. [1] See Note 3, preceding letter.
[2] (Sir) James Fitzjames Stephen (1829–94), brother of Leslie, was writing approximately half of the leaders in the *PMG* in 1872–3 (J. W. Robertson Scott, op. cit., p. 157). In Jan. 1873 his 'Liberty, Equality, and Fraternity', assailing John Stuart Mill, was appearing.

So bold and able a writer will set a balance. Only guard against a certain sombrely prognosticating tone that he has:—as in the sermon on New Year's Eve. Opposed to the artificial cheerfulness of the Journals, it's like starlight after pantomime fires. But it gives the *Pall Mall* by degrees a Mr. Toobad[3] twang.

Some one assured me that George Smith had yielded his part in the *P[all] M[all]* to Spottiswoode: not true, I hope?

I have looked at Morris's poem 'Enough for love',—'Love is enough',[4] I mean. Have you? I looked away. The look was enough. Our public seems to possess the fearful art of insensibly castrating its favourites. The songs are of the species of Fitzball's Gossamer Tree:[5] charming in melody, but there is no such thing as a gossamer tree. I hope when Swinburne publishes his 'Tristram' you will review him. Take him at his best he is by far the best—finest poet, truest artist—of the young lot—when he refrains from pointing a hand at the genitals. And I trust he has done so this time. I never see him, and have to imagine that he has taken offence—without a formal editorial letter to tell me of it, as in a famous case known to us.[6] All states of life have their privileges, and mine is to be behind the scenes of many illustrious and ringing names, and to laugh. How truly wise is so and so! I hear, and I bow. The aim of the pretenders must be but to have this homage of the public, and who would rob them of it because he happens to be behind them on the stage and peruses a dead blank instead of the pretty picture confronting the pensive? I would run on, but you are a busy man. If we can't meet, I will invite myself to you for the evening. I hope your daughter still improves.

From your loving
George Meredith

---

[3] A character in Thomas Love Peacock's *Nightmare Abbey*. He was always quoting the 12th verse of the 12th chapter of Revelation: 'Woe to the inhabiters of the earth and of the sea! for the devil is come among you, having great wrath, because he knoweth that he hath but a short time.'

[4] *Love is Enough, or the Freeing of Pharamond* (1873).

[5] Edward Ball (who adopted the name Fitzball), librettist, author, and adapter of numerous plays, says (*Thirty-Five Years of a Dramatic Author's Life*, 1859, ii. 16) that in one of his 'Songs of the Birds' appeared the line 'Now I sit on a gossamer tree'. Too late he learned that there was no such tree as the gossamer, a provincialism in his native vicinity for a species of poplar.   [6] i.e. Morley. See Letter 473.

510. *To* GEORGE SMITH

MS.: Yale.

Box Hill, Dorking
February 11, 1873

My dear Mr. Smith,

I am due to you this month, but I am all behindhand, and want an extension of time—till May fully.[1] The reason is partly that I have been slashing at my work as usual, but I was upset in France last Autumn and severely shaken. It stopped my pen for a period, though no bones were broken. I might have hurried on to keep my engagement, but I should have roughed my work, and failed of doing it in the spirit. I am sure you will understand this and tell me so, for I am uneasy.— The title of the Novel is *Beauchamp's Career*, which I think sounds as if it should have reverberation. I am

Yours ever faithfully,
George Meredith

511. *To* GEORGE SMITH

MS.: Yale.

Box Hill
February 27, 1873

My dear Mr. Smith,

Do pardon me. I postponed from day to day, thinking there was time up to the end of February: and when one is not at writing a letter is a burden like the grasshopper of Ecclesiastes. I shall be glad to renew

510. [1] Smith, Elder & Co. had published GM's last novel (*Harry Richmond*), and George Smith had advanced payment or part-payment for his next novel (*Beauchamp's Career*) against a bill of exchange as security for the delivery of the novel. And now the novel wasn't ready. Worse still, when Smith saw the MS. later, he rejected it, and GM had difficulty meeting the bill.

if you will kindly send me the paper.[1] It will be safest to say—the end
of May; for I shall desire to polish, I am sure.—Asher of Berlin has
a series coming out after the Tauchnitz pattern:[2] He has taken my
Shaving of Shagpat:—I propose *Harry Richmond*. He said he would
rather wait for my forthcoming novel: but I think he will take *HR*
sooner or later. Believe me

Yours most faithfully,
George Meredith

512. *To* GEORGE SMITH

MS.: Yale.

Box Hill, Dorking
March 5, 1873

Dear Mr. Smith,
Here is the bill accepted by me, payable at L[ondon] and W[est-
minster] Bank, St. James's Square. I am

Your very faithful
George Meredith

513. *To* AUGUSTUS JESSOPP

MS.: Yale. Excerpts published: Ellis, p. 282; Stevenson, p. 193.

Box Hill, Dorking
April 8, 1873

My dear Jessopp,
(A sudden fear is on me that my envelope address to you fails in
dignifying you correctly—forgive me!)—[1]
—If Palgrave, or any friend of yours puffed full of praises of this
and that work by you, will do me the honour to come to my cottage,
the same is welcome, for in default of seeing you, your friend is my
next best; and if he is burdened with admiration I will soon relieve
him. But I am at present too busy on *Beauchamp's Career* to spend
a day in town. I was bound to send it to the publisher not later than

511. [1] The bill of exchange alluded to in the previous letter.
   [2] Asher and Company of Berlin and Tauchnitz of Leipzig were publishers of Asher's
Collection of English Authors and Tauchnitz's Collection of British and American
Authors respectively.
513. [1] Though GM had taken note, in Letter 483, of the D.D. degree conferred on Jessopp by Oxford, he had apparently failed to do so in his last letter.

the end of May, but it will run on with me through June. And it is already full to bursting—it and I. 'The world is too much with me'[2] when I write. I cannot go on with a story and not feel that to treat of flesh and blood is to touch the sacredest;—and so it usually ends in my putting the destinies of the world about it—like an atmosphere, out of which it cannot subsist. So my work fails. I see it. But the pressure is on me with every new work. I fear that *Beauchamp* is worse than the foregoing in this respect. The central idea catches hold of the ring of the universe; the dialogues are the delivery of creatures of this world, and the writing goodish. But altogether it will only appeal (so I fear) to them that have a taste for me; it won't catch the gudgeon World, and I, though I never write for money, want it—and there's a state of stultification for you!

Have you heard from Leslie Stephen? I rather expect him next Sunday. Palgrave would make a pleasant addition. My love to your wife. Mine and the babes are well. I am ever

Your affectionate
George Meredith

[Marginal notes:]

By the way, I opened a volume of *Richard Fev*[*erel*] the other day, and had a sharp distaste. The lumpy style is offensive.

Did you chance to see in the *Morning Post* of about a month back two columns on the riots in Stuttgart?—middling well written by Arthur. He returns at Midsummer.

514. *To* MISS LOUISA LAWRENCE[1]

MS.: the Lawrence family.

Box Hill
April 10, 1873

My dear Miss Lawrence,

Will my work ever be worth what I am reduced to pay for it? Will it seem worth anything at all to you? Are you not likely to say when you come to read it (if you also should take your part of the burden)— 'For this, he, in a world like ours, refused a veritable pleasure, lost it eternally, declined to taste the cream of London with London's cream

513. [2] Cf. Wordsworth's sonnet 'The World Is Too Much With Us'.
514. [1] For the Misses Lawrence, see Biographical Section, p. 1720–21. At the time of this letter they lived at 18 Whitehall Place, and it is clear that GM is declining a second invitation, probably for an evening of music.

—and for this!'— Down go the three volumes! I see the act; the sound of it reverberates through the luckless author now. 'Surely, you say, to your alter ego,[2] the production of something great could alone have excused him:—and this! I have heard he is unreadable. Why does the man write!'—She, the other, I hope, sighs for me—is she not gentle?—and pleads (here I am bold)—'He thinks he is composing something great: I am told he has always that idea, and that sustains, that enables him to continue his self-mortification: he sits on the Hill hatching his everlasting three volumes, imagining them eaglets. It is a mania with him. He deserves pity rather than anger. Enough for the poor wretch that when his work is out Reviewers think there's rain, and lift up voices from the lowest ditch in one spontaneous chorus!'

'Still, you say, a second invitation is a mandate. Never another for him!'

Madam, my soul—do not be alarmed: an illustrious composer of novels of murderers and philosophical seducers once said to a fellow member of the House of Commons, 'Kinglake, let us meditate on Life', during a debate in the House.[3] Kinglake received a shock, and I am sure you do at the startling apparition of my soul in my first letter to you. But is a soul anywhere out of place? It is a test—is it not?—of noble housewifery to be able and to be willing to give the poor shivering thing welcome.—My soul, then, flies to you. Its corporal tenement is at the grindstone.

Was there not some Saint who resisted . . .? I forget his name and the exact temptation: but he resolutely pored on his book, and though now and then he lifted half an eyelid at Mdlle Aimée Desclée,[4] a Paternoster vigorously repeated helped him over his human frailty. He passed into the Calendar. Reflect that I have no such chance but look only for you and your sister's charity, and let me know that I have it.

> Your most melancholy, little
> musical,
> George Meredith

---

[2] Her sister, Miss Mary.

[3] ? Bulwer Lytton. Kinglake was in the House of Commons from 1857–68 and Bulwer Lytton from 1852–66 (besides an earlier period), but they were of opposite parties, and the remark could not have been made while they were in their seats.

[4] Aimée-Olympe Desclée (1836–74), French actress who became a renowned comedienne.

515. TO FREDERICK A. MAXSE

Text: typed copy, Maxse Papers.

Box Hill
May 28, 1873

My dear Fred,

The extract from the *Globe* is very funny:[1] but will that or anything stop the career of a humbug where the public is a craw fit only for stuffing? Any villany where there's no judge!—Christie writes weakly: or else I feel so strongly that Hayward ought to be trounced.[2]—No vacant room this week. What do you say to Wednesday next? and come early.—The articles on John Mill in the *Examiner* were very acceptable.[3]—I was in company with a Cubitt-Maxse Juryman some days back and hope I convinced him of his erratic verdict:—he confessed that the bullying tone of Chambers,[4] contrasted with J. Brown's[5] quiet attempts to, apparently, explain the real case, *did* affect the minds of the Jurymen.—

Nightingales have (with exception of one or two nights) been weak this year.

Have you read Browning's last?[6] We will talk over it. Oh that I had time for verse!—

I like the prospectus of the Warwickshire School and seem to take to the man and his wife; but mine pleads it is too distant!—Arthur comes back in July. Where to quarter him is the present problem of the question—What to do with him.

'Ere thou beget a son, have a path for him in thine eye.'[7]

This day you are at Epsom?—Moralist!

If it be true that we are all reduced to knaves and fools, then is the spectacle of Whalley introducing the Claimant Orton Tichborne at the Britannia Theatre,[8] significant of the courage as well as the grandeur

---

505. [1] The trial of the Tichborne Claimant was in progress, and on 24 May the *Globe* carried an advertisement addressed to counsel and jury who 'should welcome the best claimant to their verdict, in W. T. Cooper's Effervescing Lozenges, or solid thirst quenchers, which at once remove the dryness of the throat organs overtaxed by heated court and long talking', etc.

[2] A reference to W. D. Christie's *John Stuart Mill and Mr. Abraham Hayward* (1873).

[3] The 17 May issue of the *Examiner* carried twelve articles on J. S. Mill, who had died the preceding week.

[4] Possibly Sir Thomas Chambers, Q.C., or Montague Chambers, Q.C.

[5] Probably Joseph Brown, Q.C., who was of Surrey origin.

[6] *Red Cotton Night-Cap Country.*

[7] If this is really a quotation, it ought to be from *The Pilgrim's Scrip* but isn't. The sentiment, of course, is familiar enough.

[8] On 27 May *The Times* reported that Orton, the Tichborne Claimant, had asked permission to appear at theatres and that the Lord Chief Justice had refused it. G. H. Whalley, M.P., was one of Orton's public supporters.

of the race. A colossal scene. A fat knave, an intrepid ass. But still, you see, we are great in our decay.

France, Fred?

I think you have a kind of spinster Aunt's affection for a scapegrace. I will not ruffle it. I like in France what you do, and that is a plum or two; but you make much of the plums in your rapture at the discovery of them; I mourn that they should be so sadly solitary. I am

Your constantly offending

George M.

516. *To* GEORGE SMITH

MS.: Yale.

Box Hill
June 2, 1873

Dear Mr. Smith,

I will come to you on Wednesday at from 5 to a quarter past.

Please hold over the bill. If I fail next time I will meet it. But as I am rushing to the close (when I'm not harking back) you will soon have all the MS.[1]

Yours very faithfully,
George Meredith

517. *To* ?FREDERICK GREENWOOD[1]

MS.: Berg Collection, New York Public Library.

Box Hill, Dorking
October 13, [1873]

My dear [name effaced: ? Greenwood],

I send you three chapters; but you need not do more than just glance at the first and last: the middle chapter '18' is the questionable one. I fancy it would head the 2nd volume. It is called 'An Invocation, a Triad, and an Image of Impartial Dealing'—and it is very short—and might pass? but be without softness for me. I shall be ruled by you.

516. [1] See Letters 510, 511, and 512.
517. [1] I have eliminated all other logical possibilities, and surely this letter must be addressed to the same person as Letter 474. Moreover, Greenwood (with Maxse) could not have 'described the book glowingly to Morley' and persuaded him to publish it without having read it (see Stevenson, p. 194).

The Election here treated of does not fill many chapters. Beauchamp has to go through it, and I don't represent it in the hackneyed way.

Let me have the chapters back as quickly as is convenient to you, for now (at last!) in a week I shall be ready to hand all in at Waterloo Place.[2] And I fancy the time is getting favourable for the political views and sayings that come up incidentally throughout the story.

All my excuses for troubling you, and I am

Your loving
George Meredith

518. *To* [MARMADUKE J.] TEESDALE[1]

Text (excerpt): American Art Association Catalogue (8 Feb., n.y.).

Box Hill, Dorking
November 29, 1873

My fullest thanks to you for writing. I go to Eltham today. I had fears, but Miss Potts had promised to write, and not hearing from her, I hoped that things might be going on well. Now I have no hope at all. It will be an irreparable loss. But to have known so good a woman is a sorry comfort.

519. *To* CHARLES KENT

Text (excerpt): Maggs Brothers Catalogue 203 (1904), p. 27.

Garrick Club
February 3, 1874

[Interesting letter referring to a novel he had read. Also:] I have a novel, which is a story of the ideas and indication of the struggles of this time, drawn from the quick; it's called *Beauchamp's Career*, but the burden of the story is, I fear, too heavy, [etc.]

517. [2] Address of the *Cornhill.*
518. [1] A London solicitor who lived at Eltham and was known to GM through Mrs. Wood. Apparently he had written to GM of the serious illness of Mrs. Wood, who, contrary to GM's expectations, recovered and lived another fifteen years.

520. *To* MISSES LOUISA AND MARY LAWRENCE

MS.: the Lawrence family.

February 27, [1874]

Dear Miss Lawrences,
   (one and individible)
   Victor Hugo's *Quatre-Vingt-Treize* has been sent to me to review:
I have done my work, and take the liberty to send you the book,
which is worth reading and indeed has some very fine points. I should
have done myself the honour to come in person, but that I fear every
half hour of my day in town will be inexorably marked out for me.
Believe me

Your most faithful and devoted
George Meredith

   I bid my messenger wait lest perchance you should have read the
book—improbable, seeing that it has not been out more than a week.

521. *To* FREDERICK GREENWOOD

Text: *Letters*, i. 240–1.

Box Hill, Dorking
March 12, 1874

My dear Greenwood,
   I should like to review *Spain and the Spaniards* of Azamat Batuk;[1]
and also *Yu-Pe-Ya's Lute* by Mrs. Webster,[2] if I see stuff in it. Will you
leave them out for me? I want work. My poor *Beauchamp* is not
thought good for the market by George Smith, who is (as he always is)
very kind about it.

Your faithful
George Meredith

521. [1] Azamat-Batuk was the pseudonym of N. L. Thieblin, whose *Spain and the
Spaniards* was published by Hurst and Blackett. (W. M. Meredith transcribed the name as
Azamar-Batuk.)
   [2] Mrs. Augusta Webster, *Yu-Pe-Ya's Lute. A Chinese Tale.*

522. *To* JOHN MORLEY

Text: *Letters*, i. 241–2.

Box Hill, Dorking
May 22, 1874

My dear Morley,

I thank you very much for stepping over the obstruction for our mutual convenience in the matter of *Beauchamp*. Greenwood and Maxse told me that the work pleased you.[1] I need scarcely assure you that I look upon your appreciation of my labour as a good reward of it. I write for you and men like you. Consequently when the greater paymaster failed me, I hoped the work might be accepted where it would be more suitably accommodated, feeling quite certain you would allow nothing to stand in the way of your estimation of it on its merits. Your reluctance to undertake the burden of so lengthy a production, I cannot but think reasonable, and I gladly meet your kind proposal that I should cut it short as much as I can, without endangering the arteries. I will get the MS. from George Smith[2] immediately, and do my utmost upon it. It strikes me that the parts to lop will be the letters, a portion of the Visit to Normandy, the heavier of the electioneering passages, introductory paragraphs to chapters, and dialogues passim that may be considered not vital to the central idea. That, which may be stated to be the personal abnegation coming, in spite of errors here and there (as it were in spite of the man himself), of a noble devotion to politics from the roots up, I think I can retain uninjured—possibly improved by the exclusion of a host of my own reflections. At any rate they can be reprinted subsequently. Chapman will buy the book for the 3 volume issue. It rests with me that this should be brought about. I will take the liberty to let you know to what amount, and when, the task of excision has been performed.

My little ones, I am glad to say, are well, and so is my wife, whom I join in sending her compliments and regards to Mrs. Morley.

Let me add that I await the continuation of the essay on Compromise[3] with some impatience.

I am your obliged and faithful
George Meredith

522. [1] Three years earlier Morley had broken off relations with GM because of GM's rough handling of his 'opinions, ideas, and likings'. (See Letter 473 and note.) GM's dignified reply to Morley had left the way open to reconciliation at some future time, and Greenwood and Maxse now used the MS. of *Beauchamp* as a means of bringing the reconciliation about. Morley no doubt had long regretted his yielding to personal pique and was glad of an opportunity to renew relations.
[2] Smith had rejected *Beauchamp's Career* for the *Cornhill*. (See preceding letter.)
[3] 'On Compromise', *FR*, Apr., June, July, Aug. 1874.

523. *To* MONCURE D. CONWAY[1]

MS.: Yale. Published: *Letters*, i. 242–3, with variants; excerpt published: Stevenson, pp. 195–6.

Box Hill, Dorking
June 18, 1874

Dear Sir,

I have been away from home, and I regret very much that your letter of the 29th May should have remained unanswered up to this date.

I am engaged in cutting down my novel for the *Fortnightly Review*. The task is hard, for I have at least to excise a third of my work, which appears to be a full three-volumes measure. Supposing that I accomplish it to the satisfaction of the Editor, the first chapters will be published in the Sept[embe]r Number, as far as I can calculate.—Would it be of use to you to have early serial sheets?

I feel bound to warn you of the nature of my work. It is not likely to please the greater number of readers. Mr. George Smith (of Smith Elder & Co.) could not take it for the *Cornhill Magazine*. It is philosophical-political, with no powerful stream of adventure: an attempt to show the forces round a young man of the present day, in England, who would move them, and finds them unalterably solid, though it is seen in the end that he does not altogether fail, has not lived quite in vain.—Of course, this is done in the concrete. A certain drama of self-conquest is gone through, for the hero is not perfect. He is born of the upper class, and is scarcely believed in by any class, except when he vexes his own, and it is then to be hated. At the same time the mild spirit of a prosperous middle class, that is not extremely alarmed, is shown to be above persecuting; so that the unfortunate young man is in danger of being thought dull save by those who can enter his idea of the advancement of Humanity and his passion for it. In this he is a type. And I think his History a picture of the time—taking its mental action, and material ease, and indifference, to be a necessary element of the picture.

But I am afraid all this will not sound hopeful to you in the interests of an American publisher, if it should [be] on behalf of one that you do me the honour to address me.

I find myself writing to you on a matter of business.—I am indebted to your lectures for support, and have often wished to thank you for them. I beg you to pardon the liberty I take in doing so.

I am, / Dear Sir / Yours most faithfully,
George Meredith

---

523. [1] This letter is a reply to a letter from Conway about American publication of GM's books. (For Conway, see Note 1, Letter 402.)

524. *To* JOHN MORLEY

Text: *Letters*, i. 243-4.

Box Hill, Dorking
July 14, 1874

My dear Morley,

Since you are inclined generously to trust to me to cut the Novel short, I promise you that it shall be done to your satisfaction, as to quantity. The 'mutilation' does me no hurt; but hitherto I have merely looked at it to see that it could be done;—but with shudders to think how much more there was to do! The central portion, I fear, must be cut to pieces, condensed, rewritten.—I would have begun upon the MS. immediately; but Chapman had given me to suppose that you were very anxious for space for critical and attractive articles. —I fancied there was no hurry.—Today I post 3 chapters, which I fancy will come within the pages you number for me. The excisions are not so numerous here as they will be subsequently to the Venetian scenes. These also I shall be able to cut down a little. Remember that I despatch the sheets to Virtue[1] because it is your wish: I am not anxious to begin.—I will try my hand at a paragraph or two of Prologue. I see that it is wanted. It is difficult. If I had but temporary command of your style I should not fear.

The latest portion 'On Compromise' is very good indeed.[2]—Are the instances a trifle over-familiar for the dignity of the Essay? They at least give your meaning clearly and bring them home—are likely to do downright service. For that purpose it will not do to stand much aloof—among the sons of Hengist. I have just returned from Uckfield,[3] where his descendants are in the majority, though they would assume Horsa to be his wife.—Morison's 'Impossible French Republic'[4] strikes one as overwhelmingly true—as it is powerful.

525. *To* JOHN MORLEY

Text: *Letters*, i. 244-5.

Box Hill
July 23, 1874

My dear Morley,

I find I can say better what should be said of Beauchamp in a paragraph at the head of the 4th chapter—I am very shy of prefaces, and by

524. [1] Messrs. Virtue, printers of the *FR*.   [2] See Note 3, Letter 522.
[3] A dozen miles north of Seaford. Katherine Wheatcroft, whose husband had died in 1870, lived there.
[4] J. Cotter Morison, 'Is a Republic Possible in France?' *FR* (July).

introducing my one or two remarks incidentally I hope to escape from a tone that seems to avoid the apology only by some loftiness—or the reverse. I am afraid it would not be I who could put the intermediate touch. Conception rarely fails me, though ability does, and I can barely conceive of its being done in the proper tone.—I own that you might do it for one of your own works: but for a piece of fiction having a serious aim, and before a public that scorns the serious in fiction, and whose wits are chiefly trained to detect pretension, it is more than commonly difficult.

I will take care that Virtue prints the next chapter early, so that, if you will be so good as to offer it, I may have your counsel anent the paragraph.

Did I speak to you of Morison's article? It abounded in cleverness: it threw me over and silenced me:—but is it just to be writing so decisively unhopefully? Many of his illustrations are excellent. It is at any rate admirable journalism. I am

Yours very faithfully,
George Meredith

526. *To* MONCURE D. CONWAY

MS.: Berg Collection, New York Public Library.

Box Hill, Dorking
July 29, 1874

Dear Sir,

My copy of The Ordeal of R[ichar]d Feverel has been lent to some friend. It is possible that Chapman & Hall have one, and if they have, I will request them to forward it to Holt & Co.[1] Supposing the latter to be desirous to publish it in America, I should be of opinion that it would be as well for me to cut the opening chapters short, and correct here and there the lympy style.—I do not insist on it, but I think it would be better to do it.

I wish you fair weather for your vacation tour and am

Yours very faithfully,
George Meredith

526. [1] Henry Holt & Co., well-known New York publishers; now Holt, Rinehart and Winston, Inc.

527. *To* FREDERICK A. MAXSE

Text: typed copy, Maxse Papers. Published: *Letters*, i. 245–7, with omissions.

Box Hill
August 5, 1874

My dear Fred,

Probably you are in strong sunshine.[1] Here we have a chilly day, a shrouded sky, half a suspicion of light now and then, a bit of a breeze that has puffed spasmodic life into the yachts at Cowes, and shakes the rain from our junipers. The fine weather has become a Christian penitent, and makes everybody unhappy around her.—How I long to be with you! I am afraid that the doing of justice to *Beauchamp* and other work I have will nail me down (a coffiny phrase!) Or rather, I am fearing it, for I [am] still looking forward with a bit of hope.

On Sunday White arrived, in attendance upon Mr. Jacob Homburg,[2] of whom we are all very fond. He is a nice little fellow, with an addiction to hunting rabbits, that I must cure him of, and a passion for the kitchen, due to the soft influences of your cook, probably incurable. Already he has taken to his new home, follows me well and seems to like his quarters. The exception to his good conduct is, that he refuses biscuit and thinks of standing out for meat pure and simple.

You have seen the papers and meditated upon the Beecher–Tilton scandal.[3] Guilty or not, there is a sickly snuffiness about the religious fry that makes the tale of their fornications and adulteries absolutely repulsive to read of, and but for the feeding of the reptile Sarcasm in our bosoms, it would disgust one more than a chronicle of the amours of costermongers.

If Austria permits to you the *Fortnightly*, you will have seen that *Beauchamp* has made a start. It is a singularly fine number.

Do you know I have a great liking for being in Austria, and if I come I would propose a route something like this: to be at Nuremberg about the 22nd (I cannot be off before the *20th*): to proceed to Ratisbon,[4] and by steamer to Linz and Passau: thence quickly to the Salzkammergut and by any route you like to Tyrol and Lienz, for a few days among the dolomites' valleys: then by rail to Verona and by the North Italian lakes homeward anyhow.—Would such a scheme

527. [1] Maxse was in Carlsbad. [2] A dachshund given to GM by Maxse.

[3] Henry Ward Beecher (1813–87), Congregationalist minister in Brooklyn, was one of the leaders of the anti-slavery forces preceding the Civil War. He used the pulpit for discussion of public questions, and great crowds averaging 2,500 flocked to hear him.

On 30 Dec. 1870 one of Beecher's parishioners named Theodore Tilton, a journalist for whom Beecher had obtained a position, accused Beecher of improper relations with Mrs. Tilton, who had made a written confession which she later retracted. The story leaked out, but a formal charge of adultery against Beecher was not filed until 1874. The trial lasted six months and resulted in failure of the jury to agree on a verdict. Beecher remained popular but tarnished. [4] Modern Regensburg.

please you, with some small amount of knapsack walking? Tell me. For walking is the thing I must have, or it will be waste of time and money for me. Up at four a.m., a walk to breakfast, a walk to dinner, a stroll and then early to the couch.—Latterly I have been rising here at half past five, and have enjoyed the tonic morning air immensely, yet more the fresh loveliness of the downs and fields, the velvet shadows, sharp and thin, and the exquisite sky. This morning there was little of that, however. The weather seems to be making up for the jolly squalls and the gale we had crossing to Cherbourg once.[5] Changes have come since then! Where's the *Susan?* Where's the *Grebe?*[6]—By the way Betty Vulliamy would like to know whether you are a Good Templar, and if not whether you are willing to become one. I don't know the nature of the rites of initiation.

Scandal again: The Marquis of Bute off with his wife's lady's maid.[7] Madame taken home to her own family. Archb[ishop] Manning quite consternated, Rome furious.

So spins the world away.—I would not have you write, because it's better for your health's sake that you should not; but you may jot down what you think of my plan of a tour, or what your proposition is: and what, supposing we do not meet upon the date you name, your aim is likely to be. Whither you will go, and for how long, and which way homeward.—I have not abandoned the prospect of meeting you somewhere: but at this instant (and it is the reason why I did not write to you by return of post) I do not see my way out of the encircling whirr of work.—Marie and I rejoice that you should be feeling better and condescending to repose—a good sign of itself. Willie sends his love to you, with the message that Jacob Homburg is getting on very well. Marie Eveleen flourishes charmingly.

Adieu, my dear Fred. Write soon, and I will reply. Tell me your scheme. I will come if I can, and meet you, if it doesn't preclude walking somewhat. Nuremberg I have never seen and much want to. By what date is it imperative for you to be in England?

Your loving
George Meredith

<hr>

[5] In Aug. 1865.   [6] The *Susan* ... the *Grebe*: yachts formerly owned by Maxse.

[7] Something of the sort must have happened, though, if so, gossiping diarists and journalists were remarkably uninformed or discreet. Cartoons in *Punch* (1 Aug. and 22 Aug.), however, were on target: in one the subject is an unfaithful Scottish husband; in the other one Scot encounters another unexpectedly in an inn and inquires, 'What's brought you here? Where's your wife? What! have you got a divorce, or a dispensation from the Pope, or what—' The reply is, 'No, on'y a plenary indulgence.' Whatever the truth of the matter, the Marchioness bore her husband children in 1875, 1881, 1883, and 1886.

Bute, who had become a convert to Catholicism in 1868, was the prototype of Disraeli's hero in *Lothair* (1870).

528. *To* FREDERICK A. MAXSE

Text: *Letters,* i. 248–50.

Box Hill
August 10, 1874

My dear Fred,

Hail, rain, thunder, lightning:—have you anything like this at Carlsbad? This is our daily entertainment, and I don't dislike it, for it gives fine scenery.—I am glad you like the opening of *Beauchamp.* I am at work cutting down, which will necessitate some amount of fresh writing. Chapman urges me for copy, so that he may have an advance lot to forward to America for pay, otherwise he won't get the same,[1] so I am bound to go on with my work, and that fact, besides considerations of the purse, seems to forewarn me I am doomed to remain in harness. I fear so. I cannot say at present, but the outlook is bad. I may be able in September to accomplish a cheap trip of a fortnight to my wife's sister in Dauphiny, for a breath of mountain air. Switzerland gets dim as Leith Hill[2] behind the raincloud.—It is an immense relief and joy to me to think of the chance of your recovery. Perhaps the waters do something but the seclusion from work and nervous worry is the main secret, I fancy. Next year, if things are favourable with me, I might try Carlsbad myself. Obtain the best general information as to the waters, and let me know how they operate.—By the way, have you read Swinburne's *Bothwell?*[3] I am afraid it's going to be allowed to sink because of its size; and no doubt there is too much of it, but you at least are one of those who should read and support it.—Morley finishes 'Compromise', very good and bold work that cannot but be beneficial. I presume that Morison on the 'Prospects of the Republic in France' did not please you. The Positivists, he tells me, are howling still. It was well written. I am afraid it contains more truth than we care to admit, though none can deny to Gambetta[4] very honourable leadership of late. I have seen one *Lanterne.*[5] Hum. And read Rochefort's *Fortnightly* Article.[6] Have you?

528. [1] Modest payments were obtainable from American publishers at this time, when America had not subscribed to the International Copyright Agreement, in return for proofs or advance copies of foreign books.

[2] Four miles SW. of Dorking.

[3] Swinburne's *Bothwell* (1874) was sequel to *Chastelard* and precursor to *Mary Stuart.* It was much too long for stage production.

[4] Léon Gambetta (1838–82), one of the heroes of the Franco-Prussian War, was the Republican champion against Royalism.

[5] *La Lanterne*, edited by Henri Rochefort, was originally established in Paris in 1868 but was now published in Brussels. Rochefort had been banished in 1873 because of his involvement in the Communist uprising of 1871.

[6] 'The Revolution of September, 1870': a review of Jules Simon's *Souvenirs de la Révolution du 4 Septembre* in the Aug. 1874 issue.

Poor stuff.—We want from him an orderly narrative done in a certain grave pitch of tone, not carping criticisms of other men's work.

I hope to be hearing from you to-morrow, when I may have something to reply to, so I will hold this from the post for 24 hours. Jacob[7] sits at my feet, and is my constant companion—a dear little fellow.

Aug. 11.—Your letter just come: You have not yet received mine dated the 4th, and to which I calculated getting yours of this morning for an answer.—Adieu. I will write again.

Your loving
George M.

529. *To* JOHN MORLEY

Text: *Letters,* i. 247–8.

Box Hill
August 10, 1874

My dear Morley,

Pardon me if I have been causing anxiety to the Editorial bosom. Each day that I keep back my MS. I feel capable of cutting out more and more; and for the present number the more the better, for it will be as well to get over the Venetian scenes in this number as nearly as possible—according to the amount of space you can give me. The chapters are short.—You will see that the 2nd paragraph of Chapter 4 is composed of the prefatory observations. I am quite ready to defer to your judgment if you object to them, or to the way in which they are done.—To-morrow morning I send several chapters on to Virtue from Chapman's, and very shortly you shall have a volume in advance.—I need hardly say how glad I am that you approve of it so far. Maxse writes from Carlsbad that he thinks the beginning 'excellent', but the public and press may think differently. For your sake as well as mine I hope not. M[axse] confesses to feeling very much improved in tone. He wishes me to meet him at the Bel Alp on the 20th. I do not see that it is possible. I have the restless feeling for the mountains as actively as ever, but neither time nor purse.—Morison should be coming to me for a day or two, and if he does not I shall fear that things are going ill at Pitfield.[1] The conclusion of 'Compromise' gives

---

[7] See Note 2, preceding letter.

529. [1] On the advice of Mrs. Morley's physician, Morley had moved from Pitfield House in June 1873. Cotter Morison, who had returned to England from France, where he had been living, bought the lease (Hirst, i. 246).

me a bold, healthful, high-reaching Essay, practically a guide to turn to when the heart is weaker than the eye is blind. If, either owing to the casuistry pertaining to the subject, or to the desire for directly applying your meaning, you have missed the philosophical altitudes you love better (I understand Morison to hint at this), you have at least said what no one else dares or can say. I shall re-read it:—Let me add that now and then I have thought you less careful in your style than commonly. It has the good swing, but there are dissonances. That is little, but there are at the same time phrases running with sentences that are cast in a tone too purely argumentative for that proper to the essay: showing as it were the want of absolute compression of your own thought in awaiting the objections of an opponent, double-stating it.— I do not quarrel with what I like well, but what I like I wish to see perfect, and I am sure you will overlook a critical habit in me.

Your most faithful
George Meredith

530. *To* FREDERICK A. MAXSE

Text: typed copy, Maxse Papers. Published: *Letters*, i. 250-1, with omission of a sentence.

Box Hill
August 15, 1874

My dear Fred,

I write so that you may not be disappointed of a letter at Meyringen,[1] and good morning to you on your way to the Bel Alp! I am finishing a Poem 'The Nuptials of Attila'[2]—about forty pages: Jacob at my foot, an accustomed pigeon on the window-sill, bees below humming over some droppings of honeycomb just taken from them. This is pastoral and should content me, yet I wish I were with you, in sight of the Alps. Zürich I don't much care for, yet to be at Zürich would enrapture me.—Why should you return!—You have a meeting, I'll swear! Now I look at my pigeon fronting me, I remark that he is amazingly like a parson. He is on one leg, asleep, his beak in breast, all his feathers oddly ruffled to swell his size, and an eye turned on me like the eye of Falstaff heeling over with excess of Sherris. Say, a Bishop.—When I was staying with my wife's sister last June we dined one evening with the rector of the place. He said to me: 'Do you

530. [1] Meiringen, Switzerland.
      [2] Published in the *New Quarterly Magazine* (Jan. 1879).

think it true that there is a portrait of Jesus Christ extant?'—'Of
Nazareth?' said I. He blinked faintly like my sleepy pigeon.—'Certainly of Nazareth'.—'Oh! no, then', said I. 'But it is affirmed that
there is an authentic portrait of the Virgin his Mother.' 'Could one
trust it?' he asked me with a supplication in the tone. 'Decidedly not'
said I. He was (to make use of one of their distinctions) High Church.
One may be high and not see far. And now goodnight, Fred. Write
from Bel Alp.—Where you also will be high and not see so far as me,
I dare say.

Your envious
George M.

531. *To* FREDERICK A. MAXSE

Text: *Letters*, i. 251–2. Collated with typed copy in the Maxse Papers.

Box Hill, Dorking
September 3, 1874

My dear Fred,

I am reminded by Jacob von Homburg that you pass through
Geneva on the 5th, and there is just time for me to despatch you
a greeting. I know the disappointment of *not* getting a letter when one
calls at a foreign post office.—Wind S.E. with rain. For a week we
have had fine S.W. skies: yesterday was quite wonderful with scaling
clouds. I went up the hill with Will and his mother and sister (Jacob of
course) and we flew a kite and dreamed. It was on the whole as good as
Switzerland while it lasted, but it was not the shaking up of Alpine
walks and the freshening of mountain air. This is what I want and
find I certainly can't get before next year. The more I look at *Beauchamp* the more I see that the work must be almost redone—at least to
suit my taste.—Tyndall's Belfast address[1] you have seen, no doubt.
It has roused the Clergy, Fred. *They* warned away from science? *They*
excluded from the chief works of God and told to confine themselves
to the field of the emotions! They affirm that Tyndall is an atheist, and
would dare to say he is already damned if the age were in a mood to
hear that language. The man or the country that fights priestcraft and
priests is to my mind striking deeper for freedom than can be struck
anywhere at present. I foresee a perilous struggle with them. So far

---

531. [1] John Tyndall (1820–93) delivered his inaugural address as President of the
British Association at Belfast on 19 Aug. Exception was taken to his speech by the Bishop
of Manchester in consecrating the new church at Higham, near Burnley, on 29 Aug.

I am heartily with Bismarck.²—I want you to note for me what sort of weather you have had on the days when I recorded our weather here. I am noting as far as I can the general prevalence of the S. Westers at this period. Sept[embe]r is commonly a fine Swiss month; whether it shares our luck at all is what I want to learn. France, I find, has usually our weather in Spring, and not in Autumn.—I shall see you soon. The folly of your coming back affects me strangely. Necessity would have to pull hard to fetch me to these shores, had I choice of Switzerland or Italy. Write when you return—and come here.

Your loving
George Meredith

532. *To* FREDERICK SANDYS

MS.: University of Texas.

Box Hill, Dorking
September 10, 1874

My dear Sandys,

I have asked Wills¹ to come and dine with us here on Sunday week, and we shall be very glad if you can join him. You are to be taken over a Conservatory or two to look at Deadly plants.—I called on Monday. The man waved me off at 10 paces distance. It was at least some saving of a fruitless journey. Let me hear that you will serve as guide to Wills.

Yours ever,
George Meredith

533. *To* MRS. COTTERILL¹

MS.: Yale.

Box Hill
October 11, 1874

My dearest Hostess and my heart's best guest!—

I wish to come to you and carry away your good man to Paris, but

---

531. ² That is, in his struggle against the Catholic Church. (See an unsigned article [by Robert Morier], 'Prussia and the Vatican', *Macmillan's Magazine*, Jan. 1875.)

532. ¹ William Gorman Wills (1828–91), artist, novelist, playwright. As he was born in Ireland and educated at the Waterford Grammar School and Trinity College, GM may have known him through Wyse. Wills, however, became a member of the Garrick Club about 1872 (Freeman Wills, *W. G. Wills: Dramatist and Painter*, 1898, p. 54).

533. ¹ The Cotterills, former neighbours of the Merediths at Norbiton, now lived at Tongswood, Hawkhurst, Kent.

I am in this dilemma. A request came to me some time back from the Editor of the *Fortnightly Review* to begin the publication in his pages of a novel that has to be compressed because it is too long. Now the act of compression necessitates a great deal of re-writing. I thought I might get so far ahead as to be able to take a week's holiday, but I find I must have three hours' work per diem—and would Paris allow of that?— to say nothing of the Lord of Tongswood charioteering in Paris with me! So in despair I am obliged to postpone the trip. It would have been in every way delightful, owing to your forethoughtful arrangements. All promised well, and if I had seen a chance I would have made the rush. Marie was, and is, in favour of it. She prescribes it 'for my condition'. But I'm obliged to hold back.

The proof that your lord comprehends my situation and excuses me till a better season is to be given, by his making an appointment to pass an evening at the Garrick with me—that is not Tuesday or Friday. I am

> Your most loving and loyal
> George Meredith

534. *To* JOHN MORLEY

Text: *Letters*, i. 252–3.

> Box Hill, Dorking
> November 19, 1874

My dear Morley,

I gave you your 'month of freedom from editorial cares', thinking it might be wanted for a holiday on tough desk-work, then fearing that a personal affliction, to which I could not minister, urged you to keep aloof. I am very glad to have your letter. When Maxse saw you before you started he thought you were looking ruddily well—chubbily: so writing at least agrees with you. Yours is the better way. Public life, if only one can keep up to the mark of it, and know when to abandon it, is the wholesomest. You get most wisdom out of it: and it is the only path to follow to know oneself. Hermit philosophers are soon seen following the fancy as much as infants, but it is not so pretty a fancy.—I assume that objections are not yet raised against *Beauchamp*, because I have not yet had a sneer from Chapman. As far as I have seen, the Weekly Commentators are disposed to leave it alone, and I would rather have them do so.—¹ Absolute re-writing I find to be my lamentable task for the whole of it!

The *Essay on Compromise*² was put in my hands the other day in Piccadilly. I hold it a brave good book to take counsel with. The work on 'Supernatural Religion'³ comes in the way of my re-reading it immediately—thanks to your article, and another (yours, it struck me) in the *Pall Mall*—I feel to the writer as we used to towards our big boy champion against the bullies at school: that is, I admire, believe in him, feel that it is my fight, but can aid only very little—by gesticulation chiefly. He is a splendid fellow. Hitherto we have pined for one who should unite profound scholarship and cunning of fence. I like his unhasting equability of tone. I am near the end of the 1st volume, and long to get to the summing up.—You did well by *Bothwell* in *Macmillan*.⁴ I spoke of the article to the more than Scotchman, his partner⁵—the coarser bran or pure porridge Scotchman. 'Hegh, don't ye know the writer of it?' said he, and scotched your name.—The other night I saw Irving⁶ in *Hamlet*, a great pleasure that I should like to hear of your having. He listened to my criticism next day, and no doubt I thought the better of his Hamlet afterwards, but it is good acting. . . .

Your ever faithful
George Meredith

I remember—I had certain things to say of Mill upon 'Nature',⁷ but must defer it. I rejoice that you speak with regret of the weak spot elsewhere.

---

534. ¹ The only review of the serial up to this time was published in the *Sunday Times*, 9 Aug. 1874, p. 7 (Hergenhan, p. 416.).

² When Morley's series of articles on Compromise was concluded in August, the work was issued in book form.

³ *Supernatural Religion: An Inquiry into the Reality of Divine Revelation* (by Walter Richard Cassels) was published anonymously in 1874 and reviewed favourably by Morley in the October issue of the *FR*. Churchmen not unnaturally regarded it as a violent attack upon Christianity and struck back, notably Canon Lightfoot in the *Contemporary Review* (Dec. 1874, Jan., Feb., May, Aug., Oct. 1875, and Feb. 1876).

⁴ An unsigned article, 'On Mr. Swinburne's *Bothwell*', *Macmillan's Magazine* (Oct. 1874).

⁵ George Lillie Craik, husband of the novelist Dinah Mulock and partner in Macmillan's.

⁶ (Sir) Henry Irving (1838–1905), who had first acted Hamlet in 1864, was currently acting at the Lyceum Theatre, with Isabel Bateman as Ophelia.

⁷ *Nature: the Utility of Religion: Theism* (1874). Morley wrote two articles, 'Mr. Mill's Three Essays on Religion', on them (*FR*, Nov. 1874, Jan. 1875).

[*There is no Letter 535*]

536. *To* FREDERICK GREENWOOD

Text: *Letters*, i. 253–4.

Box Hill, Dorking
Last Day of '74

My dear Greenwood,

Though you are rapidly becoming insubstantial to me as well as elusive, like the very spark in the burnt sheet of my rejected manuscript, I believe in you still and will wish New Year's happiness to an Editor so deep in his retirement as to be but the animating spirit of a newspaper. Do you ever think of me? Ever imagine how much an hour of you calls me up? Do you read a bit of *Beauchamp*? I have a portion of it under me to compress and rekindle, and words can't say what a dole of criticism from you (with an interjection or two on the right side) would do to animate the finish. Do you lunch at the Garrick? Sometimes I see you glowing through the bars of the *Pall Mall*, roguish as Holbein's Harry 8th Jester at Hampton Court, or awful as Eblis with the fire at his heart. But I see you only in brilliant dots, like a score of devil's music played to a dyspeptic at night, to haunt him for the remainder of his term, integral no more.

Let nonsense be no more. Men grow grave, Editors most of all. I am troubled about various outlooks for the country, and do hope you will be at work on the subject of a conscription—your own subject years back. Our stiff-necked people must pass under this yoke.

Some day I shall call for a talk of five minutes. Meantime I salute you with all my heart.

537. *To* FREDERICK A. MAXSE

Text: typed copy, Maxse Papers. Published: *Letters*, i. 254–5, with omissions.

Box Hill
January 13, 1875

My dearest Fred,

Your letter struck like a shaft of sunlight into my bath yesterday morning, and the contents appear to me very good, Movement and bracing air—these are the specifics. I have such a vision of your pinewoods that they will henceforth be one of my points of attraction. How delightful to roam through them with your boys!—I assume that the little chaps picked up at once on landing.

Our frost broke up the night you started, and a rising wind made me think of you.—

I doubt if there will be any fresh matter this month; Morley gave only two chapters[1] last month. No doubt you will be back with the boys for their schooling before the further proofs require attention; but I shall hear from you and the proofs shall fly to you wherever you are.—Did you see in *The Times* a letter of a delicious Bishop reproving Auberon Herbert upon the subject of Prayer: Assuring us, in large type, that God answers it, upon the example of the human physician to whom we cry for aid, and are answered.[2] The proof [of] a spiritual response from the instance of the material one is finely episcopal. *The Times* printed no reply to my Lord Bishop.

I go in so dull a round that I have nothing to say. A dash over to France like yours will be youth to blood and brain of me. Tell the dear little lads I think of them and wish them well.

Your loving
George Meredith

538. *To* FREDERICK JONES

Text: *Letters,* i. 255–6.

Box Hill
January 23, 1875

My dear Jones,

It's I who am the delinquent: Marie will not touch the pen to tell it. The truth is, I am so tied down to work at this period that I cannot hope to spare two days for pleasure before the end of February. Blame, but pity me, and that will bring you round to the right feeling. Besides, our Babsie[1] is only just flinging off a catarrh, and I feel threatened with it, yet must drive my quill.

Consider, however, you, that the Birthdays occur on the 10th and 12th of next month. Will you come on the 10th to celebrate Marie's? Once you did. Be that admirable man and wife again! You will make

537. [1] Of *Beauchamp's Career* in the *FR.*
  [2] Herbert branded as superstition man's attempt to persuade God to modify the laws of nature or 'to act upon His will so as to alter his intentions in regard either of men or things, souls or bodies'. In these days of locomotion and machinery the idea of some Unseen Power suspending natural laws would be hideous (*The Times,* 2 Jan.). In reply an English Bishop (not otherwise identified) said that Herbert's letter written to contradict the belief that 'our Father in Heaven will give good things to them that ask Him . . . has not shaken my belief in my Master's word' (*The Times,* 5 Jan.).
538. [1] i.e. Marie Eveleen.

us happy. And then can be settled the time of our visit to you. I have long been wishing to see you and make you know my sympathy for you in the blows that have struck you heavily through the year. They have been a grief to us, believe me.[3]

I do hope you will come on the 10th. Write to me pardoning me and heaping anthracite on my head (a costly matter in these days) by the promise that in spite of my breaches of faith you can be generous. Willie will be so happy to see Ethel.[4] He shall have a holiday for that day. Give my warmest regards to Mrs. Jones—dashed by no cynicism of your own: and to Miss Jones: and my love to Bright-hair.

Your faithfullest
George Meredith

539. *To* MARMADUKE J. TEESDALE[1]

MS.: Yale.

Box Hill, Dorking
March 29, 1875

My dear M. Teesdale,

I have been very busy and rather unwell: pray let it be my excuse to you for delay in replying before this.

I wish you had tried pentameters, or else rhymed seven feet lines of equal length in the run of couplets. It would have given you space for many subtleties and beauties that you have had to overlook. It is a good maxim that in translations you should get the longest line possible to the temper of the poetry and avoid difficult rhyming. In your stanza here, you manage well with the first line. The second however is a dissyllable: in which words we are shockingly weak for purposes of rhyme, and the recurrence of the participle ending in 'ing' which makes the greater number of our rhyming dissyllables becomes vulgar. Then midway you are so impoverished that you have to break off and go to monosyllable terminations and this is unpleasant in a form of regular verse in which the ear has become accustomed to the finale in two notes. Nor do I much like the dancing measure in

---

[3] There is no clue to the blows.

[4] The Joneses had two daughters, Mabel and Ethel (the younger). 'Bright-hair' (below) was Ethel, the Merediths' favourite.

539. [1] See Note 1, Letter 518. In 1874 Teesdale had published a translation of Goethe's epic-idyll *Hermann and Dorothea* (2nd edn., 1875), the book for which GM is thanking him in this letter. Teesdale was making further translations from Goethe and had submitted some of them to GM for criticism.

such a poem, dactyllic or anapaestic. Here and there it has insisted on a word to suit the meter, and the word is not quite the thing. 'Amphora' comes in finely: but the girl never carried an amphora. Then the mother 'decorously *pacing*' is not Göthe's mother, who walked 'proudly beside'—*feierlich neben*. A mother must not be said to be pacing. 'Flaunt in' and 'wanting' are rhymes that echo one another horridly. I have ventured to mark in pencil a suggestion here and there, but pray take it merely as a hint on the spur of the reading; and if you think it an impertinence pardon it in the good intention. As to publication, I would not advise it until you have worked over and over it, crooned and polished, perhaps have recast it. You have a strong feeling for Göthe and for melody, but it takes time to render this Great One, and in my opinion it is right to give the whole of your author, and wrong to evade portions, as you have done in 'Alexis and Dora'. Believe me I am sympathetic with your work when I say it. —I liked the 'Hermann and Dorothea' very much. The lines were occasionally very weak from your making them quite unnecessarily start upon prepositions against a cardinal maxim to be found in your Latin Grammar: for as the rule is that the preposition gives no ictus, the line does not sail or roll at all when 'of', 'by', 'from', etc. leads it, but shambles in prose, and you reverse the fit arsis and thesis. But I like the honest translation and cordially thank you for the book. I am ever

Yours very faithfully,

George Meredith

540. *To* JOHN MORLEY

Text: *Letters*, i. 256.

Box Hill
April 12, 1875

My dear Morley,

Your letter written at Trier was a delightful surprise to me. On the Sunday following we imagined you at Rheims, gave you to the Sainted Joan for an hour, compared the wheels of your mind with the ceremonials of the Cathedral, and finally deposited you in Paris, where for your good health I trust you may even still be. I am anxious to see you here, but this weather allows of no forecast of when. Let me hear of your return. It would (weather permitting and your work) be pleasant to have your appreciation of some of the upper Frenchmen while it is new. I feel like the one who 'ploughs with pain his native lea'.[1] I go nowhere, see, hear, know nothing.—Yes, I went to see Salvini[2] on Friday. Saturday gave the newspaper criticism, and after observing the true and only Othello, you should have read them! Faint, prim, puling exceptions to this and that: Like political England they want peace—not to be disturbed. They harp on Othello's 'Tenderness'. Do you perceive much of it in reading the play?—one of the finest in action of Shakespeare, lowest of the great plays in conception.

Yours ever warmly,
George Meredith

541. To MRS. ANNA C. STEELE

MS.: University of Texas.

Box Hill
April 22, 1875

My dear Mrs. Steele,

How good of you and how amiable to think of giving me so much pleasure! But by the very post which brings your invitation I receive four stall tickets for Monday morning, when I have my wife, with two ladies (dame and damsel) of the neighbourhood, to convoy to see the Moor. She will lose her heart, but it will only be following mine, and yours. Our rendezvous is in Salvini.

Dear me, it gives one an old savour of the love of fame again, a sort of idea that it is a generous thirst instead of a capering foolishness, such as our excellent English teach us it is.

I have not read Il Gladiatore, but imagine the superb Spartacus Salvini will be.[1] M. Soumet is also unknown to me by name. The subject of the tragedy makes one envious. As it is a Frenchman's work, we shall certainly have floods of rhetoric to drown the matter.—Once more into the Gallery I! Or if you will offer to catch me on my flight upward and keep me midway, believe me I will resign ambition for the topmost seats of the house. I am

Your most faithful
George Meredith

540. [1]   Who ploughs with pain his native lea
And reaps the labour of his hands. . . .
In Memoriam, lxiv. 25–26.
[2] Tommaso Salvini (1829–1916), Italian tragedian, made his début as Othello at the Theatre Royal, Drury Lane, on 1 Apr. The Globe (2 Apr.) described him as 'a powerful and original actor... whose style is altogether new' and whose 'voice is rich and powerful'.
541. [1] The Times announced (17 Apr.) that the success of Salvini's Othello had caused postponement of Soumet's tragedy, Il Gladiatore. Soumet's plays were better known to the generation preceding GM's than to his own.

542. *To* FREDERICK SANDYS

Text: *Letters from George Meredith to Various Correspondents*, p. 7.

Box Hill
Derby Day, [May 26, 1875]

My dear Sandys,

I saw your Galopin[1] gallopin' in this afternoon, looked for you on the hill and saw a pigeon conveying the news to you of your triumph. It is evident that you have now an Income for life in the Garrick Sweepstakes. I expect a dinner. But let me order it: you and I alone. There's a dry still Champagne I know of.—I have just asked Lethbridge for a bed for two or three days. If his room is occupied, will you give me yours for Friday night and Sunday night? and you and I will knock nobs over a quiet glass on Saturday if you like.—Also what think you of *Hamlet* on Monday?[2] I rather shrink from seeing Salvini as the Dane, but I am with you. In which case take a ticket for me. Lots of treats, mind. Remember I swell your income by a pound per annum.[3]

Write by return.

Yours cordially,
George Meredith

543. *To* JOHN MORLEY

Text: *Letters*, i. 256–7.

Box Hill
June 29, 1875

My dear Morley,

Most foul! But postponements, as you justly remind me, destroy the integrity of men, and the ruins of our appointment fall in a heap on the next, and down we shall go into the dark and unknown vast if we do not lay tight hold of the nearest branch, and swear—

All or nothing! I can't endure your coming for only a night and two bits of days: a Thursday without head and a Friday without bottom. Tell me that though all London should crave for you openmouthed, you come on Wednesday week, not to leave us at least before Friday. But don't be due anywhere till that week is done.

542. [1] Winner of the Derby in 1875.
 [2] The opening night of Salvini's *Hamlet* at Drury Lane.
 [3] A jesting allusion to the Garrick Club betting pool for the Derby.

Come on Wednesday in time for a French breakfast in the garden about 1/4 past 11. You have no idea how nice it is. We tried it on Sunday with three good men and an ancient Hock, and I assure you, that staid and formal day danced to its end like an ecclesiastic that has received the promise of a bishopric. Say, then, Wednesday week, and here before 1/2 past 11. Haply we shall have majestic July weather. Write, bind thyself. From me and mine to you and yours all sweet greetings!

Yours,
George Meredith

544. *To* JOHN MORLEY

Text: *Letters*, . 257–8.

Box Hill
July 1, 1875

My dear Morley,

We stipulate for you, that we are not to expect you in soaking weather.

Because (and here lies the sting of it, only to be obliterated by our welcome of you) you come so rarely that we are anxious to make a great occasion of it: great, not grand, and much radiancy is required of the heavens when that you do come. Therefore should July continue to squeeze a sponge, again postpone. But if it promises fair on Tuesday, tell me at what early hour (writing on Tuesday, with a calculating eye aloft) I may go to the Station to meet you and bring you to

The Breakfast.

I wish I knew of conversible fellows to ask to meet you. One can meet, I am told, remarkable characters, but the speechful, the reciprocating, the sunny and unpresumptuous, who speak from the healthy breast of that dear Mother of us, the Moment,—where are they to be found?

I have looked, I forgot to tell you, at Tennyson's *Queen Mary*,[1] and I had great pleasure of my reading. I saw no trace of power, but the stateliness, the fine tone, the high tone, of some passages, hit me hard. Curiously too, in him, the prose is crisp, salient, excellent. The Songs, if we had not Shakespeare's to show what are not literary

544. [1] Tennyson's *Queen Mary*, a drama in blank verse, was published a few weeks earlier.

forcings to catch a theme to point a comparison, would do. As it is, 'Milking the cow' smells of milking the brain. Mary's 'Low-low' is an instance of public consciousness—before Victoria's people.—But the work seems to me to be good, and how glad I am to have it of him!

Your faithful

George Meredith

545. *To* JOHN MORLEY

Text: typed copy in W. M. Meredith's copy of *Letters* (Bodleian Library).

Box Hill

July 29, 1875

My dear Morley,

It's disappointing and vexing, for now we have fair nights and days to offer you; but you give good reasons, and nothing can be said. I'm tied up to be lashed again.—It's really very bracing.

Meanwhile here's the hat. And so confirmed has our habit become of standing under it to consult about you in the morning, that we have gone there again to ask ourselves whether its presence is to signify a promise that you will return to fetch it some day or that it is to be an indemnification for the everlasting absence of the head that owns it. In either case I won't have it disturbed.

My objection to 'Modern' is that in English, and to English minds, the slightest stress on the word, if it is not partly intended for ironical, has the effect of inviting irony.

'La Revue Moderne' is very well, but with us 'Modern' has not strength for a title.[1] I declare I prefer the 'Impartial' or the 'Universal': and I have only to pronounce them to shake my dubious head.

'The Review of the Time.'

This rather takes me.

I will shake my noddle further, for I am anxious that there should be a name to displace the misnomer.

I like to hear of your finding difficulties in writing. In this is the promise of the true artist.—An easy flow to a flourishing end, punctual to the predicted date, is the delight of the public, the death of the writer. He little knows how they eat him up!

Your faithfullest

George Meredith

545. [1] Apparently Morley was at last contemplating a new name for the *FR* 'to displace the misnomer'. The *FR* had issued its last mid-monthly number on 15 Nov. 1866 (Everett, p. 73), and Morley had taken over with the Jan. 1867 issue.

546. *To* RICHARD H. HORNE

Text: *Letters from GM to RHH*, pp. 12–13.

Box Hill, Dorking
August 3, 1875

My dear Horne,

I am very glad to hear from you directly. First to the business of your letter. Bonaparte Wyse told me you were somewhat hurt with me for the reason that I had not come into communication with you on your return. I chanced to mention the report concerning you: but not to justify my conduct, for I do not attend to scandal, and it had not affected me.[1] I said that I had spoken to men who seemed to be unwilling to renew their relations with you, probably upon the ground of the scandal.—The chivalry of the defence of woman by Sentimentalists has gone greater lengths.

I shall be happy to call on you when I am disengaged, but I am busy up to the blinking eyes; and an evening in London signifies a night to be passed there, which robs me of my quiet morning at home next day. Were I a dashing writer of railway prose or even a composer of poetical flimsy, this would not matter; but I write studying. I would not speak of it but that I know it must appeal to you.—However, I will certainly give myself the pleasure of calling some day about noon.—I have written to you in reply to your transmission of papers— do you know?[2] I sent the letter to your publishers. Until B[onapar]te Wyse mentioned you I had met no one who could tell me your address, and I had no time to hunt for it in London. Moreover I live in Boeotia, and have the habits of the country, and never pay complimentary visits to friends. I love them, be assured, and rejoice if I can serve them, none the less.

Believe me, my dear Horne, / Most sincerely yours,
George Meredith

546. [1] Horne had written GM that Wyse had told him of a domestic scandal 'got up' against Horne in his absence. Even had the perfect lies been perfect truths, he said, they emanated from the last man in the world who should have cast such a stone, and added: '. . . I have never followed the bad example of Dickens in parading my private grievances. . . . I c'd not make up my mind to the lasting pain that my very brief statement would have caused my self-divorced wife' (letter of Horne to GM, *Letters from GM to RHH*, pp. 10–11).
[2] Horne had sent GM a book, a letter, and a photograph in Nov. 1871. I know of nothing else.

547. *To* JOHN MORLEY

Text: *Letters*, i. 258–9.

Box Hill
August 12, 1875

My dear Morley,

I must write now, though I have little time to give a faint sketch of what I have to say of *Rousseau*.[1] It has moved me as few books have done. I had but a poor knowledge, from never having read a compact history of this period when Wit, Science and Sentiment contended, and the latter, which was to fade before the other two, struck an unsound Age with the ring of the ultimate Truth. Rousseau was the very keynote.—You have handled him with consummate mastery: and none can know the trial you have sustained better than he who as I do penetrates to the man, hating this in him, warming to that, alternately, incessantly. But here is one of the most curious and one of the grandest problems of humanity, which you have handled perfectly. How unjust I was to the printed portion in the *Fortnightly*! Or may one be pardoned for not having seen the fulness of the work there? I did not discredit you for style (excepting a point or two), but exactly for that which I find in the book—mastery of every note of that evasive heart, and a power of showing the Heroic coward complete in his contradictions. To my mind it is—and it will be to me—one of the most precious of studies. It is one of the wisest of books. For such is the nature of Rousseau that his notes are the deepest and highest within the scale of philosophy, and the very lowest. But (with an exception or two to be named when I meet you, and soon, and here, I hope) you touch all equally, delicately, fillingly,[2] with volume where needful.—I cannot exhaust my admiration. I am at times electrified by companion ideas of my own.—To me the study has a charm that flings off monotony. Speaking critically for the multitude (in the manner of modern criticism) monotony is a character of the subject and the book: wherefore it has not been popular. And with reviewers 3 things present and one absent were required: Competency of knowledge, quick sympathy for the shifting marvellous creature your theme, a comprehension of the mystery of what we are—and no prejudice. The little g for G was turned on you heavily.—[3] But such a fate befalling a book like this should be consolation, as to rewards for value, to novelists and pigmies.

547. [1] Morley had published portions of his *Rousseau* in the *FR* (Sept.–Dec. 1872); the book was published by C. & H. in Mar. 1873. No doubt composition of *Beauchamp's Career* and his estrangement from Morley at the time account for GM's delay in reading it.
[2] ? Error for *fittingly*.
[3] i.e. Morley's unconventional use of lower case *g* in *God* had brought down criticism on him. Morley argued that capital letters designated names, that God is a Trinity, that Christ said he is not a person but a spirit, etc. (Hirst, i. 246).

Can you by chance come to us next week? It will delight me infinitely. I have to talk over Rousseau with you, much to say. I made no marks, but I will at whiles, and meantime I remember enough to occupy us.

Your faithfullest
George Meredith

548. *To* RICHARD H. HORNE

MS.: Ashley Library, British Museum. Printed: *Letters from GM to RHH*, pp. 14–15.

Box Hill
September 29, 1875

My dear Horne,

I thank you warmly for electing me one of the Fifty whom you think worthy to receive this edition of *Cosmo*,[1] with the minor pieces. I have had my copy of a previous edition 'taken or detained', and cannot compare them. I remember I used to class *Pope Gregory*[2] as the more powerful of these two lofty dramas, but human sympathy is more deeply touched in *Cosmo*. Garcia at the death of Giovanni, with his continual reversion from his dead brother to himself, and backward, is in the highest degree natural and affecting, for so in such a moment, as with recurrent throbs, the heart moves.

'—*those* dreadful eyeballs
Turning *me* all to stone—'
'God make *me* a stone
Or make *him* animate . . .'
etc. etc.

Pity and self-pity are here in one outcry.

Garcia's lines: 'Ye creeping winds etc.' have the flow of settled grief—only to be attained in verse surcharged with the matter.—In no work but the greatest do I take such an impression of personal grandeur and weight, as when Cosmo speaks.—Things may be said on the other side perhaps to account for the tragedy's not having worked its way to the stage. Many of the minor poems are old favourites of mine. Among the new, the lines of Leconte de Lisle[3] come home to me warmly for I greatly admire the poet.

548. [1] *Cosmo de Medici*, a tragedy in five acts, first published in 1837.
   [2] *Gregory VII*, first published in 1840. *CHEL* says of it and *Judas Iscariot* (1848) that they 'are works of power and some grandeur, born out of due time'.
   [3] Charles Marie Leconte de Lisle (originally Leconte), 1818–94, French poet.

I have been absent yachting—just before the gales: and let this plead for my delay in writing to thank you. I leave home for three or four weeks. Afterwards perhaps you will give me the pleasure of a visit. My regret is that this diminutive cottage is not rich in a spare bed that I may offer you. It is one of the fatal causes why I see few friends, for my hatred of London keeps me out of it, except upon compulsion to go and remain for two hours. Adieu.

[Marginal note:] In the hope of seeing you soon, here or in Town, I am

> Your faithful
> George Meredith

549. *To* MR. WILLIAMS[1]

Text (excerpt): American Art Association, Anderson Galleries, Inc. Catalogue (5-6 Dec. 1934), p. 125.

> Box Hill, Dorking
> November 9, 1875

Will you do me the favour to forward immediately the remaining copy of the *Ordeal of R[ichar]d Feverel* in your possession, to 'C. Kegan Paul, Esq., care of Messrs. H. S. King & Co., publishers, 65 Cornhill'. And accept my thanks in advance for your trouble.

550. *To* (?) MR. PFALZ[1]

Text (excerpt): Anderson Galleries Catalogue (4-5 Dec. 1922), p. 40.

> Box Hill, Dorking
> November 10, 1875

My dear Pfalz,
The test of a sweet nature is its ability to bear with an old joke: so then if the weighty demands of your business permit it, will you tell your Jack and mine, that I hope to see him on Sunday if it's tolerably fine. I will take all possible care of him.

549. [1] ? Of Williams & Norgate, booksellers.
550. [1] A name unknown to English directories and found but rarely in German directories. One suspects Meredithian playfulness: quite possibly GM was addressing one of the Palgraves, the most likely being Reginald Douce. (Cf. Palsgrave, a count Palatine; Palatinate, a state of the old German empire, under the rule of the Palsgraf or Count Palatine of the Rhine.)

551. *To* (?) MR. PFALZ

Text (excerpt): American Art Association Catalogue (8 Feb. n.y.).

[Box Hill, Dorking]
November 12, 1875

I have won your heart by loving Jack. 'Twas partly my intention, but I was honest, and you know, that when cordial impulse goes with cunning, heart of woman or man will be caught and swept away. This brilliant morning makes me bolder to press for Jack to come, if only he shall be well enough to face the journey; and he is not to go out at night; he is to have Will's hammock-cot, and we quarter the boy on a neighbour, who has taken him before, on such occasions. And Jack shall have his bath in the morning beside a fire in my room, by the light of logs hewn, split and sawn by this hand of mine. He shall not be pressed to walk more than he pleases. In truth, considering that you are likely to have a fog on Sunday night, it would be well he should be here. I promise to read him ballads of mine; and I will refresh him with laughter at you; for nothing is half so sweet as laughing over them we love. Of course, if Jack prefers it, next week will do as well as this, but Brackenbury is a nice fellow, and there may not be such cheerful company the following Sunday. I suppose we cannot hope to have you? . . . but you are invariably Sunday's Grand Lama—the rival of Deans and Chapters, the mark for islands and continents to aim their choicest at.

552. *To* J. W. FRIEND[1]

MS.: University of Texas.

Box Hill, Dorking
December 1, 1875

Dear Sir,
    Your letter of the 16th of last month has come to me after some delay.—I cannot at the present moment undertake a serial story for the projected Journal, but I shall be glad to see your prospectus of it,

---

552.　[1] Unidentified. He is not listed in the *Cambridge Bibliography of English Literature* or any of the other bibliographies I have consulted as editor of any of the periodicals established at about this time.

from which I may be able to judge whether my style of writing will suit it. I am

Yours very truly,
George Meredith

553. *To* J. W. FRIEND

MS.: University of Texas.

Box Hill
December 4, 1875

Dear Sir,
I am unable to supply the story, for your new Journal. I thank you for the proposal.

Yours very truly,
George Meredith

554. *To* MISS MARY LAWRENCE

MS.: the Lawrence family.

Box Hill
December 27, 1875

Dear Miss Mary Lawrence,
I have been hoping up to the last moment that I might be presentable to you to-day: but I am the victim of a cold that has caught me with the grip of Influenza, and I carry a head I could call wooden if it ached less. I trust to have the happiness of a walk with you and your other you—W[sic][1]—before you leave Burford.[2] I am, in profound dejection,

Your most devoted
George Meredith

554. [1] The 'other you' is Louisa ('the two who are one'). The capital *W* is a kind of pun—double *u*.
[2] Burford Lodge, near Box Hill, home of Sir Trevor Lawrence.

555. *To* MISS ALICE BRANDRETH[1]

MS.: Mrs. J. G. Gordon. Published: *Letters*, i. 260–1, with inaccuracies; Lady Butcher, pp. 23–24, with variants.

Box Hill
February 11, 1876

Wife being absent, I could find
Nought to say to Rosalind.
She returns, and swift as wind
Now I write to Rosalind.
—Young Orlando, reared as hind,
Was fit mate for Rosalind,
(When his manners were refined).
He had youth like Rosalind.

—Shall a man in grey declined,
Seem the same for Rosalind?
Yea, though merely aged in rind,
Is he worthy Rosalind?
This in grave debate should bind
Parliaments and Rosalind.
—Still, if, captious, wayward, blind,
And the rest of 't, Rosalind
Should insist:—if to her mind
(If she have one) Rosalind
Thinks me (if to thought inclined
Ever): I with Rosalind
(And I say it, having dined,
Slept and dreamed of Rosalind)
I will do my best; and kind
Prove our audience, Rosalind!
Take these words for treaty signed
—No Orlando, Rosalind!
But a man with wrinkles lined,
Vows to read with Rosalind.

G.M.

555. [1] This 'letter' was in response to an invitation to read the part of Orlando in *As You Like It* (not Bassanio in *The Merchant of Venice*, as stated in *Letters*, i. 260 n.). Alice Brandreth was to have the role of Rosalind. (For a biographical sketch of Alice Brandreth, see Biographical Section, p. 1721.)

556. *To* MRS. E. L. BRANDRETH

MS.: Mrs. J. G. Gordon. Published: Lady Butcher, p. 24, without date and with the misreading *word* for *verse*.

Box Hill
March 5, 1876

Dear Mrs. Brandreth,
    After 3 nights of anxious thought!—and it may be communicated to the Professor,[1] if you think fit.

> 'Now so richly SYLVEST'RINED,
> Here's the last verse to Rosalind.'

And my compliments to her, from

Your most faithful
George Meredith

557. *To* FREDERICK GREENWOOD

Text: *Letters*, i. 261–2.

Box Hill
March 9, 1876

My dear Greenwood,
    Don't laugh at my simplicity: I'm treating you as if you really meant to come. And who knows? Faith has been rewarded and unfaith astounded before now. We have a fine South-Wester blowing, likely to hold on for some days. Will you come this Saturday early?—or will it hit you better to appoint the next? I have written it, you see, with the lovely gravity I can assume. Still, if you do come I shall celebrate the event and make a date of it. Jupiter, they say, in his Godly irony grants mortals their wishes. I don't believe in the irony, but I do in accidents, and that now and then a loaf tumbles out of Jupiter's bread basket. O tumble, come! I've a great appetite for you.

556. [1] James Joseph Sylvester (1814–97), born Joseph, was a brilliant mathematician who held professorial positions at various institutions before being called at about the time of this letter to the newly opened Johns Hopkins University at Baltimore. In 1883 he returned to England as Savilian Professor of Geometry at Oxford.
    A friend of the Brandreths, he took part in their Shakespearian readings (see preceding letter) and had composed 300-odd lines to rhyme with Rosalind. Lady Butcher says that when he sent a copy to GM, GM sent this note to Mrs. Brandreth.

558. *To* C. KEGAN PAUL[1]

MS.: Yale.

[Box Hill]
March 22, 1876

Dear Mr. Paul,

Will you come to us on Sunday, if the weather should be at all smiling?

I have asked Colonel Brackenbury and shall be able to provide for you both at the inn, whither to my regret I shall have to despatch you at night.

I beg you to reply to—Box Hill, Dorking.

There is an early train on Sunday from Victoria—about half past nine: at Clapham a little later; and one in the afternoon. Let me hear of your choice and I will meet you: but the earlier the better. You come by the L.B. & S.C. Railway to Box Hill and Burford Bridge Station: and you shall be hurled to town as early as you please on Monday.—You will give my wife and me great pleasure by coming.

Yours very faithfully,
George Meredith

559. *To* JOHN MORLEY

Text: *Letters*, i. 262.

Box Hill
March 28, 1876

My dear Morley,

For some time I have been entertaining myself with the notion that you went with the Governor-General to Rome and Naples, and so could not give me a chance of seeing you here. You partly proposed for February! Will there be a likelihood of it in April? You know the pleasure and refreshment it is to me.—I am busy, idly busy with verse: unable to let go forth that which ought not to have so much time wasted on it, therefore discontented with the work and myself. Your voice would brace me. What is it occupies you? Hard work, if you have not been absent, but what kind of work? I am particularly curious to read you this month, on the question of Empress, and as to

---

558. [1] Charles Kegan Paul (1828–1902), author of a life of William Godwin (1876), took over the publishing business of H. S. King in 1877. In 1879 he published GM's *The Egoist*.

how you interpret Disraeli's speeches.[1] Is it a genial contempt for the House, or dotage? does he laugh at the gentiles, or but flounder before them? I fancy the answer to be that he is heartily sick of the task his Imperial mistress imposed on him at a moment when he did not know the English people so well.

For the rest Radicalism will have nothing to regret in the passing of the Bill.

560. *To* MISS LOUISA SHORE[1]

Text (excerpt): Louisa Shore, '*Poems*', *with a Memoir by her Sister Arabella Shore* (1897), pp. 32–33.

Box Hill, Dorking
April 9, 1876

The poem[2] . . . a moon-sketch; it has a breath of pure melody, coming of most tender feeling, with a certain haze proper to it, reminding me of a night scene by the sea . . . a beautiful poem of, I fear, no fancied sentiment, and winding up with such grave, good hopes as I share with you, and few at this time, though more than in old times, look to.

561. *To* JOHN MORLEY

Text: *Letters*, i. 262–4.

Box Hill
April 12, 1876

My dear Morley,
The essay on Macaulay[1] is masterly, perfectly balanced, clear, sound, delightful with apt expression in the delivery of a just sentence.

559. [1] Relative to Queen Victoria's assumption of the title Empress of India. A recent visit of the Prince of Wales to India caused the Queen to regard the moment as auspicious, and Disraeli, engrossed in Eastern affairs and the Suez Canal purchase, yielded. In introducing the Royal Titles Bill, he did not announce the exact title, which was only revealed on the second reading of the bill (9 Mar.). Apprehension and resentment of the mystery were widespread, but in the end Disraeli triumphed easily.
560. [1] Louisa Shore (1824–95), minor poet who had been encouraged by John Morley several years earlier to communicate her admiration of GM's works to him. An intermittent correspondence developed, of which little has survived.
  [2] *Elegies*, which GM must have seen in MS.; it was first printed for private circulation in 1883.
561. [1] In the April *FR*. Morley disparaged Macaulay as a stylist, demonstrating his inferiority to Clarendon and Burke and then selecting Southey as a fairer standard of comparison.

I find this fault: I do not think it right that you should 'stumble' on the quotation concerning Tickell and Addison,[2] wherewith to oppose Macaulay to Southey, when you have just given the latter at his best. We all go with you in your verdict, only in a literary sense we feel that you are below your own mark here for an instant.—Of course you are not comparing him with Southey, but casting light on his style from the first lamp to hand. All the more however does it seem to me that you should in such a case be careful of your selection of an example, which you may well cry horror and thrice horror upon, as it stands where you have placed it, and which is yet inoffensive enough in its natural place. Nay, here I should defend the style of Macaulay, on whom I see the advocate's wig while I hear him thumping excusably in the advocate's manner to defend those two. Detestable as is the iterated blow on 'villany', it is only so as old Bailey eloquence is so, and appears to be vehement with the good object of wresting life or character from a stupid Jury. But if you had apposed some description of William or Luxembourg or Marlborough, I should have been better satisfied.— On this point I feel so sure, that I am anxious you should consider about it before you republish the essay. And I will not ask pardon of a great writer and student for drawing attention to what looks but little.

A minor defect, of a kind that I will direct your eye to in *Rousseau*,[3] is at 'blaze and glare', or amplication in language which is not an extension of the idea or fortification of the image. There will be a glare if there is a blaze, but that is nothing compared with the twice insisted-upon harshness of sound, in consideration that it is not necessary twice.—So fair is your work to me that I am persecuted by such generally imperceptible specks on it.

Enclosed is a poem of 3 verses for the *Fortnightly*, if you think it worthy.[4] If you can find the Sonnet to Carlyle[5] I shall be glad: I am not sure of my memory.

Ever your faithfullest
George Meredith

---

2 '. . . We open Macaulay's Essays and stumble on such sentences as this: "That Tickell should have been guilty of a villany seems to us highly improbable. That Addison should have been guilty of a villany seems to us highly improbable. But that these two men should have conspired together to commit a villany seems to us improbable in a tenfold degree." ' This, concludes Morley, is 'the very burlesque and travesty of a style'. (Thomas Tickell, 1686–1740, minor writer, was a satellite of Addison's and under-secretary in Ireland when Addison was secretary.)

3 GM had read Morley's *Rousseau* (published 1873) during the preceding summer.

4 'A Ballad of Past Meridian', *FR* (June 1876).

5 So far as I can discover, this sonnet, composed in honour of Carlyle's eightieth birthday, first appeared in *Letters*, i. 260.

562. *To* MRS. E. L. BRANDRETH

MS.: Mrs. J. G. Gordon. Excerpts published: *Letters*, i. 264, with inaccuracies; Lady Butcher, p. 24.

Box Hill, Dorking
April 13, 1876

Dear Mrs. Brandreth,

I shall be very happy to come on Thursday the 27th, and if I am not staying with a friend in town, as at this season I generally am, your offer of a bed will be very acceptable. Please to tell my dear Beatrice—Rosalind—Katharine[1] that I bear in mind the scheme of writing a play for her. Also she should in loyalty be informed that the Professor[2] has been largely corresponding with me. He starts (it was the latest announcement) on the 15th: and threatens that when at Baltimore he will bring his whole mathematical force to bear upon the Governors of the Hopkins University to make them invite me with honours to act as his colleague in the shape of lecturer on Poetry and Rhetoric. Thus you see he will insist on having one of us: I have lived near the Rose, so I am sweet to him.—I beg to be remembered to Mr. Brandreth and Katharine, and I am ever

Your most faithful and devoted
George Meredith

563. *To* WILLIAM LETHBRIDGE[1]

Text (excerpts): composite of excerpts in Sotheby Catalogue (2 June 1919), p. 15, and Anderson Galleries Catalogue (24–25 Feb. 1920), p. 35.

[Box Hill, Dorking]
May 10, 1876

I have, alas! fallen from my fine vegetarian heights! I feed now like my fellow-beasts . . . my frame has benefitted, my pride abated, and all spirituality has abandoned me. I am as low as Lowe[2] can be.

562. [1] Alice Brandreth, designated here by the names of various Shakespearian characters whose parts she had read in home theatricals.
   [2] Professor Sylvester. (See Note 1, Letter 556.)
563. [1] The Sotheby Catalogue gives Ernest Lethbridge as the addressee, but I am sure that this is an error.
   [2] ? A reference to Robert Lowe (1811–92), the Adullamite who helped to defeat the Whig reform bill in 1866.

564. *To* W. C. BONAPARTE WYSE

MS.: Yale.

[Box Hill]
May 20, 1876

My dear Félibre and Friend,

Your letter of invitation, unfortunately for me, came too late. I was bound, as I am always at this season, by all sorts of invitations of a less agreeable kind—to dine with anything but poets: and I was held a fortnight in advance. I seriously thought of coming, and I made the attempt. A week's earlier information of the *bèu jour de Santo Estello*,[1] and I should have been able to make my arrangements.—I am full of regrets. It would have delighted me to have seen you in your element, to have drunk Châteauneuf du Pape with you, and to the health of Mistral. By the way, I am going to write a full review of him. Perhaps at the festival next year I shall have an opportunity of attending. If we can be there together it will be glorious. Here is East wind of nearly a month's duration. I suppose you are not in Provence but you have clear sky, soft gales, flowers and poets. What better upon earth!

Do write me word of the circumstances of the day. Let me see in my mind's eye the picture of which I make the absent one.

And tell me when you expect to be next in London.

My wife speaks of you and yours with constant friendliness. She is not at my elbow, or she would, be sure, send her message of greeting.

All health, wealth of soul and good accidents befall you. I am

Yours most cordially,
George Meredith

565. *To* [? WALTER] WELDON[1]

Text (excerpts): composite of excerpts in The American Art Association Catalogue of the Collection of William F. Gable (n.d.) and Sotheby Catalogue (4–5 Dec. 1916), p. 41.

Box Hill, Dorking
May 24, 1876

My dear Weldon,

Here's a state of things!—I can run down on Friday night to

564. [1] The bèu jour de la Santo Estello commemorated the martyrdom of the Roman virgin Santo Estello on 21 May in the year 98. This anniversary had been kept by the Félibrists since the founding of the Félibrige on 21 May 1854. *Bèu jour* is Provençal for *fine day*. (I am indebted to my colleague Professor Raphael Levy for this note.)
565. [1] Presumably Walter Weldon (1832–85), journalist and publisher of *Weldon's Register* (1860–4) who later entered the chemical industry. At the time of his death he lived at Rede Hall, Burstow, Surrey (Boase).

Gravesend and share your fortunes till Monday, but I can't go down
with you. . . . I'm grieved at this uncompanionable scheme of mine and
really advise you to postpone the having me as a guest. Besides I'm
jealous of Wingfield[2] as a novelist and Sandys beats me amazingly as
a humourist, and I don't like Smart for getting the public to take his
Two kissing when I can't get her to accept one of mine. . . .[3] Do consider of this and how nice it will be for me to go into a barge with you
off the Tower another time!—

566. *To* MISS ALICE BRANDRETH

MS.: Mrs. J. G. Gordon. Published: *Letters*, i. 266–7 (dated *August 20*, 1876), with
inaccuracies; excerpt: Lady Butcher, pp. 47–48.

Box Hill
August 2, 1876

My dear Miss Brandreth,[1]

This, to speed you on your way with the assurance that we poor
abandoned souls look for your return—with the boots of Kazan!
(large-sized feet).[2] The spelling of your letter shows carefulness. But
what do you mean by 'sitting, not taking in much beside the rhythm'—?
do you mean, in addition to? or next neighbour to? I am sure you
enjoy that heavenly delight of young London ladies in solitude, which
consists in the poetic contemplation of themselves as looked on by the
eternal hills: and to think you incapable of this exquisite reverie is to
be unjust to you.—One topic of a serious letter to you would be the
fate of those Russian professors: for it has been remarked of you that
the professor is your natural prey; that you cannot but make him
incandescent, and are almost irresponsible in the fatality you exercise.[3]
But to say thus much is to elevate and dignify you at the cost of your
immortal nature. Wherefore I would adjure you (since these Sclavic
professors are desperate men) to commence your conversation with

565. [2] Lewis Strange Wingfield (1842–91), whose *Slippery Ground* was published in
1876. The *BMC* lists four novels by him printed at Guildford (1878, 1879, 1880, 1885),
so that GM may have known him in Surrey.
   [3] A reference to Hawley Smart's novel, *Two Kisses* (1875). C. & H. brought out a cheap
edn. of it in 1876.
566. [1] 'However much he laughed at me when we were alone or with my mother',
writes Lady Butcher (p. 17), 'he always called me "Miss Brandreth" in public, and I liked
this, being very young.'
   [2] Alice Brandreth's father was a delegate to the International Congress of Orientalists
at St. Petersburg in Sept. 1876, and his family was going along with him. Lady Butcher
(p. 47) says that this letter was in response to a 'long gushing letter about Swinburne's
Atalanta in Calydon'.
   [3] A jesting allusion to Professors A. J. Ellis and J. J. Sylvester, who took part in the
Brandreths' Shakespearian readings.

them by asking each: 'Do you keep pistols and powder?' smiling, as you ask it, and speaking with that artlessness which has done for every man Jack of a professor in old England. Should they wish to know why you ask, explain to them of course that you are anxious for their brains.

As to the Drama:[4] it is ill conceived as yet. I have been very busy: what I want is to lie fallow for a week, and I can't get the week. Pecks of poetry have been coming from me. However I will bear in mind that you wish the thing done.—May fair weather attend you! I desire you to present my compliments to your father and mother, and tell them, I pray, that my vows are most heartily offered for the comfort of their journey, and against the prediction that the drift of the Oriental Congress will be to Constantinople.

Adieu: my wife would send the warmest messages were she presiding over this pen.

Your faithfullest
George Meredith

567. *To* FREDERIC HARRISON[1]

MS.: University of Texas.

Box Hill, Dorking
August 3, 1876

My dear Mr. Harrison,

I will direct my steps to meet you with pleasure the moment I am disengaged. Unfortunately I cannot shake myself free for some days. But will you spend the day here on Sunday or Monday? The friend who will be with me is of good quality. Some day next week I shall hope to be able to offer myself, whether I see you here or not.—The plan would be for you to walk to Leatherhead either by Cobham, or Oakshott[2] (over the heath and through the village and past the Princes'

---

[4] See Letter 562.

567. [1] Frederic Harrison (1831–1923), barrister, historian, and author of numerous articles in the *FR* which GM had admired a decade before this letter, was the most prominent of the English Positivists. When the Harrisons took a house at Cobham, Morley told Harrison that 'to see Meredith in the country is to see Leviathan in his bath. Pray seek him out' (Stevenson, p. 208). Harrison did so, in a letter to which this one from GM is in answer. In his *Autobiographic Memoirs* (ii. 115) Harrison calls GM 'a man of original genius, a hearty friend, a brilliant talker'—always 'the same incomparable companion and stalwart spirit' whether in London society, a country house, or at Box Hill. But after the first half-dozen novels, he adds, he found GM's style 'too jerky and cryptic' to suit his taste.
[2] i.e. Oxshott.

covers to the descent of the hill on the high road), and about there I would meet you, and bring you on by rail, or afoot, as you please.

You are in country I call mine, if one may lay that claim upon country much described and pictured with the pen. I like it better than this about me now, though this is finer. But I have a warm love for sand and fir and gorse. I fear it is not so wild as when I knew it. A blast of withering London has blown over it since then, in the shape of a race-course, and I do not like the manliness of my countrymen in their pastimes. You are just out of this new pestilential circuit: when you walk in the firwoods beyond Claremont, facing Southward, you are where 'I meet my own image'.[3]—Last night I read Morley's *Robespierre*[4] with strong appreciation.

Yours very faithfully,
George Meredith

568. *To* MISS LOUISA SHORE[1]

MS.: University of Texas.

Box Hill, Dorking
August 11, 1876

My dear Miss Louisa Shore,

In reply to your sister's request, which strikes flattery to the author's heart, will you tell her that to hit upon Tourdestelle she must run about twelve miles n.e. of Dreux: but the landmark is Anet, the château of Diane de Poitiers, which I have called 'Dianet', and whence the valley branches up, past the château Sorel. Anet in itself is worth seeing. There lived one who did vengeance on our sex: but too much in the ancient fashion. Will you say, that I have not assumed the present situation in 'Fair Ladies', but one in which it is to be understood that the beautiful, *i.e.* the most thoughtless of the sex hitherto, turn the chief weapon of the sex to the benefit of their sisters—having learnt to say 'we' for 'I': and thus, partly by beauty, partly by earnest argument, win one champion, and make their antagonist melancholy.

567. [3]   Ere Babylon was dust
                The Magus of Zoroaster, my dead child,
                Met his own image walking in the garden.
                        —Shelley, *Prometheus Unbound*, i. 191–3.

    [4] Morley's *Robespierre* appeared in two parts in the *FR*, the first part in the August issue.

568. [1] Apparently Miss Shore had written at the instance of her sister to inquire the location of Tourdestelle in *Beauchamp's Career* and either to comment on 'A Ballad of Fair Ladies in Revolt', published in the August *FR*, or to discuss the question of women's rights apropos of it. Both sisters were ardent feminists.

Be certain that in such a combat the senses will not be excluded. Proud women may struggle against the assertion, but all experience is with that view. As to the claim for justice, it is, I repeat, waste of force to cry for it. Convenience, or in other words, the good of all, is all that is recognized by the judicial mind; and it must be proved that this movement is for the good of all. This I am of opinion will be done with time. You (for she is you) are pardonably impatient, though I recognize a wonderful patience in your toleration of one who dares to poetize about you. But it is not yet time for active measures. By spreading instruction among women, as you do, far more is accomplished than by besieging Parliament. This is a movement that, when general enough to command respect, will knock away obstruction as the lid of a pot. I have neither space nor the hour to pursue: but as I hope for the advancement of the race, and conceive that there can be none till women walk freely with men, you will not take me for a particularly deadly enemy, and should not for chilly friend. Give my warmest greetings to your sister, I beg you, and believe me

Your most faithful
George Meredith

569. *To* JOHN MORLEY

Text: *Letters*, i. 264–6.

Box Hill
August 15, 1876

My dear Morley,

Receive my thanks for the bag of golden grain. I am chained here for a time: in a few days I take Will to Pitfield[1] to find comrades with the boy and girls there, previous to his departure to school. Perhaps (for the truth is known to you, so I may as well confess it: the 'harvesters'[2] are terrific: I am spotted red mounds, I smile disdainfully at the voluptuousness that is not largely composed of scratching: I am raw: therefore there can be no chance of seeing you here before October) perhaps, then, I might come to you for a day on my way to Hawkhurst,[3] if I go there; and there is some thought of it. No mountains for me this year. But the talk I get with you is mountain atmosphere to the soul.—I have read your *Robespierre*.[4] It sent me to Carlyle. He bears the re-reading. Still that kind of thing will not do.

569. [1] Where the Cotter Morisons lived.
  [2] i.e. harvest-bugs.   [3] Where the Cotterills lived.
  [4] See Note 4 Letter 567.

It is our only History of the French Revolution, and is in as much dis-order as the Paris of Danton. Evidently this is your work to be done. —Have you not trimmed your style? The sentences are more com-pressed, not at such stretch. The 'picturing' of Robespierre seems to me the best that could be done in prose; sober, acute: the mind being all round him while the finger is upon him. You do not condemn, do not apologise for him, you explain him: and also the time. The critical and the narrative power now go well hand in hand. A little further predominance to the latter, will make yours the finest of historical styles: and as there cannot be a theme more spacious to imagination than the French Revolution, I commend you to it for a few years to come. I wish it lay as clear before me, as open to my capacity.—I shall be glad of the 2nd Part of your study.—Harrison[5] has written to me of a mid-way meeting for a walk; and written again, fearful of Phœbus' beams. I am more fearful of rousing the ire of the God by appearing to shun them; I climb the hills of mint and thyme, and can compare myself only to the Leg of Mutton stewing in herbs *à sept heures*. To say I sweat is to say an angel is holy. I am transfigured in my original elements—fire and water.—I won't talk of the East: I should run to the length of 2 leaders. I am compelled to be quite against my instincts. I cannot think very much of the Servians.[6] As to Christian against Turk;—to talk in old Tory fashion, the Turk's religion is that of a gentleman by comparison. The Christian is intended to be Russia's catspaw. Yet of course one sees that a nation cancered by the Hareem must be extinguished: it cannot live when it has ceased to live in camp and takes to the Hareem for a diversion. Where women are women but for the bed, there is dissolution, brain and heart paralysis.—Yes, Beaconsfield![7]—You were wonderfully good in allowing my ballad[8] to run to that length: I was ashamed, and yet I had to exercise restraint to keep back more verses. I will not press you, but you shall tell me if you are inclined to have other samples of my stores; and if not, be sure I cannot take offence.—One who would fain see you again— Oswald Crawfurd[9]—asked warmly of you the other day. I heard of

---

569. [5] Frederic Harrison. See Letter 567.

[6] Serbia had declared war on Turkey on 30 June, followed by Montenegro next day. In Apr. 1877 they were joined by Russia.

[7] Disraeli, now 72 and in poor health, felt unable to support the burden of the Prime Ministry in the House of Commons and was translated to the Lords as Earl of Beacons-field. The title was particularly offensive to Morley, as the biographer of Edmund Burke, because Burke had died while the patent was in course of preparation to make him Lord Beaconsfield (Hirst, ii. 19). Morley hated Disraeli and his policies and never lost an opportunity to abuse him.

[8] 'A Ballad of Fair Ladies in Revolt', *FR* (Aug. 1876), pp. 232–41.

[9] Oswald John Frederick Crawfurd (1834–1909), author, editor, and consular official. He became Chairman of the Board of Directors of C. & H., who had published several of his books, in 1894.

a lady who wanted to fortify herself in her manner of educating a son and bought *Compromise,* which strengthened her. This laurel to you—a prouder than poet's! Adieu. I wish it were this evening or to-morrow we were to meet!

570. *To* F. J. FURNIVALL[1]

MS.: Huntington Library.

Box Hill
August 24, 1876

Dear Mr. Furnivall,

I did not think the Yankees would care for lecturers this year, unless it were a saintly notoriety;—to exhibit whom engaged in the act of comfortably bagging their dollars, is as good as wit to them, and is quite in their style of wit. The Queen, John Bright, Lord Beaconsfield, Archbishop Tait, Spurgeon, they would pay at any season. I suppose Victoria would take best with them, owing to their chivalry and her family-way nature.—As to the other proposition you are so good as to suggest in my interest, let me meditate over it further.[2] I cannot spring to the thought of new work unless I feel myself gripping it. You are right in what you say of the advantages of lecturing: it pays 20 times for labour, and as it is I am not well paid for mine. But just now I am possessed of verse as of a demon, and it will not allow any diversions of prose. I will communicate with you by and by, and ask your aid, being sure that I may count on it. I have two subjects in view, one— Heine: and the other—Molière and the Idea of Pure Comedy. They will each require considerable time for the writing, as I understand them.

Accept my fullest thanks for your thoughtfulness on my behalf.

Yours very faithfully,
George Meredith

---

570. [1] (Dr.) F. J. Furnivall (1825–1910), well known for his work on Early and Middle English literature and his contributions to the *Oxford English Dictionary,* as well as for his activities in the Early English Text Society, the New Shakespeare Society, the Browning Society, and others. It is apparent from this letter that he was trying to give GM a helping hand via the lecture platform.

[2] 'The other proposition' was doubtless a proposal that he lecture in England.

571. *To* FREDERIC HARRISON

MS.: University of Texas.

Flint Cottage, Box Hill
August 30, 1876

My dear Harrison,

Encourage Mrs. Harrison to come predisposed to dine with us on Thursday. We will dine early in the afternoon to suit your hours. But you will have fine moonlight for your return. Be in time for lunch at the children's dinner, and then we shall have the afternoon for a stroll in one or other of our valleys.

The period for the invasion of Great Britain will be in the Dog days, for then is every stout islander down on his back, quite without resistance in him, more helpless than a man who has been caught in the middle by a joke when there is no wind in him to laugh. But I love sunlight and tower over my prostrate countrymen. A very short term of superiority. Summer has gone already.

You will find our cottage by turning sharp to the left when you come to Box Hill—before descending the hill of the road. You drive through Mickleham: we are about 1/2 a mile south of it. Our cottage is fifty yards up to the turning. My wife and I look forward to receiving you.

Yours very faithfully,
George Meredith

572. *To* JOHN MORLEY

Text: *Letters*, i. 267–8.

Box Hill
September 8, 1876

My dear Morley,

We must by the nature of the case be fixtures in the Hat-box.[1] My pavilion is in course of edification to receive me. But hear my proposal: There is an old farm-house,[2] long-windowed, red-bricked, Elizabethan, just far enough from us to ensure you the sense of solitude, near enough to make it possible to meet: South-west of Dorking: between the chalk hills and the sand, set in lovely rolling country:

572. [1] An allusion to the smallness of Flint House. To obtain working room and privacy for himself, GM was building a chalet (the 'pavilion' of the next sentence) up the hill a bit.
[2] The Rookery, birthplace of Malthus.

with the moral attraction to you that George Eliot has resided there; backed by a pinewood that was sown by Heaven's hand for contemplation's mood: and this used to be let for 4 guineas per week. Shall I walk to it and see if it is open? Or better, will you come down and visit it with me? It is about 2 1/2 miles from Dorking on the road to Guildford. I think this a most excellent proposal.—Let me add that our cottage would be for you at any price, were it at all in our plans to move.—I shall hope to hear from you. Harrison was here yesterday. We are of one mind in admiration of *Robespierre*. But he thinks you are almost too scathing of Disraeli.

> Your faithfullest
> George Meredith

573. *To* JOHN MORLEY

Text: *Letters*, i. 268–9.

> Box Hill
> September 13, 1876

My dear Morley,

There is no moving Marie: here she must wait, and sorely against her wish. We have no wishes left, but are the instruments of fate.

The more to confound me, the Rookery Farm is let up to the end of October.

To-morrow I take our dear old Will to his first taste of School—at Ewell, under a certain Dr. Behr, one time a master at Winchester, well recommended to me; and I like the look of the establishment.—This reminds me, Mrs. Harrison told me it was the Admiral's Mr. Lake, the 'free-thinking' schoolmaster of his boys, who wrote in the *Spectator* concerning you.[1] Ahem.—Behr simply assures me that no more than the common doses of theology will be given, and with that I must be satisfied. I do not think it well to be howking about the beds where younkers grow, to clip their roots and precipitate the natural acerbities in any given direction. Young sceptics will hardly avoid being young cynics. I burn for converse with you.—Very busy with poems.

> Your ever faithful
> George Meredith

573. [1] C. H. Lake, of Withernden, Caterham Valley, in the *Spectator* (26 Aug.) argued that no criticism of religion, politics, or society is logically tenable without regard to the education of the next generation. Morley, he said, was destroying religious faith in thousands 'by a refined destructive criticism', but had nothing to offer in its place. Lake offered the following practical rule: 'a man has no right to attack accepted views of truth by subtle and irresponsible criticism till he is prepared to offer counter-principles which are coherent, pronounceable, and verifiable—if not verified.'

574. *To* EDWARD W. B. NICHOLSON[1]

MS.: McGill University.

Box Hill, Dorking
September 27, 1876

Dear Sir,

I have to thank you for the invitation you propose to me on the part of your Board of Management, and to apologize to you for the delay in my reply, owing to my absence from home. I do not know from whom the suggestion has come or in what direction I am thought competent to hold an audience attentive for the space of an hour: still I should not be disinclined to try, if so good an opinion is entertained of me by the Board;—if only to show myself sensible of the compliment. You omitted to send the list of lectures at the London Institution, while mentioning it as enclosed. I should like to see it, that I may form an idea of my capacity to take rank in the list.—I should prefer February for my period.

As to the subjects, I could perhaps offer to lecture on one of two subjects which strike me at this moment:

'The Idea of Comedy': chiefly illustrated by Molière: and 'Characteristics of English Poetry'. But I prefer to reserve them as a proposal to you until I have seen the list. I believe you have many working men in the body of the hall of audience. I could desire nothing better.

Yours very faithfully,
George Meredith

575. *To* WILLIAM HARDMAN

MS.: Yale.

Box Hill
September 28, [1876]

Dearest Lord Mayor Tuck,

Marie wants you to do her this favour. Her lodging-housekeeper will send you a small dressing-bag empty bottle:—will you kindly leave it at your Club for me to call for it?[1]—And I have one to ask of

574. [1] Edward W. B. Nicholson, Librarian and Superintendent of the London Institution, Finsbury Circus, had written to invite GM to lecture to its members. The lecture was duly delivered on 1 Feb. 1877—the only public lecture that GM ever gave.
575. [1] There is no clue to Marie's whereabouts.

you:—this: that you will, at your leisure, write out for me briefly the case of the man Bushy, or Busby,[2] and his conflict with your board of town-councillors, aldermen, and what not; being careful to give the exact titles to them, and his position. It strikes me that I may make something of it: and no man can put such things more succinctly than you. If I am right, you will have some entertainment, and I as ever shall be bound in gratitude to you.

Your loving (with all good wishes
to D'Troïa)
George Meredith

Let me have the official title of your convenings for general, for special, and for extraordinary occasions. Also how you are attended, whether by policemen or other constables, and in what halls you meet. In fact I am desirous to have the local colouring—but not of Kingston proper, you understand.

576. *To* W. C. Bonaparte Wyse

MS.: Yale.

Box Hill, Dorking
October 6, 1876

My dear Bonaparte,

It occurred thus: I lost your letter giving your address in Avignon, and considering that you had promised me a visit on your way through London, I thought to thank you for the Provençal song when I should see you here. It then struck me likewise that I would ask you (if you and he pleased) to bring down Horne for a day. In all probability he does not understand that I am simply a laborious man working out my impressions here in solitude, and with a livelihood to get; and that I mean him no disrespect. If I were at my ease I would behave differently. Well, I was very glad to hear from you. The 'Cabeladuro D'Or'[1] is good rich thick stuff, with body and with fire, like Châteauneuf du Pape. As to the Song, my wife worked at it Trojanly and I, as it were a drum accompaniment, thumped out the Félibre lingo.—I have

---

[2] My searches in the *Surrey Comet* for this episode were unsuccessful. Jack Lindsay (*George Meredith: His Life and Work*, 1956, p. 230) is doubtless correct in saying that GM probably wanted to fill out the character of Tinman in *The House on the Beach* with elements drawn from him. Probably H. Jefferys Bushby, listed by the *ABC Court Directory and Fashionable Guide* (1871) as living at Henleaze, Kingston Hill, Kingston-on-Thames, is the person GM had in mind.

576. [1] A poem by Wyse.

been writing quantities of verse and in verse of late. I should like you to read them. I think 'The Nuptials of Attila'[2] might give you a thrill. Also I have a scheme of a Great Big Pome,—but as I see myself besieged by Butcher, Baker and Grocer if I attempt it yet, I let it rest. Once let me be free, and I'll be aloft like the stars of a rocket benignantly brightening and dying in heaven. Send me further word of yourself. Give my warm regards to your wife: my salutations to the children. Keep me informed of your address. I am sure to lose it. By the way, tell me of any essay or notice of Molière. I am going to deliver a lecture on him as the grand and unique illustrator of Comedy.

Yours ever cordially du coeur,

George M.

577. *To* EDWARD W. B. NICHOLSON

Text (excerpt): Maggs Brothers Catalogue No. 405 (1921), p. 145.

[Box Hill, Dorking]

October 6, 1876

I am afflicted for the moment with a certain hesitation as to my power of holding the attention of an audience, and the quality of my voice to fill a hall. . . .[1] My notion of the title is to make it independent of the special character that would be given it by prefixing Molière's name: and therefore I would say 'The Idea of Comedy' etc., as you have put the alternative title. [Etc.]

578. *To* MISS ALICE BRANDRETH

MS.: Mrs. J. G. Gordon. Published: *Letters*, i. 269–70, with numerous inaccuracies; excerpt: Lady Butcher, pp. 30–31.

Box Hill

November 3, 1876

My dear Miss Brandreth,

I know Palgrave Simpson,[1]—am very fond of him, and believe he

576. [2] Published in the *New Quarterly Magazine* (Jan. 1879), pp. 47–62.
577. [1] For context, see Letter 574.
578. [1] John Palgrave Simpson (1807–87), dramatist and novelist, whom GM knew at the Garrick Club. His name had been mentioned by Alice Brandreth as a possible reader of the part of Shylock in the Shakespearian readings (Lady Butcher, p. 30).

will do anything for me, until he knows you, when he will be subject to a new allegiance. If you and I do not clash, therefore, I and you may count on him. I will see him or write to him. He is of ripe age, turned of 70, very handsome, and with a consuming passion for the stage; and the dear heart of him so frankly nourishable by flattery that he will open his mouth and shut his eyes and take it in a ladle, so he will exactly suit you. How I dislike (in the abstract) men of a certain age who pretend to refuse their spoonful, and all the while their honest old lips are dribbling at the corners: as to the coming to town, let me come on the Thursday of the week after the one your Mother suggests: and go on Friday. One night of London. And besides I am very busy and shall get no work done for the next year if I cease to lash myself. And I am disturbed about my lecture and doubt if it will please. If you are mad to do kindness, have my wife the day before I come (I never knew her refuse an invitation) and whisk her to music or the play. For my part I don't like to leave my baby gal alone in the house for more than one night—one does not matter. My wife will write to your mother. I beg you to remember me warmly to your father and Mother both, and believe me for life your devoted servant and lord,

George Meredith

579. *To* MRS. E. L. BRANDRETH

MS.: Mrs. J. G. Gordon. Published: *Letters*, i. 270, with omissions and variants; Lady Butcher, pp. 48–49, with omissions and variants.

Box Hill
November 14, 1876

Dear Mrs. Brandreth,

To sit with you all three and hear of your tour[1] and of the long leashes of Russian Professors reduced by Miss Brandreth to a state of spiritual serfage, would be delightful, and what I have hoped for; but so it chances, I am under plight of promise to go to Brighton to my friend Mr. Morley on Thursday, and this involves Friday and sad am I that it should!—I think Miss Brandreth ought to be informed that our poor sample of a Professor,[2] the grey-locked, prodigious in rhyming power, returned to England during her absence—alas! for him—and was seen at the Athenaeum. I am told that he did not remain long—as why should the unhappy man, the sun being as distant and veiled as in the Black Season at the North Pole.

---

579. [1] i.e. the Russian trip.   [2] Professor Sylvester.

I hear from Eva[3] that Miss Brandreth will make an entry into our valley some time this month. How grand it would have been in the Boots of Kazan! But in any form it will be a wonderful refreshment to us. Please to give my very warm regards to Mr. Brandreth, my cordial salutes to my Katharine[4] (tamed), and believe me

Your most faithful and devoted

George Meredith

580. *To* W. C. BONAPARTE WYSE

MS.: University of Texas.

Box Hill, Dorking

December 18, 1876

My dear Wyse,

I find it is quite impossible for me to spare a morning to come to you: but you can I am sure manage to come to me. The truth is, I am very busy with divers bits of work. So come on Thursday next. If you arrive at midday I shall be able to attend on you, for I rarely write after one p.m. A train from Charing Cross will bring you to Box Hill Station on the South Eastern line.—Of course if you are tied to your friend, I would say bring him with you; but you know the small box we are cased in, and how little entertainment we can offer. On this head follow your own judgment. You do not say that your wife is with you, and I fear not. Let me hear about your coming, or what your movements are likely to be.

Yours ever,

George Meredith

Present my compliments to M. le Baron de Tourtoulon,[1] and I beg you to say that if I do not hasten to town immediately, it is because chains are on me.

579. [3] Eva Gordon.

   [4] Alice Brandreth, remembered here in her role in *The Taming of the Shrew*.

580. [1] Baron Charles de Tourtoulon (1836–1913), one of the founders of the Félibrige Society in Paris and a friend of Wyse's.

581. *To* W. C. BONAPARTE WYSE

MS.: Yale.

Box Hill
December 19, 1876

My dear Wyse,

Pray, if you think fit, ask Horne, with my compliments to him. Only, he should be made to know, as you do, that the sort of entertainment I am able to give here, is very poor, anything but attractive. I have no bed to offer, and not much of a cook to fortify a friend in winter for the long return journey.

If you come by South Eastern, your return ticket will bring you L.B. & S.C. from a station nearer our cottage. The last train is 10 to 10 p.m. We will dine at 6 1/2. Let me know the train I am to expect you by. If it is after noon, I will meet you. But in any case you know your way.

It strikes me that this long railway journey going and returning late at night is heavy work for your friend considering his age. But he will know best. Only let him be forewarned.

Yours ever,
George Meredith

582. *To* MISS ALICE BRANDRETH

Text: *Letters*, i. 271–2; published also: Lady Butcher, p. 54.

[Box Hill, Dorking]
[? End of 1876][1]

Gordon, Jim,[2]
Life and Limb
Risking, 'cause it is his whim,
Hounds to foller,
Breaks his collar-
Bone while giving a view-holler.
Ain't this news?
What's more it's true,
Then in bed the poor lad stews;

---

582. [1] Lady Butcher merely says (p. 54) that she received this rhymed letter after her return from Russia.

[2] Jim Gordon, son of Dr. and Mrs. Gordon, loved spirited horses, and the superstitious might see in this accident a foreshadowing of the one that was to cost his life in 1893.

His neck twirling
Mr. Curling[3]
Straight has set like surgeon sterling.

George Meredith

583. *To* MRS. TEESDALE[1]

MS.: University of Texas.

Eltham
January 2, 1877

Dear Mrs. Teesdale,

Mrs. Wood commissions me—GM—to say that she would have written to you before, had her ability equalled her inclination. She would have answered you better directly, but her eyes have been more than usually bad, and shall [she] has waited for my arrival, which has been of late retarded. As to the Savoyard Vicar, he appears but once in the *Nouvelle Héloise*, and it is our joint idea that this is during the 2nd absence of St. Preux, about middle of book.[2] He talks at considerable length, but there will be no difficulty in detecting the sentences reminding Mrs. Wood of J. S. Mill, when the chapter is discovered.[3] They are verging on the termination of his 'Confession de Foi'.

Mrs. Wood sends you her love.

I beg permission to send you all that season sanctions in the way of cordial good wishes for your happiness. I beg you to remember me warmly to Mr. Teesdale and the young ladies—never forgetting Edmund. When the weather is of a promising mildness I hope he will

582. [3] Presumably Thomas Blizard Curling (1811–88), consulting surgeon of the London Hospital. From 1864, however, he had a son in practice.
583. [1] Presumably the wife of Marmaduke J. Teesdale of Eltham.
[2] GM—or Mrs. Wood—has apparently confused *La Nouvelle Héloise* and *Émile*. The Vicar's Confession dwells on many ideas with which a comparison of some of Mill's views might be made: freedom and necessity (*Logic*), natural religion (*Three Essays*), freedom of thought and expression (*On Liberty*), etc.
[3] Cf:
Vicar: 'If there were but one religion upon earth, and if all beyond its pale were condemned to eternal punishment, and if there were in any corner of the world one single honest man who was not convinced by this evidence, the God of that religion would be the most unjust and cruel of tyrants' (Everyman *Émile*, p. 261).
Mill: 'If all mankind minus one were of one opinion, and only one person of the contrary opinion, mankind would be no more justified in silencing that one person, than he, if he had the power, would be justified in silencing mankind' (*On Liberty*, Ch. II). (I owe this note to Professor Francis Mineka.)

come to me and see the new study, with bachelor's bedroom I have built in my garden. I am

Your most faithful
George Meredith

N.B. Mrs. Wood trusts you will not put yourself to trouble to gratify an idle wish to know whether Mr. Mill's sentiments were original or derived, perhaps unconsciously, from Rousseau—

584. *To* WILLIAM HARDMAN

MS.: Garrick Club.

Box Hill
January 25, 1877

Dear Lord William!
    Poco—but I choke: I can hardly relate it.
    Let us be calm. Old Poco—
    Ha! ha!
    I have only just heard it, and I lose not a minute in hurrying it off to you. But perhaps you know it already? Poco of all men!
    Why not?
    Still it seizes one. It hath the mysterious nature of snuff to tickle the nerves.
    The banns are not yet up.
    I break it to you gently, you see.
    There isn't a doubt.
    She is English.
    POCO WILL BE MARRIED BY MIDSUMMER![1]
    O, Lord!—I had hoped to see you when I was last in town. I hope to come on the next occasion. I see none of my old friends, and the new world does not laugh.
    Comedy, Tuck? The hour of the Lecture[2] is unearthly: so I ask none to come.

Your affectionate
George M.

584. [1] The rumour was true, except for the date. See Note 4, Letter 603.
    [2] See following letter.

585. *To* WILLIAM HARDMAN

MS.: Yale.

Box Hill
January 27, 1877

Dear Lord William,

The Lecture is at the horrid hour of 7 p.m.: at the dreadful distance from you of Finsbury Circus, at the London Institution. I have been asked to the Royal[1] in Albemarle Street, for the afternoons, and that will be better, if I continue this kind of thing.—All my tickets are exhausted. I thought of you both, but could find no excuse for asking you to run so far for such poor fun.

I have invited Poco to come down here for a month, with sweating flannels, to get him into some training. Between ourselves—eh?—is anyone listening?

Verbum sap:

I hope my utmost. Yet is Poco somewhat advanced, a trifle wanting in what we imagine bridegroomly briskness, getting fitter for the Sage's mantle than the connubial nightshirt—one would have thought. But he knows best. He has not told me her name. I heard mention of the case, wrote to him, and had his confession.—One point you may swear to: the damsel has money. I am given to understand that there are thorns to the rose, difficulties, a mother-in-law for him of some toughness.[2]

My best love to D'Troïa. I thought Miss Hardman looking graceful but pale t'other night.

Yours ever warmly,
George Meredith

586. *To* JOHN MORLEY

Text: *Letters*, i. 270-1.

[Box Hill]
Saturday, [February 3, 1877]

Dearest M.,

One line. All went well.[1] Morison in one of his enthusiasms—which make one remember that one has word praise. Audience very attentive and indulgent. Time 1 h. 25 m. and no one left the hall, so that I may

---

585. [1] The Royal Institution, where he had also been invited to lecture.
[2] For the context of all this, see preceding letter.
586. [1] At the lecture.

imagine there was interest in the lecture. Pace moderate: but Morison thinks I was intelligible chiefly by the distinctness of articulation.

587. *To* MISS MARY LAWRENCE

MS.: the Lawrence family.

Box Hill
February 3, 1877

Dear Miss Mary Lawrence,
   I am immensely relieved to think that you had some pleasure to reward you for the pilgrimage to the East of London.[1] Be assured that the compliments of the Indivisible are very welcome. I saw you with great satisfaction.
   As to Lectures in the West,[2] I was asked, but imagined I might make a fiasco in Finsbury, and therefore declined for this Easter.
   Mariette curtsies to you becomingly.
   I hope Sir Trevor is not now unwell.

Your most faithful and devoted
George Meredith

588. *To* F. J. FURNIVALL

MS.: Huntington Library.

Box Hill
February 3, 1877

Dear Furnivall,
   The Secretary says I shot too high.[1] Still I must say that a kinder and more indulgent audience was never allowed to lecturer; and there was the best will in the world to follow me through and grant excess of time—1 hour 25 minutes. I wish it had been possible for you to be there, that I might benefit by your judgment.
   Some time back, in doubt of myself, lest I should make a frightful fiasco, I told Spottiswoode that I could not engage myself to take a course this year at the Royal.[2]
   My fullest thanks to you.

Yours very faithfully,
George Meredith

587. [1] To hear his lecture.   [2] i.e. at the Royal Institution, Albemarle St.
588. [1] See the preceding two letters.
   [2] i.e. could not engage himself to lecture at the Royal Institution. (See Letter 585.)

589. *To* EDWARD W. B. NICHOLSON

Text (excerpt): Maggs Brothers Catalogue No. 399 (1920), p. 129.

Box Hill
February 3, 1877

I have received the cheque,[1] and I thank you for it. I cannot sufficiently thank my audience for the attendance and indulgence granted me.

590. *To* MISS ALICE BRANDRETH

MS.: Mrs. J. G. Gordon. Published: *Letters*, i. 271, with omission of a sentence and with variants; Lady Butcher, p. 39, with variants.

Box Hill
February 28, 1877

My dear Miss Brandreth,

I have too much work, to be in town to-morrow, and my promise to myself to go to Dannreuther's concert[1] next time, was but my way of saying how much I liked the last. Otherwise the pleasure of being led there by you would be, as it were, to be prepared by a poet to sit with the Muses. I know you will be in full sympathy with one who chances to have said more than he meant; and indeed you should be; for by and by (yes, it must be so) a certain door will have to be broken open and a room laid bare with many Tops in it, the humming and the peg, each with his history of ONE who spun him—and how?—So innocently! in my Dannreuther fashion. On that occasion I shall come forward to plead for you.

I beg you will convey to your mother my warmest thanks for her invitation.

Your very devoted
George Meredith

589. [1] For his lecture at the London Institution.
590. [1] Edward Dannreuther (1844–1905), German pianist and writer on musical subjects, had lived in London since 1863. He was on terms of personal friendship with the Brandreths, at whose Shakespearian readings he played the piano.
The concert to which GM had been invited was one of the third series of Chamber Concerts, under the direction of Dannreuther.

591. *To* FREDERICK A. MAXSE

Text: *Letters*, i. 273.

Box Hill
March 31, 1877

My dear Admiral,[1]
    I can't but admire Mrs. Besant[2] for her courage. On the whole I must approve the publication, though to me the book is repulsive. I have a senseless shrinking from it. More horrible scenes of animal life can hardly be suggested. They effectually deprive me of appetite. The male—the female. Lord God!
    Your remarks on Odger were very good, I was glad to see them.[3]
    You talk of a Surrey walk. Once more you flash the old delusive flag of a holiday before me. Why do you not come? I am here. I have not removed from here for several years.

Yours ever warmly,
George Meredith

By the way, I am in my Chalet: well worth a visit. The second room of it contains the hammock-cot: enviable the sleeper therein!

592. *To* JOHN MORLEY

Text: *Letters*, i. 272–3.

Box Hill
March 31, 1877

My dear Morley,
    We have now a bedroom to offer you and your wife. Will you come? And can you come before the 13th April? It will rejoice us to see you, and refresh me.
    Remember that it is your habit peremptorily to cry against invitations in harvest-Bug-time. Therefore we think you due to us now.
    And I want you to see my cottage—annexe—chalet on the terrace. I think you will agree with me, that it is the prettiest to be found, the

---

591. [1] Maxse was promoted to Retired Rear-Admiral in 1875.
    [2] Mrs. Annie Besant and Charles Bradlaugh had published *Fruits of Philosophy: A Companion for Young Married Couples*, by an American physician, for sixpence. The book was directed against the evils of unduly large families, and though similar books were available at higher prices in bookstores, the two were arrested for publishing an obscene book.
    [3] George Odger, leading trades unionist, had died on 4 Mar. What Maxse's remarks were I do not know.

view is without a match in Surrey. The interior full of light, which can be moderated; and while surrounded by firs, I look over the slope of our green hill to the ridges of Leith, round to Ranmore, and the half of Norbury.

I have the hope that if you can come you will. Let it be Both of you.

I am very busy, doing little, but doing it diligently, which you know to mean well.

The article on Comedy is out:[1] cursed with misprints that make me dance gadfly-bitten.

I am greatly taken with Goldwin Smith's article.[2] I could not have written it, but the idea has been mine.

Trollope's article on Cicero[3] shows him to have a feeling for his hero. It reads curiously as though he were addressing a class of good young men. This is the effect of the style, or absence of style. One likes him for working in that mine: only,—and yet I like a certain kind of open-mindedness. By the way, in the last book noticed (by Garnett, is it?), I find 'By the first living Italian poet'.[4] The possible English of this is, that the preceding have been dead ones. Garnett has not to be taught English, but here is an example of the bad effect of writing much for journals. 'First of living Ital[ian] poets', he means.

O my dear Morley, come if only you can, for you are a great delight to me when I see you. My wife is in the cottage below, or she would send messages to yours.

593. *To* JOHN MORLEY

Text: *Letters,* i. 274.

Box Hill
April 4, [1877]

My dear Morley,
May, then![1]

But let not this be one of your lyrical postponements to a phantasm appointment: the most delusive gilded thing that ever danced between Box Hill and Brighton.

. . . There are horrid errors in the printing of the *Comic [Spirit]*,

592. [1] 'On the Idea of Comedy, and of the Uses of the Comic Spirit', in the April issue of the *New Quarterly Magazine*.
[2] 'The Political Destiny of Canada', *FR* (Apr.).
[3] Anthony Trollope, 'Cicero as a Politician', *FR* (Apr.).
[4] A review of *Bozzetti critici e discorsi letterarii* per Giosné Carducci, *FR* (Apr.).
593. [1] For Morley's visit to Box Hill.

some, I am afraid, attributable to me: I am the worst of correctors of my own writing.

I saw Myers' [article] on George Sand.[2] I took up a friend's copy of *19th Century*, and after the symposium turned to see what might be said of our favourite:—not bad, with one or two good points well done: as of the effect of a female Göthe on the ardent males.—It's wrong to be wishing April were May, for I hope to get over a great deal of work before then. But you excite the unnatural wish.

Well. The first week in May. Are you bound to me?—You will find more flowers about you—that is one advantage.—I hope your wife is better already.

Yours ever warmly,
George Meredith

594. *To* JOHN MORLEY

Text: *Letters*, i. 274–7. Excerpt published: Stevenson, p. 214.

Box Hill
April 5, 1877

My dear Morley,

I have read 'Das Göttliche'[1] this morning, and with a feeling of new strength, which is like conception in the brain. This is the very spirit of Göthe. I have many times come in contact with it and been ennobled. Fault of mine, if not more! This high discernment, this noblest of unconsidered utterance, this is the Hymn for men. This is to be really prophet-like. All other prophecy is insolence.

I had not read it last night, being very busy:—You should know, I work and sleep up in my cottage at present, and anything grander than the days and nights at my porch you will not find away from the Alps: for the dark line of my hill runs up to the stars, the valley below is a soundless gulf. There I pace like a shipman before turning in. In the day, with the S. West blowing, I have a brilliant universe rolling up to me:—well, after midnight I sat and thought of Göthe: and of the sage in him, and the youth. And, somewhat in his manner, the enclosed[2] came of it. I send it to you for your private reading. It was

---

[2] Frederic W. H. Myers (1843–1901), 'George Sand', *Nineteenth Century* (Apr. 1877).
594. [1] Morley (*Recollections*, i. 39) says, 'I once commended to Meredith (1877) Goethe's well-known and ever noble psalm of life, "Das Göttliche" ', and then quotes the first few sentences of this letter.
[2] The enclosure is printed at the end of this letter.

written off before I went to bed, and has only the merit of exactly hitting its mark. I feel it this morning a poor return to make to you for 'Das Göttliche'. But you will excuse me, for the meaning of speech is to seek an audience—if a friend, the better. By the way, some one told me the other day that he felt sure of you for Stoke.[3] He said the Address to the Miners had made a great impression. I trust so.

I am very hard at work, writing a 5 Act Comedy in verse,[4] besides tales, poems, touches of a novel, and helping my wife with a translation. But in this room of mine I should have no excuse for idleness. In truth work flows with me.—Adieu.

Yours ever most warmly,
George Meredith

[*The Enclosure.*]

MENTOR AND PUPILS

Mentor

Be warned of steps retrieved in pain.

Pupils

We have strength, we have blood, we are young.

Mentor

Youth sows the links, man wears the chain.

Pupils

Shall a sweet lyric cease to be sung?

Mentor

The song is short, the travail long.

Pupils

Shall the morning brood over her grave?

Mentor

Forge weapons now to meet the throng.

Pupils

There's a bird flying white o'er the wave.

Mentor

The torrent of the blood control.

594. [3] An idle rumour: Morley did not contest Stoke and indeed did not get into Parliament until 1883.
    [4] Doubtless the one mentioned to Alice Brandreth a year earlier (Letters 562 and 566).

Pupils
'Tis a steed bounding whither we will.

Mentor
In more than name discern the soul.

Pupils
There is love like a light on the hill.

Mentor
That light of Love is fleeting fire.

Pupils
In the deep sea of Love let us dive.

Mentor
The test of Love is in the lyre.

Pupils
Give us Love, and the lyre is alive.

Mentor
The chords are snapped by passion's touch.

Pupils
She is there, by the tall laurel-rose.

Mentor
You sway the staff—you grasp the crutch.

Pupils
She is beckoning: who shall oppose?

Mentor
Behold a giant in his prime.

Pupils
On her breasts are the beams of the day.

Mentor
A cripple he, surprised by Time!

Pupils
She has loosened her girdle: give way!

595. *To* JOHN MORLEY

Text: *Letters*, i. 277.

Box Hill
April 25, 1877

My dear Morley,

. . . At this moment your Promise for the first days in May sleeps like any other innocent in the purity of infancy. Is it fair to rob it of these hours and call it to misty delusiveness before its time?[1] I am half tempted, with a shudder, to think not; and yet we wish to know whether, as before so frequently. . . . All I can say is, that the nightingale is now in sweet song: there's not the ghost of a harvester to bite you even in fancy. I want you to see my study; I want to see you. We have a bedroom and dressing-room for you. You will be here upon the opening of the beeches. Really the sweet o' the year.[2]

596. *To* CHARLES B. BRACKENBURY

Text: *Letters*, i. 277–8.

Box Hill
April 25, 1877

My dear Brackenbury,

Overbusied, I can scarcely get time to write—I have influence with one publisher only. On reading the MS. I was forced to the conclusion that I must not recommend it.[1] Believe me, I regretted it; for I admire and could love the writer. I say earnestly it will be better to put the work by: read, meditate, and wait to produce another. She will in time do good work, for she has a head and that which spins the blood to generous fire. But it is not friendly to urge her to publish. Moreover, I doubt her getting pay for it. If I thought that she would, I might, in view of possible present needs, hesitate. Still I should not know to whom to recommend this kind of novel. She is too good to produce the popular rubbish: too young to hit higher moods.

595. [1] 'Many besides Meredith have experienced Morley's art in avoiding engagements', writes Hirst (ii. 52). 'His letters declining an invitation were often even more graceful than his acceptances.'
    [2] GM had published a poem by the title 'The Sweet o' the Year' in *Fraser's Magazine* (June 1852), p. 699. He had borrowed it from a song sung by Autolycus in *The Winter's Tale* (IV. iii. 3).
596. [1] Brackenbury, now a lieut.-colonel, had sent GM a MS.—possibly written by one of the female members of his family—in hope that GM might get it published. He himself was on the point of leaving to report the Russo-Turkish War for *The Times*.

Shall we see you in May?—War!—Ass that I was, not to go for a conscript when a lad! Soldiering is the profession of the next 15 years' future, I suppose.

Your very loving
George Meredith

597. *To* MR. TYLER[1]

MS.: Harvard College Library.

Box Hill
April 26, 1877

Dear Mr. Tyler,

Your letter did not reach me till Sunday morning, and I had a friend with me here, as at this season of the year generally upon the end of the week. I should have liked to come. I am exceedingly busy, or I would do myself the honour of leaving my card on you.—An invitation comes to me from the Philosophical Institution, Edinburgh, to deliver 2 lectures on 'The Idea of Comedy' there next session. After the lecture has been published! What does this mean? Do they expect me to read or declaim what has already appeared in print? Is it usual? But I fear the distance involves a greater loss of Time than I can spare, so I shall have to decline.

Very faithfully yours,
George Meredith

Will you not bring that nice boy of yours with you here on a Sunday?

598. *To* FREDERICK JONES

Text: *Letters*, i. 278–9, with the addressee designated simply as F—— J——s.

Box Hill
May 26, 1877

What is the meaning of this nasty silence, J[ones]! You have fallen into one of your Welsh tempers. You refuse all invitations, and you incite your good wife to gird at me and pretend that it is I who am to blame. Shame on you, Cambrian! Every Cambrian is not a shaggy

597. [1] The context suggests that Mr. Tyler may have been of Scottish origin, but I am unable to identify him.

inveterate in suspicion, susceptibility, thin-skinnedness, and malice. Why must you be, Jones? I forgave you when you slipped out of your bonded engagement to take me home with you and give me supper last February 1st. Were you insensible to my generosity? Your appointment by the seaside is a patent invention. We don't believe a word of it. Be a man, J[ones]! Drop us word that you mean to come: or if you really must go down to the melancholy widowed ocean, try a stroke of humour—not original with you, but amusing in its decorously-faced recurrence: name a day when we may expect you, after your return.—We have now a bedroom, and Will's room serves for bathroom for husbands: but if you will forego it, it will serve for a bedroom for E[thel], whom I (we all) should be very glad to see and hear. I wish we had a third room for Miss J[ones].

Good be wi' ye, ye silly sulky Taffy! Here's a muttonbone for you any day, if you'll only come and take it. Your countryman (void of their errors),

George Meredith

599. *To* MRS. CHARLES BRACKENBURY

MS.: University of Texas.

Box Hill
June 14, 1877

My dear Mrs. Brackenbury,

The reading of the letters[1] has consoled me, and I thank you for the privilege with all my heart. My hope is that we may have him home soon. He is the best man in that swarm. I think of him among the malodorous host with something like rage at his being there. It would not displease me if they were to dismiss him; and they will do so the first letter they are dissatisfied with: perhaps without waiting for evidence. Hasen Kampf[2] has been courteous to the civil correspondents.—This is a horrid war, in which one can give one's wishes to neither combatant very warmly, but I think it a crime of *lèse humanité* to put up a prayer for a Muscov.

I trust you will always have good news. The best will be that he is returning. I am

Your most faithful
George Meredith

599. [1] Letters from Brackenbury to his wife, written from the Russo-Turkish war front, where he was a correspondent for *The Times*.
  [2] Possibly Col. Kasenkamff, attached to the staff of Prince Gorchakov.

600. *To* JOHN MORLEY

Text: *Letters*, i. 279–80.

Box Hill
June 24, 1877

My dear Morley,

I hoped to hear from you that you were coming, and that I might look to a glad two or three days—more you never allow me in imagination, nor practically so much. Write on this head: and do not suppose that I ask it because I doubt your still graceful dexterity in evasion. I wish to see you, as part of my Summer. But why should I write in pathos! I foresee the grin up to the ear tips of exulting Puckery. And would the world believe it of its philosopher, were I to inform the world?

It is this knowledge, that I see deep and am discredited, which does for me.

I am as a cracking earth, and soon it will be too late for the seed in me to be raised by rain.

Whither go you this year? The pleasant book of Miss Edwards'[1] turns my eyes to France (if I can go anywhere); but Marie gives me not the best tidings of your wife, and hints at possible German Baths, and if you were sentenced to one, I might be tempted to trudge after you and sojourn in your neighbourhood a short space, just to taste German atmosphere with you and watch you divided, as no other man would be so strangely, between a certain solid intellectual approbation of the race, and disgust of their manners: admiration of their strengthiness, and a sense of their spiritual flatness: great respect for them, and a hesitancy to determine whether they are now at their full growth, or that there is light above them to conjure them higher and higher. If the latter, they are the world's masters. Adieu, my friend; I am anxious about your Rose's[2] health. I do think it would do you both some good to come here, and remember, now is our time to offer our poor inducement: this next three weeks.

Ever yours,
George Meredith

600. [1] Mathilda Betham Edwards, *A Year in Western France*, 1877 [1876].
[2] i.e. Mrs. Morley's.

601. *To* FREDERICK A. MAXSE

Text: typed copy, Maxse Papers. Published: *Letters*, i. 280–1, with omissions; excerpt: Stevenson, p. 216.

Box Hill
August 21, 1877

My dear Fred,

I heard of your return from Morley, and I received the *Index* and read 'The Cynic' and a remark on your work, rightly appreciative.[1] Morley is now on his way.[2] As for me, I fear I am again condemned to trot round my circle, like an old horse at a well, everlastingly pulling up the same buckets full of a similar fluid. I may be precipitated abroad by incapacity to continue writing; and once or twice the case has looked like it, though I have recovered in a middling fashion: but not to do the work I call good—rather the character of work one is glad to leave behind, however glad to have accomplished. Things look so bad (to apply them to my own affairs) for books that I doubt whether I ought to spend the money. Even when they are fairly good I have the doubt.

Poco Robinson, I hear, is to be married at the end of the month.[3] Ahem! The bride will clasp no lusty frame. When a man's body has been for years as it were the adopted son of a drugshop, should he, with hereditary liver-disease, think of marrying at past forty? It fills me with anxiety. For if he is a forthright honourable fellow at the tournament, he cannot last . . . ! and if not . . . . !!!—

Adieu. All the good powers be with you. Tell me when you start for Dinant alone.[4] I might . . . but no.

Yours ever warmly,
George Meredith

601. [1] An editorial in the *Index*, 'A Weekly Paper Devoted to Free Religion', viii (26 July 1877), published in Boston, quoted from Maxse's pamphlet 'Woman Suffrage / The Counterfeit and the True: Reasons for Opposing Both' and remarked that 'Nothing so wise as this has fallen under our notice for many a long day'. In later issues the pamphlet was advertised for sale at the office of the *Index* for twenty-five cents.

'The Cynic' was the self-designation of one G. E. T. [G. E. Tufts], of Binghampton, N.Y., who in the course of a long letter in the same issue announced himself the opposition party to creeds, parties, churches, cliques, and virtue as usually understood by men. Much of what he said would have been accepted by GM and Maxse.

[2] Morley and Joseph Chamberlain were spending some weeks on the Continent (Hirst, ii. 52 ff.). [3] See Note 4, Letter 603.

[4] Viscountess Milner (p. 1) says that her father and mother were wholly incompatible and separated after sixteen years. Although there have been occasional hints in earlier letters that Mrs. Maxse did not always accompany her husband on his visits to the Continent, and even of other feminine interests in his life, this may have been the time of a complete break. Henceforth Maxse lived much in France, with intervals in London and Brighton, until his mother's death in 1886. Then he sold a part of the Effingham Hill property and built himself a house, which he named Dunley Hill, on a part of the remainder.

602. *To* W. DAVENPORT ADAMS[1]

MS.: Yale.

Box Hill, Dorking
September 20, 1877

Sir,
    You are at liberty to publish the verses you have named out of my
1st volume, but I would rather not see the reappearance of 'Under
boughs of [Breathing May]', which has a tone of *niaiserie pastorale*, not
perfectly pleasant to me. The other songs do not seem to me at least to
offend in this manner. I am, Sir,

Very truly yours,
George Meredith

603. *To* WILLIAM HARDMAN

MS.: Garrick Club. Excerpt published: *Letters*, i. 281, with inaccuracies.

Box Hill
September 25, 1877

Dear and Honoured Sir William (in Sherwood Tuck),
    I have just come from a visit to Brackenbury at Aldershot, and find
your letter, glad to hear from you. Notice of your departure for Wales
had been forwarded me by my private agency. I will confess I thought
you might have given me a day on the Hill, but my friends are all free
men. Curses on him that would constrain them in aught!—I have not
seen the Notice you speak of, or heard of the same.[1] Apparently, to
judge by your hints, it is by one who has thought it necessary to go
mad to deal with me becomingly. This may be a compliment, but the
result is, that the public finds itself in the presence of not one by [but]
Two Incomprehensibles, and the impression is deepened that hard
must be the nut when the cracker falls into contortions.
    —A joke is fathered on you. Speaking of Mrs. Besant's plan,[2] Oh,
says one, my wife has long used that instrument. She's absent from
home and I'll show it you. So he takes his friend to her room and
unlocks the drawer.—Bless my soul, she's taken it away with her!

602. [1] Editor of *Latter-Day Lyrics, Being Poems of Sentiment and Reflection by Living
Writers* (1878), which included GM's 'Violets' and 'Love Within the Lover's Breast'.
603. [1] This was probably W. E. Henley's 'Living Novelists. No. V. George Meredith' in
London: The Conservative Weekly Journal (25 Aug.), p. 92. By the following June GM
was familiar with it. (See Letter 616.)
    [2] For birth control.

If you have not seen the *New Quarterly Magazine* for July last, will you commission D'Troïa to get it from Mudie's. Run your eyes over 'The Case of General Ople and Lady Camper'. I think you will recognize the General and remember the case.[3]

Poco sent in no word of the event.[4] Are we in disgrace with him? Like you I wait in awe. It is not so much a question what will come of it, as whether any remainder of our Poco will. He is however sagacious and a tactician. He hath not married a widow. On the whole we may hope.—Is there a chance of your giving us a day here—any day next month. I may go somewhere on the continent for a week of walking, but I shall soon be back (if I go) as I have much to do. My love to D'Troïa and the young ladies.

> Ever warmly yours,
> George Meredith

604. *To* JOHN MORLEY

Text: *Letters*, i. 281–2.

Box Hill
October 18, 1877

My dear Morley,

I hear you are at philosophic Pitfield.[1] I wish to see you and shake your hand, and hear of your travels. I have a country cousin's eagerness for that great relation of events. Your letter from Gmünden was pleasant to receive. Morison wrote subsequently of rain assailing you at Ischl, which I had vowed for you, but not desired. I have been nowhere during your absence excepting to Pitfield, and to Aldershot to Brackenbury home from the Russians. I am consequently dull, unrubbed, no reflector. I write, and not perfectly to my satisfaction.

We shall have a couple of beds here at the end of the month, if there is a chance of catching you and your wife—you do owe it to us.

Your stay on the Königsee, at the St. Bartolomac little inn at the end of the lake, must have been about the pleasantest time of your excursion. I did not see the lake at night, and I was with captious

603. [3] 'The case' was an episode in the life of Hardman's former neighbour at Kingston-on-Thames, General Hopkins, which GM used as the basis of the story.
   [4] Lionel Robinson was married on 4 Sept. to Katharine Lomas, daughter of Dr. John Lomas of Cheetham Hill, Manchester.
604. [1] Morley, after his holiday with Chamberlain on the Continent, had gone to visit Cotter Morison.

cockney comrades.² I still have a throb to be up the Walzmann; I propose it, and much of that region, for next year—or next. I have not been away for six!

I hope you are refreshed, furious for the pen. . . .

George Meredith

605. *To* FREDERICK JONES

Text: *Letters,* i. 196–7, with the addressee identified only as F——J——s.

Box Hill

November, Lord Guy of London

Day [5], [? 1877]¹

Friend J[ones],

It being the fashionable Season in Brighton at Brighton you are, of course. Now, your way back to Kingston lies exactly by Box Hill. Will you take us en route? Do! I have not seen you for so long that on my honour I could listen to your puns with pleasure: and who could say more? We have been most unfortunate during the summer, with first the soaking, till the Inns were full right on to October. But at present Inns gape, and we can get one room for you at the Burford or Beehive. If you are for companionship with me, J[ones], you will come. Write by return, and arrange. Bring all with you. If it rain, we'll draw the blinds, let fly the corks, and dance. If it's fair, I'll sweat you gently over the hills and home to our tobacco Parliament.² I can't say fairer.—I would send my love to Mrs. J[ones], but fear your tarnishing it in the transmission. But I kiss my hand to the heavens: and let her only look on your head, and she will see the act reflected.

Your friendliest

George Meredith

---

² ? In 1866 when he had served as correspondent for the *Morning Post.*

605. ¹ W. M. Meredith places this letter with the letters of 1869, where it almost certainly does not belong. (GM was away from England for at least six weeks during the summer and would hardly comment on the weather in his absence.) I assign it to 1877 partly on the evidence of the weather and partly on the basis of a reference in Letter 598 to a prospective visit by Jones to some seaside town.

² Carlyle applies this term to the Parliaments of Frederic I; GM probably picked it up from Carlyle but of course uses it with a different connotation.

606. *To* JOHN MORLEY

Text: *Letters*, i. 282–3.

Box Hill
November 10, 1877

My dear Morley,

Let me hear from you when you are stronger: not that I wish to ring my bell to summon you here, but that bronchitis rather alarms me. I have had reason to dread it—not on my own account, for throat and chest with me seem inexpugnable.

I am perplexed by Spottiswoode's application to me to lecture at the Royal.[1] I hate it, and it does not pay me, it makes me nervous, and I have to give up my inner mind's work to it. But I have the question going on, whether I ought to decline anything, I, unlucky, portionless, ill-paid!

France, from a knave, fallen to a fool![2]

But no, the gain has been precious in the interval. She has gained in self-knowledge, and a reasonable courage.

Judging of what MacMahon may do by his antecedents, I am inclined to think that the man who could hesitate about his paramount manifest duty toward the country when plain sense told him to save the one army of France for the defence of the capital, and a telegram from the Imperial ministry pushed him to Metz, while the enemy was in front and on his flank—this Marshal Donkey might do anything.

The situation is enough to make us all anxious, but the temperance of the French gives me some repose.

De Broglie of course is the one who makes us feel blackest.—As for the army, it would split for civil war. Very probably the Republican section would be beaten; the country thrown back for ten years. But the ten would do more harm to the cause of the winners. Honest rule must come round to a people so self-contained and intelligent.

Ever yours warmly,
George Meredith

606. [1] William Spottiswoode, LL.D., was Hon. Sec. of the Royal Institution, Albemarle St.

[2] I suppose Napoleon III to be the 'knave' and President MacMahon to be the 'fool', though the term 'knave' is equally apt for the Duc de Broglie, the premier, whose resignation on 20 Nov. was forced by the sweeping victory of the Republicans in the elections just held when this letter was written.

607. *To* JOHN MORLEY

Text: *Letters*, i. 283–4.

Box Hill
November 16, 1877

My dear Morley,

I return you Harrison's letter.[1] 'Want of courage' is no doubt often the visible gap in Celtic character; for this reason, that the Celt, if not pushing forward, will be shrinking. Movements that are impulse, either assail, or they have the tendency to contract and retreat. The French are Gallic enough to show this. Nevertheless, I see a harmonizing and solidifying of the logical brain with the mercurial blood in them. As to Gambetta and his trusting to phrases,[2] the temptation to utter them to an interviewer must be great, either to keep conversation going, or to put the sympathetic guest in better heart, or to console oneself with a trumpet sound in touching subjects vexatious. He must be judged by his public conduct, which is good.—Harrison speaks of the French in the tone of one who forgets that they have had a terrific whipping. And when he speaks of Mirabeau and Danton, let him imagine those two after the Revolution, opposed to a military chief more than probably having the army in his hand.—MacMahon might be shot by a Republican battalion, but the shot missing, he would have all the regiments. Conservatism and its friend Fear are strong enough to give him sway for a time. But the Republic is only a withdrawing tide. Back it comes ten years hence. In a third of the time it might be established by an alternation of conciliation and firmness. A Big Fool with power, we must treat like a madman on a housetop, and affectionately induce him to destroy himself for us.—I cannot clearly see what Harrison wants. His paper in the next *F[ort]nightly* may show.[3] His 'Englishman' letters were currently instructive.

Yes, I wish to see you, and have a mill-tide of talk on varieties; but do not ask me; I have to get through a wall of work that frowns on me as one on a wrong track at present. I am very grateful for fair Florence.[4]

Yours ever,
George Meredith

607. [1] Presumably a personal letter. Harrison had been in France as special correspondent of *The Times*, to which he contributed a series of letters 'By an Englishman in the Provinces' referred to *infra* by GM.

[2] Gambetta, who had been the leader of the Republicans in the recent elections, was a gifted phrase-maker. He had warned MacMahon that 'when France has spoken in her sovereign voice, you will be forced to submit or resign'. Again, 'Fear is the chief disturber of French politics'.   [3] 'The Republic and the Marshal', *FR* (Dec. 1877).

[4] It is futile to look for personal or family information in the letters or *Recollections* of Morley, but his will identifies Florence as his stepdaughter, Florence Ayling, who later became a nun. Yet the Register of Marriages in Somerset House records Morley's marriage on 28 May 1870 to Mary Ayling, *spinster*.

Cause me to be remembered in your household.

As to the sort of men who sat with Pym and Hampden, do we show them now? If not, should we pose them before the French? All countries would want a heavy shaking to bring such men to the front.— I have been pleased with the plain writing of Froude's A'Becket in the *19th Century*.[5] Your Raynal instructs me.[6] I am ashamed to say, I did not know of him. Pattison on 'Books' is perfectly correct.[7] As with India, irrigation would improve his produce.—Senior's Thiers[8] is a lasting picture to me of the Devil's own Infernal Imp. Statesman, yea, begotten by Machiavelli of the Vivandière of the Regiment! Had I time, I would compose a La Bruyère abstract of it.—Born with Satan's blessing too! His kettle-drum taps marched France to Sedan. His more than Louis Napoleon's. The Thiers-fed French really thought at the sound of the bugle that another chapter of the Windy History was to be written. Here I am pulled up: but I could talk with you over sheets.

608. *To* JOHN MORLEY

Text: *Letters*, i. 285–6.

Box Hill
November 24, 1877

My dear Morley,

The day before your enclosure of Pattison's article on you arrived, I heard of it and was longing to see it.[1] I have had great pleasure in reading it. A point is marked of what one would have prescribed for one's young ambition—and the 'more' may not be more worth having. Here is the man best entitled to sit as judge, and he hands you the laurel-crown;—of the secondary order only because the years are yet wanting that shall make you ripe for the first.—If I did not feel myself happily cut off from all ambition, I could envy you. As it is, I see you housed in a warm resting-place by the way, and I go on over frozen ruts whither we shall meet. Is that a stern forewarning to you? No, for an old master's praise is a lasting possession, the best of

607. [5] James Anthony Froude, 'The Life and Times of Thomas Becket', *Nineteenth Century* (June–Nov. 1877).
[6] Raynal's *History of the Indies*, discussed by Morley in the November *FR* as a part of his series, 'Three Books of the Eighteenth Century'.
[7] Mark Pattison, 'Books and Critics', in the November *FR*.
[8] Nassau W. Senior, 'Conversations with M. Thiers', *FR* (Oct.–Nov. 1877).
608. [1] Mark Pattison's flattering review of Morley's *Critical Miscellanies*, Second Series (1877), in the *Academy* (13 Oct.), pp. 353–4.

promptings. Nevertheless (and this is the sum of what I would say) the 'last infirmity of noble minds' is an infirmity, but susceptibility to the purest sources of Fame speaks of health. See the emptiness of it, take the passing benefit. Neither water nor wine shall give eternal life. That they invigorate for the hour is enough.—Here is a sermon to one who needs it less than most men: proof of pragmatical ineptitude in the deliverer!—I hope you are really better.—Your Black Christian of the Bloody Cross appears to have been blest by GAWD* recently.[2] If I had time I should like to write his hymn: Te Deum: with chorus of 'all the historians'.

Yours most warmly,
George Meredith

*[Footnote to letter:] Or 'Gord'.

609. *To* JOHN MORLEY

Text: *Letters*, i. 286–7.

Box Hill
November 28, 1877

My dear Morley,

When Morison sent me word of poor Bridger's ambition to enter into the Grocery line in Puttenham village, I had simultaneously a vision of a shivering bare little shop edging its way by rotation to the sparse shower of nourishing gold on that—as to grocers—arctic common. I supposed Bridger must know best; as I generally do when I am prophetic.—He would have suited me had I built stables and rooms over them; and this I cannot do for a year—or two, when I hope to prosper better.

In this valley a good gardener may sometimes command a place; or good coachman.

Can he be strongly recommended in either capacity? He has, I think, a wife and children: how many? How much does he require for his services per week?

I do not know of a place vacant; but the above particulars should be known to me. I promise not to forget him.

I go to town for a night to-morrow, and shall call on Morison. He writes in a wildly lamentable tone of France. And this when such is the

---

[2] At a guess, this means that Kars, in Turkish Armenia, had fallen to the Russians on 18 Nov., to the accompaniment of general rejoicing in England. In his article on Raynal (see preceding letter, Note 6) Morley had written of 'the native races whose blood their Christian aggressors had shed as if it had been water'.

popular feeling (including the military) toward the Republic, that a conspiracy to ruin it could not succeed beyond five years, and would displace it for that term only to endear it by proving its value to the country. That big Dunderhead[1] in the hands of the shuffling Duke[2] and the clerics may do harm for a time. But he has not got much, it is evident, by sounding the army. All depends on the Republicans making no false move. Patience! as the man says in *Mauprat*.[3] The power of taking an injury without scoring blood for it, will be of wonderful example in France.—Yours, trusting for a better account of your health,

George Meredith

I salute your wife. A kiss to Florence. A punch in the ribs to Johnson.[4]

610. *To* THE EDITOR OF THE *Dublin University Magazine*[1]

Text (excerpt): Sotheby Catalogue (18–19 Dec. 1934), p. 73.

Box Hill
November 28, 1877

[Thanking him for his reference to *The Shaving of Shagpat*.]
I am ... of your opinion that we learn much from looking Eastward.

609. [1] Marshal MacMahon.
[2] The Duc de Broglie.
[3] A novel by George Sand (1836).
[4] James Sully (*My Life and Friends: A Psychologist's Memories*, 1918), p. 132, says that he tutored Morley's stepson, but there is no mention of a stepson in Morley's will, although Clause 11 in his will bequeaths £300 to his Trustees to be held by them under the terms of a mysterious deed of trust executed by him in 1916. As John Ayling was the principal beneficiary under the terms of Viscountess Morley's will, I think it beyond reasonable doubt that he was her son and that 'Johnson' was GM's nickname for him
610. [1] Listed by the *CBEL* as J. F. Waller (1872–7) and Kenningale Cooke (1877–8). Probably Cooke is the better guess.